THE ELECTRONIC OFFICE:

Procedures & Administration

Rita Sloan Tilton, Ph.D.
Visiting Professor in Management
University of Nevada, Las Vegas

J. Howard Jackson, Ph.D., CPS
Professor, Department of Management
Virginia Commonwealth University

Sue Chappell Rigby, Ed.D.
Professor and Head of the Office Systems
and Business Education Department
Northern Michigan University

Contributing Author
Donna Cochrane
Associate Professor
Bloomsburg University

Software Consultants
Marly Bergerud
Saddleback Community College

Marcus Franklin
Cincinnati, OH

South-Western Educational Publishing

VP/Editor-in-Chief: Robert E. First	Production Editor II: Melanie A. Blair-Dillion
Developmental Editor: Inell Bolls-Gaither	Senior Designer: Elaine St. John-Lagenaur
Coordinating Editor: Angela C. McDonald	Photo Editor: Fred M. Middendorf
Production Managers: Deborah M. Luebbe and Carol Sturzenberger	Marketing Manager: Al S. Roane

Copyright © 1996

by

SOUTH-WESTERN EDUCATIONAL PUBLISHING
Cincinnati, Ohio

All Rights Reserved

ISBN: 0-538-71007-1

5 6   99 98 97

Printed in the United States of America

Library of Congress Cataloging-in-Publication Data

Tilton, Rita Sloan.
  The electronic office : procedures & administration / Rita Tilton,
J. Howard Jackson, Sue Chappell Rigby. — 11th ed.
    p.   cm.
  Includes index.
  ISBN 0-538-71007-1
  1. Office practice.   2. Office practice—Automation.   3. Word
processing.   I. Jackson, J. Howard (James Howard).
II. Rigby, D. Sue.   III. Title.
  HF5547.T57   1996
  651.8—dc20   94–37703
                                                        CIP

PHOTO CREDITS — p. xix: bottom left: Photo courtesy of Marvel, **top right:** © Walter Hodges/Westlight; **pp. xix–1:** © Pierre Kopp/Westlight; **p. 96: bottom left:** Dauphin Technology, Inc., Lombard, Illinois, **bottom right:** Photography by Erik Von Fischer/Photonics; **p. 97: top left:** Photo provided courtesy of Eastman Kodak Company, **bottom left:** Polycom, Inc.; **p. 210: bottom left:** Photography by Erik Von Fischer/Photonics, **top right:** Photography by Alan Brown/Photonics; **p. 211: bottom left:** Photograph courtesy of Dictaphone Corporation, Stratford, CT; **p. 338: top right:** Magna Visual, Inc.; **pp. 338–339:** Photography by Alan Brown/Photonics; **p. 339: top left:** © G. Fritz/SuperStock, Inc., **bottom right:** © SuperStock, Inc.; **p. 426: bottom middle:** Courtesy of Hilton Hotels Corporation; **pp. 426–427:** © David Joel/Tony Stone Images; **p. 427: top left:** Photo courtesy of Compression Labs, Inc. (CLI); **p. 498: bottom left:** © Ralph Mercer/Tony Stone Images, **top right:** © SuperStock, Inc.; **p. 499: bottom left:** © M. Taylor/SuperStock, Inc.; **p. 620: bottom left:** © R. W. Jones/Westlight, **top right:** © Chad Ehlers/Tony Stone Images

I(T)P

International Thomson Publishing
South-Western Educational Publishing is an ITP Company. The ITP trademark is used under license.

Preface

This edition of *The Electronic Office: Procedures and Administration* represents a tradition of a half century of response to the dramatic changes taking place in the office. For fifty years, this text has introduced students to exciting innovations which, at the time, made office work easier. The Selectric typewriter, the photocopier, direct distance dialing, and the Magnetic Tape Selectric Typewriter (MTST), in their day, represented quantum leaps in office technology. Many of these have disappeared. Others continue to enhance office productivity through improved design and broadened applications. Who would have dreamed in the early '50s that the manual typewriter would be replaced by the personal computer, or that the mimeograph would give way to an intelligent copier, with programmable features, that can automatically enlarge, reduce, collate, duplex, staple, and print in color? As the role of the administrative assistant has changed with the expansion of information technology, changing management styles, government regulations, opportunities for professional growth, and increasing global markets, the focus of this book has changed from preparing the secretary for the routine tasks of dictation, transcription, filing, and serving as office host/hostess to preparing administrative assistants for a broader role as professional members of the management team.

Each edition has attempted to provide state-of-the-art procedures and up-to-date information for the student preparing for a career as an administrative assistant. The book is a comprehensive classroom text adaptable to most students' needs and backgrounds. It is also a comprehensive reference tool for office professionals on the job. Students will find in-depth discussion of the procedures they will be expected to perform upon entering the world of work. Office professionals who are changing jobs, are considering study for the Certified Professional Secretary examination, or need a reference guide or manual will find the book a rich source of information.

ORGANIZATION/CONTENT OF THE TEXT

This edition follows the same logical organization as the previous edition. It has, however, been strengthened, expanded, and updated to reflect the growing influence of information technology, the expanding global marketplace, and the dramatic changes in the organizational structure of modern business.

The text consists of twenty-five chapters organized into eight parts:

Part 1, TODAY'S ELECTRONIC OFFICE, analyzes the tasks and responsibilities of the administrative assistant as well as the components of a professional image and the characteristics, personality traits, job attitudes, and office relationships of the office professional. An overview of the electronic office environment covering company organization, ergonomics, office landscaping, space management, health and safety considerations, and office security is provided. Workstation environment including lighting, heating, sound, color, and ventilation is also discussed. Office efficiency involving the organization of time and work is an integral element in Part 1. Keeping appointment records, setting priorities, managing time and stress, public relations responsibilities, and telephone etiquette are also given thorough coverage. New topics include recycling, office protocol, electronic organizers and time managers, working in a multinational office environment, and hosting international visitors.

Part 2, TECHNOLOGY AND PROCEDURES, presents a current look at office information systems and the technology and procedures that affect the administrative assistant's role. Computer hardware and software with which the administrative assistant should be familiar are presented in this section. These include software applications such as word processing, spreadsheets, and database management. Reprographic applications of photocopying, offset duplicating, desktop publishing, typesetting, and in-house printing are also explained and illustrated. Records management and telecommunications, including electronic mail, are also discussed. Coverage of portable computers, voice and pen input devices, and PIM software has been added to this edition. Information has been updated throughout this section to reflect the rapid advances in office information systems. The discussion of operating systems software has been expanded. Increased coverage of computerized records management, micrographics, and local area networks enhances the contents of Part 2.

Part 3, DOCUMENT CREATION AND DISTRIBUTION, focuses on information processing. The chapters in Part 3 incorporate the skills and procedures necessary for document creation and distribution. Editing, proofreading, formatting, working with magnetic media, and understanding the characteristics and special functions of automated equipment are addressed in the first chapters of Part 3. Taking, giving, and transcribing dictation, composing correspondence, and preparing outgoing communications and shipments and international correspondence are given in-depth coverage. A section on forms software has been added to Part 3, and all computer-related topics have been expanded to reflect the needs of the administrative assistant in the electronic office.

Part 4, RESEARCH AND ORGANIZATION OF BUSINESS REPORTS, provides a thorough coverage of the administrative assistant's role in research and organization of information. Guidelines for collecting business information, presenting statistical information, and assisting with written reports, procedures, speeches, and publications are illustrated and explained in practical terms. This part of the text contains a wealth of material on where to find information needed for day-to-day business transactions as well as the proper tools for library research, computer databases, and footnoting and bibliographic systems. Also included in Part 4 are procedures for keying speeches and a practical report-writing checklist.

Part 5, TRAVEL AND CONFERENCE PLANNING, outlines in detail the administrative assistant's role in assisting executives with travel arrangements and conference planning. The responsibilities for itinerary preparation, arrangements for reservations, travel funds, passports, visas, and the services of a travel agency are highlighted in this section of the text. Multinational meetings and the use of electronic meeting rooms are presented with a practical focus on the administrative assistant's role as a meeting planner and coordinator.

Part 6, FINANCIAL AND LEGAL PROCEDURES, discusses the financial and legal duties of the administrative assistant who is entrusted with managing money, processing investment and insurance documents, handling payroll and tax documents, and producing and processing legal documents. New tax legislation, employment regulations, and the fundamentals of social security, stock market trading, banking procedures, insurance, real estate, contract law, copyrights, wills, affidavits, and other legal documents are presented from the administrative assistant's perspective. Regulations relative to bankruptcy, civil rights, the Freedom of Information Act, and the duties of a paralegal/legal assistant are also discussed in Part 6.

Part 7, EMPLOYMENT AND CAREER ADVANCEMENT, is an orientation to placement and advancement opportunities. It presents detailed steps necessary to secure employment as an administrative assistant, including the preparation of a resume and an application letter. Tips for successful interviewing are also presented. Specific suggestions are given for planning for a professional future as an administrative assistant. Part 7 also presents the wide variety of employment opportunities available to the college-trained administrative assistant. The book concludes with a look toward a career in management. The final chapter identifies acceptable management styles, outlines the requisites of successful supervision, and explains the functions of management. This edition reflects the dramatic changes taking place in corporate structure, the opportunities for international employment, and the cultural diversity in today's work force.

Part 8, THE REFERENCE GUIDE, will help students in the clear and correct preparation of written materials. The guide identifies accepted practices for abbreviating, capitalizing, writing numbers, spelling plurals and possessives, punctuating, and using words correctly. In addition, Part 8 contains an up-to-date correspondence guide and the ARMA rules for alphabetic filing. Also included are metric weights and measures, Roman numerals, the Greek alphabet, footnote and bibliographic entries, standard proofreaders' marks, capitals and two-letter abbreviations of the U.S. and Mexican states and the Canadian provinces, and major world currencies. Students will find the information in the Reference Guide a useful addition to their professional library.

FEATURES NEW TO THIS EDITION

Marginal Notes. Marginal notes have been added to highlight the material contained in each chapter.

Learning Objectives. Each chapter begins with learning objectives. This added feature will help the student to focus on expected outcomes from having studied each chapter.

Icons. This added feature throughout the text draws attention to segments of the text that relate to tips on technology, office procedures, critical thinking, human relations, communication, and the Reference Guide.

New Topics. Topics new to this edition include the expanding global role of the administrative assistant, the culturally diverse work force, total quality management (TQM), PIM software, the changing role of corporate America, and corporate downsizing.

Template Diskette. An optional template diskette is available from South-Western Educational Publishing. Use of the template permits students to retrieve, edit, alter, store, and apply the use of spreadsheet, database, and word processing technology for computer applications correlated to the chapter text. Additional computerized activities are available with the *Work Assignments.*

Presentation Software. Electronic presentation software allows instructors to bring multimedia into class lectures. Electronic slides may be used in place of the regular transparency masters.

SPECIAL FEATURES OF THE TEXT

Summary. A summary is included at the end of each chapter to help student grasp quickly the main points of the chapter.

Discussion Questions and Problems. Each chapter includes a series of discussion questions and problems designed to stimulate an exchange of ideas.

Technology Based. The impact of information technology on the role of the administrative assistant has been updated, strengthened, and expanded. Computer-related tasks are interwoven throughout the text.

Case Problems. Cases at the end of each part are realistic human relations problems involving office ethics, work force diversity, safety and security, technology, stress management, sexual harassment, and coping with change.

Work Assignments. This supplement simulates office situations that require students to set priorities, make decisions, and execute a variety of tasks, some of which are computerized. Four in-basket simulations have been included in the *Work Assignments* in this edition, providing yet another opportunity for students to exercise critical-thinking and decision-making skills, exercise judgment, and apply the contents of the textbook in a realistic situation.

Instructor's Manual.   The manual provides lecture notes for each chapter and solutions to the questions for discussion, problems, technology applications, work assignments, simulated office situations, and tests. A set of transparency masters and suggested readings correlated to each chapter are also included in the instructor's manual.

MicroSWAT III Testing Package.   A testing program is available from the publisher. The advantages of this program for preparing, administering, and grading of tests are explained in the instructor's manual.

ACKNOWLEDGMENTS

As the book enters its fiftieth year of publication, the authors are indebted to J Marshall Hanna and the late Estelle Popham for their vision, creativity, and writing talent. We are grateful to our reviewers, who have made substantial suggestions for improvement and expansion during the writing of this edition. We are especially grateful to the thousands of teachers, students, and secretaries whose loyalty to the book has made it a classic in its field.

Reviewers for this edition were the following:

Ms. Ann Cooper
Central Carolina Technical College
Sumter, South Carolina

Dr. Eleanor Davidson
Nassau Community College
New York, New York

Ms. Carolyn S. Hayes, CPS
Delco Electronics Corporation
Kokomo, Indiana

Dr. Pamela Marino
Baruch College
The City University of New York
New York, New York

Ms. Mary Ruprecht and Associates
Management and Office Automation Consultants
Duluth, Minnesota

Ms. Marietta Spring
Glen Allen, Virginia

Ms. Ann J. Swafford
West Columbia, South Carolina

Ms. Becky L. Tassin
Louisiana State University
Baton Rouge, Louisiana

Ms. Karen Velasquez
Midland Technical College
Beltline Campus
Columbia, South Carolina

This edition represents the most comprehensive effort in a long history of revision. We hope you will enjoy using the materials to achieve your professional goals.

Rita S. Tilton　　▪　　*J. Howard Jackson*　　▪　　*Sue C. Rigby*

Brief Contents

Contents

Part 1

Today's Electronic Office

Lynn Martin, Secretary of Labor in this decade, expresses the focus of Part 1 well. In a recent report she listed five skills she believes people must master to succeed in their work lives. The first four skills are discussed in Part 1. They are

- Allocating time, money, and other resources
- Understanding and using technology
- Evaluating, processing, and using information
- Working with others

By the end of this decade the nation's work force will look completely different. By one Department of Labor estimate, 85 percent of the entrants into the job market between 1985 and the year 2000 will be women, minorities, and immigrants. As part of this culturally diversified work force, the administrative assistant must be competent in information management, oral and written communication, organizational techniques, and interpersonal skills. Part 1 introduces you to the many facets of the administrative assistant position and the skills required to be successful in the field.

Chapter 1

The Office Professional

INTRODUCTION

In today's office the administrative assistant is recognized as an independent office professional. He or she is no longer considered merely an extension of the employer. Working as a high-tech specialist, the administrative assistant operates sophisticated electronic equipment and manages complex information systems. Because of the technology available, today's administrative assistant can and often does manage the information responsibilities of several managers.

The organizational structure within business firms is changing. In order to remain competitive in today's global business climate, many firms are reducing or eliminating mid-management positions, flattening the traditional organizational pyramid. With this downsizing has come a redistribution of the work load. Qualified administrative assistants are being asked to assume responsibilities formerly held by managers, and they are actively participating in team projects. This expanded role has added to the professional stature of the administrative assistant position. Naturally, this change in job responsibilities is viewed as a plus by administrative assistants in the field. They enjoy playing a vital role in the day-to-day operations of the company.

In addition, information technology is reshaping the administrative assistant's work. The administrative assistant today has the opportunity to be at the center of the information flow in a business. The administrative assistant who has mastered the tools of information technology may be considered the company's expert in how to access, file, store, process, and send every type of information.

Although corporations are becoming leaner in managerial levels, the demand for administrative assistants has not decreased. In fact, the opposite is true. For the period 1990–2005 the U.S. Department of Labor Bureau of Labor Statistics forecasts over 500,000 new positions in the secretarial field representing a growth of 15 percent.[1] Yearly surveys of want ads by Dartnell Corporation's Institute of Business Research have found that salaries in this field are on the rise, which is encouraging information for those wanting to join the administrative assistant ranks.

You have chosen to become a part of a dynamic profession. This chapter gives you an overview of the field and sets the stage for your study of the profession.

JOB TITLES

Advances in technology have contributed to the changing role of the secretary and to the increased complexity of the position. These factors have given rise to changes in job titles and even in job descriptions. Many organizations, while perhaps not changing their formal job descriptions, have changed the job titles. Whatever the label, it is apparent that the position of secretary is regarded as one of increasing importance in today's electronic office.

Common titles for this position include executive secretary, senior secretary, administrative secretary, administrative assistant, executive assistant, and secretary. Titles such as legal secretary and medical secretary continue in these areas of specialization. Although the classification *secretary* is by far the most common in newspaper want ads, most members of the secretarial profession prefer the title *administrative assistant*.

> *Administrative assistant is the job title most secretaries prefer.*

This book, therefore, will use the title *administrative assistant* to denote the professional secretary. When discussing the person (or persons) to whom the administrative assistant reports, the titles *executive, manager, supervisor, employer,* and *principal* will be used.

JOB RESPONSIBILITIES

The specific responsibilities of the administrative assistant will depend on at least four factors: previous work experience, educational background, the nature of the employer's work, and the electronic equipment and software available. See Figure 1-1 for a listing of the basic responsibilities of the position.

The individual performing these functions may work in any of a number of environments. A physician or owner of a small business may have only

---

[1] U.S. Department of Labor, Bureau of Labor Statistics, *Occupational Outlook Quarterly*, 36, no. 1 (Spring 1992), p. 28.

BASIC JOB RESPONSIBILITIES

Keyboarding at a personal computer, dedicated word processor, or electronic typewriter

Learning and using various software systems and features: desktop publishing, graphics

Transcribing (from machine dictation or manual notes)

Participating in team projects, committees

Making decisions within authority

Solving problems within the administrative assistant role

Coordinating office communications: written, verbal, electronic

Processing and distributing mail

Telephoning

Scheduling appointments

Greeting visitors

Composing, editing, and proofreading

Researching and abstracting information

Interpreting, analyzing, and presenting data

Supervising and/or training others

Relaying staff instructions

Advising on selection of staff

Organizing time and work

Maintaining special records

Planning required information for budgets and budget forecasts

Filing (manual/electronic) and records management

Completing various administrative duties

Coordinating meetings and taking minutes

Making travel arrangements

Selecting appropriate duplication methods

Exercising effective human relations

Maintaining confidentiality

Working without direct supervision

Purchasing office supplies

Representing employer at meetings

Fig. 1-1   Specific responsibilities assigned to an administrative assistant will vary with circumstances, but certain functions are inherent to the position.

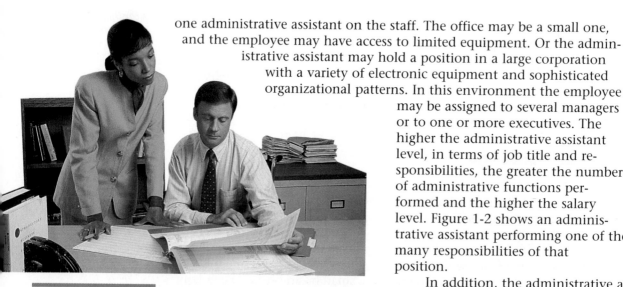

Fig. 1-2   An administrative assistant performs duties of a highly confidential nature requiring initiative, judgment, and knowledge of company practice. *Photography by Alan Brown/Photonics.*

one administrative assistant on the staff. The office may be a small one, and the employee may have access to limited equipment. Or the administrative assistant may hold a position in a large corporation with a variety of electronic equipment and sophisticated organizational patterns. In this environment the employee may be assigned to several managers or to one or more executives. The higher the administrative assistant level, in terms of job title and responsibilities, the greater the number of administrative functions performed and the higher the salary level. Figure 1-2 shows an administrative assistant performing one of the many responsibilities of that position.

In addition, the administrative assistant to one or more executives enjoys informal rank within the company according to the formal rank of the executive. This administrative assistant has access to privileged information and knowledge of official actions in an organization, and thus occupies a unique position of influence and power in the office.

A POSITIVE PROFESSIONAL IMAGE

Projecting a positive professional image is imperative for the career-minded administrative assistant. Having a positive professional image enhances success in the field. Although a description of a positive professional image could include a number of components, this section concentrates on the big three: personal appearance, knowledge, and ethical behavior (see Figure 1-3).

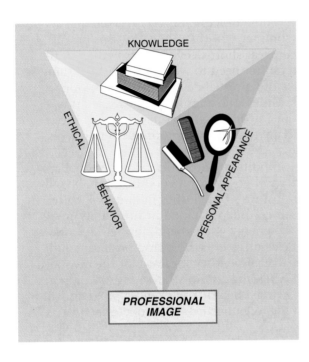

Fig. 1-3 The three most important components of a positive professional image are personal appearance, knowledge, and ethical behavior.

Personal Appearance

First impressions count. They can be negative or positive. They can be long-lasting. Successful administrative assistants know the role first impressions play in projecting a positive professional image. They take pride in their personal appearance.

Some entry-level employees do not realize that appropriate business attire and good grooming are important to their business success. Personal appearance may be a factor in decisions about salary increases and promotions. Observing the appearance of administrative assistants in an office will provide insights into what is considered proper business attire for that office.

People should remember what a person says, rather than what a person wears.

You will find that high-level administrative assistants dress conservatively for the office (see Figure 1-4).

Books have been written on proper business attire. Suits, coordinated jackets and skirts, and jacketed dresses are recommended for women; for men, the traditional business suit or, perhaps, a sport coat and slack combination. Certain colors project the proper business look: navy blue, tones of gray, tan, beige, and maroon. When selecting business attire, buy quality. Choose clothing for its durability and classic style. Use your working attire to reflect your good taste and a positive image of yourself and your employer.

Some offices observe a relaxed dress code during the summer months. Generally, this means that men can wear short-sleeved shirts without a tie and women do not need to wear hosiery. Also, some offices have a dress-casual day once a month or even once a week. Unless the administrative assistant is visiting an outside office on that day or greets the public on a daily basis, it is appropriate to follow the relaxed code.

Fig. 1-4 A suit is typical attire for the professional administrative assistant.
Right: Photo courtesy of Vogue Patterns.

Equally important contributions to personal appearance are good posture and good health habits. If you have proper posture, your clothes fit and look better. In addition, good posture suggests self-confidence. Good health habits are reflected in the way you look and the energy you expend during the workday. An administrative assistant to an executive must be in top physical condition. As pressures increase for the executive, they increase for the assistant. These pressures are compounded when the administrative assistant reports to more than one executive. Following a health and exercise program will help you maintain the control and energy needed to complete each day's work.

Knowledge

To be a professional, you must look like a professional. That is the first component of a positive professional image. To be a professional, you must also be an expert at what you do. That is the second component of a positive professional image.

Becoming an expert at what you do doesn't happen overnight. It is an evolving process; it takes time, effort, and planning on your part. The demands of the profession require that administrative assistants adapt to technological changes and take initiative on the job. This decade requires the development of certain skills (see Figure 1-5). Administrative assistants can

ESSENTIAL SKILLS FOR THIS DECADE

- Problem Solving
  —Develop experience at troubleshooting.
  —Tackle each problem that comes your way.

- Project Manager Capabilities

- Information Technology Management

- Writing Effectively and Concisely
  —Memos, letters, reports
  —Speeches, proposals, and employee awards

- Time Management Techniques

- Effective Interpersonal Relations

- Global Awareness
  —Knowledge of world geography
  —Understanding of different cultures
  —Knowledge of business environments in areas such as Africa, Asia, Europe, Japan, and Latin America

Fig. 1-5 Administrative assistants need to develop skills to meet the challenges of the '90s.

meet these challenges by enrolling in continuing education courses and seminars and by taking advantage of all training opportunities available to them. Also, administrative assistants should welcome job assignments that provide opportunities to learn the latest software and equipment.

Another suggestion is to subscribe to and read professional journals that focus on office technology, office management, and human resources. Besides reading about how you can perform your job functions more efficiently, expand your interests to include managerial topics, such as supervision and performance evaluation. This is one way you can broaden your horizons and begin to see things from management's viewpoint. Figure 1-6 is a listing of periodicals and subscription services. Begin now to build your personal library.

To develop as a professional, join and participate in Professional Secretaries International (PSI), the organization for administrative assistants. As a member of this organization, you have the opportunity to meet other administrative assistants in your local area. Meeting and sharing ideas with your counterparts in other companies are forms of networking, a way to learn from other professionals. Set as your goal the Certified Professional Secretary (CPS) rating, the certificate of excellence in your field. Study for the CPS rating gives direction to your continuing education efforts and acquiring the CPS designation attests to your professional competence. More information on PSI and the CPS rating is given in Chapter 24.

HUMAN RELATIONS

Networking means associating with colleagues in other companies and sharing mutual interests.

Fig. 1-6 Reading professional journals will broaden your horizons.

PERIODICALS AND SUBSCRIPTION SERVICES OF INTEREST TO THE ADMINISTRATIVE ASSISTANT

From Nine to Five. Semimonthly. Dartnell Corp., 4660 Ravenswood Ave., Chicago, IL 60640.

Managing Office Technology. Monthly. Penton Publishing, Inc., P.O. Box 95795, Cleveland, OH 44101.

Office Automation Report. Monthly. The Automated Office Ltd., 1123 Broadway, New York, NY 10010.

Office Guide. Semimonthly. Bureau of Business Practice, 24 Rope Ferry Rd., Waterford, CT 06386.

The Office Professional. Monthly. Professional Training Associates, Inc., 210 Commerce Blvd., Round Rock, TX 78664-2189.

Professional Secretary-Administrative Support Letter (formerly *P.S. for Professional Secretaries*). Semimonthly. Bureau of Business Practice, 24 Rope Ferry Rd., Waterford, CT 06386.

The Secretary. 9/year. Professional Secretaries International, 10502 N.W. Ambassador Drive, Kansas City, MO 64195-0404.

Via FedEx. The Magazine for Office Professionals. Quarterly. Free. Federal Express Corporation, 7628 Executive Drive, Eden Prairie, MN 55344.

Working Woman. Monthly. Working Woman, P.O. Box 3276, Harlan, IA 51593-2456.

Ethical Behavior

The third major component of a positive professional image is ethical behavior. Having a code of ethics helps the administrative assistant act correctly and consistently when faced with ethical dilemmas—situations in which management may be sending mixed signals about what behavior is appropriate and you must determine for yourself what is right and what is wrong. Your code should cover the broad areas of honesty, integrity, confidentiality, loyalty to the employer, adherence to company policies, moral behavior, and values. In following your code of ethics, recognize your priorities: your first duty is to yourself, the second to your company, and the third to your employer.

Your established code will suggest principles for you to follow. A byproduct of having and following a code of ethics as an administrative assistant is that your associates and those whom you supervise can be confident that your decisions and actions are fair and well-intentioned. Nothing attracts more respect to the administrative assistant than a reputation for doing the right thing.

Professional Secretaries International has published a code of ethics for office professionals. Use this code to develop your own code of ethical behavior. Refer to the section in Chapter 24 on how to develop a code of ethics.

INTEROFFICE RELATIONSHIPS

Being productive and happy in the work environment depends on having positive relationships with your immediate supervisor and with your co-workers. Your professionalism and the development of mutual respect are extremely important in building successful interoffice relationships (see Figure 1-7).

Fig. 1-7 Working in harmony with others requires courtesy, cooperation, and cheerfulness—the three C's of effective human relations.

Acting Professionally

Although today's office tends to be informal, with the employer and the administrative assistant often on a first-name basis, the professional office worker should encourage a professional relationship by always addressing the employer as "Mr. (or Mrs., Miss, or Ms.) Jones," as the case may be. Because this practice is generally followed in the presence of company visitors, addressing the employer in a formal manner at other times in the office could easily become automatic for you.

There is no substitute for good manners. Being rude or crude cannot enhance you professionally. Upon arriving at the office, greet your employer and coworkers with a cheerful "Good morning." At the end of the day, saying "Good night" or "Have a nice evening" is appropriate. Depending on the situation, the polite expressions "Excuse me," "Please," and "Thank you" should be used.

Successful administrative assistants make a distinction between their personal and professional lives by keeping these facets of their lives separate. They refrain from socializing with their bosses, and they keep personal matters to themselves. Conversations focus on work to be done, or perhaps national, international, or local news. Although a certain amount of discussion through the office **grapevine** (an informal communication channel concerning news of the office) is unavoidable, the professional administrative assistant should not contribute to gossip, or repeat gossip even if it is true. Certainly, the administrative assistant should not be the subject of office gossip.

Professional administrative assistants recognize the problems that can occur should an office romance develop or even be rumored. They may become distracted at work and thus less productive, not to mention the mental anguish if the romance should go sour. Although most companies do not have a written policy against such alliances, they have, instead, an unspoken, informal policy on office romances. Companies tend to discourage office romances fearing that conflicts of interest may arise.

Developing Mutual Respect

When you begin your office career, you will learn quickly that you must interact positively with employees at all levels of the organization, from the maintenance department to the executive suite. You should be aware also that you are joining a culturally diversified work force. Expect to work with people who represent a mix of Caucasians, African Americans, Hispanics, Asian Americans, Native Americans, and members of other races and cultures. Accept and value the differences that each person brings to the office. Do what you can to create a harmonious working environment so that each person can reach his or her potential. Invite mutual respect by following the golden rule: Treat others as you would like to be treated.

For instance, in conversations with others in the company, give them your full attention. Listen carefully to what the other person is saying. Speak in a friendly tone of voice with words chosen to encourage a free give-and-take discussion. If there is a strong difference of opinion between the two of you, work to avoid any put-down that could haunt you in later dealings with that person.

When your colleagues are swamped with rush assignments, offer assistance if you have time. By so simple a help as answering the phone or in some other way reducing their interruptions, you demonstrate to them that you are a team player. Also, be sure to show appreciation to others when they offer to assist you. Thank them for their help, and go one step further by mentioning their assistance to your employer.

The development of mutual respect among coworkers takes time and effort. You, the administrative assistant, should do everything you can to foster a climate of mutual respect in the office. (See Figure 1-8 for a checklist of behaviors that promote good office relationships.)

THE PROFESSIONAL ADMINISTRATIVE ASSISTANT

A Self-Evaluation

The administrative assistant's behavior in an office sets the stage for the employer–administrative assistant relationship.

	YES	NO
When I work, I work.	_____	_____
I dress appropriately for the office.	_____	_____
I address my employer or employers in a formal manner.	_____	_____
I leave my personal life at home.	_____	_____
I respect my employer.	_____	_____
I am punctual.	_____	_____
I mind my own business.	_____	_____
I execute my duties with dispatch and with accuracy.	_____	_____
I keep confidential work confidential.	_____	_____
I do not contribute or listen to office gossip about my employer.	_____	_____
I owe allegiance to the company first, then to my immediate supervisor (if in controversy).	_____	_____
I recognize that materials and equipment with which I work belong to my employer.	_____	_____
I criticize in private and compliment publicly.	_____	_____
I continue to educate myself to enhance my value to my employer.	_____	_____
I am committed to create and encourage a pleasant working atmosphere.	_____	_____
I recognize that my position is a supportive one.	_____	_____
I attempt to maintain good health to better execute my duties.	_____	_____
I am dependable.	_____	_____
I adhere to company policy.	_____	_____
I display a positive attitude toward my work.	_____	_____
I have confidence in my dealings with peers, management, and clients.	_____	_____
I accept and handle responsibility without supervision.	_____	_____

Fig. 1-8 Can you answer yes to each of these statements?

Accepting Criticism

Because administrative assistants accomplish a variety of tasks, often under the pressure of time, mistakes can and do occur. When you make a mistake, your employer may criticize your work. Being a professional means that you welcome constructive criticism as an opportunity to better your performance. React gracefully by saying, "I appreciate your calling this to my attention"; or "Thank you for your suggestion." Ask pertinent questions; for example, "What changes would you suggest?" Control any negative nonverbal behavior: mocking facial expressions, tapping feet or hands, or similar behaviors. Make a mental note that this particular error or oversight will not happen again. Be prompt in admitting an error, and do what you can to rectify it. If the situation warrants, apologize to your employer.

Learning from one's mistakes is critical. Nothing is more upsetting to an employer than to find the same mistakes repeated over and over again.

Certainly, if the criticism is unfair, discuss the matter in an amicable way with your employer. Failure to discuss the issue could breed resentment, which can only be harmful to the cordiality that must exist between you.

Recognizing Office Politics

Office politics are the informal relationships that affect power and status within an office. To some degree office politics exist in every business office, but they seem to thrive particularly in organizations where there is a lack of communication between management and employees or where the goals and mission of the organization are unclear. When employee performance measurement and reward systems are vague, generally there is political activity.

An administrative assistant needs to be aware that life in the office may include office politics. If it does, the administrative assistant must know the formal and informal power structure in the organization and how the informal communication channel (the grapevine) works. For example, a coworker who goes to lunch with your manager several times a week would be part of the informal power structure. Why? Obviously, your coworker and your manager are friends and no doubt talk freely about office matters. Recognizing this informal power link, you or others might mention information to the coworker that you think the manager should know. You can be reasonably sure that the information will be transmitted.

Office politics can be perceived as positive or negative. It is important to understand that an employee, particularly an administrative assistant, does not work in isolation. Employees need others to accomplish the work of the office. You want to convey that you are a key player and a nice person. People who stab others behind their backs seldom last long in a reputable organization. As a key player, you will have to learn the rules: work within the system yet respect lines of authority. Build a network of your peers or subordinates by encouraging team projects. Your career development may depend on your understanding of politics within your office. In office situations that may have political overtones, such as supporting or not supporting a colleague's position on an issue, you will have to learn how to make decisions without being unethical or sacrificing your self-respect.

WORKING FOR MORE THAN ONE EXECUTIVE

Working harmoniously with one executive must seem an easy task to an administrative assistant who reports to several. Instead of learning how to get along with one personality, this administrative assistant has several; instead of satisfying one set of preferences, this assistant must follow a distinct set of preferences for each executive. (See Figure 1-9.)

If one of the executives has a higher rank than the others, the administrative assistant's major responsibility is toward that individual. If all are of the same rank, the administrative assistant is responsible to all of them equally.

The administrative assistant has to be aware of the preferred work formats, the executive's goals and objectives, the pressures of each position, and each executive's work style, personal strengths, and weaknesses. Keeping all of this in balance is not easy.

Administrative assistants who work for several executives admit that setting work priorities often is a problem. Generally, the executives themselves provide this information; if not, the administrative assistant decides, either on a first-come, first-served basis, or on what the administrative assistant perceives as being more important. If a conflict of priorities occurs, the administrative assistant asks the executives to determine the order in which work will be done.

Another problem area mentioned by administrative assistants is the likelihood of showing partiality to one executive over another. For instance, if one executive is especially kind and considerate, the administrative assistant may be tempted to give that person's work preference. Ideally, the administrative assistant should view all of them equally and focus on the good qualities of each individual. Good human relations skills are a must when reporting to several different people. Treat each one with respect, conveying to each of them that his or her work is important to you. Certainly, it would be unwise to say anything derogatory about one executive to another member of the management team.

Fig. 1-9 Working for more than one executive is the norm for administrative assistants. *Photography by Alan Brown/Photonics.*

ADVANTAGES OF THE COLLEGE-TRAINED ADMINISTRATIVE ASSISTANT

Most of you reading this chapter have made office work your career choice, and wisely so. You are obtaining your training at the college level and are about to embark on your business career. You will bring to your new employer the background of business knowledge and computer skills obtained in your college program. You are well grounded in the functional areas of business—accounting, marketing, management, and so forth. Because of this study, you will have the confidence to welcome change and assume additional administrative duties when offered. At the end of your college study, you will be well qualified for today's electronic office.

As a member of the management support team, you will associate with executives at the exciting core of the company's activities. With the expanded role of the administrative assistant, you will find yourself making many decisions of an administrative nature. Your college background and your experience on the job will make you comfortable with your decisions.

For the qualified, ambitious employee, the administrative assistant position is a stepping-stone to another career. Since administrative assistants work side by side with management, the position can be viewed as a business apprenticeship. Ask any successful administrative assistant what characteristics lead to success, and you will find that working hard, assuming responsibility, continuing education, and learning every aspect of every position held are high on the list. College-trained administrative assistants know instinctively that education is a lifelong process. They recognize that continuing their education in management, computer, and supervisory skills will assist them in reaching their career goals.

Since the implementation of affirmative action programs, administrative assistants, probably more than any other group, have benefited. Many executives have looked within the firm for possible candidates for promotion. Often the executive's choice has been an administrative assistant whose quality of performance is known. Those who have a college background increase their chances for promotion to management levels.

TRENDS IN OFFICE WORK

One of the attractive features of being an administrative assistant is the relative ease with which one can become employed after years away from the field. Some former workers, anticipating reentry into business, enroll in a college course to learn new office technology and to revitalize their knowledge and skills. Those of you in this situation will find this text valuable in bringing you up-to-date on office technology and procedures.

More and more companies are offering flexible work arrangements. One example is **flextime,** a work schedule requiring employees to be on the job during specified "core hours" but providing flexibility in arrival and departure times. The flextime work schedule is approved by the employer and must total the number of hours in the company workweek. Permanent part-time work and job sharing are also possibilities. With **job sharing,** two people work at the same position, but at different times or on different shifts. Some teams work a three-day/two-day split or three days each. Some companies offer employees a **compressed workweek,** 10 hours four days a week. The 35- or 40-hour week is still considered standard.

A very popular alternative to physically being present in the office is **telecommuting.** All the electronic equipment that an employee would use in an office is installed in the employee's home. The equipment is linked to computers in a main or branch office of the company. The employee's workday is spent at home working on the automated equipment. Generally, the employee is required to attend some meetings at the company office.

Telecommuting has its advantages and disadvantages. Telecommuting is attractive to people who need to be home during the day, who may not have transportation to the office, or who may be physically disabled. On the minus side, telecommuters work in isolation. They give up the social aspects of working in an office. They risk being forgotten by management. Since they are not in day-to-day personal contact with their supervisor and colleagues, they may be overlooked for promotions.

Commuting to office work is obsolete. It is now infinitely easier, cheaper, and faster . . . to move information . . . to where people are.
—Peter R. Drucker

Summary

This chapter has described the role of the administrative assistant as an office professional. The responsibilities of the administrative assistant position range from inputting to a computer to exercising effective human relations. Technological developments have had a major impact on the profession. The role of the administrative assistant has expanded to include more administrative duties.

To be successful in the field, the administrative assistant must project a positive professional image. Three components were discussed: personal appearance, knowledge, and ethical behavior. A first impression is very important and includes professional attire, good grooming, personal hygiene, good health, and posture. A professional administrative assistant must be competent. Developing a code of ethics covering loyalty to the employer, need for confidentiality, integrity, and other areas of concern will help the administrative assistant evaluate ethical situations as they occur.

An administrative assistant works in harmony with others and makes every effort to foster a climate of mutual respect. Receiving constructive criticism is viewed by the professional as an opportunity to improve work performance. The administrative assistant most likely will work in a company with some office politics. The administrative assistant must learn how office politics affect his or her position, know the rules, and how to work within the system. Working for several executives calls for effective human relations, because each one will have a different personality and a distinct set of preferences.

The college-trained office professional has a definite advantage when entering the field. With a solid background of business course work and computer skills, the college-trained administrative assistant has the qualifications to be a partner on the administrative support team.

Administrative assistants who wish to reenter the working world continue to find opportunities for employment. To meet the special needs of some administrative assistants, a number of companies offer alternative work schedules or work-at-home arrangements. This text can serve as a valuable resource in bringing the reentering administrative assistant up-to-date on office technology and procedures.

QUESTIONS FOR DISCUSSION

1. One of the components of a positive professional image discussed in this chapter is personal appearance. What are your thoughts on face makeup, jewelry, perfume, fingernails, and their positive and/or negative influence on professional image?

2. This book recommends that the administrative assistant keep professional life and private life separate. What are your reasons for supporting or disagreeing with this recommendation?

3. Increasingly, the office work force is becoming multicultural. How will this diversity affect your behavior in the office?

4. Often administrative assistants are asked to run personal errands for the employer, serve refreshments to office visitors, and do other tasks unrelated to the technical and knowledge skills of the position. What is your opinion about doing these nontechnical tasks?

5. What do you perceive as the advantages of reporting to multiple managers? Disadvantages?

6. Rekey the following sentences using the correct form of abbreviation. Refer to the Reference Guide to correct your answers.

    a. Make no appointments for Wed., Aug. 4, but schedule an hour with Col. Ford of the U.S.M.C. on Thurs., Aug. 5.

b. The archaeologists affirmed the fact that the lost city of Akbar was built in BC 449, but the first published documentation did not appear until 1940 A.D.

c. Professor John Allen and the Rev. Alice Gray will preside at the ceremony.

d. Meet me at the Y.M.C.A. at 9 p.m.

e. The Hon. William Adams III and Professor Alfred McNabb, Jr. will speak to the student body.

*P*ROBLEMS

1. Interview an administrative assistant employed in your community to determine how office technology has changed the way in which office tasks are performed. In your discussion ask if office technology is opening up opportunities for advancement for the administrative assistant. Present your findings to the class.

2. You are about to begin your career as an administrative assistant and are in the process of completing your professional wardrobe. Your budget allows you to purchase five basic outfits. From newspaper advertisements and catalogs, prepare a display board of these outfits. Identify the style, color, and fabrics chosen. Be prepared to defend your choices.

3. From the Sunday edition of your newspaper, cut out the want ads for secretaries/administrative assistants. Compile a list of all personal requisites mentioned. Key the list at the left margin and leave room for two vertical columns to the right headed Satisfactory and Need Improvement. For each personal requisite, evaluate your personal characteristics and key an *X* in the appropriate column. If necessary, consider a plan for improvement.

*T*ECHNOLOGY APPLICATIONS

▶ TA1-1.TEM

Access the template disk, and select the TA1-1.TEM file. Complete the Basic Job Responsibilities chart shown on your screen:

1. Under "Personality Traits," key two character traits necessary to fulfill each job responsibility.

2. Under "Daily Routine," key two common tasks that are normally performed for each job responsibility.

continued

continued

3. Under "Typical Obstacles," key two routine problems you might anticipate for each job responsibility.

Use the first set of sample entries as your guide as you complete the chart.

Edit the document, proofread your final copy, and make any corrections necessary. Save the document as TA1-1.TEM, and print a hard copy for your instructor.

▶ TA1-2.TEM

Access the template disk, and select the TA1-2.TEM file. Complete The Professional Administrative Assistant Self-Evaluation Chart shown on your screen:

1. Under "Employee Behavior, Ability, or Characteristic Desired," identify each behavior that needs a solution.
2. Under "Solution Needed to Improve or Acquire Appropriate Behavior," tell briefly how you will handle the problem by completing the statement, "I will . . . " in as few words as possible.

Use the first set of sample entries as your guide as you complete the Self-Evaluation Chart.

Edit the document, proofread your final copy, and make any corrections necessary. Save the document as TA1-2.TEM, and print a hard copy for your instructor.

Chapter 2

The Office Environment

INTRODUCTION

The administrative assistant seeking employment quickly learns that opportunities exist in all types of businesses, in urban and suburban areas, and in all parts of the country. Administrative assistant positions are available in law, government, medicine, banking, manufacturing, service industries, and divisions of large corporations, such as finance or marketing. An administrative assistant interested in global business will find opportunities in multinational corporations. Another possibility is a position with the federal government in foreign service. When entering the career field, therefore, the administrative assistant is faced with a number of decisions. Some of these decisions depend simply upon personal preference, and others on the office environment, sometimes referred to as office ecology.

In making a decision about employment, there is no doubt that environmental considerations, such as the attractiveness and suitability of the workplace, play a major role. Employees want a workplace that is comfortable, safe, healthful, and pleasing to the eye. Employees who are concerned about environmental issues will want to participate in office recycling programs.

A discussion of any business office must include an analysis of the organizational structure of the firm, whether a small business or a large corporation. The organizational structure not only reveals the line of authority but also suggests the internal communication patterns. These communication patterns will have an impact on the work of the entering administrative assistant.

THE ORGANIZATIONAL STRUCTURE

As a newly hired member of the administrative-support staff, one of the first things you should do is acquaint yourself with the organizational structure of the office. You need to know the names of those who hold executive positions (the chain of command) and where your employer or group of employers fits into the management team. If you join an office that employs only one or two administrative assistants, the hierarchy will be readily apparent. If you are in a large company, however, the situation will be quite different. An organization chart like the one pictured in Figure 2-1 can give you this information.

The simplest form of organizational structure is the line organization, where authority and responsibility flow vertically from the top executive down. A variation of the line organization, known as line and staff, includes individuals in staff positions who serve as advisers or provide services to all line managers. In Chapter 1 you learned that increased competition, both domestic and international, has forced many business firms to restructure their organizational units and reduce managerial levels. This process has been referred to as **downsizing** or **flattening** of organizations. Although corporations are now experimenting with different types of organizational structures, this discussion will describe the line organization of a large manufacturing firm.

Company Officers

The administration of a company usually consists of a president (chief executive officer), an executive vice president, one or more vice presidents, a corporate secretary, and a financial officer. Each of these officers has a support staff.

The president is responsible to the board of directors for the profitable operation of the business. This position is one of liaison between the board of directors and management personnel.

The executive vice president or senior vice president is second in command in the organization. When necessary, this officer serves in place of the president and may be selected to succeed the president.

Generally there are one or more vice presidents. Each vice president is responsible for a special phase of administration, such as production or marketing.

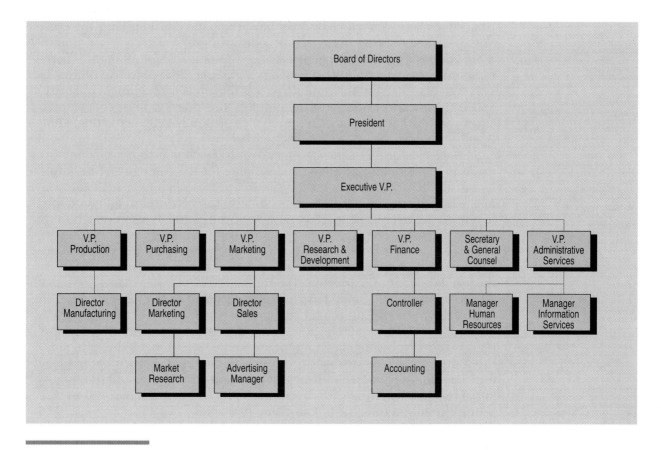

Fig. 2-1 The organization chart for the company described on these pages might look like this. Positions will, of course, vary among companies. This chart clearly identifies the levels of administrative authority in a line structure.

The corporate secretary, often an attorney, is responsible for the legal actions of the business, such as stockholders' meetings and preparing contracts. The treasurer, known in some organizations as the vice president of finance or chief financial officer, directs all monetary, budgetary, and accounting activities.

Divisions of a Company

A large company is usually organized into departments, divisions, or business units. The functions and titles of these divisions vary depending on the type of business in which the company is engaged. For example, a manufacturing firm may have such operational divisions as production, purchasing (materials management), marketing, finance, research and development, and administrative services. A retail chain may have the same divisions with the exception of a production or manufacturing department.

The Production Division controls and is responsible for all matters pertaining to the manufacture of the company's products. The objective of this division is to manufacture the product to specifications in the proper quantity and at the lowest possible cost. In addition, this division must cooperate closely with other company divisions, such as purchasing, marketing, and finance.

The Purchasing (or Materials Management) Division is responsible for procuring materials, machinery, and supplies for the company. The complexity of this division depends on the size of the company. In a small company, one person (with perhaps some clerical help) can accomplish all purchasing functions. In a very large corporation, the head of the division may be at the vice presidential level.

The Marketing Division may have two or more departments such as sales, advertising, and market research. The heads of these departments report to the vice president of marketing. The sales director (or sales manager), in addition to managing the sales department and its staff of salespeople, may be responsible for developing product policy, approving credit extensions, and preparing a sales budget. The advertising department is responsible for devising a broad advertising plan appropriate to the overall marketing program of the company. This department coordinates its advertising with the selling effort. The work of a market research department is statistical and interpretive in nature. This department gathers useful data to guide the business in marketing current products or in launching new ones.

The Finance Division handles a company's monies and accounting procedures. It records, analyzes, summarizes, and interprets the financial affairs of the company. This division is also involved in formulating company policy. The financial vice president is in charge of the finance division. This officer directs the work of the controller. The controller (sometimes spelled comptroller but always pronounced controller) usually directs all phases of accounting.

The Research and Development Division is responsible for developing better products through research. A staff of scientists and engineers works to develop new and improved products and production methods.

The Administrative Services Division serves other divisions in the internal operations of the company. The departments in this division generally report to the vice president of administrative services and include the human resources and information services departments.

In general, a human resources (or personnel) department is responsible for the interviewing, testing, hiring, training, and discharging of employees. This department also administers employee services and fringe benefits.

Some companies centralize such office functions as records management, reprographic services, mailing, and information processing by maintaining a specialized staff to perform these activities. The department is commonly called information services and the offices are located where the services are provided.

OFFICE PROTOCOL

If you are an employee in a large corporation, you will have an employee handbook that discusses company benefits, the various operating departments, company holidays, and rules by which employees must abide. A new employee is responsible for reviewing the handbook and should ask questions if a matter is not clear. A very small business or professional office would probably not have an employee handbook. You would have to ask your employer any questions you might have about employment.

In addition to written rules provided by large organizations, there is a set of unwritten rules. These rules, which have to do with certain office courtesies often involving persons of higher rank or seniority, are broadly referred to as office protocol. Consider the following examples where office protocol is a factor:

Example 1
You are a new administrative assistant in a large corporation. You recognize Mr. Alton, the president of the corporation, whom you have not met, in the hallway. He is studying a file of papers. You are about to go up to him and introduce yourself. Then it occurs to you that you should wait until your employer has the opportunity to introduce you to him.

Example 2
You and your supervisor, both women, are waiting for the elevator. You are about to enter the elevator first, then realize that your supervisor should be afforded that courtesy.

Example 3
The manager of your department has called a meeting in the conference room. You are the newest person on the staff. The manager is seated at the head of the table. You arrive five minutes early and notice that the seat to the manager's immediate right is vacant. You decide to take a seat at the middle of the table thinking a senior staff member should sit next to the manager.

Example 4
You are using the copy machine. The administrative assistant to the president of the company comes into the room and has a few copies to run. You are in the middle of your copying. You stop your copying and offer the machine to the president's administrative assistant.

In each of these situations you used good judgment in deferring to employees with higher rank or seniority. By demonstrating your respect and knowledge of office protocol, you build a foundation for positive working relationships in the office.

OFFICE DESIGN

Within the past twenty years the design of business offices has changed dramatically. Instead of the conventional office with its enclosed floor plan and heavy, traditional furniture, many companies have converted their offices to the open-plan design and use compact, modular furniture known as systems furniture. Today, in new and renovated facilities, the open-office design is the rule rather than the exception.

The Conventional Office

The traditional office is characterized by floor-to-ceiling walls, solid doors, ceiling light fixtures, and heavy wood or metal office furniture. The administrative assistant's workstation includes a wood or metal desk, chair, and credenza. Lighting, file storage, and shelving are separate components and sometimes are not easily accessible.

In a conventional office the administrative assistant's desk can be located in any one of four places. The administrative assistant assigned to an executive may have a private office, but this is becoming rare in these times of cost consciousness and space and energy conservation. It is more common to find the administrative assistant's desk either immediately inside or outside the executive's office or in a nearby location with several other administrative assistants.

The Open Plan

Instead of floor-to-ceiling walls, the open office uses movable partitions and acoustical screens as dividers. Rather than standard office furniture, colorful systems furniture with panels and panel-related components is used extensively. Individual workstations are self-contained movable units, which are far less expensive than traditional office furniture. Each station is adaptable to the particular needs of the employee and includes lighting, tools, and equipment. Paintings, thick carpets, and live or artificial plants also typify the open office. Because of the ease with which personnel and furniture can be rearranged, the reduction in square footage required by each employee, and the lower original cost outlay, the open plan makes substantial savings possible.

In addition to visible changes in the office, the open plan facilitates work flow and communication. Employees are positioned according to the flow of work and are readily visible to their supervisor. This office plan emphasizes the fact that employees are a part of a process and, thus, integral parts of the company team. An example of an open-plan office is shown in Figure 2-2.

Fig. 2-2 Open-plan office design. *Photo courtesy of TAB Products Co.*

One disadvantage of the open plan is the loss of privacy. Conversations, ringing telephones, and the humming and clicking of electronic equipment contribute to the noise level within an area. Compounding the problem is the fact that workstations are close to each other. Distractions, therefore, are frequent. One remedy is to use only established traffic patterns, such as the main aisles. Another suggestion is to rearrange the workstation furniture, placing it to face inward rather than outward from the entry to the workstation. The most effective solution, however, is for each employee to show consideration toward coworkers at all times.

Working with confidential information in an open office requires special vigilance. The administrative assistant who handles classified material should be alert to the need to turn down the display screen, place a piece of paper on the printer, and/or place working papers in a drawer when visitors or others may be close enough to read the material inadvertently.

Another disadvantage of the open office is the need for increased personal and equipment security. The greater accessibility of open spaces may require maintaining a staff of security personnel 24 hours a day.

As noted earlier, today's office is more cost-conscious than ever. In the next section you will learn how offices are responding to costs involved in waste removal and the purchase of paper products.

OFFICE RECYCLING PROGRAMS

The ecological movement of recycling papers, cans, and bottles that is increasingly common in households across the nation has reached the business office. As more Americans have become concerned about the environment and landfill shortages, businesses are seeing the merit of initiating recycling programs to benefit the environment and cut business costs.

A recent estimate by the Environmental Protection Agency is that about 80 percent of office trash is recyclable paper. Money saved from removal costs and money received from the sale of recycled materials can only improve a company's profit picture. For these reasons you can expect to be a participant in an office recycling program when you enter employment.

An effective recycling program begins with employee education on changing wasteful habits. Reducing the amount of paper used in the ordinary conduct of business is the first step. For instance, using both sides of the paper for internal memorandums and double-sided copying at the copy machine are paper reduction efforts. In the area of office supplies, refilled cartridges can be used instead of new cartridges for printers and copier toners.

Naturally, sorting and collecting paper waste and beverage cans must be part of a recycling program. Although recycling white paper (white copy paper, letterhead, and computer paper) is more profitable than colored paper, some companies do include colored paper in their program.

The key to any office recycling program, however, is employee convenience. For this reason, a dual wastebasket system is provided at each employee's workstation. Employees place white waste paper in the designated wastebasket and use the other wastebasket for all other waste.

Finally, companies must create a market for recyclable paper products by purchasing these products. As these programs grow, certainly other measures for containing and disposing of office waste will be endorsed by companies.

THE ERGONOMIC WORKSTATION

An ergonomic environment increases productivity and safeguards employee health.

Office automation has generated a number of concerns about the quality of work life for office employees. For example, most traditional office furniture is not well suited to the needs of the electronic office. Thus, a new science has been introduced which is intended to increase workers' comfort and productivity.

Ergonomics (from *ergon,* the Greek word for work) is the science of adapting equipment, work routines, and work environments to meet employees' physical and psychological needs. This science is concerned with equipment and furniture design, office layout, acoustics, color, temperature control, and other aspects of the work environment. A work area meeting the needs of employees in today's electronic office is referred to as an ergonomic workstation (see Figure 2-3).

The most important components of an ergonomic workstation are comfortable seating and proper lighting. The typical office worker sits an estimated six hours per day. The chair must distribute the weight properly, provide a backrest that will support the spine, and have short armrests that

Fig. 2-3 An ergonomic workstation.
Haworth, Inc.

are adjustable in height. Since people come in many different shapes and sizes, the chair must be adjustable; workers should be able to rest their forearms on the work tables and their feet on the floor. A chair with five legs is good for stability; for easy movement, these legs should have rolling casters. Footrests are recommended to reduce strain on the lower back and to minimize pressure on the feet and undersides of the legs.

Two systems of lighting are needed: indirect light for general lighting purposes and special lighting for the workstation. This special lighting should be adjustable for the user and is referred to as task lighting.

The desktop area should be large enough to accommodate all equipment and have an open surface for writing or reviewing references. The work surface height should be in the range of 24 inches to 33 inches. Recent developments in workstation design include a work surface height that can be changed with a flip of a button, a very important feature when a workstation is shared by several employees. A copyholder placed at eye level should be provided for ease in reading material to be keyed into the computer. To reduce static electricity prevalent in the electronic office, antistatic table and chair mats are needed at each workstation.

Workstation panels (walls) come in varying heights. Some are floor to ceiling, called movable walls. Some panels provide privacy for the seated worker. Panels should be equipped with sound-masking devices, such as special fabrics. Panels of soft colors should be selected to reduce reflections and glare. Adequate storage compartments must be included, either as part of the wall panels or as separate components of the workstation.

The workstation for a physically challenged employee must meet that employee's requirements. The Americans with Disabilities Act (ADA) requires employers to make reasonable accommodations to enable an employee with a disability to function on the job. For instance, for the employee in a wheelchair, the work surface must be an appropriate height to accommodate the wheelchair. File drawer space must be within easy reach as well. Wide aisles, appropriate entry doors, handrails, and ramp access are also necessary.

EMPLOYEE HEALTH AND SAFETY CONCERNS

Ergonomics is also concerned with the broad issues of employee health and safety in the workplace.

With the growing number of Americans using video display terminals (VDTs) during the workday, people in industry, labor, government, and science are debating the physical hazards associated with their use. Although most research studies of computer hazards discuss the possibility of radiation damage, many studies have found no problems in this respect. What constitutes a safe level of magnetic radiation exposure, however, is still uncertain. For this reason, it is recommended that VDTs be spaced at least four feet apart and that workers sit at least 28 inches from the screen. Studies conducted by the National Institute for Occupational Safety and Health (NIOSH) have found a number of health complaints among video display terminal operators.

Employees have other job-related health concerns. Office buildings today are typically constructed with fewer windows or with windows that do not open. People in these offices particularly must rely on ventilation systems to safeguard air quality. Secondhand smoke created by smoking employees is a real health concern in the office. Air quality can also be impaired by certain building insulation materials and the use of office machines that produce heat and/or emit odors. Inadequate heating and cooling systems, therefore, can affect employee health.

Other areas of concern about the effects of the work environment on employee health are office accidents and office security. Most companies take precautions to prevent accidents in the workplace, yet accidents can and do happen. To lessen accidents in the workplace, the Occupational Safety and Health Administration (OSHA) was established in 1970 to regulate safety and health standards for businesses dealing in interstate commerce. As for office security, many large companies have security systems to prevent any harm to employees or destruction of property.

Physical Ailments from the Use of VDTs

A universal complaint of video display terminal operators is eye fatigue, which is often caused by improper lighting and screen glare. The lighting in an office is often much brighter than that required for using a VDT keyboard and screen. This unnecessary brightness produces screen glare and causes eye fatigue, burning eyelids, blurred vision, and headaches. The solution to this problem is the use of adjustable task lighting, antiglare filters for display screens, and, as mentioned earlier, softer colors on walls and partitions. A 15-minute break every two hours to give operators a chance to rest their eyes is recommended. Many companies insist on a 10- to 15-minute break every hour, and some companies require eye examinations prior to employment.

A second physical complaint of operators is skeletal and muscular discomfort, such as backaches and neck aches. Complaints of wrist and finger pain are common. Keying rapidly on a computer keyboard means that you continually repeat small movements in your wrists and hands. If the wrist is incorrectly positioned at the keyboard, **carpal tunnel syndrome,** a serious wrist injury classified as a repetitive strain injury (RSI), may result. The hand, wrist, and forearm should be on the same plane. Inflammation of the tendons (tendinitis) resulting in swelling, tenderness, and weakness in the hand, elbow, or shoulder is also a frequent RSI.

In addition to using a properly adjusted chair, adjustable display screens, wrist rests, and detachable keyboards are recommended. The ideal keyboard height is 27 inches. For physical comfort, the VDT operator should look down on the screen at a 10- to 15-degree angle. For persons who use the telephone repeatedly on the job and cup the conventional receiver on the shoulder, a telephone headset will help prevent aching shoulders and sore ears. The lack of physical movement in itself can cause health problems. To combat fatigue, the VDT operator must use good posture when seated and shift positions frequently. See Figure 2-4.

Ranked third as a physical concern of workers in the automated office is noise. Word processing equipment, busy copy machines, ringing telephones,

---

ADVICE FOR VDT OPERATORS

1. Avoid working in front of a bright window.
2. Avoid working with a dark screen.
3. Take a 15-minute rest period every two hours.
4. Alternate tasks: keying, researching information, etc.
5. Stand up every half hour. Stretch.
6. Take a walk down the hall.
7. Do some exercises: turn head from one side to another, take deep breaths, make a tight fist with hands, then relax hands.
8. Look away from the screen every 15 minutes for 15–30 seconds or sit with eyes closed for a few minutes.
9. Practice good posture at your workstation.

Fig. 2-4 Ways to prevent VDT strain and fatigue.

and dot matrix and other printers contribute to the noise level in an office. Uncontrolled noise can cause headaches and earaches. Also, noise reduces the ability of employees to concentrate and increases irritability and fatigue. In fact, long exposure to noise levels over 70 decibels can permanently impair hearing. Acoustical panels and hoods on equipment, sound-absorbing ceiling tiles, floor coverings, and other sound-masking devices can reduce noise levels considerably. The use of voice–computer interaction (refer to Chapter 5) will undoubtedly compound the noise problem in the automated office.

It should be noted that not all noise in the office is offensive. A certain amount of noise is desirable, especially in open offices, to allow for speech privacy. Some companies provide piped-in music for this purpose and to serve as an aid in worker relaxation.

A Smoke-Free Environment

The right of nonsmokers in the office has been the subject of research studies and state legislation. The federal government, in passing the Occupational Safety and Health Act (OSHA, 1970), has said that employees are entitled to work in a healthful workplace. And, as a group, nonsmokers have made it known that they consider breathing secondhand smoke unhealthy. They complain of eye, nose, and throat irritations and cite research linking smoking to emphysema and lung disease. As a result, many companies are accommodating both groups—the smokers and the nonsmokers—by designating smoking and nonsmoking areas. Some companies are taking a stronger stand by instituting smoke-free buildings. More and more public buildings, such as government offices and airports, are now smoke-free environments.

Heating and Cooling Systems

For employees to be comfortable, and thus productive in their work, the office must maintain a proper balance of temperature, humidity, and air circulation. Unfortunately, there is no temperature level that will please everybody. Considering both energy conservation and employee comfort, the recommended office temperature level for heating falls in the range of 68 to 74.5 degrees Fahrenheit and for cooling 73 to 79 degrees. When determining the proper temperature level in an office, it is important to understand that normal office activities increase the production of heat. Also, the human body generates heat, and every VDT produces heat equal to that produced by one human being, not to mention the heat from office lighting systems.

How people feel at a temperature level in the office depends on the combination of temperature and humidity level, which means the relative moisture in the air. For example, a person will feel cold with a high relative humidity during the winter. The reverse is true during the summer, when a high relative humidity will make people feel warm. The comfortable range in humidity for the office is 40–60 percent moisture in the air. This moisture range also serves to reduce static electricity, a concern in the electronic office.

In addition to the right combination of temperature and humidity, the air must be circulated for employee comfort. Vent fans and blowers are used to increase air circulation. A proper filtering system is necessary to reduce air pollution caused by smoke, dust, and other undesirable elements. An optional feature of some office furniture is a desk-based air filtration system. Poor air quality leads to a tired feeling, nasal congestion, breathing difficulties, headaches, and eye itching.

Office Accidents

Although many office accidents are caused by employee carelessness, some are a result of poor company policy or company inattention to unsafe conditions.

According to Small Business Reports, one office worker out of 27 will be injured on the job at some time in his or her work career.

Falls constitute more than one-third of office accidents. Falls can occur when

1. A desk drawer or a file drawer is left open.
2. A tear in a carpet goes unnoticed.
3. An employee walks or runs on a highly waxed floor.
4. Obstructions, such as extension cords or wastebaskets, are left in the aisle.
5. Equipment is not in its regular place.
6. Hallways and stairways are poorly lighted.
7. Insecure filing ladders are used.
8. An employee rushes through a swinging door, and someone is on the other side.

Another cause of office accidents is improper lifting or overexertion. Employees suffer sprains and strains moving office equipment, furniture, office files, supplies, and so forth.

In offices where smoking is permitted, accidents involving fire can result from careless smoking habits: leaving a burning cigarette unattended or emptying an ashtray containing smoldering ashes into a paper-filled wastebasket. With the addition of computers, computer-related equipment, and small appliances to the workplace, electrical fires may occur if electrical circuits are overloaded. All small appliances, such as coffeepots, fans, and cooking appliances, should be shut off before leaving at the end of the day. The same is true for all equipment—copiers, computers, and the like.

Every office should be equipped with a sprinkler system, smoke alarms, or fire extinguishers. In the office where only a fire extinguisher is available, every employee should know where it is located and how to use it. In fact, it might be recommended that every employee have a fire extinguisher within easy reach.

Large organizations have established written procedures to follow in case of accidents. Bulletins outlining these procedures are posted where employees have access to them. Every employee should be aware of these procedures and, if necessary, follow them explicitly.

Office Security

It is not uncommon for some employees to arrive at the office very early or to stay late in order to finish a rush job, to work without interruption, or to adhere to a commuter train or car pool schedule. Working overtime (hours in addition to the regular 35- or 40-hour schedule) is standard in many offices. An hourly wage employee who is willing to work overtime is rewarded with increased income, the appreciation of management, and, frequently, a promotion to a better position.

Security guards who monitor the entrances and exits of a building are quite common in metropolitan areas and in businesses whose operation is of a classified nature. They control visitors by issuing passes; sometimes they conduct office visitors to their destinations. Security guards are on duty longer than other employees to ensure the safety of employees and property. Although the building may be monitored by television screens or by security guards, employees should not take a lax attitude about their personal property. Valuables should be kept out of sight in a safe place. Furthermore, any suspicious stranger in the office should be intercepted and questioned with "May I help you locate the proper office?"

If you are accustomed to arriving very early or expect to work late, you should inquire about the company's security measures. If there are no established procedures, you should set your own and abide by them. You may suggest to your employer the merits of an alarm system that can be activated at strategic positions in the office. Figure 2-5 provides recommendations from administrative assistants who often work after hours.

A small office or building is not likely to have a security force. If you work in such an office, avoid being the only person in the office before and after working hours and during lunch. If you must work in an unprotected office alone, particularly after hours, notify someone at your home that you are working late and call again just as you are leaving for home. If you know ahead of time that you will be working late, park your car in a well-lighted area. While working, keep all doors locked and admit no one to your office. Heighten your awareness of things around you. Be particularly sensitive to possibly dangerous situations. If you are running your printer, be aware that the sound carries, making it obvious that someone is in the office. If you hear any strange noises, call for help. Do not investigate on your own. Another suggestion is to avoid using the restroom if it is located off a hall-

Fig. 2-5 Tips for AAs who stay late (or come in early).

SECURITY RECOMMENDATIONS FROM ADMINISTRATIVE ASSISTANTS

1. Notify the guard or the human resources department that you are working late and when you expect to leave.
2. Situate yourself near others who are working late or near the alarm system.
3. Work next to a telephone and have emergency numbers handy.
4. Lock all doors leading to your work area.
5. Know when to expect custodial help and establish a cordial relationship with them.
6. Call the self-service elevator before locking your office door. Enter the elevator only after you are sure it is unoccupied. Stand next to the panel buttons.
7. Travel home in a group or have the guard escort you to your car or the source of your transportation.

way. It is not safe to enter even a locked restroom if you are the only person working late.

As you leave the building look around the parking lot before locking the building door and have your keys ready to unlock your car. Walk in lighted areas toward your car, and look in your car, especially the back seat, before getting inside. It is a safe practice always to lock your car upon entering or leaving it.

OFFICE EMERGENCIES

Office emergencies are sudden and unexpected; they require immediate attention. Delays in responding to an emergency can result in chaos, destruction of property, and/or loss of life. Large corporations have emergency policies, and employees either have a paper copy or can access it on the computer. Smaller offices post procedures for handling emergencies at conspicuous spots.

In case of fire or a bomb scare, employees must evacuate the building. Use stairways, not elevators. If you are at your desk when the alarm sounds, take your valuables with you. If you are away from your desk, do not add to the congestion by returning to your desk. Go to the nearest exit.

If you are responsible for valuable company records, put them in a safe place as quickly as possible. Supervisors leave the office last, only after they are sure all employees have vacated.

For illnesses or severe accidents, such as heart attacks, burns, or choking, emergency procedures should include a list of employees who can administer first aid. Phone numbers for the emergency squad, ambulances, physicians, the nearest hospital, and similar information should also be included. A keyed explanation of the company's location should be kept with the emergency numbers. Oxygen kits and first-aid kits are standard equipment in most offices.

If there is no established procedure for emergencies, do the research necessary and prepare a plan for your employer's approval. At the very least, take it upon yourself to (1) post emergency numbers at your desk, (2) suggest purchasing a first-aid kit, and (3) take a first-aid course.

Summary

The administrative assistant may work for a small or large firm, in an urban or suburban area, and in any type of industry or government entity. One of the first things a newly hired administrative assistant should do is become acquainted with the organizational structure of the office. This can be done by studying the organization chart and learning the names of the officers and managers of the various divisions of the firm. Newly hired administrative assistants should be aware of office protocol involving employees of higher rank or seniority.

The administrative assistant may work in a conventional office or an open-plan design. The open-plan office places the administrative assistant at a workstation that has modular furniture and panels, rather than ceiling-to-floor walls affording total privacy. In the open-plan design the administrative assistant must be considerate of other office workers with respect to noise, interruptions, and the like.

Many offices have implemented recycling programs. Administrative assistants are being asked to separate used white paper from other waste paper.

As office automation has become widely implemented, issues on the health and comfort of employees have been raised. *Ergonomics* is the science of adapting equipment, work routines, and the work environment to meet workers' physical and psychological needs. A workstation that meets the needs of employees in terms of comfort and productivity is known as an ergonomic workstation.

One of the main health concerns of employees working with video display terminals (VDTs) is eye fatigue. Another physical complaint of VDT users is skeletal or muscular discomfort. Still another is the effect of noise generated by automated equipment. A health concern for all employees in any office is air pollution from tobacco smoke, dust, and other undesirable elements. The existence of proper ventilation, heating, and cooling systems is important for employee comfort on the job.

Most offices have established safety procedures, yet office accidents do happen. In the event of an emergency, the administrative assistant should know exactly what to do and have emergency phone numbers available.

QUESTIONS FOR DISCUSSION

1. Considering your interests, abilities, and aptitudes, in which department of a business organization (production, purchasing, market research, sales, advertising, accounting, human resources, etc.) would you prefer to work? Give reasons for your choice.

2. A physically challenged employee who uses a wheelchair will be joining your department. What accommodations should be made in the workstation, electronic equipment, and accessories?

3. To avoid carpal tunnel syndrome, a repetitive strain injury, it is recommended that, when using the computer keyboard, the hand, wrist, and forearm should be on the same plane. Explain what this means. Demonstrate to the class the proper technique.

4. In view of the fact that you most likely will operate a video display terminal during your working career, how do you plan to insulate yourself from the health complaints discussed in this chapter?

5. This chapter discussed office protocol. Give other examples of violations of office protocol that occur in the office.

6. Besides those office products mentioned in this chapter, what products can you suggest that would be recyclable?

7. Punctuate the following sentences. Use your Reference Guide to correct your answers.

   a. I have worked in Dallas Texas most of my life and I believe that I do my best work here.
   b. I found the new employee to be ambitious but not offensive aggressive but not pushy and confident but not overbearing.
   c. The tests may reveal talents in music, or art, or literature.
   d. The office environment often referred to as office ecology is a subject of much discussion among managers.
   e. When an opportunity comes to serve on a committee consider it a stepping stone to promotion.

1. Interview an administrative assistant employed by a large corporation in one of its major operating divisions, such as marketing, production, or finance. Discuss how the communications within the division are channeled (hierarchy within the division), the types of communications (correspondence, memoranda, etc.), and the broad subject areas of the communications. Report your findings to the class.

2. Interview an administrative assistant who works in an open-plan office layout. Discuss any concerns about noise, distractions, lack of privacy, etc., and their effect on the administrative assistant's productivity. Report your findings to the class.

3. If you have part- or full-time employment, discuss with your employer any specific energy conservation measures being taken by the firm. Do any of these measures affect employee comfort? Discuss your findings with the class.

TECHNOLOGY APPLICATIONS

▶ TA2-1.TEM

Access the template disk, and select the TA2-1.TEM file. A summary of comments is listed from employees in your company concerning the hazards and discomforts of working overtime.

The list was prepared by your office manager, who has asked you to analyze the comments and use them to develop a set of guidelines for overtime workers—essentially, a policy for workers to follow to ensure their safety and comfort after hours.

The guidelines you develop should address the key headings in the summary. Try to pick up or adapt the keyed materials as much as possible. Save the document as TA2-1.TEM, and print a hard copy for your instructor. Your finished guidelines will be distributed to all employees and posted on all bulletin boards. *Hint:* Consider labeling it "Notice to All Employees."

▶ TA2-2.TEM

Access the template disk, and select the TA2-2.TEM file. It contains a general format that you can use to develop a set of emergency procedures for everyone in your office.

Less than ten years old, your firm is growing at a rather fast rate. As its revenues and profits have grown, so too has its personnel. Ten years ago B&G Services started with only four employees—two of them partners and co-owners—in a small office. Now B&G boasts several dozen employees and is planning to open a branch office.

continued

continued

Along with the growth has come additional responsibility. And with the responsibility, additional need for control—for the regulations, policies, and procedures that management needs to control a business enterprise and that employees need to guide them in their work. Often the most important need is also the most overlooked: *the need for emergency procedures.* By preparing for those "What if . . . ?" situations, you may save the company money and time, and you may even save lives.

On one sheet only, your final emergency procedures chart should address three types of emergencies: (1) fires, (2) bomb scares, and (3) accidents and medical crises. What should employees know, and what should they do, in the event of such disasters? Be sure to address issues such as evacuating the building, protecting company records, handling personal valuables, and having emergency telephone numbers handy. Keep in mind that some employees are physically challenged; they too must be carefully considered. And what about protecting computer information? Do you think you should advise employees to take time, in the event of fire, for example, to try to protect files?

Your instructor may provide additional directions for you to follow in developing your emergency guidelines.

Chapter 3

Time and Task Management

LEARNING OBJECTIVES

After studying this chapter and completing the activities, you will be able to:

1. Maintain a well-organized work area.
2. Describe electronic and paper methods used for calendaring and scheduling.
3. Follow principles on the proper use of time.
4. Discuss the various office memory devices.
5. Identify strategies for handling on-the-job stress.

INTRODUCTION

The responsibilities of an administrative assistant are many and varied. In addition to the variety of duties for one particular position, responsibilities also vary from one position to another. The complexity of assignments can vary as well. Working for more than one executive increases the administrative assistant's duties. An administrative assistant, therefore, must know the principles of work organization and make every minute count in the workday. A lackadaisical attitude regarding time can be a source of irritation to employers and can directly affect the performance of your work.

Software programs are available to save time and make the administrative assistant more productive. Traditional manual records such as desk calendars, appointment books, and various reminder systems can be handled electronically. These programs are discussed in this chapter along with the paper systems used as office memory devices and those used in recording appointments. Because administrative assistants often work under time pressure, this chapter also includes a section on job-related stress: its causes, symptoms, and remedies.

THE WORKING DAY

Administrative assistants may work from 8 to 5, 9 to 5, or any other variation of hours specified by an employer. They may follow a flextime schedule (refer to page 14) or work part-time, perhaps 15 to 20 hours a week. Because the administrative assistant's schedule is arranged to suit the employer's convenience, it may be different from that of other employees in the same office. At the same time, it must constitute a full workweek in terms of hours. Vacations may also be irregular, because an administrative assistant must defer to the employer's schedule by remaining on the job when the work load is heaviest. An administrative assistant to several executives must be available to all of them during regular office hours.

THE ADMINISTRATIVE ASSISTANT'S WORK AREA

An administrative assistant's work area is usually L-shaped. To work efficiently, with the least amount of time, effort, and frustration, a well-organized and well-equipped workstation is necessary. The objective is to have everything needed to accomplish daily tasks either on the desk, in the desk, or within easy reach (considered 23 inches) of the administrative assistant.

Stacks of papers are the leading cause of desk clutter.

A flat, uncluttered surface is the best work area. You should find the recommendations given below helpful. If you are left-handed, the reverse of some of the statements is true. The photograph in Figure 3-1 shows

Fig. 3-1 The arrangement of materials and equipment on traditional office furniture.

the arrangement of materials and equipment on traditional office furniture.

1. Place an in/out basket for mail on the right-hand side of the desk or work surface. A three-tiered basket is useful for papers ready to be filed. This basket can be attached to the wall panel.

2. Keep a message pad and pencil beside the telephone. Place the telephone within reach to the left of your chair. Answer the telephone with your left hand, so the right hand is free to write down messages.

3. Place reference manuals at the front of the work surface or on a shelf.

4. Keep a desk calendar, stapler, and tape dispenser at the front of the work area.

5. Place your computer and printer on a separate table, on an extension of the desk, or, if modular systems furniture is used, on the work surface.

6. Place the copyholder at eye level on either side of your keyboard.

7. Keep electric cords out of sight.

Drawer space should also be organized. Keep pencils, pens, rubber bands, paper clips, and the like in special compartments in a top drawer. Keep stationery in a deep drawer in an organizer that has slots for different types of paper. For instance, you might store company letterhead in the first bin, plain letter-quality paper in the second, memo sheets in the third, and so on. A place for envelopes is often provided at the front of a stationery organizer. Position envelopes with their flaps down and facing the front of the drawer so that they are in the proper position for placement in a typewriter or printer. Use a deeper desk drawer or, in the case of modular systems furniture, a storage compartment for files that are referred to daily. These files include work in process and other types of reference files.

Before leaving for the day, you should remove all papers from your work surface, secure or lock your computer, including diskettes, and lock your desk. In fact, some companies have a policy requiring all work surfaces be clear at the end of the day. A vacant drawer at the bottom of the desk is a good place to put unfinished work. In addition to locking the desk at the end of the day, lock the desk when you plan to be away from your workstation to safeguard any material of a confidential nature.

In the course of your day, you may work intermittently in your employer's office or another area. When working away from your desk, take all necessary materials and supplies with you so that work can be done as quickly as possible. If you do not have a telephone answering machine or a call forwarding feature on your telephone, ask a coworker to answer your phone and take any messages in your absence.

AREAS OF RESPONSIBILITY

Work as an administrative assistant can be divided into three areas: (1) routine duties, (2) assigned tasks, and (3) original work.

All positions involve some routine duties, although automation has reduced the amount of routine work necessary. Routine duties are completed without employer direction. Examples of routine work include filing, answering the telephone, operating the copy machine, sorting the mail, replenishing supplies, and locking up confidential materials at the end of the day.

Assigned tasks are given to the administrative assistant by the employer. These tasks can be simple, complex, or a mixture of both. In any event, assigned tasks are tasks that must be done, usually in a limited amount of time. Making travel reservations, making a bank deposit, or getting technical material from the library are examples of assigned tasks.

Original work is defined here as that area of responsibility in which the administrative assistant displays initiative and creativity in assisting the employer. Work that demonstrates forethought or requires following an activity through to its conclusion is typical of this category. As you handle assigned and routine tasks more efficiently, you will have more time for service of an original nature. Such service earns attention that may lead to promotion.

The administrative assistant can increase her or his scope of responsibility by demonstrating competence in initiating supportive activities. For example, an administrative assistant who wants to perform work of an original nature should anticipate requests for data that would support a business report and supply it before the employer requests it. Reviewing and evaluating software programs that will enhance job performance is an example of original work. Training a new employee on equipment or use of a software program also falls into this category. In addition, the creative administrative assistant who notices an important article in a magazine would call it to the employer's attention.

Creativity is not a trait one inherits. Creativity can be nurtured, and there are several ways this can be done. First, gather ideas and develop an "idea bank" for yourself; then brainstorm with these ideas. Second, learn to be independent in your thinking and in your assessment of office problems. Third, continue to expand your thinking by reading about office technology and the office environment. Always be curious about new developments and be ready to recommend changes that will increase your productivity.

ELECTRONIC ORGANIZERS AND TIME MANAGERS

Technology has provided the means to reduce or even eliminate the traditional paper records needed to organize work and schedule appointments. Software programs (often referred to as applications) are available that replace the paper desk calendar for making appointments and the traditional card file of names, addresses, and telephone numbers. Having these capabilities in the computer system makes it possible for the administrative assistant to save time and be more productive in maintaining this information.

For example, if a client calls and requests an appointment with your employer, and you are working at the computer, you can exit what you are doing and enter the appointment in the electronic calendar. Any notes about the appointment can be entered next to the date selected. Like a paper desk calendar, the electronic calendar can be displayed and printed for a day, a week, or a month.

A typical task for an administrative assistant has been to maintain a card file of names, addresses, and telephone numbers of persons the employer regularly contacts. Cards are filed alphabetically in a box or on a Rolodex holder. This same information can now be entered into the computer and updated as needed, ready for instant retrieval. This electronic address book is an example of a database, a feature of software commonly used by the administrative assistant. For an example of a computerized address list, see Figure 3-2.

Fig. 3-2 A computerized address list.

	File	Edit	Format	Graphing	Search	Options	Help

	Name, L	Name, F	Address	ZIP	Phone
1:	Archer	Maria	5467 Harper	78623	555-6734
2:	Carlock	Adam	735 Akron	78643	555-2727
3:	Carlson	Nancy	258 Hunt	78623	555-6938
4:	Esteban	Anna	6343 Sunset	78633	555-1438
5:	Harlan	Winston	6943 Sunset	78633	555-5586
6:	Jackson	Ben	6545 Hunt	78623	555-6846
7:	Jerrell	Chester	874 East Way	78623	555-7945
8:	Johnson	Beth	9353 Estes	78623	555-4848
9:	Li	Mark	3463 Allen	78642	555-9077
10:	Macky	Elaine	9365 Allen	78642	555-5897
11:	Morris	Robert	845 Cameron	78643	555-3645
12:	Orin	Mark	567 East Way	78633	555-1224
13:	Robinson	Ellen	2689 Erin	78643	555-2334
14:	Savoy	Sara	125 Oak	78623	555-7564
15:	Subick	Art	543 Thomas	78623	555-5954
16:	Zorn	Tom	643 Edwards	78623	555-9494
17:					
18:					

A time-management aid traditionally kept on paper by the administrative assistant and the employer is the to-do list, a list of tasks to be done. Each task on the to-do list is assigned a priority value. A personal information management (PIM) software program can be used to organize, classify tasks by priority, and track (keep track of) important parts of an employee's work. A calendar is provided for scheduling, tracking telephone calls, meetings, and to-do items. Besides replacing the traditional paper to-do list, PIMs also replace the paper tickler or reminder system. (A more complete discussion of computers and software for time management is provided in Chapter 5.) Figure 3-3 shows a typical computer screen of PIM software.

MANAGING TIME: THE PAPER PROCESS

Ask administrative assistants to describe their typical workday and chances are they will say, "We can't. No two days are alike." They will probably add

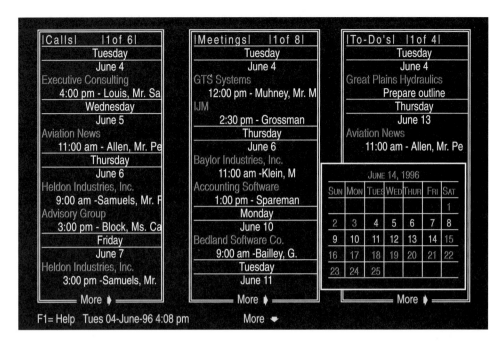

Tuesday
June 4
Executive Consulting
4:00 pm - Louis, Mr. Sa
Wednesday
June 5
Aviation News
11:00 am - Allen, Mr. Pe
Thursday
June 6
Heldon Industries, Inc.
9:00 am -Samuels, Mr. F
Advisory Group
3:00 pm - Block, Ms. Ca
Friday
June 7
Heldon Industries, Inc.
3:00 pm -Samuels, Mr.
━━ More ▶ ━━
F1= Help   Tues 04-June-96 4:08 pm

|Meetings| |1 of 8|
Tuesday
June 4
GTS Systems
12:00 pm - Muhney, Mr. M
IJM
2:30 pm - Grossman
Thursday
June 6
Baylor Industries, Inc.
11:00 am -Klein, M
Accounting Software
1:00 pm - Spareman
Monday
June 10
Bedland Software Co.
9:00 am -Bailley, G.
Tuesday
June 11
━━ More ▶ ━━
More ◄

|To-Do's| |1 of 4|
Tuesday
June 4
Great Plains Hydraulics
Prepare outline
Thursday
June 13
Aviation News
11:00 am - Allen, Mr. Pe

JUNE 14, 1996

SUN	MON	TUES	WED	THUR	FRI	SAT
						1
2	3	4	5	6	7	8
9	10	11	12	13	14	15
16	17	18	19	20	21	22
23	24	25				

━━ More ▶ ━━

Fig. 3-3 A computer screen showing calls, meetings, a to-do list, and the calendar.

that variety is what makes an administrative assistant's position so interesting. This variety, however, often brings a certain pressure of time to the position.

When your work load is heavy and there are many demands on your time, you may sense that your use of time is getting out of control. You may be having difficulty getting the important work done. Take a minute and plan a work analysis, consider what activities are time wasters, and decide to follow a daily work plan. The processes described in this section (with the exception of the daily work plan) apply also to the administrative assistant who uses a PIM software program. Administrative assistants need to know the principles and procedures involved in managing time.

Work Analysis

The first step in organizing time and work is to make an analysis of your duties. This analysis can be done on a computer or handwritten as shown in Figure 3-4. For at least two weeks keep a record of each duty you perform and the amount of time given to it, or record only those duties performed at predetermined time intervals. Establish a coding system to streamline your work analysis. For example, use "IM" for incoming mail, "K" for keying, etc. A careful study of this sheet will show you where you are not using time to the best advantage. For instance, you may see that you spend too much time searching for information or performing other routine tasks that could be delegated to someone else. Compare your work analysis to your job description. It has been estimated that most workers spend 80 percent of their time on tasks that are less important to the company and only 20 percent of their

Fig. 3-4 A work analysis classifies tasks and indicates the starting and completion times for each.

WORK ANALYSIS SHEET								
Date: _October 15_			Position _Administrative Asst. to V-P_					
TIME		TASK	CLASSIFICATION					TOTAL TIME	EVALUATION
Start	Complete		Outside Contact	Intraco. Contact	Subor-dinates	Adm. Matters	Routine		
8:00	8:10	Housekeeping duties					✓	10	Total time necessary to maintain standards
8:10	8:15	Telephone confirmation of meeting	✓					5	
8:15	9:05	Open, sort, distribute mail		✓	✓		✓	50	Train Susan to distribute
9:05	9:52	Daily Briefing		✓		✓		47	Suggest holding of telephone calls
9:53	11:30	Keying of memos, letters					✓	97	
12:30	1:00	Explanation of monthly report preparation			✓			30	No need to replicate

time on tasks that are of the greatest value. You want to give the tasks of greatest value your utmost effort and concentration.

Time Wasters

The work analysis sheet will identify weaknesses in your use of time and indicate where changes need to be made. You may find that one of the biggest robbers of time is the telephone. The trend today is for employers to answer their phones directly and use telephone answering machines or voice mail (see Chapter 8, page 199). This trend should reduce the time administrative assistants spend answering phones, taking messages, transferring calls, and the like.

Any interruption of the employer by the administrative assistant or vice versa wastes time. You can reduce interruptions by communicating with your employer via the computer or paper notes and by consulting each other only at convenient times during the day.

Socializing with coworkers is another time thief. Certainly some employee socialization is acceptable and even encouraged in offices, but it should never occur at the expense of getting work done. In open-plan offices this problem is more acute than in offices of conventional design.

Other wasters of time include:

Waiting for work

Waiting for others

Working with incomplete information

Poor instructions

Reworking documents because of errors or omissions

Lost items

Failure to delegate

Lack of a daily plan

Equipment breakdowns

Lack of proper tools

Unclear deadlines

Procrastination

Be mindful, too, of such subtle time wasters as filing papers that could be thrown away, writing unnecessarily wordy letters and memos, duplicating information on several company forms, or recording information that is no longer valid or necessary. Concentrate your energy and your time on those activities that lead to increased efficiency and work productivity, activities that are most valuable to your employer and to yourself. Learn more about your office equipment and what it can do to save you time.

Don't make things more complicated than they need to be. Simpler is usually faster.

Daily Work Plan

The real key in managing time is to manage yourself. Every administrative assistant should make and follow a daily work plan. A daily work plan is a to-do list for one day, but with time parameters added. It also provides objectives and evaluation sections. This plan should be prepared the night before or first thing in the morning.

A daily work plan requires setting objectives for the day, listing the work to be done based on the objectives, and assigning priorities to the work. A sample priority rating is "A" or "1" for work to be done immediately; "B" or "2" for work to be done today; and "C" or "3" for work to be done when convenient. Ascertain priorities according to your employer's requests or according to built-in schedules stating when weekly reports are due. Check off each item on your plan as you complete it. Figure 3-5 is an example of a handwritten daily work plan. In preparing your daily work plan, you should follow the principles on the proper use of time given in Figure 3-6 on page 47.

Most administrative assistants and employers prepare a daily work plan. Most employer/administrative assistant teams go over their respective plans at the beginning of the day and make adjustments as necessary. If the plans do not agree, usually the employer's plan is followed. Administrative assistants learn quickly that they must be flexible with their plans and adapt when emergencies arise. If your employer has no such plan, you can suggest a plan by example. For instance, you can submit your plan the first thing in the morning, and through give-and-take discussion, a daily plan for the team can be made. Then follow this practice on a daily basis.

Many office forms, such as the work analysis sheet shown in Figure 3-4 and the daily work plan in Figure 3-5, are handwritten. To ensure that your handwriting is legible, place both elbows on the desk surface and use proper

An efficient administrative assistant does the job right. An effective administrative assistant does the right job correctly.

DAILY WORK PLAN

Date: _October 16_

Priority Code:
1 – Urgent
2 – Do today
3 – Do when convenient
4 – Do when all other duties
    are accomplished

Goals 1. _Complete research for report_
2. _Select meeting time/place_
3. _Compare notification letters_
4. _____

TIME	TASK	PRIORITY	EVALUATION
8:00	Open, sort, distribute mail	2	Delegate to Susan
8:30	Library research	1	
9:00	" "	1	
9:30	Compiling data	1	
4:30	Back up active computer files		

writing tools: a sharp pencil or ballpoint pen. Write uniformly: allow proper spacing between letters and words, and make lowercase letters one-third the height of capital letters. Be a good judge of your penmanship. If you cannot read your own handwriting when it is cold (24 hours old), you can be sure that others will have a difficult time reading it.

Assignment to More Than One Executive

Most likely you will work for a team of executives, possibly four or six. You should check with each individual daily to determine his or her work priorities. Sometimes it is difficult to decide which job to do first, second, and so forth. There are guidelines, however. If one executive holds a higher position than another, generally the higher-ranked executive's work takes precedence, unless a matter is of such urgency that it must take priority. If they are at the same management level, or if you are in doubt about which work takes precedence, ask them to assign priorities as a matter of routine. Some administrative assistants use a system whereby executives complete a priority slip when assigning work so that there is no question about the order in which work is to be completed. If there appears to be a conflict, you may have to rely on your own judgment to determine priorities. If you work swiftly and are able to do work within reasonable time limits, the question of priorities is often academic.

Periodic Peak Loads

A study of the flow of work for a one-month period may indicate patterns of fluctuation. For instance, Mondays traditionally bring heavier mail and, con-

PRINCIPLES ON THE PROPER USE OF TIME

1. Plan each project thoroughly; have complete instructions before beginning. Know what is expected and when.
2. Work on the item of highest priority first. Avoid handling several projects at once.
3. Make the easy decisions quickly.
4. Initiate a plan to control interruptions.
5. Set deadlines; allow yourself a cushion of 20 percent more time than you think will be necessary.
6. Allow some time, perhaps on a weekly basis, to clear out clutter.
7. Jot down notes or make computer entries of business conversations that are essential for recall.
8. Delegate nonessential tasks, if possible.
9. Get unpleasant tasks out of the way.
10. Complete the most complex tasks during your best working time.
11. Complete routine work when your momentum is low.
12. Complete the hardest tasks in uninterrupted blocks of time, if possible.
13. Group similar tasks, such as making copies or telephone calls.
14. Stay with a task until it is completed.
15. Pick up paperwork only once and finish the task immediately. (Time managers estimate that over 50 percent of daily paperwork can be disposed of in the first handling.)
16. Divide long tasks into manageable parts and complete one part at a time.
17. Do tasks right the first time.
18. Put spare moments to work for you.
19. Coordinate your daily plan with your employer's work plan.
20. Learn to say no to tasks that do not meet your employer's objectives.
21. Reward yourself when you complete a major task.
22. To give yourself momentum, begin the day with a task you can complete quickly.

Fig. 3-6 The real key in managing time is to manage yourself.

sequently, heavier word processing assignments. Thus, other Monday plans should be light. An administrative assistant needs to anticipate work loads. Think ahead by making weekly or monthly to-do lists. Take advantage of slack times. Slack periods are ideal for transferring files, updating database files, and duplicating sets of frequently requested materials. Many administrative assistants, when overloaded with work, know someone in the office who has slack work periods and who will help get the work done. Then, when the situations are reversed, the administrative assistants return the favors. Reciprocity is not, however, a viable alternative for the administrative assistant who is always busy and cannot offer assistance to anyone else.

OUTSIDE ASSISTANCE

Even with the best planning, emergencies will occur. The unexpected absence of a staff member, for example, may upset the normal functioning of the office force. All at once you may be faced with a difficult job and not enough time in which to perform it.

You exhibit good judgment by requesting temporary help if a situation warrants such action. Obtain your supervisor's permission to contact an agency that supplies experienced temporary help. Among such agencies are Manpower, Inc.; Kelly Services, Inc.; and Olsten Temporary Services. An administrative assistant who supervises temporary workers should acquaint them with company hours, facilities, office procedures, and other office employees. An office temporary should be given a copy of the company's procedures manual and forms guide. The work for the temporary person should also be well organized so that time is not wasted waiting for information.

Sometimes work requires professional skills or abilities beyond those of the administrative assistant, or perhaps the job is of such size that it can be done more quickly and less expensively outside the office. In such cases, with the employer's permission, the administrative assistant turns to a special service agency. These agencies prepare and mail multiple copies of original letters, obtain hotel and travel reservations, take full recordings of meetings and prepare transcripts, reproduce materials, furnish and maintain mailing lists, or provide competent help for other jobs of a specialized or technical nature.

On completion of the work, the administrative assistant writes a note in the desk manual (see page 50) identifying the agency or the individuals employed. Also, a record of the total cost and a brief evaluation of the service should be kept for future guidance.

SUPERVISION OF SUBORDINATES

The administrative assistant may be assigned one or more full-time assistants or temporary helpers. With relatively inexperienced workers, the administrative assistant assumes the role of teacher. In this capacity, you must provide the worker with opportunities to develop efficient work habits and teach the proper use of equipment and facilities.

When assigning work, give thorough directions. There should be no doubt as to what is to be done. If the work is complicated, written instructions should supplement oral directions. Periodically check on the progress of the work so that mistakes are avoided. Assignments of varying difficulty give subordinates the opportunity to show their level of skill.

In addition to being a teacher, the administrative assistant is also a student—a student of human behavior. The administrative assistant studies the abilities of subordinates. It is your responsibility to motivate them so that they work to their full potential and take pride in their work. As a supervisor, you will complete an employee evaluation form similar to that shown in Figure 3-7. A supervisor gives credit and praise when due. If criticism

EMPLOYEE EVALUATION

Name of Employee _Joe A. Morgan_   Department _Human Resources_

Directions: Read over each section carefully. Appraise employee's performance by placing a check mark in the box below the comment that applies to the employee. Check only one box in each section. Appraisers are encouraged to use the remarks section for additional comments pertinent to the employee's evaluation.

KNOWLEDGE OF THE JOB

Technical job information and practical know-how	Proficient on job; makes the most of experiences--a "self-starter"	Rarely needs assistance but asks for it to save time	Knows job fairly well; regularly requires supervision and instruction	Job knowledge limited; shows little desire or ability to improve
	✓	☐	☐	☐

Remarks: _has thorough understanding of machines_

QUALITY OF WORK

	Consistently does an excellent job; errors very rare	Usually does a good job; seldom makes errors	Work is usually passable; regularly requires reminder to do a better job	Doesn't care; work is inferior in many respects
	☐	✓	☐	☐

Remarks: _proofreads thoroughly_

QUANTITY OF WORK

	Exceptionally fast; efficiency unusually high	Fast; usually does more than expected	Turns out the required amount of work–seldom more	Slow; output below minimum requirements
	☐	✓	☐	☐

Remarks: _____

ADAPTABILITY

Mental alertness; ability to meet changed conditions	Learns new duties easily; meets changed conditions quickly	Grasps new ideas if given a little time; adjusts to new conditions	Routine worker; requires detailed instructions on new duties and procedures	Slow to learn; requires repeated instructions; unable to adjust to changes
	✓	☐	☐	☐

Remarks: _____

RELIABILITY

Confidence in employee to carry out all instructions conscientiously and completely	Dependable; on time, does what you want, when you want it	Conscientious; follows instructions with little need for follow-up	Generally follows directions, but needs occasional follow-up	Requires frequent follow-up, even on routine duties; apt to put things off
	☐	☐	✓	☐

Remarks: _capable of formatting documents without instructions._

Summary Statement: _Mr. Morgan is highly productive and extremely creative in his work._

Signature and Position of Evaluator: _P.B. Schultz, Supervisor_

Fig. 3-7 A sample employee evaluation.

becomes necessary, however, a supervisor discusses the work, not the worker. For more information on supervision, refer to Chapter 25.

PAPER MEMORY DEVICES

An administrative assistant needs a good memory to maintain office efficiency. Several paper memory aids are described here.

Desk Manual

Every administrative assistant should compile a loose-leaf desk manual and keep it up-to-date. It should cover each duty, responsibility, and procedure of that particular position. It is also a useful place to keep frequently needed company information. Chapter 24 of this book explains the contents and organization of such a manual.

Desk Calendar

The employer and administrative assistant should have individual desk calendars for notes and reminders, business as well as personal. As discussed earlier in this chapter, these calendars can be electronic. To supplement the employer's calendar, an administrative assistant usually maintains an appointment book, discussed later in this chapter.

At the end of the year get next year's desk calendar ready. Using your present calendar as a guide, mark important dates, meeting times, and other similar information on the new calendar. If deadlines for projects are known or vacations set, note these on the calendar as well. Keep your employer's old calendar for one year or until you are sure its notations are of no further use.

Tickler File

The most widely used paper reminder system, filed according to dates, is the tickler. This efficient office aid derives its name from the accounting term *tick,* meaning to check off. A **tickler** is an accumulating record of items of work to be done on future days. Items are ticked off when completed. The administrative assistant's desk calendar can be used as a tickler, though calendar page space is limited. File folders can be used as a tickler system as well.

The most flexible tickler is a file box with 3-by-5-inch colored guide cards, as shown in Figure 3-8. The file box has cards for each month, one to three sets of date guides (numbered from 1 to 31), and one card labeled "Future Years." The guide for the current month is placed at the front of the file, and the set of cards for each day in that month is placed behind it.

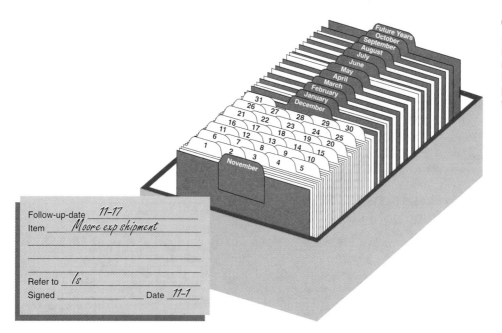

Fig. 3-8 Using this box system, the administrative assistant enters a tickler item concerning an express shipment due before the end of the week.

Follow-up-date _11–17_
Item _Moore exp shipment_
_____
_____
Refer to _Is_
Signed _____ Date _11–1_

Additional date guides may be placed behind the next one or two months. An item of future concern is written on an individual card, and the card is filed behind the guides for the proper month and date. If the item is to be followed up several months later, it is dropped behind the month guide. It will be filed according to date when the month comes to the front.

Since an item is often forwarded and reforwarded, write the follow-up date in pencil so that it can be erased and changed when necessary. In fact, since the tickler is a type of note, the entire item is usually written in pencil. Annual events, such as due dates for taxes and insurance premiums, are re-filed for next year as soon as they are ticked off.

It is the administrative assistant's responsibility to remind the employer of tickler items. An oversight can be very embarrassing and costly to the firm. You should use the tickler as a memory aid to remind yourself of work to be done, to tick off items accomplished, and to record work for a future date.

As a matter of routine, you should check the tickler file when making the next day's work plan. After this check, place that day's guide in the file at the end of the numbered guides for that month, leaving the following day's numbered guide at the front of the file. Near the end of the month, arrange tickler items for the next month behind the appropriate numbered guides.

Pending File

The pending file is another memory aid. It is a file folder in which the administrative assistant temporarily holds papers concerning matters that are undecided or unfinished. It is kept at your workstation, in the employer's desk, or in some other place nearby. Be careful not to isolate letters in the pending file that should be available in the regular files. This can be avoided by making extra copies of incoming and outgoing letters and filing the originals in their respective files. If a matter that is pending does not involve a letter, prepare a special note about the matter and place it in the pending file. Make a regular check of the pending file to determine which matters to call to the employer's attention. Make a notation regarding pending matters on the daily work plan. Any letters that have been answered should be released to the regular files and extra copies should be discarded.

Chronological File

Some administrative assistants make an extra copy of everything they key in order to maintain a complete chronological file of their work. This file is kept in the administrative assistant's desk. Copies for this file are sometimes made on colored paper for easy identification in filing. Many a problem has been solved by this ready reference file. If you are also in charge of the employer's files, it is a good practice to note the location of the employer's file copy on the chronological copy.

The length of time you keep copies in the chronological file is a matter of preference. Some administrative assistants keep copies in the chronological file in their desk file for three months. Copies of older correspondence are kept in a file cabinet nearby. (See Chapter 7, page 155, for additional information on the chronological file.)

Desk Reference Files

The administrative assistant can organize office work more efficiently by keeping desk reference files. If you need a paper file less than twice a day, it can be stored out of your reach, but still within easy access when you are at your workstation. Store the most frequently used files in drawers within easy reach. Such files include the most recent copies for the chronological file, work in process, and current project records. The administrative assistant keeps these reference files in a deep desk drawer. Desk reference files are frequently needed files; they can be planned only after you are thoroughly familiar with the job.

THE EMPLOYER'S APPOINTMENT RECORDS

A busy employer may see a number of visitors in the course of each day; therefore, in order to keep the office running smoothly, you must keep a manual (paper) or electronic record of daily appointments.

Some executives use their computers to schedule appointments and meetings. In the case of meetings, after keying in the date, time, and names of the participants, the computer system checks schedules of the participants and indicates the best date and time for the meeting. A note of confirmation is then placed in each person's electronic mailbox (see Chapter 8). The administrative assistant, however, maintains the master appointment schedule and enters any appointments and/or meeting dates the executive makes on that schedule.

Scheduling Appointments

The effective administrative assistant follows the employer's personal preferences in scheduling appointments, keeps a close watch on the employer's time, and uses good judgment in maintaining the appointment schedule. Appointments are arranged in different ways. For example:

1. Appointments may be scheduled on a recurring basis. Using a calendar from the previous year, the administrative assistant records on the current calendar at the beginning of the year the regularly scheduled conferences of boards or corporation committees at which the employer's presence is necessary. Additional recurring appointments are scheduled as new commitments are made.

2. The employer or the administrative assistant may schedule an appointment over the telephone.

3. The executive or the administrative assistant may schedule an appointment by mail.

4. The executive may ask the administrative assistant to schedule a follow-up conference with someone who is currently in the office.

5. The administrative assistant may schedule a definite appointment with a caller who happens to come in when the employer is out.

6. The administrative assistant may arrange an appointment outside the office for the executive with individuals not associated with the company.

If the office uses personal information management (PIM) software, the administrative assistant and/or the employer enters all appointments into a computer terminal. The electronic calendar keeps track of the employer's appointments. On a daily or a weekly basis, the administrative assistant depresses the appropriate keys to print a record of a specific day's or week's appointments. The administrative assistant may also view the appointment schedule on the computer screen. If electronic calendaring is not available, the administrative assistant handles appointments manually as described below.

Always obtain the telephone number of the person making an appointment so that he or she can be contacted if the appointment has to be canceled.

In most offices, an appointment book is used to record the employer's appointments (see Figure 3-9). Note that appointments are for half-hour

Fig. 3-9 An example of an appointment book.

APPOINTMENTS
FRIDAY, APRIL 9, 19--

Time	Engagements	Memorandums
9:00	Mr. Smith, ext. 245	HR - Call DC Mohr re contract
9:30		
10:00	} Meeting with sales personnel in third floor conference room	See Jane Kumar for annual sales graph
10:30		
11:00		
11:30	Mrs. Alice Carter of ABC Systems, 555-8297	annex blueprints
12:00	Dr. Pardi, ext. 131	Hampton specifications

intervals. Calendars are also available in 15-minute segments. In maintaining this book, you need to follow the four W's of scheduling appointments as shown below:

WHO the person is—the name, business affiliation, and telephone number.

WHAT the person wants—an interview for a position, an opportunity to sell a product or to discuss business, etc. (Indicate any materials that will be needed for the appointment.)

WHEN the person wants an appointment and how much time it will take.

WHERE an appointment is to be held, if other than in the executive's office. (Be sure to include the address and room number.)

If the individual making the appointment is in the office at the time of scheduling, the administrative assistant gives that person a written reminder.

The administrative assistant reminds the employer of appointment commitments the day before and the first thing the next morning to avoid any communication breakdown. Pertinent information and files concerning the appointments are placed on the employer's desk along with an appointment schedule. Some employers prefer a keyed list or computer printout of the day's appointments that also includes a list of to-do items or reminders such as that shown in Figure 3-10. This list can be placed on the employer's desk the day before or the first thing in the morning. The list may be on 8 1/2-by-11-inch paper or on a 3-by-5-inch card.

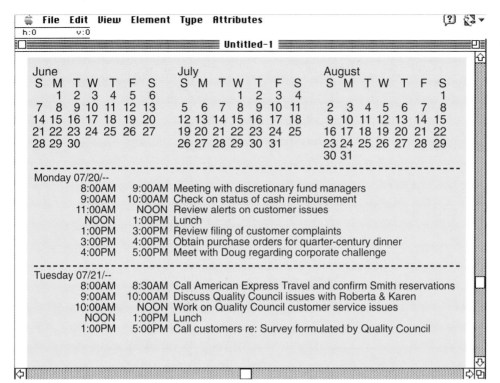

Some employers prefer a separate keyed list or computer printout of matters to be handled that day. The appropriate files are then attached to this list. Any matters not completed that day are carried over to the next day's list.

Another useful practice is to include any questions you may have on the list of reminders that you key for your employer. The executive can write the answers directly on the sheet and leave it on the desk. In this way you can get answers without disturbing your employer.

The executive generally keeps a pocket diary or a small electronic appointment calendar as a convenient reference when attending meetings or visiting outside offices. In addition to the official appointment book you maintain and the pocket calendar retained by your employer, there may also be an informal calendar on your employer's desk. To avoid conflicts in scheduling appointments, check all calendars on a daily basis. Always check with the executive after meetings held outside the office to determine if any appointments have been made.

The administrative assistant who works for several executives maintains a separate list of appointments either on a computer or in a record book for each (see Figure 3-11). The procedure for scheduling appointments for several executives is the same as that described in the foregoing paragraphs.

Keep appointment books, calendars, and/or computer printouts of your employer's appointment schedules for at least one year. They provide an ex-

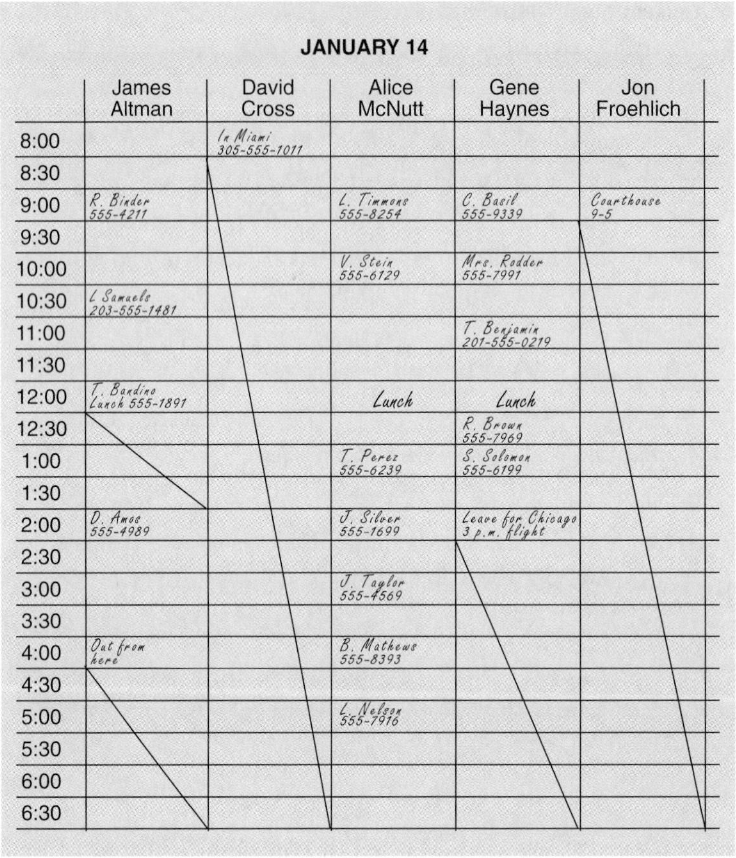

Fig. 3-11 An example of an appointment book kept by an administrative assistant for five managers.

JANUARY 14

	James Altman	David Cross	Alice McNutt	Gene Haynes	Jon Froehlich
8:00		In Miami 305-555-1011			
8:30					
9:00	R. Binder 555-4211		L. Timmons 555-8254	C. Basil 555-9339	Courthouse 9-5
9:30					
10:00			V. Stein 555-6129	Mrs. Rodder 555-7991	
10:30	L. Samuels 203-555-1481				
11:00				T. Benjamin 201-555-0219	
11:30					
12:00	T. Bandino Lunch 555-1891		Lunch	Lunch	
12:30				R. Brown 555-7969	
1:00			T. Perez 555-6239	S. Solomon 555-6199	
1:30					
2:00	D. Amos 555-4989		J. Silver 555-1699	Leave for Chicago 3 p.m. flight	
2:30					
3:00			J. Taylor 555-4569		
3:30					
4:00	Out from here		B. Mathews 555-8393		
4:30					
5:00			L. Nelson 555-7916		
5:30					
6:00					
6:30					

cellent record of names, dates, and activities. The assistance they can provide in preparing activity reports, locating addresses and phone numbers, and settling possible business differences is immeasurable.

Date and Time Preferences. In selecting the date and time for an appointment, consider the personal preferences of the employer. These are some guidelines to be considered:

1. Schedule few, if any, appointments on Monday mornings, because the weekend accumulation of mail often requires attention.
2. Provide unscheduled time between appointments so that they will not overlap.
3. Allow ample time in the schedule each day to take care of the mail.
4. Avoid late-afternoon appointments.
5. Avoid appointments just before a trip.
6. Avoid appointments on the first day the executive returns to work after an absence of several days.

7. Suggest two alternate times for the appointment rather than ask the caller when it would be convenient for an appointment.

8. Make appointments to be held away from the office at convenient times for your employer; for example, the first thing in the morning, on the way to the office, before or after lunch, or just before the end of the day are convenient times for these appointments.

Unless advised otherwise, you must seek the approval of the employer in granting appointments. Tentatively record appointments in the appointment book or key them into the computer until they are explained and approved.

Avoiding Unkept Appointments.   Nothing destroys good relations faster than not keeping an appointment. Preventing conflicting appointments is one of the administrative assistant's most difficult challenges. Sometimes the executive forgets to tell the administrative assistant about appointments made outside the office.

Experienced administrative assistants suggest setting aside some time to review the day's appointment schedule with the executive. This practice may bring to mind an unrecorded appointment. Ask to see the executive's pocket diary (or pocket electronic calendar) until the executive becomes accustomed to giving it to you for checking. At the end of the day, remind the executive of any unusual appointments. These may include a very early morning appointment or a night meeting.

Sometimes an employer may be unavoidably prevented from keeping an appointment. If so, you should notify the appropriate person(s) by telephone and, after checking calendars, suggest a later meeting time. Occasionally your employer may forget an appointment. You can be helpful by quickly locating your employer and seeing that the appointment is kept as scheduled. If the employer is suddenly called out of town, you may have to cancel an appointment or arrange for another person to see the visitor. If you must cancel an appointment, you should contact the visitor and report the cancellation without going into great detail. Be discreet and noncommittal. Comments such as "Mr. Sloan has been unavoidably detained" or "Something unexpected has come up requiring a cancellation" are all that are required.

Saying No Tactfully.   Obviously appointments should be refused as tactfully as possible. Refusals should be prefaced by a sincere "I'm very sorry, but . . ." A logical reason for the refusal should always be given. Use your employer's name rather than the impersonal-sounding "she" or "he" when explaining the situation to the caller. Other tactful ways to refuse appointments are to explain that the executive is in conference, must attend a meeting on that day, has a heavy schedule for the next two weeks, or is preparing to leave town. If a caller seems very disappointed about a refusal, you might offer to relay a message to the executive or take other appropriate, helpful action.

Canceling Appointments

If an appointment must be canceled, the administrative assistant calls and notifies the visitor of the cancellation. The executive often asks the administrative assistant to write a letter to an out-of-town visitor to confirm a cancellation to prevent embarrassment in case the telephone message was not received. If possible, the administrative assistant immediately schedules a new appointment to replace the canceled one.

STRATEGIES FOR HANDLING JOB-RELATED STRESS

It is not unusual to hear office employees complaining about the stress they experience in their work. In Chapter 2 we learned that video display operators complain of emotional stress in working with the screen on a daily basis. Their psychological stress is compounded by physical discomfort with eyestrain and muscular aches in the wrist, back, and neck. From a health standpoint, employees are concerned about job-related stress. Employers are concerned, too, because they have found that job stress leads to increased absenteeism, decreased productivity, and increased company medical costs.

Administrative assistants are not free from job-related stress. A recent survey of administrative assistants indicated that approximately 80 percent ranked their position in one of two categories: moderately stressful or very stressful. Although some stress is considered beneficial in doing one's best work and in being productive, too much stress is unhealthy and leads to eventual job burnout (reduced productivity, possible job change). Here are some office situations that can create stress for an administrative assistant.

1. Learning something new or difficult
2. Having too much work to do in too little time
3. Working with poor or incomplete instructions
4. Working with complex assignments
5. Working with frequent interruptions
6. Experiencing personality clashes with superiors or with coworkers
7. Having little or no cooperation from coworkers
8. Experiencing frequent changes in the office—for example, in policies, procedures, or personnel
9. Having undue responsibility without authority
10. Waiting for repair of necessary equipment

Some of the symptoms of excessive stress are irritability, insomnia, alcohol abuse, and food abuse. Physical changes will take place as well, including rapid breathing and heart rate, tenseness in muscles, and an upset stomach.

To realistically and maturely cope with work-related stress, the administrative assistant should have a plan to decrease stress on the job. That plan should address the three major components of stress—psychological factors, physical factors, and work load factors.

In addressing psychological factors, the administrative assistant needs to keep a proper perspective on any office problems. It is often said that 95 percent of the things people worry about never even happen. Worrying is, then, to say the least, nonproductive and should be avoided. When people worry, they experience stress. If you tend to worry, make every effort to break this habit. Another suggestion is to stay calm during periods of crisis in the office. Develop a sense of humor; learn to laugh at yourself. If possible, develop a support system with your coworkers by discussing situations that create stress. Together identify and develop steps to take to help one another when needed. One last note: believe it or not, procrastination—the big time waster—produces stress. Here, a behavioral or attitudinal change is in order.

Fig. 3-12
Administrative assistants may experience job-related stress.

Physically, the administrative assistant can cope better with stressful situations if these suggestions are followed:

1. Be well rested for each workday.
2. Follow a well-balanced diet. Keep caffeine and sugar intake down. Don't skip meals.
3. Establish a regular exercise program and follow it.
4. Take a break if you begin to feel stressed.
5. Do relaxation exercises at your workstation. Close your eyes, meditate, take deep breaths.

In regard to the stress caused by your work load, there are some actions you can take:

1. Be prepared; plan ahead for the work load.
2. Learn all the functions of your electronic equipment to become more productive in your work.
3. Exert more control over your work load; work with your employer to avoid assigning too much top priority work to be accomplished during one day. Set realistic goals for yourself. Tell your employer, "I can do these projects right away, but I can't get to the others until next week." Ask your employer, "How can we handle this situation?"
4. Make decisions so that you do not procrastinate.

Summary

This chapter has discussed the administrative assistant's important responsibilities of organizing time and work. The work of an administrative assistant has three broad classifications: routine, assigned, and original work. Original work draws attention to the administrative assistant's abilities and may lead to promotion.

Administrative assistants know the importance of time and therefore plan their work daily. They set priorities and plan ahead with weekly and sometimes monthly schedules. They anticipate their employers' requirements and observe the time management principles set forth in this chapter. Administrative assistants who work for more than one executive check with each one daily to determine the work priorities. Conflicts in priorities are either settled by the principals or sometimes by the administrative assistants themselves.

Helpful desk reference materials are the desk manual, a desk calendar, the tickler, and the chronological file. The administrative assistant's desk calendar is for personal and work reminders. For scheduling the employer's appointments, the administrative assistant keeps an appointment calendar which is either paper or electronic. Software programs offer features which can save the administrative assistant time and make him or her more productive in scheduling appointments, setting work priorities, and preparing daily to-do lists.

On the afternoon before, the administrative assistant gives the employer a keyed list of appointments for the next day, either on a 3-by-5-inch card or on standard-size paper. Prior to appointments, pertinent files and other information are put on the employer's desk.

Working with the varied and numerous responsibilities often under the pressure of time can be stressful to the employee. Advice to administrative assistants in combating job-related stress includes developing a sense of humor, staying calm in crises, being well rested for each workday, and planning ahead and being prepared for the work load.

QUESTIONS FOR DISCUSSION

THINK IT *Through*

1. One administrative assistant who works for several managers has said that she is always putting out fires. What do you think she means by that statement?

2. Assume you work in an open-office design. One of your coworkers often comes into your workstation and interrupts you while you are talking on the telephone to a customer. How would you handle this situation?

THINK IT
Through

3. What suggestions can you offer to maintain good health when faced with stress in the workplace?

4. Your employer frequently gives you rush assignments at the end of the day that you have to stay overtime to complete. What steps would you suggest to your employer to increase efficiency and reduce the need for overtime?

THINK IT
Through

5. What would you do first if all the following happened at the same time? While you were composing an urgent communication, your employer, who was talking long-distance, buzzed you to enter the office; the administrative assistant to the company president walked by your desk into your employer's office; and a subordinate was at your desk who wanted to borrow a file from your desk drawer. Explain your reasoning.

THINK IT
Through

6. If necessary correct the following sentences. Refer to the Reference Guide to check your answers.

a. When you have completed four years work on a degree you should be able to take over your father in laws business.

b. The womans coat and the childrens toys were left in the Thomases car.

c. Our firm employs four CPA's and ten CPS's.

d. Whose going to the reunion of the class of 85?

e. You will come with me to Margarets party; no ifs, ands, or buts about it.

*P*ROBLEMS

1. Before leaving work at 5 p.m., you must prepare tomorrow's daily work plan. Use Figure 3-5 as a guide. On a plain sheet of paper, key the order in which you would perform the following tasks:

Call about airline schedule for next week's proposed trip.

Verify employer's 1 p.m. crosstown appointment.

Prepare agenda for 10 a.m. staff meeting.

Obtain sales figures from marketing for the second page of a four-page report. The report is urgent.

Order flowers to be sent to an employee in the hospital.

Transcribe three letters still on transcription equipment.

Purchase a get-well card to send to an employee in the hospital.

Obtain agenda items from your employer for the staff meeting.

2. The following items are on your desk on March 2 to be marked for the tickler file. Before filing these items in the regular files, key a card for each one for the tickler file. Indicate on each card the date under which the card would be filed. Note on the card where the original material is filed. If you have access to personal information manager (PIM) software, enter these tickler items into the system. Follow your teacher's instructions for producing a printout.

   a. Notes for an article to be written for the September issue of the *Journal of Accountancy*. The deadline for an article is April 1.

   b. A note about setting up a conference with a bank official about a short-term loan to pay an invoice due April 1.

   c. A letter accepting an invitation to speak at a meeting of seniors from the College of Business and Economics on May 8.

   d. The program of the annual convention of the International Controllers Institute to be held on April 6 in Brussels. Your employer plans to attend.

   e. A notice of a March 8 meeting of the Administrative Committee. Your employer is a member.

3. It is late Friday afternoon and you are 15 minutes away from your two-week vacation. Your employer is out of town until Monday. You have a number of pending matters on your work surface. Decide which of the following tasks to handle yourself in the time remaining, which to leave locked in your employer's desk, and which to leave for your replacement to handle. Key your decisions and give the rationale behind them.

   a. Your employer's insurance premium is due the following Wednesday. You are authorized to make payment.

   b. Notification of a meeting scheduled for Thursday of the following week.

   c. Rough draft of a letter written by a staff member that needs to be rekeyed for signature and mailing.

   d. Confidential promotion papers concerning a staff member.

   e. Interoffice memorandum requesting technical data from your employer.

   f. A letter from your employer's daughter at college.

▶ **TA3-1.TEM** Access the template disk, and select the TA3-1.TEM file, which presents next month's calendar for three executives in your department. The calls and messages you've received this morning require you to make the following changes to their schedules:

1. Ms. Mendez called to change her appointment with Linda Barney *from* Monday the 4th at 11:00 a.m. *to* Wednesday the 6th at 2:15 p.m.

2. The president of your company, Beatrice Vernon, called to invite Linda, John, and Patrizia to a managers' meeting on Monday the 11th at 9:30 a.m. The meeting is expected to last until noon. All three executives will certainly attend. Note the conflict in #3 below.

3. On Monday the 11th Patrizia Glendale had a meeting scheduled with Charles Wittnauer (the Director of Purchasing) at 10:30 a.m. Now Patrizia can no longer keep that appointment; she will be meeting with the president at that time. You called Mr. Wittnauer's office to reschedule that meeting for Friday the 15th at 1:30 p.m.

4. Lyle Williamson, a sales representative, called to ask for an appointment with John Chang on Monday the 11th at 10:30. Of course, you informed Mr. Williamson that John Chang would not be available then; instead, you suggested Tuesday the 12th. Mr. Williamson asked you to make a tentative appointment for him on that day at 10:00 a.m.; he will call to confirm that time within the next day or so.

After you have entered and proofread all the necessary changes, print out a copy of the revised monthly calendar for each executive.

▶ **TA3-2.TEM** Access the template disk, and select the TA3-2.TEM file. On screen you will see column headings for a Time Analysis Chart, a form that was provided by your company's Training Department at the Time Management Workshop you recently attended.

Step A. Using your word processing software, edit or revise the chart as necessary:

1. Enter the day and today's date.

2. Adjust the column spacing as necessary.

3. Draw two horizontal lines—one above and one below the columns. Draw vertical lines to separate the columns.

continued

continued

4. Print out a sample copy of the chart. Review the copy to determine whether you need to revise the columns for any reason; if so, then revise the chart.

Step B. Now use your final copy of the Time Analysis Chart to monitor precisely how you spend your time for one full day:

1. In the Start column, enter the time you begin *every* activity and task for the entire day (that is, every activity that takes 10 minutes or more).

2. In the Activity/Task column, identify that activity briefly (for example, "Telephone w/Bill Thompson").

3. In the End column, enter the time you end that activity.

4. At the end of the day, in the Total Hours column enter the amount of time (in 1/4-hour intervals) you devoted to each activity.

5. In the Comments column, briefly describe the reason for or purpose of the activity or task (for example, "to discuss insurance").

Step C. At the end of the day (or the next day, if you prefer), analyze your entries:

1. Try to find patterns or insights into ways you might have saved time (by combining tasks, avoiding certain activities or devoting less time to them, rescheduling appointments, postponing meetings, etc.).

2. Summarize your analysis in a list.

Chapter 4

Successful Public Relations

INTRODUCTION

Ask any administrative assistant to name one of the favorite responsibilities of the position, and you are likely to hear "Receiving office visitors." It is one of the most liked responsibilities because administrative assistants are people oriented. Receiving office visitors is an important job function because the administrative assistant is often the first contact a visitor has with the company. In this public contact role, the office professional creates the first impression of the company. Needless to say, the impression must be a good one. Creating and maintaining a favorable company image requires courtesy, patience, sensitivity, tact, and the ability to get along with others.

Another public relations responsibility involves the proper use of the business telephone. The telephone is a vital communication link between the company and the public. Like receiving office visitors, representing the company over the telephone may be the first contact a caller has with the company. In addition to being proficient in handling this instrument, the administrative assistant must have a pleasant telephone personality and be well versed in telephone etiquette.

The office professional's skill in dealing with people face to face and over the telephone can be worth uncountable dollars in goodwill to the company. Some of this skill is innate to certain individuals, but for most people it comes with on-the-job experience. Being gracious to every office visitor and telephone caller is the hallmark of an experienced administrative assistant.

RECEIVING OFFICE VISITORS

Methods of receiving visitors vary among companies. Large organizations generally have a reception area near the main entrance. Here a trained receptionist assists visitors in determining which department or person to see and then calls the appropriate administrative assistant to find out whether the employer is available. If the visitor has an appointment, the receptionist gives the visitor directions to the office. In some offices, the administrative assistant personally escorts the caller to the correct location. In offices requiring security clearance, the receptionist notifies the administrative assistant after security procedures are completed, and then the administrative assistant meets the visitor in the reception area. When an administrative assistant directs a visitor to an office, he or she walks slightly ahead, opens any doors, pushes elevator buttons, and makes small talk (the weather, last night's game, etc.).

In small companies, visitors may use a telephone in the lobby to announce their arrival. Assuming the caller has an appointment, the administrative assistant may give directions or personally escort the visitor to the office.

The administrative assistant in a small office is a visitor's initial contact with the company. Callers may or may not have appointments. The administrative assistant must decide immediately whether the visitor is at the right place, whether to admit the visitor, whether to schedule an appointment for a later time, or whether to refuse an appointment.

Whatever the office organization, the administrative assistant has a twofold obligation: first, to follow the guidelines and procedures established by the employer and, second, to provide a hospitable office climate.

Guidelines and Procedures

Office visitors with or without appointments can be from outside the company, employees of the company, or personal friends. Members of the employer's family usually arrive without appointments. As a new administrative assistant or as an administrative assistant with a new employer, you need guidelines for handling office visitors. You will need to know the employer's preferences in receiving callers and those you can admit without appointments. You will also have to determine whether you are to keep a record of office visitors.

The Employer's Preferences.   Your predecessor, if available, can give you information on how the employer wants office visitors received. If the former administrative assistant is unavailable, or if your employer is new, you should ask your employer general questions about how to take care of office visitors and learn through experience. If you report to several executives, you need to determine each one's preferences by asking questions. Here are some questions about employer preferences and comments regarding them:

Questions	**Comments**
1. Does your employer want to see everyone who calls?	Many employers pride themselves on their open-door policy, meaning they will see any caller during office hours. You should ask this question.
2. Does your employer prefer to see certain callers (salespersons, for instance) at specified times only?	Some employers find this policy useful in making the best use of their time. Learn the answer to this question.
3. Which personal friends and relatives are likely to call? Which of these should be sent in without announcement? Who else should be admitted without appointments?	Do not ask these questions directly as you may appear too inquisitive. You will soon sense the answer. Certain persons can always enter the employer's office without first obtaining your permission: top executives to whom your employer is responsible and their administrative assistants; co-executives and their administrative assistants; and the employer's immediate staff. Special-privilege callers come in with confidence. They know they are welcome and usually introduce themselves to a new administrative assistant.
4. How should callers be announced?	You may use the telephone or go directly into the office to announce a caller. Procedure may differ depending on the caller or the work the employer is doing at the time. You may have to learn from experience how to announce visitors. Observe your employer's reactions to the way you approach different circumstances.
5. When should you attempt to terminate visits?	For some appointments, your employer will instruct you when and how to initiate a termination. When an appointment is running overtime and another caller is waiting, you should inform your employer that the next appointment is waiting. You can do so with a note or by using the telephone.
6. Are there callers that your employer prefers to avoid?	Feel free to ask this question. Often an employer is plagued by overzealous salespersons.

Office Etiquette.   Some administrative assistants are very adept at greeting visitors. They have personal characteristics that make them feel comfortable meeting strangers, and they have a knack for recognizing visitors who have been in the office previously. Their courteous manner makes the visitor feel welcome. Experience teaches this very important public relations function. As a new administrative assistant, you should learn to be gracious and to follow proper office etiquette.

Procedure

Office visitors should not be treated as interruptions of your work.

Attitude plays an important role in developing good office manners. Visitors to your office should be considered office guests, not interruptions. In other words, when a visitor comes to your workstation, courtesy requires that you stop what you are doing, look directly at the person, smile, and speak immediately. Your greeting should be friendly and cheerful. A simple, pleasant "Good morning" or "Good afternoon" sets the stage for effective communication. Making the visitor wait while you finish keying a line, file another three letters, or continue chatting with another employee is rude. If you are on the telephone, acknowledge the caller with a nod or a smile, indicating that you will be free momentarily.

When addressing the visitor, use *Mr., Miss, Mrs., Ms.,* or a professional title and the last name. In conversations with visitors or when addressing your employer in the presence of guests, always refer to your employer by his or her last name, for instance, *Mrs. Alexander.* Using a courtesy or professional title in addressing your employer is an important mark of respect.

If the caller has an appointment, greeting the person by name adds a personal touch to the welcome. After the usual pleasantries, the administrative assistant escorts the visitor into the executive's office and makes any necessary introductions in a courteous manner.

If an unscheduled visitor wishes to see your employer, you should identify yourself and ask the caller's name, the company the caller represents, and the purpose of the visit. A greeting such as the following is appropriate: "Good morning. May I help you? I am Alice Brown, Mrs. Alexander's administrative assistant." Then, if the caller insists on speaking with Mrs. Alexander, continue with, "May I tell her who is calling?" The caller's business card provides this information and may give a clue to the reason for the visit. However, actually questioning the caller about the purpose of the visit may be necessary. In this case, tact and patience often are important. An experienced administrative assistant handles the situation graciously and obtains the information for the employer.

The visitor on legitimate business is accustomed to making office calls. She or he will approach you, provide identification, state the purpose of the visit, and ask to see your employer. Occasionally, however, it may be necessary for you to ask: "May I tell Mrs. Alexander the nature (subject) of your visit?" If you need clarification from the visitor, ask questions. The easiest way to be sure that you have the information correct is to repeat what has been said. State it as you understand it.

Clients and customers are always given cordial and gracious treatment. Marketing representatives from businesses that supply materials and services related to the employer's work are treated with courtesy and attentiveness. It is helpful to marketing representatives to suggest appointment times that you know are good for your employer.

The Decision About Whom to Admit. Scheduled appointments generally do not pose a problem. These visitors are admitted readily. For unscheduled appointments or in making appointments, some administrative assistants are inclined to become too protective of their employer's time. Often they turn away visitors the employer should see. Engage in a conversation with the caller long enough to determine if he or she should be admitted. When in doubt, ask whether your employer wants to see the visitor.

A caller's business may involve a matter outside the scope of your employer's duties. You will save everyone's time by determining the nature of the visit first and, if necessary, referring the caller to the proper person. Project yourself as a person who wishes to be helpful and accommodating to the visitor. Telephone a person in the appropriate office and explain the situation. If an appointment is made at once, direct the caller to the correct office. If an appointment must be made for another day, confer with the visitor and set a mutually convenient time. In most cases your helpfulness in arranging this appointment will more than offset any inconvenience the visitor may experience.

Names and Faces. One extremely valuable public relations skill is remembering names and faces so that you may greet callers in a sincere and natural manner. Listen carefully without interruption when the name is pronounced. If in doubt, ask the person how to pronounce it or spell it. You can train yourself to remember a person's name by repeating it when you first hear it and using it when addressing the person.

The ability to remember faces is another attribute of the superior administrative assistant. Keep a file of business cards. Before filing a card, make notes that will help you associate the name on the card with the face of the caller. Figure 4-1 is an example of how you can use business cards to remember names and faces. To recognize the employer's colleagues, you should watch carefully for their pictures in company publications, newspapers, or magazines.

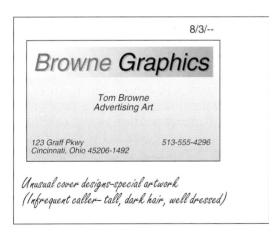

Fig. 4-1 Make notations directly on the caller's business card to help you associate the name with the face.

A Record of Visitors. Some offices maintain a register of office visitors as a matter of record or for security reasons. In a large company this register may be kept at a receptionist's desk; in a small office the administrative assistant may keep this information. A register includes names, dates of visits, business affiliations, purposes of visits, and other pertinent information. This information may be recorded manually in a register kept for this purpose (see Figure 4-2) or maintained electronically by using software such as personal information manager (see Chapter 5).

If the flow of visitors is small, the efficient administrative assistant can keep a simple record of visitors conveniently and permanently on a desk calendar.

REGISTER OF OFFICE VISITORS

Date	Time	Name and Affiliation	Person Asked For	Person Seen	Purpose of Call
6/8/--	9:30	H. Horton, Cove Lighting Fix.	S.G.	✓	sales rep
6/8/--	10:30	L. Alton, Standard Printing	R.B.	✓	sales rep
6/8/--	11:45	R. Krause, luncheon appt.	R.B.	✓	Merrill cont.
6/8/--	1:40	J. Keller, Flexwood consultant	S.G.	✓	Merrill cont.
6/8/--	3:50	Flexwood delivery driver	—	—	Brought samp.

The Administrative Assistant's Contributions

The individual administrative assistant's personality, maturity, and knowledge of office etiquette set the stage for the employer to develop a positive rapport with the office visitor. A receptive climate includes making the visitor comfortable, making introductions, and using good judgment in interrupting the visitor's conference with the employer.

Preparing for Visitors. If the office has a receptionist (or a security officer), the administrative assistant gives that person the caller's name, the time of the appointment, and any special instructions in anticipation of the caller's arrival. If several visitors will be meeting with the employer at the same time, the administrative assistant arranges for extra seating and places notepads and pencils at convenient locations in the office. If you are aware that a caller is disabled, make preparations for special accommodation.

Prior to an appointment, place all applicable files and documents on your employer's desk. Make your workstation and your employer's office presentable by removing extra papers, folders, and newspapers. Remove used cups, soft drink bottles, and the like.

Discuss with your employer guidelines for handling interruptions and any other matters you think might come up during the appointment. Ask whether you should remain at your workstation during the conference. Do not hesitate to pose these questions. You should have a clear understanding of your employer's preferences.

When an important out-of-town client or executive is expected, you may be asked to make hotel reservations, order a rental car, and arrange for the visitor to be met at the airport. If the visitor is to see several members in the firm, notify each member of the visitor's expected arrival time and, if appropriate, provide a brief description of the purpose of the visit. Some administrative assistants make a practice of sending visitors a city map with the office location and major travel routes marked on it. Visitors should also be informed of the location of visitor parking at the office.

A special situation arises when a visitor will be in the office for an extended period. You may be asked to find an office and a temporary administrative assistant, or you may assume additional responsibilities. Look upon this additional duty as an opportunity to learn more about your employer's work and the company.

Receiving International Visitors.   In the global marketplace environment that exists today, your employer may host foreign visitors. Your welcome and your cordiality will definitely influence their attitudes toward your employer and the company. Before their arrival, research their culture, social customs, and protocol. For instance, in some cultures personal space is closer than we are used to. If a visitor stands closer to you than you are comfortable with, try not to back away. Be aware, too, that international visitors expect a degree of formality, and personal questions should be avoided. In some cultures rank and protocol are very important. Administrative assistants should determine quickly who the senior person of the group is and show deference to that person while in the office. Some foreign visitors place a great deal of importance on the exchange of business cards. If you are offered a business card, read it carefully and indicate that you will keep it in an appropriate file.

If your employer expects visitors who do not speak English, you will have to arrange for an interpreter to attend the meeting with your employer and to assist you in greeting them upon their arrival. Even when an international visitor does speak English, in your conversation avoid unusual words, and without being too obvious about it, speak at a slower than usual pace. Also, use short, direct sentences and, if appropriate, ask questions to determine if you are being understood. Be careful that you do not appear condescending.

Other services, such as arranging hotel reservations and securing guides and transportation, may be necessary. If your employer has visited the international callers in their country, take cues from how your employer was received and entertained. Comparable welcoming services and social events are expected as indications of esteem and respect.

Making the Wait Pleasant.   In your role as a public relations representative for your employer, you should make a visitor's wait comfortable and pleasant. In order to accomplish this objective, attend to the visitor's hat and coat, offer a beverage, and provide current magazines or the daily newspaper.

Always check with your employer before ushering a visitor into the office. If a visitor is early for an appointment, ask your employer for instructions. Perhaps the appointment time can be changed. If it is not convenient to change the time of the appointment, and the visitor must wait, give the visitor some indication of how long the wait will be.

After an unduly long wait, you may remind your employer that the caller is still waiting. If the employer indicates that it will be only a few more minutes, you may report this to the caller.

You are not expected to entertain office visitors. After exchanging pleasantries about the weather, travel time, and so forth, return to your duties. If the visitor persists in talking, avoid any discussion about company business or your employer.

If several visitors are waiting, admit each in proper turn. You are under no obligation to introduce them to each other unless all are attending the same conference.

Handling the Actual Appointment.   Appointment records tell the administrative assistant when to expect a person's arrival. If an individual within the company is late for an appointment, it is entirely proper for you to telephone that person's office to ask about the delay.

Often more than one person is involved in a meeting. When the first person arrives, should you inform the executive of the arrival or wait until the entire group has assembled? There is no hard-and-fast rule. The decision depends on the visitor's status, the employer's activity at the time, and individual preference. If the first visitor is very important, you may not only inform the employer of the arrival but also may notify the other conferees to assemble at once. Otherwise, it is appropriate to wait until the entire group is assembled before informing the employer.

When your employer is going to another office for a meeting, anticipate what papers and files will be required and place them in her or his briefcase.

Admitting the Visitor.   If this is the visitor's first call, you should lead the way to the employer's office. Before leaving your workstation, cover your work or unobtrusively slip it into a folder. If the employer's door is closed, knock. After a slight pause, enter the office with the visitor. When the proper introductions have been made, leave and close the door quietly.

In some instances you will not be able to leave your workstation to escort the visitor to your employer's office. If this is the case, a simple gesture will indicate that the visitor may enter.

Sometimes the employer walks out to greet the caller. Should there be two callers waiting, indicate to your employer who is first.

Should voices carry from your employer's office, close the door or turn on soft music. If your employer has a speakerphone (see Chapter 8), be sure that it is off.

Making Introductions.   Self-introductions are common in business, but occasionally the administrative assistant is responsible for making introductions.

Remember this rule when making introductions: The person given the greater courtesy is named first. In business introductions, the name of the person of higher position is given first. Include titles, such as *Doctor, Captain,* and *Bishop,* if known, and affiliation. For instance, an administrative assistant to Harold Jenkins would introduce a new administrative assistant, Mrs. Linda Dorion, to Mr. Jenkins in this fashion: "Mr. Jenkins, this is Mrs. Dorion, administrative assistant to Ms. Elsworth." In introducing Bishop Manning to Mr. Jenkins, the administrative assistant would say: "Bishop Manning, this is Mr. Jenkins." When introducing a sales representative of Horton Manufacturing Company, the administrative assistant would say: "Mr. Jenkins, this is Miss Flemming of Horton Manufacturing Company." With group introductions, the administrative assistant introduces the most recent arrival to the group by saying the person's name, title, and affiliation, and then giving the name of each member of the group, if self-introductions are not forthcoming. If a person has a hard-to-pronounce last name, practice saying the name several times to yourself before making the actual introduction.

When your employer introduces you to a client, business position takes precedence; therefore, the client is addressed first. Respond to introductions in a natural way. Say "I am glad to meet you" or simply "Hello." "How do you do?" is sometimes used, but it may sound a bit stilted in today's business world. Stand when greeting visitors or when being introduced to show respect, particularly if the visitor is considerably older than you or of great importance.

You should be aware of the following situations where gender, age, and rank, rather than strict business position, are factors in making an introduction:

Introduction	Factor in Presentation	First Named
1. Woman to man (in a social setting)	Gender (usually)	Woman
2. Woman to man (in a business setting)	Rank	Person with higher rank
3. An officer of the company and a manager in the same company	Rank	Officer
4. Dignitary (head of state or church dignitary) to your employer	Rank	Dignitary (out of respect)
5. Young person to mature person	Age	Mature person
6. Member of the armed forces or of a college faculty to your employer (who is a member of that group)	Rank	Person with higher rank
7. A customer of the company to your employer	Rank	Customer (customer is life-blood of company)
8. An individual to a group	Convenience	The individual, then each person in the group

Handshaking.   The practice of shaking hands reduces barriers between people. It is said that the way a person shakes hands reveals a great deal about that person. An enthusiastic handshake, for example, can signify that the person is sincere in offering the greeting.

Handshaking is customary and almost automatic between men. More and more, professional women shake hands. When a man and a woman shake hands, usually the woman offers her hand first. In a business office, the position of the other person may preclude the administrative assistant from taking the initiative. One always accepts an extended hand. To do otherwise is a slight and will probably cause embarrassment.

Handshaking is also an acceptable method of greeting for most cultures. There are some differences, however. For instance, in Spain a handshake should last five to seven strokes; in France, a single stroke is proper.

Handling the Difficult Visitor.   Being courteous to certain visitors may require considerable discipline and restraint. Some callers are gruff; some are condescending; some are self-important or aggressive; some are even rude. To be gracious to these persons requires strong willpower and will test your public relations skills.

A nuisance visitor can resort to all sorts of ruses to get past the administrative assistant's workstation. In such cases you must exercise tact and firmness. Be wary of a person who, without giving a name, says, "I'm a personal friend" or "I have a personal matter to discuss with Miss Jones." The caller with legitimate, important business has everything to gain by providing a name and stating the purpose of the visit. You may explain to the caller that you are not permitted to admit visitors unannounced. You may also suggest that the caller write to your employer to request an appointment at a later date. If that fails, and the caller still refuses to give you a name or to state the purpose of the visit, offer a piece of paper and request that a short note be written. Enclose this note in an envelope and take it to your employer, who can then decide whether to admit the caller.

Some callers try to obtain information from the administrative assistant either about the executive, other employees, or the company. Be wary of prying questions. Do not answer them, except in generalities. A remark such as "I really don't know" or "I'm not at liberty to disclose that information" will ordinarily stop such inquiries.

Interrupting a Conference.   Most employers do not like to be interrupted during a conference. Interruptions are distracting and waste the time of all participants. For certain conferences you will be told that there are to be absolutely no interruptions. Most of the time, however, employers realize that an interruption is sometimes necessary. You and your employer should come to an understanding on what kinds of matters warrant an interruption and also the best method of handling them—with a written note or a telephone call, for instance.

An unobtrusive way to handle an interruption is to key or handwrite the message on a slip of paper and take it into the office, usually without knocking. Give the message directly to the person. If it requires a reply, wait for the answer.

When there is a telephone call for the visitor, ask if you can take the message. If so, key or handwrite the message along with the caller's name, the date, and the time of the call; give the message to the visitor after the conference. If the one calling insists on speaking to the visitor, go into the conference room and either hand the visitor a note or say something like this: "Mr. Lawrence, Mrs. Rowett is on the telephone and wants to speak with you. Would you like to take the call here [*indicating which telephone he is to use*] or would you prefer using the telephone on my desk?" If the latter is chosen, the administrative assistant takes care of other business away from the desk to afford the visitor privacy. Two examples of written messages appear in Figure 4-3.

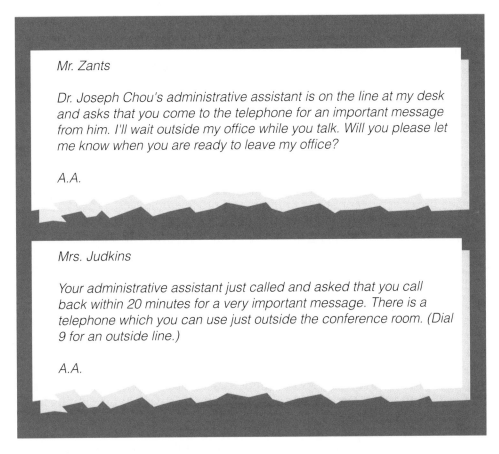

Mr. Zants

Dr. Joseph Chou's administrative assistant is on the line at my desk and asks that you come to the telephone for an important message from him. I'll wait outside my office while you talk. Will you please let me know when you are ready to leave my office?

A.A.

Mrs. Judkins

Your administrative assistant just called and asked that you call back within 20 minutes for a very important message. There is a telephone which you can use just outside the conference room. (Dial 9 for an outside line.)

A.A.

Fig. 4-3 Shown here are two acceptable ways of handling typical interruptions of business conferences. Before acting, the administrative assistant decides which procedure will make the interruption as unobtrusive as possible.

Some inconsiderate visitors do not know when to leave. Always check with your employer to determine if your assistance is needed in this area. Usually the employer rises to indicate that the conference is over, but occasionally a caller will not take the hint. You may help by taking a note in to the executive. This gives your employer an opportunity to announce apologetically that it is time for another meeting. In order to free your employer, you may telephone from another person's desk to ask if an interruption is required. Often answering the telephone affords a sufficient break in the conversation to make the caller realize that the visit is over. You can also reduce overlong visits by informing the visitor upon entering that your employer has another appointment scheduled in ten minutes.

OPERATING THE OFFICE TELEPHONE

Some phase of at least 90 percent of all business transactions is conducted by telephone. The telephone often serves as a client's or customer's first contact with the company. In fact, research shows that 75 percent of those who decide not to do business with a firm made that decision as a result of that first contact with the company. The administrative assistant who answers that call must be proficient not only in operating the telephone, but also in expediting the call to the proper party. At the same time, the administrative assistant must be courteous to every caller and thus build goodwill for the company. The telephone is an important public relations tool for the administrative assistant.

Special Skills

Because the telephone plays such a vital part in business, many companies provide in-service telephone training for all office employees. What you say during a telephone call makes a difference. The tactful choice of words in contrast to a blunt statement; an offer of help in contrast to a plain "no"; a complaint handled effectively; and pleasant, businesslike conversations conducted with ease come with experience and proper training. Accommodating each caller creates goodwill for the company.

Telephone Voice Personality. Your voice over the phone reflects your personality. Make it attractive to callers. (See Figure 4-4.) If you consider each call an annoying interruption, your voice will reflect a negative attitude. You really cannot afford to answer the telephone in an indifferent or uninterested way. It is possible that the person calling may be very important—your employer, for instance. Here are six simple rules to assist you in developing a pleasant telephone voice:

1. Speak at a normal speed; use rising and falling inflections to avoid monotony.
2. Use a tone suitable for face-to-face-conversation; keep your voice low-pitched.
3. Speak directly into the transmitter; hold it between half an inch and an inch from your lips.

4. Try to visualize and speak directly to the person calling, not at the telephone.

5. Try to convey a friendly, intelligent interest.

6. Use simple, nontechnical language and avoid slang.

Enunciation. Administrative assistants give and take information over the telephone frequently. Enunciation, then, becomes very important. Watch for these frequent causes of inaccuracy: *F* and *S* are often confused, as are *P* and *B*, *T* and *D*, and *M* and *N*. To prevent mistakes, use any simple, easy-to-understand word to identify a letter, such as *D as in David, A as in Alice, V as in Victor,* and so on. Make it a practice to spell difficult names. It is particularly important that the listener understand any numbers; therefore, the speaker should slightly exaggerate their enunciation. Repeat all numbers. If there is still a question about one digit, give its preceding sequence, as "three, four, five," emphasizing the proper number.

The American Telephone and Telegraph Company recommends the following sentences to improve your diction. *Read them aloud slowly, giving every sound its proper value.* Think about them, too.

Fig. 4-4 The voice with a smile.

1. For distinct enunciation, every word, every syllable, every sound must be given its proper form and values.

2. Think of the mouth chamber as a mold in which the correct form must be given to every sound.

3. Move your lips noticeably.

4. Your teeth should never be kept closed while you are talking.

Telephone Etiquette. Rudeness that would never occur in a face-to-face encounter too often occurs in telephone conversations. Answering the telephone in a courteous manner is essential to good business practice. These guidelines for telephone etiquette are strongly recommended:

Good manners mean good business.

1. *Answer* the telephone before the third ring, even if you are in the midst of an important job. Answer with a friendly greeting and identify the company (or department) and provide your name.

2. *Listen* until you know definitely what the caller wants. If in doubt, ask for a confirmation of your understanding.

3. Do not eat, drink, chew gum, smoke, or file papers while talking on the telephone. These noises are quickly picked up over telephone lines and can be misinterpreted as showing a lack of interest on your part.

4. Avoid using the words *not, can't, don't, won't.* Be courteous as well as helpful. Use positive, rather than negative, words or phrases.

5. Sprinkle your conversations with "Thank you" and "Please." Do not be superficial in your use of these expressions; be genuine. The proper response to "Thank you" is "You're welcome."

6. Never assume the identity of a caller. Use the caller's name only if you recognize the voice.

7. Follow through. Either get the information, transfer the call, or arrange for someone (maybe you) to call back; then *do so.* Return calls as promptly as you can.

8. Do not place callers on hold without their permission.

9. If your employer is unable to talk on the telephone, record the message on a telephone message form. (See Figure 4-5 on page 82.) Don't trust the message to memory.

10. Treat internal calls (within the company) with the same courtesy as outside calls.

11. If you are making the call, identify yourself immediately by giving your name, company affiliation, and the purpose of your call.

12. Keep calls short. Plan conversations before placing calls.

13. If you must leave a message using *voice mail* (see Chapter 8) or a typical telephone answering machine, make the message as brief as possible.

14. When closing a telephone conversation, do so courteously and graciously. End the call by simply saying "Goodbye." Saying "Bye-bye" at the end of a conversation is unbusinesslike and leaves a distinctly bad impression. Suggested wording of your last sentence might be
    a. Thank you for calling, Ms. Levinson.
    b. I'm glad I was able to help you. Goodbye.
    c. You're welcome, Mr. Rogers. Goodbye.

15. If you must terminate a conversation suddenly for any of several reasons, give a plausible, tactfully worded explanation. Examples include: "I'm sorry, Ms. Allen has just buzzed for me to come into her office"; "I'm sorry, someone is waiting for me in the reception room"; or "I'm sorry, I must get out a rush letter for Mr. Barkley." Finally, place the receiver in its holder gently. A slammed receiver at the very least is rude and may be interpreted incorrectly.

Incoming Calls

There are specific techniques to follow in handling incoming calls. Some offices require that a telephone log be kept of all incoming calls. If so, there are special books for this purpose. Also, every executive has preferences about how calls are to be handled. Although the trend today is for executives to answer their telephones directly, many executives prefer to have their calls screened. If you are working with several executives who are frequently out of the office, it is especially important to learn the preferences of each one. Armed with this information, you can then adopt appropriate procedures. When you must be away from your desk, use the call-forwarding feature of your telephone system (see Chapter 8) or arrange for a coworker to answer your phone.

Asking for Identification.   How you answer your telephone depends upon whether it is connected directly to an outside line or to the company switchboard. In general, you should answer with a courteous greeting, give the name of the company (department, or individual's office), and follow with your name. You should never answer by simply saying "Hello" or "Yes." If your telephone is on an outside line, you may answer in the following manner:

> National Supply Company, Sales Department, Miss Ruiz speaking.
>   *or*
> National Supply Company, Mr. Brandt's office, Miss Ruiz speaking.

If the call comes through the company switchboard, the switchboard attendant has already identified the company. Answer these calls and internal calls as follows:

> Sales Department, Miss Ruiz speaking.
>   *or*
> Mr. Brandt's office, Miss Ruiz speaking.
>   *or*
> This is Miss Ruiz speaking. May I help you?

Most executives and professional people answer their telephones by saying their entire names (first and surname) or surnames only, while administrative assistants answer by using a courtesy title and their last names. For security reasons, some offices instruct their female employees to use their first names only in answering calls. In this case, you would answer, "Mr. Brandt's office, this is Susan" or "Mr. Brandt's office, Susan speaking."

Screening Calls.   Some employers prefer that the administrative assistant screen all telephone calls. They realize that many calls can be handled by the administrative assistant. Also, by following this practice, they are relieved from dealing with unwanted calls. Even if the employer normally answers his or her own telephone, when someone is in the employer's office the administrative assistant should answer all calls. If you answer a call from someone that you recognize as a VIP (very important person), tell your employer who is calling either by using the interoffice line or writing a note, and then follow the employer's directions. When the caller provides no identification and you do not recognize the voice, find out who is calling. The abrupt question

"Who is calling?" sounds rude and discriminating. Tactful administrative assistants phrase their questions like this:

> May I ask who is calling, please?
> *or*
> May I tell Miss Wong who is calling, please?
> *or*
> Miss Wong is in, may I tell her who is calling, please?

The buzzer system on the telephone and the interoffice line or a handwritten note are used to notify the executive of the caller. Identify the caller to the executive in this manner: "Mr. Deal of Armstrong Company is on line X" and then put the call through if you are directed to do so. Some executives prefer this kind of screening so that they can immediately address callers by name.

If a caller refuses to provide identification, ask the executive for instructions or ask the caller for a telephone number so that the executive can return the call later in the day.

An angry customer is a challenge. An angry customer provides you the opportunity to be a problem solver.

Appeasing an Angry Caller. An angry caller cannot see you, so it is important that you project a friendly, caring attitude. Consider such a call an opportunity to remedy a customer's complaint and maintain the company's goodwill. Keep in mind that the person is not angry at you; the person is angry about a problem or a situation. The first thing for you to do is listen to what the caller has to say. Even if you want to clarify an issue as the caller unfolds the story, do not interrupt at this point. Take notes as necessary. At an appropriate time indicate that you understand the caller's situation. Comments such as "I understand how you feel" have a tendency to defuse the anger.

After you have heard the problem and have indicated empathy with the caller, ask questions that will help you understand what happened to make the caller angry. If it is within your authority, solve the problem. If it is not, take personal responsibility by connecting the caller to a person who can.

Make your closing remarks positive. For example, "Thank you, Mrs. Boni, for calling this matter to our attention. We appreciate your business and we want to keep you as a valued customer."

Reporting the Unavailability of the Executive. The administrative assistant has three responsibilities regarding incoming calls when the executive is not available to answer the telephone:

1. To give helpful but not explicit information to the caller about the executive's schedule and activities.
2. To get information from hesitant callers.
3. To take messages and keep a record of incoming calls.

Giving Information. When the executive is not available to answer a phone call, give a plausible explanation, suggest a time when the caller might call back, or possibly suggest that the caller talk to another person. A typical explanation might be:

> Mr. Graham, Mrs. Allen is attending a conference. May I help you or transfer you to someone who can?
>
> *or*
>
> Mr. Graham, Mrs. Allen is away from her desk at the moment. May I help you?

Avoid dead-end replies such as "Mrs. Allen is not here." Notice in the two preceding examples that the information that was given was not explicit. An executive may not want anything specific communicated to certain callers. *When in doubt, don't be explicit.* Unless you have reason to be explicit, try to be helpful without being too specific. Note the differences in the following responses:

Specific	*Helpful but Not Explicit*
Miss Ettinger hasn't come in yet.	Miss Ettinger isn't at her desk. I expect her at ten o'clock.
Mr. Santiago is in Chicago on business.	Mr. Santiago is out of the city today.
Mr. Hubbard left early today to play golf.	Mr. Hubbard won't be in until tomorrow.

Getting Information.   Getting information from an unidentified caller is often a challenge. How can you get both the name of the caller and the purpose of the call before the person says, "I'll call back," and then hangs up? You may have to use an oblique approach. The conversation might develop something like this:

> You answer the call and say, "Ms. Allen is away today. I am her administrative assistant, perhaps I can help you." (Notice that you do not abruptly ask who is calling or what is wanted.) If the caller is hesitant, you might ask, "May I have her call you tomorrow?" If the answer is "Yes, will you? This is Helen Fox, 555-6412," you might then ask, "Shall I give her any special message, Ms. Fox?" Or you might ask, "Will Ms. Allen know the reason for your call?"

Another approach to take with callers who are hesitant about identifying themselves is to delay stating whether the employer is available to take the call until after the caller has been identified. For example, if the caller asks to speak to your employer, Ms. Smith, you may respond by saying "May I tell Ms. Smith who is calling?" Then follow through by asking the purpose of the call. When you have this information, you can then reveal that your employer is out of the office for the day. Suggest that the caller speak with someone else or indicate that your employer will return the call. Phrase your requests for identification in a courteous and positive way. Examine the following:

Discourteous Requests	Tactful Requests
She wants to know who's calling.	May I say who's calling, please?
If you'll tell me who's calling, I'll see if I can locate her.	She's in a meeting. May I take a message?
Ms. Smith isn't taking any calls this morning.	Will you please wait while I see if she is in?

Taking Messages.　As you answer your telephone, pick up a pencil and a telephone message pad. *Keep these supplies handy at all times.* Some firms use small printed slips for this purpose. It is possible to buy books of telephone message forms that are interleaved with carbon sheets. The original message can be put on the executive's desk, and the administrative assistant retains the carbon copy for reference. This particular system is useful for reminding the employer to return calls. If a call back is requested, do not promise that your employer will return the call. This may not be the case. Rather say, "I'll ask Mrs. McDuff to call you when she is free," or "I'll give Mrs. McDuff your message." Messages left on a telephone answering machine should be written on telephone message forms also. An example of a telephone message form appears in Figure 4-5.

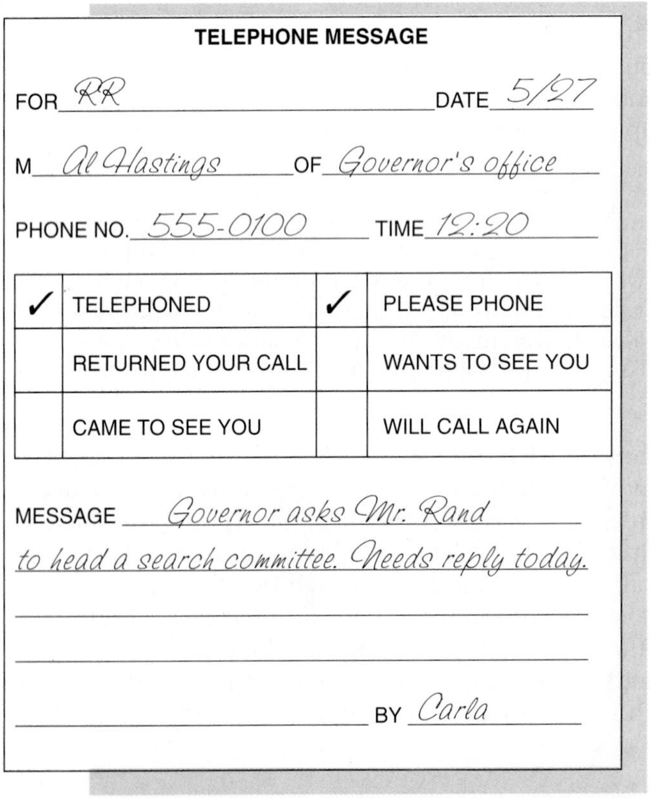

Fig. 4-5 Telephone messages should contain all pertinent data.

```
                    TELEPHONE MESSAGE

FOR  RR                           DATE  5/27

M  Al Hastings        OF  Governor's office

PHONE NO.  555-0100      TIME  12:20

  ✓  | TELEPHONED          | ✓ | PLEASE PHONE
     | RETURNED YOUR CALL  |   | WANTS TO SEE YOU
     | CAME TO SEE YOU     |   | WILL CALL AGAIN

MESSAGE   Governor asks Mr. Rand
to head a search committee. Needs reply today.


                              BY  Carla
```

After you have recorded the message, add the date, the time, the name and company affiliation of the caller, and your initials. Place telephone messages in order of importance on the executive's desk beside the telephone or in another conspicuous spot. An administrative assistant to several executives may establish a *message island* (a message holder or message box system) which each executive can regularly check.

If your employer uses a voice mail box (see Chapter 8), he or she will personally access any telephone messages. If the executive uses a computer to store messages, enter the telephone message on the computer so that it may be called up by the executive and read from the screen. An example of a telephone message stored electronically is shown in Figure 4-6.

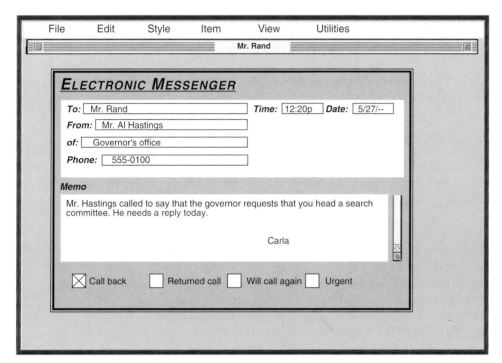

Fig. 4-6 A telephone message stored electronically.

Always relay messages promptly. If there is no message to report, make a record of the call for the executive's information. When the executive is out of town, especially for an extended time, an administrative assistant may keep a telephone diary, similar to the one shown in Figure 4-7, of all calls and messages.

Transferring Calls. When you receive a call that is not for your extension, or if you believe that someone other than yourself or your employer could better handle the call, transfer it; but avoid giving the caller the runaround. (It is possible that the caller has already been transferred to several extensions.) The following techniques can be used to demonstrate to callers that you and your organization want to be helpful.

				Disposition	
Time	Name of Caller	Affiliation	Message or Purpose	Spoke With	(Call Back) Telephone
9:15	Mr. E. Jones	sales dept.	product manager's meeting postponed	E.J.M.	

TELEPHONE DIARY OF INCOMING CALLS
August 6, 19--

1. Be sure that the person to whom you transfer the call can actually supply the information the caller seeks. This is your opportunity to demonstrate your understanding of your company's organization and to show that you know who knows what.

2. Look up the extension to which you are transferring the call in the company directory. Tell the caller the number of the extension you are transferring the call to and the name of the person at that extension. Stay on the line until the call is answered. If the matter is important, follow up with a telephone call to the company employee.

3. Rather than transferring a call, consider the possibility of getting the information for the caller yourself and returning the call.

Recording Complete or Summarized Telephone Conversations. If your employer wishes to record crucial telephone conversations, the recorder must be equipped with a sound device that emits intermittent beeps to warn the other person that the call is being recorded. You may be asked to key a full transcript or a summary of these telephone conversations. The transcript may be condensed, but it should be keyed in dialogue form, as shown below.

Telephone call, 6/10/95, 2:50 p.m., Mr. Alan King to Mr. Willis Burt.

K Hello, Willis, how are you?
B Fine, Alan. What can I do for you?

Note that it is not necessary to use quotation marks when keying a word-for-word telephone conversation since the identification of the speaker precedes each comment.

At other times you may be asked to get on the line and take notes during a conversation. Your employer should introduce you to the caller or mention that you are on the line to record parts of the conversation.

Answering a Second Telephone. A telephone with one line probably will have a call-waiting feature that allows the administrative assistant to take a second call without disconnecting the first call. Some executives, however, have multiline telephones. If two lines ring at the same time, you answer one and ask the caller for permission to place the caller on hold while you answer the other call. If the second call is local, get the number and offer to call back, placing the call immediately after completing the first call. If the second call is long distance or from a mobile telephone (there are additional charges for these types of calls), explain that you are handling another call and excuse yourself long enough to tell the first caller, "I'll be with you in a minute." Complete the long-distance or mobile-telephone call as quickly as possible. When you get back to the first call, thank the caller for waiting and apologize for the delay.

When a caller is on hold, make an attempt to get back on the line every 30 seconds to report any additional delay. If there will be a long wait, suggest that you return the call as soon as possible so that company lines are not tied up.

In the event you are on the telephone when the second call comes in, follow the same procedure. Your main concern is to dispatch each call efficiently and courteously.

If you are answering calls for another administrative assistant, answer them with the same smile and competency that you display with your own calls. Record all messages and leave them in a readily accessible place. Later double-check with the administrative assistant to make sure the messages were received and understood.

Receiving Long-Distance Calls (Precautions).   Many telephone calls you receive will be long-distance calls. To reduce waiting time, a well-trained caller immediately announces that the call is long distance. Special efforts should be made to get the person for whom a long-distance call is intended on the line without delay. Before you accept a long-distance collect call, be sure that you have your employer's permission.

If the executive is not available to take a long-distance call, listen carefully and record the message completely and accurately. Repeat the area code and phone number to assure that you have recorded them correctly. If you receive a person-to-person call for your employer, give the long-distance operator full information on when the call should be returned. The operator may ask you to have the executive return the call and give you details about completing the return call. If your employer can be reached at another telephone, either locally or in another city, and you believe that your employer will have no objection to receiving a call there, tell the operator where the call can be transferred. If your telephone is equipped with a call-forwarding feature, transfer the call yourself.

Outgoing Calls

Administrative assistants mention two problems that make things difficult when they are trying to put through outgoing calls for their employers. The first concerns the calling executive who, after requesting that a call be placed

Procedure

Always get approval before placing a caller on hold.

and the administrative assistant gets the person on the line, suddenly is nowhere to be found. At this point the administrative assistant must apologize and place the call again later. A second problem occurs when the party being called is unavailable. A message is then left to have the call returned or the administrative assistant agrees to try the call again at a time specified. This situation sets the stage for "telephone tag," a very time-consuming process in which both administrative assistants place and re-place the call until it is finally completed. These problems occur with local, interoffice, and long-distance calls. The following sections offer recommendations for making outgoing calls.

Local and Interoffice Calls. The procedure for placing local calls varies with the kind of telephone equipment in use. If the desk telephone is a direct outside line, simply dial the telephone number. If the line goes through a switchboard, either dial 9 for an outside line or ask the switchboard attendant for a line by saying, "Outside, please." When you get a dial tone, dial the number. When making an interoffice call, dial the extension number listed in the company telephone directory.

Administrative assistants regularly make two kinds of local calls. They will either phone someone with whom the employer will talk, or they place their own calls. Generally employers make their own interoffice calls, but on occasion and especially with executives, administrative assistants are asked to get the party on the line for the executive. When a senior executive is calling a junior executive in the firm, the administrative assistant waits until the junior executive is on the line before connecting with the senior executive. This is another example of office protocol.

When placing an outside call for your employer that goes through a switchboard, ask for the person and/or extension number. When you are connected, indicate the person with whom your employer wishes to speak and immediately identify your employer by name, affiliation, and purpose of the call, if known. Say something like: "Ms. Norman, please. Mr. Allen of Allen and Lovell calling." If Ms. Norman is unavailable, ask for a convenient time when Ms. Norman can be reached or leave a message for Ms. Norman to call Mr. Allen back, mentioning a time when Mr. Allen will be in his office. Follow the same technique when placing an interoffice call by saying the name of the person called and identifying your employer as the caller, such as, "Mr. Ellison, please, Mr. Allen calling."

Before placing a call for your employer, be sure that your employer has access to a needed file or other source of information. If the switchboard operator or an administrative assistant asks you to put your employer on the line first, be gracious and follow the request. When rank is not involved or when making outside calls, the person who originates the call should wait for the other person to get on the line.

You should jot down what you want to say before you place a phone call. This will help you avoid the embarrassment of having to call back because you forgot something. You will speak with more confidence and effectiveness and make a better impression by knowing in advance what you are going to say.

Introduce yourself properly. Upon being connected, give your own name and your firm's name: "This is Susan Baer of Allen and Lovell." Making a good impression on people over the telephone is just as important as making a good impression in person. When you initiate a call, telephone etiquette requires that you end the call. Do so pleasantly by saying, "Thank you for the information. Goodbye."

Long-Distance Calls.   Long-distance calls may be made by direct distance dialing (station-to-station) or through a long-distance operator. Telephone companies charge for use of out-of-state directory assistance. You will not want to make a habit of using this service instead of keeping telephone number records. When placing a call for an employer, follow the same process of identification by naming the person called, the person calling, and the affiliation. If the call is station-to-station, indicate that the call is long distance by saying the city and state where you are located, for instance, "Mr. Ellison, please. Mr. Allen of Allen and Lovell, Kansas City, Missouri, calling."

As with other telephone calls, the person calling should either be on the line or readily available when the connection is made. For a complete discussion of the types of long-distance calls including international calls and the procedures to follow in making these calls, see Chapter 8.

SPECIAL FUNCTIONS

Administrative assistants, particularly those who work for executives, may be responsible for planning special events held on the company premises or at a hotel or restaurant. A weekly luncheon in the executive dining room, a reception for a new client, a sit-down dinner, an employee retirement party are occasions when the administrative assistant's public relations skills are used.

Before making any commitments for an event, the administrative assistant must know the objectives of the function, the budget allowed, the method of payment, and the names and/or the number of guests who are to attend.

For instance, if you are asked to plan a special luncheon on the company premises for guests from another country, you may research menus of that country and make suggestions for the food served. Or, you may have the luncheon catered by a restaurant in your area, and you select the menu. For a large number of guests, you may have to provide place cards. If the luncheon is at a hotel or restaurant, your responsibilities will include making the initial contact, requesting the right table location or room, and reconfirming each person's reservation. Whether a credit card is used in payment or the company is billed directly, your employer must sign for the service, and you will be asked to verify the reservations and the amounts charged. It is a good idea to develop a task list immediately so that progress of the event can be tracked.

It is unlikely that you would attend a corporate luncheon or dinner; therefore, your duties would be limited to those of planning and verification. For such functions as retirement parties, receptions, and other companywide events in which you are involved in the planning process, you would be expected to attend. Your responsibilities would be expanded to include seeing that everything runs smoothly during the function. If the presentation of a gift is part of the function, you may be expected to determine the type of gift and make the actual purchase.

An administrative assistant who knows the social graces and is a good conversationalist makes a good impression on others and is a definite asset to the employer. When circulating and talking with guests, suggested topics of conversation are business events, sports topics, mutual experiences, travel, and hobbies. Avoid discussing business or company gossip of any type.

A helpful guide to every administrative assistant in a public relations role is a book of business etiquette. For information on planning meetings and conferences, refer to Chapter 17.

Summary

A very important responsibility of an administrative assistant is successful public relations. The administrative assistant is often the first contact a customer or client has with a company. This first contact can be face-to-face or over the telephone.

When welcoming office visitors, the administrative assistant becomes the public relations representative for the employer and for the company. The same is true when the administrative assistant answers the telephone or places a call for the employer. Recognizing frequent visitors—their faces and names—is an important aspect of this responsibility. Another is providing a receptive and hospitable office climate by treating each visitor with respect and courtesy.

Every employer has a set of preferences which the administrative assistant must consider in scheduling appointments. The administrative assistant must know these preferences and follow the employer's instructions.

A valuable asset to any office is the employee who displays an attractive telephone personality. Ease in conducting pleasant, effective telephone conversations comes with experience, proper training, and knowledge of telephone etiquette. Distinct enunciation is a necessity.

When answering incoming calls, some executives prefer that the administrative assistant screen all calls. The administrative assistant must learn the identification of the caller before putting the employer on the line. When the executive is unavailable to take phone calls, the administrative assistant completes a telephone message form. Messages left on voice mail or the typical telephone answering machine are recorded on telephone message forms as well. Long-distance calls have priority over other calls. A call from an angry customer is considered an opportunity to maintain the company's goodwill, and the administrative assistant conducts the call accordingly.

When placing outgoing calls, the administrative assistant identifies the name of the person being called and the name and affiliation of the caller.

As part of their public relations responsibilities, some administrative assistants are asked to plan special functions sponsored by the company. Examples of these events are weekly executive luncheons, receptions, and retirement parties.

QUESTIONS FOR DISCUSSION

1. You have read in this chapter that an administrative assistant is often the first contact a customer has with a company. What responsibilities does an administrative assistant have to make this a successful experience for the administrative assistant, the employer, and the customer?

2. In the following situations, you are asked to introduce the two persons specified. Which person would you afford the greater courtesy by naming first?

   a. Your employer's 14-year-old daughter and an administrative assistant in the office

   b. A well-known politician and your employer, president of the company

   c. Your elderly mother and your employer, Carl Samson

   d. Miss Alvarez, a business product sales representative, and your employer, Ralph Hazelton

   e. Rabbi Harold Silverman and your employer, Ms. Fishburg

   f. Professor James Ford and Alfred Bostick, Dean, College of Business

3. What special considerations or arrangements should be made for international visitors to the office?

THINK IT *Through*

4. Generally employers do not like to be interrupted during a conference. Yet, as an administrative assistant, you may have to talk with your employer. How would you proceed to do this?

THINK IT *Through*

5. Reword the following sentences to reflect better telephone usage.

   a. Sorry, I don't know where Miss Schwartz is. She should be at her desk.

   b. We don't give that information out to the public.

   c. You should have called the purchasing department for that information.

   d. I don't know who handles employee insurance, but Mr. Wallenstein doesn't.

e. Miss Lombardi is in a conference with the tax consultant.

f. I haven't got time to look it up, Mr. Kenyon. I have to get this report ready for the committee in 20 minutes.

g. I haven't the foggiest. I'll ask Marge to fill me in on what happened at that meeting.

h. Oh, I gave you the wrong information. I thought you were Professor Milligan of New York State College. She is writing a book on the same subject.

6. Select the correct word in parentheses. Refer to the Reference Guide to correct your answers.

a. Nancy's (fiance, fiancee) was (formally, formerly) employed by the Textor Company.

b. The attorney was selected because he is (an uninterested, a disinterested) expert on cases involving political corruption.

c. You should (insure, ensure) the package and wrap it securely to (insure, ensure) safe delivery.

d. Ice cream is an easy (desert, dessert) to prepare, and one that is appreciated by a large (number, amount) of people.

e. Mary is an (alumnus, alumna, alumni, alumnae) of St. Catherine's, and her brother is an (alumni, alumnus, alumnae, alumna) of Clemson. Both are (alumni, alumnae, alumnus, alumna) of State Community College.

*P*ROBLEMS

1. Analyze the following situations. How would you handle each of them? If the solution requires a conversation or note, indicate exactly what you would say. On a piece of paper, key your answer to each situation.

a. A visitor, while waiting for a scheduled appointment, makes the following statement: "I understand your employer was in New York last week."

b. A visitor on crutches is expected in ten minutes. You think the visitor will be bringing a carton of materials for your employer.

c. Your employer has called an important meeting in the office for 10:30 a.m. The company's most important customer arrives fifteen minutes early for this meeting.

d. Two important visitors are in the office with your employer. It is time for your coffee break.

e. A visitor is in your employer's office, and it is closing time.

f. A visitor whose appointment you forgot to cancel arrives as scheduled. Your employer is working under pressure to complete an important contract.

g. Your employer's daughter has called the office three times within the last hour. Your employer is in a meeting with other officers of the company.

h. An unscheduled visitor comes into the office to talk with your employer.

i. A caller who has failed to keep two appointments telephones for a third one.

2. You are an administrative assistant to Edward Finlay, an executive with True Products. Below are four telephone situations in which correct procedures were not followed. Key the recommendations you would make for handling each of these calls.

a. Mrs. Jones calls for your employer. Mr. Findlay is out of the office and you take the message to return the call. Mrs. Jones says that Mr. Findlay has her telephone number. You complete the message form and place it on your employer's desk.

b. Mrs. Jones calls and Mr. Findlay is out of the office. A call back is requested and all the information is provided to complete the message form. You promise to have Mr. Findlay return the call.

c. Mr. Findlay requests that you call Mrs. Jones for him. When the phone is answered, you say, "Mrs. Jones, please, Ed calling."

d. Mr. Findlay asks that you call Mrs. Jones. He wants to talk about one of the points outlined in a memorandum he received. You get Mrs. Jones on the line. Several minutes later, Mr. Findlay buzzes you to please bring in the file.

TECHNOLOGY APPLICATIONS

▶ **TA4-1.TEM**   Access the template disk, and select the TA4-1.TEM file, which presents a draft document for a Register of Office Visitors.

Revise the draft as follows:

1. Add a new column, "Time," to follow the "Date" column (and the same size as the "Date" column).

2. Relabel the "Name" column to read "Name & Affiliation."

3. Center the title REGISTER OF OFFICE VISITORS over the chart.

Save your revised draft document, print a second copy, and submit the revised Register to your instructor.

continued

continued

▶ TA4-2.TEM

Access the template disk, and select the TA4-2.TEM file, which duplicates one page from the manufacturer's instructions for using your firm's telephone system. The information is accurate, but it is far too wordy to be helpful! While employees are on the phone, they fumble through the wordy instructions in an effort to find the information they need.

You have been asked to create a short "reference card" that all employees can use to quickly find appropriate instructions while they are using the telephone. A sample of a helpful "reference card" is also shown on the template.

Develop the reference card. Use headings, as shown in the sample, and create a very concise list under each heading. Use numbers or symbols, whichever you consider appropriate, to highlight the items in your list. (Vary the typeface and type size, if possible.)

Case Problems

C

**Case 1-1
UNDERSTANDING
THE CULTURE**

Genevieve McCoy is a senior administrative assistant in the research and development department of a large manufacturing company. She, along with the six administrative assistants under her supervision, handles the information responsibilities of 30 engineers. The administrative assistants are located in an open-plan office and each has a self-contained workstation enclosed with panels. The work load is heavy and very technical in nature. Shorthand knowledge is not a requirement of the position. One of the administrative assistants, Pearl Watamabe, joined the department six weeks ago. Of Japanese descent, Pearl learned her administrative assistant skills at the local community college. Pearl is a very conscientious worker. She volunteers to help others when her time and work permit. One of her employers, Alan Scales, always prints his memos and reports for her to key. No matter how hard she tries, every document she keys for him has to be revised. She becomes very discouraged because she believes these revisions are a reflection on her ability. Mr. Scales is aware that she has trouble reading his printing and takes extra time to print as clearly as he can. Although Mr. Scales has always been nice to her and has never complained to Ms. McCoy, Pearl decides to ask for a transfer. According to company procedures, this is done through the human resources department. When Ms. McCoy learns that Pearl is transferring, she cannot understand what happened. She is concerned that as a supervisor she was not told something was wrong. She also wonders why she didn't sense that a problem existed.

What should Mr. Scales have done to rectify this situation? How should Ms. McCoy evaluate her supervisory responsibilities?

**Case 1-2
NOT IN MY JOB
DESCRIPTION**

Marjorie Whitman has been an administrative assistant for many years. She has recently been employed by a new company and is assigned to Benjamin Henry, manager of public relations. She is very happy with her immediate employer and her work, but has one major problem. An officer of the company, Estelle Ruggles, continues to ask her to do personal work for her. Mrs. Ruggles asks her to do her income taxes, prepare apartment leases, and make her coffee. This last task is particularly irksome to Marjorie because in the first place she doesn't even like coffee and, in the second place, being a maid is not in her job description. Mr. Henry says Marjorie is to assist Mrs. Ruggles in any way she can. Marjorie wants to tell Mrs. Ruggles to make her own coffee, but she fears that might jeopardize her job and possibly a future reference.

What should Marjorie do?

Case 1-3 WORKING WITH DIFFICULT PEOPLE

Sondra Howard has been on the job for six weeks. She and another administrative assistant, Karen Slaughter, are assigned to six employers. One manager, Reuben Kozary, has a limited background in English, and, therefore, his written communications take considerably more time and effort by the administrative assistant. Karen has let Sondra know that she does not want to do Mr. Kozary's work. Their supervisor is unaware of this situation, and Sondra decides that it is not her place to say anything. Because of Mr. Kozary's background, he makes a number of changes in the documents he prepares. On the last document six printings had to be run. He made 25 changes on the first printing, 50 changes on the second, 14 changes on the third, etc. Within the past two weeks, he has been blaming Sondra in private for the long time it takes her to prepare his work. His vocal complaints are having an effect on the work she does for her other managers. Sondra empathizes with Mr. Kozary's language problem, but she is beginning to assume a defensive attitude. She considers him a very difficult person. Otherwise, she is very happy with her position and would like to stay there.

What should Sondra do to keep her position?

Case 1-4 KEEPING A PROFESSIONAL DISTANCE

Ellen Poppin, an experienced administrative assistant, is a new hire at Andrews, Warden, Sullivan Advertising in New York City. She reports to David Sullivan, account executive for the three biggest accounts with the agency. For some, life in New York City can be in the fast lane, but Ellen's life away from the office revolves around her husband and her two young children. After her first week on the job, she felt confident that her relationship with Mr. Sullivan was going well. During the second week, however, the atmosphere seemed to change. Mr. Sullivan began to insist that he and Ellen be on a first-name basis. He liked that kind of informality. Ellen was somewhat concerned about professional distance, but decided she would go with his preference. One afternoon Mr. Sullivan called Ellen into his office, commented that it was time for them to become better acquainted, and said that there is no better way to do that than to have a drink together after closing hours. Ellen felt uneasy with the way Mr. Sullivan was looking at her. She immediately said she had a long train ride home and that she had to pick up the children no later than 6 p.m. She discerned the obvious disappointment on his face. The next morning, Mr. Sullivan suggested that they go to lunch, again stressing the fact that they needed to become better acquainted. Here, she thought, was the second danger signal. Is my job in jeopardy if I refuse his invitation? Should I go to lunch and see if my fears are really justified? What are his invitations leading to?

▬▬▬ **What should Ellen do in this situation?**

Case 1-5 COOPERATING WITH YOUR COLLEAGUES

Kathy Mathison's desk is located outside her employer's office along with two other administrative assistants. Kathy's work load is often extremely heavy, so much so that she often misses taking a coffee break. Her colleagues, Mary Alice and Sue, go to coffee together at regularly scheduled times, and have long since stopped inviting Kathy to go with them. Kathy is left to answer the phones. Kathy has always done her best to answer their phones the same way she does her own phone, with a pleasant voice and helpful attitude. Up to this time, there have been no complaints. Today, they had no sooner left for coffee when Kathy's employer, Samuel Green, called her into his office. He said he had an important memo to get out. And, as luck would have it, the phones started to ring. Kathy excused herself and said that she must answer the phone, that the others had gone to coffee. In a harsh voice Mr. Green said, "Ignore those rings, we have more important things to do than answer their phones." Without a word Kathy returned to the computer terminal and continued to key in Mr. Green's notes. When Mary Alice and Sue returned to the office, both phones were ringing. Kathy and Mr. Green couldn't help overhear Mary Alice's and Sue's remarks when they returned. "You would think Kathy could at least answer these phones. I suppose she just can't be bothered. Some people just have to act so important and so darned busy." Kathy was hurt by these remarks. She always considered herself a co-operative worker. Mr. Green offered no comment.

▬▬▬ **What should Kathy say when she returns to her desk?**

Case 1-6 TOO MANY BOSSES

Robert Slocum is administrative assistant to Bertram Wine, manager of administrative services for Advance Advertising Company. In addition to Mr. Wine, Robert works for three other individuals, all of whom have different demands and schedules. Robert's job duties include general tasks such as sorting the mail, answering the telephone, and greeting the public. Within the last month, Robert has felt increasing stress in trying to complete all of his work during the regular workday. Coming to work a half hour early and leaving later in the day has not helped the situation. When he mentioned the work overload to Mr. Wine, Mr. Wine told Robert to discuss the problem with his three other employers because his (Mr. Wine's) work takes priority. Feeling caught in the middle further increased the stress Robert was feeling. Being company-minded, Robert realized that the work of all his employers must get done, and he decided not to bring up the matter with them.

▬▬▬ **How can Robert convince Mr. Wine that additional staff is needed?**

Part 2

Technology and Procedures

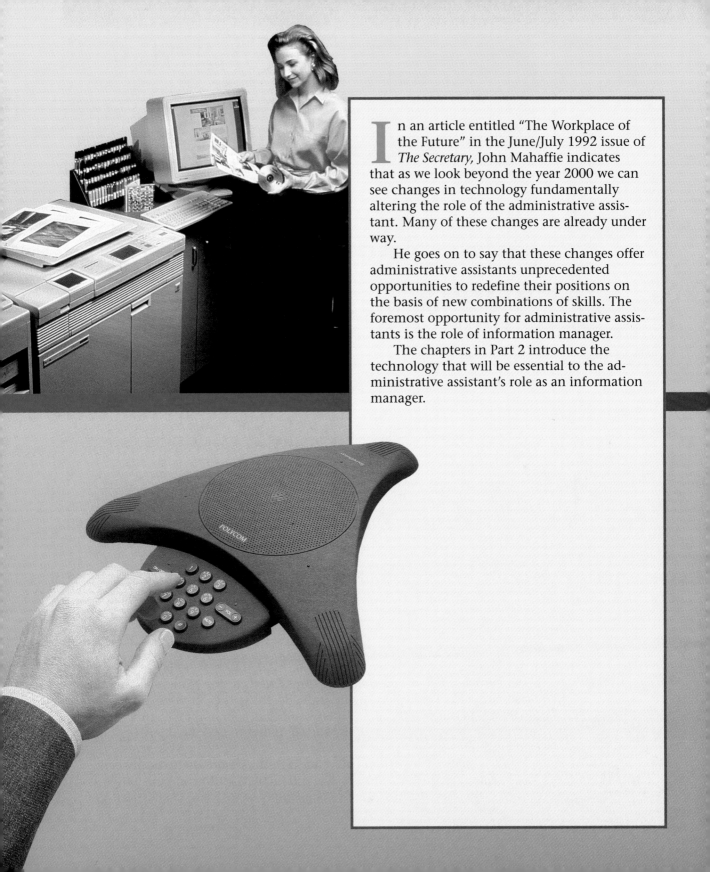

I n an article entitled "The Workplace of the Future" in the June/July 1992 issue of *The Secretary*, John Mahaffie indicates that as we look beyond the year 2000 we can see changes in technology fundamentally altering the role of the administrative assistant. Many of these changes are already under way.

He goes on to say that these changes offer administrative assistants unprecedented opportunities to redefine their positions on the basis of new combinations of skills. The foremost opportunity for administrative assistants is the role of information manager.

The chapters in Part 2 introduce the technology that will be essential to the administrative assistant's role as an information manager.

Chapter 5

Hardware and Software Systems

LEARNING OBJECTIVES

After studying this chapter and completing the activities, you will be able to:

1. Describe the impact of computer hardware and software on the administrative assistant's job responsibilities.
2. Identify the computer hardware components and explain their functions.
3. Explain the differences in the categories of computers: mainframe, mini, micro, and portable.
4. Explain the purpose of computer operating systems software.
5. Identify the various applications software and explain the functions of each.
6. Identify criteria that should be used when evaluating and selecting software.
7. Describe security procedures that can be used to protect computer hardware and software.
8. Understand the possibilities of future applications of computer hardware and software that will affect the administrative assistant's position.

INTRODUCTION

Today computers affect every facet of our lives. In our everyday lives we interact with computers when making transactions at the bank, making purchases at retail stores, checking in at the doctor's office or at hospitals, and frequently in our own homes. When you begin your employment as an administrative assistant, you will use the computer to execute many of your job responsibilities.

The explosive growth of computer technology has dramatically benefited the administrative assistant. The productivity of the administrative assistant has increased through the use of a variety of software applications that are available for computer systems. However, the computer skills of today's administrative assistants must go beyond the use of the microcomputer for basic word processing, spreadsheet, and database applications. These skills must include use of sophisticated graphics, desktop publishing, interactive video, and an understanding of computer networks.

Many administrative assistants also are being required to become adept at installation and customization of software and at hardware repair. Others must acquire an understanding of computer operating systems and sophisticated *macro creation* (a series of keystrokes that can be entered under a specific name enabling the operator to use fewer keystrokes). The administrative assistant can become a valuable member of the management team by utilizing the full power of the hardware and software available.

COMPUTER HARDWARE COMPONENTS

The physical devices, referred to as hardware, that make up a computer system include four components: input devices, the central processing unit, storage devices, and output devices (see Figure 5-1). Input devices such as the keyboard are used to enter information into the computer. The central processing unit (CPU) processes the information entered into the computer into a desirable form. The information that has been inputted and processed is

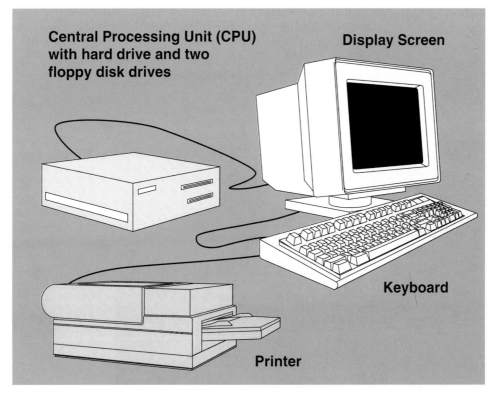

Central Processing Unit (CPU) with hard drive and two floppy disk drives

Display Screen

Keyboard

Printer

Fig. 5-1 This computer system illustrates the basic components of a computer hardware system including an input device, a central processing unit (CPU), a storage device, and an output device.

then saved on one of the storage devices available. Output devices display or print out information from the computer. Software, which provides the instructions for the operation of the hardware, enables the computer system to perform many different tasks. Applications of computer systems in the office environment today include the preparation of documents, manipulation and management of financial reports, and management of stored information such as mailing addresses and personnel records.

Input Devices

Information is entered into the computer by using a variety of input devices. The keyboard is the most widely used input device; however, other mechanisms such as the mouse, the optical character reader, the voice, and the light pen are also used. Each of these will be described in more detail below.

Keyboard. The keyboards used with most computer systems are separate units connected to the computer system by a cable. Keyboards for computer systems will vary in size, shape, and location of features. A standard keyboard includes alphanumeric keys, movement keys, numeric keys, and function keys. Keyboards are discussed in more detail in Chapter 9.

Optical Character Reader (OCR). Optical character readers, also referred to as scanners, scan and capture typed, printed, or handwritten information from paper and transfer this information to the computer (see Figure 5-2). Information transferred from the original document to the computer includes instructions for positioning tabs, indentions, and underscores. The OCR is used frequently as an economical means of inputting draft material into the computer because it eliminates the need to rekey information. In addition it is used when preparing material using desktop publishing and graphics software packages.

Fig. 5-2 An optical character reader (OCR) transfers printed material to magnetic media for use in computer systems. *Courtesy of International Business Machines Corporation.*

Mouse. Many computers use an input device called a mouse in addition to the keyboard. A **mouse** is a small, hand-operated attachment to the computer used as an electronic pointer (see Figure 5-3). By using the mouse the operator can give input processing commands and move the **cursor** (a beam of light on the computer screen that shows the place for entering text or making a change) without using the keyboard. When the mouse is manipulated on the top of the workstation, the cursor moves on the screen. The mouse can also be used to select functions to be performed from a **menu** (a listing of options). Once a menu option is selected and the button on the mouse is depressed, the function chosen will then be executed.

Voice. Voice-recognition technology enables the computer to recognize spoken words and phrases. Great strides are being made to perfect this form of input. Many current systems recognize single words or phrases from a limited vocabulary spoken by an individual. This type of input is used to give simple commands to computer programs or to enter specific data such as numbers.

Other types of voice-recognition systems are essentially voice-driven computers. They can interactively learn a user's vocabulary and speaking style (up to 30,000 words) and respond to natural language rather than limited sets of words spoken in a predetermined order. Users of this type of system can create a text at a speed of 30 to over 40 words per minute. The increased use of this type of system will eliminate the need for many of the traditional dictation and transcription functions currently performed in the office.

Pen. Rather than entering data via the keyboard or voice, many computer users prefer to write into them. The pen, or stylus, which is a pencil-like device, can be used to point, draw, or write on a computer screen. The pen may be attached to a regular microcomputer for artwork and graphic designs. In addition, handheld "pen" computers weighing as little as eight ounces are used for data entry by sales representatives, construction supervisors, and others who frequently need to collect information when working outside the office (see Figure 5-4). Users also can fill in on-screen forms with data.

Fig. 5-3 The administrative assistant is using the mouse to move the cursor on the screen.
Courtesy of International Business Machines Corporation.

TECHNOLOGY

Users of general-purpose, voice-driven computers can create text at a speed of 30 to 40 words per minute.

TECHNOLOGY

The electronic pen can either replace the keyboard or work with it.

Central Processing Unit

The central processing unit (CPU) is the "brains" of the computer. The CPU in most computers is in the form of electronic circuitry which performs the *mathematical, logic,* and *control functions* of the computer. In microcomputers much of the work of the CPU is performed by a *microprocessor* chip. The *microprocessors* found in computers today are physically about the size of postage stamps. These small devices contain enough circuitry to perform many of the complicated tasks required by a computer.

The CPU consists of (1) an internal storage or memory component, (2) an arithmetic/logic component, and (3) a control unit. The CPU accepts data from various input devices, processes the data according to the operator's instructions, and sends results to storage or to an output device. The relationship between the various components of a computer system is shown in Figure 5-5. The administrative assistant must understand these components in order to communicate effectively with other personnel in the company or when purchasing equipment.

Storage or Memory. **Storage** (frequently called *memory*) is the place where computer data and programs are stored. Storage is organized into thousands of individual locations, each with a unique "address." The speed with which the processing unit can locate an address and transfer the data to the arithmetic/logic component is referred to as **access time.**

Most computers have two types of storage: internal (also called primary) and external (secondary). **Internal storage** is quick-access storage. It holds data that are being used at a given time. **External storage** consists of de-

Fig. 5-4 Employees who work away from the office environment can gather data by using the pen to input information into the computer.
Dauphin Technology, Inc., Lombard, Illinois.

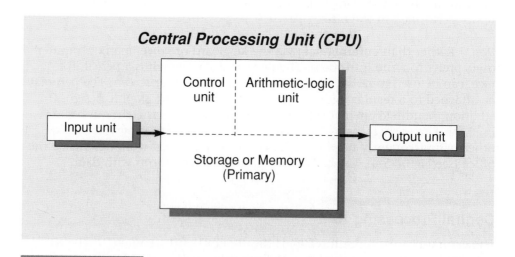

Central Processing Unit (CPU)

| Control unit | Arithmetic-logic unit |

Input unit →

Output unit

Storage or Memory (Primary)

Fig. 5-5 The relationship of the central processing unit (CPU) to other major parts of the computer.

vices, such as magnetic disks, that hold data until needed. Storing data on external or secondary media is less expensive than storing it internally in the CPU.

Arithmetic/Logic Component.   The arithmetic/logic section of the computer is like an electronic calculator that performs addition, subtraction, multiplication, and division. It can also logically compare and select alternate courses of action.

Control Unit.   The control unit directs the many functions of the computer system. It seeks instructions from stored information and then interprets and executes this data. It internally controls operations of input devices, the storage unit, the arithmetic/logic unit, and output devices.

Storage Devices

The most common method of storing information is on magnetic media. Typically data and programs are stored on magnetic media. **Data** consist of words, symbols, and numbers in an unprocessed form. A **program** is a group of instructions that cause the computer to perform desired functions. From magnetic media the programs or data can be retrieved from storage when needed. Magnetic media can take several forms: floppy disks, hard disks, and, occasionally, magnetic tape.

In all cases, the storage of the program or data on media involves the use of a storage device, usually a **disk drive.** The disk drive is designed to read program instructions or data from a disk into computer memory and to transfer instructions or data from the memory onto the disk for storage purposes. The type of disk drive used in a computer will vary with the cost of the computer and the intended applications. A floppy disk drive uses a floppy disk, while a hard disk drive uses an internal, nonremovable disk for storage. Optical disks are also used for storage of information.

Floppy Disks.   Floppy disks are a convenient method of storing information on a magnetic medium. They can be transferred between like computers, placed in a cabinet for safekeeping, and easily erased when the need to retain stored documents or data has passed.

As computer technology has changed, floppy disk sizes have changed. Today, two common sizes of floppy disks are available along with two variations in storage capacity for each disk size. Floppy disks are manufactured for computers in a 5 1/4" or 3 1/2" size.

When purchasing new disks, it is important to know which type of disks are to be used with your computer so that the maximum amount of information can be stored on each disk. The choice between a 3 1/2" disk or a 5 1/4" disk is governed by the physical size of the floppy disk drive in your computer. A quick glance at the computer will confirm which size of floppy disk is needed. The smaller, 3 1/2" floppy disk is the more modern size. It utilizes a disk housed in a fairly rigid plastic case that provides a measure of protection for the internal magnetic material and the programs and data stored on the magnetic medium. The more pliable (floppier) 5 1/4" floppy disk comes in a removable lightweight cardboard or paper jacket that provides minimal protection for the magnetic material. These disks are easily bent, soiled, or otherwise damaged and should be handled with extreme care.

Hard Disks. Like a floppy disk, a hard disk uses a magnetic medium to store programs and data for retrieval at a later time. However, the hard disk cannot be removed from the hard disk drive. The hard disk drive is an integral part of the computer and can be removed only by computer service personnel. Although the ability to transfer data or programs to external storage media, called **archiving,** is less convenient with a hard disk drive than with a floppy disk drive, a hard disk drive has much greater storage capacity. A typical floppy disk can contain approximately 300 pages of text; a typical hard disk drive can hold approximately 6,000 pages.

The hard disk drive also allows quicker access to stored information than the floppy disk drive. A variety of software programs can be stored and accessed on the hard disk drive, eliminating the need to handle floppy disks. The advantages of speed and storage capacity make the hard disk drive an essential part of a contemporary computer. (See Figure 5-6.)

Optical Disks. The optical disk is a new storage and retrieval technique that involves the use of **laser** technology coupled with a rotating disk, much like the audio compact disc (CD) commonly used with stereo systems. **Laser**

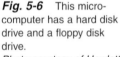

Fig. 5-6 This micro-computer has a hard disk drive and a floppy disk drive.
Photo courtesy of Hewlett-Packard Company.

technology makes use of a focused beam of light which reads information stored on the rotating plastic disk. Rather than using a conventional magnetic medium to write or read information onto or from the disk, a laser beam reads information from the rotating disk. This technology will have a great impact on the automated office because many new applications will be available through the use of optical disks.

One form of optical disk, the compact-disc read only memory (CD-ROM) can contain upwards of 700 megabytes (MB) of data which may consist of text, image, animation, video, and sound. The CD-ROM is a convenient method of distributing large volumes of information such as databases, instruction manuals, telephone directories, and other records. The large amount of information contained within a CD-ROM makes this technology a very cost-effective way of providing large amounts of information to many computer users.

Magnetic Tape.   Magnetic tape has been used as a storage medium for computer information for many years. Over the past ten years the popularity of floppy disks and hard disks has relegated magnetic tape to a smaller segment of the computer field. Software backup is the only remaining application that utilizes magnetic tape. In this application, a tape cartridge is inserted into a cartridge recorder, which is either built into the computer or connected to the computer. A copy is made of the software contained on the hard disk. This archiving or storage process assures that a permanent copy of the contents will be stored on the hard disk. If the hard disk drive should malfunction, a copy of its contents is on the tape and can be reloaded into the computer. Archiving of a computer's hard disk using a magnetic tape unit is generally done on a regular basis, perhaps once a week or month, to ensure that up-to-date information is always on file in a safe location.

Output Devices

When you think of output devices, you normally think of printers. However, the display monitor, also known as the cathode ray tube (CRT) or video display terminal (VDT), should be considered an output device.

Display Monitors.   The display monitor, which looks like a television screen, enables the administrative assistant to view the data being keyed into the computer. (See the display monitor in Figure 5-6.) In addition, information stored in the computer can be called from memory to the screen for changes and corrections. Output on the display monitor is called "soft copy" because it is viewed but not printed. Display monitors can vary in size. The 24-line display monitor is the one in most common use. However, full-page, 66-line monitors are gaining in popularity, especially for desktop publishing applications. The quality of text displayed on a monitor can vary. Today most monitors are identified as VGA (video graphics array) or Super VGA. Monitors are available in monochrome or color.

Printers. Nearly all office computers use a printer as an output device. These printers use a variety of printing technologies. They come in many styles and sizes and are often selected for printing specific software applications.

One of the most important decisions to make when purchasing a computer system, other than selecting the computer itself, is the selection of a printer. This decision is important as it may affect the appearance and quality of the printed page and may limit the types of software that can be used with the printer. Thought also should be given to any anticipated changes in the future printing needs of the computer user as well as the effect of technological improvements.

Printer output generally can be grouped into three categories—word processing, data presentation, and graphics, as well as a combination of any of these three categories. **Word processing** output typically consists of correspondence, reports, and manuscripts. **Data presentation** output generally takes the form of numerical tables such as financial reports. **Graphics** output includes drawings, charts, and graphs. The administrative assistant must understand the printing output needs of the office in order to choose the correct printer for the intended applications.

COMPUTER SYSTEMS

The administrative assistant in today's office will encounter many types of computer systems. The systems may include mainframe computers, minicomputers, microcomputers, and portable computers. This section will focus on the characteristics of some of the most common computer systems.

Mainframe Computers

The mainframe computer, which is large in size, has the greatest capacity to store and process information rapidly. These computers also have the ability to communicate with a number of users simultaneously. In some instances, the mainframe computer is superior to minicomputers or microcomputers for high-volume or sophisticated applications.

Mainframe computers are used in large organizations such as government offices, hospitals, corporations, universities, and companies that sell computer time to smaller companies. An office that uses a mainframe computer will certainly employ a staff of computer technicians to monitor the operation of the computer and to ensure that it is working properly. These staff members can be of help when communication or software difficulties arise.

Minicomputers

The minicomputer is used in offices where the capacity of a mainframe computer is too large, but more computing power is needed than can be provided by a microcomputer. A number of workstations can be connected to the minicomputer. It is really a smaller version of the mainframe. The minicomputer is especially useful in engineering offices, scientific laboratories, or architectural companies where a large amount of mathematical calculating is done or where computer-aided design (CAD) is a significant part of the work load. In these environments, the minicomputer allows the simultaneous use of a variety of software applications by a number of users. (See Figure 5-7.)

Microcomputers

By far the most popular computer system used in the office today is the microcomputer. The microcomputer has made computing power available to administrative assistants and management personnel. The microcomputer,

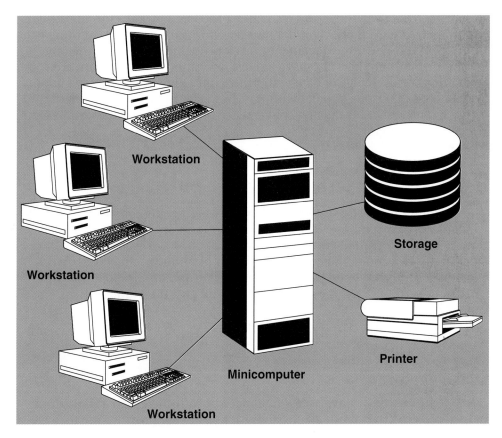

Fig. 5-7 A number of users can access the minicomputer at the same time.

Workstation

Workstation

Workstation

Minicomputer

Storage

Printer

Fig. 5-8 The microcomputer enables the administrative assistant to complete a variety of tasks more efficiently.
Courtesy of International Business Machines Corporation.

which gets its name from the microchip that made it possible, is small enough to sit on an office workstation. The typical microcomputer system in an office today has both floppy and hard disk drives, a printer, and possibly a cable connection to a network which links the microcomputer to other microcomputers, a mainframe computer, or a minicomputer. (See Figure 5-8.)

Portable Computers

A fast-growing segment of the microcomputer market is the portable computer. This type of microcomputer is popular in situations when computing capabilities are needed away from the office or in any situation not requiring a permanent computer workstation. Portable computers can be divided into three categories according to weight and size. These include laptop, notebook, and palmtop computers.

Portable computers are battery operated and generally contain a floppy disk drive, a hard disk drive, a screen, and a keyboard. Connectors are available on the computer so that, when the traveler returns to the office, a printer can be connected for printing documents developed while away from the office. Most portable computers also have a plug connection for a **modem,** a device permitting the exchange of data with other computers over telephone lines. Portable computers are popular with traveling sales representatives, accountants, and others who value the convenience of a computer while away from the office. (See Figure 5-9.)

COMPUTER SOFTWARE

The computer hardware systems discussed earlier in this chapter are complicated pieces of machinery. However, this hardware only becomes functional when used in conjunction with software. Software provides the step-by-step directions the machine needs to perform specific tasks. Two types of software are operating systems software and applications software. This section will discuss these types of software and the purposes they serve.

Operating Systems Software

Every computer must have access to a piece of software called a **disk operating system (DOS).** The operating system software provides the management of the floppy disk drive, the hard disk drive, the keyboard, and the display monitor. This software normally is resident within the computer on the hard disk drive. In general, the operating system controls the interaction of the hardware components of the computer system. When the computer is turned on, the operating system software is loaded from the hard disk drive into the computer memory. This initial loading of the operating system must occur before applications software, such as word processing and spreadsheets, can be loaded into the computer.

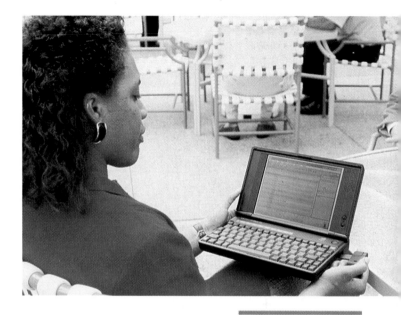

If an attempt is made to load a floppy disk into a computer before the operating system is loaded, an error message similar to the following will appear on the computer screen:

**NON-SYSTEM DISK OR DISK ERROR
REPLACE AND STRIKE ANY KEY WHEN READY**

In addition to managing the hardware components of a microcomputer, the DOS allows the computer to perform a number of disk-related functions; for example:

Format or initialize a disk.

Copy the contents of one disk to another disk.

Copy one document (file) from one disk to another disk.

List a catalog or directory of all the documents (files) on disk.

A variety of operating systems are used in computers. The three most popular operating systems are MS-DOS/PC-DOS, Windows, and OS/2.

MS-DOS/PC-DOS. The most popular operating system found in the office today is MS-DOS, often called PC-DOS. This product, which is produced by Microsoft® Corporation, is used by most IBM and IBM-compatible microcomputers. This is a *command-driven* operating system.

Windows. Windows™ is a special type of software that is used on IBM and IBM-compatible computers. This software, produced by Microsoft®

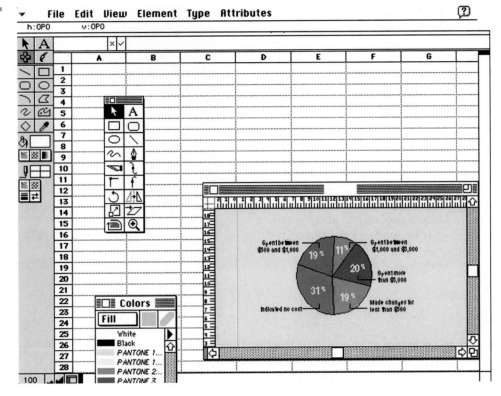

TECHNOLOGY

The goal of Windows is to spare the computer user from having to master the command structure of the computer's operating system.

Corporation, is an enhancement to DOS that frees the user from the complexity of the DOS command structure. Windows provides little pictures, called **icons** (see Figure 5-10). Working with a mouse, the user can "click on" an icon to accomplish DOS functions instead of keying on the command line. When using desktop publishing software, it is desirable to have access to the Windows environment.

This approach is called "graphical user interface"or GUI (pronounced "gooey") for short. A graphical user interface and a mouse-driven operation greatly simplify the operation of a microcomputer in many ways. Icons, for example, make the selection of applications software or DOS functions easy since complex command sequences are no longer needed.

Compared with the traditional MS-DOS operating system, Windows requires computer systems that are equipped with considerably more memory and hard disk space. If adequate memory is not provided in the computer system, Windows will cause application programs and DOS functions to operate a good deal more slowly.

OS/2. The operating system OS/2, produced by IBM Corporation, also incorporates a GUI in its operation. OS/2 is a true graphical operating system intended to replace MS-DOS and Windows. OS/2 excels at handling multiple applications at the same time. For example, running a word processor and a database in different windows on the computer screen at the same time is easily accomplished with OS/2. OS/2 requires powerful computers with significant amounts of memory and hard disk storage space.

Other Operating Systems.   Other operating systems in use today include DR-DOS, NT, UNIX, Pen-Point, XENIX, and Apple Computer System 7. Each operating system has its own unique method of operation and its own strengths and weaknesses. However, they all accomplish the same task of managing the input and output of the computer along with storage and retrieval of data from disk storage.

Applications Software

Applications software lets you perform specific tasks on your computer. The demand for applications software is huge, and there are thousands of applications software programs to choose from to handle business operations. This section will discuss the following categories of software packages that you as an administrative assistant are likely to use: word processing, spreadsheets, database management, graphics, communications, integrated packages, desktop publishing, and personal information management (PIM).

Word Processing.   Word processing software is the most widely used applications software on the market today. In fact, word processing software brought the computer to the administrative assistant's workstation by increasing productivity and efficiency in preparing written communications. This software enables you to create, store, retrieve, edit, and print a wide range of documents. A more detailed description of the features of word processing software is provided in Chapter 9, Processing Documents.

Because word processing software users are becoming more sophisticated, newer word processing programs offer more advanced features. These features include:

Operating at much faster speeds

Indexing capability

Graphics capability

Spelling checker

Thesaurus

Dictionary

Grammar checker

Word processing software packages can vary from basic applications to very sophisticated applications including desktop publishing capabilities. Therefore, before purchasing new word processing software, you must determine your specific needs and evaluate the features available on a number of software packages. See Figure 5-11 for an example of word processing applications.

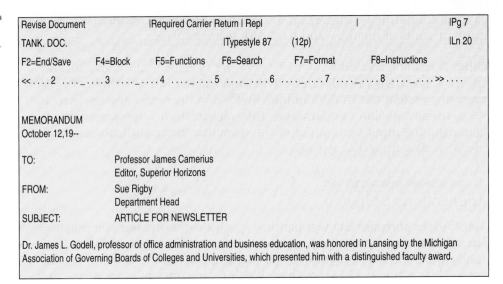

Fig. 5-11 Word processing software has revolutionized the way written documents are prepared in the office today.

Spreadsheets. Spreadsheets have been prepared manually for years using columns and rows on ruled accounting paper. Similarly, spreadsheets on the computer are set up in columns and rows. These columns and rows form a series of cells where numerical data are stored. In addition, spreadsheets can store entire formulas that enable the spreadsheet to be recalculated immediately any time a number is changed. While the initial development of the spreadsheet can be time-consuming and must be done with skill and accuracy, its ability to automatically calculate has eliminated tedious tasks that once had to be done manually and has dramatically increased productivity in the office.

After word processing, the use of spreadsheet software for financial analysis functions is the most popular application for microcomputers. Spreadsheets are used not only for routine accounting but also for "what-if" inquiries with a proposed plan or budget. You can experiment with different situations because the computer will recalculate the formulas in the entire spreadsheet whenever a number is changed. In addition, spreadsheets can be used for:

Analyzing sales data

Preparing financial forecasts

Budgeting

The development and manipulation of spreadsheets can provide management with information needed to support business decisions. See Figure 5-12 for an example of a spreadsheet application.

Databases. Database software is used as a very powerful electronic filing cabinet. Just as in a manual filing system, data are entered and stored in a specific format requested by the user. The data then can be retrieved or manipulated by identifying the specific format in which the data are to be

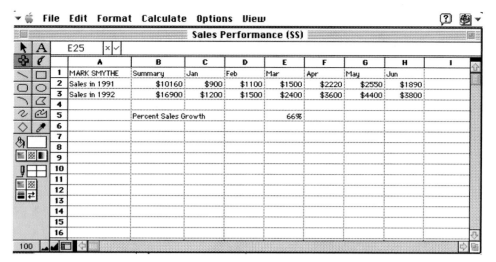

Fig. 5-12 The spreadsheet is used for financial analysis and as supporting information for management decisions.

presented. Basically, database software stores information and helps you find the information you need. By using the computer to store information, the amount of physical filing storage space needed is greatly reduced, and the speed with which the information can be retrieved can be greatly increased.

All databases are made up of sets of **records.** As an example, a personnel office maintains a record for every employee in the company. Within each employee record, a number of fields contain information such as the address, social security number, phone number, years of employment, department of employment, salary, vacation days available, sick days available, etc. Most databases are set up in columns and rows similar to a spreadsheet. Each record is made up of one row of fields. See Figure 5-13 for an example of a database application.

Graphics.   Frequently, the printed word is the best way to communicate information. However, as you become more inundated with the information produced by the computer, you need help to interpret and digest the information more quickly. The old saying that a picture is worth a thousand words certainly applies to the use of graphics software in illustrating information produced by the computer.

Usually you will use graphics software to prepare analytical graphs (such as line graphs, bar charts, and pie charts) to help the reader analyze and understand specific information being presented. The graphics information may be integrated into a written report, or it may be used separately for presentation at a meeting. Many graphics software packages are available for use in the office. You must be careful when selecting a program to be sure that the software meets your needs relating to such factors as your computer system, the type of graphics you want to produce, and the cost. Figure 5-14 shows a chart prepared using graphics software. More information is provided about graphics software in Chapter 15.

A1: [W7] 'TITLE

READY

	A	B	C	D	E	F	G	H	I
1	TITLE	FIRST NAME	LAST NAME	SCHOOL	SCHOOL STREET	SCHOOL CITY	ST	ZIP	
2	Mr.	Joseph	Simmons	A.D. Johnston High School	Moore Street	Bessemer	MI	49911	
3	Ms.	Anne	Stone	Baraga Township High School	210 Lyons Street	Baraga	MI	49908	
4	Ms.	Emi	Kato	Bark River-Harris High School	U.S. 2 & 41	Harris	MI	49845	
5	Ms.	Karen	Anderson	Bay de Noc Community College	2001 N. Lincoln Rd.	Escanaba	MI	49829	
6	Ms.	Linda	Baines	Bay de Noc Community College	2001 N. Lincoln Rd.	Escanaba	MI	49829	
7	Mr.	Milton	Cateel	Bay de Noc Community College	2001 N. Lincoln Rd.	Escanaba	MI	49829	
8	Ms.	Susan	Dover	Bay de Noc Community College	2001 N. Lincoln Rd.	Escanaba	MI	49829	
9	Mr.	Doug	Ganney	Bay de Noc Community College	2001 N. Lincoln Rd.	Escanaba	MI	49829	
10	Mr.	Roberto	Mendez	Bay de Noc Community College	2001 N. Lincoln Rd.	Escanaba	MI	49829	
11	Ms.	Dolores	Thorne	Bay de Noc Community College	2001 N. Lincoln Rd.	Escanaba	MI	49829	
12	Ms.	Carol	Hartwig	Big Bay de Noc School District	Highway M-183	Cooks	MI	49817	
13	Mrs.	Susan	Weymouth	Big Bay de Noc School District	Highway M-183	Cooks	MI	49817	
14	Mr.	Charles	Mattson	Brimley High School		Brimley	MI	49715	
15	Mr.	Milt	Southern	Brimley High School		Brimley	MI	49715	
16	Ms.	Carla	Kotten	Burt Township High School	Box 296	Grand Marais	MI	49839	
17	Mr.	Eva	Tramble	Calumet High School	Calumet Avenue	Calumet	MI	49813	
18	Ms.	Kathryn	Wattson	Calumet High School	Calumet Avenue	Calumet	MI	49813	
19	Mr.	Tom	Brown	Carney-Nadeau Public School	P.O. Box 68	Carney	MI	49812	
20	Ms.	Carol	Van Able	Carney-Nadeau Public School	P.O. Box 68	Carney	MI	49812	

01/Jan/19--

Fig. 5-13   This database program is made up of rows and columns. Each record is made up of a row of fields.

Fig. 5-14 A graphic presentation of business data can assist the reader in analyzing and under-standing the information.

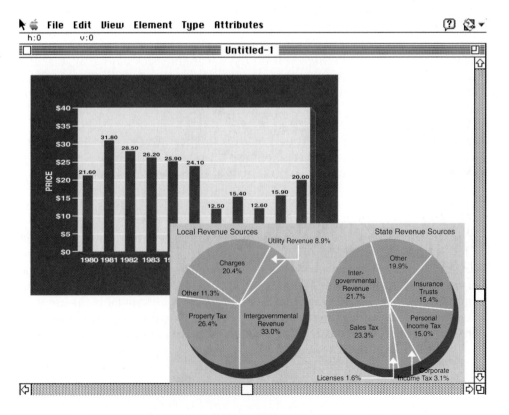

Communications.   Communications software enables the user of a micro-computer to receive and transmit information to and from other computers in other locations. Information also can be obtained from information retrieval services or public databases using communications software. Other applications include sending mail or data electronically. The user must have access to a modem and telephone lines to use the communications software. These communications applications will be discussed in detail in Chapter 8.

Integrated Packages.   Integrated software packages combine applications such as word processing, database management, spreadsheets, graphics, and communications into a single group of programs. In the past, software pack-ages were designed to perform only one of these functions at a time. Because these software programs were not designed to share information, the user constantly had to exit one program and enter another to retrieve informa-tion. The integrated software programs that offer two or more applications in one program provide a solution to this problem.

An integrated software package provides many advantages. Because these programs allow you to perform a variety of applications, you eliminate the need to constantly enter and exit programs and to change disks. When information is entered into one application of the software, such as the spreadsheet, it can be used in all of the other applications of the software. This saves a tremendous amount of time. Because the same commands are used to perform various functions, the user develops proficiency in operating the software.

Desktop Publishing.   The use of desktop publishing software in the office frequently is the responsibility of the administrative assistant. A **desktop publishing program** allows you to transfer text created by a word process-ing program into professional-looking documents such as:

Customer newsletters

Employee newsletters

Policies and procedures manuals

Sales brochures

Business forms

Money can be saved by doing design and layout in your own office. This software enables you to experiment with various types of design and lay-out. Type sizes and styles can be mixed, ruled lines can be added, and graph-ics can be inserted. Typeset-quality copy is then produced on a high-quality printer. This process eliminates the many "cut-and-paste" steps required to prepare material for printing. Instead, the layout is done on a computer, and the screen display takes the place of a drawing board.

Most computer systems are capable of using desktop publishing soft-ware. Regardless of the computer used, most desktop publishing systems will use a laser printer. Some may also use a scanner or optical character reader to read material into the computer which can then be edited and reprinted.

TECHNOLOGY

Administrative assistants equipped with a computer and a laser printer can take advantage of desktop publishing's numerous software packages.

The use of this software in the office has moved the preparation of publishable documents squarely into the office environment. Many offices now do much of their preparation of materials for printing within the company rather than sending it out. The administrative assistant now has additional responsibilities in connection with the use of this software in preparing manuals, brochures, and other published documents.

Personal Information Management (PIM). Personal information management software, often referred to as PIM software, is a program that assists in managing people, projects, and a variety of information sources. Typical software features include the following:

1. To-do lists which track daily, weekly, and monthly activities.
2. Phone lists for a personal telephone directory.
3. Notepads to keep various notes on activities and projects.
4. Card files containing vital data on clients.
5. Calendars to record short- and long-term calendaring events.
6. Calculators to complete basic math functions.
7. Project lists to identify outstanding projects and their due dates.

The traditional tools of the office such as yellow sticky notes, to-do lists, calendars and schedules, Rolodex cards, tickler files, and in-baskets are giving way to the PIM software. By using this software, you can substantially increase your productivity. A PIM software screen is illustrated in Figure 3-3 on page 43.

Multimedia Software. Multimedia software combines a variety of technologies to enhance computer-based presentations. These presentations can include text, data, graphics, animation, audio, and video that can be viewed on a computer screen or other output screen such as a television set. Most current multimedia applications are geared towards entertainment, education, and reference. However, these applications now are being incorporated into software programs such as word processing and spreadsheets.

Recent studies by the Wharton School of Business and 3M conclude that audiences retain approximately 10 percent of what they hear. However, when visuals are added, the retention rate increases to 50 percent. The use of multimedia presentations will enable the user to provide more effective, people-oriented communication. Figure 5-15 shows a multimedia software application.

Fig. 5-15 Multimedia applications enable the user to integrate video, audio, and animation into traditional computer applications.
Courtesy of International Business Machines Corporation.

Software Evaluation and Selection

Choosing the appropriate software for use with microcomputers is a difficult task. Most people have a favorite software package and are happy to recommend it to you. However, software that meets the needs of one company may not be appropriate for your company.

Several important factors should be taken into consideration when purchasing software. You first should determine your company's needs and then only buy software that meets those needs. You should always try out the software before you buy it. Most computer software sales outlets will allow you to try out your applications on the software before final purchase.

The software must be compatible with your computer system; this includes the operating system as well as the hardware. Because some software packages require the use of more memory than others, you must be sure that your computer has sufficient memory to run the software. Compatibility of other components such as the display monitor, the printer, and the disk drives is also important.

Many software packages are available for every application you may need. Therefore, you should compare like features of several of these packages before making a selection. Important features to consider are:

Ease of use

Documentation

Safeguards

Service

Compatibility

Calling software "user-friendly" means that a person with very little computer experience can understand how to use it. When trying out software, you should look at such features as the *menus, commands,* and *help screens.* The menus are important to the software user because they identify the choice of functions available. On software that does not use menus, functions are performed by using command words. Help screens provide the user with additional information or instructions when using the software. In addition, the instruction manual, also called documentation, should be written so that it is easy to understand. Step-by-step instructions should make the operation of the software clear to you. Safeguards should be embedded in the program that allow you to recover information when mistakes are made. Software developers who stand behind their products usually provide emergency numbers you can call for help. Other services that should be investigated include replacement of damaged software and the ability to update the software at a nominal cost when an improved version is issued.

LOCAL AREA NETWORKS (LANs)

Local area networks, often called LANs, connect microcomputers located near each other so they can share information and resources in an effective, cost-efficient way. LANs provide many services and capabilities that can enhance the administrative assistant's work. They allow expensive peripherals such as high-speed laser printers, large disk drives, CD-ROMs, modems, and micro-computer-based facsimile (FAX) equipment to be shared as easily by all net-work users as if they were part of each user's own microcomputer.

LANs provide information sharing and communications not possible with stand-alone microcomputers. By using a networked server, departmental and corporate information can be shared by all appropriate users, and docu-ments can be sent within work groups for review and comments. Electronic mail, which is available on the LAN, also allows users to send and receive messages and information in ways not feasible with paper or voice.

LANs are for small companies as well as large ones. Low-cost, easy-to-use LANs are now available that bring the benefits of networking to groups as small as two or three users. Networking technology will continue to advance in the future offering higher performance and more flexibility.

SECURITY CONSIDERATIONS

As the use of microcomputers has increased, more people have developed an increasingly sophisticated knowledge of computer systems in general. Some of these more knowledgeable people are gaining access illegally to private in-formation stored on company computers. As a result, greater emphasis is being placed on developing policies that minimize or prevent data loss due to theft, accident, or equipment failure.

Security Procedures

Many experts believe that nearly 95 percent of all computer security breaches go undetected. While most mainframe computer systems have elaborate secu-rity procedures, many microcomputer users have not addressed this problem. With the increased integration of microcomputers with mainframe systems and networks, the need for security procedures has increased. Information stored on any magnetic media is easy to copy, and microcomputer magnetic media such as disks are portable and easy to conceal or steal. In addition, a security problem occurs when only one copy of a document exists and is erased. If the microcomputer is connected to any type of communications system, security problems increase.

A number of steps can be taken to prevent theft or destruction of hard-ware or software. Equipment can be bolted down, or locking computer furni-ture can be purchased. Precautions such as locking doors to equipment rooms and the use of security guards can be effective precautions. You can arrange for backup computer facilities if your equipment should be stolen or mal-function.

The most important precaution you can take for security of data stored on the computer is to arrange for a backup of all material that you have on magnetic media. This information should be stored in a separate location. Administrative assistants should lock up floppy disks when they are away from their desks and when they leave for the day. Software that provides a locking feature for the hard drive of a microcomputer also is available. Frequently access to computer programs is limited by assigning a password or access code to individuals who should have access to classified information on the computer. The password or access code must be entered into the computer each time the individual uses the computer system before the program can be accessed. Another precaution to use in protecting access to software is frequently changing the password or access code for individuals who have access to classified information. Individuals who have access to classified information on a computer system can be searched as they enter and leave their place of employment each day. The company should periodically review the security policies and procedures to be sure that security needs are being met.

Computer Viruses

Computer viruses are a serious threat to computer security. A **computer virus** is a program introduced into the computer without the permission or knowledge of management. It invades computer processors and disrupts normal operation of the computer in much the same way that a biological virus disrupts living cells and causes disease in a human being. A computer virus is a computer program that carries in its code instructions for reproducing itself perfectly. When it invades a computer, the virus temporarily takes control of the operating system, which is the program that enables the computer to run applications software programs. The virus spreads into other programs and then spreads from one computer to the next as users share disks and link their computers via telephone lines.

Computer viruses, which are usually spread by pranksters and criminals, have the potential to wreak havoc by destroying data or impeding computers that are vital to business and government. As a result new security measures are increasing to guard against this potential.

Antivirus programs have been developed that can check your computer software for viruses; this software can eradicate any virus that is found. Guidelines that can be used to help prevent or control viruses include the following:

1. Purchase all software from known, reputable sources.

2. Test new software on an isolated computer before introducing it into a computer system or sharing it with other users.

3. Back up all master software and computer data at least once a month so that the backups can be used if current versions are invaded by a virus.

4. Periodically scan hard disk drives on your computers for viruses.

THE FUTURE OF COMPUTER SYSTEMS

The future holds the promise of continued change in computer systems used in the office. During the past 20 years administrative assistants have seen phenomenal changes in office technology. Only your imagination will limit the vision of changes that will occur during the next 15 years.

Engineers and other technological experts agree that continued research in electronics, computers, and software will produce new and improved products for the office. The graphical user interface (GUI) will become the most dominant operating system because it greatly simplifies the operation of the microcomputer.

High on the list of products that will be widely used are computers that recognize voice input so that initial keyboarding can be eliminated. New developments have overcome the problem of dialects. Computers that recognize handwriting when written with a special pen will be used frequently in work situations away from the office environment. Variations in handwriting style and appearance are now recognized and understood by the computer. While these methods of input of text and data will not replace the keyboard, they will offer the computer user options. Some of these technologies will be mentioned in later chapters.

During the next ten years electronic miniaturization will reduce the size of computers to systems that will fit in the palm of your hand. The highly portable computers will be able to recognize voice and handwriting, as well as incorporate keyboards, display screens, telephones, and FAX machines. In the future, you may be wearing a personal computer like clothing!

The technologies of telecommunications and computers are converging so that linking computers to other computers will be as commonplace as talking on the telephone is today. Picture phones as well as other applications for the telephone will be available at the office and at home.

The use of multimedia for presentations and records management will be commonplace by the year 2000. The result will be more people-oriented communications using all facets of technology available.

The challenge you face as an administrative assistant is to be prepared to accept the new technology. If you use the new technology to its full potential, you will not only be a more productive employee; you will also find your work more interesting and challenging.

Summary

The explosive growth of computer systems technology has dramatically enhanced the productivity of the administrative assistant. Computer systems are increasingly being used in today's office to classify, sort, merge, record, retrieve, transmit, and report large quantities of information.

The components of a computer system include input devices, the central processing unit (CPU), storage devices, and output devices. These component parts are referred to as the computer system's hardware. Computer hardware systems may include mainframe computers, minicomputers, microcomputers, portable computers, or a combination of these computers. When increased capabilities are needed, microcomputers can be interconnected with a mainframe computer, a minicomputer, or other microcomputers. The microcomputer can be expanded to include the capabilities of sharing information and sharing printers as well as accessing the storage capacity and computing power of other computers.

Computer software is required to operate computer hardware systems. Operating systems software is a group of special software that provides for the management of the floppy disk drive, the hard disk drive, the keyboard, and the display monitor. Applications software lets you perform specific tasks on your computer. Many applications software programs are used by the administrative assistant. These programs include word processing, spreadsheets, database management, graphics, communications software, integrated software packages, desktop publishing, personal information management (PIM) software, and multimedia software.

Care must be taken to prevent the theft or destruction of computer hardware and software. The most important precaution you can take for security of data stored on the computer is to arrange for a backup of all material that you have stored. Precautions should also be taken to avoid contamination of your data by computer viruses. The use of antivirus programs can assist in checking your software for viruses.

The future for computer systems will include continued research in electronics, computers, and software that will produce new and improved products for the office. If you use the new technology to its full potential, you will not only be a more productive employee, but you will also find your work more interesting and challenging.

QUESTIONS FOR DISCUSSION

1. Why is it important for an administrative assistant entering the office today to have a background in computer technology?

2. The use of computer systems enables the administrative assistant to work more efficiently. Do you think this assistance from office automation improves job satisfaction for the administrative assistant?

3. How can companies combat the loss of computer equipment as well as the data and information stored on computer equipment?

THINK IT
Through

4. Predictions indicate that many changes and improvements in technology will take place in the next 20 years. How can the administrative assistant prepare for these changes?

5. Rekey the following sentences using the correct punctuation. Use the Reference Guide to correct your answers.

    a. We lost the election it was held too soon.

    b. I ordered the book in May however it was not mailed until July.

    c. Make your letters attractive for example leave at least a one inch margin at the bottom.

    d. The stock dividend was declared on May 4, 1994 August 4, 1994 and June 4, 1995.

    e. I have scheduled flights for Boston Philadelphia and New York but the strike will delay all three.

PROBLEMS

1. Visit an office that uses microcomputers or computer terminals connected to a mainframe or minicomputer. Interview administrative assistants to determine how their job responsibilities have changed as a result of using the computer to complete many of their tasks. Prepare a report analyzing the changes that have taken place in the responsibilities of these administrative assistants.

2. Visit a computer retail sales store. Compare and evaluate two brands of microcomputer systems. Include the following components in the computer system: central processing unit with a 120-megabyte hard disk drive and a floppy disk drive, a keyboard, a color display monitor, and a dot matrix printer. Prepare a report that compares and evaluates the systems according to the functions they can perform, the cost, the ease of use, and the service provided by the vendors. Include a recommendation for purchase of a specific system based on your analysis.

▶ **TA5-1.TEM**

Access the template disk, and select the TA5-1.TEM file. On screen you will see the shell document for a form letter used to inform clients that our catalog is currently backordered.

Using your word processing software, enter the codes you will need to use this file for mail merging. Then use the merge feature to print out a copy of this letter to each of the following clients:

1. Dr. Nancy Nash
   1101 Kings Mill Drive
   Richmond, VA
   23225-0012

2. Mrs. Blair Cosby
   270 Palmer Court
   Warren, PA
   16365-4592

3. Mr. Paul Franklin
   4400 West Avenue
   Statesboro, GA
   30458-9876

4. Mr. Luis Medina
   71 Hanna Lane
   Maywood, NJ
   07607-3730

Use block format for all letters, and use today's date.

Chapter 6

Reprographics

LEARNING OBJECTIVES

After studying this chapter and completing the activities, you will be able to:

1. Discuss the advantages and disadvantages of each reprographic method.
2. Identify the components of copying, and formulate a strategy to set a copying policy.
3. List the major criteria for selection of a copier.
4. Describe the basic components needed for desktop publishing.
5. Explain the potential legal implications of copying certain documents.
6. Discuss the major advantages and disadvantages of using desktop publishing software.
7. List the steps in using desktop publishing software.

INTRODUCTION

TECHNOLOGY

Reprographics is the multiple reproduction of images.

Image processing is the technology related to photocopying, duplicating, image printing, optical character recognition (scanning), and desktop publishing.

For years experts have been predicting the shift towards the "paperless office"; however, the paperless office has not yet arrived. As long as paper is still the preferred means of exchanging information in the business world, machines will be needed to reproduce hard copy. The administrative assistant will have to select an efficient, cost-effective method to reproduce documents. **Reprographics** is the term used for the multiple reproduction of images. In the information processing cycle, reprographics comes under the key technology called **image processing.**

When we think of reprographics we normally think of copying and duplicating machines; however, image processing also includes optical character recognition (scanning), intelligent copiers, and desktop publishing. Reprographics today is not limited to the reproduction of a hard copy. For example, computers can now be connected directly to copiers, and the copies can be produced directly from the information shown on the computer screen.

124

The administrative assistant should be familiar with reprographic equipment and be able to prepare originals for copying. A knowledge of desktop publishing software is necessary. In many offices, the administrative assistant determines the type of reprographic equipment to purchase and also assumes responsibility for its control. A thorough knowledge of reprographic equipment and supplies can reduce the expense and delays often associated with producing multiple copies. It is vital that you understand reprographic equipment and the processes that will allow you to use the equipment most effectively.

COPYING MACHINES

Copiers (also called photocopiers) use an image-forming process to create reproductions of originals. In recent years, the copier industry has been characterized by a flurry of technological innovations designed to make the task of reproducing images faster, easier, cleaner, and less expensive. For example, the use of microprocessors simplified the design, maintenance, and operation of copiers. The application of microprocessors to this industry also allowed manufacturers to increase the work-saving features of their machines and reduce the number of operating parts. Major copier manufacturers, such as Xerox, Canon, and Sharp, continue to focus on the needs of users in simplifying the reproduction process.

TECHNOLOGY

Copiers use an image-forming process to create reproductions of originals.

Copier Volume Levels/Speeds

Low-volume copiers, often called **convenience copiers,** are simple and easy to operate. Low-volume copiers are placed in readily accessible locations throughout an organization. Time spent traveling to and from the machines is greatly reduced as a result of their accessibility, and no special skills are required to operate them.

Today's low-volume copiers are small (often tabletop units), relatively inexpensive to purchase, and virtually maintenance-free. Low-volume copiers are capable of producing up to 20,000 copies per month at speeds of up to 20 copies per minute. These machines offer a broad range of features and are used in large as well as small organizations.

For offices that require 20,000 to 50,000 copies per month, the **mid-volume copier** has become popular in the past few years. It operates at speeds of 21 to 60 copies per minute. The modular design of many mid-volume copiers permits users to customize their machines. When the need arises for a special feature, it can be added easily and inexpensively to an existing machine.

In some organizations high-volume copiers are used. These machines are usually operated by trained employees and are equipped with many special features. **High-volume copiers** operate at speeds of 61 to 125 copies per minute and are recommended for volume levels of 50,000 to 100,000 copies per month.

Copier Image Processing

Copiers seem to be such simple machines. You place the original on a glass surface, select the desired number of copies, and push a button marked "Print" or "Start." Seconds later, copies of the original are released from the machine one after another. From the standpoint of the imaging process used, however, most commonly used copiers are far from simple.

Fig. 6-1 The xerographic copier, like this plain paper convenience copier, is popular in many offices. *Photo courtesy of Xerox Corporation.*

Xerographic Process. Most office copiers, like the one shown in Figure 6-1, use the xerographic process to produce images and are **plain paper copiers** (PPCs). In plain paper copying, a camera throws an image of the original onto a positively charged drum. When a sheet of plain (untreated), negatively charged paper is passed over the drum, the image adheres to the paper and is permanently fixed with heat. A **toner** (ink in powdered or liquid form) is used to develop the image on the exposed paper.

If you share the responsibility for selecting copying equipment, you should be aware that there will be recurring expenses for paper, toner, and maintenance. When making an assessment of different copiers, these expenses should be a factor in the cost comparison.

Fiber-Optic Process. The fiber-optic process uses an array of tiny, hairlike strands of glass to replace the lenses and mirrors of xerographic copiers. These tiny strands of glass transmit images in the form of pulsating light.

The use of fiber optics in place of conventional lens and mirror assemblies has occurred mostly in low-volume or convenience copiers. Copiers using fiber optics are slower than conventional copiers because the optics (light source) must remain fixed while paper on a moving platen moves past the light.

Intelligent Copier/Printers

The intelligent copier/printer represents one of the most exciting and versatile advances in copying technology. An intelligent copier/printer can scan hard-copy originals and convert them to digital masters. These masters can then be changed—pages resequenced, images enhanced or revised—and then printed, all from computer instructions. An intelligent copier/printer can also communicate with other intelligent copier/printers and receive digital images directly.

Intelligent copier/printers often use laser technology. A beam of red light (laser) is used to transmit the original image onto a sensitized surface; the image is then transferred from that surface to a plain sheet of paper. Because of its speed, laser technology is growing in popularity for producing high-volume jobs like telephone directories.

Intelligent copiers currently on the market can perform the following operations:

1. Reproduce hard copy at local or distant locations without operator intervention.
2. Communicate with other intelligent copier/printers.
3. Print up to 135 pages a minute with 600 dpi (dots per inch) resolution.
4. Merge data from various electronic sources.
5. Depict line art, photographs, and text.
6. Print high-quality copy.
7. Operate at a low noise level.

Various kinds of finishing operations such as stitching and thermal binding can be added to this intelligent copier/printer to produce a finished booklet. More information is provided on page 131. The intelligent copier is the first step toward integrating document creation with production publishing using electronic documents prepared with desktop publishing tools.

Because the intelligent copier/printer is a hybrid, combining copier and printer capabilities, it is relatively expensive. You will find its major applications in large company in-house print shops producing high-volume jobs. An example of an intelligent copier/printer appears in Figure 6-2.

Fig. 6-2 Intelligent copier/printers use laser technology to produce high-volume jobs like telephone directories.
Photo courtesy of Xerox Corporation.

Copier Features

Major developments in copier technology have produced a number of significant features that make the copying task easier. Although many of these features once were available only on expensive high-volume machines, they are now available on a wide range of low- and mid-volume copiers.

If you have a voice in the selection of reprographic equipment for your office, you should consider the desirability of certain features as they apply to your job. Some of the many features available on today's copiers are outlined in the following paragraphs.

Automatic Document Feed. The automatic document feed holds a stack of originals and feeds them one at a time over the lighted glass surface for copying. This device is a great time saver, eliminating the need to raise the copier cover, position the original on the glass surface, and press the button to print each time a copy is made. Most automatic feeders hold up to 50 originals. Another version, called a **stream feeder,** takes originals from the operator's hand and feeds them over the glass one at a time.

Automatic Duplexing. Duplexing is copying on both sides of the page. With automatic duplexing, the operator does not have to reload paper to copy on the other side. On low-volume convenience copiers, however, it is usually necessary to reload the paper manually for the second pass. Copiers that are not designed for duplexing are likely to produce slightly burnt, smudged copies, and excessive duplexing may damage a machine. Although duplexing saves paper and reduces paper handling, it should be done only on machines equipped with this feature.

Automatic Exposure Control. This feature controls the lightness and darkness of copies. It is especially useful when copying from newspapers or other darker-than-normal originals. The operator also has the option to manually adjust the exposure control setting.

Copy Counter. The copy counter presets the desired number of copies, a help in minimizing the number of excess copies made.

Copy Auditor. The copy auditor controls copier access and accounts for all copies made on photocopiers to facilitate chargebacks to departments or clients. Each user is required to input a code before access to the equipment is allowed. Some systems will allow the inputting of up to 300 user codes. Accumulated totals are shown on the screen while new copying is taking place. Add-on features can include an impact printer to generate transaction receipts. Other types of auditing systems supply users with a magnetic card to gain access to the copier.

Roll Feeding. This feature permits a variety of copies in different sizes to be reproduced. The copier is fitted with a roll of continuous-feed paper that can be cut into various lengths as it is fed through the machine.

Finishing. This feature enables the copier to produce collated sets of multi-page documents. A stapler can be added to this feature to finish the collating process by stapling the assembled sets.

Color Copying. Color copying in a choice of toner colors has become commonplace in low- and mid-volume copiers and is moving into the high-volume copier market. Interchangeable color toner cartridges enable the user to switch easily from one color to another. Some copiers house more than one toner color, with each available at the touch of a key on the control panel of the copier. An attachment to some color copiers makes color "prints" by enlarging color slides on paper. For example, color prints might be made from a transparency and distributed to an audience after a management presentation. (Transparencies are discussed in detail on pages 139–140.)

Full-color copying is still out of reach for most businesses because of its high price. The demand for this type of color copying will remain in specialized areas such as engineering departments, quick printers, ad agencies, and design houses until the price comes down. An example is shown in Figure 6-3.

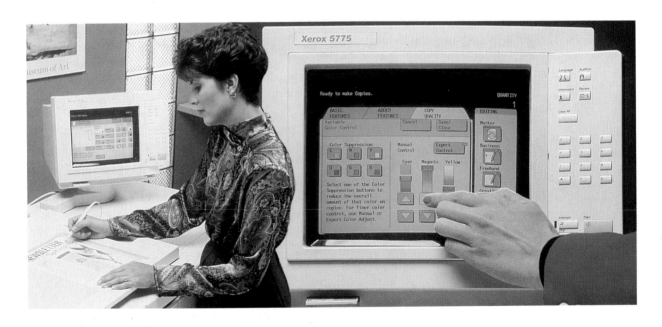

Fig. 6-3 Color copiers are used in specialized businesses such as ad agencies and design studios. *Photos courtesy of Xerox Corporation.*

Job Recovery. It is sometimes necessary to interrupt a "run" to make a few copies of something urgent or to allow someone else to use the machine. When this happens, if your machine is equipped with a job recovery feature, the machine will remember where it was interrupted and, afterward, will return to its place automatically.

Reset Key or Return to Position.   This is a money-saving feature that prevents overcopying. For example, if you are making 20 copies of a document, once you have completed the last copy, the copy counter will automatically return to 1. This prevents the next user from making 20 copies in error.

Reduction and Enlargement.   Many copiers are capable of reducing and/or enlarging the size of originals. Varying degrees of reduction and enlargement are available. This feature is useful in reducing computer printouts, drawings, and ledger sheets that are too large to fit into the files. The enlargement feature permits operators to produce copies larger than the originals; it is useful for sharpening details and making copy more readable. Most manufacturers are offering this feature now and are expanding the number of ratios available for enlargements and reductions.

Electronic Editing.   Electronic image manipulation is available on a number of copiers; built-in functions accessed by controls located on the copier's console panel or a separate image-editing board control this process. Image-editing, such as copying or deleting portions of the original document, can be achieved on many machines. More advanced editing capabilities give users the ability to move, center, overlay, and reduce or enlarge images in addition to copying and deleting portions of the original document.

Instant On.   This feature eliminates the need for warm-up time. The copier can be used the minute it is activated.

Interrupt Key.   The interrupt key permits the operator to stop the machine at any point in the copying process. This is useful in emergency situations when the operator wishes to discontinue the copy cycle.

Automatic Diagnosis.   This feature will diagnose copy status and malfunctions. Machines display words or icons to signal this information. For example, paper jams are located by the position of a lighted dot in a graphic on the copier.

Help Button.   A feature designed to help inexperienced operators, the help button flashes understandable instructions in step-by-step order so that an operator can produce copies correctly. This is probably the most "user friendly" of all the features.

VOLUME COPIER/DUPLICATORS

TECHNOLOGY

Duplicators make copies from prepared masters.

Duplicators make copies from prepared masters, and one of the most cost-effective developments in office reprographics is the *copier/duplicator*. These machines use the xerographic imaging process and are designed for high-volume production (100,000 to 200,000 copies per month).

A copier/duplicator offers the convenience of a copier and the speed and cost advantages of a duplicator; also included are certain desirable automated features, such as a sorter. The **on-line sorter** of a copier/duplicator allows copies to proceed directly from the copier/duplicator to the sorter without operator intervention. As multiple copies of the first page of the original come off the copier/duplicator, they are automatically separated into a series of bins, one bin for each copy. This process is repeated until all pages of the original have been copied. Each bin will then contain one complete, copied set of the original. In addition to assembly, some copier/duplicators carry the process one step further to include **on-line finishing.** The assembling unit receives the copies and jogs, staples, and deposits each set in a removable tray.

Most copier/duplicators produce the number of desired copies of page one before proceeding to page two. Others, however, produce one copy of each page of a report; assemble and finish set one; then proceed to repeat the process and complete set two. The advantage of the latter system is that it is not necessary to wait until all sets have been duplicated before getting the first finished set.

AUTOMATED DUPLICATORS

The automated duplicator offers the convenience of reproducing copy directly from an original. Manufacturers of offset duplicators have produced highly automated machines for high-volume users. Basically, the automated duplicator combines three machines into an on-line assembly process including: (1) an automatic master-making machine, (2) a high-speed duplicating machine, and (3) a sorter to provide assembled copies. The operator produces the master on the automatic master maker and transfers the master to the duplicator. The duplicated copies are fed automatically into a sorter, and the operator receives assembled copies.

The operation is automated further by some manufacturers. The master moves via conveyor belt directly from the master maker to the duplicator; the operator does not have to intervene to transfer the master to the duplicator. The operator's function is to feed the original into the master maker and to set the duplicator for the desired number of copies. These highly automated duplicators are also known as continuous copy offset systems. An example appears in Figure 6-4. See Figure 6-5 for a checklist on copy quality.

COPYING ABUSES

The ease with which copies can be made on reprographics equipment has led to the tendency to make more copies than needed. According to a nationwide survey of corporations, unnecessary photocopies cost American corporations at least $2.6 billion a year and account for nearly two out of every five photocopies made on office machines. In addition to overcopying, there is

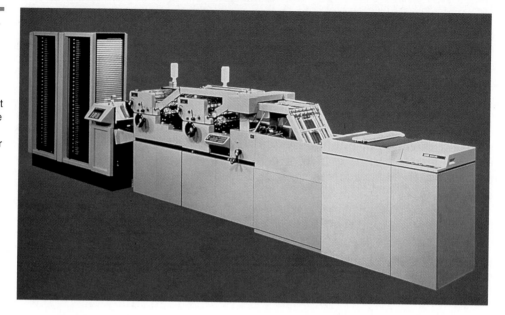

Fig. 6-4 In the continuous copy offset system, originals are fed into the duplicator at the right and an offset master is prepared. The master moves on a belt to a machine that processes the master. The master automatically attaches itself to the cylinder of the offset duplicator, where many copies are duplicated very rapidly. *Photo courtesy of AM Multigraphics.*

also the cost of unauthorized personal copies: recipes, bowling scores, personal letters, and the like. The copier industry estimates that 8 percent of the 400 billion copies made each year in the United States are for personal use and are of no benefit to the company paying for the machines and their supplies. Although each copy costs only a few pennies, the cumulative total adds many dollars to the monthly copying bill.

Fig. 6-5 If you answer no to any of these questions, you are not obtaining the highest quality of reproduction from your copying machine.

COPY QUALITY CHECKLIST

1. Is the background as white as on the original?
2. Is the copy free of specks or spots?
3. Is the copy free of streaks?
4. Is the intensity of the ink-like impression similar to that of the original copy?
5. Does the copier compensate for less-than-perfect originals, such as those with dark backgrounds or light images?
6. Does the copier reproduce a pencil original into readable copy?
7. Does the copier adjust to the reproduction of originals on colored paper?
8. Do both black-and-white and color photographs reproduce clearly?
9. Can the copier produce good copies from such items as labels, card stock, transparencies, vellum, and specialty papers?

To address the problems of overcopying and unauthorized copying, some companies centralize all copiers in a reprographic department, assigning full-time operators to the machines. A reprographic requisition form must be submitted with each original. This system has been known to decrease the volume of unnecessary copying by 20 percent. Other companies, however, contend that centralizing copiers increases the time it takes to get copies, takes the administrative assistant away from the workstation, and causes delays. The cost of lost time far exceeds the savings gained by eliminating unauthorized copying and overcopying.

Copiers can be equipped with a device to ensure that only authorized personnel use the machines. Such devices also make it possible to charge copying costs to departments or individuals. One such unit employs a counter that cannot be reset by the user. The operator must have a key to activate the machine. When a key is inserted in the lock activating the machine, the counter corresponding to that key records the number of copies made.

Today many companies are adopting computer-driven copier control units to make users accountable for their output. These control units may be in the form of a keypad attachment or a magnetic strip card. In the keypad system, a keypad copy controller is mounted on the copy machine. Each user receives an account number, which might be the user's phone number, social security number, or a specific number supplied by the company. At the same time, the machine supervisor has a code for entering or closing new accounts. The personal magnetic strip card is used in much the same way as credit cards and automatic teller machine cards. A personal identification number lets the user activate and use the machine. When the machine is accessed with the card, accounts can be automatically tallied, sorted, and charged back to users. A supervisor can enter the system and examine and delete accounts as needed.

Some companies are now providing employees with limited access to the copiers for personal use at their own expense. They are issued magnetic strip debit cards. For example, an employee with a $20 debit card makes ten personal copies at ten cents per copy and still has $19 left for private use. When the debit card is used up, a recharge unit on the machine can put a dollar amount of the employee's choice back on the magnetic strip. The use of these more sophisticated copier control units provides a number of advantages, including greatly reduced costs, tighter control over budgets, simplification of chargeback billing, reduction and sometimes elimination of unauthorized use, reduced maintenance costs, complete machine security, and less wasted time going to and from machines.

Because of the ease of making photocopies and the availability of copiers in the office, there is a temptation to make copies of valuable personal papers and to use or carry them in place of the originals. There are rules against and penalties for copying certain papers. These papers include drivers' licenses, automobile registrations, passports, citizenship papers, naturalization papers, immigration papers, postage stamps, copyrighted materials, and securities of the United States government.

DESKTOP PUBLISHING

The administrative assistant needs to become familiar with desktop publishing software, one of today's most-used categories of applications software. The software combines text and graphics to produce many types of business publications on a personal computer—hence the name "desktop publishing." Typical desktop publishing hardware/software components as shown in Figure 6-6 include a personal computer with a hard disk, a laser printer or other printer capable of high-quality graphics, and software to do word processing, graphics, and page makeup. Mouse-based software makes desktop publishing easier to accomplish. A more powerful and sophisticated system, called a workstation publishing system, involves a minicomputer or mainframe computer. Dedicated publishing systems are those in professional publishing environments.

Fig. 6-6 Desktop publishing components include a personal computer with a mouse, laser printer, and applications software for word processing, graphics, and page makeup software. *Photos courtesy of Hewlett-Packard Company.*

Desktop Publishing Software

There are a number of popular page makeup software packages. Even traditional word processing programs offer many features of page composition software programs. For projects that do not require a complex page layout, the administrative assistant can prepare documents having a professional, typeset-look without learning how to use anything more complicated than an advanced word processor. For example, the user has the capability of changing print size and appearance, drawing lines and borders, and adding clip art to a document. **Clip art** is public domain art, either in books or on disks, that can be used free of charge without credit in a publication. Using clip art is a fast way to get graphics onto a page, especially when there is no time or money to hire an artist. Most line drawings and technical illustrations in newsletters and advertisements are taken from clip-art catalogs.

Traditional Method of Layout

To fully appreciate the capabilities of desktop publishing software, examine the production of a company brochure without using desktop publishing software. First, the author provides a typewritten manuscript. The editor corrects it in pencil and sends it back to the author for review. After the author has okayed the corrections, the editor marks it with instructions regarding margins, type sizes, and other aspects of the design and submits the marked manuscript to a typesetting service, where it is retyped and special formatting codes reflecting the design are added. A printed proof of the manuscript (called a galley) typeset in a single column is sent back to the author and editor to proofread. In the meantime, an artist prepares any artwork. Using the galleys and art, a designer lays out each page of the document, cutting and pasting blocks of type and art for fit and sensible placement on the page. The proofread galleys, art, and layout go back to the typesetting service, where the galley corrections are made, the pages are assembled, and a new proof is sent to author and editor for review. Turnaround time becomes a key consideration when there is a deadline, and delays are common when material must be typeset by an outside vendor. The function of the administrative assistant during this process may be only to coordinate the activities and revisions. Figure 6-7 illustrates the traditional layout process.

Layout with Desktop Publishing

When you substitute desktop publishing software for the manual layout process, the production of the company brochure becomes streamlined, fast, and less expensive. Using desktop publishing software the administrative assistant can create not only text but also headlines, captions, and/or computer graphics. Electronically scanned-in logos, graphics, or photographs can be "cut" to fit the page on the screen. This process is actually called cropping, the trimming away of unimportant background without shrinking the central image. For example, you could trim a photograph of a person to just include the head. Clip art can be imported into the document, multiplied, shaded, rotated, flipped, tilted, or altered. The size and style of the type can be changed. In other words, the screen becomes the page layout without a drafting table, scissors, glue, rulers, or paper, making changes easier. A copy is printed only after the user is satisfied with the on-screen display. One of the characteristics of this software is the WYSIWYG (pronounced "wizzywig") display—"What you see is what you get," meaning that the appearance of the printed page is shown as accurately as possible on the computer screen. There are four major steps to desktop publishing:

1. Prepare the text and illustrations with a word processing program and graphics package. Optical scanners can be used to input text and graphics.

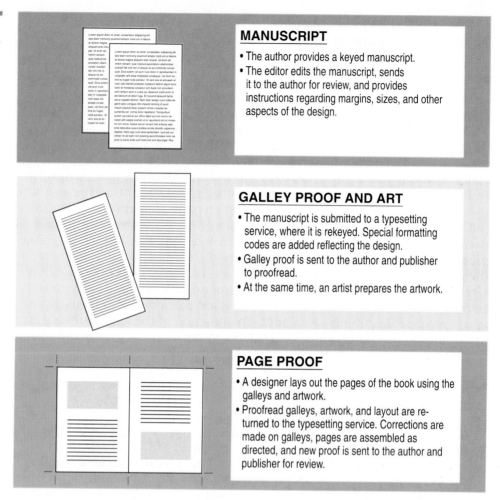

Fig. 6-7 The traditional method of preparing material for publication.

MANUSCRIPT

- The author provides a keyed manuscript.
- The editor edits the manuscript, sends it to the author for review, and provides instructions regarding margins, sizes, and other aspects of the design.

GALLEY PROOF AND ART

- The manuscript is submitted to a typesetting service, where it is rekeyed. Special formatting codes are added reflecting the design.
- Galley proof is sent to the author and publisher to proofread.
- At the same time, an artist prepares the artwork.

PAGE PROOF

- A designer lays out the pages of the book using the galleys and artwork.
- Proofread galleys, artwork, and layout are returned to the typesetting service. Corrections are made on galleys, pages are assembled as directed, and new proof is sent to the author and publisher for review.

2. Use the page makeup program to develop the format for each page. It is in this step that the desktop publishing software earns its name. The screen provides rulers, column guides, and other page design aids to allow the user to lay out the page.

3. Step three allows the merging of text and illustrations into the page format. For example, the page makeup software will automatically move excess text to another column or page and help size and place illustrations and headings.

4. When pages are formatted the way you want, they are stored electronically on the hard disk ready to print.

Desktop publishing does not replace full-service print shops capable of producing high-resolution graphics and color. It does, however, have a place in the production of a number of documents for a company of any size. Small or medium-size companies can produce attractive materials quite reasonably, and they will look professional. Some typical business desktop publishing applications include advertising flyers, newsletters, forms, circulars, price lists, manuals, and brochures.

Advantages of Desktop Publishing

There are definite advantages to using desktop publishing software. Desktop publishing is far less expensive than typesetting. Desktop publishing is an efficient way to control common documents in-house where turnaround time is especially important. Where the security of a document is important, desktop publishing in-house avoids the loss or misuse of information. Finally, the overall quality of documents improves in the organization. Not only will desktop publishing software enable the administrative assistant to create a more eye-pleasing and more professional-looking product, but it will get read. We are a visual society. Arranging information so that it is easy to read, with eye-catching type and graphics, will encourage people to read and digest the message. Customers will also react favorably to desktop publishing materials.

Skills Required in Desktop Publishing

Desktop publishing software is not the answer to every publishing problem. Skill is definitely needed to lay out a document. Putting the software into the hands of an inexperienced user may produce the "ransom note" effect, a document with a distracting jumble of too many different sizes and styles of type. It will take time and some study to learn the style conventions to produce certain types of documents. A casual user may become frustrated because consistent use is necessary to become comfortable with the software.

Using desktop publishing software requires an understanding of the specialized language of printing. For example, the administrative assistant needs to be familiar with the notion of point size, typefaces, typestyles, and fonts in order to create a pleasing document. Figure 6-8 illustrates the distinction be-

Palatino	Helvetica
Palatino Bold	**Helvetica Bold**
Palatino Italic	*Helvetica Oblique*
Palatino Bold Italic	Helvetica Narrow
Palatino Outline	***Helvetica Narrow Bold Oblique***

Fig. 6-8 Examples of typeface, typestyle, font, and point. A *typeface* is a specific type design, such as the Palatino and Helvetica typefaces shown here. Typefaces come in families of related *typestyles*, such as bold or italic, that are carefully designed to complement one another and work well together. A *font* is a particular typestyle and size of characters, such as Palatino 18-point type.

tween these four terms. Other desktop publishing vocabulary can be found in Figure 6-9.

Fig. 6-9 The administrative assistant who uses desktop publishing software needs to learn a new vocabulary.

COMMON DESKTOP PUBLISHING TERMS

Justified means all lines are the same length, spaced to come out even at the righthand margin.

Kerning in typography is adjusted spacing between letters.

Leading is the space between the baselines of two lines of print.

Line spacing is the blank spacing between the lines of a typeset page.

Pica is a standard measure of line length and depth; 1 pica equals 12 points, or about 1/6 inch.

Point is a standard measure of type size; 1 point equals about 1/72 inch.

Proportional spacing is spacing that takes into account the varying width of characters in a line of type; for example, the letter *w* is given more space than the letter *i*.

Serifs are the small flares that project from the main strokes of the letters in some typefaces, like Palatino in Figure 6-8.

Sans-serif designates a typeface with no serifs, like Helvetica in Figure 6-8.

Typography refers to the shape, style, or appearance of printed alphabetic and numeric characters.

Whether or not an administrative assistant is called upon to use desktop publishing software, a knowledge of its potential is necessary. All businesses are concerned with the quality and cost of documents. It will be up to the administrative assistant to see that documents are produced in an efficient, cost-effective manner, whether in-house or by an outside printer.

COMMERCIAL AND IN-HOUSE DUPLICATION

According to BIS Strategic Decisions of Norwell, Massachusetts, worldwide consultants on information technology, the demand for duplicating increases at the rate of 200 billion copies every five years. Many companies are meeting this demand with their own in-house reprographics shops. This growing trend challenges the administrative assistant to provide high-quality originals in an acceptable format to the reprographics department.

Some firms will continue to use commercial print shops in situations when jobs cannot be produced in-house or the volume of work does not justify the purchase of large-scale reprographics equipment. In every city there are commercial shops that specialize in reprographics. These businesses are usually listed in the Yellow Pages under "Letter Shop Service," "Copying and Duplicating," or "Photocopying." Such shops will prepare masters, run copies, address envelopes, and fold and insert enclosures. They will do an entire job or any phase of it.

If the office does not have adequate reprographic equipment or if time is short, the administrative assistant may need to turn to an outside shop. Factors that must be investigated and compared in choosing a shop include (1) rates charged per copy, (2) quality of prepared copy, (3) cost for collating, (4) cost for binding, and (5) time needed for completion. The administrative assistant should maintain a file of information about available shops.

SELECTING THE REPROGRAPHIC METHOD

The administrative assistant usually makes the decision whether copies are to be produced by a copier, a copier/duplicator, a centralized in-house duplicating service, or a commercial shop. Several factors enter into this decision: the number of copies required; the urgency; copying and duplicating facilities available in-company and from outside agencies; the quality of reproduction desired; and the cost per copy.

If the number of copies required is 15 or fewer, the convenience copier is the least expensive, fastest, and most convenient method. If the number required is 100 or more, the high-speed copier or the copier/duplicator is the fastest method, provides the highest quality reproduction, and usually results in the lowest per-copy cost. However, when the number of copies required falls between 15 and 100, the choice falls within the *gray zone,* meaning that your decision is not clearly weighted for copying or for duplicating. The copier/duplicator is economical in this range, but it is a high-volume machine and is usually available only in larger companies with a centralized reprographics department. The commercial shop may be the most economical in the 15-to-100-and-above copy range, but inconvenience and the shop's slow turnaround time may preclude its use. Because of these factors, many companies choose to make most copies on a copier or copier/duplicator because of convenience and fast turnaround.

PREPARING TRANSPARENCIES

Making a transparency is a quick process. Before attempting to make a transparency, be sure you have the right film for the machine you are using. You can damage your copier if the film you use is designed for another type of machine. Special film has been produced for plain paper copiers that enables you to make a transparency in much the same way you make a paper copy. Substitute the film for the paper in the copier's paper feed tray, place your original on the platen of the copier, and press the print button.

One type of transparency film is made for desktop convenience copiers, and another type is manufactured for the high-volume copier/duplicator systems. There are also many transparency films on the market capable of producing color transparencies on clear film in bright purple, red, blue, or green. Film is also available that produces white-frosted images that project black against clear or colored backgrounds. The following tips should help you produce perfect transparencies on your first try:

1. If the transparency film becomes separated from its backing sheet, re-assemble the sheets by matching the rounded corners.
2. To write or draw on an original, use a No. 2 pencil or a black marking pen.
3. If the transparency is too light or too dark, adjust the exposure dial.
4. If the backing sheet does not peel away easily, the machine is too hot.
5. Some copiers (such as those that use the thermographic process) have a screen carrier to move the original and film through the machine. A screen carrier consists of two sheets of special paper fastened at the top. The original and the film are placed in the carrier before insertion into the copier. The screen carrier transports the packet through the machine.

When your employer is called upon to make an oral presentation, your ability to prepare the proper supporting visuals will not only enhance the presentation, but also provide an opportunity to demonstrate your creative talents. Consider creating transparencies using a software package designed specifically for the production of presentation materials.

In preparing a transparency or a similar visual to be used before an audience, remember to:

1. Keep the content of the transparency simple. Put only one idea on a transparency; complex visuals tend to confuse rather than clarify.
2. Use print that is about 1/4-inch high so it is large enough to be read from any point in the room.
3. Use about four words per line and around six lines per transparency.
4. Make full use of color, graphics, and diagrams to enhance the content.
5. Proofread the copy carefully; a printing error can often kill the effectiveness of a presentation and embarrass the presenter.
6. Mount transparencies in suitable frames and label them for easy handling.

THE FUTURE OF REPROGRAPHICS

The information processing technologies, once distinct and separate, are converging. Image technology is no exception. A facsimile (FAX) machine transmits a copy of an image whether a picture, text, or graphics to another machine via telephone lines or other electronic means. The receiving FAX machine prints out the image on paper. The sending and receiving FAX machines can be located in the same building or in another country. A FAX machine doubles as a copier because you can produce an exact duplicate of a document without sending it (see Figure 6-10). A laser printer is also comparable to a photocopier. Many companies make both machines from essentially the same base technology. Computer scanners are similar in many ways to both copier and FAX machines. Images are scanned and digitized. Digital technology converts information into language that a computer can process. Once digitized, the images can be displayed, stored, retrieved, altered, merged with text, and communicated. Copier technology is moving towards digital technology. The nature of work is changing; there are small work groups linked together with a local area network (LAN), making copies among themselves and sending or receiving FAX messages. A local area network is an interlinked arrangement of computers within a limited geographic area that share information and electronic equipment with the other computers in the network. This is the perfect environment for the possibility of a multifunction machine dedicated to that work group.

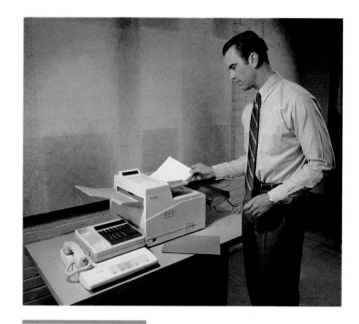

Fig. 6-10 FAX machines have the capacity of making copies, if needed.
Photo courtesy of Xerox Corporation.

As the demand for full-color copiers increases, there should be a decrease in prices enabling more offices to take advantage of this technology. Another factor in the growth of full-color copiers is **digital laser technology,** which allows users to network color copies into personal computers and workstations. An office will be able to purchase one copier offering both black-and-white and full-color capabilities. Laser color machines are the wave of the future that will produce the highest quality output.

Summary

Reprographics is a classification of office work that emerged with the advent of copier technology. Reprographics is the multiple reproduction of images. It involves the use of two primary types of equipment: copiers and duplicators.

Copiers use an image-forming process similar to a camera to create copies directly from existing originals. Duplicators, on the other hand, make copies from masters that must be prepared before copies are reproduced.

The demand for more and better copies has brought about a dramatic change in the field of reprographics. A continuous flow of technological advances has enabled the administrative assistant to produce faster, easier, cleaner, and less expensive copies.

Numerous features are now standard equipment on low-volume convenience copiers as well as high-volume copiers. These features may include copy reduction, enlargement, automatic duplexing, automatic document feed, electronic editing, and color copying.

Copiers are commonplace in most offices; but because of easy access, they are often abused by employees who copy personal materials at company expense. Various controls have been developed to prevent this abuse.

Typesetting equipment has been used traditionally to produce professional-quality documents. Today, however, desktop publishing software enables the administrative assistant to prepare camera-ready copy on the computer. While this software will lead to more in-house copy preparation and printing, it will not eliminate the use of commercial printing shops.

In order to produce professional-looking copies, administrative assistants need to know how to make transparencies and camera-ready copy. It is also essential to know which reprographics process will produce the highest quality copy at the lowest cost in the shortest time.

QUESTIONS FOR DISCUSSION

1. If you were charged with the selection of a new convenience copier, what would you need to learn? Which aspects would you consider most important?

2. In what ways has the photocopier changed office practices? Would life be more difficult without it? Explain.

THINK IT *Through*

3. Compare and contrast decentralized convenience copying systems with centralized copying systems.

4. Most office workers do not give a second thought to copying material for personal use. Do you agree with this statement? If you agree, how might you change an employee's point of view?

THINK IT *Through*

5. What procedures can be used to reduce or eliminate the abuse of copying machines in the office?

6. How has the use of desktop publishing software affected the reprographics function in the office of today?

7. Select the word or phrase which properly completes each sentence. Use the Reference Guide to check your answers.

    a. All of us _____ Phillip will attend. (accept, except)

    b. I am not _____ to asking questions when I am lost. (averse, adverse)

    c. He will _____ to his military experience in his address to the association. (allude, elude)

    d. I cannot _____ the course of the committee after they have voted. (altar, alter)

    e. Her shoes were the perfect _____ for the new tweed suit. (compliment, complement)

    f. The sample is _____ the ones we were shown at the market. (different than, different from)

PROBLEMS

1. Because of the recent merger of your company with another firm, copying requirements have increased from 15,000 to approximately 50,000 copies per month. Your employer has been given the task of restructuring reprographic services in your company. You have been asked to provide a list of the major manufacturers of copying equipment suitable for this higher range and to indicate which manufacturers maintain local showrooms or sales and service offices. Secure materials from at least two of these vendors and prepare a list comparing features of each manufacturer.

2. Interview an administrative assistant in a business of your choice and find out how the business designs and prints some of its documents, such as the company newsletter and advertising brochures. Be prepared to discuss the reasons for the choices that the company makes when choosing a reprographic method.

3. Collect several company samples of desktop publishing and analyze each on the basis of artistic attractiveness, text placement, art work, and size and style of type.

▶ TA6-1.TEM

Access the template disk, and select the TA6-1.TEM file. On screen you will see in rough-draft form a *copy instruction sheet.*

Your firm recently entered into an intern program with a local high school. Selected interns will work part-time in your office, performing many routine tasks in an effort to help you and your coworkers. One common task will be to operate the copy machines; in essence, the student-interns will form a small copy department.

In an effort to ensure that staff members instruct students precisely, your manager has asked you to revise the rough draft so that the copy instruction sheet will be easy for employees to complete and easy for interns to understand.

Revise and format the copy instruction sheet so that you will be able to fit *four* originals on one 8 1/2 x 11 sheet:

1. Reduce the left and right margins to 0.3 or 0.5 inch, if possible.
2. Use a smaller typeface.
3. Arrange the copy so that everything fits on roughly one-quarter of a full page.
4. Delete colons after entries (to save space).
5. Change "Date" to "Submitted on," and then add "Needed by."
6. Combine related information.
7. Add a space for Remarks (that is, for comments *from* the copy department).
8. Print and then review your first revision. What more can you do to "squeeze" copy and yet keep the form clear and easy to read?

Save your revised and formatted document. Print one copy and submit it to your instructor.

▶ TA6-2.TEM

Access the template disk, and select the TA6-2.TEM file. On screen you will find three quotations that your manager wants to show as transparencies in an upcoming presentation to the sales department. Do you have the hardware and software necessary to format and print these quotations in very large, very distinct, very clear type?

If you do, then proceed as follows:

1. Arrange each quotation on one full page with the quote first, followed by the name of the person quoted on the last line. (Delete the colon that now follows each name.)

continued

continued

2. Use 36-point Helvetica Bold or some similar face and size for each quotation.

3. Arrange the page in landscape style, that is, so that the finished transparency sits across the 11-inch (not the 8 1/2-inch) side of the sheet.

4. Add quotation marks to the beginning and the end of each quotation.

5. Add a dash (--) before the name of each person quoted (with no space between hyphens or after the dash), and begin the name at the *center* of each sheet.

6. Proofread your work; then print one copy of each page.

7. If you have blank transparency (acetate) sheets, copy the transparencies onto the acetates using a standard copy machine.

Submit the final transparencies to your instructor.

Chapter 7

Records and Image Management

LEARNING OBJECTIVES

After studying this chapter and completing the activities, you will be able to:

1. Identify and use the five basic filing methods.
2. Explain the computerized records management systems available.
3. Describe the applications of micrographics.
4. Identify the types of filing equipment used in the office.
5. Explain and use appropriate filing procedures.
6. Describe appropriate records management practices.

INTRODUCTION

Advances in technology have moved business into an information society. This increased need for information has generated new ways of thinking about the necessity of filing the millions of paper documents created each day. Despite earlier predictions of a "paperless office," over 90 percent of all filing in the United States is still completed using paper. Paper records continue to increase at a rate of 8 percent annually. Approximately 100 billion documents are created each year.

Micrographics (creating, using, and storing images and data on film) and imaging (converting images to digitized electronic data) are used for records management applications in many of today's offices. As more records are produced, the need for easy access when they are needed in decision making grows. At the same time, the need for easy disposal when they are no longer useful grows. As a result, the use of these technologies will increase so that records management can become more effective and efficient.

Because records and image management has taken on increasing importance, the administrative assistant must not only observe correct filing practices but also initiate the use of new technologies available to enhance the records management process. This chapter discusses the administrative assistant's filing responsibilities, various methods of electronic and manual filing, filing equipment and supplies, procedures for filing and retrieving records, the mechanics of good filing, retention and transfer of files, and building company archives (historical records).

THE ADMINISTRATIVE ASSISTANT'S FILING RESPONSIBILITIES

Files, whether handled electronically or manually, are the memory of a business. Depending on the size of the company, the files may be *centralized* in one location or *decentralized* in various departments or branches. Most administrative assistants maintain decentralized (in-office) files and also send materials to and secure materials from large central files. In-office files relate not only to the company business for which the executive is responsible; they also contain a number of personal files such as expenses of the executive and professional associations of which the executive is a member. The executive's personal files should be kept separate from those pertaining to company business.

If the company has a records management program, the administrative assistant receives instructions about which materials are to be sent to the central files, which materials may be retained in the executive's files, and how long to keep certain records before destroying them or sending them to a low-cost storage area.

Records managers are concerned primarily with reducing the amount of paper in files. Since office space is expensive and personnel costs are high, records managers want to avoid filing documents with no reference value, to reduce duplication of copies, and to ensure that superseded material is destroyed when replacements are filed. In an effort to streamline the records management process, document management software is being used to track in-and-out filing activity, to locate filed information quickly, to reduce the number of lost or misplaced records, and to analyze filing activity and costs. Thus, the administrative assistant needs to understand the in-office filing procedures and the centralized filing procedures thoroughly.

Designing the Files

When most people think of files, they think of the typical vertical file cabinet so conspicuous in every office. Actually, the administrative assistant works with many different types of files. In addition to the traditional drawer files with alphabetic, numeric, geographic, and subject captions, there are file-card files, project files, files of catalogs, magazine files, blueprint or other oversized material files, tape cassette files, transparency files, files of computer printouts, microform files, open-shelf files, and computerized files. Each type of file has a unique function.

The administrative assistant's filing responsibilities usually go beyond maintaining existing files to include the design and installation of the various types of files that will best serve the executive's need for information. In planning files, three factors must always be considered: findability, confidentiality, and safety.

Findability. The criterion for judging any file system is findability. Therefore, files should be thought of not as places to put materials but as places to find materials. The efficient administrative assistant makes decisions about where to file an item after considering the following questions:

How will it be requested?

How can I find it?

Materials must be located quickly, and only those materials actually wanted should be removed from a complete file. To do this, the administrative assistant must understand what the executive needs. Safely filing materials is important, but being able to find them promptly is vital.

Confidentiality. The administrative assistant is also responsible for the confidentiality of the employer's files. The degree of security required varies. Tight surveillance is required for files and papers marked *confidential, secret, vital,* or *personal.* In addition, great care must be exercised to maintain security over confidential information stored on computer disks and microforms. Reasonable protection over less sensitive materials also should be exercised.

If an executive works in a highly sensitive area or industry, there should be a company policy regarding access to confidential and secret materials. Confidential records usually do not leave the executive's office. Before releasing a confidential record (even to your executive's superior), obtain your employer's permission, unless there is a company policy to the contrary. Access to personnel records is regulated by the Privacy Act (see page 611).

Safety. Allied to the need for confidentiality is the administrative assistant's ultimate responsibility for the safety of the records in the executive's office. Many records may be irreplaceable. Administrative assistants should lock all confidential material in a filing cabinet or vault before leaving the office as a safeguard against prying eyes and exposure to fire or water damage. Security systems are built into many new files that automatically lock them when not in use. In addition, information stored on a computer or optical disk should be "backed up" (an additional copy made) at regular intervals.

Developing an Index

Developing an index that indicates how the files are arranged should be a priority of the administrative assistant. The index can be maintained manually or with the use of records management software. Even after an administrative assistant is quite familiar with the files, an index will prove its usefulness: It will help anyone (including an executive or a new assistant) locate material. Do not underestimate its value. A simple index for locating filed material appears in Figure 7-1.

Often communication between the administrative assistant and executive seems particularly weak in the filing area. Since the administrative assis-

FILE INDEX NO. 89 CHEMICAL		
	Location	
	File No.	Drawer No.
Correspondence		
Company	2	1
Government	2	2
Patents	2	3
Personnel Work		
Applications	1	2
Medical	1	3
Security	1	6
Reports		
Company	5	1
Outside	5	3

Fig. 7-1 An index helps locate filed material.

tant oversees the files, there is the tendency to consider the files the administrative assistant's private domain. Yet the filing system is a joint responsibility. If an administrative assistant and an executive work together in planning the system, the transfer of either of them to another office will not destroy the continuity of the files. A new administrative assistant should not attempt to reorganize the files until considerable insight into the information needs of the office has been acquired.

Ideas for setting up files may be obtained from professional organizations, publications, and equipment vendors. Manuals have been published and entire filing systems have been developed to manage the records of insurance, legal, municipal, medical, accounting, and other offices.

FILING METHODS

Material should be filed according to how it is identified and how it is called for, and according to standardized rules of filing. The five basic filing methods are alphabetic, subject, numeric, geographic, and chronological.

Manufacturers of filing equipment have devised and patented improvements upon these five fundamental filing methods. For example, manufacturers have devised color schemes to expedite sorting, filing, and finding procedures. Techniques for grouping names spelled differently but pronounced alike also have been developed.

Paper remains the method of choice for over 90 percent of all filing in the United States.

Alphabetic Filing

Most of all manual filing done in the office, possibly as much as 80 percent, is **alphabetic;** that is, the files are sequenced alphabetically. Furthermore, all filing systems are directly or indirectly based on the alphabetic system. Alphabetic filing is understood by everyone, and the filing is direct. It is not necessary to consult a subordinate file before filing or finding material in an alphabetic file. The method is based on strict guides for alphabetic indexing as presented in the Reference Guide (refer to pages 738–746). An example of an alphabetic file is shown in Figure 7-2.

Phonetic indexing is a modification of alphabetic indexing. In **phonetic** indexing, names are arranged not by their spelling but by their sound. Thus, *Burke* and its variants—*Burck, Berk, Berke, Birk, Bourke, Bork, Borck,* and others—are filed together. Filing phonetically eliminates problems found in other systems. Errors occurring because of misspellings and poor handwriting are reduced. Phonetic filing is used most effectively with files containing thousands of proper names.

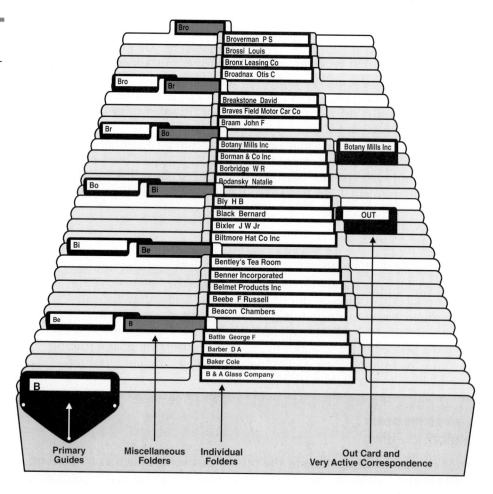

Fig. 7-2 In this representation of an alphabetic file, four types of file markers are used.

Subject Filing

The nature of some executives' work makes filing some correspondence, reports, and documents under **subject headings** particularly useful. A subject file is actually an alphabetic file. Captions are the key words used in locating filed material. The use of clear, concise, and mutually exclusive subject captions is essential to successful subject files.

To get an idea of the subjects used in subject filing, examine the Yellow Pages of your local telephone directory. You will see Employment Agencies cross-referenced to Employment Contractors and Temporary Help, and Loans cross-referenced to Banks, Financing, Credit Unions, Mortgages, Savings and Loan Associations, and Pawnbrokers.

Each piece of material is filed under one subject caption, but a **relative index** is prepared to support the subject file. This index is basically a cross-reference system; it lists all captions under which an item may be filed. To obtain an item from a subject file for which the subject caption is not known, the searcher first consults the relative index to identify all possible headings under which it may be stored.

The time it takes an executive and an administrative assistant to develop a relative index will be saved later when material under a number of captions must be retrieved. If, for example, the executive asks for the file on the wage-incentive plans of a rival company, the Green Corporation, it may have been filed under: (1) fringe benefits, (2) incentive plans, (3) personnel, or (4) Green Corporation. The relative index will help locate the appropriate file.

A description of a portion of a subject file is shown in Figure 7-3. This figure shows one major subject file heading and its subdivisions.

Notice that the main heading (OFFICE EQUIPMENT) has a number of subheadings. OFFICE EQUIPMENT is subdivided into several categories:

OFFICE EQUIPMENT: Copiers
OFFICE EQUIPMENT: Microcomputers
OFFICE EQUIPMENT: Printers

Some of these subdivisions may be further subdivided. For example, *OFFICE EQUIPMENT: Microcomputers* is subdivided by manufacturer: Compaq, Gateway, and IBM.

Microcomputers is further subdivided by a special classification guide in the fourth position for repairs. Additional classifications depend on the needs of the user.

Subject filing presents special retrieval problems because material may be requested under any one of many titles. For this reason one management consultant has said, "To do subject filing well, the administrative assistant must think like the executive." File folders must be identified with the correct and complete name of the item rather than a shortened version that may have been adopted in the office. No area of filing requires the exercise of better judgment than the arranging of materials by subjects that best indicate their content.

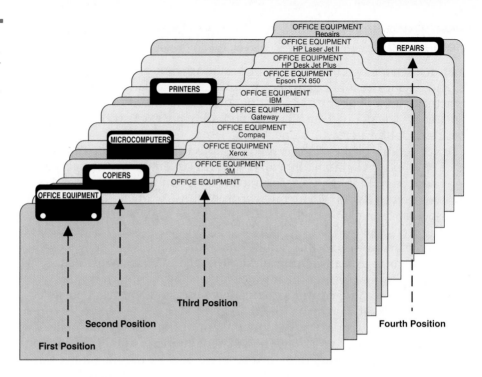

Fig. 7-3 This subject file would be suitable for a purchasing agent or an office manager.

OFFICE EQUIPMENT
Repairs

OFFICE EQUIPMENT
HP Laser Jet II

REPAIRS

OFFICE EQUIPMENT
HP Desk Jet Plus

OFFICE EQUIPMENT
Epson FX 850

PRINTERS

OFFICE EQUIPMENT
IBM

OFFICE EQUIPMENT
Gateway

OFFICE EQUIPMENT
Compaq

MICROCOMPUTERS

OFFICE EQUIPMENT
Xerox

OFFICE EQUIPMENT
3M

COPIERS

OFFICE EQUIPMENT

OFFICE EQUIPMENT

Third Position

Second Position

First Position

Fourth Position

Numeric Filing

Lawyers, doctors, architects, engineers, accountants, real estate agents, insurance brokers, and contractors often assign numbers to their projects and clients. For example, law firms frequently assign case numbers to their work. These numbers become the basis for the **numeric file.** Because anonymity is desired, records of confidential material commonly are filed numerically. A numeric filing plan has four parts:

1. Alphabetic card index
2. Main numeric file
3. Miscellaneous alphabetic file
4. Accession or number book (a record of numbers already assigned)

In numeric filing, the alphabetic card index is consulted first to obtain the file number. The item is then located by file number in the main numeric file. If a name or subject is not in the card index, the miscellaneous alphabetic file is searched. It should be obvious from this explanation of numeric filing that it is an indirect system. One must search the alphabetic card index before searching the main numeric file for materials.

If the subject file for a small operation (see Figure 7-3) were converted to a numeric subject file, the main heading for office equipment in the first position might be assigned the number 100. The numeric assignments for each subdivision would then correspond to the numbers shown in Figure 7-4.

NUMBER	MAIN HEADING First Position	DIVISION Second Position	SUBDIVISION Third Position	SECOND SUBDIVISION Fourth Position
100	Office Equipment			
110		Copiers		
112			3M	
114			Xerox	
116				
118				
120		Microcomputers		
122			Compaq	
124			Gateway	
126			IBM	
128				
130		Printers		
132			Epson FX 850	
134			HP Desk Jet Plus	
136			HP Laser Jet II	
138				Repairs

Fig. 7-4 In this numeric subject file, alternate rather than consecutive numbers are assigned. Intervening numbers can be used when a machine from another manufacturer is purchased.

Terminal and Middle Digit Filing.   In straight numeric filing, as the files increase, the numbers assigned to them become higher. Because most filing work deals with recent dates, it involves high numbers. In a numeric file of insurance policies, for instance, the most recent policies would have the highest numbers. The higher a number is, the more difficult it is to file. **Terminal digit filing** avoids this problem. This filing method divides a number into pairs of digits. For example, insurance policy No. 412010 would be identified as 41 20 10. The last two (terminal) digits identify the drawer number; the middle pair of digits indicate the guide number in the drawer; and the beginning two digits indicate the sequence of the folder behind the guide. Thus, policy No. 41 20 10 would be filed in Drawer 10, behind Guide 20, and 41st in sequence behind the guide (between policy No. 40 20 10 and policy No. 42 20 10). Figure 7-5 shows a records technician retrieving folders from a terminal digit filing system.

To appreciate the advantage of terminal digit filing, visualize 100 file drawers, each labeled with a two-digit number (00, 01, 02, and so on through 99). Policy No. 2 12 00 would go in Drawer 00, while policy No. 2 12 01 would go in Drawer 01, and so on. As consecutive new policy numbers were assigned, the policy materials would be distributed throughout 100 drawers.

Research shows that terminal digit filing saves up to 40 percent of file operation costs by assuring a uniform work load, better employee relations, unlimited expansion facilities, and fewer misfiles. This system has been modified into triple terminal digit filing (using the last three digits as the drawer number).

Fig. 7-5 Research shows that records technicians make fewer filing errors when terminal digit rather than basic numeric filing is used.
Kardex Systems, Inc.—Marietta, Ohio.

Decimal-Numeric Filing. When used with subject filing, a decimal-numeric classification permits more expansion than does a simple numeric arrangement. The decimal arrangement lends itself to any subject that can be subdivided.

Main headings, major divisions, and first divisions are assigned a number just as they are in the simple numeric arrangement; but a decimal point followed by one or more digits is placed after the number of the first subdivision. The decimal point indicates that there are additional subdivisions. For example, a shoe manufacturer might assign number 444 to women's shoes. A decimal point and a single digit would be added to identify the following:

444	Women's Shoes
444.1	Dress Pumps
444.2	Orthopedic
444.3	Sandals

A second digit after the decimal point indicates an additional subdivision, such as

444.10	Open-Toe Dress Pumps
444.11	Open-Toe, Open Heel Dress Pumps

Some libraries use a decimal-numeric system, known as the *Dewey decimal system,* which is used internationally and has been around for almost a century. Engineering firms, governmental agencies, and large pharmaceutical houses also use decimal-numeric filing.

Advantages and Disadvantages. Numeric filing has both advantages and disadvantages. It is easy to learn. Misfiling is reduced because numbers are easier to locate and are less confusing to file than spelled names. Furthermore, the alphabetic card index makes extensive cross-referencing possible. A disadvantage of numeric filing is the time it takes to consult the alphabetic card index before material can be located.

Geographic Filing

Geographic filing is used to arrange records by geographic units or territories. Divisions are made in a logical sequence: nations, states or provinces, cities, and so on. Guides are used for large divisions and subdivisions. Behind each guide, material is filed in miscellaneous folders alphabetically, usually by name of city and then by name of correspondent. Individual folders are filed alphabetically by location, then by name. An example of a geographic file appears in Figure 7-6.

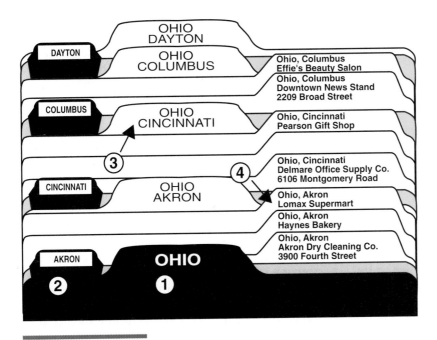

Fig. 7-6 In this geographic file, papers are filed alphabetically by geographic areas as indicated by guides and folders (see No. 1 and No. 2). In the miscellaneous folders for each city (see No. 3) papers are filed alphabetically by the names of correspondents. Individual folders are used for correspondents who have enough communications to warrant separate folders (see No. 4).

The geographic file frequently is supported by a card index in which names of companies are filed alphabetically. If the location of a company is forgotten, it may be obtained by referring to the alphabetic card index.

Chronological Filing

When records are filed chronologically, they are arranged in date sequence with the most recent date at the front. There are three major types of chronological files: transaction files, pending files, and reading (or chron) files.

Transaction Files. Transaction files store records according to the date of transaction. They are useful when records, such as purchase orders or invoices, occur on a daily basis.

Pending Files. Pending files serve as reminders of items pending. Items filed in the pending action file should never become a part of an individual file until the pending action has been completed or a response has been received. Administrative assistants often maintain a pending file for busy executives that chronicles the executive's daily activities for a one-month period. Each morning, the administrative assistant pulls the chronological pending file and reviews it to see what the employer must do that day. Wise administrative assistants check a week or two ahead in order to get signatures, decisions, and so forth before the executive leaves on an extended trip. Remembering to check the pending file must become a habit. Failure to do so can result in lost discounts (if bills are not paid on time), missed appointments, and poor relations with customers and clients.

Reading Files. An administrative assistant who periodically must send material to a central file usually keeps a chronological file as a ready in-office reference. This file, sometimes called a **reading** (or **chron**) **file,** consists of a copy of each *outgoing* item, filed in chronological order in a ring binder or in a topbound folder. Such a file can answer many questions—was a letter mailed, to whom was it addressed, when was it mailed, what price was quoted, and was an enclosure mentioned—all without the delay of consulting the central file.

A reading file does not use an index. As a result, if a record is requested without reference to its date, a search of the records is required, a time-consuming and sometimes frustrating task. To speed locating material in the reading file, some administrative assistants place a sheet with a dated index tab between copies to separate each day's work. It also is recommended that a notation be placed on each copy in the reading file showing where the original correspondence concerning that item is filed. The administrative assistant retains materials in this file for a limited time only, perhaps six months to a year; each month the materials for the earliest month are discarded.

Selecting a Method

The basic filing methods used in your office should depend on how materials are identified. If they are identified by name (either personal or company), an alphabetic file system will probably be used. If each client, job, or project is identified by number, a numeric system is appropriate. When the identifying name for the item is a territory or a geographic location, the geographic method will be best. When items are categorized by subject, then a subject file should meet your office needs. When records are stored by the date of completion, such as a reading file, a chronological file is appropriate.

COMPUTERIZED RECORDS MANAGEMENT

The processing capabilities and storage capacity of computers have made electronic storage and retrieval of information a common practice in the modern office. Automated filing equipment that provides rapid access to large quantities of data is available from many sources. A number of methods, such as computer-generated document management, records management software, and imaging, are used to help the administrative assistant.

Management of Computer-Generated Documents

The management of computer files (documents) is just as important as the organization, filing, and retrieval of paper documents. In most offices, computer files are stored on the hard disk drive of the computer.

The disk drive can be thought of as a multidrawer filing cabinet with labeled drawers and labeled file folders stored within each drawer. The same organizational format is used with computer files. In computer terminology the drive (file cabinet) is referred to as the root directory. The root directory is divided into subdirectories which are equivalent to drawers in the filing cabinet. Just as the filing cabinet drawer contains a number of file folders, the subdirectories are divided into subdirectories (subdirectories of subdirectories).

To assist in the location and retrieval of computer files, a tree-structured directory system is used. This organization plan resembles a tree's root system. An example of a tree-structured directory is shown in Figure 7-7.

U.S. businesses alone produce more than one billion pieces of paper a year; the use of computerized records management technology can assist in managing this paper flow.

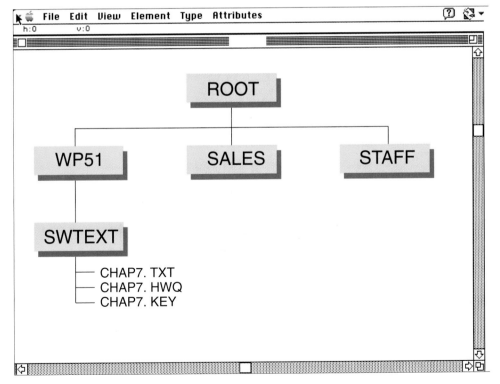

Fig. 7-7 This tree-structured directory illustrates the organization of computer subdirectories.

The starting point (origin) of the root system is the root directory. Radiating out from the root directory are subdirectories (1st subdirectories) and further subdirectories (2nd subdirectories). Documents relating to specific topics are stored within a particular subdirectory (the equivalent of a file folder in a filing cabinet). The DOS directory path shown below illustrates the subdirectory names and the path the computer follows when an individual document is stored or retrieved from the computer's disk storage.

C:\WP51\SWTEXT

> **2nd Subdirectory.** This subdirectory label (SWTEXT) is equivalent to identifying the heading on a particular file folder within the file cabinet drawer.

> **1st Subdirectory.** This subdirectory name (WP51) must be limited to eight characters. This is equivalent to labeling the file cabinet drawer.

> **Disk drive identification letter (C:)** and root directory identifer (\). This is equivalent to identifying a particular file cabinet in an office.

Just as a file folder can contain a number of pieces of correspondence, the subdirectories within a computer can contain a number of files. Figure 7-8 illustrates the use of the directory (dir) DOS command to provide a listing of all of the files (documents) in the subdirectory named SWTEXT. The directory path that identifies the "route" to the documents is shown in this figure.

Fig. 7-8 This directory shows the names of the files within the second subdirectory (SWTEXT).

```
C: \ WP51 \ SWTEXT>dir

Volume in drive C is DOS400
Volume Serial Number is 342C-17CE
Directory of  C: \ WP51 \ SWTEXT


.                      <DIR>            09-10-95        3:22p
. .                    <DIR>            09-10-95        3:22p
CHAP7   HWQ                    984      09-12-95        7:08a
CHAP7   KEY                   1626      09-23-95        4:10p
CHAP7   TXT                  30937      09-24-95        4:51p
              5 Files(s)       4501504 bytes free
```

Records Management Software

Records management software automates the tracking of in-and-out filing activity, assists in locating filed information quickly, and reduces the number of lost or misplaced records. The use of such an automated system can also analyze filing activity and costs.

Some companies use records management software developed in-house to meet highly specialized requirements. These companies may write their own programs or use readily available database software such as dBase. However, most companies use ready-made programs designed to automate the records management system. This software ranges from single applications to integrated packages. The integrated packages address active records, inactive records, micrographic records, computer assisted retrieval (CAR), barcode tracking, retention schedules, and disposal cycles.

Many advantages to using this software are apparent. Most systems provide a near-automatic method of checking records in and out of a file, usually by means of a bar code system. The number of misplaced or lost files is reduced and a means of following up on overdue files is provided. In addition, a complete inventory of records is maintained, as well as historical data such as the activity of a document file, the department using the file, and the specific individual using the file.

Imaging

Imaging is a new process of handling information and the media that convey that information. An imaging system can convert all types of documents, such as letters, forms, drawings, maps, charts, and photographs, to digitized electronic data that can be stored and retrieved immediately. Electronic-based image systems include a scanner that converts the paper document to a digitized form, a processor that compresses the image, a storage medium to retain the image, a retrieval mechanism to convert the image for viewing on a monitor, and an output device that processes the image to hard copy format.

Imaging systems came into being as a direct result of the development of **laser optical disk** technology. The optical disk is well suited for high-volume records management because of its extremely high capacity and durability. The optical disk media can be a write-once/read-many (WORM) disk or an erasable disk. Write-once optical disks record information that cannot be changed; erasable optical disks are more like magnetic disks that permit recording over used portions of the disk.

Imaging systems are dramatically altering the workplace by reducing paper processing, streamlining work flow, and making files instantly accessible. As the cost of imaging systems decreases, the number of companies using these systems will increase. Imaging systems should be used in companies that have high volumes of documents and high activity in the files, when a company cannot afford a misfile or lost file, when high security is required, when space is a consideration, and when the company needs to maximize the efficiency of personnel.

The administrative assistant must become familiar with the capabilities of imaging systems, as much filing in the future will be handled through imaging.

MICROGRAPHICS

Micrographics, the process of creating, using, and storing images and data in *microform,* has merged with computer technology to decrease filing space, reduce misfilings, and increase document retrieval speed. Records managers use microforms extensively, reducing records to a very small size for a safe, secure, and cost-efficient method of storing needed business documents over an extended period of time. **Microfilm** is a fine-grain, high-resolution film. It is the most common type of microform. Images, considerably reduced in size, are stored on reels, in cartridges, on cassettes, on aperture cards, on microfiche, and in jackets.

It is possible to convert information stored in a computer to microfilm. **Computer output microfilm (COM)** is imaged directly from magnetic media. The electrical impulses on the media are converted to visual images and stored on microfilm. **Computer input microfilm (CIM)** can be converted to electrical impulses, stored on magnetic media, and used as input. CIM is a relatively low cost method of rapidly introducing information from a large microfilm file, such as census data, into a computer for processing.

Types of Microforms

A wide variety of user needs and applications has given rise to a number of different forms in which microfilm is made, stored, and used.

- Microfilm can be wound onto large **reels** that occupy relatively little space. The disadvantage of storing microfilm on reels is that material cannot be located easily and, therefore, cannot be updated easily.

- **Cartridges** are more convenient than reels for filing microfilm since each roll of film may be wound onto a single cartridge. It is easier to retrieve material from a cartridge than from a reel. Microfilm on cartridges also is protected from fingerprints and other damage.

- **Cassettes** are frequently used for filing microfilm. Each cassette contains two spools, the feed and the take-up spool, so that film that has been viewed can be rewound easily.

- Microfilm may be more convenient to use if the images are clipped from the film roll and mounted on cards. These are called *aperture cards.* Data may be written on the card or coded by punched holes that permit the card to be filed and retrieved manually.

- A sheet of film containing multiple images is called **microfiche** (pronounced "microfeesh"). Many images can be stored on one sheet. For example, a long report can be recorded on one 6-by-4-inch microfiche. Microfiche can be filed in a card file or in a specially designed book binder.

- Strips of film can also be stored in plastic **sleeves** (or **jackets**). Jackets can be updated easily. The images on a single strip of film can be replaced more quickly and more easily than an entire roll of film. Images in a jacket can be copied or read directly from the jacket without removing the film.

Microfilm Readers

There are four basic types of readers available for viewing or reading microforms. The choice of a reader will depend upon the office environment, the user's needs, the microform used, and the cost.

- **Lap readers** are designed for compactness and personal use. They are available only as microfiche readers.
- **Portable readers** are lightweight. They may be inserted or folded into a case similar to a portable typewriter case.
- **Desk readers** are designed for use on a table or stand. An example appears in Figure 7-9.
- **Reader-printers** allow users to view a microform on a screen and produce a hard copy reproduction of the image as well.

Retrieval Systems

A number of retrieval techniques (manual, semiautomated, and automated) that direct the searcher to information on microfilm have evolved over the years. High-speed microform indexing and retrieval systems use computers. **Computer-assisted retrieval (CAR)** has the capability of locating or iden-

Fig. 7-9 This desktop reader-printer accepts a variety of microforms and produces high-quality prints.
Photo provided courtesy of Eastman Kodak Company.

tifying a microimage (a unit of information, such as a page of text, too small to be read without magnification) by commands initiated through a computer terminal. The computer manipulates an index at very high speeds and provides information for retrieving a desired document. An index serves not only to guide users to the location of the information being sought but also to aid in screening or selecting information. The operator of a terminal need only query the computer, and the image is presented automatically to the operator in a matter of seconds. In some systems, information can be displayed at the terminal or printed out as hard copy.

FILING EQUIPMENT

Copies of printed records are most often filed in drawers or on shelves. The records may be placed in folders that rest on the bottom of a drawer or in suspension folders that hang from a metal frame within the drawer or shelf. Two advantages of the suspension folder are that heavy folders do not sag and that folders open wide and slide smoothly on hanger rails. Cards are filed in several ways: in drawers, in boxes, in trays, or in panels, where the captions are immediately visible.

Vertical and Lateral Files

For many years the vertical file was the most popular type of filing equipment. This equipment is available in one- to six-drawer units in a wide variety of colors. One important disadvantage of vertical files is that opening a drawer requires at least three to four feet of space in front of the cabinet.

The lateral file is rapidly replacing the conventional vertical file cabinet. Lateral files use 50 percent less aisle space and provide up to 100 percent greater accessibility and visibility. The lateral file may be a drawer file that rolls forward or sideways, or it may be an open-shelf file. In executive offices where attractive surroundings are important, the type of lateral file chosen most often has a closed front. Lateral files have drawers that close or cabinets with doors that lift up, slide to one side, or pull down.

Open-Shelf Files

In open-shelf filing, folders are placed vertically on open shelves. No drawers are involved. Folders are accessed from the front. Since open shelves can extend to the ceiling, they can accommodate more material per square foot of floor space than drawer files can. They also require less floor and aisle space, cost less, and require less time when filing and finding records. In central filing departments like the one shown in Figure 7-10, open-shelf filing is used more often than other kinds of filing equipment.

Fig. 7-10 Open-shelf files make it easier for administrative assistants and other office personnel to file and find records. *Kardex Systems, Inc.— Marietta, Ohio.*

Tabs identifying the contents of an open-shelf file folder project from the side of the folder. Captions are written on both the front and the back of the tab so that the searcher can locate a folder from either side. Color coding is frequently used with open-shelf files for increased visibility. If a whole section is color-coded red, a folder with a green caption is obviously misfiled.

High-Density Mobile Files

Many businesses have large volumes of active documents that must be readily accessible. Often the actual paperwork must be present for legal reasons. To handle this volume, companies are investing in high-density mobile filing systems. These systems are growing in popularity because they can increase the total file space by as much as 200 percent in less than half the floor space currently used for paper filing.

The high-density mobile filing system can save this tremendous amount of space because it uses vertical space rather than horizontal space to store the files. In addition, rather than separating each row of file units with individual aisles, each unit moves on a set of tracks so that only a single aisle is needed at any one time. These units can be designed for paper, magnetic media, books, artifacts, drawings, and odd-sized materials. These systems can be powered electrically, mechanically, or manually. The controlled access to filed materials leads to increased productivity and improved records management. An example of a high-density mobile filing system is shown in Figure 7-11.

Fig. 7-11 High-density mobile filing systems increase file space tremendously while reducing floor space needed. *Kardex Systems, Inc.— Marietta, Ohio.*

Files for Magnetic Media

The array of equipment for housing magnetic media is almost as varied as it is for housing paper documents. Magnetic media, such as floppy disks, often are filed in desktop modular units which can be kept on or close to the computer workstation. When the unit is closed, the disks are protected against environmental contamination such as dust, water, or excessive handling.

Desktop modular stands or rotary stands, designed to house flat magnetic media, generally hold large amounts of material. Examples of desktop files for magnetic media appear in Figure 7-12. One such file holds ten floppy disks in a notebook-like arrangement for easy indexing and accessing by the operator.

Horizontal Files

Horizontal files store materials such as maps, drawings, and blueprints in a flat position. These materials are normally much larger than materials filed in a vertical file drawer. They are found most commonly in engineering and architectural offices.

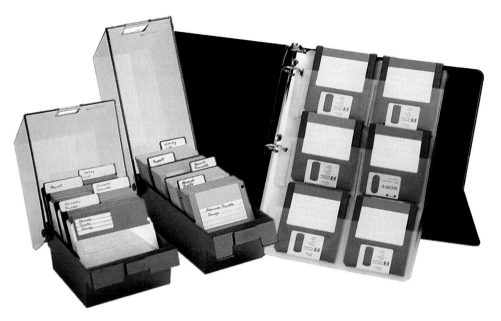

Fig. 7-12 Magnetic media may be housed in a variety of desktop files. *Left photo: Fellowes Manufacturing Co.; right photo: Ring King Visibles, Inc.—a HON INDUSTRIES company.*

Rotary-Wheel Files

Rotary-wheel files were designed to make a limited amount of information available within arm's reach. Rotary wheels vary in size from small desktop units, such as the Rolodex, to large motorized floor models.

FILING SUPPLIES FOR PAPER DOCUMENTS

Filing supplies include many items, such as file guides, file folders, suspension or hanging folders, expandable files, labels, index cards, and storage boxes. Many of these products are updated regularly to keep pace with the changing needs of business.

Expandable or accordion files are replacing the manila folder in many cases. The expandable folder is suited well to shelf files since it has closed sides that prevent records from falling out.

Color coding of filing supplies is being used increasingly to improve efficiency and reduce misfiles. Color coding also enables the user to set up visual cues that communicate more quickly and effectively than typewritten labels. A break in the color bar of a color-coded system highlights a misfile immediately. While small filing systems may not need color coding, for the large file user it can be essential when accuracy, speed, and efficiency are important.

Some administrative assistants purchase their own filing supplies; some requisition them from a stockroom. In either case, an administrative assistant

The choice of appropriate filing supplies may mean the difference between a filing system that merely retains information and one that will improve information management and productivity.

needs to know what types of filing supplies are available and how to select the supplies that best meet the needs of a particular filing system.

FILING PROCEDURES FOR PAPER DOCUMENTS

Many papers that should be destroyed often are filed instead. Letters of acknowledgment, letters of transmittal, announcements of meetings (previously noted on the desk calendar), forms and reports already filed in another location, duplicate copies, and routine requests for catalogs and information fall into this category. Any document superseded by another document in the file should be removed.

A temporary file may be kept for materials having no permanent value. Papers in this file are marked with a "T" and destroyed when the action involved is completed.

The government has developed its removal technique to a high level. In many departments of the government, every document receives a date-of-destruction notation before it goes into the file. By continually purging (removing) the files of outdated materials, an administrative assistant can reduce volume and keep the files up-to-date.

Preparing Paper Documents for Filing

Filing routines vary with the system used, but appropriate indexing and coding and adequate cross-referencing are at the heart of any successful system. The term **indexing** refers to the decision regarding where to file a document; **coding** refers to the actual labeling of a document. These procedures ensure that a document will always be placed in the same location when refiled.

The increase in the amount of information being filed has led to the development of index entries that include multiple keywords, such as document name, number, author, date, subject, operator, comments, and revision level. Cross-references may be listed either on cross-reference sheets or on the document itself in order to prevent misfiles and retrieval problems. Key words and other captions should be used freely. A good administrative assistant follows this rule: When in doubt, cross-reference.

In alphabetic filing, a document is usually filed according to the most important name appearing on it. A letter to or from a business is usually coded and filed according to the name of that business. If the correspondent is an individual, that person's name is ordinarily used. If, however, an individual is writing as an agent of a business and the name of that business is known, the business name is used instead. Similarly, if a business letterhead is used by an individual to write a personal letter, the name of the individual is coded rather than the name of the business. (Complete rules for alphabetic filing sequence are given in the Reference Guide.)

In subject filing, the subject title must be determined from the body of the document. It is then coded according to that subject or according to a number that represents that subject. In numeric filing, the number to be used as a code is determined from the alphabetic card index. In geographic filing, coding is usually done by state and city. Detailed steps for filing papers are given in the following paragraphs.

Preparing Materials. To ready paper documents for filing, remove all pins and paper clips; staple related materials together with a single staple. Place staples in the upper left corner and place papers in the file with the staple up. Clippings or other materials smaller than page size should be attached to a regular sheet of paper. Damaged records should be mended or reinforced with tape. If they are not filed in a special place, oversize papers should be folded to the dimensions of the folder and labeled.

Releasing Materials. When an incoming letter is placed in the filing basket, it should bear a release mark indicating that it has been acted on and is ready for filing. This mark may be in the form of the executive's initials, a stamp, the administrative assistant's initials, a code or check mark, or other agreed-upon designation. A check of all attachments will indicate whether they belong to the document. A release mark is not necessary on the file copy of an outgoing letter or on an original letter to which a copy of a reply is attached.

Indexing and Coding. Once the administrative assistant has indexed a document (decided where to file it), coding may be done either by underlining or by marking on the document the name, word, or number that is to be used as a basis for filing. A colored pencil is commonly used for this purpose. In geographic filing, coding may be done merely by underlining the city and state in the letterhead or in the letter address.

Cross-Referencing. If there is a possibility that a filed document may be sought under another caption, a cross-reference is made and filed in the second location. Cross-reference forms may be colored or tabbed sheets or cards on which the cross-references are listed. A photocopy or an extra copy of the letter (usually on paper of a different color from the file copy) can also be used as a cross-reference sheet.

An example of a cross-reference sheet appears in Figure 7-13. The cross-reference sheet indicates that on May 3 a letter from the Modern Office Equipment Company regarding an exhibit at the Eastern Office Equipment Association convention in Baltimore was received. All correspondence about this convention was filed under Eastern Office Equipment Association. This cross-reference sheet was made and filed under Modern Office Equipment Company. Placing an *X* (for cross-reference) near the name on the original letter indicates that a cross-reference sheet has been filed.

Documents that should be filed under more than one name need to be cross-referenced. For instance, a letter from Allen Vincent Company poses a problem. Is Allen a given name or a surname? A regular file should be set up for Vincent, Allen. A cross-reference should be made to Allen, Vincent.

Documents can be cross-referenced by subject. If inquiries have been mailed to several printers asking for quotations on new letterheads, a cross-reference sheet labeled "Letterhead Quotations" may be filed under *L*, listing each of the printers' names. Correspondence with the printers may be filed alphabetically according to their names.

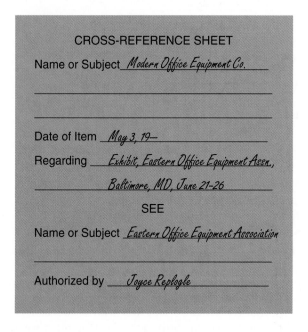

Fig. 7-13 Commercially available cross-reference sheets are often colored sheets imprinted with fill-ins. They may also be tabbed, colored cards on which cross-references are listed.

Sorting.   *Sorting* is arranging papers, including cross-reference sheets, in sequence for filing. When sorting material, the administrative assistant should use a sorter that has alphabetic or numeric divisions or a combination of both, depending on the filing system used. Each of the letter or numeric groups can be put into correct sequence.

Keying Labels.   The one rule that should be observed when keying file labels is the rule of uniformity. See Figure 7-14.

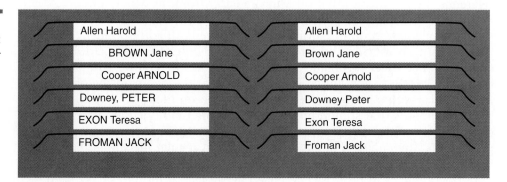

Fig. 7-14 The captions on the left are inconsistent in capitalization and placement. Captions should be keyed in uppercase and lowercase letters as shown at the right.

Requesting Material from the Central Files

When the administrative assistant releases material to the central files that will be needed at a definite future date, the item is marked or stamped with the notation *Follow-Up*. The date on which it will be needed is also noted. Its file folder may also be tabbed with the follow-up date. Frequently, however, the administrative assistant will not know when material will be needed. In these cases, material is requested from the central files when needed by following the usual routine; requests may be made by telephone, in person, or by a requisition card sent to the filing department. If a records management computer tracking system is used, the request may be made directly to the central file computer.

An administrative assistant who is familiar with the central filing system or systems can provide additional leads as to where to locate specific material. The more information the administrative assistant can give to records technicians (names, dates, subjects, addresses, file numbers, etc.), the more quickly material can be located and delivered.

Materials should be returned promptly to the central files. A special problem arises when files checked out to one person are transferred to someone in another department before they are returned to the central files. In some companies, transfers are reported to the filing department on a special form. In any case, records technicians should be informed of the location of all files.

Reducing Misfiles

Manufacturers of filing equipment report that the typical office has a 3 percent rate of misfiled records, though in some cases the rate is as high as 7 percent. The waste of executive, administrative assistant, and clerical time due to misfiling is expensive and frustrating, with a significant impact upon office productivity. Administrative assistants should vow to avoid misfiles.

A number of causes of misfiling are identified below.

1. One cause of misfiling is carelessness. Placing a record in a folder without scanning its contents to see if they are related to the document being filed, using paper clips to fasten materials together and picking up unrelated papers in the process, or putting one folder inside another are all careless filing mistakes.

2. Another cause of misfiling is failure to use supplies and equipment as recommended.

3. The final cause of misfiling lies in coding. Using captions that are not mutually exclusive, choosing a wrong title, or using too few cross-references are typical coding errors that lead to misfiles.

If only one paper is lost, it is probably in the incorrect folder. Check the folders in front and in back of the correct folder, check between folders, and check the bottom of the drawer. Search out- and in-baskets. Don't overlook your employer's desk and your own. Look in the index of files transferred to storage areas. Look under alternate spellings of names and under similar numbers or titles. For instance, if the name you are looking for is Brooks Allen, look under Allen Brooks. If 2309 is lost, look under 2390. Look in the relative index for other possible captions. If the file is not under CE, look under CA, CO, CU, since the second letter may have been misread.

If an exhaustive search does not locate an item, key all information known about the missing item and the date when the loss was discovered on a sheet of paper. File the sheet where the missing item should be. This practice forestalls a later search for the same item. Also, consider the possibility of obtaining a copy of the lost item from its sender or source.

GOOD RECORDS MANAGEMENT PRACTICES

Records management involves the systematic control of records from creation to final disposition. The purpose of records management is to identify, preserve, and protect a company's important documents and to eliminate temporary, useless records with the least possible delay. Experience has shown that as many as 85 percent of some companies' filed records are never retrieved, not even once.

The emphasis in records management, however, is not only on the destruction of useless records but also on records preservation and protection. The upsurge in government investigations of corporations, antitrust suits, and price-fixing court cases has made it necessary for companies to be certain they have retained adequate records and that there are no gaps in their documentation.

Archives

In addition to the files required for good management, companies also preserve historical records, or **archives.** These records will include such documents as incorporation papers and minutes of meetings of the board of directors and stockholders. An administrative assistant to a top executive is frequently responsible for overseeing archives. Usually an organization's archives are kept separate from other records essential for conducting day-to-day business operations.

Materials transferred from the central files to the archives still should be indexed in the central files so that they can be located in remote storage. A microfilm copy often serves as a backup to paper archives of historical significance.

Retention Schedules for Paper Documents

The most efficiently operated companies often have an overall file retention plan for administrative assistants to follow. Companies use retention schedules to specify how long a document can remain in the office flow; if and when it should be removed to a separate, low-cost records center; and when it should be destroyed. Professionally organized retention plans recommend the following practices:

1. File general correspondence requiring no follow-up for one month.

2. File expired insurance policies and incoming and outgoing correspondence concerning customers and vendors on routine, promptly settled business for three months.

3. File bank statements, duplicate deposit slips (except as noted below), work sheets for financial statements, internal reports and summaries (including printouts from data processing equipment and all magnetic tapes and disks), and physical inventories for two years.

4. File canceled payroll checks and summaries, invoices to customers and from vendors, employee data (including accident reports), and completed contracts and leases (as well as similar legal papers) in compliance with the statute of limitations in affected states.

5. Permanently file books of accounts; minutes of stockholders' meetings; capital stock ledgers and transfer records; corporate election records; certificates of incorporation and corporate charters, constitutions, and bylaws; canceled checks, vouchers, and complete cost data on capital improvements; tax returns and rebated papers; perpetual agreements about pensions, group insurance, and other fringe benefits; deeds; maps, specifications, and plans; patents, trademark registrations, and copyrights; annual reports; organization charts and procedures manuals; and CPA-certified financial statements.

Transferring Materials

Plans for storing files are made in relation to the importance of the material; costs can be reduced by storing infrequently needed documents in low-priced filing equipment in low-cost rental areas. The danger that vital records might be destroyed in a disaster has raised concerns for safe storage; storage in mountain vaults and caves as well as in widely dispersed units are possible solutions. Some companies build their own storage centers, while others rent file storage space from companies specializing in providing ready access to stored materials.

Certain types of files can be handled under a **perpetual transfer** plan. When an undertaking is terminated or a project is finished, the file is closed and transferred. Since it is all but impossible to avoid having to consult some transferred records, a two-period transfer method may be adopted. With a two-period transfer, the middle drawers of a file cabinet are used for active materials; the upper and lower drawers, for semiactive materials. Semiactive materials are transferred at a set date to the inactive files in a storage center.

Summary

Every year businesses generate more and more information that must be stored, retrieved, processed, and, in some cases, ultimately destroyed. Consequently, the administrative assistant needs to understand and observe good filing practices.

Findability, confidentiality, and the safety of the records should be considered when designing a new filing system. An index should be developed that will indicate where to look in the files for materials.

Materials should be filed according to how they will be identified and requested and according to the rules for the filing method chosen. There are five basic filing methods: alphabetic, subject, numeric, geographic, and chronological. Each filing method has particular advantages depending upon how materials are identified.

Automated filing equipment that provides rapid access to large quantities of data is available. A number of automated filing methods such as computer-generated document management, records management software, and imaging are used to assist the administrative assistant in maintaining large volumes of records.

Microfilm can save space and improve records management efficiency. Computers have made the electronic storage and retrieval of information a common practice in today's offices.

Filing equipment is another important facet of records management. The administrative assistant should be familiar with such items as vertical and lateral files, open-shelf files, high-density mobile files, horizontal files, and rotary card files.

Numerous supplies are available to enhance the efficiency of the records handling task for paper documents. File folders, guides, labels, and cross-reference sheets should be familiar to the administrative assistant.

The administrative assistant should be able to prepare paper documents for filing in the proper manner, should use the proper filing procedures to avoid misfilings, and should be familiar with procedures for requesting information from central files.

Good records management practices include the establishment of complete archives (historical records), the development of sound retention schedules, and the arrangement for transfer of infrequently needed records to permanent storage.

QUESTIONS FOR DISCUSSION

1. How do you think computerized files will alter your responsibilities as an administrative assistant?

2. What are some of the advantages of using imaging technology for storage and retrieval of records?

3. Do you agree with the concept that developing office files is a joint responsibility of the administrative assistant and the executive, or do you think this is the administrative assistant's responsibility alone? Explain your response.

4. Any communication having reference value should be retained and filed. What are some of the communications that come into or are generated in an office that should be discarded with relative promptness?

5. Companies centralize files for economy and efficiency. Executives, however, tend to resist releasing materials to the central files, preferring to build up their in-office files. What can the administrative assistant do to help resolve this conflict?

THINK IT *Through*

6. Provide the appropriate capitalization in the following sentences. Use your Reference Guide to check your answers.

   a. Catherine the great, father flanagan, and richard the lion-hearted are the subjects of interesting biographies.

   b. The xyrode corporation has model 12 on display in room 22 at the commander hotel.

   c. A panama hat and a manila envelope containing samples of nylon carpet were found at the cabin on the clinch river.

   d. The department of history at browder university is sponsoring an exhibit of the papers of general marshall and the treaties that ended world war II.

   e. The office in the crump tower on second avenue overlooks the morgan house hotel.

PROBLEMS

1. You are the administrative assistant to the sales manager in an organization that has no automated filing equipment. The following items have been seen by the manager and are ready for action. Indicate what disposition you would make of each one. If an item is retained, indicate under

what name or subject it would be filed. (A separate file is kept for the manager's personal items.)

    a. A reminder notice for the next weekly meeting of the Sales Executives' Club.

    b. A new catalog from Brown and Brown, a firm that provides sales incentive plans. (The old catalog is in the files.)

    c. An application from Wanda Higel for a sales position.

    d. Copy for the weekly sales newsletter, which is sent to the sales manager by Lloyd Giroux, editor, for final approval before it goes to the reprographics department.

    e. A letter from an applicant for a sales position thanking the manager for the initial interview.

    f. A notice that the sales manager's office subscription to *Sales Management* has expired.

    g. A letter from Rosa Di Lorenzo asking to change her appointment from Wednesday to Friday at the same hour.

    h. A copy of the manager's expense account for the preceding week.

    i. A requisition for a new dictating unit for the manager's use.

    j. A quarterly report of XY Corporation, in which the manager holds stock.

    k. An interoffice memo from the president of the company approving the manager's request to hold a sales training conference at Lake Crystal on September 18–20.

    l. A letter from an irate customer complaining about the treatment received from the Little Rock area sales representative, Herman Beckwith.

2. On July 18 your employer, Maria Martinez (credit manager), dictated the following letter to be sent to Mr. Sam W. LaScola, 421 East Oak Street, Columbus, OH 43210-3223.

Dear Mr. LaScola: On June 4 you wrote us that you had purchased the Oak Street Market in Columbus and that you would assume all the market's obligations. At that time the market owed us $86.15 on Invoice No. 3310. On June 13 you ordered more goods for $52.60 at 2/10, n/30. The old bill incurred by the Oak Street Market is now 60 days overdue and your own order of $52.60 remains unpaid. We wonder if something is wrong, Mr. Russo. Won't you write us at once, either enclosing your check for the two invoices or letting us know when we may expect payment. Yours very truly.

You are then told by the credit manager to follow up in ten days with Form Letter 5, if the account is still unpaid. If no action has been secured in 20 days, you are to send Form Letter 8.

a. Key the letter in an appropriate format and prepare one copy for filing.

b. Prepare a cross-reference sheet (see page 168) and cross-reference the letter.

c. Release the letter for filing.

d. Prepare a follow-up card for the tickler file.

TECHNOLOGY APPLICATIONS

▶ **TA7-1**

Access the template disk, and get a directory listing of the files on disk. At the A>: or B>: prompt, key:

A>:Dir[Enter]

or

B>:Dir[Enter]

Use your software to print a hard copy of the screen information, which lists all the directories, subdirectories, and files on your template disk.

Now identify each directory, subdirectory, and file by writing the letter D for directory, S for subdirectory, or F for file next to each entry. Your instructor may collect or discuss your marked printout.

▶ **TA7-2**

On your template disk, create a subdirectory for storing all your Technology Applications assignments. In this way, you can separate the files you create from the files that were provided on the original disk.

Before you proceed, think of a directory name. What name will quickly and easily identify this group of files? How about TA_KEYS as a directory name? [Then you can name your individual files TA7-1.KEY, TA7-2.KEY, and so on. The *path* for such files would be A>:\TA_KEYS\TA7-1.KEY, for example.]

1. Create the directory.

    a. Use your word processing software to create the directory.

continued

continued

b. Use DOS to create the directory. At the A>: or the B>: prompt, key:

A>:MD TA_KEYS

or

B>:MD TA_KEYS

MD is the DOS command for "make directory." Leave 1 space after MD, then key the directory name of your choice—in the example above, TA_KEYS.

2. After you have created the directory, key Dir to see the full directory listing on screen.

3. Print out a hard copy of the screen listing showing the disk's contents and the new directory.

Chapter 8

Telecommunications

LEARNING OBJECTIVES

After studying this chapter and completing the activities, you will be able to:

1. Define telecommunications.
2. Describe the various kinds of telephone systems.
3. Identify special services and equipment available with telephone systems.
4. Follow the proper procedures for placing long-distance calls.
5. Identify and describe the advantages and disadvantages of various types of electronic mail.
6. Discuss teleconferencing.

INTRODUCTION

Because business and industry are demanding the services offered through telecommunications, this industry continues to grow at a very rapid rate. Technological advances are constantly being made in the transmission of communications via telecommunications facilities. The administrative assistant must understand this technology in order to function effectively in the office environment. Because so many companies manufacture a wide variety of equipment that performs unique tasks and also offer a variety of services to consumers and businesses, the administrative assistant is challenged to make decisions that will provide the office with the most efficient and cost-effective communication system available.

This chapter begins with a definition of telecommunications and includes a discussion of communication networks and transmission technology. Specific telephone systems are discussed as well as a variety of special services and equipment available with these telephone systems. The various types of electronic mail are also explained in this chapter.

TELECOMMUNICATIONS DEFINED

In its broadest sense, **telecommunications** is the electronic transmission of communications from one location to another. Electronically transmitted communications can take five different forms: data, text, image (maps, graphics, pictures), voice, and video.

Information Technologies and Communication Networks

Developments in the field of electronics have created new and efficient ways of circulating business information. When automation was introduced to the business office, each piece of equipment performed only one function with its own separate technology. The telephone, for instance, only transmitted voices. The computer only processed digital (numeric) data. Administrative assistants keyed material dictated by the executives in one area and sent transcripts by conventional means to another location. Reprographic equipment served to reproduce information at only one location.

Today, information technologies are integrated. Machines that formerly performed only one function have been merged with others. Electronically generated messages can now be composed, edited, transmitted, reproduced, distributed, and filed in a fraction of the time it once took to send a conventional business letter through the mail or to complete a typical telephone conversation. Mail can be electronically "picked up" from the equipment in which it is stored at the convenience of the recipient. It is possible not only to transmit voice, data, image, and text to one or several locations electronically, but to merge all four kinds of information at one receiving point.

Messages appearing on a computer screen may be read, stored in a computer's memory for later recall, or printed. With the appropriate equipment, all forms of information (handwritten or keyed messages, processed or unprocessed data, charts, or voice messages) can be transmitted from the point of origin to any distant point or points equipped with the appropriate receiving equipment.

The integration of information technologies, which permits separate technologies to communicate with each other, is often made possible by networking. **Networking,** the linking of computers and peripheral equipment across distances through various communication carriers, occurs on a local and a global scale.

Local Area Networks. Individual (stand-alone) microcomputers, which were introduced into the office environment in the late 1970s, can now be connected electronically by cable. This cable system, called a **local area network (LAN),** provides a path for the transfer of documents and data between and among computers connected to the LAN. Local area networks have changed the organization and operation of offices, providing a level of information sharing not possible with individual microcomputers. Through networks, information can be accessed by departments within a single building or by many departments located in various nearby buildings. LANs provide the path through which electronic mail (E-mail) (see page 198) can be routed to computers connected to the network.

The heart of any LAN is the network server, often called a file server. The network server is a computer that controls the flow of information between computers and other devices connected to the network. The network server also stores most of the software programs, files, and data that will be accessed by the LAN users.

Many network configurations are available. The dominant LAN configurations are ARCnet, Ethernet, and Token Ring. See the drawing of a network configuration in Figure 8-1. Regardless of which type of LAN is used, the re-

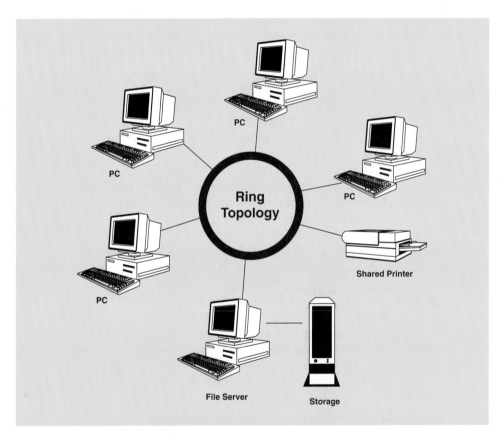

Fig. 8-1 Diagram of a Token Ring network showing connected computers, printers, copier, and file server.

sults will be the same. Office productivity will be increased through the sharing of information among offices, and time will be saved because employees seeking correspondence and other information will make fewer trips to file storage areas. In addition, communication will be increased between offices through the use of E-mail. A number of devices can be connected into a network. Figure 8-2 is a list of the configurations that can exist in a local area network.

CONFIGURATIONS FOR A LOCAL AREA NETWORK

Computer to computer. Microcomputers can be connected to other microcomputers as well as being connected to mainframe computers.

Computer to printer. Computers are often connected via a LAN to a common printer.

Computer to copier. Computers may be connected to a high-volume, high-speed copier.

Computer to telecommunications equipment. If telecommunications equipment is included in the network, it is possible for messages created on a computer to be transmitted via telephone lines to computers in other cities or countries.

Networking is not limited to large offices. The cost of local area networks is within the budgets of small offices having as few as two or three microcomputers.

Wide Area Networks.   In addition to an internal communication system, many businesses also need access to an external or global communication system. Local area networks can tie into a larger network to enable a business to communicate over a greater geographic region. With a **wide area** or **global network,** electronic equipment can communicate within a given city, to another city, or to a foreign country. A business can communicate with its branch offices and with other business firms as well. Satellite and microwave communication systems make wide area networks possible.

Transmission Technologies

Methods of electronic transmission include the following technologies: analog and digital transmission, cable and fiber optics, and microwave and satellite communication. While any detailed discussion of these methods is certain to be highly technical, the descriptions that follow will acquaint you with the processes.

Analog and Digital Transmission.   Certain communication networks transmit information in either an analog or a digital mode. **Analog signals** transmit data in continuous, smooth sound waves. Voice communication networks such as telephone lines are in analog mode. Computer information, on the other hand, is transmitted in the form of **digital signals;** that is, discrete (unconnected) on/off signals. In order for voice and data transmissions to be sent over the same network, analog signals must be converted to digital signals and vice versa. A device called a **modem** (from *mo*dulator and *dem*odulator) makes such conversions possible. For instance, an office with only analog transmission (voice) facilities would use a modem to convert digital signals from a computer to analog mode for transmission over its analog line. At the receiving location, a modem would convert the analog signals back to digital form for use by another computer. Figure 8-3 depicts this exchange of signals.

Digital transmission is regarded as more efficient because it has the capability of sending large quantities of information at very rapid speeds. Most businesses are replacing old analog lines with digital lines. Forecast for the future is the development of digital systems for simultaneous voice and data transmission.

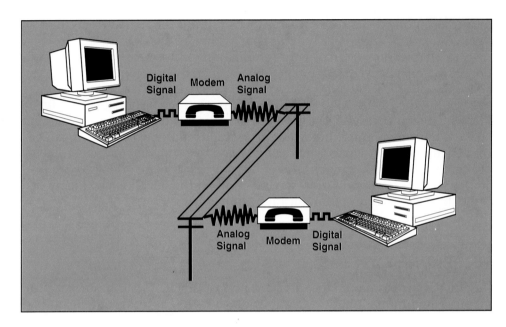

Fig. 8-3 Modems are used to convert digital signals into analog signals for transmission over telephone lines.

Copper Wire and Fiber Optics. The most popular medium through which electrical signals for voice and data communication are transmitted is the traditional copper wire. Telephone lines are composed of many copper wire pairs, bundled together to form a cable. Limitations of copper wires have led to the development of fiber-optic cables, the newest medium for the transmission of voice and data.

Fiber-optic cables are very popular because of their small size and their ability to transmit large amounts of information. By using fiber optics, not only can voice and data be transmitted simultaneously, but many different users can be transmitting over the same fiber cable at the same time.

Unlike copper wires, which carry electricity between users of the cable, fiber-optic cables are clusters of clear, flexible tubes that carry beams of light. At the beginning of the cable, an electronic device called a **transmitter** takes the electrical information coming from a telephone, computer, or similar device and converts it into a light beam. The light beam is then transmitted through the cable to a receiver that converts the light beam back into electrical signals for connection to telephones, computers, printers, or other electrical office systems.

Telephone companies and others installing new cables to connect computers, telephones, and other data-carrying wires are currently in the process of converting from traditional copper wires to fiber-optic cables. The advantages of fiber cables are well worth the effort.

Microwave and Satellite Communication.   Long-distance, high-speed transmission of information is made possible by microwave and satellite technologies. Microwave communications are sent by transmission towers, which are strategically located 30 miles apart all the way across the country. Signals are relayed from one tower's antenna to another's until the signals reach their final destination.

To offer worldwide transfer of information, orbiting satellites use a variation of the microwave relay tower system. Generally positioned 23,000 miles above the earth, the satellites transmit signals in space. Today many satellites are orbiting the earth. Digital signals are sent from earth stations to a satellite, which rebroadcasts the signals for transmission to another earth station. Like the transmission technologies discussed previously, voice signals can be converted to digital signals when sending and receiving microwave or satellite communication. Many businesses lease or rent the use of microwave and/or satellite communication services through the telephone company or through other satellite communication companies.

TELEPHONE SYSTEMS

Despite the increasing number of alternatives available to businesses for communicating information, the telephone remains the most popular means of communication between two or more persons. High levels of competition among manufacturers to provide sophisticated telephone systems has offered businesses a wide choice of telephone equipment and systems.

Key Systems

The **key system** links a group of key telephones. As the name implies, each key on a multibutton telephone ties into a separate telephone trunk line, rather than running through pooled trunk lines of a larger PBX (private branch exchange) system. Each key telephone permits the user to select an outside line or an intercom (internal communication) line. Each individual key telephone also has the same capability of receiving, initiating, and holding calls. Intercom lines can be used both for conversations and for paging. Key systems are popular with small businesses that need a limited number of telephone stations.

AT&T's Spirit Communication System is an example of an electronic key system. This system has an ultimate capacity of 16 stations, 6 outside lines, and 2 intercom lines. Some of the standard features of the Spirit System include a *speakerphone,* which allows hands-free operation instead of using the handset; *speed dialing,* which can dial frequently called numbers with the press of single button; *last number redial,* which enables a number to be re-dialed without dialing the number again; *conference calling* for up to four people at a time; *intercom conference calling;* and *voice mail,* which allows callers to leave a message on an automated answering machine. Other features may be programmed into the system.

A sophisticated system developed by AT&T is the Partner Communication System (see Figure 8-4). This system can handle up to 8 outside lines and 24 stations. Each telephone has buttons for outside lines and buttons for programming Partner's features. In addition to the features included in the Spirit System, the Partner includes such programmable features as privacy, which prevents others from listening in on or interrupting your call, and *do not disturb,* which, when turned on, prevents calls from ringing on that phone. The *busy redial* feature automatically redials a busy number for you (up to 15 attempts) and alerts you as soon as the call goes through. *Call forwarding* lets you redirect calls from your office so that they will actually ring at another telephone number you choose. *Remote line access* gives you access to the

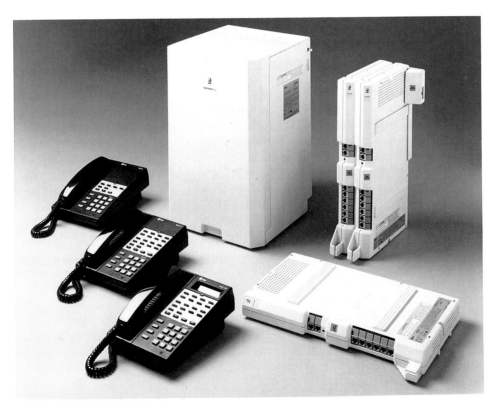

Fig. 8-4 AT&T's Partner Communication System permits users to select a number of intercom lines and a number of outside lines as well as many automated features. *Permission of AT&T Archives.*

system lines from another location, allowing you to make business calls while on the road. *System answer* enables the system to automatically answer calls during periods of high call volume, deliver a recorded announcement, and put the caller on hold until someone can handle the call. Many other optional features make Partner a very sophisticated communication system.

PBX (Private Branch Exchange) Systems

Many businesses have sufficient phone traffic to justify some type of central switchboard system. A **PBX (private branch exchange) system** is used in organizations that have more than 25 telephone extensions. The phone attendant answers incoming calls and forwards them by touching a button on an electronic console (switchboard). However, many of today's PBX systems have the **direct inward dialing (DID)** feature, which gives each person an individual extension. Every telephone in a company has its own seven-digit telephone number. Any caller can direct-dial this number from an outside telephone, bypassing the switchboard. Direct calls can be made within the company to any extension by dialing the last four or five digits of the telephone number. Using direct inward dialing can vastly reduce the number of calls coming into the business through the central switchboard.

Another feature of PBX systems is **direct outward dialing (DOD).** To place outgoing calls, the caller dials 9 (or another code) to get an outside line, then dials the desired phone number. The assistance of a phone attendant is not needed in making outgoing or internal calls.

Additional options available with a PBX system include *directory services,* which allow users to enter employees' names and get their extension; *call coverage,* which allows calls to be transferred to another telephone when you are away from your desk; *speed dialing;* and *voice mail.* Another feature designed to improve phone management is rollover, which allows an incoming call that is not answered in a certain number of rings to be automatically transferred to another extension. Most PBX systems also can be designed to block certain outbound calls (900-number calls, for example) and keep track of the phone numbers each employee is calling. These recordkeeping functions provide both basic billing information and detailed management reports.

Today's PBX systems are computer controlled. They can be purchased or leased from any number of equipment manufacturers, such as AT&T. A computerized telephone system permits a company to acquire new features through periodic enhancements to the computer program. These add-on features can be customized to fit telephone needs and existing arrangements in each organization.

Most PBX systems accept and transmit only analog (voice) signals. Another type of PBX system is the **digital PBX,** which has integrated voice and data transmission capabilities. The digital PBX is regarded as a major support component to local area networks. An example of a digital PBX console appears in Figure 8-5.

Fig. 8-5 Modern PBX systems incorporate digital technology to provide administrative assistants and executives with a host of information and communication capabilities. *Permission of AT&T Archives.*

Centrex (Central Exchange) Systems

Centrex is a central-office-based equivalent of a PBX service which is offered by regional telephone companies. Telecommunications companies are trying to enhance the appeal of Centrex service by offering a number of added features normally found only on advanced systems. Such features as automatic call distribution (ACD), call forwarding, and station message detail recording are frequently sold as on-premises additions to Centrex service. These additional features make Centrex an attractive alternative to a key system or PBX system.

The major advantages of Centrex include a single point of contact for service calls, monthly leasing rather than capital outlays, quick installation, no ties to aging technology, and savings on support costs and office space. However, there are some disadvantages such as the loss of control of the service, difficulty in meeting special needs, and problems with assuring adequate service from the phone company.

SPECIAL SERVICES/EQUIPMENT

Many telecommunication companies and other equipment manufacturers offer a variety of services that directly affect the administrative assistant. Some special services and equipment represent significant advances in the communications market and have resulted in considerable savings in time and costs.

Incoming Toll-Free Calling

Through its 800 service, AT&T offers subscribers volume-discounted long-distance service for *incoming* calls on an intrastate or interstate basis. For the caller, 800 service represents toll-free calling by dialing 1 + 800 + the designated phone number. This service is particularly attractive to businesses that want their customers to have easy access to them and their services.

Subscribers choose from six levels of coverage based on geographic zones, known as service areas. Service area 6, which is the broadest service area, includes the continental United States, Alaska, Puerto Rico, and the Virgin Islands. Lower-numbered service areas provide service to narrower geographic zones and offer a lower cost per unit of use. All AT&T 800 service customers are entitled to a free listing in either the business or consumer edition of the *AT&T 800 Service Directory*.

Wide Area Telecommunications Service (WATS)

AT&T also offers volume-discounted long-distance service for outgoing calls via its **wide area telecommunications service (WATS).** In addition to a tapered discount based on usage, WATS provides time-of-day and day-of-week price discounts. WATS offers the same six levels of geographic coverage as 800 service, with cost per unit of use based on breadth of coverage. In addition to transmitting voices, WATS can be used to transmit data and graphics. Similar WATS-like services are also available through other long-distance carriers.

Leased (or Private) Lines

It is possible for a company to lease telephone lines for its exclusive use. Special *tie lines* can be used to connect various locations of a business complex in different parts of the same city or in different cities. They provide direct voice contact and data transmission capabilities between separate units of a business. A tie line can connect switchboards, key telephones, and regular telephones. Usually, unlimited calling is provided at a fixed monthly charge, with tie lines always being reserved for the exclusive use of the subscriber.

Many organizations lease private telephone channels for calling their foreign branches or other companies. The volume of calls determines whether leasing lines is cost effective.

Foreign Exchange Service (FX)

With **foreign exchange service (FX)** a local telephone number can be listed in the directory of a city that is remote from a company's location. With this service, clients, rather than placing a long-distance call to the company, can place a local call to the listed number. For example, the New York

City directory might carry the number of a firm located in New Brunswick, New Jersey. The company's New York City clients can, in effect, make local calls to New Brunswick, because the New Brunswick company picks up the long-distance charge. FX does *not* refer to international calls.

Cellular (Mobile) Service

The cellular telephone, once only a science fiction appliance, is now a fact of life. Cellular telephones use radio signals to transmit conversations between individuals in locations remote from the traditional office setting (in trucks and cars, for example). The equipment is made by a number of manufacturers and is sold primarily through cellular-service carriers. Anyone can make a call to a mobile phone from any telephone, and any telephone can receive a call from a mobile unit. Conversations travel partway by radio waves and partway by telephone wire through given geographical areas called **cells.** Each cell has a radio transmitter and control equipment linking mobile telephones to computers and the local telephone system.

▼ **TECHNOLOGY**

About 25 percent of new telephone numbers are going to cellular phones.

Cellular telephones include mobile models that are permanently installed in cars, transportable units that are powered by separate battery packs, and truly portable self-contained handheld units. An example of a cellular phone appears in Figure 8-6. Each type has advantages and disadvantages. The mobile cellular phone is the most common type. These phones do not require a separate battery pack since their power is drawn from the car's electrical system. The transportable phone may be used in remote locations. A battery is included, so it can be used virtually anywhere. The handheld, portable phone is the most convenient and versatile cellular phone. As such, it is also the most expensive type. It requires no external power source because it has a rechargeable internal battery. The low output of the handheld phone limits the strength of the signal transmitted, which in turn limits the effective range of this phone.

Pagers

Unlike cellular phones, which permit two-way conversations, **pagers** are signaling devices that alert the holder to contact a predetermined phone number for messages. Pagers are small units that can be attached to a belt or kept in a pocket, briefcase, or handbag. A caller activates the pager by dialing the pager's telephone number. The vibrating signal or beeping sound of the pager signals the holder to

Fig. 8-6 Cellular phones help people increase productivity by providing telephone access at remote locations. *Ameritech Cellular Services.*

call for a message. Some voice units are capable of giving short messages. Others can display the caller's phone number. Pagers are very popular with executives and salespeople who are often away from the office, yet must keep in contact with office personnel for messages and/or instructions.

Touch-Tone Service

Touch-tone service utilizes the 12-key pushbutton telephone. Ten keys are reserved for dialing numbers zero to nine; two additional buttons (* and #) allow direct access to a computer center, a dictating center, or other service centers. Touch-tone service permits data to be entered into computers via tone transmission.

The Speakerphone

The **speakerphone** has a built-in transmitter and volume control to permit both sides of a telephone conversation to be amplified and played over a speaker. The administrative assistant can leave the telephone, walk to the opposite side of the room, look up information in a file, and read it to the caller from this location. Users are not tied to the telephone receiver. The speakerphone allows for more productive and less complicated conference calls. Speakerphones also make it possible to deliver lectures over the telephone and have them amplified to classes or conference groups. An example of a speakerphone appears in Figure 8-7.

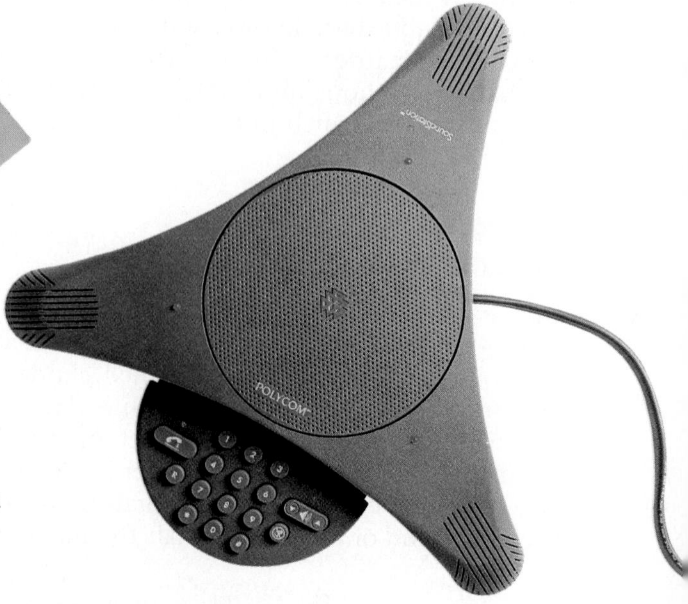

Fig. 8-7 Conference calls that include several people at each site are a cost-effective means of communication.
Polycom, Inc.

Conference Calls

The amount of time executives spend traveling to and from meetings, combined with the increasing expense of airfare and lodging, makes **conference calls** a particularly cost-effective communication tool. Recent innovations have made it possible to set up conference calls without the assistance of an operator. But if your company does not have an electronic switchboard with conference call capability, it is still possible to set up conference calls. For example, if your employer wants to discuss a marketing strategy with associates in several branch offices across the country, a conference call can be arranged by using the following steps:

1. Notify the conference call participants of the time the call will be made.
2. Call the long-distance operator and ask for the conference operator.
3. Specify to the conference operator the names, locations, and phone numbers of the persons to be included in the call.
4. Indicate when the call should be placed. The conference operator will call back when all of the parties are connected.

A conference operator may also help you set up a **one-way conference call.** In a one-way conference call, only the voice of the caller is transmitted to a specified audience. Another conference call feature allows you to add a third caller to a conversation that is already in progress.

International Telephone Service

If your company's long-distance carrier provides international service, overseas telephone calls can be dialed directly. If you know the local number of the company being called and have a directory with access codes for international calls, you may use **international direct distance dialing** (IDDD) to reach your overseas party using the steps shown in Figure 8-8. Special

1. If a long-distance carrier other than your company's designated long-distance company is used, that carrier's five-digit number must be dialed before step #2.
2. Dial 011 (the international access code)
3. Plus 44 (the country code)
4. Plus 1 (the city routing code)
5. Plus 123456 (the local number)
6. If a push-button telephone is used, depress the # button after dialing the number to save connecting time.
7. After dialing the call, allow at least 45 seconds for the call to start.

Fig. 8-8 Steps to follow when making a direct-dial international call to London from the United States.

pamphlets available from your telephone company can keep you up-to-date on international rates and special conditions in various countries.

If your telephone is not capable of handling IDDD calls, dial the operator and give the name of the country, the name of the company, and the name of the person you are calling. Of course, it is essential to consider time zones and to check times during which various overseas rates apply. Consulting a world time zone map, as shown in Figure 8-9, will help you decide when to place international calls.

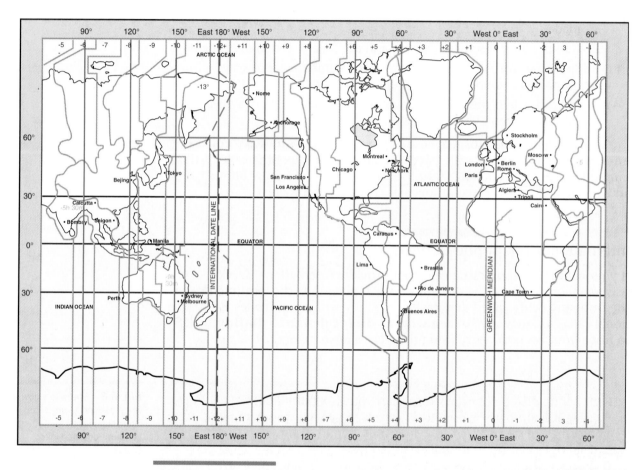

Fig. 8-9 Zones in east longitude are numbered in sequence from 1 to 12 and labeled *minus;* zones in west longitude are numbered 1 to 12 and labeled *plus.* To obtain Greenwich time, the zone number in each zone is either added to or subtracted from the standard time in accordance with its plus or minus sign. For example, Chicago is in the +6 zone. When it is 9:00 a.m. in Chicago, add six hours to determine the Greenwich time of 3:00 p.m. Tokyo is in the −9 zone. When it is 10:00 a.m. in Tokyo, subtract nine hours to determine the Greenwich time of 1:00 a.m.

Message-Taking Equipment and Services

Equipment and services are available to ensure that telephone calls are always answered, even when no one is able to cover the phones. The quality and performance of these products and services are key business concerns.

Answering, Recording, and Switching Devices. Automatic answering equipment delivers a prerecorded message. The user makes a recording, asking callers to leave a message. Upon returning to the office, an administrative assistant copies the machine's messages onto telephone message forms and gives them to the executive.

Many answering machines allow their owners to call in from outside the office, revise their recordings, and listen to their messages. While small businesses such as real estate and insurance offices find these answering devices especially advantageous, this equipment is helpful to large businesses as well.

Telephone Answering Services. Unlike automatic answering devices that merely recite impersonal prerecorded messages, the attendant for a telephone answering service is able to exercise judgment and understanding, personally assisting callers. Many businesses invest in answering services as a way of personalizing their offices during the hours they are not open. The administrative assistant in an office using such a service should establish friendly relations with answering service personnel, always checking with the service immediately upon coming into the office and providing complete information to attendants when the answering service takes office calls.

Taped Announcements. Almost every telephone user is familiar with taped announcements that report the time of day, the weather, flight information, market information, movie schedules, and the like. It is possible for a business to develop similar announcements, possibly specifying office hours, mailing address, or other general information. Some organizations make taped announcements of advertising messages to play to callers who are waiting on hold.

Telephone Directories

In addition to answering the telephone, the administrative assistant sometimes places local and long-distance calls. To do this efficiently, an administrative assistant must know how to get maximum service from telephone directories and telephone operators and how to make the appropriate choices regarding directory services that are available.

The telephone directory has two major parts. The alphabetical directory (the White Pages) is divided into residential and business sections. Each section contains an alphabetical listing of phone service subscribers, their addresses, and telephone numbers. The classified directory (the Yellow Pages) is divided into a "fast-finding index" and the regular listing of businesses under headings arranged by product or service.

The telephone directory is a rich source of information. The introductory pages of directories for most metropolitan areas contain the following information:

Emergency numbers

Community service numbers

Instructions for telephoning locally, nationally, and overseas

Area codes for major cities in the United States

A map showing area code distribution

A local ZIP Code

Long-distance rates to major cities and hours during which rates apply

Facts about telephone services and their costs

Helpful hints for finding numbers quickly and easily

Explanations of billing

Money-saving tips

Area maps with street guides

Community profiles

Some of these explanations may be repeated in a foreign language if enough people in the area use that language.

A corporation may find it advantageous to keep in a central location a collection of telephone directories from cities in which it conducts a large volume of business. If you are unable to secure an out-of-town directory, it is also possible to find them in some hotels, major travel terminals, and public libraries.

The Alphabetical Directory. You can usually locate numbers in the alphabetical directory quickly, but the exceptions make it necessary for the administrative assistant to know the rules for arranging names in alphabetic sequence. For example, there are 21 columns of the surname *Miller* in one metropolitan directory.

Identical main entries (*Miller, Jeff,* for example) are listed in alphabetic order according to street names. Numbered streets are listed after named streets in numeric rather than alphabetic order. (Thus, *Eighth Street* would follow rather than precede *Second Street.*)

Locating various government offices and public services also requires an understanding of alphabetic listings. These offices or services are generally listed under their proper political subdivisions. City offices are found under the name of the municipality; county offices, under the name of the county; state offices, under the name of the state; and federal offices, under *United States Government.* (Government listings are sometimes found in a special blue-colored section in some directories.) Public schools are usually listed under the municipality, then under a *Board of Education* subentry. Parochial schools are listed individually by name.

The Yellow Pages Directory. The Yellow Pages directory is a very helpful reference for the administrative assistant. In metropolitan areas, this classified directory of products and services is usually bound separately from the White Pages. If an executive wants to talk with "that air conditioning firm on Church Street," an alert administrative assistant might start by looking in the Yellow Pages under *Air Conditioning Equipment & Systems—Supplies & Parts* and looking for companies located on Church Street.

You should circle every frequently called telephone number in the directory. You should also jot down numbers you look up just in case you get a busy signal when you first dial them. List new or changed numbers on the proper directory page or in a desk directory.

Personal Telephone Directory. Large organizations may provide employees with a company telephone directory that lists the telephone numbers of employees. In addition to this directory, every administrative assistant should keep a personal, up-to-date directory of outside telephone numbers for the executive. (You can look up a number in a personal telephone directory in ten seconds, about a third of the time required to search a larger directory.) In a personal directory, the names of frequently called persons and firms are listed alphabetically. A thoughtful administrative assistant places a condensed list of these numbers either at the back of the executive's daily calendar or beside the telephone.

For your personal directory, it is better to use some kind of card or tab insertion scheme rather than a keyed list that makes no provision for adding names or making name changes. Any list quickly becomes out-of-date unless a system is devised that provides for additions and deletions. Most administrative assistants use a small rotary wheel for mounting their personal directories. For making corrections, some use stick-on labels. A personal telephone booklet may be obtained from the telephone company; blank pages at the back of a phone directory can also be used to list the names and numbers of persons frequently called. Electronic telephone directories are also being used by administrative assistants to keep track of important numbers. The electronic directory may be maintained on a computer or an electronic organizer, a pocket-size device designed to store addresses, telephone numbers, and appointments.

Some people prefer not to have their telephone numbers listed in the city directory. Usually, the city's directory assistance (information) operators will not have these unlisted numbers on record. Only in exceptional circumstances (with the customer's consent) will the telephone company arrange to complete directory-assisted calls to unlisted numbers. Keeping unlisted numbers in a personal directory becomes doubly important since they cannot be found elsewhere.

Business Promotion Listings. A company you need to reach may list its telephone number in a directory in several ways to promote business. One way to promote business is to list a special reverse-charge toll number, an 800 number. With an 800 number, charges are automatically billed to the party receiving the call. A company may also incorporate its toll-free 800 number into its advertising. To determine if a company you want to call has an 800 listing, dial 1-800-555-1212 and give the operator the name of the company. The operator will give this information to you if it is available. A directory of 800 numbers is also available for those who use such numbers frequently. Hotels and motels often list their 800 numbers nationally with listings that look like this:

SHERATON HOTELS & MOTOR INNS—
Reservation Office StLouisMo
No Charge To Calling Party 1-800-555-3535

Some companies also list their out-of-town numbers in local directories in the hope that they will promote business even if the caller has to pay for the call.

LONG-DISTANCE CALLS

Every time you pick up your phone, you enter a vast $150-billion system that connects nearly 200 million telephones in the United States. Long-distance calls can be made to all telephones in this country and to most other countries and territories throughout the world.

Station-to-Station/Direct-Distance Dialing (DDD)

Because of the time and money saved through direct-distance dialing, businesses tend to use station-to-station, long-distance service, except in cases when it is known that the person to be reached may not be readily located. Dial station-to-station when you are willing to talk with anyone who answers the telephone or when you are reasonably sure that the person you want to talk to is nearby. Charges begin when the telephone or the switchboard is answered. If the person you are trying to reach is not immediately available to take the call, charges are assessed while you wait for that person to get on the line. For example, if you are trying to reach someone registered at a hotel, the hotel operator may page the lobby or the hotel restaurant if that person is not in his or her room. If the operator cannot locate the guest, the call is still fully chargeable to you.

Most station-to-station long-distance calls are dialed directly. Usually you dial 1 plus the three-digit area code, then the telephone number. In some locations when dialing a long-distance number within your own area code you must still include the area code number. However, in most locations when dialing a long-distance number within your own area code you need to dial only 1 plus the number.

Specific directions for DDD may be found in the front section of your telephone directory. You can obtain the area code from the letterhead of the company you are calling (it is often included with the address), your personal telephone directory, the front of the telephone directory, or the operator. If you have the area code but do not know the telephone number, dial the pre-fix 1, the area code, and the number 555-1212 to reach directory assistance. Tell the directory assistance operator the city and the individual or business you wish to call, and you will be given the number. If there is even a remote possibility of calling this same number in the future, record both the area code and the telephone number in your personal directory.

Dial the number carefully. If you reach the wrong number on any DDD call, promptly report the error to the operator to avoid all charges for the call. If your connection fails during a call, inform the operator so that the charges can be adjusted. Sometimes you may dial a number and get a recorded mes-sage telling you that your call has not been completed and asking you to ini-tiate it again. If it is evident that, for some reason, your call is not going through, dial the operator for help.

Person-to-Person

A person-to-person call requires operator assistance and is made when you must talk to a particular person or extension. Charges begin when that per-son or extension answers.

If you know the area code and telephone number but wish to call person-to-person, collect, or on a credit card (also known as a calling card), or if you wish to have the call charged to another number, you need only rou-tine operator assistance. Dial 0, the area code, and the telephone number. When the operator answers, either:

1. Say, "Person-to-person call to [give the name of the person you are calling]."
2. Say, "Collect call from [give your name]."
3. Say, "Credit card call billed to [give your credit card number]."
4. Say, "Bill to [give the area code and telephone number to which the call is to be billed]."

For the convenience of credit card customers, touch-tone telephones can handle credit card calls without operator assistance. Press 0, the area code, and the telephone number. When the tone sounds, use the phone keys to enter the credit card number and the call will be put through automatically. In addition, special public telephones for credit card users are now increas-ingly available at major airports, some hotels, and other heavy-traffic areas throughout the country. The user simply inserts the card into a slot, enters 0, then dials the desired number.

If you require special assistance, dial 0, state your problem, and give the operator whatever information you have. One administrative assistant had to call an official in Washington, D.C., at 2 p.m. on behalf of an employer who expected to be in the local courthouse near another telephone at that time. The administrative assistant explained the situation to the operator, who placed the call at 2 p.m. to the courthouse telephone and charged the call to the employer's office telephone. Another administrative assistant was asked to get in touch with a client who was staying at a Pittsburgh hotel. The administrative assistant told the long-distance operator that the only clue to the person's whereabouts was that lodging would be at one of Pittsburgh's better hotels. The operator checked the hotels until the person was located. Although not every operator will put forth a superhuman effort, they can be of great help and the administrative assistant with no other alternatives may have to ask for this kind of service.

Time Zones

Time zones are very important to the administrative assistant who must make long-distance calls. A New York office would not call San Francisco before 12 noon New York time because there would be little likelihood of reaching anyone in the San Francisco office before 9 a.m. San Francisco time. Conversely, an administrative assistant in Los Angeles would not place a call to Boston after 2 p.m. Los Angeles time because that office would probably close around 5 p.m. Boston time. Administrative assistants who place overseas calls should also become familiar with international time zones.

The map in Figure 8-10 indicates time zones and area codes for the continental United States and adjacent Canadian provinces. A person placing a long-distance call should plan the call to coincide with the business day in the city called. The time where the call originates determines whether day, evening, or night rates apply.

Relative Costs

Calls dialed directly are much cheaper than person-to-person calls. Having a number at hand and dialing it yourself saves a great deal of money. Calling at night or on weekends is cheaper than calling during the business day. Knowing the relative costs of different services enables customers to use the telephone economically.

Businesses have several options for controlling the costs of long-distance telephoning. Some computer-controlled telephone systems automatically select the least expensive long-distance line for a call. If the least costly outside line is busy, the computer dials the caller back when the line is available and then dials the number automatically. Other telephones automatically give priority for long-distance lines to the caller holding the highest rank so that executive time spent on long-distance calls is reduced.

Paying for Long Distance

An administrative assistant may be responsible for accepting, accounting for, and reversing long-distance charges, or for obtaining a credit card on which

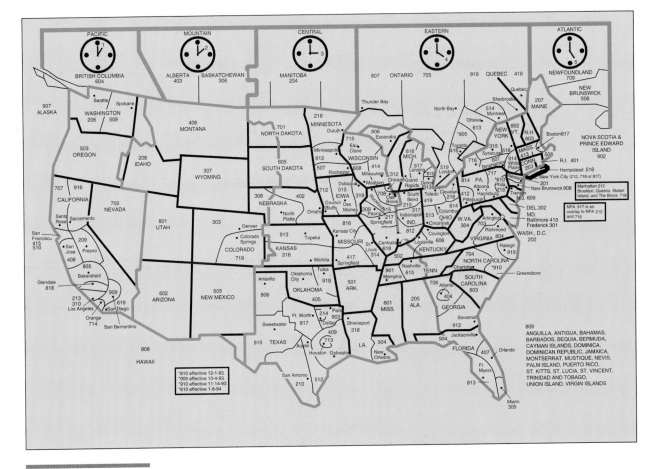

Fig. 8-10 This map shows area codes and standard time zones for the continental United States and Canada. © 1992 Cincinnati Bell Directory.

an executive can charge calls. Many administrative assistants keep a record of outgoing long-distance calls to assist in verifying calls and charges.

Cost Records of Toll Calls. For accounting purposes, most companies charge toll calls to specific departments, clients, or jobs. Modern telephone equipment automatically performs this accounting function. However, if the telephone system does not have this accounting capability, the administrative assistant may be expected to keep records of the toll charges to be checked against a bill and charged to the proper departments.

The federal government levies an excise tax on long-distance calls. The telephone company collects this tax from subscribers. Tax rates are shown on the customer's bill. A cost record of each long-distance call for accounting purposes requires that this tax be computed and added to each toll charge.

Collect Calls. Long-distance calls can be made collect; that is, charges for person-to-person and station-to-station calls can be reversed (or charged) to the number called rather than to the caller. The request to reverse charges, however, must be made at the time the call is placed so that the person called can have an opportunity to accept or refuse the charges. Because collect calls are operator assisted, they are more expensive than direct-distance dialing calls.

Telephone Credit Cards. Executives who make telephone calls while away from the office may carry telephone credit cards, allowing them to charge calls to their companies. These cards use a code number to initiate calls through the operator or through special credit card telephones. Monthly telephone bills identify credit card calls as such.

ELECTRONIC MAIL

The Electronic Mail Association, a trade association for the communications industry, defines **electronic mail** as the generic term for the noninteractive communication of text, data, images, or voice messages between a sender and designated recipient by systems utilizing telecommunications links. Rather than using the U.S. Postal Service, office support personnel frequently send communications electronically via communicating computers and copiers, electronic mail (computer-based message systems), voice messaging, and facsimile machines. Each of these types of electronic message systems is described in this section.

Communicating Computers and Copiers

A **communicating computer** can exchange information with a compatible computer via telephone lines. The functions of sending and receiving information are under operator control and supervision. Information is keyed, stored on a magnetic medium (such as a disk drive), and then transmitted over telephone lines. At the receiving location, the information is received by a computer, and it can be stored or printed. Because the data transmitted can be stored at the receiver's location, information can be received after office hours, thus taking advantage of lower night telephone rates. In addition, a communicating computer can be a component of a computer-based message system.

Another electronic device that plays a key role in electronic messaging is the *intelligent copier/printer*. This machine can produce hard copies from input received from various devices, including computers.

Electronic Mail (E-Mail)

Electronic mail is a computer-based message system. E-mail systems, as they are frequently called, have become popular with executives because they increase communication efficiency between and among executives and office support staff (administrative assistants and clerical personnel). With this type of system, on-line computers (computers connected to each other through a network) exchange information. Messages are keyed and transmitted through telephone wires or satellites to receiving terminals. The equipment required to establish a computer-based message system at a typical workstation is a microcomputer with a keyboard and screen, a modem, and electronic mail software. The message system accepts messages for registered users, storing them in files called mailboxes, for later pickup by the addressee. The recipient of the message can print a copy, address a response to the sender, forward the message to another person, or delete the message from the system. In addition, messages can be filed by "downloading" (transferring) the message from the E-mail system to a diskette or the hard disk drive on a microcomputer. Conversely, documents or messages can be created on the microcomputer and "uploaded" (transferred) to the E-mail system for sharing with someone else.

While the cost of sending messages by this system is more expensive than a postage stamp, it has many advantages. The message, whether it is one line or 50 pages, can be sent around the world in a matter of seconds. Messages can be sent to multiple recipients simultaneously from one original by using a distribution list. Reading the mail and responding immediately or forwarding it to someone else saves a tremendous amount of time.

Voice Messages (Voice Mail)

Voice message systems, also called voice mail, can help reduce the wasted time and expense that telephone communication frequently involves. These systems enable the user to receive, send, store, forward, or delete telephone messages. As a result, voice message systems help eliminate the multiple call-back game called "telephone tag."

When you reach an unattended phone that is connected to a voice message system, you hear a message, often recorded by the person you are calling. The message will include prompts that tell you how to leave a message or reach another extension or an attendant by pressing particular keys on the telephone keypad. If you decide to leave a message, it is digitized and stored in the recipient's personal "mailbox," a section of computer memory that is reserved for that individual. The system will then inform the user that a message is waiting, sometimes through a blinking indicator light on the phone. To access the message, the recipient follows the prompts and presses the appropriate keys on the telephone keypad. The message is then played back. The recipient can reply to the message or send a copy of the message to someone else.

Voice message systems have a number of advantages. The systems can now be integrated with computer-controlled PBX central telephone systems and also can interface with the microcomputer. The system is available to answer calls 24 hours a day, 7 days a week. The ability to store and forward messages provides confidentiality, so private information can be left on the system. In addition, it is a time saver. A normal phone conversation lasts four or five minutes; a voice message that imparts the same information averages

TECHNOLOGY

Half of all calls are for one-way transfers of information. With voice mail, the call is made once and the transaction is done.

only 30 seconds to a minute. For the frequent business traveler, voice message systems offer convenient one-way communication with the home office as well as the ability to receive stored messages that may have been left on the system.

Facsimile Equipment

The **facsimile (FAX) machine** is the most popular form of electronic messaging today and is found in large offices, small offices, and home offices. It is the most flexible and inexpensive form of electronic messaging. The FAX machine is essentially a blend of telephone, copier, and document reader. FAX machines read a document that has been inserted into the machine and transmit images of the document over telephone cables to another FAX machine, which receives the image signals and prints a hard copy of the transmitted document. Thus, hard copy is transmitted over the telephone wires, eliminating the need to rekey the document. Photographs, printed matter, and drawings can be transmitted via FAX with remarkable clarity and resolution. See Figure 8-11. Facsimile equipment is easy to use and requires only minimal operator training.

For best results in sending documents via FAX, clear, legible material is essential. Keyed material generally transmits quite well, as does material handwritten in black ballpoint pen or dark pencil. Drawings should be

Fig. 8-11 Facsimile equipment can transmit photographs, printed material, and drawings. *Lanier Worldwide, Inc.*

done in dark pencil or ink and should not contain extremely small printing or diagrams.

As the use of FAX machines has increased, so have the types of machines and the features found on these machines. A variety of small, inexpensive FAX machines are now available. This enables small offices, home offices, and other locations to purchase a FAX even though only occasional use is required. More expensive FAX systems incorporate a telephone, a telephone answering machine, and perhaps a plain paper copier in addition to the facsimile function. This integration of systems results in a single piece of office automation equipment that copies documents, transmits and receives documents, and handles traditional telephone functions in one desktop piece of equipment.

For those business executives and sales representatives who travel extensively, portable FAX systems allow the transmission of documents by mobile telephone. Portable FAX machines can be connected to the mobile telephone in a car, allowing documents such as sales orders, drawings, or other printed items to be transmitted from the automobile.

A growing number of add-on products give computers the ability to transmit via FAX. These accessories allow the computer user to transmit a document directly from the computer via the telephone lines to a FAX machine. A limitation of using this type of FAX is that the document must be generated in the computer's memory. This limits the types of documents or forms that can be transmitted.

Care must be taken when using FAX systems. The document is likely to be received by a FAX that is shared by an entire office, so it may be read by persons other than the addressee. Obviously, security is a concern. The transmission of confidential documents should be handled with care. The following procedures may be helpful when transmitting sensitive documents via FAX:

1. Alert the addressee by telephone that a sensitive FAX document is being transmitted. The recipient of the document may be able to stand by the FAX and pick up the document before others have a chance to see it.

2. Be certain of the correct telephone number for the intended FAX equipment. If the receiving FAX telephone number is misdialed, the document could be sent to a FAX machine other than the one intended.

3. Use a cover sheet (see Figure 8-12). The use of a cover sheet will provide a

FACSIMILE COVER PAGE

DATE: November 4, 19--

TO: John E. Dorsett, Vice President
Chemical Power Company

PHONE NUMBER: (204) 555-1604

FAX NUMBER: (204) 555-2361

NUMBER OF PAGES INCLUDING COVER: 2

FROM: Christina Ostwald
James River Power Company

PHONE NUMBER: (316) 555-8925

FAX NUMBER: (316) 555-5671

REMARKS: Please FAX your approval of this document as soon as possible

Fig. 8-12 Use of a FAX cover sheet when sending a document provides a measure of security.

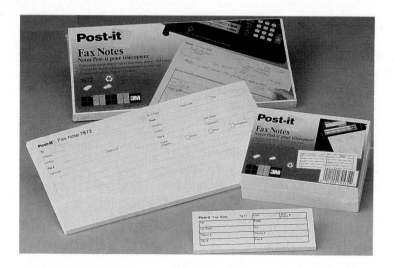

Fig. 8-13 If confidentiality is not essential when sending a FAX message, a "Post-it" transmittal form can be attached to the top of the document. This saves the cost of sending an additional cover sheet.
Reprinted with permission of 3M Co.

modest measure of security at the receiving FAX station and help ensure that the document reaches the desk of the intended recipient. However, if security is not a concern, a small "Post-it" brand transmittal form, such as those shown in Figure 8-13, can be used.

TELECONFERENCING

Another example of telecommunications technology is **teleconferencing.** Using telecommunications systems, an executive can conduct and/or attend a meeting without traveling to a distant location. Avoiding travel expenses and time lost in traveling makes teleconferencing attractive to business organizations. Meeting participants communicate electronically using two-way voice, text, or video communication. For a detailed discussion of teleconferencing, refer to Chapter 18, Meetings and Conferences.

THE ADMINISTRATIVE ASSISTANT AND COMMUNICATIONS SYSTEMS

The preceding discussion has provided a look at the developments in communication systems that affect how business offices exchange information. What does this chapter mean to you in performing your day-to-day duties?

Administrative assistants have decision-making responsibilities for sending messages that are consistent with office policy and executive preferences. Evaluate each message-sending situation by asking yourself the following questions:

1. How urgent is the message?
2. Is it important to make a special impact on the recipient?
3. Are documentation or reference copies needed?
4. Can another method save costly overtime?
5. What is the least expensive, most appropriate way to send the message?

You will compose many types of communications. In addition to originating documents, you will edit them; therefore, you must sharpen your communication skills. All communications should represent your best efforts at clarity and brevity.

Communication channels bring you in contact with more and more people. Realize that your professional image in representing your organization and your employer will extend beyond the confines of a single office.

You will utilize many of the components of communications systems. Your job will change as new components are added. You must keep up by learning to operate new components and understanding the functions of others.

In the future, there will be increased executive use of communication systems. More executives will work both at home and while traveling, as more sophisticated equipment becomes available. The executive will input material to the administrative assistant's workstation, and the administrative assistant will be responsible for operating workstations at both the executive's and the administrative assistant's desk. If you have your eye on advancing your career, your experiences as an administrative assistant can help you acquire the background necessary to become an information manager.

Summary

Telecommunications is broadly defined as the electronic transmission of communications from one location to another. These communications can be in the form of data, text, image, voice, or video.

When automation was introduced to the office, each piece of equipment had its own separate technology. Today, such functions as data processing, word processing, and communications are now integrated. Integration is made possible by networks. A local area network (LAN) uses cable to connect computers, copiers, and printers in an office complex. A local area network can also tie into a wide area network, thus expanding the communication to another city or another country. Wide area networks are made possible by satellite communication.

Voice communication networks are in analog (voice) mode; computer data, on the other hand, consist of digital (data) signals. In order for digital and analog signals to be sent over the same network, one must be converted to the other. A modem is used to perform these conversions. Cable is the main transmission medium of voice and data communication. Fiber optics, the use of thin glass-like tubes to transmit data as light, is replacing copper cabling as the major transmission medium. Microwave and satellite communication provide high-speed transmission of information over great distances. Satellite communication offers a global network opportunity for business organizations.

The telephone continues to be the most popular means of communication between two or more persons. The three types of telephone systems available today are the key system, the PBX system, and the Centrex system. The telephone system used will depend on the size and the needs of each office.

Special time-saving and cost-saving services and equipment are available for telephone subscribers. They include wide area telecommunications service (WATS), AT&T's 800 service, leased lines, foreign exchange service, cellular (mobile) service, pagers, touch-tone service, speakerphones, conference calls, overseas telephone service, message-taking equipment and service, and telephone directories.

Long-distance telephone calls can be made by calling station-to-station or person-to-person, depending on the situation. Calls may be placed through direct-distance dialing (DDD) or with the assistance of the operator.

Electronic messaging refers to communication sent to a destination by electronic means. Electronic messages can be sent by communicating computers and copiers, electronic mail (computer-based message systems), voice messages, and facsimile equipment.

Teleconferencing allows businesspeople to attend meetings electronically. Meeting participants communicate using two-way voice, text, or video communication. A more detailed discussion of teleconferencing is provided in Chapter 18.

The administrative assistant in a highly technical office environment needs to be extremely knowledgeable about telecommunications. The administrative assistant will make many of the decisions regarding efficient methods of sending communications.

QUESTIONS FOR DISCUSSION

1. Describe two types of documents that would be appropriate to send via a facsimile (FAX) machine and two types of documents that would not be appropriate to send via a FAX machine.

2. Distinguish between local area networks and wide area networks.

3. What applications can you think of for cellular phone service in a business organization?

4. Examine your local telephone directory. What information is found in its introductory pages? in the Yellow Pages?

THINK IT
Through

5. Your office is located in New York City and you are asked to call the accounting division of a company in Paris, France. You are to dial the number directly. During what hours of your business day (9 a.m. to 5 p.m.) would you attempt to dial this call?

6. How can an administrative assistant use a voice message system to increase his or her productivity?

7. A *redundancy* is the needless repetition of two meanings. Two words that are joined by a conjunction but have the same meaning are called *doublets*. Rekey the following sentences and eliminate the redundancies and doublets.

   a. If you live in close proximity to a school, it is easy to continue on in your program without repeating again the application for admission.

   b. During the month of June, it is our customary practice to reduce down prices on all merchandise that has depreciated in value.

   c. The two twin beds are too small in size for the room.

   d. This material is basic and fundamental to each and every employee's performance evaluation.

   e. First and foremost, I must point out that the true facts will not be repeated again when this case is over and done with.

PROBLEMS

1. If you were employed by a well-equipped corporation, which type of communication would you probably choose to use in the following situations? Give reasons for your choices.

   a. A message to three sales managers in different locations. (A reaction is necessary from each.)

   b. A message informing the payroll department in a branch office that data required for issuing paychecks have not been received.

   c. A message containing detailed information about a branch factory's production schedules for the next two months.

   d. A message to inquire about prices of a well-known office machine manufactured in a nearby suburb.

   e. A message to the production manager in a distant branch factory.

   f. A message that must reach 12 sales representatives in different locations by the following morning.

   g. A message that will be received after closing hours but must be available when the office opens the following morning.

   h. A graph to be used tomorrow in a national sales meeting.

2. Visit a technologically up-to-date office and make an oral report to the class on either of the following topics: the company's internal and external telephone system or its electronic message system. Include reasons why the company selected a particular system. Discuss what kind of equipment is used.

3. Locate phone numbers for the following places in your local telephone directory. Key a list in tabular form including the organization or department as it appears below, the name under which the telephone number is listed, and the telephone number for each item.

   a. City hall

   b. Fire department

   c. Park or recreation department

   d. Police department

   e. Post office

   f. Public library

   g. A local college or university

   h. The local office of the state employment service

   i. Telephone repair service

   j. Weather information

*T*ECHNOLOGY APPLICATIONS

▶ **TA8-1.TEM**

Access the template disk, and select the TA8-1.TEM file, which shows the FAX cover sheet now used by B&C Industries. The cover sheet needs to be updated.

1. Include B&C's new FAX number (555-9876) and its new phone number (555-9000).

2. Include an entry for Company in the Sent To column and an entry for Division in the Sent By column.

3. Change Date to Today's Date.

4. Note that this FAX sheet is a half-page sheet. Before you print out a copy, duplicate the form so that you will fit two forms on one sheet.

5. Insert a dotted line between the top and bottom halves to show where to cut the form.

Print out a hard copy of the new "two-up sheet" and submit it to your instructor.

Part 2

Case Problems

Case 2-1
CHECK AND DOUBLE-CHECK

Calvin Hedges is office manager for a large transportation company. His administrative assistant, Colleen Cauley, often sends revenue forecasts to the executive vice president in New York. These forecasts are sent over a computer network. To save time, Mr. Hedges suggested that Colleen key the reports, proof them on the screen, and then transmit them. On two recent occasions, the reports contained serious errors: $10,000 was transmitted as $100,000 and $5,000 was transmitted as $50,000. Although these errors were caught "at the top," numerous telephone calls ensued, resulting in embarrassment for the local vice president. Colleen was blamed for the errors; however, after checking the originals, she discovered that the first error was made by Mr. Hedges, and the second was her keying error.

How should Colleen handle this situation? Should she confront Mr. Hedges about his error? Or should she assume the blame for both errors, apologize to Mr. Hedges, and develop safeguards so that similar errors won't happen again?

Case 2-2
CAUGHT IN THE MIDDLE— EMPLOYER'S REQUEST FOR PREFERENTIAL TREATMENT

Theresa Sadak, a copywriter for an advertising agency, handed a 24-page market analysis to her administrative assistant, Montgomery Dale, saying, "Take this down to reprographics and tell them that this is a rush job. We have to have ten copies, collated and bound, by 4 p.m. tomorrow, even if they have to let some of their other work go until later."

Aware that his employer had a reputation for making everything a rush job, Montgomery approached Joe Santini, supervisor of reprographics, with the written job order in hand and said cautiously, "Listen, Joe, Ms. Sadak is really in a bind. She has to have ten bound copies of this market analysis by 4 p.m. tomorrow, and she knows that she can depend on you to get her out of this crisis."

Joe was unimpressed. "You tell that boss of yours that she has to learn that there are other people in this company who need copies. She just has to wait her turn. Look at that pile of work orders. Do you think she has any right to ask to be put ahead of those requisitions? I've done my last rush job for Madam Sadak."

▰▰▰ Montgomery considered his alternatives. Should he try again by revealing confidential information that a million-dollar contract was riding on that report? Should he accept Joe's refusal? If so, what should he say to Ms. Sadak? What else might he suggest to get the report finished by the deadline?

Case 2-3
TELEPHONE
ABUSE

Raymond Hein is the administrative assistant to Dennis Williams, president of Westland Industries, located in San Francisco. As part of his duties, Raymond supervises three employees located in a room adjoining his office. He reviews communications and copying expenses and often makes recommendations concerning office procedures. For some time, he has been concerned about the rising costs of WATS calls. This month his telephone line (one of two company lines) was charged with over 40 hours of use, an increase of 20 hours. Since the company is charged for all calls over 10 hours per month, the bill was substantial. To Raymond's dismay, 10 of the hours were reported after 5 p.m., when the office was closed. Considering that Westland Industries is in the Pacific Time Zone, it is unlikely that use of the WATS line after 5 p.m. could be for business purposes. Raymond suspects that one or all of the employees he supervises could be making long-distance calls on the WATS line after business hours.

▰▰▰ What should be Raymond's plan to control the use of the WATS line? Should he confront the employees in his section?

Case 2-4
BUILDING A
GOOD
RELATIONSHIP
WITH RECORDS
MANAGEMENT
PERSONNEL

Marty Bymes is administrative assistant to Ying Pai, an attorney in charge of shareholders' relations. Marty is usually annoyed by the type of service she receives from the records management administrator, Phyllis Downe. She feels that the records department is inefficient and frequently slow, and she often says so.

One day a crisis developed for Mr. Pai because of the possibility of a lawsuit instigated by a shareholder. Marty telephoned Ms. Downe to request records that had not been referred to in ten years. Ms. Downe told her that the files were, of course, on microfilm and that it would be impossible to get them in fewer than four days. Prior requests for records had to be taken care of first. The department was shorthanded and nobody was immediately available to locate the records by reading the microfilm.

Marty said, "But this is an emergency. Mr. Pai wants those records by 4 p.m. today." Ms. Downe replied, "Sorry, but that will be impossible unless you or Mr. Pai would like to go 50 miles to the microfilm records center and get them yourselves."

▰▰▰ What short-term action can be taken? What long-term action? What principles are involved?

Case 2-5
ELIMINATING PERSONAL USE OF THE FAX MACHINE

Sidney Meravi's desk is located directly across from the office facsimile machine. Although it is not his responsibility to monitor the employees' use of the FAX machine, he often overhears coworkers discussing items that they are sending on the FAX machine. In the past few months, it has become apparent that several employees are using the machine for personal reasons.

While Sidney doubts that his coworkers realize that using the FAX machine for personal reasons is the same as stealing, he feels that he should bring the situation to his employer's attention. However, if he does talk to his employer about it, his coworkers will know he was the one who told her. This could make working with his coworkers unpleasant.

What principle is involved? What steps should Sidney take in this situation?

Part 3

Document Creation and Distribution

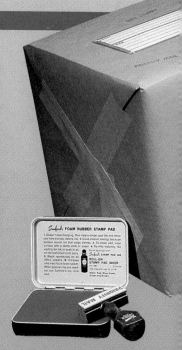

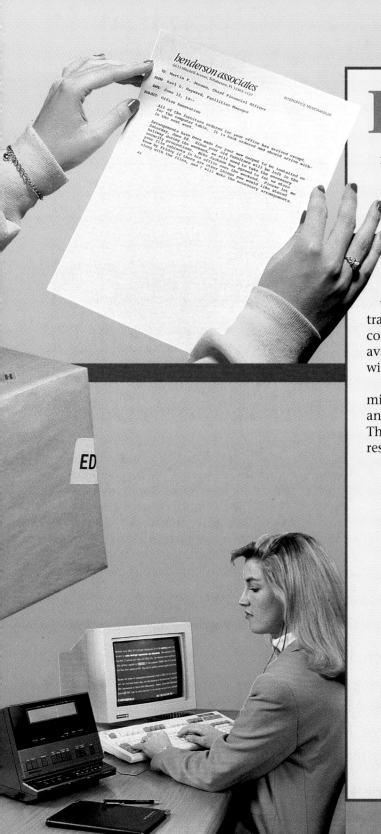

In *Office Technology Management,* Angela Cody points out that the wide use of computers and other office systems has generated an incredible demand for business forms and paper—and that this flood of paper must be managed! The way an office is organized to handle information, from origination to final distribution, contributes to the effective processing and management of information.

Preparing high-quality written communications is a primary responsibility for the administrative assistant. The administrative assistant who applies good written communication skills and adapts to and uses available computer equipment and software will be an asset to the executive.

Another major responsibility of the administrative assistant is handling incoming and outgoing mail effectively and efficiently. The chapters in Part 3 will discuss all of these responsibilities.

Chapter 9

Equipment and Supplies

LEARNING OBJECTIVES

After studying this chapter and completing the activities, you will be able to:

1. Select the appropriate equipment to use when creating and processing documents.
2. Design and use forms for a variety of applications in the office.
3. Identify the various types of office supplies needed to complete the administrative assistant's responsibilities efficiently and effectively.
4. Use appropriate criteria to purchase office supplies in a cost-efficient manner.

INTRODUCTION

Many kinds of written and electronic communications are produced and distributed daily in the electronic office. Letters are received and sent, memos are dictated, and reports are analyzed. The ability to produce error-free, attractive documents is a basic requirement of the administrative assistant. This chapter focuses on the characteristics of the equipment used to produce these documents and the supplies associated with document preparation. Familiarity with the equipment and supplies will help make your job easier and the documents you produce more attractive.

EQUIPMENT CHARACTERISTICS

At the core of document processing is the equipment used. In preparing documents, one or more types of equipment may be used: electronic typewriters, computers, or terminals connected to minicomputers or mainframe computers. This section will briefly explain the characteristics common to all or most of these pieces of equipment.

Keyboards

The **keyboard** is the most universally applicable inputting device used for work that is primarily text oriented. Additional inputting devices are available for use with the computer, such as the mouse and light pen. The keyboards for electronic typewriters are usually attached to the processing units. However, most personal computers and terminals connected to a mainframe have detached keyboards, similar to the personal computer shown in Figure 9-1, so they can be adjusted to the comfort of the operator.

Fig. 9-1 This personal computer shows a detached keyboard.

Alphanumeric Keys.   Most keyboards use a standard arrangement of keys referred to as the *QWERTY* arrangement. This keyboard was originally designed to place the most-used characters as far apart as possible to avoid clashing typebars. This basic arrangement has been the standard keyboard for over 100 years. These keys include the letters, numbers, and basic symbols. Many keyboards include a separate ten-key **numeric pad** located to the right of the keyboard for more efficient inputting of numbers, as shown in Figure 9-2.

Fig. 9-2 This keyboard shows the separate ten-key numeric pad on the right.

Cursor Keys.   **Cursor keys** on computer keyboards enable the user to locate specific portions of a document on the screen; when the cursor is moved to the appropriate point, a specific action such as inserting or deleting material can occur. These keys, which are usually separate from the numeric keypad, are also referred to as **directional keys** because arrows are positioned on the keys to indicate movement up, down, left, or right. The cursor keys are usually located to the right of the alphanumeric keyboard. Directly above the arrow keys are six keys labeled Insert, Delete, Home, End, Page Up, and Page Down.

Function Keys. **Function keys** are used to perform formatting and editing functions such as inserting, deleting, and moving copy. Frequently these keys are used in conjunction with keys on the alphanumeric keyboard to perform specific tasks. The function keys are located to the left of the alphanumeric keyboard or across the top of the keyboard above the numbers and symbols. On an electronic typewriter the function keys are labeled according to the function or functions they perform. Many people think that the function keys numbered F1 through F12 on computer terminal keyboards are the only function keys. However, any key that does not generate a character can be considered a function key, such as the Alt, Ctrl, Shift, and Esc keys. The difference between the F keys and the other function keys is that the F keys can execute a function when pressed by themselves; the other function keys work only in combination with other letter or number keys, or in combination with other function keys. For example, when using WordPerfect 6.0 software, the F7 key executes an exit from the document on the screen. However, when the F7 is struck in conjunction with the Shift key, the document on the screen is printed.

WordPerfect® for DOS 6.0
for IBM® Personal Computers

Bold	Ctrl + B	Page Number	Ctrl + P
Compose	Ctrl + A	Paste	Ctrl + V
Copy	Ctrl + C	Play Sound Clip	Ctrl + S
Cut	Ctrl + X	Repeat	Ctrl + R
Cycle	Ctrl + Y	Set QuickMark	Ctrl + Q
Find QuickMark	Ctrl + F	Toggle Text	Ctrl + T
Italics	Ctrl + I	Undo	Ctrl + Z
Outline Edit	Ctrl + O	WP Characters	Ctrl + W

				Ctrl				Ctrl				
Shell	Speller	Screen	Move		Outline	Decimal Tab	Notes	Font		Merge/Sort	Record Macro	Tab Set	Save
Writing Tools	Replace	Reveal Codes	Block	Alt	Mark Text	Flush Right	Columns/Table	Styles	Alt	Graphics	Play Macro	Table Edit	Envelope
Setup	◆Search	Switch	◆Indent◆	Shift	Date	Center	Print/Fax	Format	Shift	Merge Codes	Open/Retrieve	WP Characters	Bookmark
Help	◆Search	Switch To	◆Indent		File Manager	Bold	Exit	Underline		End Field	Save As	Reveal Codes	Block
F1	F2	F3	F4		F5	F6	F7	F8		F9	F10	F11	F12

Fig. 9-3 This template identifies the command codes for the function keys for WordPerfect 6.0 software.
Courtesy of International Business Machines Corporation.

The administrative assistant must understand how each software program used regularly controls the keys on the keyboard. Only then can the keyboard be used for maximum efficiency. Templates identifying the command codes for the function keys, similar to the one shown in Figure 9-3, usually are provided with software used on computers. These templates are very handy as you learn all the shortcuts built into your software programs.

Memory

The **memory** unit of any type of electronic equipment stores the operating system, program, and data during processing. The memory size controls the number and complexity of functions that can be performed. On an electronic typewriter, for example, the small memory capacity limits the functions it can carry out. Computer memories vary in capacity but usually can store large amounts of information, sometimes as much as 100 pages. As the computer memory is filled, the computer will notify the administrative assistant to delete files or store them on external media such as floppy disks.

Display Monitors

The **display monitor** allows the user to view information about the software being used as well as the material as it is being keyed into the computer. Changes and corrections can thus be made easily before the material is printed. On most electronic typewriters a one- or two-line display enables the administrative assistant to view a limited number of characters as they are keyed; some models may have a partial page display. On a personal computer the display monitor is usually a half-page displaying 24 lines; full-page displays are also available. The display monitor can be monochrome (typically black and white or green and white) or color. With the decrease in the cost of color monitors, most monitors purchased today are color.

Disk Drives

The **disk drive** is a device that reads information from and writes information to a disk. The disk drive is either built into the computer or located in a separate box attached to the computer. Most equipment has two disk drives. The floppy disk drive is used to store data on a floppy disk or retrieve data that has been stored previously on a floppy disk. Both disk drives may be used for floppy disks, or a hard disk drive may be used when a large amount of storage is needed for data. The capacity of the hard disk far exceeds that of the floppy disk. In addition to the hard disk drive, a floppy disk drive may also be included in the computer system (see Figure 9-4).

Fig. 9-4 Computer with detached keyboard, mouse, color monitor, floppy disk drive, and hard disk drive. *Courtesy of International Business Machines Corporation.*

Printers

Printers used in document processing are of two types, impact and nonimpact. **Impact printers** employ a mechanism such as a daisywheel or a character bar to strike a ribbon against paper to produce a printed character. **Nonimpact printers** produce images without any physical contact.

The electronic typewriter, which has the printer built into it, uses an impact printer. The personal computer uses a separate printer connected by cable.

Impact Printers. An impact printer is any printer that uses a mechanical mechanism to strike a ribbon against paper, imprinting a character on the paper. The dot matrix printer and the daisywheel printer are the two most popular types of impact printers.

The **dot matrix printer** is the most widely used impact printer in the office today. (See Figure 9-5.) It receives its name from the type of mechanism used to strike the ribbon against the paper. Most dot matrix printers use an array of tiny wires that force the ribbon against the paper. The number of wires, which ranges from 9 to 24, determines the quality of the final printed image. The 9-wire printers are the least expensive and produce a minimal-quality image; the 24-wire printers produce the highest-quality image but are more expensive.

The dot matrix printer is ideally suited for text applications, data processing applications, numerical data tables, invoices, graphics illustrations, and other situations in which "letter quality" print is not needed. This type of printer is reliable, prints at a fast rate, and is available at a relatively low cost. Printing speeds for the dot matrix printer range from 50 characters per second (CPS) to approximately 500 CPS. The fast printers are more expensive, but the higher cost can be justified by the time saved when printing lengthy documents.

In an effort to provide a higher quality of print, some dot matrix printers offer a "near letter quality" (NLQ) mode of print. The improved print quality is achieved by causing the printer to print over characters two or three times. The NLQ mode generally is accessed on the printer by a switch or button. Print speed is, of course, reduced significantly when a dot matrix printer is printing in the NLQ mode.

The **daisywheel printer** uses a rotating print wheel and a hammer that strikes the wheel to print the character on paper. This printing method is similar to the traditional rotating print head on an electric or electronic typewriter.

The daisywheel printer produces high-quality print and is ideally suited for the office that requires most documents to be letter quality. However, these printers print at a slower rate than the dot matrix printers, cannot print graphics, and are more expensive. The daisywheel printer offers the flexibility of changing type styles and pitches by replacing one daisywheel with another.

Nonimpact Printers. Nonimpact printers are the most popular form of printer used in the office today as the price is now competitive with that of impact printers. The nonimpact printer uses the latest technology to deposit the printed image on the paper without impacting the paper with a hammer or print head. The nonimpact printers use laser technology, light emitting diodes (LEDS), ink jet, thermal (heat), or other electronic means to print characters on paper. These methods of printing offer very high quality printing, equal to that of offset printing; reasonable printing speed; and the option of choosing a variety of type styles and graphics.

The **laser printer** is the most popular nonimpact printer. This printer uses a beam of laser light to electronically expose a rotating drum inside the printer. When the page is fully exposed on the drum, the image is then transferred to the paper. This process operates much like the standard plain paper copier used in offices. Laser printers print at a speed of 12 to 20 pages per minute and can print graphics as well as a variety of type styles and sizes. (See Figure 9-5.)

The **ink-jet printer** sprays ink directly onto the paper to produce the characters. The characters are produced as patterns of dots on the paper and are letter quality or near letter quality. The ink-jet printer is inexpensive to operate, very quiet, and fast. It can also produce a variety of type styles and sizes.

Fig. 9-5 A dot matrix (impact) printer is shown on the left, and a laser (nonimpact) printer is shown on the right.
Left: Courtesy of EPSON; right: Photo courtesy of Hewlett-Packard Company.

Color Printers. Businesses looking for a more effective way to communicate to clients and employees are purchasing color printers. The improved quality and lower prices, combined with the proven benefits of color documents, have made desktop color printers a critical tool for producing more effective business documents. Marketing research reports identify the many advantages of color output for reports, marketing, proposals, and presentations. One such study indicates that information emphasized with color was recalled by the reader twice as often as the same material without color highlights. Another research report showed a 52 percent higher response from a two-color mailing than from an identical black-and-white mailing. A wide choice in color printing technologies is available, including dot matrix, thermal transfer, ink jet, and color laser. The decision regarding the appropriate technology to choose when purchasing a color printer will depend on the specific applications needed by the purchaser.

Printer Accessories.   Most printers, impact or nonimpact, can be equipped with a variety of accessories, including cut paper sheet feeders, continuous form feeders, package label feeders, and different-colored ribbons. The cut sheet feeder allows one or more different sizes of paper to be fed automatically to the printer from a paper tray or bin without the need to manually change from one size of paper to another.

Continuous form feeders are used for processing a large number of like documents. Invoices, checks, shipping documents, or labels are fed into the printer in a continuous stream, speeding up the paper handling process greatly.

OFFICE FORMS

American business *runs* on paper forms. In fact, every business function involves some type of business form at some point in its operation. A function is either initiated by, authorized by, recorded on, or summarized on a form. Everyone in a business organization is involved with paperwork, and the administrative assistant is no exception. A significant portion of the administrative assistant's time is spent completing forms, copying information onto forms, reading forms, interpreting forms, routing forms, filing forms, and using forms for reference. Furthermore, the administrative assistant is not only a user of forms, but may be a designer of them as well.

Types of Forms

Modern technology and business ingenuity have provided many types of business forms in different configurations that include many timesaving features. Some of the more widely used types are described below.

Single-Copy Forms.   Single-copy forms are used today more than any other type of form. The nonimpact printers so prevalent in offices today use only single sheets of paper; however, they can print any number of copies desired. The form can also be reproduced on a copier. Another reason for the growth in single-copy forms is that multiple copies of the form are not needed when the document can be stored on a disk and called up on the computer when needed.

Carbonless Forms.   The carbonless form permits impressions from copy to copy through dyes and chemicals built into the paper. This type of form saves time, is smudge-free, and provides less bulk, increasing the number of copies that can be made at one time. For companies that still need multipart forms, the carbonless type continues to have the largest share of the market.

Unit Sets and Snap-Out Forms.   Also called carbon sets or carbon packs, unit sets and snap-out forms are preassembled with interleaved one-time carbons. Each unit is self-contained. This type of form permits easy one-motion removal of carbons, saves time, and is convenient. Use of these forms will continue to decline as the use of other types of forms increases.

Continuous Forms.   Continuous forms are joined in a series of accordion-pleated folds. These forms are used for quantity work, such as processing invoices, statements, purchase orders, and payroll checks.

Spot Carbon Coated Forms.   Carbon is applied at designated spots on the back of each form in the pack. This permits production of a number of different forms at one sitting. For example, packing slips, shipping orders, address labels, inventory withdrawal slips, and invoices—each containing only the data appropriate to that form—can be processed at the same time.

Forms Control and Design

As a business expands, the number of forms that it needs seems to multiply at an astonishing rate. Consequently, most large business and government organizations have established systems for forms control. Such systems periodically review forms and discontinue those that have become useless or obsolete. Provision is also made for the establishment of definite procedures to prepare and approve new forms.

The administrative assistant may be expected to exercise similar control over forms originating in the executive's office. This would include a systematic review of all forms with an eye to possible improvement, the elimination of unneeded forms, and the design of new forms to expedite the work of the office. In designing new forms, consider the following factors:

Necessity.   Is a separate form really needed? Could it be combined with an existing form? In what ways will a new form save time?

Wording.   Does the title clearly indicate the purpose of the form? Does it contain a code number for filing reference? Does the form contain all necessary information? Does it provide only necessary information? (Example: The company name is not needed on intracompany forms.) Does the form mechanize the writing of repetitive data? Are code numbers and check boxes used to eliminate unnecessary keying?

Disposition.   Does each copy of the form clearly indicate its disposition? Is color coding or other appropriate means used to facilitate distribution?

Arrangement.   Is the form compatible with the equipment on which it is to be used? (Example: If it is to be filled in on a typewriter, do the type lines conform to typewriter vertical line spacing and require a minimum of tabulator stops?) Does the sequence in which the data are to be inserted follow the sequence of information on the data source? Does the form allow sufficient space to fill in information? Will the arrangement of the form speed operations?

Retention.   If the form is to be retained, how and where? Does the form size fit the filing system?

Forms Software

Forms software programs enable computer users to design, fill in, print, and store forms electronically. Basically, forms software automates manual methods of forms processing, such as handwriting and typing, and is replacing the use of traditional preprinted, standardized forms. These programs generally fall into three categories: forms design, forms fill-in, and forms processing programs.

Forms Design Software.   This software enables the user to create a customized form that can serve as a master for making copies. The user can draw lines and boxes and refine the form until the design is appropriate to the needs.

Forms Fill-in Software.   This software provides a template that prints input information in the appropriate spaces on a standardized form. The administrative assistant enters only the variable data into the computer. Advantages of using this software are the speed at which forms can be completed and execution of any calculations that must be performed and included on the form.

Forms Processing Software.   The features of forms design and forms fill-in software are combined in forms processing software. The user can design, fill in, and print forms as well as link the software to databases to access information. This software enables the user to share the variable fill-in data on a form with other documents that use the same information.

TYPES OF OFFICE SUPPLIES NEEDED

The range in quality of most supplies used by an administrative assistant is wide. Many factors, particularly use and quality, must be considered in the selection of supplies. Figure 9-6 on pages 222 and 223 summarizes the features of some of the paper and supplies administrative assistants use frequently.

Printer Ribbons and Ink Cartridges

The quality of the final copy of a document is dependent on the printer and the type of ribbon or ink cartridge used. Nearly all ribbons or inks designed for use with any type of computer printer are enclosed in self-contained cases called cartridges. Electronic typewriters and impact printers use ribbon cartridges, while nonimpact printers use ink cartridges. Laser printers, another form of nonimpact printer, use a toner cartridge. A description of these major types of ribbons and cartridges follows.

Ribbon Cartridges.   Two types of ribbons are used in impact printers: *fabric* and *film*. Most fabric ribbons are made of nylon, which is relatively inexpensive and long-lasting. The nylon ribbon is ideally suited for use in high-speed line printers and dot matrix printers. It can also be used in daisywheel printers. Correct ribbon specifications must be matched with particular models of printers. The ribbons come in a variety of ink consistencies and nylon densities; cartridges are constructed to fit specific printers.

Film ribbons, which are made of carbon-coated mylar or polyethylene, are generally used in daisywheel printers and electronic typewriters because they provide the high-quality print required for letter-quality copy. Film ribbons can be either multistrike or single-strike ribbons. *Multistrike* ribbons allow the type element to strike overlapping areas on the ribbon. *Single-strike* ribbons allow the printer element to strike an area of the ribbon only once. The single-strike ribbon creates the best possible character impression on the paper. The single-strike ribbon also is more expensive and is used up more rapidly than the multistrike ribbon. Film ribbons are also available in cartridges manufactured to fit specific printers.

Ink/Toner Cartridges.   Nonimpact printers use ink cartridges, as the characters are created on the paper without physical contact. Ink-jet printers use an ink cartridge that sprays a fast-drying ink onto the paper in a dot matrix format. Laser printers use a toner cartridge. The toner is attracted to an image on the printer drum and then transfers the image to paper.

Bond Paper

Bond paper is so called because it was originally used for printing bonds, which had to be durable. Bond paper can be made of all-cotton fiber (sometimes called *rag*), of sulfite (a wood pulp), or of any proportion of the two. High-cotton fiber bond suggests quality and prestige, and it ages without deterioration or chemical breakdown. It has a good, crisp crackle. It is hard to the pencil touch and difficult to tear. High-sulfite bond is limp, soft to the pencil touch, and easy to tear.

There are excellent all-sulfite papers in crepelike, ripple, or pebble finishes that many companies use exclusively. Letterhead is usually made of 25 percent or more cotton fiber. Forms for business records are usually made entirely of sulfite or a high percentage of sulfite.

Paper that is 100 percent cotton content imparts an importance to a corporate communication.

Watermarks.   Hold a piece of paper up to the light. See the design or words? That is the *watermark*. It can be the name or trademark of the company using

Fig. 9-6 Features of frequently used paper office supplies.

LETTERHEADS, ENVELOPES, AND OTHER PAPER SUPPLIES

Letterheads	Standard company use. Business size (8 1/2" × 11"); usually 16-, 20-, or 24-pound with 25 percent cotton fiber content (rag). Also available in continuous-feed format for use with computer printer.
	Top executive use. Business size and Monarch size (7 1/4" × 10"); usually 24-pound bond with 100 percent cotton fiber content.
Matching Envelopes	Standard company use. No. 10 (9 1/2" × 4 1/8") of same weight and cotton fiber content as letterhead.
	Top executive use. No. 10 and No. 7 (7 1/2" × 3 3/8") of same weight and fiber content as letterhead.
Color	Usually white; however, tinted pastel shades are increasing in popularity.
Plain Sheets to Match Letterheads	Same weight, cotton fiber content, color, and size as letterhead. (Never use a letterhead for the second or subsequent pages of a letter.)
Interoffice Letterheads	Business size or half size (8 1/2" × 5 1/2"); usually 16- or 18-pound bond with high sulfite content.
Interoffice Envelopes	Oversized, strong, perforated, reusable envelopes with many ruled lines for the names of successive addressees.
Oversize Envelopes	Strong white or manila envelopes with gummed flaps and/or metal clasps (9 1/2" × 12" or 10" ×

the paper or the brand name of the paper. Since only better bond paper is watermarked, the mark is a sign of quality.

There is a right side and a top edge to plain watermarked sheets. Always have the watermark read across the sheet in the same direction as the printing. Put watermarked sheets in your stationery drawer in a way that puts them in the right orientation for insertion in the electronic typewriter or printer.

Substance. The weight of paper is designated by a substance number. The number is based on the weight of a ream consisting of approximately 500 sheets of 17-by-22-inch paper. If the ream weighs 20 pounds, the paper is said to be of substance 20, or 20-pound weight. Two thousand sheets of

	13") that allow letters and reports to be mailed unfolded.
Forms	Usually in pads to prevent waste. Multicopy forms may be continuous-feed. After the "chain" is inserted in the electronic typewriter or computer printer, key the first set; the forms feed through automatically. To eliminate handling interleaved carbons, continuous-feed forms often have spot carbon coating on the back of each copy only where the keyed information is to appear on the copy underneath.
Labels and Return Addresses	Usually gummed on the back; packaged in sheets or strips; printed with the company's return address.
Legal Paper	Top-quality bond; legal size (8 1/2" × 13" or 14"); plain or with ruled margins.
Plain Sheets	Business size; usually 13- to 16-pound. Most often used for reports and general typing. Also used for copying machines.
Computer Paper	Continuous-feed paper designed for use with a tractor-feed printer. Quality and cost can vary depending upon use; size of paper will vary depending on the type of printer used and the number of characters per line.
Reprographics Paper	Business and legal size; various colors and substances.
Writing Pads	Ruled paper; business or legal size; usually yellow.
Scratch	Assorted sizes; usually sold by the pound.

8 1/2-by-11-inch paper can be cut from one ream. Paper is produced in a wide range of weights. Letterhead and envelopes are usually of substance 16, 20, or 24. Airmail stationery, now used primarily for overseas correspondence, is usually of substance 9 or 11.

Letterheads

Letterheads vary widely, depending on individual taste and the nature of the company's business. Most large companies have a standard company letterhead that includes the company's name, address, telephone number (including area code), FAX number, and sometimes the name and title of an individual. The letterhead may contain information about the company's product or display the company's trademark. All letterheads may be ordered with matching envelopes and blank sheets for multipage letters.

Top management usually has prestige letterheads that differ from the standard company letterhead in style, printing process, weight, and cotton fiber content. The letterhead of top management usually shows only the company name, address (no phone number), and the executive's name and title. In addition, the executive may have a personal letterhead used mainly for outside work with foundations or charity organizations. Personal letterheads may show only the executive's name and address or only the name. In general, as an individual is elevated in the company, his or her letterhead acquires simplicity and dignity befitting the position. The trend in all letterheads is toward simplicity.

Computer-Related Supplies

Additional supplies are needed if you are working with computers. An adequate inventory of these supplies must be maintained if you are to operate the equipment efficiently.

Disks. Floppy disks are used for external storage of data keyed into the computer. The disk is made of a flat, round sheet of plastic that is magnetically treated and covered with a rigid plastic shell for protection. The amount of storage on a disk will vary; the double-sided, high-density disk can store the largest amount of information. The disks for the computer are 5 1/4 inches and 3 1/2 inches. The 3 1/2-inch disk is the most popular size as it can store more information.

Other Computer Supplies. A variety of supplies are needed for working with computers such as static-reducing chair mats and desk mats, covers for the computer and keyboard, and glare filters for the computer monitors. Cleaning kits are also needed for regular cleaning of the equipment. Additional supplies needed for working with disks include disk labels, marking pens that will not damage the surface of the disks, and disk storage cabinets.

Miscellaneous Office Supplies

The administrative assistant must be sure that a wide variety of miscellaneous supplies are on hand at all times. The specific items needed will depend on the functions of the office. However, the following list includes office supplies that are needed in every office.

Paper clips
Post-it Notes
Pencils
Pens in a variety of colors

Staplers, staples, and staple removers
Writing pads
Highlighter pens
File folders and labels
Adhesive labels of various sizes
Address labels
Adhesive tape
Glue stick/waxer

An inventory checklist should be maintained so that additional supplies can be ordered before the current supplies are depleted.

PURCHASING OF OFFICE SUPPLIES

The executive usually delegates to the administrative assistant the responsibility of procuring office supplies. Unless the executive has a special need or unless high costs are involved, the administrative assistant uses personal judgment to make selections. The procedures for obtaining office supplies differ for the administrative assistant in a large office and the administrative assistant in a small office; however, both must have a knowledge of supplies in order to choose those that best fill executive and office needs.

The administrative assistant in a small office is a direct buyer. In a large office, however, the administrative assistant may request forms and supplies from a central stock or requisition them from a purchasing department. The administrative assistant who has supervisory responsibilities may select and purchase supplies for an entire department or company. In this case, the administrative assistant must use sources of product information to compare supplies and find dependable vendors.

Quality of Supplies

Some businesspeople believe it is important to use only the highest-quality stationery, forms, and office supplies; others find medium quality adequate. Every office uses a pride factor and an economic factor to determine the level of quality it pursues. You will not find this quality level precisely stated or written out for you, nor is there a question you can tactfully ask to determine it. You can deduce it, though, by observing the characteristics of supplies currently being used in your office and by examining cost records.

Sources of Supplies

Many sources of supplies are available to the administrative assistant. These include the local office supply store, sales representatives, and mail-order catalogs. Each source has its advantages and disadvantages.

Local Office Supply Stores.   Local office supply stores are the most convenient source of office supplies. However, the typical store cannot carry all varieties of all brands of all office supplies. Each store carries one or two brands of an item in the varieties most commonly sold, none of which may exactly fill your needs. Even though your selection may be limited, the local store can often order the supplies you need and have them available within a few days.

In metropolitan areas a number of large office supply discount stores have made a much wider variety of products available. Because of their size, these discount stores offer a much larger selection of products at a lower price. If you live in an area that has such discount stores, you should check their products and prices on a regular basis.

Sales Representatives.   Representatives of office supply agencies may call on you with samples and price catalogs. They, too, limit themselves in brands and varieties, so choice is again restricted. Since you cannot possibly know everything about all supplies that a particular sales representative carries, it is helpful to have a dependable sales representative of whom you can ask advice. When you are in the market for an item, explain your exact needs. Sales representatives are trained to help you make a wise selection. After you have made a selection, you will probably order your supplies directly from a sales office over the telephone.

Mail-Order Catalogs.   The mail-order catalog offers the administrative assistant the opportunity to purchase office supplies conveniently from the office. In addition, when you want a specific variety of a specific brand that is not sold locally, you can order it from a mail-order catalog. While ordering from the catalog may save time, it usually takes several days to receive the supplies. This delay may eliminate this option if the supplies are needed immediately.

Collecting Information

Collect specific information about each kind of office supply you use. Suppliers often furnish helpful literature. Sales representatives can also provide you with information. Often descriptive, informative brochures are given away at exhibits of office equipment and supplies. Frequently, advertisements in professional magazines offer to send more detailed information about specific products.

Keep records of the specific products purchased, how often they are purchased, and the price. This information will be useful when placing future orders.

Choosing Supplies

Choose supplies that are in keeping with the quality range in your office. There is no economy in cheap supplies. Unknown brands may contain inferior materials or may be odd-sized. Consequently, they may be more expensive in the long run than the better grades. *Usually you get just about what you pay for.*

There is no reason to shift from one brand of supply to another as long as the one in use is satisfactory and fair in price. On the other hand, supplies are constantly being changed. A product may be greatly improved since the last time you examined it.

When contemplating a change in brand, get samples of competing products and test them all under the same circumstances. Compare prices and quality. Analyze claims made regarding extra service or added efficiency. If the price is higher, you should decide whether the difference is justified.

Overbuying Supplies

Some office supplies deteriorate when they are held in stock too long. For example, printer ribbons dry out, some paper yellows, and liquids evaporate. New products may be preferable to those you have stocked. It is better, then, to err on the side of underbuying than to overbuy. Repeat orders can always be placed shortly before supplies are needed.

You may tend to overbuy because of quantity discounts. An item that costs 50 cents a unit in small quantities usually costs appreciably less when bought in large quantities. Consequently, it may seem to be economical to order in large amounts. Monetary savings are not always the prime consideration, however.

Some paper suppliers have arrangements whereby a year's supply may be purchased at one time. While you obtain the price advantage of a bulk purchase, the paper is delivered in specific lots at designated intervals throughout the year. Such a plan provides a price advantage without the problems of storing the paper until it is needed.

Requisitions and Invoices

In a large company, most supplies are kept in stock and are obtained by submitting either a supply requisition or a written request. Items not carried in stock must be requested by submitting a purchase requisition to the purchasing department giving the most detailed description you can provide of the needed item.

An administrative assistant or supervisor who has the authority to purchase supplies has added responsibilities. These include making a careful record of each item purchased, checking deliveries, and verifying the accuracy of the items and extensions on the invoice or bill that accompanies or follows delivery.

When an item is invoiced (included and charged on an invoice) but is omitted from the shipment or is substituted or defective, the administrative assistant notes that fact on the invoice and requests an adjustment.

Storing Supplies

If you wish to determine how efficient an administrative assistant really is, examine the supply cabinet. A storage cabinet that presents a jumble of boxes, packages, and articles in no apparent order is no recommendation for efficiency.

The well-arranged storage cabinet has several characteristics. Similar materials are placed together. Materials used more frequently are placed at the front of the cabinet at the most convenient level for reaching. Small items are placed at eye level; bulk supplies and reserve stock are placed on the lower shelves. Shelf depths should be adjustable to fit supplies and conserve space.

All packages are identified by oversized lettering made with a marking pen or by a sample of the contents affixed to the front. Unpadded stationery is kept in flip-up, open-end boxes. (There are no carelessly opened, paper-wrapped packages.) Loose supplies, such as paper clips, are kept separately in open, marked boxes. A list of all supplies by shelves is often posted on the inside of the door.

YOU AND YOUR EQUIPMENT

Keying competence is more than speed with accuracy; it is economy in using time and supplies and knowing how to organize your work. It is also discovering ways to increase your output and efficiency. Competence comes only with experience. Become comfortable with your equipment by exploring its features and learning its capabilities; then give it the care it requires.

Instruction Booklets

Every piece of equipment or software has a helpful, reassuring booklet of instructions on its use. The booklet accompanies the equipment or software (see Figure 9-7) on delivery, but often disappears before the equipment does. If your predecessor has not left an instruction booklet for you, request one from the vendor. It will save you time and give you confident know-how. There is nothing worse than struggling with strange equipment or software.

Learn the capabilities of your equipment and software. It may have useful features you are not aware of. The special features of your equipment and software are illustrated and explained in the instruction booklet.

Equipment Care

Even though most equipment is sturdy and almost self-sufficient, it does require attention from you. Regular cleaning of your computer equipment is es-

Fig. 9-7 Software instructional manuals assist the administrative assistant in using software efficiently and effectively.
© David Joel/Tony Stone Images.

sential for uninterrupted, efficient use. Dust, dirt, and contaminants can interfere with the processing and printing of data and cause damage to your equipment. Regular, periodic cleaning can prevent expensive equipment failure and downtime. Read the equipment care section of your instruction booklet carefully. No amount of skill is going to produce good copy if the equipment is not kept in excellent working condition.

Summary

The preparation of error-free, attractive documents continues to be an important requirement for the administrative assistant. The equipment and supplies available to assist with this task are continually improving.

Electronic typewriters and personal computers are used widely in preparing documents. The configuration of these electronic systems will vary from office to office. Administrative assistants must understand these various configurations in order to assist in selecting the appropriate equipment needed to prepare written documents.

Business forms are used in most business transactions. The administrative assistant must be able to use these forms efficiently. Forms control, which includes a review of forms for possible improvement, elimination of unnecessary forms, and the design of new forms, expedites the work of the office and may be the responsibility of the administrative assistant. Forms software is being used to assist in the design, fill-in, and processing of forms. Use of this kind of software is replacing the traditional preprinted, standardized form.

Because administrative assistants frequently have the responsibility of ordering office supplies, they must be knowledgeable about the type and quality of supplies available, from printer ribbons to letterheads. A good working relationship with the local office supply store and a collection of information from various vendors about each kind of office supply available will enable an administrative assistant to make wise purchases for an employer.

If equipment and software are to be used to maximum efficiency, the administrative assistant must know how to operate all the features. Instructional booklets that accompany the equipment and software should be studied so that the administrative assistant becomes knowledgeable about the capabilities and care of the equipment and software.

QUESTIONS FOR DISCUSSION

1. If your office is located in a small town without a nearby office supply company, explain how you would obtain information about the latest products available for the office.

THINK IT *Through*

2. If your employer allowed you to select your own equipment for the production of final documents, what are some of the features you would want in a personal computer and printer, and how would you determine what equipment to purchase?

THINK IT *Through*

3. You are employed as administrative assistant to the manager of the R&D (research and development) division. This is a highly sensitive area and thus under strict control for security leaks. A major security leak was traced to your wastebasket and to the snap-out carbon forms you have been using.

   a. Explain how this could happen.

   b. Specify possible solutions to this problem.

4. Office costs are a high percentage of a company's total costs, especially in service-oriented businesses such as insurance companies. The cost of producing a business letter continues to rise. Identify the things an administrative assistant can do to help curb the spiraling costs of a business letter.

5. When two or more sentence parts are joined by one or more conjunctions, the parts should be of like kinds; that is, all single words of the same part of speech, all phrases, or all clauses. This is called parallelism. Rekey the following sentences making the parts parallel.

   a. He likes keyboarding, editing, and to proofread.

   b. The employment process consists of recruiting, screening, interviewing, and selection.

   c. Ms. Colby attended the board meeting in the morning, conducting a survey during her lunch hour, and enjoyed a concert in the evening.

   d. Girls pay more attention to housekeeping than boys.

   e. Last summer they went to France, Switzerland, and to Italy.

PROBLEMS

1. Administrative assistants must be knowledgeable about many types of office supplies, from paper clips to quality of stationery. Visit an office supply store or study an office supply catalog to determine the variety and quality of supplies available. Prepare a report comparing two brands of each of the following items and indicate which brand you would purchase based on the features of the product, the quality, and the price:

   3 1/2-inch computer disks, double-sided, high-density

   14 reams of paper, 16 pound with 25 percent cotton content

   Continuous-feed computer paper designed for use with a tractor-feed printer, 8 1/2 × 11 inches

   Writing pads, ruled paper, business size, yellow

2. The quality of print produced by printers varies considerably. Collect samples of documents produced on a dot matrix printer, a daisywheel printer, and a laser or ink-jet printer. Prepare a report analyzing the quality of the documents produced by each of the printers and the advantages and disadvantages of each type. Also indicate in this report the types of correspondence and reports for which each printer is best suited.

▶ **TA9-1.TEM** Access the template disk, and select the TA9-1.TEM file, which shows an outline for a *routing slip,* a special form used to direct ("route") a magazine or other publication among several or many employees.

The routing slip is stapled to the cover of the publication by the librarian or assistant who begins the routing process. Two, three, or more forms are pasted onto one master sheet; then the sheet is cut, and the forms are saved, then used as each edition arrives. (The actual number of forms that fit on one 8 1/2″ × 11″ sheet depends on the number of names in the list.)

Complete the routing slip as follows:

1. Fill in a publication name. Use *U.S. News & World Report.*
2. Number the three steps in the process listed under "Please Route."
3. Use multiple columns to format the names in the second step (and thereby save space).
4. Do whatever else you believe is necessary to make the form attractive.

Save your document file, print a copy of your finished form, proofread it carefully, and submit the final form to your instructor.

▶ **TA9-2.TEM** Access the template disk, and select the TA9-2.TEM file, which shows an outline for a *requisition form,* used in offices to request materials and supplies.

Your manager has asked you to complete this requisition. Create a ruled chart for all the column headings. Position the footnote *below* the chart, and leave room for all the fill-in information that follows.

Save your document file, print a copy of your finished form, proofread it carefully, and submit the final form to your instructor.

Chapter 10

Document Origination and Preparation

LEARNING OBJECTIVES

After studying this chapter and completing the activities, you will be able to:

1. Identify the methods of dictation used in the office.
2. Define the various forms of word origination.
3. Dictate effectively.
4. Use appropriate transcription skills.
5. Use proper procedures for processing a document.
6. Prepare completed documents for mailing.

INTRODUCTION

The administrative assistant is involved in the origination and processing of most of the written communication in the office. In addition, the administrative assistant handles many of the employer's electronic communications. A document, as referred to in this chapter, is any written, printed, or electronically prepared business communication that conveys information. The most common type of business communication is correspondence: letters and memos. Other kinds of documents include reports, forms, statistical tables, and envelopes.

It is very likely that the administrative assistant will transcribe from machine dictation on a regular basis when producing new documents. Manual shorthand dictation is still used in some offices. A number of skills such as gathering and organizing necessary materials, scheduling your time, and applying basic language fundamentals must be applied to produce mailable documents.

This chapter begins with a discussion of the administrative assistant's responsibilities in the dictation process. Various methods and types of dictation are presented. Since many administrative assistants are beginning to dictate for their employers, instructions for giving easily transcribed dictation are included. The procedures and techniques used by administrative assistants to create, format, input, and edit documents are also discussed.

PREDICTATION RESPONSIBILITIES

Regardless of how dictation is given, the administrative assistant has several predictation responsibilities to perform. Among them are preparing a list of action items for the attention of the executive, replenishing the executive's supplies, and assembling materials from the files that will be needed for dictation.

Action Items

A preliminary step to dictation is the collection of **action** items (items to be acted upon). Early each morning the administrative assistant prepares a list of items that should be acted upon by the executive that day. Some of the items will require dictation; others may or may not consume part of the executive's available dictation time. Overdue letters, reports, and shipments, or letters and reports that must meet deadlines, all require dictating attention. The day's appointments, conferences, and meetings will affect the time available for dictation.

Prepare in brief form, in duplicate, a list of action items. Or, if you prefer, prepare a separate note for each action item. Retain a copy and use it in transferring unfinished work to tomorrow's list. Clip the list (or separate notes for each item) to the edge of a portfolio or file folder, as shown in Figure 10-1. When an item has been attended to, the dictator can either check it off the list or discard the corresponding note. Take this collection of items to the dictator's desk as early in the day as possible before dictation begins.

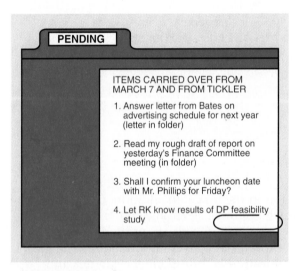

Fig. 10-1 Folder containing carry-over correspondence and attached list of items requiring action.

Your Dictation Vocabulary

An administrative assistant has to experience only once the embarrassment of using *iniquity* for *integrity, impetuous* for *impervious,* or *ambitious* for *ambiguous* to learn the meaning, spelling, and pronunciation of words that sound alike in dictation and look alike in shorthand. To learn the executive's vocabulary quickly, read file copies of recent letters and appropriate technical and trade publications. From these sources make a list of words new to you. Learn the meanings, spellings, and pronunciations of the words. In other words, compile your own glossary.

Several handbooks in special fields such as law, accounting, medicine, and real estate have word lists to help you increase your vocabulary.

METHODS OF DICTATION

To initiate the written communication process, the executive, sometimes referred to as the *word originator,* must provide dictation for the administrative assistant. Dictation can take one of the following forms: machine dictation, manual shorthand, or machine shorthand.

Machine Dictation

Because executives' time is so valuable and the nature of their work so critical, the use of dictation equipment is no longer an option but a necessity in most offices. Dictation equipment assists the executive and the administrative assistant in processing communications in the fastest, most economical way.

Portable and Desk Models.   The hand-sized, battery-operated portable dictation unit is a boon to the traveling salesperson or executive. It allows the word originator to mail recorded material to the administrative assistant for transcription. A portable unit can be used in a car or on an airplane, wherever it is convenient for the word originator. Many executives who like to work at home find this dictation unit indispensable.

A desktop dictation unit is often located at the dictator's desk. The unit saves time because the originator dictates to a desktop machine while the administrative assistant is free to perform other tasks. Some desktop units also may be used for transcribing. However, only one operation—either transcribing or dictating—can be performed at a time on a combination unit.

Centralized Dictation.   Central systems are distinguished from other types of dictation machines by the fact that recorders are grouped in a central location. An example appears in Figure 10-2. With the most sophisticated systems, a recorder not in use is automatically selected and put into operation to process incoming dictation from executives. The medium on which dictation is recorded varies. Cassettes, continuous loops of magnetic tape, and magnetically coated disks all may be used in a centralized dictation system.

Dictation to a centralized system is transmitted by the word originator via public or private telephone connections. Connection to a dictation system by public telephone lines enables any telephone on or off the premises to serve as a dictation unit; thus, dictation may take place from an executive's office, home, hotel room, or even a telephone booth. The advantage of a private telephone line is that the dictation system does not tie up the pub-

▼ **TECHNOLOGY**

Dictation equipment enables the executive to make much more efficient use of valuable time.

Fig. 10-2 The centralized system groups all records in one location so that a number of dictators and transcribers can have access to the system.
Photograph courtesy of Dictaphone Corporation, Stratford, CT.

lic telephone lines of the dictator or centralized office. Also, after it is installed, the expense of a private telephone line is diminished.

Endless Loop or Continuous Flow Systems.   All of the dictation machines described to this point have used a specific receiving medium, such as a disk or cassette. These types of receiving mediums are called **discrete media.** Discrete media can be stored, mailed, or switched from dictation machines to transcription machines. Most portable and desktop dictation units use discrete media that allow the dictator to play back the dictation and make changes and corrections by dictating over the recording.

The endless loop-based system is an alternative to cassettes or disks. Loops of magnetic tape, which are sealed inside a case or tank, go round and round for hours of use and reuse. Dictation is recorded on one head while another head plays out the dictation for the administrative assistant to transcribe. Since the magnetic tape does not have to be removed from the machine for transcription, it is possible for the administrative assistant to start transcribing while the dictator continues recording. This feature proves invaluable when processing rush work. Another advantage of the endless loop system is that the encased tape requires no reloading.

In a centralized system, monitoring panels with visible dials show the word processing supervisor at a glance which machines are in use, which are idle, and how much untranscribed dictation has yet to be assigned to a specialist. Some endless loop systems automatically send priority items to the front of the line to be transcribed first. Others indicate the length of items to be transcribed.

Digital Dictation Systems.   All of the dictation systems described to this point use an analog recording system which is very similar to the traditional tape recorder. With the analog system it is difficult to insert or edit material once it is recorded because the insertion can only be as long as the material being replaced.

The digital dictation system converts the dictator's voice to a digital signal. It is then stored on a computer hard disk. The storage capacity of hard disks varies, but normally 80 hours of voice can be stored on an 80-megabyte hard disk. The digital system will automatically assign an identifying code to each dictation job. Other information can be added to jobs as they are stored, including routing and priority instructions. The dictated document becomes a voice file, similar to a data file in a computer. After a document is dictated, it can be randomly accessed and edited. Words can be added or deleted without recording over material already dictated. Just as on a computer disk, material on the disk adjusts as changes are made so that none of the information is lost. Most digital systems in use today are centralized systems so that they can be shared by multiple users.

Digital technology is expected to revolutionize the dictation industry during the next ten years. Voice-file manipulation, random access of dictated information, and voice-mail integration are now possible on digital dictation systems. A small telephone coupler can be used to connect the telephone and a transcription machine to enable the administrative assistant to transfer voice mail to a tape which can then be transcribed. In effect, a message recorded on a voice-mail system can be processed in the same way as other dictated material. In addition, some digital dictation equipment can be integrated with personal computers.

Manual Shorthand

Shorthand dictation, dictation by the executive to the administrative assistant in a face-to-face situation, continues to be used in some offices for several reasons. Many executives prefer to work on a regular basis with one person who is familiar with their routines and can assist them while they are dictating. In addition to traditional dictated correspondence such as letters and memos, shorthand dictation is often used for complex documents requiring extensive explanation. Shorthand is also the preferred method for recording instructions, telephone messages, minutes of meetings, and ideas exchanged during informal meetings.

While shorthand no longer is used widely for extended face-to-face dictation, it remains an extremely useful skill for the administrative assistant; and some employers will continue to require shorthand skills for employment.

Machine Shorthand

The standard shorthand machine, which enables a person to take notes in excess of 300 words per minute, has been used for years, primarily by court reporters. Such rapid speeds are possible because words are recorded by depressing one or more keys at a time.

A new process involving shorthand machines is called **electronic shorthand.** This technology enables machines to record keystrokes on both paper tape and magnetic tape simultaneously. The paper tape can be used to read back notes, immediately if necessary. The magnetic tape is read into a computer and transcribed into words. The transcript is displayed on a screen for editing and revising. The final copy then can be printed or stored for retrieval at a later date. With this technology, material that formerly would have taken weeks to transcribe can be transcribed immediately at extremely high speeds—over 500 pages per hour.

Voice Recognition Systems

Voice recognition systems for office dictation are currently being used in isolated markets such as medical labs, where the person dictating needs both hands to perform the action being described and cannot activate a dictation machine. These systems recognize human speech patterns and translate them into printed words on a computer screen.

Voice recognition systems are either speaker dependent or speaker independent. The speaker-dependent system requires a sample of how the speaker pronounces each vocabulary word before it can recognize that speaker. A speaker-independent system can recognize the vocabulary within its memory without having a sample of each speaker's voice. Recent advances have improved these systems. Many systems now have a vocabulary in excess of 5,000 words and can recognize natural language. Some voice recognition systems can "learn" words that are specific to each user's needs. Dragon Systems markets a very sophisticated system with a vocabulary of 30,000 words. The system consists of a speech recognition board for the computer and software.

The voice recognition systems that allow a dictator's words to be keyed as they are spoken will certainly change the way that an administrative assistant prepares the hard copy of a communication. Even though the dictated material will not have to be transcribed, it is anticipated that documents inputted in this manner will still need to be edited by the administrative assistant. Use of the independent voice input system will greatly speed production time for a final document.

FORMS OF WORD ORIGINATION

In addition to business communications, dictation transcribed by the administrative assistant may include instructions, reminders, and requests. Various types of dictation may be intermingled, depending on the executive's preferences. Whether transcribing from a machine or taking dictation by shorthand, the administrative assistant should record instructions on paper rather than relying on memory. Dictation falls into several categories.

Communications

The bulk of dictation falls into the category of communications. This category includes letters, memos, reports, outlines, drafts, and electronic communications such as voice mail and computer messaging systems. Electronic messages are first transcribed and then sent via telecommunications. The equipment used to send these messages is fully discussed in Chapter 8.

Instructions

The executive will frequently dictate instructions for a variety of tasks while dictating regular communications. *All instructions should be written down.* When transcribing from a machine, jot down the instructions on a notepad. When using shorthand, take down the instructions in your notebook as they are given.

Directions for Transcribing. The dictator will often give directions for transcribing a document after it has been dictated. Directions for transcribing a document include instructions for handling rush documents, for complying with special stationery requests, for supplying the number of copies needed, or for gathering additional information from special resources.

An electronic or manual index on the front of the dictation machine allows the administrative assistant to identify the beginning and end of documents as well as the location of specific instructions. The administrative assistant can scan the tape for instructions before beginning the transcription process.

Directions for Composing. The executive often delegates the composing of a letter to the administrative assistant. The administrative assistant may be asked to compose a letter in response to a letter at hand, or to originate an item of correspondence. Complete directions for composing a letter must be taken in writing to be sure that all points are covered. Often, the administrative assistant can use the information provided by the executive almost verbatim in composing the correspondence. Refer to Chapter 11 for detailed information about letter composition.

Specific/General Work Instructions. Any specific instructions, such as canceling one of the executive's appointments, planning an itinerary, or writing and cashing a check, should be written down. When the executive explains office routines or preferences concerning procedures, write them down. As time permits, transcribe them and insert them in your desk manual for reference.

Highly Confidential Material

In a large office there are likely to be several persons who are inquisitive about what is currently happening in the executive offices. Transcripts on an administrative assistant's desk (such as finished letters waiting to be signed), letters being keyed, and copies in viewing range are often fruitful sources of information.

If possible, transcribe highly confidential dictation when it is unlikely that anyone will be nearby. However, if someone comes to your desk while you are transcribing, clear your computer screen, making your action as unobtrusive as possible. Keep transcribed letters covered with a sheet of paper, face down or inside a file folder. Destroy the dictated notes or erase the machine dictation immediately. Give the original and any copies to the executive as soon as possible. Copies are just as informative as originals, so treat them with the same respect. If imperfect copies are made on the photocopy machine, destroy them by shredding. Many executives now use electric wastebaskets to shred paper that might reveal company secrets.

Telephone Dictation

Keep a separate notebook near the telephone to take telephone dictation. Since the dictator cannot see how fast you are taking notes, it helps if you say "yes" after you have completed each phrase. To avoid errors, read the entire set of notes back to the dictator.

Occasionally the executive may request that you monitor a telephone conversation and take notes. Unless you are unusually speedy, you cannot hope to get every word; but you can take down the main points in the same way one takes lecture notes. Transcribe such notes at once while they are still fresh in your mind.

Both sides of a telephone call can be recorded on a dictating machine placed near the telephone. Legally, however, the other person must be told that the conversation is being recorded. The recording may be kept for reference, or you may be asked to transcribe the entire conversation or to abstract its important points.

On-the-Spot Dictation

In Figure 10-3, an administrative assistant has been asked to take notes during an impromptu meeting. At times it is necessary to take dictation within a split second, while standing or working at a desk where there is no cleared space. You may even have to take notes on scratch paper. In order to become accustomed to the awkwardness of rush work, practice taking notes with a notebook on your knee or while standing using a scratch pad. After transcription, date the notes and keep them for reference until the document has been approved by the executive.

Fig. 10-3 During an impromptu conference, the executive has asked the administrative assistant to come in and record comments made during their discussion.

At the Keyboard

Occasionally, the executive may ask you to key something as it is being dictated to you. It helps to ask before starting whether the dictation will be long or short so you can determine the placement of the item on the page. Do not stop to correct errors as they are made. It is better to correct errors when the executive has finished dictating and has left your desk. If the dictation is keyed on an electronic typewriter, rekeying is often required as the placement is often unsatisfactory and insertions or corrections usually are necessary.

Printed Forms

The answers to questions on a printed form are frequently dictated. The executive usually works from the form; therefore, the information given will seem sketchy and incomplete. Make a photocopy of the form prior to dictation so that you can use it for reference during dictation. If the dictator does not identify the numbers or letters of the items corresponding to the information being given, ask for them so that you can key the information on the proper lines.

If only one copy of a form is furnished, make a photocopy of the completed form for the files. If completing printed forms is a new experience for you, or if you are unsure of the line spacing, you could make a photocopy of the blank form and practice on it.

Fig. 10-4 When dictating, speak slowly and distinctly and give explicit instructions.

LEARNING TO DICTATE

The administrative assistant will find that taking, giving, and transcribing dictation can be done more efficiently if dictation equipment is used. A deterrent to using dictation equipment is the reluctance of the dictator to organize thoughts and materials before starting to speak. Although all equipment provides for playback and correction of dictation and is equipped with some type of control to alert the transcriber to a transcription problem, a dictator may also fear that the dictation will be imperfect. Some administrative assistants, accustomed to transcribing and to speaking slowly and distinctly with logical phrasing, have less difficulty in dictating efficiently than some executives do. Refer to Figure 10-4.

To prepare for giving dictation that will be easy to transcribe, first study the instruction book for the equipment until you can operate all of its controls. Dictate a practice item that contains tricky words and figures. After a short interval, play back the dictation and see whether you can distinguish every word and figure. To produce dictation of which you can be proud, it helps to make an outline; the more complex the communication, the more necessary the outline.

TRANSCRIPTION FUNDAMENTALS

Transcription is a high-level skill. It is often performed under rush conditions and involves competency in keying, English usage, punctuation, and decision making. The ultimate test of your ability to perform this complicated process is the production of a quality transcript.

Language Skills

The fundamental tool of the administrative assistant is the English language—spelling, punctuation, and word usage. Formatting style and the ability to use reference books are also important skills for the administrative assistant. You must master these fundamentals so that you can transmit the dictator's ideas flawlessly. You—not the dictator—have to be the expert in the areas of spelling, punctuation, and word usage. You are responsible for generating error-free communications.

To strengthen your spelling skills, compile and maintain your own list of troublesome words. If you make it a practice to write down any misspelling that occurs in your transcriptions and any word that you have to check in a dictionary, you will have a custom-made list for instant reference.

An administrative assistant must know the rules of punctuation as they apply to formal writing. A paper that is to appear in print or a report to the board of directors must be punctuated with formal correctness. Comprehensive punctuation rules are given in the Reference Guide.

Grammar and usage are based on relatively fixed standards used in communicating at a formal or educated level. Since most of the executive's writing is at that level, the administrative assistant must have a mastery of grammar—a knowledge of the system of rules for speaking and writing correctly.

Reference Sources

Dictionaries vary. Compare the very British and formal *Oxford English Dictionary* to *Webster's Third New International Dictionary of the English Language*. *Webster's* aroused a great furor when it first appeared because it seemed to be giving the stamp of approval to word usage and spellings that scholars did not consider correct.

Three recommended desk-size dictionaries that have recently been revised are *Webster's New Collegiate Dictionary*, *The American Heritage Dictionary* (College Edition), and *Random House College Dictionary*. A desk dictionary should be replaced with a current edition every five years or so. You should turn to the dictionary at transcribing time to learn:

1. The correct spelling of a word, such as *neophyte*.
2. The correct spelling of an inflectional form, such as the past tense of *benefit*.
3. The preferred form to use when there are variant spellings of a word, such as *acknowledgment* or *acknowledgement, judgment* or *judgement*.
4. Whether to use one word or two words, such as *highlight* or *high light*.
5. Whether to treat a word as foreign and underline it, such as *bon voyage* and *carte blanche*.

6. How to divide a word at the end of a line; *committee,* for example.

7. Whether to use a hyphen to join a suffix or prefix to a word or to form one complete word without a hyphen, such as *pre-Socratic* and *preview*; *selfsame* and *self-control*; *businesslike* and *doll-like.*

Dictionaries indicate the correct solution to each of these seven situations in different ways. The key to how they are indicated in your dictionary is given in the explanatory notes at the front of the dictionary. (Sometimes this section has an explicit title, such as "Guide to the Use of the Dictionary.") One administrative assistant continually hyphenated compound words incorrectly because of confusing the mark denoting syllabication with the one indicating a hyphen. Careful reference to the explanatory notes will prevent such embarrassing mistakes. When you do locate an important point in the explanatory notes, underline it or enclose it in a frame with pencil for easy reference.

A current and comprehensive office handbook will help you with many transcription problems. Manuals for special fields such as law, medicine, and science are also available to help you if your work involves specialization.

In addition to these comprehensive reference sources, a number of manuals are available that can help you in efficiently and effectively producing mailable documents. Several quick-reference manuals are shown in Figure 10-5. Some of these references include the *Reference Manual for the Office,* 8th edition, by House and Sigler; the *Word Division Manual,* 4th edition, by Perry; and the *National ZIP Code and Post Office Directory.* Reference books are discussed more fully in Chapter 14.

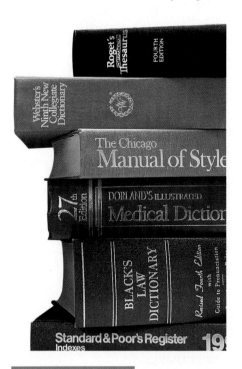

Fig. 10-5 These reference manuals enable the administrative assistant to check for specific applications of correct English usage as well as specialized medical and legal terms.

Transcription Instructions

Before you begin to transcribe, check any instructions at the beginning of a machine-dictated item or in your notes regarding format, number of copies, distribution, additions on certain copies, enclosures to be prepared, or the preparation of final or rough draft copy. In making a rough draft, use wide margins and double or triple spacing to allow for editorial changes.

Order of Transcription

Transcribe rush and top-priority items in order of most immediate importance as indicated by your notes, instructions on the dictating equipment, or your supervisor. Electronic communications must get first attention. Letters to be sent by express mail should be attended to next; they should be presented immediately for signing and mailing. If there is an extremely important interoffice memo, it may take precedence over other transcription items. Show your employer that you can make the right decisions regarding priorities. Store any transcription items that must be carried over until the next day in one designated location.

Number and Kinds of Copies

Some companies require two copies of every letter, one for the individual correspondence file and another for a chronological file of all letters mailed each day. Materials in this chronological file are kept at least a month for quick reference. Whether copies are produced by a copy machine or computer printer will depend on your organization's equipment and methods.

You will be asked to make and furnish certain individuals and departments with copies of every letter you transcribe relating to subjects of mutual interest. List in your desk manual the persons who should receive copies for each general subject. You can then make the correct number of copies and distribute them properly each time you key a letter. Your notes or dictated instructions for each item usually will tell you the number of copies needed.

Dating Transcription

Use the date of transcription if it differs from that of the dictation. It may be necessary to edit the dictation to make it conform to the date of transcription. For example, you might key "your visit *yesterday*" rather than "your visit *this morning*" if you are transcribing dictation that was given the preceding day.

Letter and Envelope Styles

Many companies furnish style manuals for use with their correspondence. If you do not receive one, compile your own models from previous correspondence and from style authorities. Study the model letters and envelopes shown in the Reference Guide.

The modified block letter is used most often because of its attractive layout. However, many administrative assistants use the block style letter because of its timesaving features. If you have the choice, you may want to use the simplified letter style. Study the post office's recommended format for envelopes (shown in Chapter 13). Use the latest forms of nonsexist salutations, or omit the salutation altogether. Note the new ways of indicating reference initials, especially those used for documents entered by computer. Using whatever decision-making authority you have, try to modernize the format of your transcription; but never forget that the dictator makes the final decision.

PROCEDURES FOR PROCESSING A DOCUMENT

Much of the processing time the administrative assistant spends on a document will be spent in the preparation of that document. While the equipment and software used to produce documents may differ, the basic procedures for creating, formatting, and editing the documents are similar. These procedures are explained below in more detail.

Creating a Document

The procedures for creating a document using an electronic typewriter are similar to those used with a traditional electric typewriter. Formatting features, which are used to establish the layout of the document, must be set before a document is created because the document is printed as it is keyed. A number of automatic features, such as automatic carriage return, automatic word wrap, automatic decimal tab, center, underline, and automatic relocate, enhance the capabilities of the electronic typewriter.

Computers use an applications software program. If the machine has a hard disk, the applications program initially can be "installed" on the hard disk and activated when the machine is turned on. If the machine has two floppy disk drives, the program disk is normally activated by inserting the disk in the disk drive and turning on the machine. The administrative assistant should always follow the steps outlined in the procedures manual that accompanies the software program disk.

After the application software program is loaded, the administrative assistant will enter appropriate commands or select the desired functions to create a document. Some software programs allow the administrative assistant to assign a specific name to each document, while other programs assign a file name automatically. After the document is keyed, it can be saved on either a floppy disk or a hard disk drive. Once the document has been named and stored, it can be retrieved from storage for editing or printing.

Formatting a Document

Formatting a document enables the administrative assistant to make the necessary adjustments to equipment or software to achieve an attractive layout of text on a page. Reference manuals are available to assist in determining appropriate formats. In addition, many companies establish standard formats for frequently prepared documents.

When using a computer, formatting selections are usually made prior to keying the document but can be changed if desired after the document has been keyed because printing is a separate function. The most frequently used format features establish left and right margins, tabs, page length, line spacing, headers and footers, page numbering, and type style. While the procedures for making formatting selections will vary with equipment and software, the main formatting features remain the same. Most equipment or software establishes formats called **defaults.** If the administrative assistant does not change the format features, the established defaults are used.

A *format line* (or lines) may be displayed at the top or the bottom of the screen, identifying the format features, the name of the document, and other valuable information about the task you are performing. This line of information is also called the status line or lines. Figure 10-6 shows typical format lines for a word processing program. Directions for changing formatting features on any equipment or software can be found in the user's manual. With practice, the administrative assistant will become familiar with the keying of frequently used formatting features.

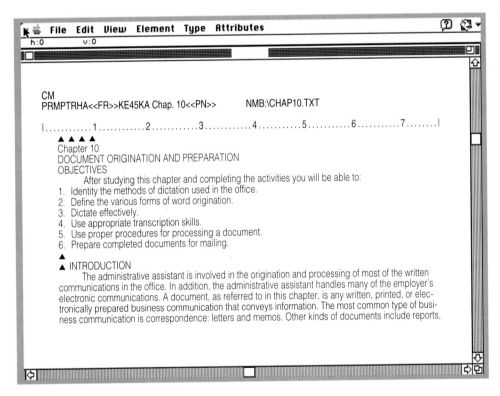

Fig. 10-6 The format or status lines identify the format features in use when processing a document.

Inputting and Editing a Document

Once the format features have been set, the administrative assistant begins to key the document. This process is called **inputting.** The document may be changed several times between the original composition and the final copy. Making these changes is called **editing.** Editing may be done by the author of the document or by the administrative assistant who is processing the document.

Most word processing software programs provide similar inputting and editing functions. The specific steps to be used may differ, however, so it is important that the user's manual or a training tutorial be reviewed before beginning to use the editing functions. While the names may vary depending on the software used, the major editing functions are identified below.

Center. Text will be centered automatically between left and right margins.

Copy. Text can be reproduced in another location within the document while the designated text remains in its original position.

Delete. A character, word, or block of text can be removed from the document.

Global Search/Replace. The text can be searched for a specific word or phrase, which can then be replaced with a different word or phrase. The word or phrase will be replaced each time it appears in the text. For example, the word *executive* might replace *employer* in a long document.

Indent. A temporary left margin can be set to indent specific material within a document.

Insert. A character, word, or block of text can be inserted in a document without altering previously keyed material.

Merge. Merge enables a document that has been stored to be inserted into another document. An example is a list of addresses of customers that has been stored and is then inserted as the letter addressee of sales letters, resulting in an individualized letter for each customer.

Prompts and Messages. Prompts and messages appear on the screen while editing functions are being completed. They help to guide the operator through the editing functions.

Save/Store. Text will be stored on a disk as a separate document when the operator has completed the keying and editing process. The document can be recalled for additional editing.

Scrolling. Documents can be scanned vertically and horizontally to locate the desired text for editing or reviewing purposes.

Proofreading a Document

After a document has been keyed, it should be reviewed on the screen before it is printed. Checks should be made for keying, spelling, and grammatical errors. Many word processing software packages have aids to assist you in checking for spelling and grammar errors, and some even provide a thesaurus. However, these aids cannot substitute for careful proofreading on the part of the operator. No matter how beautiful a document looks, if it contains any proofreading errors, the desired reaction is destroyed.

Spell Checks. Most word processing packages include an *electronic dictionary* that compares the words in a document with the electronic dictionary to verify spellings. If a word does not match any of the words in the dictionary, the word is highlighted on the screen so that the operator can check the spelling. For an example of what a spell check looks like, see Figure 10-7. Since the dictionary does not include all words, especially names of companies and proper names, some words may be highlighted that are spelled correctly. Frequently used words can be added to the electronic dictionary.

Spell checks do have limitations. If a word is spelled correctly but is used incorrectly in a sentence, the spell check does not recognize this as an error. An example of such a mistake is "Thank you for *you* letter." Operators must recognize that a spell check of a document is not a substitute for careful proofreading.

COMMUNICATION

An error that led to the loss of a valuable customer was a reference to a dump truck driver *as a* dumb truck driver.

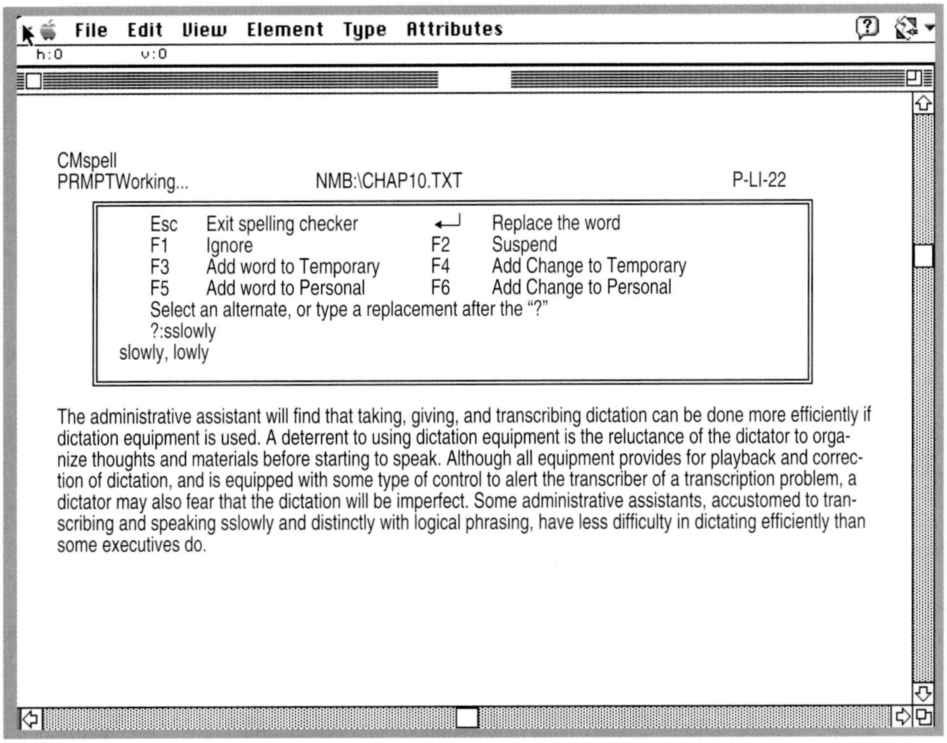

Fig. 10-7 The misspelled word is highlighted with spell check providing alternative spellings.

Grammar Checks. *Grammar checks* assist the operator in avoiding common grammatical errors such as disagreement of subject and verb. However, it will not check for all types of grammatical errors, so proofreading by the operator is important.

Thesaurus. Some word processing packages include a *thesaurus,* a list of synonyms (words with similar meanings) for a specific word organized by parts of speech and by meaning. The operator can review the list and replace the word with one of the synonyms if desired or retain the word in the text. The thesaurus is especially useful when preparing long reports and manuscripts.

Common Transcription Errors.   The top ten transcription errors are omitted letters, substitutions (*-ing* for *-ed,* for instance), omitted space, omitted punctuation (such as failure to close a quote), transposed letters, omitted words, a small letter for a capital letter, a full line omitted, a spelling error, or a capital letter for a small letter. Watch for these errors.

Good Proofreading Techniques.   The following proofreading techniques are recommended:

1. Before printing, when using a computer, scroll up one line at a time on the screen and use the top of the screen to guide your eye as you read line by line.
2. Read the material once for content.
3. Read again for mechanical errors: grammar, spelling, and punctuation.
4. Read from right to left.
5. Wait 30 minutes and reread.
6. Check numbers, especially decimals, and names and addresses with extreme care.

If you are unsure of the accuracy of your proofreading, ask someone else to read aloud from the original as you proofread, or ask someone else to proofread your work.

Reference Notations

Several types of information may be keyed below the final signature line. This information, in the order it appears on the correspondence, includes reference initials, enclosure notations, copy notations, and filing codes.

Reference Initials.   Reference initials are keyed a double space below the last keyed line in an interoffice memorandum or below the signature area of a letter in any of several ways.

ty or *TY* or *t* (transcriber only)
MP:TY or *MP:ty* or *mp/t* (dictator and transcriber)
MP:AG:TY or *mp:ag:ty* (executive, actual composer of document, and transcriber)

Enclosure or Attachment Notations.   Key enclosure or attachment notations a double space below the reference initials at the left margin. Be sure the wording in the body of the letter agrees with the notation. For example, when the letter states "Enclosed are . . .", the word *Enclosures* should be used. When the letter states "Attached is a copy of . . .", the word *Attachment* should be used.

Copy Notations.   Key the names or initials of copy recipients a double space below the enclosure notation. (The sender need not sign copies.) If the sender does not want the recipient of the original correspondence to know that a copy is being sent to someone else, the transcriber should make the appropriate number of photocopies of the correspondence and then key *bc* (blind copy) on the recipient's copy and the file copy. The notation *c* stands for copy and *pc* stands for photocopy.

Word Processing Codes.   Filing codes are reference notations that identify documents so that they can be located on magnetic media or hard copy. The following example shows one possible method of notation:

LM/a2.4

LM is the document originator; *a* is the document processor; *2* identifies Tuesday, the second day of the week. The *4* can indicate the fourth document keyed by *a* on Tuesday, that the document is stored on the fourth magnetic disk, or that it is the fourth hard copy filed behind *Tuesday* in the files.

Envelopes

When you are using an electronic typewriter, before removing a letter drop its envelope between the letter and the platen. When you remove the letter, the envelope will be positioned for addressing. Before removing the envelope from the electronic typewriter, check the address against the original source document for accuracy. When using a computer, the envelopes will be fed into the printer automatically; or you will feed the envelope into the printer manually. Slip the addressed envelope, flap side up, over the top of the letter and enclosures. The accumulated stack of correspondence is easy to handle, and your employer will find it easy to read and sign the letters. However, in order to reduce addressing errors, some employers prefer to have the addressed side of the envelope showing to match the letter address. On some electronic typewriters and computers, letter addresses, once keyed, can be stored in memory for addressing envelopes automatically.

Enclosures

Whenever an enclosure is mentioned in a letter, there is an implied instruction to the administrative assistant to obtain the enclosure and attach it to the letter before submitting it for signature. If possible, collect all enclosures at the same time. Be sure the enclosures all face the same direction. A page printed across the longer dimension should be turned so that its top edge is at the left edge of a letter printed in the usual way on 8 1/2-by-11-inch paper. If the enclosure refers to a previous letter between the correspondents, do not use the file copy or the original letter as the enclosure. Instead, make a photocopy of the document and identify it as such.

If an enclosure is small enough and does not cover the body of the letter, attach the enclosure to the face. If the enclosure is larger, place it behind the letter.

Should it be necessary to submit a letter for signature without its enclosures, clip a note to the letter listing the missing enclosures. Refer to the example in Figure 10-8. The note will serve a dual purpose: it will inform the executive that you have not forgotten the items to be enclosed, and it will remind you not to mail the letter until the enclosures are at hand.

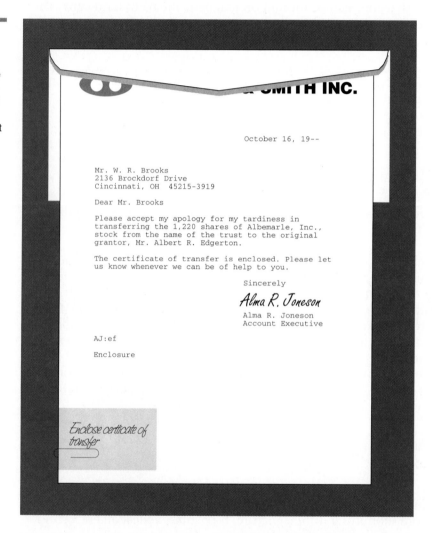

Fig. 10-8 If an enclosure will be bulky or difficult for the signer to handle, the administrative assistant attaches a note to the letter as a signal of awareness of the enclosure and as a reminder at mailing time.

Submitting the Correspondence for Signature

If rush items are involved, they are submitted as soon as completed. Some executives like to sign the mail at least twice a day. In other cases, the mail is signed in the afternoon in time to meet mail schedules (with which the administrative assistant must become familiar). Learn and follow the executive's preferences in these matters.

The correct arrangement of transcribed material is as follows: the letter and envelope are on top, followed by the enclosures, any extra copies, and the file copy with its notations. If the executive is there, present the letters face-up. If not, turn the letters face-down or insert them in a folder to keep them clean and to prevent them from being read by onlookers.

Most administrative assistants arrange to be at the executive's desk for the signing session. If questions or concerns arise about the items to be signed, the administrative assistant can respond immediately.

A frequent point of irritation between an executive and a transcriber is the difference between what the executive thinks was dictated and what has been transcribed. There is only one gracious way to handle these differences of opinion. The administrative assistant accepts responsibility for making all corrections and changes. It really does not make any difference who made the mistake. The important thing is to go about correcting it at once, cheerfully and willingly.

Preparing the Correspondence for Filing

The administrative assistant prepares transcribed dictation for filing by stapling the copy of each reply to the top of the incoming letter it answers. Place pertinent letters requiring follow-up in the pending file, or make tickler entries from the copies. Write each follow-up date on the file copy or on the original letter to show that the date has been set and recorded. Add the filing notation before laying the correspondence aside. The matter of designating where to file letters is addressed in Chapter 7. Increasingly, the file notation is made by the dictator or transcriber and keyed on the document at transcription time.

PREPARATION OF SIGNED MAIL

Before mailing, the administrative assistant makes a final check of all materials. The following questions should be answered.

1. Has the document been signed? Are all enclosures attached?
2. Is the envelope address the same as the letter address?
3. Is the amount of postage correct?
4. If stamps are used, are they securely affixed?

In some large offices, administrative assistants are relieved of the final work of sending out correspondence. Mail clerks collect the sealed and unsealed envelopes, determine the proper postage, and send all the mail to the post office. In small offices, the administrative assistant attends to every step of this routine. Modern office equipment, such as the folding machine, makes the routine faster and easier. However, the administrative assistant should know the most efficient manual procedures as well.

Folding and Inserting Letters Manually

A letter is ready for mailing when it is signed and all enclosures are assembled. An administrative assistant often folds and inserts the letters while waiting at the desk for the executive to read and sign the rest of the mail. Every letter should be folded in such a way that it will unfold naturally into reading position. The proper methods are shown in Figure 10-9.

Fig. 10-9 Examples of ways to fold letters into envelopes.

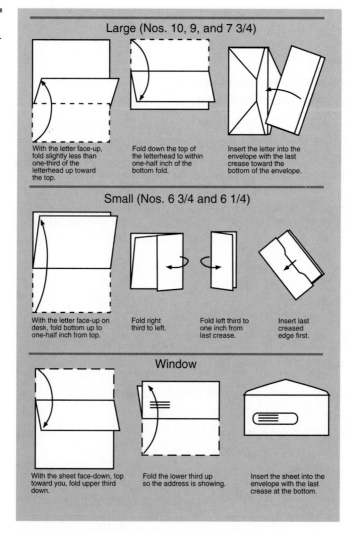

Large (Nos. 10, 9, and 7 3/4)

With the letter face-up, fold slightly less than one-third of the letterhead up toward the top.

Fold down the top of the letterhead to within one-half inch of the bottom fold.

Insert the letter into the envelope with the last crease toward the bottom of the envelope.

Small (Nos. 6 3/4 and 6 1/4)

With the letter face-up on desk, fold bottom up to one-half inch from top.

Fold right third to left.

Fold left third to one inch from last crease.

Insert last creased edge first.

Window

With the sheet face-down, top toward you, fold upper third down.

Fold the lower third up so the address is showing.

Insert the sheet into the envelope with the last crease at the bottom.

Sealing and Stamping Envelopes

When all letters are enclosed, jog the envelopes into a neat stack with all the address sides down and the flaps opened out. Now pick up the stack, grasp the flaps, and bend them back to make them flatter. Holding the side edges of the stack of envelopes between your hands, fan them out onto the desk so that only the gummed part of the flap of each envelope is visible. Then take a moistening tube, sponge, or wet paper towel and, with one swing of the arm, moisten all the flaps at once. Lay the tube aside on a blotter and start sealing the envelope nearest you by folding over the flap. Continue up the column. As you seal each envelope, pick it up and lay it flap side up in a stack.

If the sealed envelopes are to be stamped by hand, first remove all those that require special stamping. Lay the rest of them out with the address side up, leaving enough depth for the stamps to be pasted. Take a strip of stamps that are joined at the sides, moisten one stamp at a time on a nearby sponge or moistener, and affix the stamp to an envelope, working down from the top envelope. For strip stamps that are attached at the top, as rolled stamps are, lay the envelopes across the desk.

Envelopes requiring special stamping should be given individual attention. Those that are to be sent special delivery or to other countries and those that are too heavy for the minimum postage should be handled separately. Write in pencil in the stamp position the amount of postage needed. This penciled figure is later covered by the stamp.

Considerable loss is incurred from using excess postage. Every office should have some kind of postal scale. Weigh every piece of mail. When in doubt, weigh! Small scales for first-class mail are sensitive to fractions of an ounce. Check the accuracy of your scale periodically by placing nine new pennies on it; adjust the scale until they weigh exactly one ounce. The post office no longer delivers unstamped mail, so check carefully to be sure all mail is stamped.

Summary

Because the administrative assistant is involved in the processing of most written documents in the office, it is imperative that you have the skills necessary to produce quality written communications efficiently.

The executive has the option of using a number of types of equipment for dictation including portable or desk machines, centralized dictation units, endless loop or continuous flow systems, and digital dictation systems. Voice recognition systems for office dictation are being used in isolated markets; however, as the price of this type of system decreases, its use will increase. Shorthand dictation (dictation by the executive to the administrative assistant in a face-to-face situation) is seldom used in the office today.

The administrative assistant will encounter many types of dictation in the office including routine letters, memos, reports, and drafts; instructions for transcribing and composing documents; highly confidential material; telephone communications; on-the-spot dictation; dictation at the keyboard; and dictated answers to questions on printed forms.

Because the administrative assistant may be asked to dictate, he or she must know how to use dictation equipment. The instruction booklet for the equipment should be studied, and dictation should be practiced until efficiency is achieved.

Transcription skills are critical to the written communication process. The administrative assistant must have excellent English language skills. These skills include spelling, punctuation, and word usage. Formatting style and the ability to use reference books are also requisites for the administrative assistant. The ability to determine priority of transcription and the number and kinds of copies needed is also important.

To complete document processing in the most accurate and efficient manner, the administrative assistant must follow a number of procedures. These include creating the document, formatting the document, inputting and editing the document, and proofreading the document; using appropriate reference and enclosure notations; submitting the correspondence for signature; and preparing the correspondence for filing.

After the administrative assistant has made a final check to see that everything is in order, correspondence is folded, inserted in the appropriate envelope, and sealed. Envelopes are then stamped. Large offices may have a mail room to handle these procedures.

QUESTIONS FOR DISCUSSION

1. As the new administrative assistant to the director of an electronic engineering research laboratory, how would you familiarize yourself with the lab's highly technical vocabulary?

2. As an administrative assistant responsible for processing many long reports, what aids can you use on your computer software to assist you in proofreading these reports?

3. How would you handle the situation if the dictator:

   a. Habitually uses out-of-date, stereotyped phrases.

   b. Makes obvious errors in grammar.

THINK IT
Through

    c. Repeats the same conspicuous word several times in one business letter.

    d. Dictates even the most obvious punctuation, although much of it is questionable.

    e. Mumbles.

4. How would you proceed if you dictated a letter which was transcribed in a format that did not conform to your instructions?

THINK IT *Through*

5. Some prefixes are joined to the root word; others are hyphenated. Rekey the following sentences using the appropriate treatment of the prefixes. Use your Reference Guide to check your answers.

    a. As an exmanager of the team, she is often non-committal about their prospects for an allstate championship.

    b. When you receive a bi-weekly statement, do not be overanxious about the charge for the semi-circular braces.

    c. She has served for four years as the co-planner of the extra curricular activities that made the students self-supporting.

    d. The super-structure of the trans-continental plan is sub-standard in so many ways that inter-national competition will not permit pro-Canadian designers to out-distance the MX22.

PROBLEMS

1. Your executive hands you a letter of invitation to speak at a chamber of commerce meeting on December 10. The letter is from David Atchison, president of the chamber. His address is 1610 Northway Drive, your city. Your employer asks you to reply stating that the pressure of business makes it impossible to prepare adequately for such a presentation and suggests a substitute, Maria Savitsky of the Springer Corporation. Prepare an outline for the reply and dictate it to a dictation machine. Ask either a classmate or your instructor to critique your work.

2. Administrative assistants use word processing software on computers extensively because it enables them to produce error-free documents more efficiently. Many brands of word processing software are on the market. Assume that your employer is interested in purchasing new word processing software for your computer. Prepare a report comparing two word processing software packages and indicate the features available with each. Based on your evaluation, identify the software package you would purchase and give your reasons for selecting that particular package.

*T*ECHNOLOGY APPLICATIONS

▶ **TA10-1.TEM**   Access the template disk and select the TA10-1.TEM file, which shows a draft of a letter that Shirlene Edwards, one of your coworkers, keyed hastily yesterday for your manager. Because Shirlene is out of the office today, she called to ask you to edit her draft, print a final copy of it, and submit the final copy to your manager, who is expecting you to submit the final letter.

Edit Shirlene's draft copy, as follows:

1. Print a hard copy of the draft.
2. On the hard copy, correct any errors in spelling, grammar, punctuation, and style (number, abbreviation, and capitalization usage). Do not revise or rewrite unnecessarily.
3. Enter all your hard-copy corrections in the TA10-1.TEM file.
4. Save the updated document file.
5. Print out a "final" copy of the revised document.
6. Read the final copy "just to make sure."

Submit both the marked-up draft copy and the final copy to your instructor. (*Hint:* Can you find 10 distinct errors?)

▶ **TA10-2.TEM**   Access the letter on template file TA10-2.TEM. Proofread this draft to correct all errors. (*Hint:* There are 18 errors in the draft.)

Refer to the Reference Guide as needed. Produce a mailable copy for your instructor.

Chapter 11

Composition of Business Correspondence

LEARNING OBJECTIVES

After studying this chapter and completing the activities, you will be able to:

1. Define the basic writing principles for writing business correspondence.
2. Compose business correspondence for an employer.
3. Process international correspondence in the correct way.
4. Compose personal correspondence, when appropriate, for an employer.

INTRODUCTION

COMMUNICATION

The public perception of a company is influenced by the company's written communications.

Often the written word is the most effective way to communicate ideas in business. Because electronic technology is being used increasingly to transmit communications in the office, more information is being transmitted in written form. Written communications may be the only contact others have with your firm. Your ability to compose effective messages, either on paper or electronically, will contribute significantly to your employer's success and to your advancement.

Your ability to express your ideas clearly, concisely, and correctly will make you an invaluable employee. Whether you are asked to formulate a simple reply to a request for a catalog or to send a message to an applicant who does not qualify for a position with your firm, these kinds of composing assignments provide opportunities to display your writing ability and your creativity. Each composing assignment tests your educational background and experience.

To help perfect your composing skills, this chapter presents in capsule form the principles involved in producing communications that express personal concern, build goodwill, and solve business problems. Examples of typical business and personal correspondence you may be asked to compose are also included.

THE BASICS

When your employer says, "Prepare a reply for my signature" or "Send an electronic message for me," he or she shows confidence in your writing ability. Before undertaking a composing assignment, organize your thoughts in a logical fashion. A simple outline of what you want to say will help achieve this goal.

Written messages often become permanent records and, therefore, have more impact upon the reader than the spoken word has upon the listener. Today, because of the administrative assistant's access to electronic technology, you may be asked to compose electronic messages as well as printed messages. It is essential to use as much care in preparing electronic messages as in preparing all other types of business communications. In certain situations, it may be necessary to revise a document several times until just the right combination of ideas, words, and sentences produces a lasting, favorable impression.

The writing principles presented in this chapter represent a modern approach. A review of basic writing principles will help you recall the do's and don'ts of composing clear, concise, and correct communications. Before beginning any composing assignment, you should:

1. Review what you believe are the reader's expectations.
2. Isolate the main purpose of the communication and build the message around it.
3. Focus on the reader by writing about his or her interests.
4. Gather and verify facts.
5. Outline major points and place them in an effective order.

Finally, after completing the steps identified above, draft the document, making sure that every sentence is clear and that complete and correct information has been supplied.

Set the Proper Tone

Tone conveys the attitude of the writer and should be used to make a message cordial, tactful, positive, and courteous. By ignoring the importance of tone, you may give the reader the feeling that you are blunt, impolite, unfriendly, or given to high-pressure sales tactics. The effective writer controls tone by the careful choice of words. The reader's interpretation of your words will determine the nature of the response to your correspondence.

Personalize Your Message. Even if your letter is written for a mass audience, make each reader feel that it was written to one person—the recipient.

Personal Tone

To help you plan a pleas-
ant vacation, we are
enclosing a copy of our
new travel brochure.

Impersonal Tone

Our new travel brochure
has been published to
help clients plan their
vacations.

Most business communications suffer from too much attention to the writer's point of view and very little emphasis on the reader. Such letters lack the *you* attitude. Instead of beginning a paragraph with *I* or *we,* reverse the order and begin with *you.*

Emphasis on the Reader

For your convenience, we
are enclosing a Banktime
Credit Card to help you
establish credit in our
city.

Emphasis on the Writer

We are enclosing a Bank-
time Credit Card to help
you establish credit in
our city.

Using the reader's name is another way to put your reader in the picture. Don't overdo this, however; some readers may be irritated by being addressed with false familiarity.

COMMUNICATION

Your communication should be directed toward the reader.

Personal

You will be glad to
know, Mrs. Lane, that
the Bank of Grundy has
raised the interest rate
on passbook savings to
7 percent.

Impersonal

The Bank of Grundy has
raised the interest rate
on passbook savings to
7 percent.

Humanize Your Message.   Relax and let your letters reflect your personality. Business communications need not be dull and mechanical.

Friendly, Human Tone

Thanks for your order.
We are pleased that you
chose our firm to fur-
nish linens for your new
hotel. I have instructed
our shipping department
to fill your order
promptly, and you should
receive your first ship-
ment of linens within
two weeks.

Dull, Monotonous Tone

We are in receipt of
your recent order for
linens. I have instructed
our shipping department
to process the order
immediately. The first
shipment should arrive
in due course.

Encourage Your Reader.   Accent the positive elements in your message. Tell your reader what you *can* do, not what you *can't* do. Bring out points favorable to your reader. Present good news in the first sentence. When writing bad news, avoid dwelling on negative terms such as *error, mistake, inconvenience,* and *trouble.* These words merely emphasize the problems.

Positive Tone	Negative Tone
Because you take pride in owning a Prestige car, we are making a special effort to restore the paint to its original luster. By carefully mixing the proper colors, we can spray the car on Friday and let it dry over the weekend. You can drive away on Monday in a car that looks like new.	The problem you reported in your complaint of October 6 resulted from an unfortunate error in mixing the paint. It will be necessary to repaint the car, and we regret that we must keep it over the weekend. We apologize for the inconvenience; but as you know, errors like this are bound to occur.

Be Natural—Write the Way You Talk.   A business message functions as a substitute for a visit or personal call and should be written in a conversational tone. If your letters or electronic messages or those of your employer contain dull, hackneyed expressions, substitute natural expressions.

Natural Expressions	Hackneyed Expressions
immediately, soon *[or supply the specific date]*	at an early date, in the near future, at your earliest convenience
as you requested, as you stated	as per your letter, in accordance with your request
here is, enclosed is	enclosed herewith please find
this is to let you know	please be advised that
later	at a later date
today *[or supply the specific date or time]*	in due course
because or since	in view of the fact, due to the fact that, owing to the fact that
Thank you for your letter of *[supply the specific date]*	I have your recent letter

as you instructed	pursuant to your instructions
this, that, these, those	the above named, the above mentioned
omit "thanking you in advance" *[never take your reader for granted]*	thanking you in advance

Practice Tact. Tact is knowing what to do or say to maintain good relations with others. It is essential that a letter informing the reader that a claim has been denied, a promotion has been disapproved, or employment is being terminated is tactful.

Tactful Tone	**Tactless Tone**
Another box of brochures is being mailed to you today. If the lost brochures do eventually arrive, please return them to us. Your first shipment was mailed on October 6 to your Oakland address. We would appreciate your checking with your local post office to see if they are holding the shipment.	We cannot understand why you failed to receive the brochures we mailed on October 6. They were sent to you at your Oakland address. Check with your local post office to see if they are holding the shipment. In the meantime, we will mail you another box of brochures. If the lost brochures should turn up, return them to us immediately.

Never Write in Anger. No matter how hard you try to disguise anger, your words and expressions will give you away. Writing letters that destroy customer relations is something no business can afford to do. The best advice to follow is to cool off and wait a few days before responding. (If your employer violates this principle, you may take it upon yourself to hold the angry letter a few hours or until the next day. Your employer knows this rule of thumb, too, and will appreciate your good judgment.)

Improve Sentence Quality

Today's busy reader has little time for wasted words that do not contribute to the message. In addition, wasted words increase the cost of sending electronic communications. Every word should work. Your writing will improve considerably if you let each sentence express one idea.

Keep Your Sentences Short. Sentences containing fewer than 15 words will give your message impact. They also carry your reader's interest from one set of ideas to another. Caution should be exercised, however, not to put too many short sentences together. Such an arrangement gives your writing a monotonous, unbalanced effect. Compound sentences and transitional words and phrases can relieve this monotony.

A sentence that expresses a thought briefly and clearly is concise. A concise sentence is stripped of unnecessary words and, thus, is easy to read and understand. Conciseness is a mark of finesse and skill. It is an important quality for business communications because it saves time—the writer's time, the administrative assistant's time, and the reader's time. It can also save paper. To achieve conciseness, state a fact only once. Cut out superfluous words and phrases in each sentence. At the same time, however, beware of conveying a brusque tone. For instance, "Be here at five" lacks the graciousness of "I'm looking forward to seeing you at five."

Keep Your Paragraphs Short.   Your reader will be less likely to ignore your ideas if you present them in short paragraphs. Remember to begin a new paragraph when you change subjects.

Prefer the Short Word.   A good vocabulary is essential to precise expression. As a general rule, however, a simple word will have a more powerful effect than a long word that your reader might have to look up. Small words can express big ideas—*sun, sea, sky, joy, war.* A waiter is more likely to grasp your meaning if you ask, "Is the *tip* included in the price of the meal?" than if you ask, "Is the *gratuity* included in the price of the meal?"

The trend in business letters and electronic messages is toward short, informal words. These words usually create a friendly, personal relationship between the writer and the reader; they also help the writer relax and write naturally.

If a word is long, chances are you should change it to a shorter, more familiar word so that its meaning is clear. Some readers are, however, scholarly and intellectual. Visualize your reader and choose words suitable to that person.

In the list that follows, examine the words commonly used in business writing and their short, less formal counterparts. Would you say that the short words are always preferable to the long words? that the long words are always preferable to the short words?

approximately	about	inevitable	sure
ascertain	learn	inform	tell
commence	begin	inquire	ask
communication	letter	peruse	read
conflagration	fire	procure	get
demonstrate	show	purchase	buy
encounter	meet	remuneration	pay
endeavor	try	residence	home

A handy reference for the administrative assistant's desk, *Roget's International Thesaurus in Dictionary Form,* lists synonyms, antonyms, and related phrases. When a word seems too long, too impressive, or is used too often, check a thesaurus for a substitute.

Avoid Redundant Expressions.   Too many words unnecessarily lengthen a communication and sap its vitality. When two or three words are used to express a thought that could be expressed with one word, your writing becomes redundant, causing readers to lose interest.

Some examples of redundant expressions that frequently occur in business communications are presented below. In each of these examples, only one of the words is needed. To avoid redundancy, build a *watch list* of needless words that creep into your correspondence:

mutual cooperation	attach together	at the hour of 9
widow woman	hot water heater	free gratis
close proximity	general public	both alike
future prospect	local resident	is now currently
definite decision	intent and purpose	if and when
continue on	future planning	circle around
refer back	serious danger	settle up
matinee performance	commute to and from	never before in past history
prominent and leading	last remaining	repeat again
penetrate into	seldom ever	total destruction
each and every	day dawned in the East	vital necessity
vital and essential	end result	violent explosion
	regular weekly report	lonely isolation

A related error often made by business writers is using comparative forms of words that have no degrees of comparison. If a task is *impossible,* it cannot be *most impossible.* Words such as *honest, fatal, mortal, final,* and *hazardous* are concepts that cannot be compared. Such expressions as *completely honest, very fatal,* and *rather obvious* waste your reader's time.

Strive for Clarity.   It is difficult to estimate the cost of unclear statements—statements that leave the reader confused. The statement, "All the citizens had a part in appointing the members of the committee, and they think that the project should continue," leaves doubt as to whether *they* refers to the citizens or to the members of the committee. Such statements baffle even the brightest readers and could lead to serious misinterpretation. If there is any possibility that what you have written could be misinterpreted, rewrite it.

Use Active Verbs.   To make a forceful impression, writers have found that the active rather than the passive voice is helpful. In the active voice, the subject is the doer of the action; whereas in the passive voice, the subject is acted upon. Therefore, the passive voice tends to weaken a sentence. When forcefulness is not a factor, however, and the writer wants to concentrate on the *you* attitude, the passive voice may be used to avoid *we* and *I*. The passive voice is also effective in eliminating the generic use of masculine pronouns in describing occupations, lifestyles, and so forth. The following sentences illustrate each of these principles:

Forceful	**Weak**
We have approved your loan and have notified your agent.	The loan was approved by us and your agent has been notified.

Nonsexist	**Sexist**
A premium will be given when the customer buys.	When a customer buys, give him the premium.

Use Concrete Expressions. Vague expressions and ambiguous references cloud your meaning and detract from your message. Precise, specific terms improve the clarity of your writing and make your sentences more forceful. Expressions such as a *good* salary, a *large* crowd, a *few* hours, a *big* sale, and *several* errors are vague. One reader may visualize a good salary as $25,000, while another would consider $50,000 a good salary. After you have written your first draft, check it for fuzzy expressions.

Avoid Negative Expressions. In every kind of communication, words with negative connotations should be avoided. As one business communicator put it, negative words can turn a letter into a brink-of-war communique. Negative words in their kindest usage still have an unpleasant tinge. A list of negative reaction words is given here. You can undoubtedly add others—and you should!

abandoned	claim	failure	misfortune
abuse	collapse	fault	mistake
alibi	collusion	fear	muddled
adverse	complaint	flagrant	regret
apology	criticize	flat	reject
bankrupt	deadlock	hardship	scheme
blame	decline	hazy	so-called
biased	desert	impossible	sorry
beware	disaster	inconvenient	useless
calamity	error	insist	won't
can't	evict	meager	wrong
cheap			

Words with positive connotations improve tone. Use them whenever possible. Compiling your own reference list of positive reaction words will help you become alert to using them. Here are a few:

ability	conscientious	gracious	please
abundant	dependable	gratifying	poised
achieve	desirable	happy	praise
active	determined	kind	progress
admirable	distinctive	lasting	prominent
advantage	diversity	majority	punctual
benefit	effective	merit	steady
beautiful	enjoy	perfect	study
capable	faith	permanent	thorough
cooperate	good	pleasant	thoughtful
cheer	glad		

Avoid Sexist Words. Sexist words are words that discriminate against both men and women. You should avoid using these sexist words where possible. Some suggestions follow.

Sexist	**Nonsexist**
If a customer charges an item, he is sent a bill.	A customer who charges an item is sent a bill.
A supervisor is not responsible for the accident if he is not negligent.	A supervisor who is not negligent is not responsible for the accident.
When an employee is absent from work on a regular basis, he is subject to dismissal.	An employee who is absent from work on a regular basis is subject to dismissal.
manpower	personnel, workers
businessman	business executive
policeman	police officer
housewife	homemaker

Use a Forceful Beginning Sentence. Getting started is often the most difficult part of the letter-writing task. Your first sentence should be gracious and establish a point of contact with your reader. *Thank you* is always a good beginning when it is used appropriately and sincerely. When your reader has had previous correspondence with you and is expecting a specific reply, a good way to begin is to assure your reader in the first sentence that a specific action has been taken. Consider the following examples:

Forceful	**Weak**
Thank you for your letter of October 15 requesting a copy of our fall catalog. Because of high demand, we are temporarily out of catalogs, but we will mail yours when our new edition comes off the press next month.	Due to excessive demand, we regret we cannot comply with your request for a copy of our fall catalog. We have had to request an additional printing and will mail you a copy of this edition when it becomes available.
Your check for $85 in payment of claim No. 4577 was mailed today.	As you requested, we have instructed our accounting department to mail you a check for $85.
A copy of our brochure, "Modern Technology," is on its way to you with our compliments.	Your request for a copy of our brochure, "Modern Technology," has been received; and we are forwarding a copy to you today.

Although the use of *Dear Mr., Miss, Mrs.,* or *Ms.* combined with a last name is still the most popular form of salutation, many business writers are adopting the *dearless salutation* and the *salute opening* to begin their letters. (Most electronic communications eliminate the salutation completely.) Because of increased awareness of sexual stereotyping, *Dear Sir, Gentlemen,* and *Dear Madam* are disappearing from salutations. The dearless salutation substitutes some other word for *dear,* and the salute opening incorporates the salutation in the first few words of the opening sentence as illustrated in the following examples:

Dearless Salutation

```
Ladies and Gentlemen:
Hello, Mrs. Wilkins:
Good Morning, Dr. Cortez:
```

Salute Opening

```
You are right, Mrs. Wilkins,
in assuming that the shipment
was prepaid.
```
```
Congratulations, Dr. Cortez,
on your recent appointment
to the Finance Committee.
```

Use a Gracious Ending.   The closing lines are your last chance to make a good impression and achieve a favorable reaction. Some important pointers on writing effective closing sentences follow:

1. *Make the last sentence independent of the complimentary close.* Avoid fragmented endings such as "Hoping to hear from you soon, I remain." Fragmented endings are considered outmoded and add nothing to your message.

2. *Omit meaningless phrases.* If you have turned down an application for credit, it is meaningless to say, "Call on me again when I can be helpful."

3. *Make it easy for your reader to reply to a specific request.* Use statements such as "Return the postage-free card" or "Sign the enclosed card, and we'll bill you later."

4. *Look to the future.* Resell your company, its products, and its people. For example, a retail clothing store might close its letters by saying, "You are special to all of us at Martin's, and we will work hard to provide you with courteous service and quality merchandise."

5. *Ask for the action you want.* If you want your reader to respond in a certain way, don't imply your expectations. When you can, point out the advantages the reader will gain by reacting favorably to your request. For example, you might say: "Send no money now. Just complete the enclosed order form and you can enjoy the comfort and beauty of your new furniture today. We'll bill you after January 1."

6. *End on a positive note.* If you are answering a letter asking for an adjustment, don't apologize. Apologies and negative endings only remind the reader of inconvenience and error. A frank admission of error on your part may win your point, but too many negative words weaken your message. Instead of writing "We regret the inconvenience this error has caused you, but mistakes are bound to occur in an organization as large as ours," use a positive approach: "The situation you described in your letter of October 15 has been corrected, and we look forward to working with you when you again need furniture for your new home."

7. *Don't thank in advance.* This is discourteous: it presumes the reader's willingness to cooperate. It is appropriate to show appreciation in a closing sentence, but never make a statement such as "Thank you in advance."

8. *Stop when you've said enough.* In an attempt to be courteous, many letter writers drag their readers through a maze of words that add nothing to the message. Statements such as "Again, let me thank you for . . ." are redundant and weaken the effect of your letter.

Use Letter-Writing Basics

This section covered the basic principles of effective letter writing. Your adherence to the recommended guidelines should help you avoid the most common pitfalls that make letter writing unclear and uninteresting. The next time you compose a letter, analyze it using the checklist in Figure 11-1. If you can answer yes to these questions, your letter conforms to writing techniques that will make a favorable impression on your reader.

Fig. 11-1 If you can answer yes to most of these questions, your writing ability is above average.

CHECKLIST FOR EFFECTIVE WRITING

Can you answer yes to these questions?

____ Is your message long enough to give complete information but short enough to assure a thorough reading?

____ Is it clear and easy to read?

____ Does it present advantages to the reader that encourage the action you desire?

____ Is it natural, friendly, and conversational?

____ Is it neat and attractive, indicating that you care about the impression it makes?

____ Does it indicate a desire to help the reader?

____ Is it courteous and free of unpleasant, negative, or superior words and phrases that belittle the reader?

____ Is it forceful and interesting? Is it free from dull, hackneyed expressions? Have you used a variety of words and sentence structures?

____ Is it personalized? Did you use the reader's name and incorporate the reader's interests?

____ Does it focus on the reader by avoiding too many sentences beginning with *I, we, our,* and *my?* Does it have the *you* attitude?

____ Is it free from sexist language and stereotypes?

TYPICAL CORRESPONDENCE COMPOSED BY THE ADMINISTRATIVE ASSISTANT

The occasions when an administrative assistant is asked to compose material for the employer fall into two categories—assignments of a business nature and assignments of a personal nature. No matter what the orientation may be, a request to compose a message for the employer is to be regarded as a compliment—a compliment to your ability to do this high-level task.

Business Correspondence

Experienced administrative assistants generally are asked to write drafts of reports, speeches, minutes of meetings, difficult letters, and memos. This material probably requires the employer's signature or approval. Routine assignments, such as replies to requests for information, transmittal letters, special requests, short messages, reservations, appointment letters, or acknowledgments, might appropriately be written and signed by the administrative assistant.

If you are just beginning to assume these correspondence duties, you may wish to prepare a suggested reply to a letter and give it to your employer for editing. This is a good way to familiarize your employer with your ability as a correspondent.

In the course of transcribing your employer's dictation or keying from rough drafts, you may find it necessary to correct grammar, dates, amounts, and sentence structure. Of course, you will do so tactfully and courteously. This is an instance in which your knowledge of English fundamentals can be brought to your employer's attention. If you become recognized as an expert in these fundamentals, you may find yourself putting the finishing touches on much of your employer's business correspondence.

Acknowledgments.   In general, every letter or electronic message should be answered or acknowledged promptly, preferably the day it is received. In responding, discuss the points raised by the letter. In acknowledging a letter or other materials, merely inform the sender of its receipt and add any other necessary information. Acknowledgment letters or electronic messages may be sent to notify a customer that an order or a request for an appointment has been received. An effective acknowledgment letter will show appreciation; refer to the major points in the letter received; explain the action to be taken in the future; and resell the customer on your firm, its products, and its service. Notice how the body of the letter in the sample below incorporates the four important features of an effective acknowledgment:

COMMUNICATION

Individualized letters of acknowledgment are appreciated and provide a personal touch.

```
              Mr. Thomas Osier
              Osier Hobby and Craft Shop
              2612 Vernon Boulevard
              Nashville, TN  37201-6921
```

Appreciation	Thank you, Mr. Osier, for your letter of October 4 indicating that your order was shipped to Memphis instead of Nashville as you requested.
Major Point	Your concern about receiving your merchandise in time for pre-Christmas sales is understandable.
Specific Action	Mr. Andrews, our sales manager, is in Atlanta this week; and I will notify him

today to authorize a shipment to you from our Atlanta warehouse.

Resale of Company Service We will make every effort to provide you with prompt and courteous service to ensure that you receive your merchandise in time for your pre-Christmas promotions.

Sincerely

Evelyn Paltzer

Cover Letters. A universal business practice is to inform recipients when money or material is being sent separately. A cover letter tells what is being sent, why, when, and how.

A letter of transmittal is also a form of cover letter. It states that the material is enclosed and usually includes pertinent remarks about the enclosure.

When material is to be sent separately, the cover letter should start with the direct approach. Indicate what is being sent and why. Tie in the reader's personal interest if possible.

Ms. Susan Hedges
2615 Pebbleshire Drive
Birmingham, MI 48321-5734

Dear Ms. Hedges

What Is Being Sent and Why Today we mailed separately a complete set of swatches from our latest collection of decorator fabrics.

Reader's Personal Interest These swatches should help you select draperies for your new home. When you have selected the fabric, please contact us to place your order.

Cordially

Rita Lawton, Designer

Requests and Inquiries. Letters or electronic messages that request personal favors, information, or free materials should be courteous and complete in every detail. Let the reader know exactly what you want; give sound reasons why the reader should comply with your requests. Don't write in a demanding tone; keep in mind that you are the one who wants the favor. Make it easy for the recipient to reply to your letter or message, and express your gratitude and your willingness to return the favor.

Editor
<u>Office Issues</u>
5521 Avenue of the Americas
New York, NY 10034-6125

REPRINT OF ARTICLE

In the November issue of <u>Office Issues</u>, I noticed an
article outlining the many opportunities available
to male administrative assistants. The article was
both informative and timely, and I would like to
have reprints for students who come to me for career
counseling. I will need 23 copies.

Enclosed is an addressed envelope. If there is a
charge for these reprints, please bill me.

I appreciate your help in providing copies of this
informative article. Your magazine often is a helpful aid as I assist students in planning their careers.

JAMES TINDALE, COUNSELOR

Answers to Inquiries.   When writing a letter or sending an electronic message in reply to an inquiry, try to give a satisfactory answer that will make
your reader think you are giving personal attention to the request. If you cannot provide the information requested (for whatever reason), tactfully state
your refusal so that your reader will not be offended; don't make excuses.
Express appreciation for the letter and offer additional help when appropriate—this is an excellent public relations tool. Double-check before mailing
the letter to be sure that you have answered all of the reader's questions.

Ms. Letitia DuMoulin
Business Women of Louisville
584 Hilltop Road
Louisville, MN 55642-1629

Dear Ms. DuMoulin

Thank you for your letter of January 4 asking for a
complimentary copy of our booklet on fund raising.
The demand for this publication has been so great
that our supply of copies was exhausted before the
end of the year. This booklet is being reprinted and
will be available by February 1.

In the meantime, if you would like to have our Fund
Raiser's Kit, which contains much of the same information plus some of the materials you will need to

get started, just write your order on the bottom of
this letter. Enclose $3 to cover mailing costs, and
we will get a kit in the mail to you.

Sincerely

Jeffery VanAble

Reminder Letters.   Every administrative assistant keeps a tickler file of pending items. Replies anticipated, reports due, and goods to be received all are recorded in this file. When an item is overdue, the administrative assistant sends a reminder. This is a routine procedure, and the administrative assistant sends the communication without being instructed to do so. Tactful phrasing is imperative, for no one likes to be reminded of negligence or lack of promptness.

To ensure that you are writing tactful reminder communications, never write in an accusing tone. Don't imply forgetfulness on the reader's part. Give complete information and close with a positive look to the future.

Mr. Firooz Mirbaha
Midstate Piping Company
2150 Sundell Road
Peoria, IL   61600-1538

Dear Mr. Mirbaha

By July 24 we must complete our bids on the new
construction on Highway 77 North. We need the quotations we requested on June 1 to submit our bids on
time. Could you have this information sent to our
Chicago office by the first of next week? A stamped
envelope is enclosed for your convenience.

Your help in securing this contract is greatly appreciated, and we look forward to working with you
as the project progresses.

Yours truly

Mark Makowski
Project Engineer

Letters of Recommendation.   In writing a letter of recommendation, your employer is putting the stamp of approval on an employee or on a former employee who is seeking another position. Letters of recommendation usually give the reason for writing the letter, outline the duties performed by the employee, state the employee's qualifications for the job, and include the recommendation of the writer, as shown in the following example:

Mr. David Chambers
Ohio Insurance Company
2957 Garfield Road
Dayton, OH 45401-2477

Dear Mr. Chambers

I understand that Mr. J. A. Brandt has applied for
the position of branch manager in your Dayton office. Mr. Brandt worked for us from his senior year
in college until about a month ago. Although his duties were not supervisory in nature, he was thorough
and accurate in all his work. He is very efficient,
and his pleasant disposition made him very popular
among his coworkers.

We regret that he has left us, but we are delighted
that he has found a position that will offer him the
opportunity he deserves. It is a pleasure to recommend him to you. We are confident that he will prove
himself capable of performing any responsibilities
you assign him.

Sincerely yours

Juanita Alvarez

Letters of Introduction.   A letter of introduction is usually written to assist
a former employee, customer, business associate, or acquaintance. This letter
should establish the relationship between your employer and the person
being introduced, state the reasons for the introduction, and politely ask
the reader for help. Your employer may be called upon to write a letter of
introduction to someone that neither the employer nor the person being
introduced knows. The letter may be hand-carried and presented to someone whose identity is unknown at the time the letter is written. It is not
necessary to begin the letter with the outdated TO WHOM IT MAY CON-
CERN. Simply begin the letter with the introduction and omit any form of
salutation.

LETTER OF INTRODUCTION FOR NANCY ADAMS

This letter will introduce Ms. Nancy Adams, who
served as my administrative assistant from October
1990 until May 1994. Ms. Adams is a professional in
every sense of the word. She is dependable, loyal,
honest, and hardworking. She is leaving us to accompany her husband to Milwaukee; he has accepted a position with AMB Corporation.

I heartily recommend Ms. Adams to you. Any help you can give her in locating a suitable position will be appreciated.

ANDREA IWINSKI

A sample letter of introduction for a business associate follows:

Mr. Ronald Morehouse
Morehouse Manufacturing Company
6987 Midway Boulevard
Chicago, IL   60681-9137

Dear Ron

Some time next month a young engineer, Donna Maxey, will call on you in Chicago. Our firm has worked with Donna for the past five years, and we find her to be an outstanding authority on metal design. She is now traveling throughout the Midwest to establish herself in a line of work that she will explain to you.

Please make her feel welcome and extend to her any help you can give.

Sincerely

Henry E. Starzyk

Negative Letters.   Often a letter must be written about unpleasant subjects: *complaints, refusals,* and *mistakes.* These letters require special care.

Complaint Letters.   As a company employee, any complaint letter you receive that is antagonistic toward your company must not be taken lightly. A prompt, thorough investigation of the complaint is necessary. Often a company does not even know there is a reason for dissatisfaction, so a genuine complaint letter is usually appreciated.

But what if *you* have a complaint? A good formula to follow in writing your letter is to begin with a positive reference to the trouble, continue with a detailed explanation, and end with a courteous request for an adjustment. See if the following paragraphs meet these criteria:

Sales Manager
Springer Furniture Company
2173 Cardinal Drive
Fairfax, VA   22049-2843

ORDER NO. 91653

On October 16 I ordered a solid cherry nightstand to match the Provantique bedroom grouping I purchased from you on August 29. The nightstand was delivered this morning in the carton in which it was originally packed. Upon opening the carton, I discovered that the nightstand had been packed before the finish had completely dried. The cardboard packing left impressions on the top of the stand and cleaning cannot remove them.

I am expecting guests for the Thanksgiving holidays and am eager to have the room completed before their arrival. Will you please have your truck pick up the nightstand, have it refinished, and return it to me before Thanksgiving? If this is not possible, could I please have another nightstand shipped from the factory?

I realize that this error was made at the factory, but I know you will take care of it before my guests arrive.

ANTHONY BERTUCCI

Refusal Letters.   One of the most severe tests of your ability to compose an effective letter will come when your employer asks you to write a letter of refusal. Banks often have to reject loans, and employers have to turn down job applicants and refuse requests for favors. Since it is difficult to maintain the reader's goodwill when you must refuse a request, letters of this type require special care.

When it is necessary to refuse a request, use the sandwich technique. Place the refusal between a positive opening statement and a positive closing statement. A positive opening statement softens the impact of bad news. It should contain at least one element upon which both you and your reader agree, but it will not be effective if it sounds artificial or contrived. You should give a detailed explanation leading to the refusal; keep it practical and sympathetic. Avoid general statements that substitute for detailed explanations. State the refusal, or imply it strongly. Leave no doubt in your reader's mind. Offer an alternative action if possible and resell your company, its products, and its services. An example of a refusal that uses the sandwich technique follows:

Mr. Anthony Bertucci
356 Laurel Drive
Fairfax, VA 22041-4042

Dear Mr. Bertucci

Positive Point of Agreement	The Provantique bedroom suite you purchased from us on August 29 is indeed one of the finest groupings that has been carried by our store. We are

	sure it is especially beautiful in your new home. However, the Provantique grouping has been discontinued by the manufacturer, and no matching pieces are available. Our refinishing
Explanation Leading to the Refusal	specialist tells us that all attempts to match the finish on the Provantique grouping have proved unsuccessful.
Alternative Suggestion	May we have John Hendricks, A.S.I.D., our interior designer, visit you at your convenience? We have explained your concern to him, and we are confident his suggestions will enable you to select a compatible piece of furniture to complement your Provantique grouping and enhance your guest bedroom.
Resale of Merchandise	Our adjustment department will call you to make arrangements to pick up the nightstand. Of course, the full purchase price will be refunded, and we will offer you our most attractive price on any item you select as a replacement.
Positive Closing	We appreciate the opportunity you have given us to help furnish your new home. With the holidays approaching, we look forward to helping you select any accent pieces you may wish to acquire to beautify your home at this festive time of the year.
	Sincerely
	Marie Albornoz

Mistake Letters. As long as people and computers handle the affairs of business, mistakes will occur. These errors require letters that are tactful enough to soothe feelings and maintain harmonious relationships. When you write a letter about a mistake, admit that you are at fault without the use of pompous phrases and long words. If you forgot to put an enclosure in a letter, write a brief note of explanation to the addressee, include the enclosure, and send a copy of the message with the rest of the day's mail to be signed. This procedure lets your employer know that the enclosure was omitted from the original correspondence.

It is human nature to want to help a person who admits a mistake, unless that person's mistakes occur too frequently and have severe consequences. Compare your reactions to the mistake letters which follow.

Acceptable

After you called yesterday, I checked our file of advertisements and found that we neglected to include yours in the October issue of <u>Edwardian Times</u>. We are sorry that this happened, and we will give your advertisement preferred placement in our November issue.

Unacceptable

Pursuant to your telephone call of October 10, we immediately searched our records to determine what disposition had been made of your ad submitted for publication in the October issue of <u>Edwardian Times</u>. Apparently, through some inadvertent oversight on the part of our editorial department, your ad was omitted from this issue. We hope hope that delaying the ad for another month will not seriously inconvenience you.

Interoffice Correspondence

Written communication among the staff of a company takes the form of an interoffice memo or electronic communication, a style less formal than a traditional letter. (See the illustration of an interoffice memorandum in the Reference Guide.) The administrative assistant will have many opportunities to compose messages for intracompany distribution. For an example of an interoffice electronic message, see Figure 11-2.

Ordering supplies, requesting temporary help, and setting the time and place for a meeting are examples of occasions when an interoffice message might be used. Your approach in writing these communications should be direct and concise. If your employer requests that you send a memorandum to the staff scheduling a meeting, your memo might read as follows:

TO: Sales Staff

FROM: John Breese

DATE: November 10, 19—

SUBJECT: Staff Meeting

The meeting of the sales staff will be held in my office at 10:00 a.m. on May 4. The items for discussion include the establishment of sales districts and quotas. Please bring . . .

> **COMMUNICATION**
>
> *Within an organization, the memorandum is the most widely used written communication.*

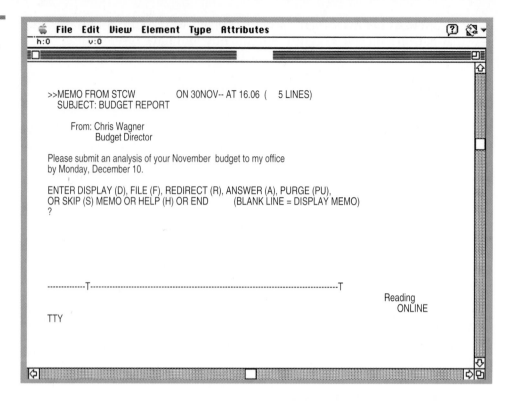

Fig. 11-2 An example of how an electronic message looks on the computer screen.

Standard Letters and Paragraphs

You will soon discover that certain letter-writing situations recur frequently. Many of the letters you compose will address similar circumstances. When you find an especially effective sentence or term, preserve it for another letter. You can do this by compiling a letter reference manual. The manual should contain samples of letters that reflect your employer's language and typical reactions. Although the preparation of such a reference takes time, it will become one of your greatest time-savers. Here is how to do it:

1. Keep an extra copy of all outgoing letters for a month.
2. Reread all of them at the end of the month in one sitting. As you read them, you will recognize words, phrases, and ideas that frequently recur.
3. Separate the letters into categories; make extra copies of letters that fit several classifications; underline favorite phrases and other keys to your employer's ways of handling situations; set up a file folder for each classification. Ask yourself the reasons for variations among the letters in the amount of detail used, degree of cordiality, language, tone, and style.

4. Make an outline of the points usually covered by the letters in each category.

5. Pick out the best opening and closing sentences and the best key points tailored to specific situations.

6. Compile a letter guide, using a loose-leaf notebook. Prepare an outline for model responses to letters in each category and place on dividers that separate the categories of letters. Prepare model opening and closing sentences and model paragraphs for each category on separate sheets.

7. When you compose a letter, compare it with the model outline to be sure that you have included all necessary parts.

8. Keep a record of the form used for each letter sent so that you do not send the same letter to the same person twice.

One of the advantages of the computer is the ability to store standard sentences, paragraphs, or letters. Once you have established a letter reference manual, you should store standard sentences, paragraphs, or letters as documents. Then record in the reference manual the code or name under which each one is stored. When you are asked to compose a letter that incorporates standard information, all you will need to do is retrieve the stored information. This combination of a letter reference manual and stored information can increase greatly the efficiency of the administrative assistant.

International Correspondence

Now that many U.S. corporations are multinational and many foreign companies have major offices or plants in the United States, the business community is indeed global in nature. Within this global environment, employees must develop a better understanding of international business communications. A major key to better communications at the international level is to develop an understanding of cultural differences and to become aware of the nature of these differences. The differences will vary from country to country and may include customs, values, language barriers, religion, art, education, decision-making processes, manners, and status. As the administrative assistant, you may be expected to assist your employer in obtaining information about the cultural differences of a country in which your company is conducting business. This information will help to avoid miscommunication either orally or in written correspondence.

Language style for international correspondence is much more formal and traditional than for domestic correspondence. Social amenities must be observed meticulously. Although you may not compose many letters to foreign companies, you will very likely prepare correspondence dictated by your employer to business executives in foreign countries. Your knowledge of that country's customs can assist your employer in developing a clear, concise communication. While English is becoming the international language of

HUMAN RELATIONS

When interacting with an international client, the most successful managers assume the decision-making patterns of the client's culture.

business, occasionally you may be asked to have messages translated into a foreign language.

When addressing a letter to a foreign recipient, copy the address exactly as it is given, as style differs from country to country. In European and South American countries, the street number follows the street name: Nassaustraat 7, not 7 Nassaustraat. In Japanese addresses, many other designations in addition to the street name and number are used to locate the prefecture and the section of the city; all are essential. If you are asked to compose or critique your employer's international correspondence, this list of ten tips for writing international correspondence will be helpful:

1. Use formal or "correct" English. Avoid colloquial expressions, regional expressions, and slang, as this may lead to misunderstanding and the loss of business. References to Hollywood, Wall Street, or Watergate may leave your reader at a loss. Using a saying like "You can't teach an old dog new tricks" could offend a reader in a country where dogs are considered vile animals.

2. Use simple language and short sentences and paragraphs. Make only one point in each sentence. Punctuate your writing generously. Use the "dictionary" meaning of the word as much as possible. Put all figures in writing and confirm oral discussions. Use charts, graphs, and pictures to help clarify your message.

3. Do not be too familiar. Using first names and inquiring into personal business is sometimes regarded as disrespectful by people in other countries. Proceed slowly in writing to your overseas clients on a first-name basis.

4. Avoid a condescending tone. Your reader will be quick to detect a superior tone in your letter. Never mention in correspondence that a country is a "developing nation," part of the Third World, or dependent upon the United States for aid.

5. Do not discuss religion or politics unless religion or politics is the business at hand.

6. Expect and give formal courtesy. Although the writer of foreign correspondence may convey "most sincere compliments" or ask "your esteemed favor," it is not necessary for you to respond in kind. It is essential that "please," "thank you," and other courteous expressions be used generously in international correspondence. Stick to formal styles; use full titles and spell all names correctly.

7. Question tactfully. If you need to know whether the person to whom you are writing has the authority to approve or sign a contract, be very tactful in determining this. Do not in any way question the status of your reader. Position and status are immensely important in many foreign countries.

8. Respect the social customs, religion, and mores of your reader. Be prepared for different standards of conduct. For example, time is essential in most of the correspondence of Americans. However, if you

insist upon prompt replies, you may offend your reader unless the request is phrased tactfully.

9. Do not compete with your reader. Although you may be quite knowledgeable about Belgian lace, Chinese porcelain, Swiss watches, or French wines, don't pit your acquired expertise against that of your reader. It is not wrong to let your reader know that you have knowledge of such things, but don't try to be an expert.

10. Eliminate all forms of humor. With the exception of a few countries, American humor is misunderstood overseas.

Personal Correspondence

Occasionally your employer will ask you to write personal letters or send electronic messages of a personal nature to business acquaintances. Some of these communications may be written without dictation or instruction and submitted to your employer for signature or approval. It is especially important that these communications sound as though your employer had written them. Use the same salutation, complimentary close, and writing style that your employer uses. Personal correspondence should be printed on executive-size stationery or on the executive's personal stationery, if available; otherwise, it should be printed on plain bond paper. Submit your first draft for approval.

The types of personal communications your employer may send are almost limitless. They may be messages of appreciation, sympathy, recognition, congratulations, introduction, or formal acceptances and regrets. Often, because of their personal nature, your employer will dictate these communications; however, should she or he ask you to compose such a message, consult an etiquette book or an up-to-date handbook on communications.

Letters of Appreciation. An executive busy in the office is usually just as busy outside the office with community activities. For instance, after a year of work on a civic project, your employer may ask you to write a note to committee members acknowledging the contributions they made to the project. For example:

```
Ms. Bettie Ahola
1206 Broadway Drive
Ann Arbor, MI  48104-2157

Dear Bettie

The work is finally concluded, and it is through
your efforts and those of the other members of the
committee that we can consider this project com-
plete.

Watching our dream become a reality will be gratify-
ing to each of us. I hope we will have the opportu-
```

nity to work together on another project for the
betterment of our community.

Sincerely

Roger Jordan, Chairperson
United Community Fund Campaign

Letters of Recognition. In the course of your employment, you will come
to know many of your employer's friends and will recognize their names
when you see them in print. If one of them has an article in a current magazine, you may be asked to scan the article and draft a communication com-
plimenting the friend, using the executive's writing style, as in the following
example:

Mr. Phillip Winsier
610 Sunrise Boulevard
Orlando, FL 32801-9571

Dear Phil

I have just read your interesting, informative article in the current issue of <u>Dynamics</u>. It reflects
your skill in organizing ideas into a clear, bal-
anced presentation, allowing readers to draw valid
conclusions. Your readers, I know, will commend you
for your treatment of this complex subject.

Sincerely

Bryn Kaster

Letters of Sympathy. If death or tragedy occurs in the family of one of the
executive's friends, you can draft a sympathy note to be copied in longhand
by the executive. A personal note is more thoughtful than a commercial card;
it is sincere and usually brief. The words "die" and "death" are usually
avoided in sympathy notes. Two examples follow.

Mrs. Merle Cramer
2140 Elder Drive
Lincoln, NE 68501-3619

Dear Mrs. Cramer

We were distressed to read in this morning's <u>Times</u>
of the passing of Dr. Cramer. All of us extend to
you our sincere sympathy for the loss of a good
friend, a respected associate, and a great citizen.

Sincerely

Sally Gravedoni

Mr. James L. Carter
258 Riverside Drive
Flemington, NJ   08822-7531

Dear Mr. Carter

All of us at Benson's extend our sincere sympathy to
you and your family. Mrs. Carter's loss will be
keenly felt here in the office by those of us who
worked with her. Her personal integrity and good
judgment made her invaluable to us.

We send you our sincere sympathy and affection.

Sincerely

Martin Sweeney

Letters of Congratulations.   If there is publicity about the promotion or professional achievement of one of your employer's friends, you may draft a letter of congratulations. For example:

Mr. Keith Sibilsky
Cober College
526 Main Street
Cober, MN   56511-9572

Dear Keith

Congratulations, Keith, on your appointment as
President of Cober College. Having you as president
will be a great source of satisfaction to alumni and
friends of the college.

Please accept my sincere good wishes for a productive presidency.

Sincerely

John Lucy

Letters Accepting Invitations.   Letters accepting invitations should convey appreciation and enthusiasm. Details of the invitation might be repeated to assure the person issuing the invitation that the time, place, date, and other arrangements are clear. If your employer receives frequent invitations to speak, it might be wise to put together a packet to include with letters of acceptance. The packet might include a biographical sketch (to be used in introducing your employer), a list of the special equipment your employer will need to make the presentation (projectors, recorders, screens, etc.), and a publicity photograph (to be sent only when requested). If a spouse or other special guests will accompany the employer, this information should be included in the letter of acceptance. Give your reader as much information as possible. This will eliminate the need for additional correspondence requesting a biographical sketch, a photograph, and a list of audiovisual equipment needed for the presentation. Use the following example as a guide to compose acceptances:

```
Mr. Lawrence Duvall
Fidelity Mutual Company
2451 6th Avenue
New York, NY   10361-1452

Dear Mr. Duvall

Thank you for including me in your plans for the an-
nual employees' banquet to be held at the Mario Hotel
in New Orleans on Monday, November 14, at 7:00 p.m.

In keeping with your banquet theme, I have entitled
my remarks, "The Five A's of Job Satisfaction." I
will do my best to give your employees an interest-
ing 20 minutes.

My wife will accompany me and, as you suggested, we
will meet you in the lobby of the hotel at 6:00
p.m.

I look forward to meeting you in New Orleans.

Sincerely


Eric Cauley
```

Letters Declining an Invitation.   Letters declining an invitation should express appreciation for the invitation but, at the same time, express regret. A specific explanation of the circumstances that prevent acceptance should be given. Specific reasons are more sincere than statements such as "due to circumstances beyond my control," or "because of a previous engagement." These are flimsy excuses and have a ring of insincerity.

Suitable	Unsuitable
Thank you for inviting me to be your keynote speaker at the artists' forum on August 23 in Portland, Maine.	I regret exceedingly that I must decline your invitation to speak at the artists' forum on August 23.
I regret that a teaching assignment at a print-making workshop during the entire month of August makes it impossible for me to accept.	Circumstances beyond my control make it impossible for me to accept.

```
It was thoughtful of you
to include me in your
plans, and I hope you
will keep me in mind for
next summer's forum; I
will not be teaching
that semester.
```

Letters Canceling Previously Accepted Engagements.   Canceling engagements often causes inconvenience, frustration, and ill will and should be done only when a genuine emergency arises. Despite careful planning, occasions may arise when it will be necessary for your employer to cancel a previously accepted engagement. The following model should be helpful in drafting a letter of this type:

```
Ms. Amy Milken
5500 Indian Trails Road
Santa Fe, NM  87501-2112

Dear Ms. Milken

This is a difficult letter to write as I know it
can cause you only worry and inconvenience.

On Monday morning I was awakened at home to learn
that our North Brattenborough plant had lost thou-
sands of gallons of milk because of a leak in the
filtering system. This morning our home office or-
dered a massive project to correct the situation.
This unexpected emergency will, of course, make it
impossible for me to speak before the national sym-
posium in Santa Fe next Saturday.

Sincerely


Sam Cohodas
```

Summary

One of the most important contributions you can make to your employer will come from your ability to write effectively. Your willingness to compose business and personal correspondence and electronic messages for your employer will make you an invaluable employee.

The letter is the most personal form of written communication. As an administrative assistant, you must know the fundamentals of effective letter writing as well as the proper forms of many kinds of communications—business and personal.

The most important part of any message is its tone. Tone makes the communication human. It reflects the attitude of the writer, encourages the reader to react favorably, and conveys tact, courtesy, and care.

Effective writers use a natural style that avoids monotonous, hackneyed expressions which sap the vitality of the message. Short words, short sentences, short paragraphs, the elimination of redundant expressions, and the use of active verbs will improve the clarity of your communications. Concrete words give your writing precision.

Using a forceful beginning sentence, preparing a gracious ending, and avoiding negative expressions and sexist language will also lead to a more favorable reaction from your reader.

Typical business communications composed by administrative assistants include acknowledgments, cover letters, requests, inquiries, answers to inquiries, reminders, letters of recommendation, reference letters, letters of introduction, negative letters, complaint letters, refusals, and mistake letters. Other areas in which your expertise will be helpful are interoffice correspondence and international correspondence. Letters require special care in composition if they are to make the right impression and evoke favorable responses.

You may also be called upon to compose personal correspondence for your employer. This correspondence may include letters of appreciation, recognition, and sympathy; letters accepting or declining invitations; and letters canceling previously accepted engagements.

To cover situations that frequently recur, you may develop standard sentences, paragraphs, and letters which can be stored on a computer. This stored information can increase your efficiency in preparing repetitive responses.

Keep in mind that the essentials of effective communications are completeness; clarity; conciseness; courtesy; concreteness; conversational, unbiased tone; and forceful and interesting style.

Effective composition takes work. A well-structured communication of any type omits nothing essential to the message and includes nothing superfluous.

QUESTIONS FOR DISCUSSION

1. When you were hired, your employer told you that every letter was an opportunity to build goodwill for the company. What are some of the steps you can take to ensure that the letters you compose build goodwill for the company?

2. Your employer has been invited to be the keynote speaker for the state convention of Executive Women International. The date of May 5 conflicts with a scheduled presentation of a new line of products to a group

THINK IT
Through

of buyers in New York. Your employer asks you to respond. What information should you include in your letter?

3. If your employer's position involves international business, how can you help write international business letters that build goodwill for your company?

4. Your employer says, "Subscribe to *Business Week* for me, please." These are the only details you have. How would you handle this task?

THINK IT *Through*

5. Your employer has asked you to write a letter of introduction for an employee who is leaving the company to go to Phoenix, Arizona. Neither your employer nor the employee has any contacts in Phoenix. How should you begin the letter, and what should be included?

6. Many foreign words have been anglicized in their plural form. When given a choice, use the English plural. Rekey the following sentences and use the English plural of the italicized word.

    a. Several *appendices* are included with the report.

    b. *Memoranda* from several administrators were included in the file.

    c. Modern technology has changed all college *curricula*.

    d. The *indices* of several books were examined before selecting a text.

    e. The artist used several *media* in the composition of the mural.

PROBLEMS

1. At a recent writing workshop, the participants were asked to reduce the text of the following letter to the smallest possible number of words. One administrative assistant got it down to eight words. Can you do as well?

```
A copy of your pamphlet of "The Human Side" has been
handed to the undersigned, and in reading the con-
tent we have been very much impressed and are won-
dering if this pamphlet can be secured by
subscription and, if so, what are the charges for
such subscription. Might we hear from you in this
regard at your earliest convenience?
```

2. Your employer, Ms. Perry, has just been promoted to the position of personnel manager for your firm. Ms. Perry, a recent college graduate, has a tendency to be wordy. On your return from a workshop on effective let-

ter writing, you are asked to revise the following letter to conform to good letter-writing practices. Rewrite this letter.

```
Mr. Gerald Harris
2650 Pamlico Road
Greenville, SC  29601-8502

Dear Mr. Harris

We have your letter of March 16 for which we express
our sincere thanks and appreciation. The information
your office has kindly supplied us will be most
helpful in helping us decide upon the choice of the
individual who will make the most substantial con-
tribution to this company.

In the event that any other information should come
to your attention regarding the qualifications of
this individual, we should appreciate your sending
it along to us immediately.

We look forward with sincere pleasure to hearing
from you further. In the meantime, if we can return
your generous favor, please do not hesitate to call
on us.

Sincerely


Carl Sullivan
```

TECHNOLOGY APPLICATIONS

▶ TA11-1.TEM   The two letters stored on your word processing template in the file named TA11-1.TEM have been intercepted by Mr. Stanley. They were written by his assistant. You are asked to rewrite them into an acceptable format. Key each on a half sheet of simulated letterhead.

▶ TA11-2   One of the important facets of good writing is effective organization. There are four paragraphs on page 291. Use them in writing a letter in proper format and rearrange them to create the most effective message.
Your letter will be addressed to Dr. Phillip Vandament, 1420 Center Street, Long Beach, CA 90805-3318. Provide the appropriate salutation and complimentary close. Sign your name to the letter.

continued

continued

Paragraphs:

a. The next time you are downtown, drop by our office. A few minutes of careful planning can help you protect your family against the unexpected.

b. At Providence Mutual, our counselors can help you set aside a portion of your income for your retirement, the education of your children, a vacation home, or the protection of your family for as little as $75 a month. If you wish, this amount can be deducted from your payroll check.

c. Have you often stayed awake at night wondering what would happen to your family if something happened to you?

d. Just call me at 555-1349, and I'll be glad to introduce you to one of our financial planning specialists.

Chapter 12

Procedures for Incoming Communications

LEARNING OBJECTIVES

After studying this chapter and completing the activities, you will be able to:

1. Understand the operation of the mail room.
2. Sort incoming mail properly.
3. Send and receive electronic mail.
4. Use proper procedures to process mail.
5. Handle mail appropriately during your employer's absence.

INTRODUCTION

Although electronic-based technologies, such as FAX and electronic mail (E-mail), are used by most executives, the delivery of hard copy and original documents has slowed very little. If anything, these alternative technologies have generated additional mail volume.

Handling incoming mail, both electronic-based and hard copy, is a visible means of demonstrating the efficiency and decision-making ability of the administrative assistant. Usually, the largest portion of the mail arrives from the mail room early in the morning. Many administrative assistants plan to process the mail (prepare it for the employer's attention) before the employer arrives so that action can be taken immediately. Additional mail may arrive throughout the day and must be handled in terms of its importance. Electronic-based mail should be handled as soon as it is received.

This chapter describes the techniques for processing mail: sorting, opening, recording, accumulating supporting information required for handling, reading and annotating contents, and arranging for presentation. Disposition of mail when the executive is absent from the office and when the administrative assistant works for several persons also is discussed.

MAIL-PROCESSING PERSONNEL

The first step in processing mail is sorting envelopes into groups for expeditious handling. The personnel involved in this function differ according to the way the mail is addressed and according to the size of the company.

The Mail Room

Mail room personnel receive mail from the post office, from an air express service company (see Figure 12-1), from a company mail service, or from a private mail service. It is not unusual for an organization to develop an internal mail service among its branches and its most frequent correspondents. This service can speed delivery by at least a day. The administrative assistant should become familiar with such services and their schedules.

If a letter is addressed to the company and not to an individual in the company, the envelope is opened in the mail room. The mail clerk follows established procedures for assigning the mail to the appropriate department.

The mail room is prepared for quantity handling of mail and contains equipment more elaborate than that found in individual offices. For instance, the mail room may include a mail opener that feeds, transports, removes envelope edges, disposes of waste, and stacks and counts opened envelopes all in a single operation. Another mail opener automatically processes mail of mixed sizes. Still another opens envelopes on two sides, the long end and one side; thus, contents of the envelopes are completely exposed, making their removal effortless.

In large companies, mail may be distributed from the mail room by a messenger who has an established route through the office. The messenger normally follows a fixed schedule for deliveries and pickup.

▼ TECHNOLOGY

Technological improvements in the mail room necessitate that mail room employees have a thorough knowledge of computers and other electronic equipment.

Fig. 12-1 Mail room personnel receive packages from a variety of sources, including air express service companies. *Photo courtesy of Federal Express Corporation.*

Automatic Delivery Cart. Many newer office buildings are equipped with automated delivery systems that bring mail to the administrative assistant's desk. Self-powered, unattended, robot-like carts move through the office on tracks or on an invisible path. They are programmed to make stops for mail pickup and delivery at specific locations in the office. An example of an automated delivery cart appears in Figure 12-2.

Fig. 12-2 This automated delivery cart is programmed to make stops for mail delivery and pickup.
Bell & Howell Mailmobile Company.

Computer-Controlled Vertical Conveyor. Computer-controlled selective vertical conveyor systems are being installed in newer office buildings to further automate mail services. This type of system moves heavy-duty containers in a continuous vertical loop throughout the building's floors. The system's computer directs the containers' movements and monitors all activity. Once the mail reaches the proper floor, it is delivered to a mini-mailroom and is delivered by a mail attendant.

The Administrative Assistant's Responsibilities

If letters are addressed to specific employees or departments, the mail room delivers the envelopes unopened. The administrative assistant usually gives the unopened envelopes to the addressees, with the exception of the employer's mail. The employer's mail is sorted, opened, and processed in ways that will expedite its handling when it is presented to the employer for action. In a small office, the administrative assistant opens all mail that is not addressed to a specific employee, gives it to the appropriate person for answering, and prepares the employer's mail for action.

ELECTRONIC MAIL

Electronic mail uses computer and telecommunication links to distribute messages to users of computer systems. The technology of electronic mail is discussed in detail in Chapter 8. When electronic mail is used, you will receive mail directly and may be given the capability to receive the executive's mail. The process of receiving electronic mail is similar to receiving printed mail. However, a number of the procedures such as date- and time-stamping are done automatically.

E-Mail Systems

Each person on the electronic mail system has a private mailbox that must be accessed with a specific code. Some executives choose to give their administrative assistants access to their codes so that messages can be received and processed in their absence. However, other executives may prefer to keep the access codes to their private mailboxes confidential. The administrative assistant must be careful to maintain the confidentiality of the executive's access code.

Incoming electronic messages can be viewed on the screen, as shown in Figure 12-3. If necessary, a copy of the message can be printed from the screen. Replies to messages can be sent via the electronic mail system. Most systems allow for electronic filing of the message so that it can be recalled at a later time. Messages also can be forwarded to others on the mailing list.

FI Mailbox	F2 Create	F3 System	F10 Help
From	Subject	Date	Time
MILLER	Files	10/19/XX	8:43a
LEWIS	Meeting	10/19/XX	9:12a
SINGER	Claims Info	10/19/XX	10:20a
THOMPSON	Proposal	10/19/XX	11:56a
Mailbox:	ROGERS		

Fig. 12-3 E-mail can be accessed by the administrative assistant on the computer screen as shown. A hard copy of the message can also be printed from the screen.

The electronic mailbox should be checked frequently during the day. Some systems can be programmed to automatically show a prompt on your computer screen when a message is waiting for you. Urgent messages should be processed immediately. These messages usually take precedence over other categories of mail.

Facsimiles

The facsimile (FAX) is another type of electronic communication that the administrative assistant will process frequently. If you have access to the FAX machine in your immediate office, you will be responsible for receiving the communications as they come in. However, if your company has only one FAX machine for the use of everyone, the FAX communication may be delivered to you by the administrative assistant responsible for the machine. You may be expected to retrieve the FAX for your employer when you are notified of its receipt.

Security Considerations

The increased use of electronic mail to communicate has raised new security considerations for the administrative assistant. Many confidential messages are sent via E-mail and FAX. However, it may be unwise to send confidential information using either medium unless the recipient is previously notified that the communication is being sent. Access to an E-mail box usually is controlled by a password. If you have access to your own E-mail box or your employer's, it is critical that you keep the password(s) secure. The best security measure is to memorize the password so that it is not recorded in writing. Many E-mail systems change the password of each user periodically to protect against security breaches.

Be aware that a number of people may have access to the FAX machine. It may be unwise to send confidential information using this medium unless you previously notify the recipient that a message is coming. If you are aware that material of a confidential nature is being sent to your employer, check the FAX machine frequently for messages. Do not leave incoming FAX communications where they can be read by those who should not have access to the information.

PROCEDURES FOR PROCESSING MAIL

The administrative assistant's role in processing the mail is a very sensitive one. Some executives want to see every piece of mail that comes in. Others want to give attention to only the most important communications and will appreciate the administrative assistant who takes on the burden of handling the routine pieces. Determine your employer's preferences and work style. Then demonstrate that you can assume responsibility for routine matters, but be careful not to assume unassigned authority. Steps to follow in sorting, opening, reading, and expediting the handling of incoming mail are discussed here.

Classifying and Sorting the Mail

Mail falls into seven categories:

1. Electronically delivered communications: facsimiles, hard copy printouts of electronic mail, and telegrams

2. Express mail, certified mail, priority mail, and registered letters and packages
3. First-class letters, including bills and statements, and personal mail
4. Interoffice communications
5. Newspapers and periodicals
6. Booklets, catalogs, and advertising material
7. Packages

The first four groups are delivered throughout the day and usually should receive first attention. However, some first-class mail may be put aside until all other priority communications have been processed. Electronic communications are delivered directly to you as soon as they are received. Someone, possibly you, has to sign for express, certified, and registered mail.

Express mail, a service provided by the post office, guarantees next-day delivery.

Certified mail is so designated on the envelope and is signed for on a form that is returned to the sender as proof of delivery.

Registered mail contains valuables, either papers or small articles, and involves special security measures to ensure safe delivery.

You can recognize first-class letters in regular envelopes by the amount of postage they carry and the dated postmark. Oversize first-class mail is sent in large manila envelopes with distinctive borders or is labeled *First Class* in a conspicuous way. As you become familiar with the employer's business activities and personal associations, noting the sender's return address and the postmark will help you identify business and personal correspondence of special interest.

First Sorting. On the first sorting select all electronically delivered communications, special-class mail, and important-looking first-class and interoffice mail for immediate processing. Put a large *X* on the back of any incorrectly addressed or odd-looking envelopes for the executive's attention. Unless you are authorized to open personal mail, leave these letters unopened (even though they are not marked *PERSONAL* or *CONFIDENTIAL*) and submit them with the processed mail. While you scan the mail, distinguish between urgent and routine items, putting the important items in the first group to be processed.

After completing the first sorting, stop and process the important mail according to the steps described in the Opening the Mail section on pages 298–301. Keep in mind that including something unimportant is preferable to missing something important.

Second Sorting. Sort the mail by kind in a second sorting. First process routine electronic and first-class mail. Sort it into like kinds—mail from branch offices, from the home office, from customers or clients, from traveling associates, from suppliers, from advertisers, and so on. Group first-class window envelopes; they usually contain invoices or statements. If instructed to do so, accumulate bills and statements for a specific bill-paying day. Otherwise they are submitted each day.

To get attention, *advertising mail* comes in envelopes of all sizes, shapes, and colors. You can easily spot it, although advertisers try hard to mislead you. The envelopes rarely, if ever, carry first-class postage. Open advertising mail when you have time, after other mail has been processed and handed to the executive. Do not destroy it. Executives like to keep up with *direct mail,* as it is called in the advertising profession, to know what is being advertised and whether to return the enclosed postcards.

Because of their bulkiness, put aside publications; later on, open, scan, and stamp or initial them as your employer's copies.

Opening the Mail

You need special supplies for opening mail. Place them on your desk before you start to work, arranging them within convenient reach.

You need:
An envelope opener
A stapler or clips
Pencils (several colors)
The tickler
A memo pad for *action* items

You may also need:
A date or time stamp
Adhesive notes
An action stamp or slips
Transparent tape for mending

You can save two-thirds of your envelope-opening time if you use either a hand operated or an electrically operated envelope-opening machine like the one pictured in Figure 12-4. Tap the lower edges of envelopes on the desk before opening them so that the contents fall to the bottom; then cut along the top edge. Keep the mail in the order in which it was sorted. Open all envelopes before removing the contents.

Fig. 12-4 An electrically driven mail opener can save two-thirds of your envelope-opening time. *Martin Yale/Wabash, IN (Model 6200 Letter Opener).*

Removing the Contents.   Remove the contents, flatten them, and stack them face-down at your right. If necessary, mend any cuts with transparent tape.

Hold the envelopes to the light to double-check for enclosures. Stack the opened envelopes to your left with open edges to the right and flap side up, in the same order as the contents to your right.

Use both hands to unfold and flatten letters; attach enclosures with staples or paper clips. Scan the letter to see if it contains the sender's address; if not, retrieve the envelope and attach it to the letter. Scan also to see if the letter mentions enclosures and whether those you found agree with the letter. If not, after checking inside the envelope again, underline the enclosure notation or the mention of the enclosure in the body of the letter; write *No* nearby. Attach any envelopes with missing enclosures to the letter, especially if the missing enclosures relate to forms of payment such as checks or money orders.

The interoffice chain envelope should always be saved. Draw a line through the last name on the envelope and reuse it. You will notice that these envelopes are usually perforated with holes so that all enclosures can be detected easily.

Registering, Dating, and Time-Stamping.   It is often desirable for the administrative assistant to keep a mail register of important mail should follow-up or tracing be necessary. The mail register is used to record special incoming mail (such as registered, certified, express, or insured mail) and expected (separate cover) mail. For expected bulk mail, it may be necessary to use a memo to inform the mail clerk or the receiving clerk that a package is coming.

The **mail register** is a protective record that verifies the receipt and disposition of mail. Only a few minutes are needed to record entries since abbreviations are used freely. A ruled form similar to the one shown in Figure 12-5 may be used. The blank space in the "Sep. Cov. Received" column, for example, indicates that the executive's banquet tickets have not yet arrived. As an aid in tracing lost mail, the administrative assistant usually indicates on the face of the item the number assigned to that item in the mail register. The date on which each piece of mail is received is important for several reasons:

Procedure

Administrative assistants say that a mail register is worth its weight in gold.

1. It furnishes a record of the date of receipt.
2. It furnishes an impetus to answer the mail promptly. (Each reply should be regarded as a builder of goodwill; no reply that is unduly delayed—no matter how courteous it may be—will promote good public relations.)
3. A letter may arrive too late to take care of the matter to which it refers. The date of receipt authenticates that inability.
4. The letter itself may be undated. The only clue to its date is the date of receipt. (You may find it hard to believe, but undated letters are frequently mailed—even letters prepared by administrative assistants.)

Fig. 12-5 Administrative assistants rely on the mail register to verify the receipt and disposition of mail.

MAIL REGISTER

Name _Craig Hedges_
Dates this page _3/14/--_

	RECEIVED Date	RECEIVED Time	FROM Name/Address	DATED	ADDRESSED TO Dept.	ADDRESSED TO Person	DESCRIPTION Kind of mail/enc/sep cov.	SEP. COV. RECEIVED	REFERRED To	REFERRED Date	WHERE FILED	FOLLOW-UP DATED
1	3/14	9:15 am	T. Gapinsky New York	3/12	Adv.		Ad pamphlet-layout		Adv.	3/14	Adv.	
2	3/18	9:00 am	Steel Equipment Co. Chicago	3/11		MLA	Expected catalogs file cabinets	3/21	Purch.	3/22	Purch.	
3	3/20	1:00 pm	G.N. Sims New York	3/19		MLA	ACA Banquet tickets					3/24
4	3/22	3:00 pm	L. Cox Lima, Ohio	3/18	Adv.		Book-- typefaces	4/10	Adv.	4/11	Adv.	
5	3/23	2:00 pm	D. Schmidt Chicago	3/22		MLA	Special delivery - rush order		Sales	3/23		
6	3/24	9:00 am	IRS- local	3/23		K. Logan	Quarterly taxes- forms enclosed		KL	3/24		4/1
7	3/26	2:00 pm	Jones, Inc. local	3/26	Acctg.		Registered Ch. #345		Cashier	3/26		
8	3/28	9:20 am	R. Fugazzi Denver	3/26		O. Miller	Insured package		Sales	3/28		

If the mail has not been date- and time-stamped in the mail room, do it at this point, either by hand or with a stamp. Show both the date and the time of day if the hour of receipt is important. Some administrative assistants use a date-time recorder to stamp the mail. An example appears in Figure 12-6. The date stamp is especially important if the communication is undated. It is also necessary because of the legal implications for some mail,

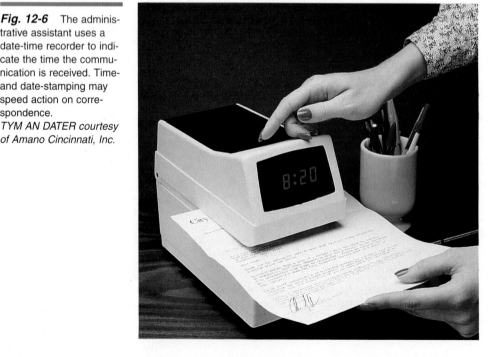

Fig. 12-6 The administrative assistant uses a date-time recorder to indicate the time the communication is received. Time- and date-stamping may speed action on correspondence.
TYM AN DATER courtesy of Amano Cincinnati, Inc.

such as bids. Occasionally, mail may be delayed in transit so long that the addressee needs the protection of the stamped date to determine where the time lag occurred. Stamping may also speed action on correspondence, especially in organizations that target replies for a same-day or a next-day response.

Reading, Underlining, and Annotating

After opening envelopes and dating the contents, you begin the interesting part of handling the mail. Follow these steps:

1. Read each communication through once, scanning for important facts. Make notes on your calendar and notes to yourself about getting needed information.

2. Underline or highlight words and phrases that tell the story as you read the correspondence again. Be thrifty with underlining and highlighting. Call attention only to what is necessary.

3. Annotate communications by writing any necessary or helpful notes in the margin or on Post-it Notes that can be attached to the correspondence. Refer to Figure 12-7.

4. Color-code your markings (if your employer approves this procedure) for those communications the employer must handle, those you can answer, and those to be referred to someone else.

Annotations come under two headings:

1. *Suggested disposition of routine correspondence.* The administrative assistant anticipates the executive's decision regarding the disposition of a communication by writing *File, Ack.* (for acknowledge), or *Give to Sales Department,* for example, in the margin or on a Post-it Note attached to the correspondence. However, the executive may overrule the administrative assistant's suggestion.

2. *Special notes.* These notes are usually reminders of some type. For example, the administrative assistant

Procedure

Post-it Notes provide the administrative assistant with a convenient means of attaching annotations to correspondence.

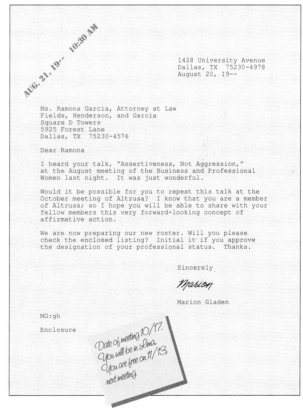

Fig. 12-7 The annotations and the date-time stamp indicate that this letter is ready for presentation to the executive.

might write *When Mr. B was here, you agreed to give this talk* to remind the executive of a commitment. If the communication is a follow-up, the administrative assistant might remove an item of correspondence from the files, attach it to the communication, and note *See our last correspondence attached* in the margin or on a Post-it Note. The administrative assistant may also annotate the message by providing a brief who's who of the sender.

You may ask, "Should I, as a new administrative assistant, read, underline, and annotate my employer's mail if my predecessor did not?" The answer is yes. Act as if it is a part of your understanding of a professional administrative assistant's service. If the employer questions the routine, abide by his or her decision. The employer is more likely to praise the practice, however, than to question it. If underlining and annotating are done intelligently, they save the employer time.

Notations for Filing.   As you open the mail, add filing notations on the communications that do not require replies. For example, if a reply to a communication can be filed without further correspondence, put the filing notation on the communication during processing. (Methods of determining where to file correspondence and when and how to make filing notations are presented in Chapter 7.)

Limiting Annotations.   Since original communications are sometimes copied on machines and sent outside the organization, an executive may ask you to avoid writing on the face of correspondence and to add annotations only on the back. Removable Post-it Notes are available in a variety of sizes and colors for annotating correspondence. These can be removed prior to copying. On the other hand, many executives want notations copied to achieve compact yet comprehensive records.

Expediting the Executive's Handling of Mail

You can expedite the executive's handling of specific communications by anticipating and preparing for certain procedural steps that will be taken. You can be of help by adopting the suggestions that follow.

Correspondence Requiring Background Information.   In many cases a communication cannot be answered unless additional information is at hand. For instance, correspondence about a real estate sale, a building project, or an insurance policy may require additional information before a response can be sent. You can look up and attach all pertinent information to the communication. You may have to judge how much background information to supply.

Correspondence Referring to Previous Communication.   When there is need to refer to a previous communication, attach the document to the current correspondence. Write *See attached* in the margin or on a Post-it Note. If the previous correspondence involves a bound file, clip the communication to the file and insert paper markers in the file to indicate pertinent points.

Correspondence Requiring Follow-Up.   Often a communication may refer to mail that will follow in a separate mailing, or it may contain a request that requires an action other than a routine answer. Sometimes a communication must be answered within a certain time. In such cases, follow these steps:

1. Select the earliest date when action should be taken.
2. Write the date on the face of the communication with a key (like *T* for *tickler*, or *FD* for *follow-up date*) so that the executive and you know that a reminder has been recorded.
3. Make a tickler entry under the selected date, and write the follow-up date in the mail register.
4. If material is expected in a separate mailing, write a note on your calendar and send a memo to the mail room describing the expected item. Indicate separate mailing notifications in the margin of the letter.

Correspondence to Be Referred to an Associate.   Often an executive passes along a piece of mail to an associate for either action or information. If you can anticipate your employer's preferences, you might fill out a Post-it Note for routing or an action slip (Figure 12-8), lightly penciling in both the associate's name and the action needed. Give the communication and the slip to your employer. If the suggested routing is approved, attach the slip to a copy of the communication, and forward it. The trend in most offices is to send photocopies to the attention of several persons at one time, as it speeds up the dissemination of information. Note the name(s) of the person(s) to whom you sent a copy, the action taken, and your own follow-up date.

Misaddressed Correspondence.   If a communication addressed to the executive actually should have been sent to another person, note the correct name in the top margin or on a Post-it Note and put the communication with the employer's other mail. Although you will probably be asked to forward the letter to

| DATE _____ |
| TO _____ |

Refer to the attached material and
- ☐ Please note.
- ☐ Please note and file.
- ☐ Please note and return to me.
- ☐ Please mail to _____
- ☐ Please note and talk to me
      this a.m._____; p.m._____
- ☐ Please answer, sending me a copy.
- ☐ Please write a reply for my signature.
- ☐ Please handle.
- ☐ Please have _____ photocopies made for
      _____
- ☐ Please sign.
- ☐ Please let me have your comments.
- ☐ Please RUSH – immediate action desired.
- ☐ Please make follow-up for_____
      _____

REMARKS:

Signed _____

Fig. 12-8 An administrative assistant devised this check-off slip to save the executive's time in distributing information to and requesting action from associates. There is room for a signature at the bottom of the slip because an initialed or signed request is more personal than a printed name.

someone else, you should give the addressee the right to see the communication first.

Personal Correspondence Opened Inadvertently.   If you should inadvertently open a personal letter addressed to your employer, stop reading the letter as soon as you discover that it is not office business. Refold the letter, replace it in its envelope, and attach a short note to the face of the envelope bearing your initials and *Sorry, opened by mistake.*

Enclosed Bill or Invoice.   When an envelope contains a bill or an invoice, if possible compare the prices and the terms with those quoted. Always check the mathematical accuracy of the extensions and the total. Write *OK* on the face of the bill or the invoice if it is correct, or note any discrepancies. Any computations in a letter should be checked for accuracy as well.

Enclosed Check or Money Order.   Compare the amount of an enclosed check or money order with the amount mentioned in the letter of transmittal or on the statement or invoice. If mailed alone, examine the check or money order against the file copy of the bill to verify the correctness of the amount. Handle the remittance according to the procedure of your office. If it is to be forwarded immediately to a cashier, indicate the amount in the margin of the letter or invoice; or prepare a memo for the executive, reporting the amount and the date of receipt.

Packages.   Packages should be processed before newspapers, periodicals, and advertisements. In some cases your mail register will alert you to watch for the arrival of a package. If you are handling a package marked *Letter Enclosed,* or if a first-class letter is attached, check the package contents before separating the letter from the package. Always examine the contents of a package at the time it is opened. If the contents are bulky and represent a quantity of like items, put a sample on the employer's desk and store the rest.

Publications.   Permanently identify each publication with the executive's name or initials. Scan the table of contents and indicate any item(s) that might be of interest to the executive. Attach a note to the front cover calling attention to the item(s).

Final Arrangement of the Mail

Arrangement of mail for presentation to the executive depends on preferences, daily schedule, or even mood. In general, though, the mail is separated into these five categories:

1. *For immediate action.* Possible order of precedence: electronic communications, important business letters, unopened personal letters, letters containing remittances, pleasant letters, unpleasant letters.

2. *To be answered.* Routine communications having no great priority.

3. *To be answered by administrative assistant.* Communications usually turned over to you for handling. (Don't preempt the executive's right to make this decision.)

4. *To be answered by someone else.* Communications usually routed to someone else.

5. *For your information.* Advertisements, publications, routine announcements.

One successful administrative assistant recommends the use of a five-pocket organizer for submitting mail, with each pocket clearly identified as to its contents. Another possibility is to separate the mail into color-coded folders, with a different-colored folder for each of the categories mentioned. Either method keeps the mail confidential. In any case, the mail should be covered if the executive is not at the desk when you present the processed communications.

HANDLING MAIL DURING THE EMPLOYER'S ABSENCE

Some executives spend a great deal of their time in travel. When they are away from the office, crises may occur in handling the mail. Simply forwarding personal mail or sending photocopies of incoming business mail will not always meet the situations that arise. The administrative assistant is in a decision-making role and must evaluate each piece of mail before giving it routine treatment. Before the executive leaves on an extended trip, the administrative assistant should get explicit instructions for handling such items as rent, telephone or utility bills, and other items that cannot wait until the executive returns.

The same caution is required for business mail. The employer should not receive a photocopy, forwarded and reforwarded, of correspondence that may be of a confidential nature. This kind of information should be transmitted by express mail. The administrative assistant must assume full responsibility for making the right decisions about handling mail in the employer's absence.

If the executive is traveling abroad, make copies of incoming mail and forward them overseas in packets. Number the packets. Overseas mail is not always dependable. If a packet goes astray, the numbering system helps the executive know whether all mail has been received. If 1 and 3 are the only packets received, 2 is obviously missing.

If the executive is traveling with a portable computer, the administrative assistant can send messages by electronic mail daily about important correspondence or matters that need the executive's attention. The executive can then forward appropriate instructions to the administrative assistant via E-mail for handling urgent situations.

When the executive is out of the office, you will be expected to do the following with the mail:

1. Maintain the mail register meticulously.
2. Communicate with the executive immediately when mail of vital importance arrives that no one else can handle.
3. Set aside communications that can await the executive's return, but acknowledge their receipt if the answer may be delayed for several days.
4. Give associates or superiors communications that must have immediate executive action. Make a photocopy of each one for the executive's information, noting to whom you gave it and stating the action taken.
5. Send copies (not originals) of communications that contain information of interest or importance, or that require the executive's personal attention, if they will arrive in time.
6. Answer or take personal action on communications that fall within your province of responsibility.
7. Prepare a digest of mail and either send it to the executive or keep it in the office to discuss when the executive calls, depending on circumstances (see Figure 12-9).

Fig. 12-9 When handling mail during the employer's absence, prepare a digest and either send it to the executive or keep it in the office to discuss when the executive calls.

DIGEST OF INCOMING MAIL

Date Rec'd	From	Description	Disposition
8/16	Clark Oil	Notice of Board of Directors meeting 9/4 in Chicago at 9.	Marked calendar.
8/16	Syracuse U.	Request to give telephone interview to School of Business students 11/13 at 10. Conflicts with staff meeting.	I wrote declining request.
8/16	J. K. Smith	Wants conference on proposed budget cuts.	Confirmed date and time; marked calendar.
8/16	Forbes	Wants more info on overseas operations.	Referred to MJB.
8/16	M. Mason	Wants conference on patent application for Project 117.	Confirmed date and time; marked calendar.

8. Collect in a folder labeled *Mail Received* (a) all original communications awaiting attention, (b) copies of all communications given to

others for action, and (c) both the originals of and answers to communications to which you have responded. Before giving the file to the executive, sort the correspondence into logical sequence, with the most important on top.

9. Hold the advertising mail in a separate large envelope. Sort it and give it to the executive after the trip is over and the pressure of accumulated work has lessened.

WORKING FOR MORE THAN ONE EXECUTIVE

For the administrative assistant who works for more than one executive, the mail processing routine is basically the same. Probably a higher level of decision making is required, because several employers' preferences and spheres of responsibility must be kept in mind and materials must be kept flowing to each one.

The administrative assistant will, of course, keep mail in separate stacks for each executive. If one executive obviously is waiting for the mail, that individual should get the first delivery of processed mail.

The value of the mail register increases when the administrative assistant is responsible for mail to several addresses. The register supplies proof of receipt for many different items of mail.

Summary

Processing incoming communications efficiently and effectively is a primary responsibility of the administrative assistant. In large organizations, mail room personnel handle the initial processing of incoming mail. In smaller offices, the administrative assistant opens all mail not addressed to a specific employee and distributes it to the appropriate people.

Classifying and sorting is the first step in processing mail. Incoming mail is classified into seven categories: electronic communications, special-class mail, first-class mail, interoffice communications, newspapers and periodicals, catalogs and advertising materials, and packages. The most important mail in the first four categories is processed after the first sorting. Routine mail is processed after the second sorting.

When opening the mail, the administrative assistant must remove all contents from the envelope, check for enclosures, and attach envelopes to appropriate correspondence for identification. All mail must be stamped with the date and time received.

Unless it is personal, the administrative assistant should read each letter for facts, make calendar notations, and underline or annotate helpful information for the executive. Filing notations should also be added. The administrative assistant can expedite the executive's handling of specific letters by anticipating steps that should be taken and preparing for them.

After the mail has been processed, it should be presented to the executive in the order of priority; mail that needs immediate action should be presented first.

When an executive travels a great deal, the administrative assistant must accept greater decision-making responsibility for the mail. This includes deciding which correspondence requires immediate communication with the executive, which can be handled by others in the office, and which should be handled by the administrative assistant.

QUESTIONS FOR DISCUSSION

1. What security precautions can you take when handling electronic communications?

2. Your employer frequently picks up the mail from your desk before you have an opportunity to process the mail as suggested in this chapter. What would you do?

3. The executive, Mr. Charles Yi, is away on a two-week trip. Decide what you would do with a letter that:

   a. Asks him to give a talk five months from now.

   b. Requires immediate management action.

   c. Is from his mother, whose handwriting you recognize.

4. In processing the morning mail for the president of a corporation, decide what you would do if:

   a. A letter refers to a letter the executive wrote nine months ago.

   b. A customer's letter complains about a sales representative who was discourteous.

   c. A letter asks that certain material be prepared and sent before the first of the month.

   d. A letter requests a photograph, the responsibility for which is in the public relations department.

   e. A letter contains important information for three department heads.

   f. An envelope obviously contains a bill from an engraver who recently supplied personal stationery for the executive.

5. What steps could you take to obtain the address of a person who keyed a request for product information and prices on a plain sheet of paper? No address was given on either the letter or the envelope.

6. If the executive is out of town but expects to return tomorrow, what action would you take to record receipt of the following communications? How would you handle each situation?

THINK IT *Through*

   a. An overnight delivery letter requesting an estimate on a large quantity of coated paper

   b. An electronic message from one of your branch sales representatives sending in a rush order for a customer

   c. A letter about a shipment of card stock complaining that one-fourth of the blue is two shades lighter than the rest (samples are enclosed as proof)

   d. A letter asking for the length of time a Mr. Edwards was employed as a sales representative by your company, his reason for leaving, and a reference

7. Punctuate the following sentences containing quotation marks. Use your Reference Guide to check your answers.

   a. "Stand on your own two feet", he snapped.

   b. The executive said "An attitude adjustment would help most of us".

   c. Have you ever heard a successful executive say, "I don't get much done in a day?"

   d. "Are you ready for the interview"? he inquired.

   e. The supervisor said "We are all working for the same purpose;" however, he did not realize that the schedule was unfair.

PROBLEMS

1. While your employer is on an extended business trip abroad, you make copies of incoming mail and forward the mail overseas in numbered packets. Your employer has received packets 1 and 3 but not packet 2. What would you do?

2. Mari Rodriguez is an administrative assistant with responsibility for processing incoming mail. Prepare your comments and suggestions for improving the steps she follows in performing this task.

   a. Ms. Rodriguez arranges all the mail in a stack and proceeds to open it and to remove the contents of each envelope in regular sequence.

   b. She flattens out the letters and enclosures and discards the envelopes.

   c. After all the letters have been removed, she checks them for stated enclosures. Pertinent enclosures she separates from the letters and sends to those concerned (such as orders for the order department). She discards the advertising.

d. She then time-stamps, reads, underlines, and annotates all letters. She prepares a routing slip for letters requiring the attention of more than one person, and she fastens each routing slip to the proper letter with a paper clip.

e. She then places the letters, in the order in which they were processed, on the executive's desk face-up for immediate attention.

TECHNOLOGY APPLICATIONS

▶ **TA12-1.TEM**   Using your word processing software, access the template disk and select the TA12-1.TEM file, which contains four letters received by your employer, Ms. Mary Jane Schmidt, as well as a mail digest form.

As you will see, you need to gather information so that Ms. Schmidt can respond to the letters. Where would you locate this information?

Proceed as follows:

1. Print out the letters and read them.

2. In each letter, underline and annotate the information needed for your response.

3. Read the letters critically; for example, check to see that amounts are accurate, that dates pose no conflicts, etc.

4. For each letter, key an entry on the mail digest form that will inform Ms. Schmidt of the response needed.

Chapter 13

Procedures for Outgoing Communications and Shipments

LEARNING OBJECTIVES

After studying this chapter and completing the activities, you will be able to:

1. Use appropriate domestic mail classifications when processing outgoing mail.
2. Identify and use special mail services that are available.
3. Use the recommended U.S. Postal Service procedures when addressing mail.
4. Purchase a domestic or international money order.
5. Identify the classifications of international mail and international air postal services.
6. Understand the advantages of each type of shipping service available and select the appropriate one for your company's shipping needs.

INTRODUCTION

The delivery of documents by mail services provided by the U.S. Postal Service and private carriers continues at about the same level as in the past.

Mailing costs are a major expense in every company. In a large organization, the administrative assistant sends much of the outgoing mail to a mail department for dispatch; but the administrative assistant may also bypass this department by preparing and sending business mail, including packages, directly. In a small office, though, the administrative assistant has complete responsibility for the mail.

With the continuing increases in postal rates, businesses are making every effort to reduce these costs and to improve postal delivery service. Transmittal expenses can be reduced greatly by the administrative assistant who is familiar with postal information and services and keeps up-to-date with changes in postal regulations and procedures.

This chapter describes domestic and international mail classifications and explains special mail services. It discusses mail collection and delivery, and the use of money orders. In addition, this chapter offers suggestions for speeding mail delivery and reducing postal expense.

DOMESTIC MAIL CLASSIFICATIONS

Domestic mail includes mail transmitted within, among, and between the United States, its territories and possessions, the Military Postal Service, and the United Nations in New York City.

The U.S. Postal Service divides domestic mail into the following general classes: first class, priority mail, express mail, second class, third class, fourth class, official and free mail, and mail for the visually handicapped. The best source of mailing information is the *Domestic Mail Manual,* which is updated regularly and may be purchased from the Superintendent of Documents, U.S. Government Printing Office, Washington, DC 20402-9371. General descriptions of each mail classification, taken from this manual, are given in this chapter. Rates and fees are not provided since they are subject to change. For current information, consult the publications available from your local post office.

First-Class Mail

All first-class mail is sent by air where available. If air service is not available, first-class mail is sent by the fastest means available. First-class mail refers to items weighing no more than 11 ounces. Items weighing more than 11 ounces that are to be sent by the fastest available means are classified as priority mail.

First-class mail includes letters, postcards, business reply mail, and bills and checks. All first-class envelopes should be sealed.

Because mail has to conform to automated sorting machine measurements, a surcharge (a fee in addition to applicable postage) is assessed on each piece of nonstandard-sized mail. Items subject to this surcharge are first-class letters and postcards more than 6 1/8 inches high, 11 1/2 inches long, or 1/4 inch thick. Mail that is less than 0.007 inches thick, 3 1/2 inches high, or 5 inches long is also surcharged. All envelopes must be rectangular in shape.

Postage for first-class items is charged on the first ounce. If mail weighs more than one ounce, the rate for the second ounce is less than for the first—a fact that many mailers are not aware of.

Priority Mail

Priority mail is given a separate classification by the Postal Service. Priority mail consists of first-class mail weighing more than 11 ounces and, at the option of the mailer, any other mail matter (including regular first-class mail) weighing 11 ounces or less. The maximum weight for priority mail is 70 pounds; the maximum size and girth (distance around) combined is 108 inches. Packages sent by priority mail are given preferential handling and are shipped by air or by selected ground transportation. Packages, either sealed or unsealed, can be mailed at any post office (not in mail collection boxes). Delivery is made within two or three days. Charges are assessed by zones: the longer the travel distance, the higher the rate. Priority mail is often less expensive than overnight express service.

The mailer who wants to send a large envelope by either first-class or priority mail should designate the class on both the front and the back of the envelope to ensure it is not handled as third-class mail. Special oversized envelopes with green diamond borders for first-class mail and red diamond borders for priority mail are available to make the mailer's preferences known.

Express Mail

Express mail is the fastest, most reliable postal service available for sending both letters and packages in most metropolitan areas. There are five service offerings: Express Mail Next Day Service, Express Mail Second Day Service, Express Mail Custom Designed Service, Express Mail Same Day Airport Service, and Express Mail International Service.

- *Express Mail Next Day Service* is designed for mailers whose needs for reliable overnight delivery do not recur on a regular basis. Mail deposited by a certain time (usually 5 p.m.) at a designated post office or collection box is delivered by 3 p.m. the next day, including weekends and holidays.

- *Express Mail Second Day Service* is designed for mailers who need faster service than first-class or priority mail provides, but do not need overnight delivery. Mail deposited by a certain time (usually 5 p.m.) at a designated post office or collection box is delivered by 3 p.m. the second day after mailing, including weekends and holidays.

- *Express Mail Custom Designed Service* is offered under an agreement to customers who make regularly scheduled shipments. Agreements are tailored to meet customers' individual needs.

- *Express Mail Same Day Airport Service* provides service between major airports within the United States. The customer takes letters or packages to the airport mail facility (AMF), and they are dispatched on the next available flight to the destination airport. The letters or packages are made available for claim by the addressee according to times determined when the items are deposited at the originating airport.

- *Express Mail International Service* is offered under a service agreement to many countries. On Demand Service, similar to Next Day Service, is available to some countries without a service agreement for the occasional user. International service is constantly expanding with the addition of new countries.

Second-Class Mail

Second-class mail includes newspapers and periodicals. Publishers and news agencies are granted second-class rates if they file the proper forms (obtained from their local post offices), pay the required fees, and comply with the regulations. Such mail must bear notice of second-class entry and be mailed in bulk lots. As an administrative assistant, you may not be responsible for bulk mailings, but you may mail single copies of a publication in the second-class category.

Third-Class Mail

Third-class mail weighs less than 16 ounces and is used for matter that cannot be classified as first- or second-class mail. The same matter in parcels weighing 16 ounces or more is considered fourth-class mail. More than half of all mail falls into the third-class category. Mail that may be sent third class includes merchandise and bound or printed matter such as catalogs, circulars, and postcards. Special rates also apply to books, manuscripts, music, sound recordings, films, and the like.

Rates charged vary for single piece and bulk third-class mailings. The bulk third-class rate applies to mailings that meet the following requirements:

1. The mailing weight must be at least 50 pounds or include 200 pieces of mail.

2. All pieces in each mailing must belong to the same category. You may not do a bulk mailing of 50 postcards, 50 small packages, and 100 circulars.

3. Bulk mail must contain only a general message directed at everyone who receives it and not a personal message directed at a specific individual.

4. All mail in the bulk mailing must be sent to a destination within the United States.

Fourth-Class Mail

The more common term for fourth-class service is *parcel post*. It includes all mailable matter not in first, second, or third class weighing 16 ounces or more.

Parcel post rates are scaled according to the weight of the parcel and the distance it is being transported. Every local post office charts the country into eight zones. Zone charts showing the parcel post zone of any domestic post office in relation to the sender's post office may be obtained free from the sender's post office.

Fourth-class parcels mailed for delivery in the United States may not weigh more than 70 pounds and may not exceed 108 inches in length and girth combined. Figure 13-1 illustrates the steps to follow when computing the size of a parcel. There are also special rates according to weight and zone for bound printed matter weighing 16 ounces or more.

It is a good idea to include the name and address of both the addressee and the sender inside a parcel post package just in case the outside address is damaged or becomes unreadable. Also, if the contents of the package are perishable or fragile, put a label on the wrapper that says either *Perishable* or *Fragile*.

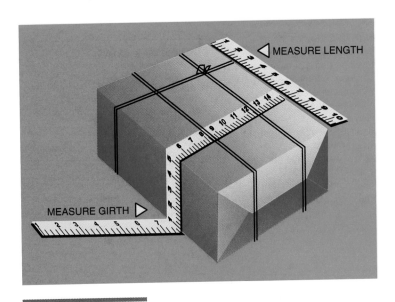

Fig. 13-1 To determine the size of a parcel, measure the longest side to get the length; measure the distance around the parcel at its thickest part to get the girth; add the two figures together. For example, a parcel 10 inches long, 8 inches wide, and 4½ inches high measures 35 inches, length and girth combined (10 inches + 4½ inches + 8 inches + 4½ inches + 8 inches). A free pamphlet, "Packaging for Mailing," may be obtained from your post office.

Official and Free Mail

Federal government offices and personnel send out official mail without affixing postage. There are two kinds of official mail: franked mail and penalty mail.

A *franked* piece of mail must have a real or facsimile signature of the sender in place of the stamp, and the words *Official Business* must appear on the address side. Only a few persons, such as the Vice President of the United States, members and members-elect of Congress, the Secretary of the Senate, and the Sergeant at Arms of the Senate, are authorized to use the frank.

Penalty mail is used for official government correspondence. It travels in penalty envelopes or under penalty labels marked *Official Business—Penalty for Private Use.* Examples of a franked piece of mail and penalty mail appear in Figure 13-2.

Free mail is sent without postage by the public. It is limited to a few items, such as census mail and absentee ballot envelopes from members of the armed forces.

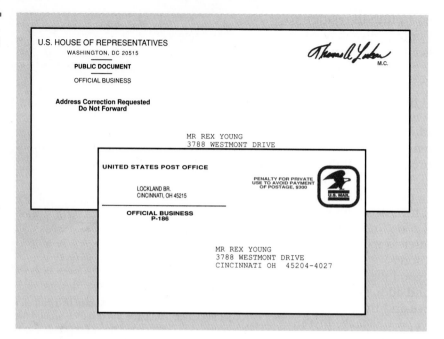

Fig. 13-2 Notice the difference between a franked envelope and a penalty envelope. A franked envelope must show a real or facsimile signature and carry the words OFFICIAL BUSINESS. A penalty envelope must carry the penalty warning and the words OFFICIAL BUSINESS under a return address.

Mail for the Visually Handicapped

Some kinds of mail to and from the blind may be mailed at no charge; other kinds of mail may be sent at nominal rates. If, as an administrative assistant, your work involves sending letters and parcels to or from the blind, consult your local post office.

Mixed Classes of Mail

When you want two pieces of mail of different classes to reach the recipient at the same time, sometimes it is better to send them together in a single mailing by labeling the package *First-Class Mail Enclosed* or by attaching the first-class letter to the outside of the package. Delivery time is determined by the mail classification of the package; therefore, a first-class letter attached to a four-pound package will go as fourth-class mail.

Electronic Messages

The administrative assistant frequently will be required to send electronic messages. These messages may be sent in a number of ways, including facsimile and electronic mail. A detailed discussion of each of these electronic message systems is presented in Chapter 8.

The administrative assistant must decide the most appropriate system to use when sending electronic messages. Factors to consider are whether the recipient has the appropriate electronic equipment, the cost, the speed with which the message must be delivered, and the type of document being sent.

SPECIAL MAIL SERVICES

In addition to transmitting mail, the post office provides many special services. The sender should be aware, however, that fees for such services may be high.

Registered and Insured Mail

▶ *Procedure*

If you must send packages or documents that are particularly valuable or important, you can use one of several tracking and documentation services offered by the U.S. Postal Service.

A piece of important or valuable mail can be registered or insured, depending on its nature. These special services are described in this section.

Registering Mail.   First-class or priority mail can be registered. It is the safest way to send valuables through the mail system. This service provides a record of when the material was mailed, where it traveled, and when it was delivered. In addition, items sent via registered mail can be insured for up to $25,000. The fee charged is based on the worth of the items.

Insuring Mail.   A piece of third- or fourth-class mail, or priority mail containing third- or fourth-class matter, may be insured up to a specific amount (check with the post office for the current amount). The package is taken to the post office window where the clerk makes out a receipt for it, stamps the package *Insured,* and puts the receipt number on it. After placing the regular and insured postage on the package, the clerk gives the receipt to the sender for filing. If the package is lost or damaged, the post office reimburses the sender according to the amount of its insured value.

First-class mail cannot be insured because it is sealed against inspection. Therefore, if first-class mail needs special protection because of its importance or value, it should be sent via registered mail.

Return Receipts and Restricted Delivery.   The sender is always furnished with a receipt showing that the post office accepted a piece of insured or registered mail for transmittal and delivery. However, the sender often wants legal evidence that the piece of mail was also received by the addressee. For an added fee, the sender may obtain a signed receipt, commonly called a *return receipt,* on any piece of certified or registered mail or on any piece of mail insured for more than $50.

Business Reply Mail

Business reply mail is used by businesses to encourage responses to their mailings by paying the postage for those responses. This mail is returned to

Fig. 13-3 A business reply envelope with a bar code.

any valid address in the United States. The mailer guarantees to pay the postage for all replies which are returned. The postage per piece is the regular first-class rate plus a fee. See Figure 13-3 for an example.

COD Service

Merchandise may be sent to a purchaser *COD*—that is, *collect on delivery*—if the shipment is based on a bona fide order or on an agreement made with the addressee by the sender. The sender often prepays the postage and the COD fees, but the postage and fees may be included in the amount to be collected if this arrangement is agreeable to the addressee. Otherwise, the addressee pays the amount due on the merchandise, plus the fee for the money order to return the money collected to the sender. The maximum amount collectible on a COD transaction is $600.

Certificates of Mailing

Proof that a piece of mail has been taken to the post office for dispatching may be obtained for a few cents for any kind of mail. The sender fills in the required information on a certificate blank, pastes on the appropriate stamp, and hands this certificate to the postal clerk with the piece of mail. The clerk cancels the stamp and hands the certificate back to the sender as evidence that the piece of mail was received.

This is an economical service when someone is mailing something of value to the addressee but has no obligation or responsibility to pay to have the material insured, registered, or certified. It also furnishes senders with inexpensive proof that they have mailed tax returns.

Certified Mail

Certified mail requires that the addressee's post office maintain a record of delivery for two years. In addition to the regular postage, the sender pays to have the mail carrier obtain a signature from the addressee upon delivery. Certified mail is appropriate for first-class mail that has no monetary value, such as letters, bills, contracts, or tax returns. It carries no insurance. If a sender requests a return receipt, an additional fee is charged (see Figure 13-4).

Special Delivery and Special Handling

The delivery of a piece of mail may be hurried along by the use of *special delivery* or *special handling* services. These services are described in the following paragraphs.

Special Delivery.   *Special delivery* service may be purchased for all classes of mail, except express mail, to provide for prompt delivery. Mail must be marked **Special Delivery** above the address. Immediate delivery is by messenger during prescribed hours to points within certain limits of any post office or delivery station. Special delivery mail should not be sent to post office box addresses, military installations, or other places where mail delivery will not be expedited after arrival.

Special Handling.   Many people are not aware that a service called *special handling* is available for third- and fourth-class mail. The fee for this service, which provides the most expeditious handling and ground transportation practicable, is less expensive than the fee for special delivery. Parcels move with first-class mail, but they do not receive immediate delivery when they reach the destination post office.

Stamps and Other Supplies

Ordinary postage stamps are available in sheet, coil, or booklet form. Postage stamps can be exchanged at full value if stamps of the wrong denomination were purchased or if damaged stamps were received. Envelopes with imprinted stamps are also available. *Precanceled stamps* and *precanceled stamped envelopes* may be used only by persons or companies that have been issued a permit to use them. Also, they may be used only on letters or parcels presented at the post office where the precanceled stamps or envelopes were purchased. The advantage of precanceled stamps and precanceled stamped envelopes is the saving of canceling time at the post office.

To facilitate in-company printing of standard messages in batches, postal cards are available from the post office in continuous sheets. The post

P 989 038 337
RECEIPT FOR CERTIFIED MAIL
NO INSURANCE COVERAGE PROVIDED
NOT FOR INTERNATIONAL MAIL
(SEE REVERSE SIDE)

Sent to *Mr. William Strong*

Street and No. *19785 Henry Road*

P.O., State and ZIP Code *Cleveland, Ohio 44126-3117*

Postage	$	29
Certified Fee		1.00
Special Delivery Fee		
Restricted Delivery Fee		
Return Receipt showing to whom and Date Delivered		1.00
Return Receipt showing to whom, Date, and Address of Delivery		
TOTAL Postage and Fees	$	2.29
Postmark or Date		

PS Form 3800, June 19--

CINCINNATI OH APR 13 19 LOVELAND BR

Fold at line over top of envelope to the right of the return address

CERTIFIED

P 989 038 337

MAIL

Fig. 13-4 A receipt for certified mail shows the itemized charges for the service including the regular postage fee, the certified fee, and the return receipt service fee.

office also sells other mail supplies such as shipping containers and packaging materials.

Metered Postage

TECHNOLOGY

The electronic postage scale and meter can streamline the processing of mail.

One of the quickest and most efficient ways of affixing postage to mail of any class is by means of a *postage meter.* The meter prints the postmark and the proper amount of postage on each piece of mail. Metered mail need not be canceled or postmarked when it reaches the post office. As a result, it often catches earlier trains, trucks, or planes than does nonmetered mail.

The postage meter may be fully automatic, not only printing the postage, postmark, and date of mailing but also feeding, sealing, and stacking the stamped envelopes. Figure 13-5 shows an automated mailing system that includes a postage meter. Some models can also print the postage on gummed tape that can be pasted onto packages. The meter registers the amount of postage used on each piece of mail, the amount of postage remaining in the meter, and the number of pieces that have passed through the machine.

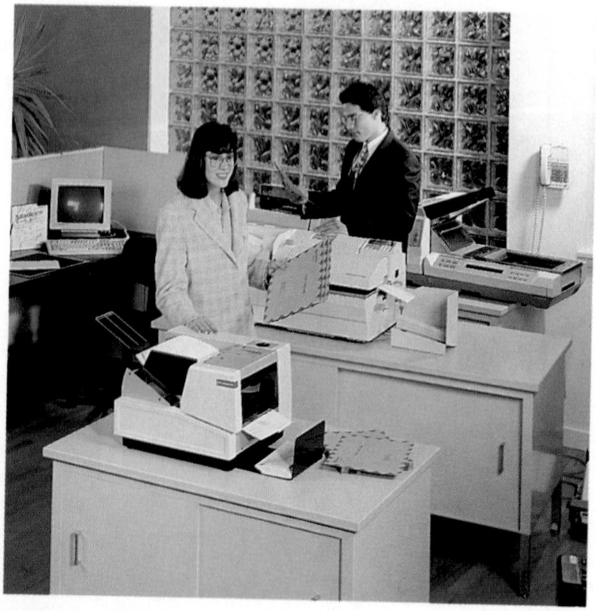

Fig. 13-5 The automated mailing system that includes a postage meter can calculate the exact postage cost and charge the cost to the appropriate department.
Pitney Bowes Mailing Systems.

The machine itself is purchased outright, but the meter mechanism is leased. In order to use a postage meter, a company first must obtain a meter license by filing an application with the post office where the company's mail is handled. The application must tell the make and model of the meter. A record of use must be maintained in a *Meter Record Book* supplied by the post office.

Postage must be purchased for the meter machines from the post office before the machine can be used. Some meter mechanisms must be carried physically to the post office so that the postage can be replenished. However, the newer meter machines can be replenished via telephone line connections to the post office.

Forwarded, Returned, and Remailed Mail

Unfortunately, mail does not always reach its final destination on first mailing. Some pieces must be forwarded, returned to the sender, or remailed. Additional postage may or may not be required.

Forwarding Mail.   The administrative assistant is often required to forward mail. First-class mail up to 11 ounces can be forwarded with no additional postage. Second-class, third-class, or fourth-class mail requires additional postage to forward mail to a new address.

Registered, certified, insured, COD, and special handling mail can be forwarded without payment of additional registry insurance, COD, or special handling fees; however, ordinary forwarding postage charges, if any, must be paid. Special delivery service will not receive special delivery mailings at a second address unless a change-of-address card has been filed.

Return of Undeliverable Mail.   An undeliverable first-class letter will be returned to the sender free of charge. For undeliverable third- or fourth-class parcels, the sender must pay full postage for the return service. To assure that third- and fourth-class packages are returned, *Return Postage Guaranteed* should be conspicuously placed below the return address.

Remailing Returned Mail.   The administrative assistant is always chagrined when mail is returned. Any piece of mail returned that has been rubber-stamped *RETURN TO SENDER* with the reason indicated by a "pointing finger" must be put in a fresh, correctly addressed envelope; and postage must be paid again.

Change of Address

The post office serving you must be notified officially by letter or by a post office form when you change your address. The old and new addresses and the date when the new address is effective must be given. Correspondents should be notified of a new address promptly by special notices or by stickers attached to all outgoing mail. The post office supplies new address cards free of charge for personal and business use.

Recalled Mail

Occasionally, it may be necessary to recall a piece of mail that has been posted. This calls for fast action. Type an addressed envelope that duplicates the one mailed. Go to the post office in your mailing zone if the letter is local or to the central post office if the letter is an out-of-town mailing. Fill in a *Sender's Application for Recall of Mail.*

If the mail is an undelivered local letter, on-the-spot return will be made. If the letter has left the post office for an out-of-town address, the post office (at the sender's request and expense) will wire or telephone the addressee's post office and ask that the letter be returned. If the mail has already been delivered, the sender is notified, but the addressee is not informed that a recall was requested.

MAIL COLLECTION AND DELIVERY

A number of plans have been inaugurated by the Postal Service to improve operations and reduce costs. An explanation of some of these plans follows.

Proper Addresses for Mail

Procedure

ZIP + 4 is a constantly changing process, so it is necessary to update address software lists on a regular basis.

The ZIP (Zone Improvement Plan) Code was designed to speed mail deliveries and to facilitate the use of automated equipment in the processing of mail. The ZIP Code originally conceived by the U.S. Postal Service in 1963 was five digits. In 1981 the Postal Service introduced a nine-digit ZIP Code. The ZIP + 4 Code includes the original five digits plus four additional digits preceded by a hyphen. For example, a ZIP + 4 Code might be 45227-1035. With four more digits, the Postal Service can pinpoint mail delivery, permitting the fine sorting of mail down to an individual carrier's route. Use of the ZIP + 4 Code is voluntary.

All bulk mailers of second- or third-class mail are required to use ZIP Codes. Failure to do so may subject the mail to a postal rate penalty. When the mail is being sorted, an item with no ZIP Code goes into the reject slot, delaying the sorting operation.

A *National ZIP Code and Post Office Directory* can be purchased from the Postal Service. The directory is updated regularly. Other sources of ZIP Codes are available from a variety of publishers.

To permit the use of scanning machines with limited capabilities for scanning spaces per line, the Postal Service has designed and approved a two-letter abbreviation for each state and abbreviations for cities with long names. These abbreviations should be used on all mail. The list of approved state abbreviations is presented on pages 799–801 of this book.

Optical character readers that electronically scan addresses are used in most post offices. They are programmed to scan a specific area on all envelopes, so the address must be completely within this read zone, single-spaced, in all capital letters, without punctuation, using the blocked style. The two-letter state abbreviations must be used. Acceptable placement for an address is shown in Figure 13-6. Optical character readers are discussed in more detail in Chapter 5.

Bar Codes

Procedure

You can obtain postage discounts by bar coding your outgoing mail.

The post office uses bar code readers to automate the sorting of mail. A series of bars and half-bars, representing an address, can be electronically scanned and sorted at amazing speed. The bar code contains the ZIP Code and certain letters and numbers from the address. The code is imprinted as well as the address. Bar coding is always used on business reply envelopes, as shown in Figure 13-3. In addition, companies are bar coding their outgoing mail in order to obtain additional postage discounts.

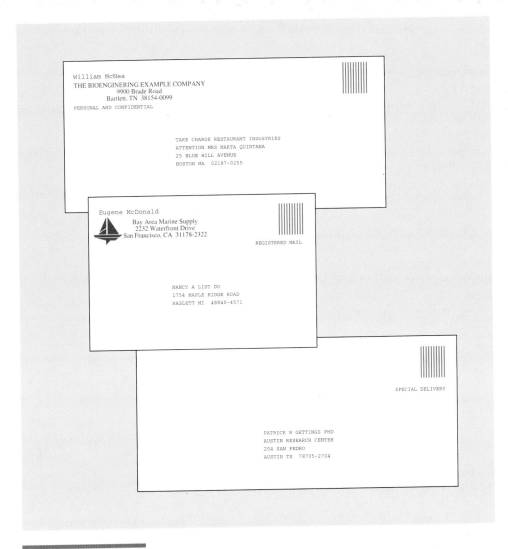

Fig. 13-6 Post office optical character readers are designed to scan a specific area on all envelopes. The illustration shows the proper location of the address as well as the proper format for addresses.

Mail Presorting

To encourage those mailing large quantities to presort mail before depositing it, the Postal Service grants a reduction of a few cents in postage on each presorted piece. To qualify for the reduction, a minimum of 500 first-class pieces must be included in each mailing. For the specifics on presorting, contact your local post office.

Postal regulations require five or more pieces of metered mail to be bundled and identified. Presorted bundles of metered mail are indicated by color-coded labels. For example, mail for the same state would be coded with an orange label bearing an *S,* and all mail for the same firm would carry a blue label with an *F* on it.

Presorting large amounts of mail is a complicated procedure that involves sorting customers for particular subsets; producing a mailing list; sorting the list by ZIP Code; printing the list in order on envelopes or labels; stuffing and sealing envelopes; and preparing the mail for the Postal Service. This procedure is not possible without some level of automation. Most companies that send out these large amounts of mail now use address software. This address software must be updated on a regular basis. The software vendor gets the updated addresses from the Postal Service and provides these updates to its customers.

The administrative assistant who is responsible for mailing smaller amounts of mail also should presort mail for speedier handling by the post office. Before depositing mail, separate it into major categories, such as local, out-of-town, precanceled, and metered. It can then bypass one or more preliminary handlings in the post office. Types of presorting vary with the types of individual mailings. For instance, if most of the mail goes to in-state addresses, this mail may be kept separate and identified as "All for [State]," thus eliminating one sorting operation.

Post Office Boxes

Renting a post office box allows you to pick up mail at any time the post office building is open. Mail can be obtained faster from post office boxes than from carriers.

General Delivery

Mail may be addressed to individuals in care of the *General Delivery* window of main post offices. This service is convenient to transients and to individuals who have no definite address in a city. Such mail is held for a specified number of days and, if not called for, is returned to the sender. Executives on touring vacations or sales representatives who are on the road for several days and do not have specific hotel addresses frequently ask to have mail addressed in care of *General Delivery* to a city on their itinerary.

Mailing List Updates

The mailer can do a great deal to obtain information about changes of address by using first-class mail marked *Address Correction Requested* and guaranteeing return postage. The postmaster also will update any list of local mailing addresses at the expense of the mailer. If the company uses address software, the addresses must be updated through the software vendor.

Private Mail Delivery

Private carriers also transport mail. Several companies provide overnight letter delivery to most major United States markets. The maximum weight for an overnight letter is two ounces or the equivalent of ten 8 1/2-by-11-inch folded pages. A special pouch is used to deliver an overnight letter.

Some companies use their own employees to deliver unstamped letters to companies with whom they conduct a large volume of business.

Automated Mail Room Equipment

Saving money on the cost of postage and the operation of the mail room is high on most every company's list of priorities. Businesses are increasing the efficiency of the mail room by using a number of electronic mail-handling devices.

An electronic postage scale can compute domestic and international mailing rates and shipping fees. Any weight restrictions that might prevent mailing are also indicated. The scale interfaces (connects) with a postage meter. An operator can place the scale in letter mode for envelope processing or in parcel mode for dispensing gummed meter tapes for packages. Electronic accounting devices can be attached to mailing equipment to record and print a daily record of postage totals and piece counts for each department in a company. Accounting devices that interface with mailing equipment enable a company to keep an accurate record of postage expenditures.

Other equipment related to mail room operation, such as folding and inserting machines, bar code printers, electronic embossers, collators, and copiers, is also being automated. The use of this equipment enables mail room personnel to keep up with the increasing flow of mail being produced in the office. An electronic mailing system weighs letters and packages, computes the most efficient rate for mailing, and makes a record of the transaction in one operation. Figure 13-7 shows electronic mailing equipment in use.

▶ *Procedure*

Companies that automate their own mail processing assume some of the most time- and labor-intensive tasks of the Postal Service. In exchange, they qualify for discounts in postage, offsetting some of the effects of rate increases.

POSTAL MONEY ORDERS

Money may be transferred from one person or business to another with the use of a *money order*. There are instances in which money orders are the requested form of payment. They are also a convenience to individuals who do not have a checking account.

Fig. 13-7 Electronic mailing equipment. *Pitney Bowes Mailing Systems.*

Domestic Money Orders

Postal money orders may be purchased at all post offices, branches, and stations. The maximum amount for a single *domestic money order* is $700. However, several money orders may be purchased at one time with a sales limit of $10,000 in face value on any day. Money orders are also available at a low rate to savings bank depositors and at other businesses, such as drugstores and supermarkets.

International Money Orders

Money may be sent to a foreign country by means of an *international money order* procurable at local post offices. When buying such an order, you are given a receipt by the postal clerk, who then arranges to send the money order abroad. Exact information is required regarding the payee and the payee's address. If the payee is a woman, you must state whether she is single, married, or widowed. The purpose of the payment should also be stated. Limits on the maximum amount of an international money order vary with the individual country.

INTERNATIONAL MAIL

The Postal Service participates in an international communications network that provides surface and air mail services for correspondence, printed material, and merchandise to almost any destination in the world. Correspondence and other documents may be transmitted electronically to some countries through the Postal Service's INTELPOST service.

Classifications of International Mail

International postal service provides postal union mail, parcel post, and express mail international service. These services are described in the following paragraphs.

Postal Union Mail.   Postal union mail is divided into two categories. *LC Mail* (letters and cards) consists of letters, letter packages, air letters (aerogrammes), and postcards; *AO Mail* (other articles) consists of printed matter, merchandise samples without salable value, commercial papers, small packets, and matter for the blind.

The postage for letters and postal cards mailed to other countries varies. The rates are normally higher than U.S. rates, and weights are limited. Specific information can be obtained from the Postal Service by the administrative assistant when correspondence is mailed. However, if your company handles a significant amount of international correspondence, you should obtain a copy of the *International Mail Manual* from the Postal Service.

Parcel Post.   Parcels for transmission overseas are mailed by parcel post. These packages may be registered or insured. Special handling services are also available. There is no international COD service. Since rates, weight limitations, and other regulations are not the same for all countries, the administrative assistant should obtain information from the post office about requirements for a particular shipment.

Express Mail International Service.   Express mail international service is exchanged with other countries under agreements and memorandums of understanding with the postal administrations of other countries. The two types available are custom-designed service and on-demand service.

International Air Postal Services

Rates on letters by air to foreign countries are charged at a fixed rate for a half ounce. International air postal services include air letters and air parcel post.

Air Letters (Aerogrammes).   For less than the cost of sending a regular air letter, the post office sells an *air letter* sheet that may be mailed to any country with which the United States maintains airmail service. Prestamped airmail, it is a lightweight single sheet that folds into an envelope for sealing and mailing. No enclosures, either paper or other kinds, are permitted. Subject to prior approval of the Postal Service, firms engaged in international trade may print their own aerogramme letterheads.

International Air Parcel Post.   A Parcel Post Customs Declaration form must be completed for all *international air parcel post* shipments. This service is available to nearly all countries and is priced according to the first four ounces and each additional four ounces according to the country of destination.

SHIPPING SERVICES

Shipments can be made by air, rail, ship, bus, truck, and van. The administrative assistant needs to know the advantages of each and the sources to investigate for current information. The following discussion deals with two shipping services: parcel delivery and freight.

Parcel Delivery Services

A number of companies deliver packages to all 50 states either by air or by truck. Delivery times vary, from overnight to four or five days, depending on the distance from point of origin to delivery. In some cases parcels are limited in weight and size. Delivery policies vary from company to company. Refused or undeliverable packages are returned to the sender. Rates are based on weights and delivery zones.

Most parcel delivery companies offer overnight or second-day delivery service. This service is similar to Express Mail Service provided by the U.S. Postal Service.

Air Service.   Air service is the fastest and most expensive means of transporting letters and packages. Many companies provide express air service for letters at a flat rate. The charge for packages varies with the size and weight of the package. Pickup and delivery is included in the fee. Next-day delivery is assured to most points in the United States. Some companies guarantee delivery to every address in the 48 contiguous states. Companies such as Emery Air Freight Corp., Federal Express Corp., Purolator Courier Corp., and United Parcel Service, Inc., own their own air fleets and can provide faster service than those using commercial planes. Some airlines also offer express air service for small parcels.

Van Service.   Some companies offer van service within metropolitan areas or to points not easily accessible by air. For example, Purolator supplements its air express service by using vans to ship packages up to 70 pounds and 108 inches in combined length and girth.

Bus Service.   If speedy delivery of a package to a small town in another part of the state is necessary, the administrative assistant may consider bus service. This service is useful particularly when destination points are not located in the vicinity of airports. Round-the-clock service is offered, including service on Sundays and holidays. Between many points, same-day bus service is available.

Choosing a Service.   With so many choices, the shipper needs to make constant comparisons of costs and services. For current service and rates, call the agencies listed in the Yellow Pages that offer courier or delivery service.

Freight Services

Freight is generally thought of as a shipment sent by any method other than mail or courier. It is the most economical service used to transport heavy, bulky goods in large quantities. Because freight shipping is the most complex of all methods, the administrative assistant will probably not be required to select the carrier and to route the shipments. Still, it is good to know a few of the salient facts.

Railroad Freight.   Ordinarily, when goods are shipped by railroad freight, they must be delivered by the shipper (consignor) to the local freight office. When the shipment arrives at its destination, the addressee (consignee) must arrange for delivery or must call for the shipment.

It is becoming more and more common for the shipper to load goods into containers at the home location and take them to the carrier, which transports and delivers the shipment to the consignee with no further handling. Containerized shipping, as this method is called, also offers the advantage of better security.

A service called *piggyback* is offered by the railroads to trucking firms for long-distance hauls. Loaded truck trailers are driven to the railway depot in one city, detached from the tractor, placed on railroad flatcars, and moved by rail to another city where they can be unloaded and driven to their destinations. Thus, areas not on the regular railroad lines can be reached.

Many railroads accept only carload lots of freight for shipment. To provide freight service for shipments not requiring a full car, freight-forwarding companies assemble shipments from several consignors that are less than a carload and are going to the same destination. This service allows shippers of small quantities to ship by rail.

Motor Freight.   Motor freight is used for both local and long-distance hauls. Truck companies operate coast-to-coast service and have connecting services with local trucking lines. As described previously, they often work in conjunction with railroads.

Air Freight. Air freight is the most expensive method of shipping freight. Businesses find that the high cost of air freight is partly offset by reduced costs in inventory and in warehouse space. Packing costs are also reduced, since air shipments do not require the sturdy crating that surface shipments frequently demand. Delivery service is provided without charge; however, there is a small charge for pickup service.

Water Freight. Water freight usually is considerably cheaper than any other means of freight transportation. River barges and other vessels on the inland waterways of the United States carry such commodities as lumber, coal, iron ore, and chemicals. Information on services and rates can be obtained from shipping companies.

International Shipments

The market for American products is worldwide. International air cargo service makes it possible to deliver goods to most places in the world within a matter of hours. The bulk of tonnage to foreign markets, however, still moves via *surface* (ships).

International shipments present special challenges such as special packing, complicated shipping procedures, marine insurance, and foreign exchange rates. Communications with a foreign business firm also present a challenge when handling international shipments.

Shipping Procedures. A foreign shipment involves the preparation of a number of documents, such as *ocean bill of lading, certificate of origin,* and *export customs declaration.* Large manufacturers doing extensive business abroad usually establish export departments (1) to market their products, (2) to execute required export and shipping forms, and (3) to arrange for the actual shipments. Many small firms use the services of an export broker or combination export management (CEM) firm. This type of firm performs the same functions as an export department—namely, marketing, processing, and shipping goods. International airlines and steamship companies also maintain departments that assist customers with their overseas shipments.

International Air Cargo. To send a shipment by international air cargo, whether you are sending one package or a carload, contact the office of an international airline. The airline will provide instructions for packaging and addressing the shipment and for completing necessary documents, such as bills of lading and customs declarations. In many cases air freight or air express is less expensive than international parcel post.

Summary

Postal costs continue to be a major expense for businesses. Administrative assistants who are familiar with postal information and services can contribute to the reduction of these expenses.

Domestic mail includes mail transmitted within, among, and between the United States, its territories and possessions, the Military Postal Service, and the United Nations in New York. Domestic mail is divided into the following general classes: first-class mail, priority mail, express mail, second-class mail, third-class mail, fourth-class mail, official and free mail, and mail for the visually handicapped.

Electronic message systems, such as facsimiles and electronic mail, are being used increasingly to send messages formerly sent as letters via the U.S. Postal Service.

Important mail can be registered or insured, depending on the contents. Other special services provided by the Postal Service include business reply mail; COD (collect on delivery) service; certificates of mailing; certified mail; special delivery and special handling; purchase of stamps and metered postage; forwarding, returning, and remailing of mail; and change of address forms. These services all require an additional charge.

The ZIP (Zone Improvement Plan) Code was designed to facilitate the use of automated equipment in processing mail. The ZIP + 4 Code is being used to further pinpoint delivery. Bar code readers are also used to automate the sorting of mail.

The Postal Service participates in an international communications network that provides surface and airmail services to almost any destination in the world. Correspondence also may be transmitted electronically to some countries through the INTELPOST service.

In addition to the post office, many other companies provide shipping services. These services include parcel delivery services, courier services, and freight services.

Because international shipments often present special problems, many organizations have specific departments to handle arrangements for international shipping.

QUESTIONS FOR DISCUSSION

1. How can automation of the mail room assist a company in decreasing mailing and shipping costs?
2. Discuss precautions that must be taken in the placement of the address on an envelope. Why are these precautions necessary?

THINK IT
Through

3. What alternative methods of sending mail have developed to compete with the U.S. Postal Service? How is the Postal Service attempting to combat this competition?

4. Your employer gives you an addressed, sealed envelope containing an income tax return and asks you to mail it. What method will you use to mail this document so that your employer will have legal evidence that the income tax return was mailed? (The federal government will prosecute a taxpayer whose return is not received, even though the taxpayer has a copy of the return and makes a verbal claim that the return was filed by mail.)

THINK IT
Through

5. Your employer asked you to mail an important letter to Germany. You are chagrined when it is returned for insufficient postage. The letter weighed one ounce, and you had affixed domestic postage. Why was it returned? How can you prevent the recurrence of such an error?

6. Mail from your home office reaches your city post office around 2 a.m. every day. However, it is not delivered to your office until the time of the regular mail delivery at 10:30 a.m. Your employer wants to have the home office mail as early as possible so that district sales representatives can be told of price changes. What do you suggest to solve this problem?

7. Under what conditions would you choose express mail over priority mail?

8. Rekey the following sentences capitalizing the appropriate words. Use the Reference Guide to check your answers.

   a. The republican party will hold its convention in july; the democratic party will meet in october.

   b. The smoky mountains and Mirage lake were visible as we drove south on I-81.

   c. The college of medicine at vikram university is located in the city of indore, india.

   d. We enjoyed mexican music on the grounds of the catholic mission near san miguel.

   e. In the distance, fall had woven a beautiful tapestry on the hills.

*P*ROBLEMS

1. Assume that your employer is out of the city on an extended business trip. Decide which pieces of mail you would forward and which you would retain. Indicate how you would send each piece of mail that must be forwarded.

   a. A personal letter

b. A piece of registered mail requiring a signed return receipt

c. A letter mailed by your office to the employer but returned because of an insufficient address

d. A special delivery letter

e. A parcel post package

2. Which service would you recommend to someone living in a metropolitan area in sending the following goods?

   a. An engine part for factory equipment that has broken down

   b. One thousand copies of a convention program for distribution in two weeks

   c. An antique desk inherited by an heir in New Orleans from a relative in St. Louis

   d. Ten dozen summer shirts ready for shipment

   e. A year's supply of letterheads for a branch office in Osaka

   f. Photographs for a resident of a town 30 miles away; the recipient is to take them on a vacation trip the following day

TECHNOLOGY APPLICATIONS

▶ **TA13-1.TEM**   Because of the high cost of shipping, Mr. Long has asked you to review costs and report on the best and most economical way to ship a variety of items.

Using your word processor, access the TA13-1.TEM file, which lists the shipping charges for the U.S. Postal Service, United Parcel Service, and Airborne Express. With this data, prepare a memo for Mr. Long explaining the best way to send the following items:

Domestic Letter—Overnight

Domestic Letter—Second Day

Domestic 2-pound box—Overnight

Domestic 2-pound box—Second Day

International Letter (Europe)—Overnight

International 2-pound package (Europe)

Domestic 5-pound package

Case Problems

When Hilma Adair came to work on Tuesday morning, she was amazed to find that a new word processing software package had been installed on her computer. She would have been delighted except for the fact that her employer, Elena Seblonka, had left a 30-page report on her desk with the request that Hilma have it ready when Elena returned from an out-of-town trip, in time for a 2 p.m. meeting that afternoon. She found that all the administrative assistants on the floor had received the same new software and that the instruction manuals had not been left for the users.

Hilma stormed into the office of the manager of administrative services and announced that she was taking the report to an outside agency for preparation, would bring it back in time for Ms. Seblonka's meeting, and in the meanwhile would attend a training session given by the software vendor on the use of the software.

▬▬▬ **What principle has been violated by the administrative services manager? by Hilma? Do you approve of Hilma's short-term solution? What long-range action do you recommend?**

Ida Morgan was in a particularly sensitive position as administrative assistant to Dr. Bryan Barton, director of research and development. She had been warned that the dictation she transcribed often involved confidential information about new processes or products, test results, and analyses of competitors' products.

She was shocked one day when Dr. Barton told her that information about a new product had been leaked to another corporation and would cause the loss of millions of dollars to the company. All employees, even she, were under suspicion. She was so shocked by the implication of her guilt that she could think of no reply.

In trying to assess the blame, she reviewed her relationships with the rest of the staff and remembered that when she returned from lunch one day she surprised Al Johnson, a recently hired junior chemist, as he was rummaging through her desk. His explanation was that he had misplaced the schedule of projects and knew she had another in her desk.

She also remembered that, although she usually kept the top drawer of her desk locked and the key in her purse, she had neglected to lock the drawer that day. She was so sure that she knew the culprit that she decided to confront Al Johnson and insist that he tell Dr. Barton about his involvement and take full responsibility.

▬▬▬ **What steps would you take in this situation?**

Case 3-3
CARELESSNESS
IN MAILING
CORRESPON-
DENCE

D. D. VanLandschoot, branch sales manager of a large national corporation, was concerned about the disappointing performance of a sales representative under his supervision. He and the corporate sales manager discussed termination of the sales representative's employment.

Mr. VanLandschoot then dictated a stern but courteous memo to the sales representative telling him that he must meet next month's sales quota and increase the number of daily calls if he hoped to stay with the company. At the bottom of the photocopy that was to be sent to the corporate sales manager, he wrote in longhand, "Hope I wasn't too hard on him, but he has been goofing off long enough. I'll keep you informed of developments."

Two days later Jim Protzman, the administrative assistant who had transcribed the memo, was confronted by an irate Mr. VanLandschoot: "Just look at this. See what you have done! You put the memos in the wrong envelopes." Jim was handed the memo intended for the corporate sales manager. A second notation at the bottom read: "I resign. I never 'goofed off' in my life."

Jim now remembers that when Mr. VanLandschoot sent him on an emergency errand at 4:45, he gave the day's mail to a subordinate and asked him to insert the transcribed materials in the envelopes and see that they were dispatched.

▬▬▬ **What should Jim say to Mr. VanLandschoot? How should he handle the error with the subordinate? What principle is involved?**

Case 3-4
NECESSITY
FOR LEARNING
ABOUT MAIL
SERVICES

Louis Tuccini had been an administrative assistant for an accounting firm for two weeks when he was given these four items to mail on his way home from work: a client's signed income tax return, a package of 200 handouts to be distributed by one of the partners when delivering a speech at a convention three days from now, a letter containing a check, and two magazines that had been borrowed from a colleague by a member accountant.

He sent the tax return and the check by first-class mail and the magazines and handouts by special handling. When he was reprimanded by his employer for his decisions, he said, "You didn't tell me how you wanted the items sent, and besides I was working overtime to get them in the mail anyway."

▬▬▬ **How should the materials have been sent? Why? What principles did Louis violate by his actions?**

Case 3-5
COMMUNICATING WITH INTERNATIONAL CLIENTS

Just before John Dorsett, vice president of sales, is to leave on a week-long business trip to visit three of the regional sales offices, he discusses plans for an important appointment with a group of clients from Japan with Jo Bennett, his administrative assistant. The appointment is three weeks from today. He indicates that two of the three clients who will be at the meeting do not speak or read English fluently.

Mr. Dorsett asks Jo to finalize the preparation of the paperwork for the appointment from the rough drafts he gives her. The rough drafts include the last two years of repair and maintenance call records for the model of equipment the clients are interested in purchasing, and the final letter of agreement that Mr. Dorsett hopes to have signed at this meeting. He also asks Jo to compose a letter to the clients confirming the appointment date and location, and to mail it as soon as possible.

After Mr. Dorsett leaves for his trip, Jo composes and finalizes the letter to the clients, being very careful to use formal language, and puts it in today's mail. In the next few days she types the final draft of the repair and maintenance call records and the final letter of agreement. Jo believes all of the necessary preparations for the appointment have been made. When Mr. Dorsett returns, he is upset that all of the necessary preparations have not been made by Jo.

▬▬▬ **What additional steps should Jo take to ensure the success of this important sales conference?**

Part 4

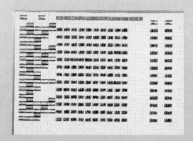

Research and Organization of Business Reports

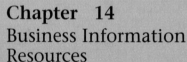

Businesses depend upon reliable and accurate information. In his book *Powershift*, Alvin Toffler observes that businesses today are collecting and storing more information than any other generation in history. One of the most challenging tasks administrative assistants will undertake is performing business research—gathering, organizing, and evaluating information to produce a business report. To accomplish these tasks, administrative assistants must have a knowledge of information sources and be able to determine which ones are appropriate to the research. Administrative assistants must be able to efficiently use traditional research methods as well as computer research systems.

Finally, administrative assistants must develop skill at preparing visually attractive documents, often incorporating tables, charts, and other graphics. A person with these responsibilities, therefore, must be current on technological advances in the acquisition of business information and in the presentation of this information in the office. Part 4 introduces you to the research and organization of business reports.

Chapter 14

Business Information Resources

LEARNING OBJECTIVES

After studying this chapter and completing the activities, you will be able to:

1. Explain the information research process.
2. Use the numerous library and computer resources for collecting secondary data.
3. Evaluate the appropriateness of information sources based upon the research problem.
4. Prepare bibliography cards and note cards.
5. Prepare an abstract of a business article.

INTRODUCTION

Earlier chapters have described the wide range of tasks associated with the position of administrative assistant. Some of the tasks, such as keying, are performed on a daily basis. Other responsibilities—such as researching information for business reports, the subject of this chapter—may be completed on a weekly, monthly, or even yearly timetable. Researching and organizing business data gives the administrative assistant the opportunity to show initiative and to work without supervision—two qualities that often lead to recognition and promotion. The key to becoming a successful researcher is knowing where to look for the information. College-trained administrative assistants should be particularly adept at finding information and, for this reason, should welcome research assignments that ask them to do the following:

- Verify the accuracy of data submitted in support of a proposal.
- Gather data an executive needs to prepare a proposal.
- Examine possible solutions to a problem, the advantages and disadvantages of certain solutions, and the opinions of authorities.
- Gather and organize information the executive will need in preparing a speech, in writing an article for a professional magazine, or in contributing to a project.

- Review personnel needs resulting from increased work load.
- Research the financial condition of certain companies.
- Compare product sales in specified categories or territories.
- Update information for a report or proposal.
- Review information sources on a continuing basis.

To accomplish these activities, the administrative assistant locates information and presents it in a proper format. This chapter will assist you in becoming a knowledgeable researcher of business information. Chapters 15 and 16 discuss ways of organizing data for effective presentation.

INFORMATION RESEARCH PROCESS

The administrative assistant has just received an assignment to research one of the areas named above. Before any information gathering can take place, the administrative assistant should approach the assignment in an organized manner.

Research Objectives

In researching a business problem, the administrative assistant must understand the objective(s) of the research. All aspects of the information research process should be conducted with the objectives in mind. It is important for the administrative assistant to answer the following questions:

1. What is the scope and nature of the request?
2. How will the report be used, and who will read it?
3. Will the sources need to be current or go back a number of years?
4. How much time is allowed to complete the project?

Narrowing the scope of the research report is probably one of the most difficult tasks because the first-time researcher usually attempts to find out everything about a subject. This is where careful attention to and clarification of the objective(s) can aid the administrative assistant in limiting the topic. Understanding who will read the report also serves to focus the administrative assistant's research efforts. The timeliness of the information determines whether sources can be one year or many years old. The project due date imposes search limitations because the time you will have to find information determines how you go about searching.

Selecting Reference Sources

The business information resources an administrative assistant will use will, most likely, be secondary data. **Secondary data** is information that has already been gathered and reported by someone else in print or electronic media. Data can be either primary or secondary; however, it is beyond the scope of this text to discuss methods of collecting **primary data,** which is the actual collection of data for the first time.

Once you are ready to locate sources of information, limit your search for materials to the best sources for the type of information you are seeking. For each source being considered, ask yourself: Is the material authoritative? Do I need articles or just essential facts and figures to fulfill the objective of the report? The answers to these questions will determine the type of sources you will use.

WHERE TO LOOK FOR INFORMATION

Information may be found in the executive's office, in the office files, in a company library, in an outside library, or in a computer database. An executive undoubtedly subscribes to technical publications, belongs to trade or professional organizations, and acquires specialized reference books for a personal office library; these are also good sources of business information. If the company you work for provides administrative assistants with desk reference materials, you have additional sources for checking facts.

Libraries

The location of most secondary sources, or at least information about them, will be a library. Many large corporations maintain a company library and have a technically trained librarian on staff. In addition to a librarian, many companies have a research staff that locates information on request. In this case, your task would be to provide accurate and carefully thought-out requests for information. In other situations, you would locate information in the company library without assistance.

It may be necessary to go outside the organization for information. The first logical outside source is the public library. A number of cities have public libraries with specialized business departments able to provide invaluable assistance to business patrons. The next logical source for information is a local college or university library. Usually the library facilities are available to the public. Business school libraries, for example, tend to have a more extensive collection of current research publications than public libraries have.

The *specialized library* is another source of information. The *Directory of Special Libraries and Information Centers,* published by Gale Research Company of Detroit, lists the location, size, and specialty of these libraries. For example, local chambers of commerce frequently maintain libraries on commercial and industrial subjects. Many business, technical, and professional societies also maintain excellent libraries, although access is generally limited to members. County and federal court buildings and university law schools often house extensive law libraries. Many cities provide municipal reference libraries for the public as well as for city employees. Hospitals and colleges of medicine maintain medical libraries. Art, history, and natural history museums have specialized libraries, as do colleges and universities. Some newspapers have large library collections that are open to the public. The U.S. Department of Commerce maintains regional offices in principal cities, making its publications available for public use through these offices.

Computer Databases

Computer databases are collections of data (databases) on many different subjects stored in large central computers. Computer databases are like electronic libraries, giving the user quicker and more complete access to secondary sources of information than a manual search can provide. With a computer database the user has the flexibility of searching for information by author, date of publication, subject, document title, or title of publication.

Databases can be updated weekly, biweekly, or monthly and serve as the computerized counterpart to printed abstracts and indexes providing the most up-to-date information. Often the information is on the database *before* it is in hard copy. In fact, some databases have information that can only be accessed in electronic form. A bibliographic database is the most common type of database, providing bibliographic citations and abstracts. Other types of databases provide full text or numeric or statistical data.

TECHNOLOGY

Computer databases give the user access to secondary sources of information more quickly and thoroughly than traditional manual methods.

USING THE LIBRARY

When a subject requires extensive research, the administrative assistant usually goes to the library to do the work. For purposes of review, a library has the following sections:

A circulation desk, where books are checked in and out

A reference area, where noncirculating reference materials are shelved

Card, microform, or computer catalogs

Book collections

Reserve collections

Periodical collections

Vertical files

A media/audiovisual center

A sound recordings collection

A microform reading center

Computer-assisted reference area

If you are unfamiliar with the library, a brief stop at the information reference desk to outline the purpose of your visit can save considerable time.

Some libraries offer tours to acquaint users with their facilities. A library tour undoubtedly would prove helpful to a new user. The librarian at the reference desk is usually very willing to assist researchers in locating the information sources they need.

While librarians can help answer specific questions, the administrative assistant should not expect the librarian to perform in-depth investigations. The administrative assistant must be willing to learn to use the basic reference tools and perform the research process.

Telephone Reference

Reference librarians provide a very valuable service to the business community. A phone call to the specialists can give you the answer to most questions, trivial or practical. The telephone numbers for the reference desks of most libraries are listed in the telephone directory. In order to save time, callers should get straight to the point. Ask for the source of information, if the librarian does not supply it. If your question is too specialized or too technical, ask to be referred to another library division or to an outside source for assistance. Administrative assistants who use the library frequently should become personally acquainted with the reference librarian. Asking for the librarian by name, particularly during rush periods, may allow your request to be handled more promptly.

Fig. 14-1 The administrative assistant, dressed informally on a dress-casual day, uses a computer terminal to search a database for information.
Courtesy of International Business Machines Corporation.

Computer-Assisted Reference

A company or library with a personal computer and modem can subscribe to an information service vendor that maintains many databases. There are over 3,000 databases in use today. By keying in a special code, subscribers can access different databases. The requested information either appears on a CRT or is printed; this is known as an on-line database search. Some libraries can provide electronic facsimiles of documents (FAX services) accessed through database searches. Figure 14-1 shows an administrative assistant performing an electronic search.

Searching Fees. For some searches, the administrative assistant may be able to use the service at no charge or for a minimal charge. For more complicated searches, however, a library staff member performs the search and an hourly fee is charged. An **on-line search** is an interactive, computerized method of accessing bibliographic citations and complete abstracts. The fee is usually based upon the amount of time spent on the on-line system, the number of titles found, and the number of abstracts requested. Fees can range from about $50 to $150 per hour. The cost is well worth it because one hour of on-line searching will yield sources that could take weeks if done manually. These sources can include all the information available on a given topic including books, periodicals, newspapers, government documents, doctoral dissertations, conference papers, and patents. If the computer searches its database after a researcher has signed off the computer, or if the desired citations or abstracts are sent to the researcher through the mail, the search is **off line.** Generally off-line searches are less expensive than on-line searches.

Accessing Database Information. Information is obtained from a database by means of a structured searching procedure. After logging onto a database system, you must enter a word or phrase that describes as precisely as possible the subject you are researching. Picking the appropriate term(s) requires some skill. To avoid wasting time and money using an inefficient searching procedure, it is recommended that the administrative assistant enlist the help of someone who is experienced at working with database searches.

Capturing Database Information. Once the search has been conducted, the researcher has several options in getting the information. The sources can be printed from the screen, or you may be able to store the information directly to electronic media for access later. This list of sources becomes your working bibliography. Often a researcher will examine the bibliographic citations first and then request abstracts (short summaries) for only those sources specifically related to the topic. This saves time and money when evaluating sources. If the information looks appropriate from the abstract, the administrative assistant can examine the full text by obtaining it from the library, from a database service, or from interlibrary loan. Figure 14-2 shows a database abstract for an article.

Database Services. Research libraries, university libraries, and most public libraries subscribe to one or more information services. You can access a database in one of two ways. You might access it directly through the company that owns the database—for example, Dow Jones, Dun & Bradstreet, or Predicasts—or work through a vendor that sells access to a range of databases. Examples of such vendors are Dialog Information Systems (DIALOG) and Bibliographic Retrieval System (BRS). There are three categories of database services:

Current Information and Services. Current information and services databases offer information such as stock quotes and news wire services.

Information Banks. Information banks offer a collection of data banks that are accessed through a single organization. These vendors give the user the opportunity to access many different databases.

Fig. 14-2 Abstract from a database reference provides a summary of the article's contents.

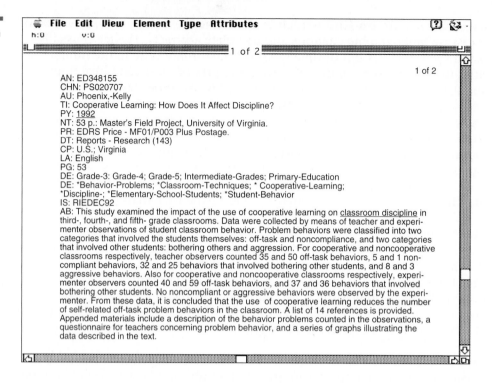

```
 🍎  File  Edit  View  Element  Type  Attributes                    ⑦ 🐌 ·
 h:0      v:0
 ▉▐▉▉▉▉▉▉▉▉▉▉▉▉▉▉▉▉▉▉▉▉▉ 1 of 2 ▉▉▉▉▉▉▉▉▉▉▉▉▉▉▉▉▉▉▉▉
                                                                         ⇧
                                                              1 of 2
     AN: ED348155
     CHN: PS020707
     AU: Phoenix,-Kelly
     TI: Cooperative Learning: How Does It Affect Discipline?
     PY: 1992
     NT: 53 p.: Master's Field Project, University of Virginia.
     PR: EDRS Price - MF01/P003 Plus Postage.
     DT: Reports - Research (143)
     CP: U.S.; Virginia
     LA: English
     PG: 53
     DE: Grade-3: Grade-4; Grade-5; Intermediate-Grades; Primary-Education
     DE: *Behavior-Problems; *Classroom-Techniques; * Cooperative-Learning;
     *Discipline-; *Elementary-School-Students; *Student-Behavior
     IS: RIEDEC92
     AB: This study examined the impact of the use of cooperative learning on classroom discipline in
     third-, fourth-, and fifth- grade classrooms. Data were collected by means of teacher and experi-
     menter observations of student classroom behavior. Problem behaviors were classified into two
     categories that involved the students themselves: off-task and noncompliance, and two categories
     that involved other students: bothering others and aggression. For cooperative and noncooperative
     classrooms respectively, teacher observers counted 35 and 50 off-task behaviors, 5 and 1 non-
     compliant behaviors, 32 and 25 behaviors that involved bothering other students, and 8 and 3
     aggressive behaviors. Also for cooperative and noncooperative classrooms respectively, experi-
     menter observers counted 40 and 59 off-task behaviors, and 37 and 36 behaviors that involved
     bothering other students. No noncompliant or aggressive behaviors were observed by the experi-
     menter. From these data, it is concluded that the use  of cooperative learning reduces the number
     of self-related off-task problem behaviors in the classroom. A list of 14 references is provided.
     Appended materials include a description of the behavior problems counted in the observations, a
     questionnaire for teachers concerning problem behavior, and a series of graphs illustrating the
     data described in the text.
                                                                         ⇩
```

Specialized Databases.   Databases offering concentrated information on a subject or profession, such as law, are called specialized databases.

Examples of on-line database services are *Dow Jones News/Retrieval* (stock quotations, financial information, news), *DIALOG* (general news, science, and business information), *CompuServe* (financial, news, and other services), *NewsNet* (business newsletters and press releases), *Lexis* (legal references), *Westlaw* (legal references), *Bibliographic Retrieval Services* (BRS) (physical and social sciences, business, medicine, humanities, education), and *Wilsonline* (business or academic research information).

Directories of on-line databases can be found in most libraries. Examples of these references include *Directory of On-line Databases* and *Datapro Directory of On-line Services.*

Limitations of Database Searches.   There is no doubt that electronic searching has the advantage of speed and convenience; however, database searches do have some limitations that the administrative assistant should be aware of. Since electronic databases are relatively new, the resources stored may not go as far back as the researcher would like to go. Another limitation, addressed earlier, is the need to use proper terms in conducting the search. If the researcher is not familiar enough with a topic to select appropriate words or phrases, this can impair the search output. Finally, an electronic search should not replace manual searching of traditional sources. Sometimes just browsing through an index or books on a shelf will yield unexpected ideas and research materials not considered before.

x

CD-ROM. CD-ROM stands for compact disc, read-only memory. It is a data publication and retrieval medium for use with computer systems. Each compact disc stores over 150,000 pages of text. Because of the savings in space, more and more references are being stored in this manner. With a CD-ROM-based index, for example, the administrative assistant simply types in the desired search word. The program may present the titles of a dozen articles that contain references to the topic. An article is chosen by pressing a key, and the program displays the article on the screen. If the user wants to quote from an article, the text is highlighted and copied to a floppy disk file for later use. If a database has been published on CD-ROM, users can perform the equivalent of on-line searching without having to actually go on-line.

TECHNOLOGY

CD-ROM is a compact disc storage medium that is read by a computer. A single disc can store over 150,000 pages of text.

Finding Information

The experienced researcher consults library indexes, guides, and catalogs as the first step in the process of finding information. These sources generally are located near the reference desk.

Books. The library's **card catalog** indexes books by subject, title, and author. The card catalog may be in card form, in microform, or stored in a computer. The card catalog indexes the contents of the library just as a book's index lists its topics. Many cards contain cross-references that tell researchers where similar or related information may be found. Catalog cards usually are printed uniformly and are available to libraries from the Library of Congress.

When using a computerized card catalog, key the author, title, or subject, and a listing of books will appear on the screen. An example of a reference from a computerized card catalog appears in Figure 14-3. Printouts of the references can be obtained from the screen, saving the user time. Some computerized systems will inform the user of the availability of the selected references.

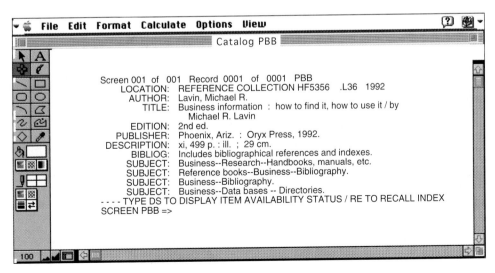

Fig. 14-3 This author card in an electronic card catalog contains many kinds of information.

As more and more libraries run out of space, there will be a switch to electronic books. Libraries scan the pages of books, storing the images in a computer. Users search for material in a computerized card catalog and retrieve the book through a computer.

Dewey Decimal System. The Dewey decimal system classifies library collections by subject. Subjects are divided into ten general classifications, numbered from 000 to 900. Each major class can be subdivided indefinitely by using the decimal point: 126.1, 126.2, 126.21, 126.211 are subdivisions of one class. Under this system, business information is found in the 650s.

Library of Congress System. Some research libraries use the Library of Congress system to classify their collections. This system uses a combination of letters and numbers. With this system, business information is found under the social sciences category, *H*.

Published Indexes. An annual publication in several volumes, *Books in Print,* lists all books included in publishers' catalogs by author, title, and subject. The listings by subject are particularly helpful in developing a bibliography of current books on a given topic. These books are normally shelved in the reference section of the library.

The Cumulative Book Index (or the *CBI,* as it is familiarly identified) is an index of books printed in English from all over the world that are still available from publishers. The CBI lists books by author, title, and subject. These extra-large volumes are normally shelved in the catalog department of the library or at a reference desk. Other indexes that list sources of current information in special fields are the *Business Periodicals Index, Education Index,* and *Social Sciences Index.*

Pamphlets and Booklets. Valuable information is often published in pamphlet, booklet, or leaflet form. Such material is cataloged by subject and title in the *Vertical File Index of Pamphlets* (a subject and title index to selected pamphlets), published monthly. Library holdings of these materials are generally kept in file cabinets. A typical entry from this index appears in Figure 14-4.

Fig. 14-4 Much valuable information is published in pamphlet, booklet, or leaflet form.

JOB hunting
How to get your first job. 24p nd Inst of food technologists 221 N LaSalle st Chicago IL 60601 $5 send payment with order
Booklet offers pointers for job-hunters. Sections include: writing resumes, networking, typical questions asked by employers during interviews (such as "Why should I hire you?" and "What do you know about our company?"), "negative factors evaluated during an employment interview frequently leading to rejection of the applicant," and a list of further readings.

News.   Summaries of newspaper and magazine reports from over 50 domestic and foreign sources are published in a one-volume, loose-leaf booklet, *Facts on File Weekly World News Digest.*

The *New York Times Index* is another valuable reference for locating sources of information published in that newspaper. Entries are arranged alphabetically under subjects. For example, suppose you wanted articles about international etiquette. You would find in the index titles and dates of articles in the *Times* on that subject. Supplements to this index are published monthly; cumulative editions, annually. The *Wall Street Journal* publishes a similar index for its publication.

Magazines.   The best index on general magazines is the *Reader's Guide to Periodical Literature.* This guide is a cumulative author and subject index to articles appearing in popular periodicals. Many libraries provide this index on computer.

Preparing Bibliography Cards

The first consideration in selecting material for examination is the *date of publication.* If current information is desired, an article on laser beams published ten years ago would be of little value. The second consideration is content. Some indexes describe the types of information found in publications. Such descriptions help researchers to focus their search.

You should prepare a bibliography card (3-by-5-inch) for each reference you choose to examine. This preliminary list of sources is called a **working bibliography.** By recording each reference on a separate card, you can easily prepare the final bibliography by sorting and rearranging the cards. When entering information about books, record the library call number, the author's name, the title of the publication, the edition (if appropriate), the publisher's name and location, and the date of publication. For periodicals, record the author's name, the title of the article, the title of the publication, the volume number, the date of publication, and the inclusive (from/to) pages in the reference.

> *A working bibliography is a preliminary list of sources that need to be examined.*

Number the cards in sequence in the upper right corner as shown in Figure 14-5. The number that is assigned to a source is used to identify all notes taken from that source. This method saves a great deal of time when you are assembling the report. If you are using a printout from a database search, number each appropriate reference next to the source. Bibliography cards serve as a permanent and detailed record of a researcher's sources.

Notetaking

After you have found the reference sources containing the required information and obtained the books, magazines, or articles you need, you are ready to begin the notetaking process. You are ready to study, evaluate, accept or

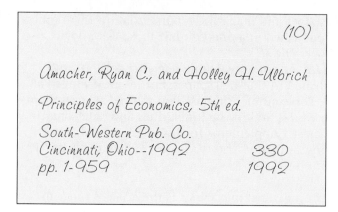

Fig. 14-5 Bibliography cards provide researchers with a permanent record of their sources.

(10)

Amacher, Ryan C., and Holley H. Ulbrich

Principles of Economics, 5th ed.

South-Western Pub. Co.
Cincinnati, Ohio--1992   330
pp. 1-959   1992

reject material, and record references on individual sheets or cards, 4-by-6 inches or larger. By using cards or sheets of uniform size instead of a shorthand notebook, the information from a complete set of references can be sorted for use in drafting the outline and writing the report.

Save time during this process of evaluating materials by learning to first scan materials. When evaluating a book, develop the habit of looking first at the table of contents, the introduction, and the index to verify if the materials are relevant to your research objectives. For shorter references, look at the introduction, conclusions, and information that is underlined or italicized. Scan each paragraph by reading just the topic sentences. Expect to take more notes than you will eventually use in the report. Get all the information you need the first time so you will not have to go back and relocate the source.

Compiling Reference Cards.   Each reference card should list the following information in a standard form.

1. Page numbers should be written in the upper left corner. (Do this first to avoid forgetting to include them.)

2. A source should be cited according to the number on its bibliography card.

3. Topics should be noted in a conspicuous position.

4. Information can be quoted, paraphrased, or summarized. A direct quotation is written word for word and enclosed in quotation marks, and any omissions from the original are indicated by ellipses. Be careful when using ellipses not to distort the original meaning or intent of the passage. (Reproducing an author's work without express permission is in violation of copyright laws.) When you put the author's ideas into your own words, you are paraphrasing. If these ideas are unique to the author, then you must indicate the source as you would with a direct quote but without quotation marks. A summary is a distillation or condensation of information from the source.

Abstracting. It may be more convenient to provide notes in abstract form rather than on reference cards. Abstracting is the process of taking the important ideas in a document and recording them in your own words. To prepare good abstracts, you must develop the ability to pick out the important points, including conclusions and recommendations, and to express them in summary form. By grouping key ideas and condensing material into manageable size, skillfully prepared abstracts can save the employer a great deal of reading time. A reference in abstract form should be identified as such. The source and page numbers also should be identified. Abstracts may be prepared in single-spaced or double-spaced form. An example appears in Figure 14-6. Before starting to prepare an abstract, check first with the library to see if its computer database service provides abstracts of your reference sources.

ABSTRACT

Murphy, Alma A. "Information Processing in the Mechanized Office."
The Mechanized Office (October 10, 1994), p. 42.[†]

Office work involves inputting, processing, and outputting information. Information is frequently inputted at the keyboard of a word processor or computer-linked terminal. Information is processed through the use of hardware (computers and word processors) and software. Printed material, also called hard copy, is by far the most common form of output. Information can also be displayed on a VDT. Other forms of output include microfilm, magnetic tape, and magnetic disks. This article gives further evidence of the merger of data and word processing. More and more manufacturers are introducing equipment that performs both data and word processing functions.

[†] CITATION GIVEN IS FICTITIOUS

Fig. 14-6   To prepare an effective abstract, you must be able to pick out important points and express them in summary form.

Photocopying Material.   Most libraries provide either photocopy service or access to photocopy machines for a minimal cost. Making photocopies is the easiest way to record secondary information. By having a copy of the document, the administrative assistant can review the wording of the original work at a later time and make notes when it is convenient. Because recording numerical data is prone to errors, statistical tables should also be copied by machine. When library publications can be borrowed, take material to the office to reproduce numerical data. Librarians will sometimes lend a noncirculating reference book for a limited time. Libraries are eager to cooperate with businesspeople and want them to make full use of library resources.

Highlighting Material. Consider using a special colored marker and highlighting key words or ideas on copies or printouts of reference sources. Highlighting replaces underlining; it lets the reader focus on the important points in the article and can save the researcher time by avoiding recopying information onto reference cards.

SOURCES OF GENERAL INFORMATION

Information sources are updated and revised constantly, and new materials are published regularly. It is necessary, therefore, to update references (including this chapter) with current sources.

Atlases

An atlas is a collection of maps and statistical information regarding populations and geographic areas. *Rand McNally Commercial Atlas and Marketing Guide,* revised and updated annually and available in most libraries, contains not only geographic maps but also many economic maps. Its primary emphasis is the United States. Other atlases include sections on the solar system, world climate, and world energy resources.

Dictionaries

One naturally would expect that administrative assistants frequently use reference sources. Even though the office may have a large unabridged dictionary, you need to have an up-to-date desk-size dictionary within arm's reach. *Webster's Tenth New Collegiate Dictionary,* for example, is a valuable addition to your reference shelf.

There are also innumerable specialized dictionaries: bilingual dictionaries for use in writing and translating foreign correspondence and technical dictionaries that focus on specialized business subjects, such as accounting, economics, data processing, telecommunications, and insurance.

New developments outdate technical dictionaries rapidly. Only the most recent editions can be considered dependably up-to-date.

Directories

Hundreds of directories are shelved in the reference section of the library. Some directories are available through computer database services. One type of directory, the city directory, is especially useful to local business firms. Most directories, however, are national in scope and serve special industrial and professional fields. For a listing of more than 10,000 American and foreign directories, consult *Directories in Print.*

City Directories. A city directory typically provides a listing of people and companies of a city by name, by address, and by telephone number. There is also a classified business section. These directories are published by private concerns for a profit, not by the municipality they serve. Not all large cities have a city directory. Unlike the telephone directory, city directories list telephone numbers in numerical order with addresses and occupants' names indicated. Current and back issues of city directories are kept at libraries for the convenience of business users. A local library's collection of directories may contain that city's directory and also the directories of other cities in the state as well as major cities throughout the country.

Special Directories. Among the better-known and most frequently used special directories are the following:

- *American Medical Directory* lists the names of physicians in the United States, Puerto Rico, and the Virgin Islands. It provides information on the year licensed, medical school attended, board certifications, etc.

- *Who's Who in America* is a biographical directory of notable living Americans from the fields of science, politics, sports, education, etc. There are also selective *Who's Who* references, such as *Who's Who of American Women* and *Who's Who in American Politics*. A one-volume biographical reference giving background information on significant Americans, both living and dead, is *Webster's New Biographical Dictionary*.

- The *National Directory of Addresses and Telephone Numbers* lists alphabetically and by categories 75,000-plus U.S. corporations, giving full names, street addresses, ZIP Codes, area codes, and telephone numbers. The multivolume *Thomas Register of American Manufacturers* and *The Million Dollar Directory* (five volumes) index names of businesses involved in similar enterprises.

- The *Directory of American Firms Operating in Foreign Countries* and *Major Companies of Europe* list businesses and office addresses of companies doing business overseas.

- The *Encyclopedia of Associations* lists the names, addresses, and officers of trade, business, labor, legal, educational, religious, and cultural organizations.

- The *National Directory of State Agencies* is organized by states and identifies primary elected state officials and administrative officers.

- The *Worldwide Government Directory* is organized by countries and enumerates government officials and government entities. It provides complete addresses and telephone numbers and general information about the country such as language, currency, political parties, and so forth.

Encyclopedias

An encyclopedia is an excellent reference source. Many encyclopedias contain essay-type articles giving important information on a specific field. Articles are usually enhanced with bibliographies, pictures, diagrams, and maps. Only two are mentioned here. In addition to general information, the *Encyclopedia Americana* provides information on American history, geography, scientific, and technical topics. The *New Encyclopaedia Britannica* has undergone extensive revisions in text and format. Special emphasis is given to science, social science and humanities, biographical, and geographical articles.

Government Publications

The U.S. government is a prolific publisher and a major source of information for the business executive. Some government publications may be subscribed to and purchased. Others are found on file in the reference department or business section of the public library or in a municipal reference library. Large cities usually have a depository library. Depository libraries are designated by law to receive all or part of the material published by the government. Refer to *A Directory of U.S. Government Depository Libraries* available from the Superintendent of Documents (U.S. Government Printing Office, Washington, DC 20402) for a complete listing of depository libraries. The reference librarian at your local library can tell you the location of the nearest depository.

For a comprehensive list of all publications issued by the various departments and agencies of the United States government, consult the *Monthly Catalog of U.S. Government Publications.* Included in this comprehensive list of government publications are those for sale by the Superintendent of Documents and those for official use only.

Proceedings and debates of Congress are given in the *Congressional Record.* The official directory of the United States Congress, the *Congressional Directory,* provides information on the legislative, judicial, and executive branches of the federal government. The *Congressional Staff Directory* publishes the names of the Washington staff personnel of members of Congress and those serving on committees and subcommittees. The *United States Government Manual,* the official handbook of the federal government, provides information on the purposes and programs of most government agencies and lists the top personnel of those agencies.

Publications of the Bureau of the Census are based on data from censuses taken in various years. They include information on population, housing, business, manufacturing, and agriculture. Full census reports provide complete information. The *Statistical Abstract of the United States* (annual) summarizes statistics about area and population, vital statistics, education, climate, employment, military affairs, social security, income, prices, banking, transportation, agriculture, forests, fisheries, mining, manufacturing, and related fields.

The U.S. Department of Commerce publishes the *Survey of Current Business* (issued monthly), which reports on industrial and business activities in the United States. Publications of the Department of Agriculture provide agricultural and marketing statistics and information for increasing production and agricultural efficiency. Department of Labor publications deal primarily with labor statistics, standards, and employment trends. The Department's official publication is the *Monthly Labor Review.*

Economic and agricultural data on many subjects may be obtained from various state governments. You should address inquiries to the departments of health, geology or conservation, and highways; to the divisions of banks, insurance, and statistics; to industrial and public utilities commissions; or to the research bureaus of state universities. Pertinent information about executive, legislative, and judicial branches of state governments is given in the *Book of the States,* which is published every two years by the Council of State Governments.

Yearbooks

Yearbooks are annual summaries of statistics and facts. The *World Almanac and Book of Facts,* the most popular book of this type, contains many pages of statistics and facts preceded by an excellent index. One reference librarian has said, "Give me a good dictionary and the *World Almanac,* and I can answer 80 percent of all questions asked of me." The almanac covers such items as stock and bond markets; notable events; political and financial statistics on states and cities; statistics on population, farm crops, prices, trade, and commerce; educational data; and information on postal services. Because of its wide coverage and low price, you might ask your employer to purchase a copy of the *World Almanac* each year for office use. Another yearbook of this type is the *Information Please Almanac.*

The *International Yearbook* and *Statesmen's Who's Who* include biographical sketches of over 10,000 political leaders and general information on international affairs and foreign relations.

SOURCES OF BUSINESS INFORMATION

Sources of business information are revised constantly, and new materials are published regularly. The list of specific business sources that appears in this chapter, therefore, should be supplemented with new sources as they appear.

General Subscription Information Services

Management often subscribes to information services relating to general business conditions. These services present information from sources that are more direct and specialized than those found in popular publications. A service may publish information in loose-leaf form so that superseded pages can be destroyed and new and additional ones inserted easily. It may be your responsibility to see that the new pages are filed in their proper place. Information services also provide data through computer database systems. Examples of these information services include the following:

- Babson-United Investment Advisors, Inc., publishes a weekly bulletin, *United & Babson Investment Report.*
- Bureau of National Affairs, Inc., in its *Daily Report for Executives* reports government actions that affect management, labor, law, taxes, finance, federal contracts, antitrust and trade regulations, international trade, and patent law.
- The Kiplinger Washington Editors publish a weekly newsletter, the *Kiplinger Washington Letter,* that analyzes and condenses economic and political news.
- Predicasts, Inc., publishes three indexes of literature appearing in hundreds of worldwide trade and financial journals, newspapers, and government reports. These indexes are published monthly; cumulative indexes are compiled quarterly and annually.

Specialized Subscription Information Services

The administrative assistant also should be acquainted with some of the specialized subscription services for business fields.

Credit.   Dun & Bradstreet Credit Rating Service collects, analyzes, and distributes credit information on retail, wholesale, and manufacturing companies.

Financial.   Most brokerage houses provide investment information to prospective and present customers. Moody's Investors Service, Inc., produces a number of financial publications, such as *Moody's Bond Survey* and *Moody's Handbook of Common Stocks.* Standard & Poor's Corporation publishes a number of handbooks and guides, such as *Standard & Poor's Register of Corporations, Directors, and Executives* and *Stock Reports.* Information is also available from Standard & Poor's through computer database services.

Information Technology.   The *Information Industry Bulletin* published by Digital Information Group provides information on the distribution and storage technologies, markets, and actions taken by companies in the information industry. The bulletin is intended for information industry executives.

Labor.   The Bureau of National Affairs, Inc., publishes a number of labor statistics in its *Labor Relations Reporter.*

Law/Tax.   Commerce Clearing House Product Systems publishes *Topical Law Reports* in loose-leaf format. A few of the topics covered are federal tax, labor, state tax, social security, trusts, and aviation.

Prentice-Hall Information Services publishes information in loose-leaf format on laws, rules, and regulations with interpretations and comments. Examples are *Corporate Acquisitions, Mergers and Divestitures,* and *Divorce Taxation.*

The Kiplinger Washington Editors publish a biweekly *Kiplinger Tax Letter* giving up-to-the-minute information on tax laws.

Management.   *Management Contents,* published biweekly by The Information Clearinghouse, Inc., provides tables of contents of 350 business and management journals and other information services.

Microcomputer Hardware and Software.   Datapro Computers & Communications Information Group, Inc., publishes *Datapro Directories* on computer and peripheral technology and software; the publication is revised monthly.

Trade.   The Bureau of National Affairs, Inc., is most noted for its coverage of labor law, international trade law, environment, and safety.

Newspapers and Periodicals for Executives

Two newspapers are of particular interest to the business community. The *New York Times,* a daily newspaper covering world, domestic, and financial news, contains a special section on business in daily editions. The *Wall Street Journal,* primarily an investor's newspaper, covers current business news and lists daily stock reports.

Countless periodicals of interest to business executives exist. For this discussion, periodicals are divided into two categories: general and specialized.

General Periodicals.   The alert administrative assistant scans general business magazines received at the office for material that may be of immediate or possible interest to the executive. Examples of general business magazines that your office may subscribe to include the following:

- *Barron's* is a national business and financial weekly published by Dow Jones & Company, Inc.
- *Business Month* (formerly *Dun's Business Month* and *Dun's Review*) is published by Dun & Bradstreet Publications Corporation. It covers finance, credit, production, labor, sales, and distribution.
- *Business Week* is published weekly by McGraw-Hill, Inc. It covers topics of national and international interest to business executives. Statistics reflect current trends.

- *Forbes,* a magazine of corporate management for top executives, is published by Forbes, Inc.
- *Fortune* is published biweekly by Time Inc. It features articles on specific industries and business leaders. It also analyzes current business problems.
- *Industry Week,* published by Penton Publishing, Inc., is written for executives with management responsibilities in administration or finance, production, engineering, purchasing, or marketing. Although selectively distributed, it is available on a subscription basis.
- *Nation's Business* is published monthly by the U.S. Chamber of Commerce. This business magazine focuses on political and general topics.

Specialized Periodicals.   It is common for a company to belong to several trade associations. In addition, the executive may belong to several professional associations. These associations issue regular magazines to their members, publishing articles and statistics of current interest. The *Standard Periodical Directory* lists 70,000 American and Canadian periodicals. The *Business Periodicals Index* is the primary source of information on a wide range of articles appearing in business periodicals.

When seeking data on a specific magazine or newspaper, you might consult Gale's *Directory of Publications* (newspapers and periodicals) or *Ulrich's International Periodicals Directory.* They provide information on the names of publications, editors, publishers, dates established, technical data, and geographic areas served. Another source for specialized magazines is the *Reader's Guide to Periodical Literature* (see page 349). More than 100 well-known magazines, such as *Business Week, Changing Times, Consumer Reports, Fortune,* and *Time,* are indexed in each issue. Articles are cataloged by author and appropriate subject headings.

Handbooks

Handbooks are published in many areas of business. They are highly factual surveys of particular fields and serve as reference sources in these fields. A few of the many handbooks published in the business area are *Personnel Administration Handbook, Office Administration Handbook, Sales Manager's Handbook,* and *Handbook for Business and Economics.*

A number of handbooks have been written for administrative assistants in legal, medical, real estate, and other specialized fields. Some examples of specialized handbooks are *How to Run a Real Estate Office, The Modern Medical Office: A Reference Manual,* and *The Career Legal Secretary.*

The Administrative Assistant's Reference Shelf

The administrative assistant may collect many worthwhile reference books, or the executive may purchase them for office use. A useful, inexpensive reference, *How to Use the Business Library,* is a valuable adjunct to any business library. Other sources of information to which you should have easy access include the following:

- An abridged encyclopedia. The *Concise Columbia Encyclopedia* in one volume is particularly strong in the areas of biography and geography.

- An annual book of statistics. The *Statistical Abstract of the United States,* the *World Almanac & Book of Facts,* and the *Guinness Book of World Records* are good sources of statistical information.

- An atlas or gazetteer. The *Rand McNally World Atlas* or *Webster's New Geographical Dictionary* are good choices.

- A thesaurus. *Webster's Collegiate Thesaurus* is quite thorough.

- A book of quotations. *Bartlett's Familiar Quotations* or *The Home Book of Quotations: Classical and Modern* are good sources for locating memorable quotations.

- A book of etiquette. *Letitia Baldrige's Complete Guide to Executive Manners.* Add one on international etiquette. *At Ease Professionally: An Etiquette Guide for the Business World (at home and abroad)* by Hilka Klinkenberg or *The Do's and Taboos of Hosting Visitors* by Roger E. Axtrell.

- A ZIP Code directory. *National Directory of ZIP Codes and Post Offices* is the standard reference for this information.

- A handbook of parliamentary procedures. *Robert's Rules of Order* is a comprehensive guide for parliamentarians.

- A manual of style. *The Elements of Style with Index* by Strunk and White is a favorite with all types of writers.

- A communications manual. *Webster's Guide to Business Correspondence* published by Merriam-Webster Inc., or *Executive's Business Letter Book* published by Enterprise Publishing, Inc., are good references.

- A toll-free business directory. *AT&T's Toll-Free 800 Business Directory* is ideal for this purpose.

- A technical handbook that relates to the executive's work. For example, the *Handbook of Modern Accounting* by Davidson and Weil would be a good choice for an accountant's office.

Summary

When researching business information, the administrative assistant may use the company library, the local public library, a specialized library, and/or a computer database service. Libraries generally subscribe to at least one database service; companies that need current sources of information are likely to subscribe to a database service as well. Searching computer databases saves the administrative assistant time in locating relevant sources of information.

The administrative assistant should be familiar with the various sections of the library. A stop at the information desk or at the reference desk is enough to direct a researcher to needed information. The index of books in a library is the card catalog. The card catalog can be on cards, microform, or computer. Library collections are classified under the Dewey decimal system or the Library of Congress system. Business information is found in the *650s* under the Dewey decimal system and in the major category of *H* under the Library of Congress system. The annual publication, *Books in Print,* lists all books included in publishers' catalogs by author, title, and subject. Pamphlets and booklets are cataloged in the *Vertical File Index of Pamphlets.* Magazines are listed in the *Reader's Guide to Periodical Literature,* which is available in book form or on computer.

When taking notes, prepare a bibliography card for each reference source. Separate reference cards are then written for each topic. A distinction should be made on reference cards between direct quotes and summary statements.

Atlases, dictionaries, directories, encyclopedias, government publications, and yearbooks are sources of general information. Business information also can be found through specialized subscription information services, such as the *Kiplinger Washington Letter.* Specialized subscription information services also are available in the areas of credit, finance, information technology, law, tax, management, computer hardware and software, real estate, and trade.

Two newspapers are of particular interest to the business community: the *New York Times,* with its special daily section on business, and the *Wall Street Journal.* Numerous general periodicals appeal to business executives. These include *Business Week, Fortune,* and *Nation's Business.* The *Business Periodicals Index* indexes a wide range of articles appearing in business periodicals.

A number of business handbooks can be found in the reference section of most libraries. A popular handbook among office managers is the *Office Administration Handbook.*

In addition to office handbooks and a dictionary, the administrative assistant should have access to a copy of the *Statistical Abstract of the United States,* a book of etiquette, and a ZIP Code directory.

1. What personal characteristics do you think are needed to be a good researcher of information?

2. Why is it important to understand the problem before you begin to look for information? What questions do you need to have answered before you begin to find sources?

3. How would your approach differ in taking notes on a magazine article available on a library shelf and taking notes on a magazine available only in a computer database to which you have access?

4. What are the advantages of using a computer database service in researching information as opposed to traditional sources such as periodicals, books, and standard reference works?

5. In your new position as administrative assistant to the vice president of a business consulting firm, you have been given the assignment to purchase five desk reference books. Which five books would you choose? By what criteria would you make these choices?

6. Name the various libraries that are nearest to your school and discuss their collections.

7. Do you agree with the statement that the administrative assistant should not expect the librarian to perform in-depth investigations? Why or why not?

8. If your employer is involved in scientific research and gives highly technical dictation, where would you turn for help in learning the vocabulary?

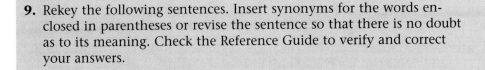

9. Rekey the following sentences. Insert synonyms for the words enclosed in parentheses or revise the sentence so that there is no doubt as to its meaning. Check the Reference Guide to verify and correct your answers.

    a. We send a report to the board _____ (twice a year).

    b. The license is renewable _____ (every two years).

    c. The state budget is approved _____ (every year).

    d. The committee meets _____ (every six months).

    e. A performance by the International String Quartet has been a _____ event on our campus since 1980 (once in two years).

1. Problem 4 in Chapter 16 will ask you to prepare a business report. In preparation, you are now to do the necessary reading, prepare bibliography cards, and take notes. Choose one of the following topics as the subject of your report:

   a. Business Ethics: A Revived Interest in the Business Community

   b. The Law in the Workplace

   c. Ergonomic Considerations in Office Design

   d. Improving Computer Security in the Office

   e. The Paperless Office: Myth or Reality

   f. Orientation Training for Office Workers

   g. The Use of Job-Related Tests in the Selection of Office Employees

   h. Privacy Laws and Office Records

   i. How to Supervise Office Workers Effectively

   j. Carpal Tunnel Syndrome—An Office Occupation Hazard?

   k. Office Technology in the Year 2005

   l. Sexual Harassment in the Workplace

   m. Mentoring

   n. Diversity

   o. Downsizing

2. Assume that you are secretary to Randolph Parker, general counsel for a subsidiary of a major manufacturing firm. Your employer has just been transferred to the home office. He tells you that he has at least ten crates of books to be unpacked and arranged on his bookshelves. You are to supervise the arrangement of the books on the shelves and to devise a system of control, since Mr. Parker expects that many of the staff will want to use his materials. What is your plan of action for arranging the books on the shelves? Explain your system of control.

3. Prepare a list of answers and your sources of information to the following:

   a. Who is the author(s) of the book *Megatrends 2000,* copyrighted 1990 and published by William Morrow and Company, Inc.?

   b. What is the ZIP Code for Searchlight, Nevada?

   c. What is the latest estimate of the population of Tulsa, Oklahoma?

   d. Who are the members of the Washington office staff of a senator from your state?

   e. Where will you find a magazine article published in May 1992 entitled "How Well Do You Speak?"

   f. Where was Elvis Presley born?

g. What are the five principal business centers located in the state of Illinois?

h. What is the London address of NCR Corporation?

i. Cite a quotation on the importance of listening.

TECHNOLOGY APPLICATIONS

▶ **TA14-1**

On-line databases are available in many local libraries. Does your library have any such database available?

Prepare a short report to your instructor. Proceed as follows:

1. Find out specifically which databases, if any, are available through your local library.

2. If databases are available, what is the charge for using each database service?

3. Using your word processing software, load the MEMO.TMP (the interoffice memo form) and prepare a memo to your instructor reporting your findings.

4. Save the document as TA14-1, and print a copy for your instructor.

5. As always, proofread your memo carefully before you submit the final copy to your instructor.

▶ **TA14-2**

You are the administrative assistant to Edna Hoover, the vice president of administrative services for an office furniture company. Ms. Hoover asks you to compile a list of periodicals that will provide up-to-date articles on procedures for the automated office.

Using your word processing software, load the MEMO.TMP file (the interoffice memo form) and provide the information to Ms. Hoover. (Refer also to "Periodicals and Subscription Services," supplied by your instructor from the instructor's manual.)

▶ **TA14-3**

Your employer, Marcos Valdez, asks you to visit the library to locate a recent comprehensive article on how to run meetings more effectively. Because he wants to discuss this topic at the next staff meeting, Mr. Valdez asks you to key an abstract of the article. Save the document as TA14-3, and print a copy for your instructor.

Hint: Refer to Figure 14-6 in the text, and use this illustration as a guide.

Chapter 15

Presentation of Statistical Information

INTRODUCTION

The process of compiling, presenting, and analyzing statistical information is standard practice in businesses and government organizations. In large companies, for instance, employees in accounting, research, manufacturing, and marketing departments work with numerical information daily. Business executives have numerical information at their fingertips—as close as their personal computer—and use this information to make business decisions. Administrative assistants also work with statistical data.

To make numerical data more readily understood, companies use tables, charts, and graphs to convey information. A well-constructed table or graph can communicate a statistical concept more quickly and more clearly than a list or a textual summary of numerical values. For this reason, publications such as annual reports, proposals, and advertising brochures, as well as oral presentations, make generous use of tables, charts, and graphs to present statistical information. Tables and graphics are also essential to business reports.

With the use of computer graphics, the capability of producing professional-looking charts and graphs is now within the financial means of even the smallest business firm. Computer graphics technology will continue to be a major growth area in business in this decade.

THE ADMINISTRATIVE ASSISTANT'S ROLE

The extent of your role in preparing and presenting statistical information will depend on your specific job responsibilities. In assisting with written reports, the administrative assistant can count on being responsible for converting statistical information, possibly compiled from spreadsheet applications, into well-planned tables, pie charts, bar graphs, or line graphs. In addition to graphics for written reports, the administrative assistant can expect to prepare or oversee the production of quality graphics for oral presentations.

With today's software technology, an administrative assistant would not be expected to prepare a chart or graph freehand. You will, however, be expected to know how to compile, organize, and classify numerical data. In addition, you should know the proper use of tables and graphs and which type of graphic will best display the data. In addition, the administrative assistant should consider whether the reader or viewer will understand the graphic. The administrative assistant's contributions in selecting the best medium for display and determining the readability of the graphic will add to the credibility of the report or oral presentation.

The most common uses of computer graphics applications are reports and oral presentations.

COMPILING AND ORGANIZING DATA

The data used by administrative assistants come from many sources. Some data compiled within a company are provided in the form of computer printouts. Other information is obtained from such secondary sources as magazines, yearbooks, and reports of outside agencies. In order to organize data from several sources into an easy-to-read format so that totals can be obtained, averages and percentages calculated, and information summarized, administrative assistants use working forms. The process of transferring facts from source documents to working forms is called **compiling** data. The simplest compilation of data is a tabulation. An example of a tabulation appears in Figure 15-1.

METHODS OF CLASSIFYING DATA

The objective of compiling data is to organize information into meaningful classifications. Data can be classified in any of five ways: (1) in alphabetic sequence, (2) by kind, (3) by size, (4) by location, or (5) by time.

1. An *alphabetic sequence* of data is often used when comparisons are being made between distinct units. For instance, in a summary of total sales by individual sales representatives, the names of the sales representatives are likely to be presented in alphabetic order.

The Leisure and Recreation Corp.
Summary of Operations
For the Year Ended December 31, 19—

Sales and Revenues
(In Thousands)

Divisions	First Quarter	Second Quarter	Third Quarter	Fourth Quarter	Total for Year
Recreation					
Lawn and Garden	$25.6	$30.2	$39.4	$42.7	$137.9
Bicycles/Motorcycles	20.5	29.4	36.4	46.2	132.5
Sporting Goods	19.5	23.6	33.0	45.0	121.1
Marine Products	29.6	32.7	33.2	33.0	128.5
Total	$95.2	$115.9	$142.0	$166.9	$520.0
Recreational Vehicles					
Campers	$42.9	$45.2	$70.5	$90.2	$248.8

From Annual Report of the L & R Corp.
Compiled by R.C. 1/31/— Checked by D.N.

2. A grouping of data by *kind* is used when information about different categories of things is being presented. An example of a grouping by kind would be a table that classified retail trade into several main groups, such as food stores, apparel stores, and hardware stores. Data would then be listed for individual stores falling into the various groups.

3. *Size variations* may be shown in two ways. In an *array,* data are listed in ascending or descending order. A table of the fifty-largest ports in the world arranged in descending order of net tonnage would be an array. In a *frequency distribution,* data are arranged according to each size class. A frequency distribution is used instead of an array when data can be grouped advantageously in classes. For example, tables of age distribution may be grouped according to the number of persons between the ages of 10 to 14 and 15 to 19 instead of listing data for each age (10, 11, 12, etc.) individually.

4. A *location listing* is used to show data by geographic units, such as cities, states, and countries. Real estate data are often listed this way, as are commodity sales on a national scale.

5. *Time-of-occurrence or time series listings* are very common. A listing may be made by days, weeks, months, years, decades, and so on. Figure 15-2 combines an alphabetic sequence of data in a time series listing by years.

After data have been collected, they may be translated into averages or percentages so that comparisons can be made. To say that sales in Dallas were 35 percent greater this month than last month is easier to interpret than to say that sales last month were $50,000 and this month, $67,500. Or it may be more helpful to know the average salary of employees in the purchasing office than to know the highest and the lowest salary paid. The use to be

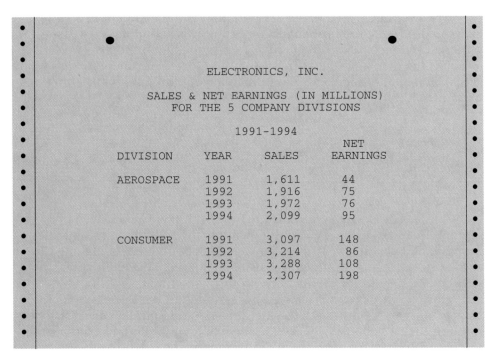

Fig. 15-2 A computer printout illustrating a combination of alphabetic sequence of data presented in a time series listing by years.

```
                    ELECTRONICS, INC.

            SALES & NET EARNINGS (IN MILLIONS)
                FOR THE 5 COMPANY DIVISIONS

                        1991-1994
                                         NET
        DIVISION     YEAR     SALES     EARNINGS

        AEROSPACE    1991     1,611        44
                     1992     1,916        75
                     1993     1,972        76
                     1994     2,099        95

        CONSUMER     1991     3,097       148
                     1992     3,214        86
                     1993     3,288       108
                     1994     3,307       198
```

made of the data determines whether an average or a percentage will be of more value.

Averages

One way to help the reader understand a set of numbers is to compute an average. (An **average** is a single value used to represent a group.) But which of the three averages in common use should you choose? The one used most often is the arithmetic average or, more technically, the **arithmetic mean.** It is the sum of two or more quantities divided by the number of quantities. If the weekly payroll for 120 employees is $48,000, for example, the average pay is $400.

The **mode** is a second kind of average. It is the value that recurs the greatest number of times in a given series. The data are arranged in a frequency distribution to determine the mode. For example, the mode in the following distribution is the class interval $260.01 to $270.00, because the greatest number of salaries falls in that range.

Weekly Earnings	Number of Employees
$250.01–$260.00	2
$260.01–$270.00	26 ← MODE
$270.01–$280.00	19
$280.01–$290.00	9
$290.01–$300.00	5

The **median** is an average of position; it is the midpoint in an array. In order to determine the median, data must be arranged in an array; that is, in either ascending or descending order. To find the median it is necessary only to count the number of items in an array and locate the midpoint. For example, assume that five students have the following amounts in their checking accounts:

Student A	$1,500
Student B	$ 750
Student C	$ 500 ← *MEDIAN*
Student D	$ 100
Student E	$ 20

The *median* is $500, but the *mean* is $574. If there are an even number of items in an array, the median is determined by adding the two middle numbers and dividing by two. In the example above, considering only the accounts of Students A through D, the *median* is $625 ($750 plus $500 divided by 2); the mean of those four accounts is $712.50.

Obviously the mean is affected by extremes. In the first example, the student with an abnormally large checking account and the one with almost nothing have a significant impact on the mean. In the second example the student with the large checking account impacts the mean. When there are extreme cases in the data, the median is usually selected as the average that comes nearest to indicating the true state of affairs.

Percentages

Percentages make it easy to grasp the relationship of various quantities to one another. For example, to say that 900 consumers were satisfied with their new color televisions has less significance than saying "900 consumers, or 30 percent of 3,000 consumers, were satisfied with their color TV purchases."

Percentage relatives or *index numbers* are used to compare the extent or the degree of change. They are relative because they are based on a clearly defined value at a specific time. An example of a percentage relative is the consumer price index (CPI). It measures the average change in price over time for a fixed market basket of goods and services. For example, assume that the base year is 1984 (expressed as 100) and prices have increased 150 percent for those specific goods and services. The CPI is then expressed as 250 (100 plus 150).

PRESENTING DATA EFFECTIVELY

When given numerical data to display in a report or oral presentation, the administrative assistant must determine the most effective presentation of the information. Tables are preferred over graphs when the numerical data contain so many points of information that a graph or chart would be unreadable or confusing. Tables are also preferred when many exact numbers are used. When well constructed, tables are easy to read and aid in reaching conclusions. Charts and graphs are better for highlighting comparisons and trends when quick identification of relationships is important.

In keying written reports, the pattern for using tables, charts, and graphs is (1) introduce, (2) display, and (3) discuss. It is unthinkable to present a table or graphic in a report before it is introduced. Doing so may lead the reader to reach some false conclusions. A thorough discussion follows the presentation of the table or graphic. The administrative assistant should ensure that this pattern is followed.

TABLES

Three types of tables are used in business reports: *general-purpose* tables, *special-purpose* tables, and *spot* (or informal) tables. General-purpose and special-purpose tables are considered formal tables; they have a number, caption, column heads, and so on. Because general-purpose tables cover a broad area of information, they are usually placed in an appendix. Special-purpose tables, on the other hand, display a particular part of the report and are placed within the text discussion. Most tables of statistical data in business reports are special-purpose tables, like the one shown in Figure 15-3 on page 370. The tables in the discussion of computing averages on pages 367 and 368 are spot tables. Spot tables are unnumbered and untitled, and appear within paragraphs of a report.

A table should be self-explanatory. It should be simple and designed for rapid reading. Incorporating too many elements in one table detracts from its readability and effectiveness. When planning a table, keep one question in mind: Precisely what is this table to show? All data that do not apply should be excluded.

After a table has been developed, a chart or graph may be used to dramatize the material presented in it. In other words, the chart does not replace the table; it supplements it. *Tables provide details; charts present relationships.* Charts alone will not satisfy readers who seek exact data. Charts and graphs are discussed later in this chapter.

Suggestions for Keying Tables

Before keying a table, you should check the accuracy of all numbers in a column and column totals if manually developed; then review the rules governing table construction. For example, columns must be arranged attractively and logically; numbers must be aligned exactly. If you are using a computer, an electronic typewriter, or a word processor, the automatic features of the equipment will make producing a perfect table on the first try much easier.

Captions. Most tables include a table number, a main title, a secondary heading, column or boxed headings, and stub (left column) headings. The table title and all headings must identify exactly what is being presented. Only the main title is keyed in all capital letters; the other headings are keyed with initial capital letters only. A secondary heading is centered and is keyed a double space below the main title. Both the main title and the secondary heading can be keyed in boldface. Figure 15-3 shows the important parts of a table.

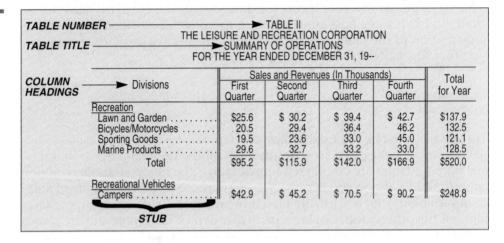

Fig. 15-3 This table was keyed from the working form shown in Figure 15-1. Leaders and additional blank lines between some entries have been used to improve readability. Note that numbers are shown in thousands; thus $95,200 is shown as $95.2.

Numbers. Tables should be numbered consecutively throughout a report. Arabic or Roman numerals can be used. Numerals follow the word *table* keyed in all capital letters or with an initial cap only (TABLE 2, TABLE II, Table 2, Table II). The table number is the first caption line; the main table title is the second. Both can be keyed in boldface and both precede the body of the table.

Main Title. The title should be complete and clearly worded. The main title of a table and its other headings should make the table self-contained. If the data represent a period of time, the title or secondary headings should indicate the period covered. Include internal punctuation in the title, but no terminal period.

If a title requires more than one line, break at a division of thought and single-space to begin the second line. Avoid ending a line with a preposition. The title should be divided so that second and third lines are shorter than the preceding line(s), forming an inverted pyramid. The table title should not extend beyond the margins of the table.

Poor Title Construction

THE ANNUAL CONVENTION OF
THE AMERICAN MANAGEMENT ASSOCIATION
HYATT REGENCY HOTEL, HOUSTON, TEXAS
MAY 19–23, 19—

Good Title Construction

THE ANNUAL CONVENTION OF THE AMERICAN MANAGEMENT ASSOCIATION
HYATT REGENCY HOTEL, HOUSTON, TEXAS

Abbreviations. In order to save space, standard abbreviations may be used in column headings, but they should never be used in titles or secondary headings. If an abbreviation may be unclear, provide a key or a footnote at the bottom of the table.

Columns. Each vertical column must have a heading. Column headings must clearly identify items in the column and be centered or blocked over the column.

Column headings may be numbered consecutively from left to right with the numbers enclosed in parentheses. Columns of related data should be placed closer together than other columns. Large groupings of columns can be indicated by wider spaces separating the columns or by double vertical rules between columns.

Alignment. The left margins of tabulated material, such as line headings and column entries in a table, should be kept even. Whole numbers in columns are aligned on the right. When decimal fractions with varying numbers of places to the right of the decimal point are listed, numbers are aligned vertically at the decimal point. Key +, –, and @ signs close to figures at the left. Use dashes, leader dots, or a blank space to indicate omissions in a column.

Incorrect Alignment

MULTIPLY	BY	TO OBTAIN METRIC
Miles per hour	1.6	Kilometers per hour
Pounds	0.45	Kilograms
Square feet	0.09	Square meters
Ounces	28.35	Grams

Correct Alignment

MULTIPLY	BY	TO OBTAIN METRIC
Miles per hour	1.6	Kilometers per hour
Pounds	0.45	Kilograms
Square feet	0.09	Square meters
Ounces	28.35	Grams

Amounts. A comma should be used to separate each set of three digits in amounts, but should not be used to separate digits after a decimal point. For example, *1,125.50161* is correct; *1,125.501,61* is not.

Dollar signs should be used with the first amount in a column and with each total and subtotal. If columns include dollar amounts and other categories of numbers, key the dollar sign at each dollar amount. Format columns with percentages or like symbols (pounds, kilograms, etc.) in the same manner.

Incorrect	Correct
$1,456.26	$1,456.26
$ 362.35	362.35
$ 18.46	18.46
$1,837.07	$1,837.07

Leaders.   Lines of periods, or *leaders,* aid readers by guiding their eyes across the expanse of space between columns. Solid leaders (a period in every space) or open leaders (a space between consecutive periods) can be used. Solid leaders are more common because they are easier to key. When open leaders are used, periods on successive lines must align vertically. Achieving this may make it necessary to leave an extra horizontal space between a column entry and the first period, as shown in the example below. With computer software, leaders can be keyed automatically. Your finished copy should look like this:

> Night school classes 45
> Art classes   47
> Fashion design and clothing   52

Spacing.   Tables can be entirely single-spaced or double-spaced, or can feature a combination of single and double spacing. When long columns are single-spaced, leaving a line blank after every three, four, or five entries improves readability.

Rulings.   The appearance and readability of a table are vastly improved by the use of horizontal rulings made with the underline key. When formatting a ruled table, key (or use command to add) a single ruling the entire width of the table a double space below the title. A single ruling the width of the table separates column headings from the entries below. This ruling is keyed a single space below the column headings. A single ruling of the same width should appear a single space below the last entry in the table. If used, vertical rulings are placed at the midpoint between columns and extend from the single ruling at the top to the single ruling at the bottom, as shown in Figure 15-4. A formal table without rulings is called an open table.

Units.   The unit designation of data (inches, pounds, and so forth) must be given. Generally this information is provided in the main heading or subheading.

Footnotes.   If the meaning of any item in a table is not clear or must be qualified, an explanation should be given in a footnote. Footnotes are also sometimes used to indicate the source of the data. Footnotes are single-spaced. A *source* footnote is keyed first followed by any footnotes referring to specific items in the table. To identify footnote references in numerical data, use symbols (*, #, †) or lowercase letters. A number used to reference a footnote in a table could be confused as being part of the numerical data. Figure 15-4 shows proper footnoting.

Reference.   The name of the person responsible for the preparation of the table should be indicated on a file copy. When data are extracted from secondary sources, such as publications, the sources should be footnoted.

Fig. 15-4 A ruled table with sources, a note, and footnotes identified by lowercase letters *a* and *b*.

Table V
ESTIMATED COVERAGE AND CONTRIBUTION
OF EMPLOYEE-BENEFIT PLANS

(In Millions, Except Percent)

Type of Benefit	Coverage			Contribution[a]	
	Employees				
	Number	Percent of Employed Wage and Salary Workers	Dependents	Amount	Percent of Total Wages and Salaries
	(1)	(2)	(3)	(4)	(5)
Private and public employees:					
Life insurance and death benefits	40	63.3%	5	$2,039	0.63%
Accidental death	26	42.1	...	99	.03
Hospitalization[b]	46	72.8	72	3,801	.18
Regular medical	37	58.1	56	1,840	.57
Major medical expense	16	24.8	27	965	.30
Private employees only:					
Temporary disability	26	50.0	...	1,387	.52
Supplemental unemployment benefits	6	3.7	...	147	.04
Retirement	25	46.5	...	6,890	0.56
Total	218	...	...	$17,168	...

Sources: Based on data from various life insurance agencies and trade union and industry reports.

Note: Coverage data refer to civilian wage and salary workers and their dependents.

[a] Excludes dividends in group insurance.

[b] Coverage data include persons covered by group comprehensive major medical expense insurance as well as those with basic benefits.

Proofreading the Table

Every table must be checked for accuracy. Proofreading requires the help of another person. One person should read from the source document while the administrative assistant checks the completed original. For copy in columnar form, read down a column rather than across the page. Reading numbers aloud follows a prescribed routine. The words in the following examples that are connected by a hyphen should be read as a group; the commas indicate pauses:

718	seven-one-eight
98,302	nine-eight, comma, three-zero-two
24.76	two-four, point, seven-six
$313.00	three-one-three even (*or* no cents) dollars
77,000	seventy-seven thousand even

After the accuracy of the completed table has been verified and errors have been corrected, the original draft of the table and its source copy should be filed in a personal folder kept by the administrative assistant or attached to and filed with the file copy of the final draft. If anyone who reads the table discovers an error, checking the filed copy of the original data will enable you to determine whether the error originated in the source copy or was made in the process of keying the table.

COMPUTER GRAPHICS TECHNOLOGY

Graphics with a professional appearance can be produced with a personal computer. The administrative assistant who has a personal computer equipped with a graphics memory card, graphics software, a monitor, and an output device can prepare high-resolution paper graphics, slide graphics, overhead transparencies, photographs, and many other office applications. The software can be integrated with three or more types of programs, such as word processing, spreadsheet, and database, or can be a dedicated graphics software package. The monitor can be either monochrome or color (requiring a color graphics interface card). Output devices include dot matrix printers, plotters (pen-like devices that draw on paper), ink jet printers, and laser printers.

A computer graphics system permits people and machines to exchange graphic information at electronic speeds. Information presented graphically can be reviewed rapidly. An operator can work directly with charts, curves, sketches, and drawings on VDTs. An image can be reviewed, moved, redrawn, altered, erased, recorded in memory, and/or printed out on a printer/plotter, film recorder, or video projector.

Bar, pie, line, and organization charts can be produced in a myriad of colors, patterns, and type styles depending on the equipment and software package. After the operator keys the commands specified by the software package, the computer processes the numerical data into the specified graphic. Graphic software packages differ in their options. For instance, some graphics software will compute percentages before preparing a pie chart and may have the capability to explode (set apart) a piece of a pie chart.

Computer graphic technology has significantly increased the use of graphic aids in business reports and oral presentations (see Figure 15-5). In the past, internal graphics departments or outside service firms prepared the professional visual aids needed for reports and presentations. The use of computer graphics technology, however, has shifted much of this responsibility to the report or speech writer with a personal computer and ultimately to the writer's administrative assistant.

Just because a computer produced the graphic does not mean that the graphic is correct for the data shown.

An administrative assistant, therefore, must know how to operate the computer graphics system used by the business to select, display, and produce the most appropriate graphic for the data at hand. In making this selection, the administrative assistant cannot lose sight of the objective of graphics aids: simplicity, clarity, and service to the reader.

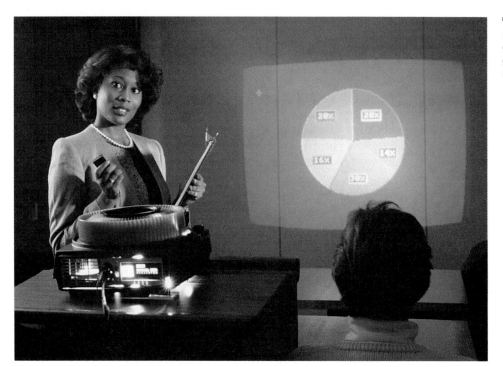

Fig. 15-5 Slides can be created with computer graphics technology for use in oral presentations.

CHARTS AND GRAPHS

A graph or a chart is a statistical picture. It presents numerical data in a visual form that is easy to analyze and remember. Taking hard facts and organizing them in visual form to make comparisons, to emphasize contrasts, and to bring out the full force of a message is a challenging opportunity.

Each type of graph or chart is used for a specific kind of comparison. Before selecting a graphic to display the data, you must first identify the message you want to convey and then determine the type of comparison (time, parts, items, frequency, or correlation) to be made. The most common graphics are line graphs, bar graphs, and circle charts. These and other types of graphics are discussed in this section.

In preparing a report having several charts or graphs, it is common practice to number them consecutively. A chart or graph is labeled "Figure" to distinguish it from a table. The word "Figure" is typed with an initial capital letter followed by an Arabic numeral. The title of the chart or graph follows the figure number. The caption is generally typed below the chart or graph, but can appear above the illustration. Numbering may not be necessary for an isolated chart or one used as a transparency during a presentation.

A chart or graph is labeled Figure *to distinguish it from a table.*

The source of the data and the date of compilation are placed below the chart. While this information may be omitted from the presentation copy, it must be recorded on the file copy.

Line Graphs

A commonly used type of graph is the line graph. *The line graph is most effective in showing fluctuations in a value or a quantity over a period of time.* Numeric variations in production, sales, costs, or profits over a period of months or years can be effectively illustrated with line graphs. The line graph shown in Figure 15-6 emphasizes the relationship between the total sales of foreign and domestic branches of a company over a five-year period. To avoid distortions or misleading the reader, always show the *zero* point.

Fig. 15-6 Although this line graph only shows two curves, as many as four or five could be plotted.

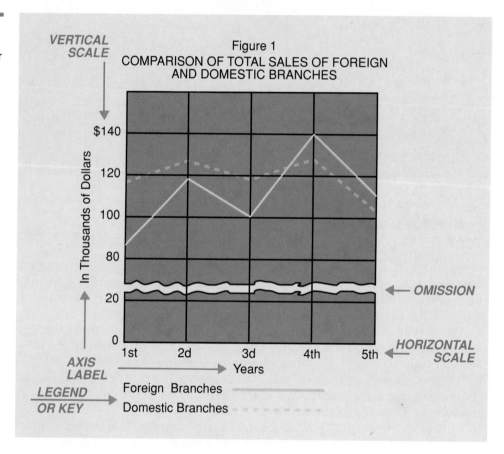

VERTICAL SCALE

Figure 1
COMPARISON OF TOTAL SALES OF FOREIGN AND DOMESTIC BRANCHES

In Thousands of Dollars

$140

120

100

80

20

0

1st   2d   3d   4th   5th

Years

← OMISSION

HORIZONTAL SCALE

AXIS LABEL

LEGEND OR KEY

Foreign Branches

Domestic Branches

Bar Graphs

The bar graph presents quantities by means of horizontal or vertical bars. Variations in numeric values are indicated by the lengths of the bars. The width of the bars is constant. Bars can be separated by spaces or can be contiguous. This latter type of bar graph is called a **histogram.**

A bar can represent a single value or be stacked; that is, with segments of the bar representing different components of the whole bar. The bar graph is most effectively used to compare a limited number of values, generally not more than four or five. *Bar graphs are often used in time series, frequency distributions, and comparisons among different sizes and different amounts.* With the exception of time series, the quantities indicated on bar graphs should begin with zero. Also, when possible, bars should be arranged in ascending or descending order according to lengths. If the bars are arranged according to time, the earliest period should be first. Figure 15-7 is an example of a bar graph.

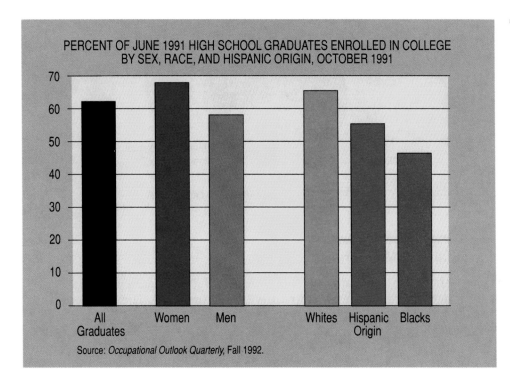

PERCENT OF JUNE 1991 HIGH SCHOOL GRADUATES ENROLLED IN COLLEGE BY SEX, RACE, AND HISPANIC ORIGIN, OCTOBER 1991

Source: *Occupational Outlook Quarterly,* Fall 1992.

Fig. 15-7 This bar graph was prepared for a transparency. Note that the chart is unnumbered and that the caption is at the top.

Circle Charts

The circle chart, sometimes called a *pie chart,* is an effective way to show the manner in which a given quantity is divided into parts. Data for circle charts must be converted into percentage form. In this type of chart, the complete area of the circle represents the whole quantity (100 percent), while the segments within the circle represent the parts, often referred to as wedges. Thus, the chart shows not only the relationship of each part to the whole but also of each part to every other part. Each part is identified by title, color, or other designation. The largest segment is generally plotted at the top of the circle (at 12 o'clock); moving clockwise, the rest of the segments are plotted in descending order of size. The sequence of parts may be changed, however, to give emphasis to a specific element.

The circle chart may be used to present such data as how the sales dollar is spent; how taxes paid by a firm are divided among local, state, and federal governments; or the percentage of store purchases made by men compared with those made by women. A circle chart is shown in Figure 15-8.

Fig. 15-8 Circle charts illustrate the relationship of each part to the whole.

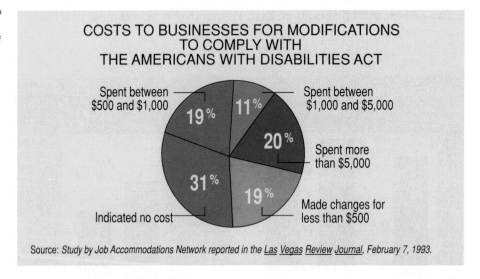

Pictorial and Map Charts

One of the more interesting developments in graphic representation is the use of pictorial charts, or **pictographs** (see Figure 15-9). They are generally an adaptation of one of the other types of graphs, using drawn symbols to represent the types of data being charted. For example, a bar chart showing losses due to fire might feature a streaming fire hose; the length of the stream would vary to indicate the amount of the loss. Growth in telephone service might be shown with drawings of telephones arranged in a line; each telephone would represent, for example, 1,000 telephones. To avoid distorting their values, all symbols used in the chart must be the same size.

Maps are often used to depict quantitative information, particularly when comparisons are made between geographic areas. Map charts range from simple sketches to detailed displays. If color is used to outline geographic areas, a legend will be needed to explain the meanings given to each color. If quantities are involved, figures can be placed inside geographic areas. Other symbols representing quantities, such as dots, also may be used. An example of a map chart is shown in Figure 15-10 on page 380.

Limitations of Charts and Graphs

Although charts and graphs are useful in presenting comparative data, they do have certain limitations. The number of facts presented on any one graph

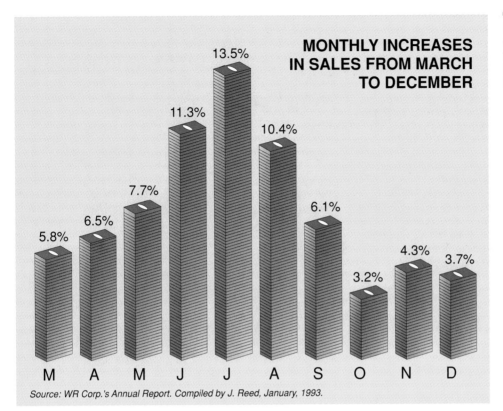

MONTHLY INCREASES IN SALES FROM MARCH TO DECEMBER

Source: WR Corp.'s Annual Report. Compiled by J. Reed, January, 1993.

Fig. 15-9 This pictorial chart uses money to illustrate the rise in WR Corporation's sales from March to December.

is usually limited to four or five. It is best to use a table when six or more elements are involved. A second limitation of most charts and graphs is that sometimes only approximate values are shown. Some graphics, however, do provide the specific value within the drawing. A third limitation is that it is possible for a graph to be drawn with mathematical accuracy and still give a distorted picture of the facts. For example, the overall width of a line graph determines the angles of the plotted curves. A graph that is too narrow may indicate much sharper rises and falls than the data indicate. In the same way, a line graph that is too wide may give the impression of gradual fluctuations between plotted points when the data indicate sharp increases.

A word of caution: A person can use numerical information to prove almost anything.

Interpreting Charts and Graphs

Poorly prepared graphics can create false or misleading impressions. To guard against arriving at inaccurate conclusions, the reader should examine a graphic critically, checking the following points:

- *Horizontal and vertical axes.* Are they appropriate for the data?

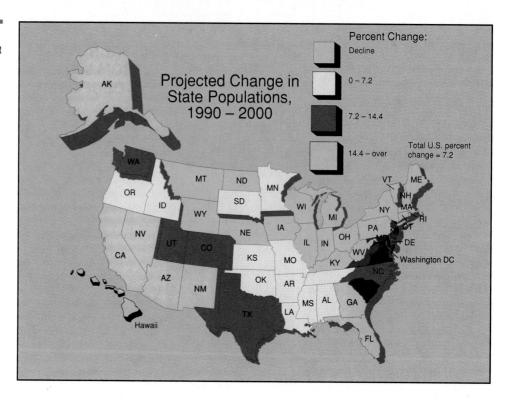

- *Plotting of data.* Are the increments uniform?
- *Zero point.* Is the quantitative axis at zero?
- *Type of chart or graph.* Is the graphic the right type for the data?
- *Legends and explanatory notes.* Do they describe the purpose and content of the graphic?

Report writers and presenters of speeches understand the importance of illustrating differences that make a difference.

After reviewing the mechanics of the graphic, the reader should interpret the information carefully. Some questions may be appropriate. For example, How was the data collected? Are the sample sizes (number of observations) large enough? Are the samples (observations) representative of the population being described? Is the information from unbiased sources? Does the evidence support the conclusions given? A careful evaluation of the information presented in a graphic is necessary to avoid conveying misinformation to a naive reader.

MISCELLANEOUS GRAPHIC AIDS

Other forms of graphic aids important in the business arena are flowcharts, organization charts, and wall charts. These graphics are discussed here.

Flowcharts

One of the most widely used tools in office management is the flowchart. It traces a unit of work as it flows through the office. Symbols with connecting lines are used to trace a step-by-step sequence of the work from point of origin to point of completion. Basic flowchart symbols are shown in Figure 15-11. A template can be purchased for drawing these symbols, or computer

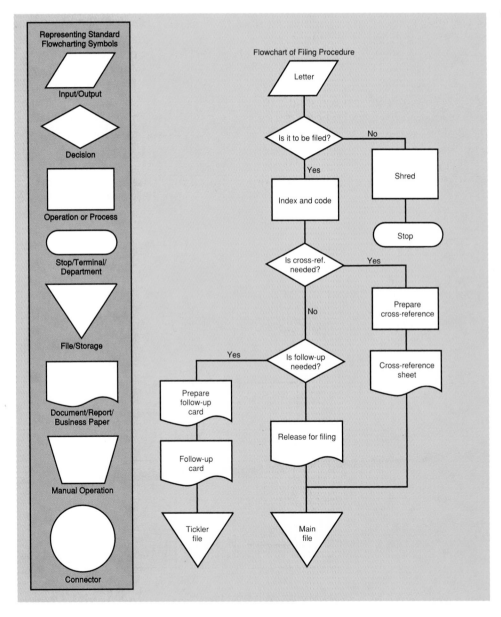

Fig. 15-11 A flowchart traces a unit of work as it flows through the office.

software can be used to create them. While the meaning of each flowchart symbol has become fairly standardized, a key can be provided to prevent any misunderstanding.

Organization Charts

An organization chart is a graphic presentation of the structure of a business. It points out the relationship of responsibilities and answers two basic questions: (1) What are the lines of authority (who reports to whom)? and (2) What are the functions of each unit (who is responsible for what)? Figure 15-12 answers these questions.

A business organization is seldom static. New personnel, new divisions, new responsibilities, and the realignment of old responsibilities create change. The organization chart, therefore, is frequently revised. In preparing or updating an organization chart, the administrative assistant must be aware that responsibility should flow downward and each level must be clearly defined. Also, different symbols differentiate policy-making positions (line) from support positions (staff).

The organization chart in Figure 15-12 shows line and staff relationships. Such a chart is supplemented with a functions chart on which the responsibilities of each position are identified. Showing both authority relationships and functional responsibilities on one organization chart would detract from its visual simplicity.

Fig. 15-12 On this organization chart, four levels of administrative authority are clearly identified, and the administrative staff is differentiated from the support staff. Note that the administrative assistant to the president is not under the supervision of the office manager.

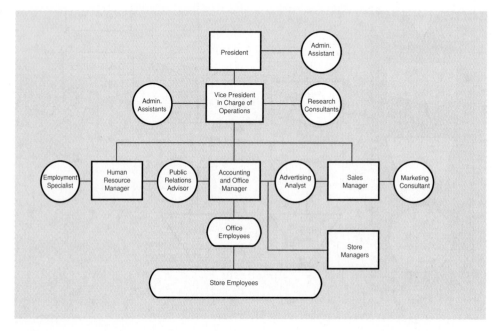

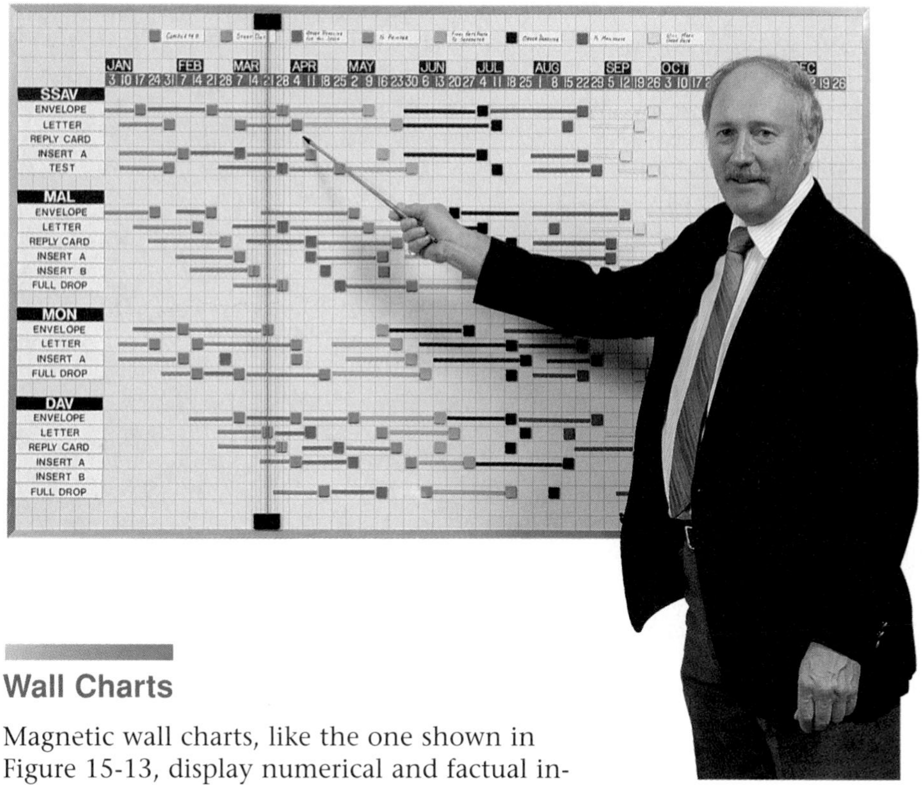

Fig. 15-13 This wall chart is used for tracking jobs in process. *Magna Visual, Inc.*

Wall Charts

Magnetic wall charts, like the one shown in Figure 15-13, display numerical and factual information, such as schedules, production gains, and equipment utilization. Wall charts, magnetic and nonmagnetic, can also be used to plot the progress of important projects.

A scheduling device still used by many organizations is the Gantt chart, developed by Henry L. Gantt in the late 1800s. Basically a bar chart, the Gantt chart plots time to be allocated on the horizontal axis and the resource to be scheduled (such as workers and equipment) on the vertical axis.

Summary

Data, whether in reports, advertising brochures, annual reports, or speeches, must be presented so that numbers are easily understood by the reader or the listener. The use of tables, charts, and graphs enhances comprehension. Computer graphics technology provides the capability for improving communication at all levels. Charts and graphs can be produced in color on paper, on film, or on transparencies. In addition to knowing how to operate the equipment and the software package, the administrative assistant working with computer graphics must know what graphic will best display the designated data and, at the same time, be understood by the reader.

The administrative assistant in today's office environment works with numerical information on a daily basis. If the administrative assistant is asked to compile data from source documents, it must be organized so that totals, averages, and percentages can be obtained. Data can be classified in any of five ways: in alphabetic sequence, by kind, by size, by location, or by time.

When exact numbers are required for a study, tables are preferable to charts or graphs. Charts and graphs are better to show comparisons and trends when quick identification of relationships is important.

Producing a well-balanced table requires careful planning. Following the rules of table construction is imperative. Most tables include a table number, a main title, a secondary heading, column or boxed headings, and a stub (left column).

A chart or graph presents numerical information in picture form. A commonly used graph is the *line graph*. It is most effective in showing fluctuations in a value or a quantity over a period of time. The *bar graph* illustrates quantities by means of horizontal or vertical bars. It is used in time series, frequency distributions, and comparisons. When a given quantity is divided into parts, the *circle or pie chart* is an effective graphic. The circle represents the whole quantity while the segments within the circle represent the parts. When preparing a chart or graph, the administrative assistant should keep in mind that these visuals have limitations: The number of elements that can be shown is limited to four or five and their values generally are shown as approximations. Further, although mathematically accurate, a chart can give a distorted picture of the data. The reader interpreting charts or graphs must look carefully at the mechanics of chart preparation and at the methods used in gathering the information. Other kinds of charts include pictorial charts, map charts, flowcharts, organization charts, and wall charts.

QUESTIONS FOR DISCUSSION

THINK IT
Through

1. Your employer gives you a handwritten list of numerical data having five columns with totals. You are to key the table on an electronic typewriter or computer. Is it a part of your responsibility to check the accuracy of these figures? Why or why not?

2. How has computer graphics technology shifted the responsibility for preparing visual aids from in-house graphics departments or outside sources to report writers and presenters?

3. What kind of graph should be prepared to present data in each of the following situations:

   a. Proof that a company has initiated affirmative action programs within the past three years

b. The total yearly cost of going to college during the past five years

c. Tuition rates at state-supported and private colleges over the past ten years

d. Amounts spent on research in six divisions of a large corporation over the past three years

e. The division of energy costs among five departments of a firm

f. The number of male employees compared with the number of female employees of a company for each year of a five-year period

g. The locations of ten manufacturing plants in the United States

h. The monthly schedule of assignments for 20 employees

4. Corporations usually use graphs extensively in their annual reports to stockholders. Financial tables and statements, however, are generally used in presenting data to boards of directors and to banks. Why are graphs used in the one case and tables in the other?

5. A consulting firm with a total of 50 employees reported in a community wage study that its average wage (arithmetic mean) was $20,000. An examination of the records revealed that the firm had ten executives, each receiving $70,000 a year. What would be your criticism of the reported average wage figure?

THINK IT
Through

6. Rekey the following sentences. Select the correct word from those in parentheses. Check the Reference Guide to correct your work.

a. An executive assistant should be able to (sight, cite, site) the rules for alphabetic filing.

b. This copy is (different than, different from) the one you signed in April.

c. Atlanta is (further, farther) from the office than it is from the factory.

d. An effective assistant will (accept, except) decision-making responsibilities.

e. I cannot go (any place, anywhere) without my computer.

PROBLEMS

1. Consult recent issues of business magazines. Find a visual aid that you believe distorts the data or misleads the reader. Prepare a transparency of the graphic. Discuss with the class the reasons why you believe as you do.

2. Prepare an organization chart depicting the structure of the company where you now work or have worked.

3. Before establishing a policy on sick leave, your employer asks you to make a study of the number of days 70 employees in the Des Moines office were absent from work because of illness and other causes (excluding vacations). You obtain the total number of days each employee was absent. They are as follows:

26	8	17	15	17	14	13
16	7	5	47	20	25	19
12	20	11	15	9	4	41
18	27	19	11	19	12	13
8	3	44	18	24	17	15
18	14	13	10	2	37	20
28	16	15	15	14	11	9
1	32	19	30	18	11	12
10	6	13	15	33	17	21
16	11	13	8	7	14	12

a. Prepare a frequency distribution of the days absent. Use a classification interval of five days (one workweek), such as 1 to 5, 6 to 10, and so forth. Determine the percentage of employees who were absent in each frequency interval.

b. Using this information, prepare a table with an appropriate title and column headings using an electronic typewriter or computer.

4. The following amounts are sales per day of a product for 25 days in April:

$118.23	$ 9.61	$107.16	$ 10.66
$ 41.32	$ 18.23	$ 26.31	$ 94.33
$ 91.73	$ 27.11	$ 83.17	$101.09
$ 63.24	$ 16.94	$ 67.92	$ 89.31
$ 36.74	$ 78.26	$ 74.26	
$ 18.92	$124.36	$ 68.31	
$ 87.65	$ 97.08	$ 17.08	

a. Prepare a tabulation in pencil of the sales so that you can determine the median. What is the median sale for April?

b. Calculate the arithmetic average or mean of the April sales.

Note: If you have computer capabilities, complete this problem using a spreadsheet.

▶ **TA15-1.TEM** Using your template disk, access the TA15-1.TEM file. The spreadsheet shows the total sales (divided among four product lines) for a women's wear company.

Proceed as follows:

1. Develop a spreadsheet showing not only (a) total sales in dollars and (b) individual product line sales in dollars but also (c) sales in percent (that is, product line sales as a percent of total sales).
2. Prepare a circle chart or pie chart showing sales in percent for each product line.
3. Prepare a bar chart of the same sales data.
4. Review the spreadsheet, the pie chart, and the bar chart before you submit them to your instructor.

   Note: If you do not have computer graphics capability, manually draw the pie chart and bar chart.

▶ **TA15-2.TEM** Using your template disk, access the TA15-2.TEM file. This file shows the sales volume for Innovative Products by month for a two-year period.

Proceed as follows:

1. Using your computer graphics, prepare a line graph of the spreadsheet data. Remember to use titles and legends.
2. Print the line graph, check it for accuracy, and then submit the final graph to your instructor.

   Note: If you do not have computer graphics capabilities, draw the line graph by hand.

What does the graph imply about seasonal fluctuations and general performance for this two-year period?

R

eports and Written Documents

INTRODUCTION

Every year millions of business reports are written, and the majority of these reports are written for management personnel. Executives rely on business reports not only to provide them with information but also to assist them in solving business problems.

An administrative assistant who works for a report writer will be involved from the preliminary stages of report preparation to the binding of the report. The initial keying responsibilities are the tentative outline and successive drafts of the report. When final approval is given, the administrative assistant makes any corrections requested in the body of the report; keys, proofreads, and corrects the introductory and supplementary sections; and then prints, collates, and binds the manuscript. The equipment and the software used will determine the ease with which the report is prepared.

When a paper is written for publication, special formatting is required. The same is true for keying speeches and writing company procedures. This chapter provides useful information for the administrative assistant responsible for keying these kinds of documents.

REPORT WRITING

A business report transmits objective information to one or more persons and is written for a specific business purpose. A report is used to plan, organize, and implement business operations. It contains factual information presented in clear, concise language. It can be written by an employee of a firm for internal use, or for a business client; it can also be prepared for a company by an independent authority.

Written reports for internal use may be circulated either vertically (up and down the company ranks) or horizontally (across management lines). A written report may take the form of an interoffice memorandum, a letter, or a bound manuscript.

Report-Writing Routine

The routine for writing a report differs considerably from the routine for writing a letter. The report writer follows these steps in preparing a business report:

1. Prepares a tentative outline.
2. Collects information.
3. Formulates an outline of the contents.
4. Writes the report.
5. Checks logic of content organization.
6. Submits the report for first keying.
7. Rechecks the organization of material and edits sentence by sentence for clarity and correctness. Rewrites sections as necessary.
8. Presents report for second printing.
9. Checks the organization and editing again before final printing.

In gathering information for a report, the writer reviews both *primary* and *secondary* information sources. Primary sources include personal observations, questionnaires, surveys, interviews, and experiments. Secondary sources refer to previously published documents, such as books, articles in magazines, and so forth.

The language of reports is objective, emphasizes factual information, and is free of any personal bias or opinion. Reports are generally written in formal writing style (in the third person) without *I*'s, *we*'s, and *you*'s. Substitutes for these first-person and second-person pronouns, such as "the writer" or "the researcher," are also frowned upon. Reports written in informal style use first- and second-person pronouns. Illustrations of formal and informal writing styles follow:

Formal Style	**Informal Style**
A study of office correspondence at Henderson Associates supports the need for more computers.	After making a study of office correspondence at Henderson Associates, we recommend purchasing more computers.

The present verb tense or a combination of present and past tense is used for report writing. For example, a discussion of how a study was conducted or when investigations were made is written in the past tense, because these actions are no longer in process. Some reports discuss all actions as having taken place in the past, in which case the past tense is used throughout the report.

Report writers vary in their skill at preparing reports. Every writer, however, edits and polishes successive drafts until the final report is as clear, concise, and logical as possible.

The Administrative Assistant's Responsibility

The administrative assistant plays an important role in the preparation of business reports. It is not unusual for an administrative assistant to be involved in each step of the report-writing routine, from collecting information to the final printing of the report. In addition, the administrative assistant is responsible for editing reports for clear language, correct spelling and punctuation, and accuracy of numbers and computations. Producing attractive reports is made easier through the use of the many automatic features of computers and word processing and/or graphics software.

The Form of the Report

Depending on the nature and circulation of a report, its form may be a letter, an interoffice memorandum, or a formal, bound manuscript. Some companies have style sheets for all three forms or for special reports. Style sheets standardize report formats. If a style sheet is not available, the writer follows a consistent pattern.

Letter Reports.   Letter reports are external reports prepared for clients outside the firm. These reports follow a letter format and include all letter parts. They are prepared on letterhead stationery, single-spaced, with one-inch side margins. Special headings, such as an introduction, a summary and/or conclusions, and recommendations, are common in letter reports. These headings are keyed at the center or at the left margin and may be underscored. If boldfacing is used, headings can be keyed without an underscore. Tables and/or graphics are used to display numerical data and are referenced in the text. Tables should begin and end on the same page. As with most reports, the language is objective, written in the third person (formal writing style), and free of statements that show personal bias.

Interoffice Memorandum Reports.   Memorandum reports are internal communications formatted in memo style. An example of a memorandum report appears in Figure 16-1. These reports are single-spaced and may include side headings for the introduction, discussion, summary, conclusions, and recom-

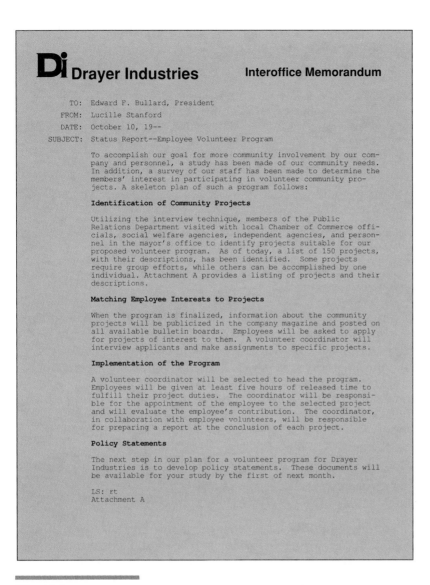

Di Drayer Industries　　　　　　**Interoffice Memorandum**

TO: Edward F. Bullard, President
FROM: Lucille Stanford
DATE: October 10, 19--
SUBJECT: Status Report--Employee Volunteer Program

To accomplish our goal for more community involvement by our company and personnel, a study has been made of our community needs. In addition, a survey of our staff has been made to determine the members' interest in participating in volunteer community projects. A skeleton plan of such a program follows:

Identification of Community Projects

Utilizing the interview technique, members of the Public Relations Department visited with local Chamber of Commerce officials, social welfare agencies, independent agencies, and personnel in the mayor's office to identify projects suitable for our proposed volunteer program. As of today, a list of 150 projects, with their descriptions, has been identified. Some projects require group efforts, while others can be accomplished by one individual. Attachment A provides a listing of projects and their descriptions.

Matching Employee Interests to Projects

When the program is finalized, information about the community projects will be publicized in the company magazine and posted on all available bulletin boards. Employees will be asked to apply for projects of interest to them. A volunteer coordinator will interview applicants and make assignments to specific projects.

Implementation of the Program

A volunteer coordinator will be selected to head the program. Employees will be given at least five hours of released time to fulfill their project duties. The coordinator will be responsible for the appointment of the employee to the selected project and will evaluate the employee's contribution. The coordinator, in collaboration with employee volunteers, will be responsible for preparing a report at the conclusion of each project.

Policy Statements

The next step in our plan for a volunteer program for Drayer Industries is to develop policy statements. These documents will be available for your study by the first of next month.

LS: rt
Attachment A

Fig. 16-1 Interoffice memorandum reports are single-spaced documents. They may be written in first, second, or third person, depending upon their circulation.

mendations. Tables and supporting data generally are attached to the memorandum. Memorandum reports may be written in a combination of first, second, and third person. The circulation of the report determines the writing style. For instance, a report for upward distribution would probably be written in objective, third-person (formal writing) style; one being distributed horizontally could be more informal.

Formal Reports.　　A formal report is identified by its format and its impersonal tone. The appearance of the manuscript and the formality of its language convey that the subject is important. A short formal report may consist of only the body or informative text. A long formal report may have, in addition to the body, various introductory parts and supplements including:

Introductory Parts	Sturdy cover or title page (or both)
	Preface, letter or memorandum of transmittal, including acknowledgment
	Table of contents
	List of tables, charts, and illustrations
	Summary (can follow Conclusions and Recommendations)
Body of the Report	Introduction, including purpose of the report
	Main body of the report
	Conclusions and recommendations
Supplementary Parts	Endnotes (if used instead of footnotes)
	Bibliography
	Appendix
	Index

Notice that the summary can precede the main body of the report. This arrangement benefits the busy executive who has time to read only a synopsis. Those who need or want complete information will read the entire report. Also, while the appendix generally follows the bibliography in a report, it can precede the bibliography.

Of the three main parts of a report (introductory, body, and supplementary), the body is usually developed first and keyed in all but final form before the other parts are prepared. For this reason, this chapter discusses the development of the body of a report first.

DEVELOPING THE BODY OF THE FORMAL REPORT

The writer of a report is responsible for what the report says and what it implies. It makes sense for the writer who has the help of an administrative assistant to work closely with that individual as a team member in the preparation of a report.

The Outline

A methodical writer first makes a topic outline or framework containing all the important points to be covered in the report. This outline later may serve as the table of contents. Headings for a report may also be taken from the outline.

There are two outline numbering systems: alphanumeric and decimal. In an alphanumeric outline, numbers and letters alternate. For instance, main headings begin with Roman numerals (I., II., III., etc.) and are keyed with all capital letters. First-level subheadings begin with capital letters (A.,

B., C., etc.) and are keyed with initial capital letters. Second-level subheadings are also keyed with initial capital letters and begin with Arabic numerals (1., 2., 3., etc.). The decimal outline system found mainly in scientific reports, manuals, and some business reports uses Arabic numerals and decimals. Figure 16-2 shows the alphanumeric and decimal outline systems.

```
          DESIGNING A BUSINESS FORM

I.   PURPOSE OF THE FORM

     A.  Systems Analysis

         1.  Definition of the Problem
         2.  Discussion of the Facts
         3.  Analysis of the Results of the
             Study
         4.  Recommendation

     B.  Preparation of the Proposal

         1.  Rationale for the Study
         2.  Discussion of the Systems Analysis

II.  FORM DESIGN

     A.  Type of Information
     B.  Space Requirements
     C.  Sequence of Information
```

```
          DESIGNING A BUSINESS FORM

1.   PURPOSE OF THE FORM

     1.1.  Systems Analysis

           1.1.1.  Definition of the Problem
           1.1.2.  Discussion of the Facts
           1.1.3.  Analysis of the Results
                   of the Study
           1.1.4.  Recommendation

     1.2.  Preparation of the Proposal

           1.2.1.  Rationale for the Study
           1.2.2.  Discussion of the Systems
                   Analysis

2.   FORM DESIGN

     2.1.  Type of Information
     2.2.  Space Requirements
     2.3.  Sequence of Information
```

Fig. 16-2 Notice the alphanumeric and decimal systems and that the headings are parallel in wording.

In constructing an outline, there are general guidelines to follow concerning main and subheadings. No main heading or subheading in an outline ever stands alone. For every *I* there is at least a *II*, for every *A* a *B*. (If an outline contains a single heading, it is probably part of another point, or misplaced, or irrelevant.) Headings should be worded concisely in parallel style. For example, in Figure 16-2, the main headings *I* and *II* are both noun phrases. Subheadings under the same main heading should be parallel. For example, under one main heading, the subheadings may be noun phrases, while the subheadings under another major heading may be verb phrases. Headings can be short constructions beginning with nouns, verbal nouns, or verbs; long constructions that tell the story; or complete sentences. Once a style for headings is established, it must be consistent and parallel throughout.

C O M M U N I C A T I O N

In outlines no main heading or subheading ever stands alone. For every I there is at least a II; for every A a B.

The Draft

A carefully written formal report is printed at least once in draft form. A draft is generously spaced. Although accurately keyed, drafts give little thought to final form. The purpose of a draft is to get the writer's thoughts on paper, to provide something tangible to edit and improve. Preparing a draft is not a waste of time; rather, it is a vital step in report preparation. In keying all drafts, you should follow these practices:

1. Use paper that is less than letterhead quality. Continuous-feed computer paper can be used for this purpose. Some offices use colored paper for drafts.

2. Provide plenty of room for edits. Use triple or quadruple spacing and wide margins on all four sides. Indent paragraphs five spaces.

3. If a quotation is several lines in length, single-space and indent it in the same form as it will appear in the final copy, because changes in quoted matter are unlikely to be made.

4. If following the traditional (academic) style of documentation, key footnotes at the bottom of the page, on a separate sheet, or as shown in Figure 16-3.

5. Material for an appendix should be keyed in final form and labeled Appendix (or Exhibit) A, B, and so forth. Keep this material in a file folder for safekeeping until the report is completed.

6. Key insertions in subsequent printings at the proper place in the document and reprint affected pages of the document.

7. Electronically save each draft. Keep a paper copy of each draft at your desk for easy reference. Number each successive draft and date it. Each page is numbered in sequence and sometimes carries the draft number and the date.

8. Carefully check and proofread each successive draft so that subsequent drafts contain valid material. Be sure to make all changes that appear on the draft paper copy on your electronic media. Have the paper copy and the screen at the same place in the document while making corrections or updating the document.

9. Save paper and electronic copies of all drafts until the report is completed and presented. Even though it has been superseded, a writer may decide to use material from an earlier draft.

A simple method of incorporating a footnote into a draft is to type the footnote immediately below the line in which the reference number appears.[1] Separate the footnote from the

---

[1]Rita Sloan Tilton, J. Howard Jackson, and Sue C. Rigby, The Electronic Office: Procedures and Administration (Cincinnati: South-Western Educational Publishing, 1996), p. 394.

---

text by keying lines across the page above and below it.

Fig. 16-3 Footnotes keyed by this method are retained in correct position if copy is rearranged during editing.

COMPUTER SOFTWARE AND REPORT FORMATTING

A number of word processing software programs with various options are available to make report preparation a challenging and interesting experience for the administrative assistant. For the prewriting stage, there are outline programs that construct outlines as a writer inputs ideas. For use during the draft process, a thesaurus is an option offered by many word processing programs. With several keystrokes an operator can look up a word or a phrase; a list of synonyms then appears on the monitor. Punctuation, style, and grammar check modules of some programs identify errors such as wordiness or the omission of a quotation mark. The spell checker option is an excellent aid, but the administrative assistant must be aware that some words with very different meanings are pronounced the same. A spell checker cannot always detect an error in proper word usage. A good example is "principal" and "principle"; both spelled correctly, but perhaps misused in the manuscript. Another option to aid in report preparation, discussed in Chapter 15, is a computer graphics software program. A feature of great interest to the administrative assistant—footnoting and bibliography presentations—is included with most word processing programs. Having this option makes keying traditional (academic) style footnotes at the bottom of manuscript pages a relatively easy task.

Integrated software provides several programs in one software package; generally included are word processing, spreadsheet, and database management. Some integrated programs include graphics, outlining, indexing, and/or a spell checker. For a more thorough discussion of software, refer to Chapter 5.

An advanced report preparation system is desktop publishing. A full desktop system offers low-cost publishing capability to a company. Desktop publishing integrates word processing software, graphics software, clip art software (enables the user to incorporate standard drawings into the document), and page composition software (accepts materials created by other programs and controls font size, spacing, page breaks, etc.) to produce professional-looking newsletters, brochures, reports, and the like. A laser printer is an important component of the system. An administrative assistant using desktop publishing will need to practice using the software to lay out pages, choose type sizes and styles, and create drawings before attempting a major project.

KEYING THE BODY OF THE FORMAL REPORT

The final version of a report measures the originator's skill in concise, logical writing and the administrative assistant's skill in sustained, attractive, meticulous keying and in proofreading. The administrative assistant must follow an accepted manual of style for formal report preparation. Page layout and a system of footnoting must be determined. These topics are discussed in this section.

Also, it is generally necessary to provide multiple copies of reports. Most office managers prefer that report originals be prepared on good quality paper and photocopied for distribution.

Page Layout

The page layout of a business report looks much like a printed page from a standard textbook. Although double spacing is preferred, reports can be single-spaced. To be sure that each page is uniformly keyed, the administrative assistant carefully studies the company's report style sheet or, if one is not available, an accepted manual of style for report preparation. A widely used style manual is *The Chicago Manual of Style,* published by The University of Chicago Press and now in its fourteenth edition. With the preferred style in mind, the administrative assistant then designs a page layout covering margins, indentations, and line spacing. If the administrative assistant uses a word processor, instructions can be programmed into the machine. If using a computer, the administrative assistant follows the instructions in the software manual. When the report is very detailed or lengthy or when several operators are sharing the responsibility for keying the report, the administrative assistant prepares a job instruction sheet.

Job Instructions.   The keying and printing of a report of many pages must be organized in advance and controlled while in process. To accomplish this task, prepare a job instruction sheet. Cover every point about type style, form, placement, and format. Try to anticipate in advance every question that will be raised. Figure 16-4 provides a listing of information required to ensure consistency in keying and printing a report.

Indentations.   Paragraphs may be keyed flush with the left margin or indented 5, 10, 15, or even 20 spaces. Formal reports are usually double-spaced with paragraph indentations. For single-spaced reports, double-space between paragraphs. In blocked double-spaced work, quadruple-space between paragraphs. Indentations make for easy reading, regardless of the line length of the body.

Margins.   The top margin of the first page of a part or section of a report can be 1 1/2 or 2 inches (the writer's choice); the bottom margin is 1 inch. The top and bottom margins of subsequent pages of the report are 1 inch. The left margin is either 1 inch or 1 1/2 inches (if the report is to be bound at the left), and the right margin is 1 inch.

Headings and Subheadings.   Headings and subheadings are used to guide a reader through a report. (Headings and subheadings are often referred to as *degree headings*—first, second, and third degree, for example.) Two questions should be considered in creating and evaluating headings: Do they clarify

COMMUNICATION

Between consecutive headings intervening text is needed.

INFORMATION REQUIRED FOR A JOB INSTRUCTION SHEET

1. Kind and size of paper to be used
2. Kind, type style, and pitch (l0, 12) or font of word processor or computer/software/printer to be used
3. Page format, including:
   Left margin
   Right margin
   Top margin (specify for first page and following pages)
   Bottom margin
   Vertical spacing (single, double, or other)
   Paragraph indentation (specify number of spaces)
   Tabulation indentation (specify number of spaces)
   Tabulation indentation (specify for outline level I., A., 1., a., etc.)
   Tabulation spacing (single or double)
   Headings (provide examples and indicate placement and the vertical spacing before and after each level heading [see page 396])
   Subheadings (provide examples and indicate placement and the vertical spacing before and after each level heading [see page 396])
4. Placement of computer printouts, tables, and graphs (see page 401)
5. Quotations (see page 398)
6. Enumerations (see page 400)
7. Footnotes (see page 398)
8. Numbering pages (see page 401)
9. Handling of keyed (printed) pages awaiting assembly
10. Instructions for final proofreading (see page 409)
11. Number of copies required
12. Instructions for collating (see page 409)
13. Instructions for binding (see page 412)
14. Distribution of copies
15. Disposition of original draft(s) and/or electronic media

Fig. 16-4 Preparing a job instruction sheet ensures consistency of style and format in the finished report.

content and increase readability? Are the headings parallel according to outline construction?

In general, headings and subheadings parallel the outline. (Note the arrangement of headings in this book. They cue the reader to the relative importance of subject matter.) Centered and capitalized headings are superior to centered headings with capitals and lowercase letters. Also, centered headings are superior to side headings. If boldface is used, key headings without underscoring following this same hierarchy of keying and placement. See Figure 16-5 for the traditional placement of headings and subheadings.

COMMUNICATIO**N**

Long reports are more readable if headings and subheadings are used.

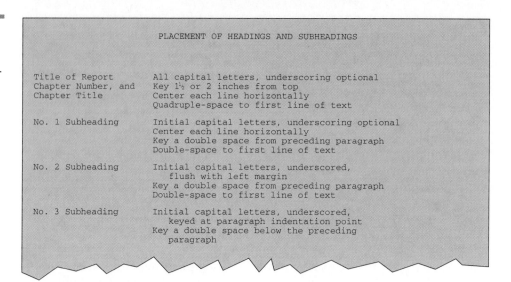

Fig. 16-5 In a formal report headings and subheadings are keyed and placed according to a system of hierarchy. If boldfacing is used, follow this same system without underscoring.

```
                          PLACEMENT OF HEADINGS AND SUBHEADINGS


    Title of Report         All capital letters, underscoring optional
    Chapter Number, and     Key 1½ or 2 inches from top
    Chapter Title           Center each line horizontally
                            Quadruple-space to first line of text

    No. 1 Subheading        Initial capital letters, underscoring optional
                            Center each line horizontally
                            Key a double space from preceding paragraph
                            Double-space to first line of text

    No. 2 Subheading        Initial capital letters, underscored,
                                 flush with left margin
                            Key a double space from preceding paragraph
                            Double-space to first line of text

    No. 3 Subheading        Initial capital letters, underscored,
                                 keyed at paragraph indentation point
                            Key a double space below the preceding
                                 paragraph
```

Quoted Matter

Reports often quote material from other sources, either directly or indirectly, and must give credit to these sources. For indirect quotations or references, a footnote providing the source suffices. Figure 16-6 shows how direct quotations can be handled in business reports.

Permission to quote copyrighted material must be obtained from the copyright holder when reports are to be printed or duplicated for public circulation. (Material published by a governmental agency is not copyrighted.) Full information, including the following, should be sent to the copyright holder with the request to reprint:

1. The text leading up to the quotation or a copy of the page that includes the quotation
2. The lines to be quoted (underscore or highlight the lines on the copy)
3. The source line or the complete footnote
4. The title, publisher, and date of publication in which the quoted matter will appear

Footnotes

Three methods of footnoting are used in business reports. They are the traditional (academic) method, the textual citation/reference method (in-text citation), and the scientific/technical method.

Traditional footnotes are keyed at the foot of the page on which the citation appears or at the end of the article or chapter. When footnotes are

KEYING DIRECT QUOTATIONS

1. Quotations of *fewer than four lines* are keyed in the body of the paragraph and enclosed in quotation marks.

2. Quotations of *four or more lines* are usually keyed without quotation marks, single-spaced, and indented from the left margin or from both margins.

3. When a quotation of *several paragraphs* is not indented, quotation marks precede each paragraph and follow the final word in the last paragraph only.

4. A *quotation within a quotation* is enclosed in single quotation marks.

5. *Italicized words* in a quotation are italicized or underscored.

6. Omissions are shown by ellipses—three periods with a space before, after, and between each period (. . .) within a sentence. Use four periods if the omission comes at the end of a sentence.

7. *Inserted words (interpolations)* are enclosed in brackets. Parentheses cannot be used. Since they often occur naturally in the text, the reader will be unable to identify interpolations if parentheses are used.

8. If a quotation has an error in grammar, spelling, word usage, or the like, indicate the report writer's knowledge of the error by using the word *sic* enclosed in brackets immediately following the error.

9. A source for a quotation should be footnoted, unless the source is identified adequately in the text.

grouped at the end of a chapter or report, they are referred to as *endnotes*. In paging the report, endnotes precede the bibliography. Footnotes are numbered in sequence throughout each section or throughout the entire report. Footnote numbers, called *superscript* numbers, are raised slightly above the line of print at the citation point and at the footnote location.

Administrative assistants using electronic equipment that does not have a superscript feature can key the footnote number between slashes (for example, /2/, indicating footnote 2) at the citation point and the number on the line of typing at the footnote location.

The placement of traditional (academic) footnotes at the bottom of the page makes it easy for the reader to check source material. Alternatives to the traditional method of footnoting have been created to make it easier for the person keying the manuscript. Now that computer software is available to make footnoting placement automatic, however, the report writer's paramount concern should be the convenience of the reader.

The keying of traditional footnotes may be reviewed in the Reference Guide on page 760. A guide for keying the bibliography in traditional style also can be found in the Reference Guide.

One alternative to the traditional (academic) system is the textual citation/reference method. The American Psychological Association (APA) and the Modern Language Association (MLA) style sheets for report writers use the textual citation/reference method. In APA style, at the citation point in the body of the report, the name(s) of the author(s), the publication date, and the page number are enclosed in parentheses; for instance: (Tilton, Jackson & Rigby, 1995, p. 35). In MLA style the name(s) of the author(s) and the page number are enclosed in parentheses at the citation point: (Tilton, Jackson, Rigby, 35). In most respects, the bibliography follows the same format as the traditional bibliography, and is entitled "Reference List" (APA) or "Works Cited" (MLA). If you use either of these styles of footnoting/bibliography formatting, you will need to consult the appropriate manual.

Another method of footnoting, often used in scientific and technical publications, is a number system linked to the bibliography. Footnotes are numbered consecutively and are followed by a colon and the page number of the reference listed in the bibliography. These footnote citations are enclosed in parentheses. For example, (15:30) indicates page 30 of the fifteenth reference. The bibliography is arranged in numerical sequence according to the order in which footnotes appear in the body of the report. A variation of this method is to arrange the references in the bibliography in alphabetical order by last name of author and number them. Footnotes are then numbered according to the numbers assigned to them in the bibliography. The bibliography is keyed in the traditional (academic) style.

Enumerations

There are two ways to key enumerations, with a hanging indent or flush left. In the hanging-indent style, the first word of the second line is aligned with the first word in the previous line. For example:

```
1. Our recruiting program will begin in September,
   and our objective will be to hire as many quali-
   fied young women as we can find for the vacan-
   cies.

2. Our training program will run for one full year.
   The first three months will be devoted to the
   orientation of new employees.
```

The other method of keying enumerations calls for keying the number and all lines flush with the left margin, as shown below:

```
1. Our recruiting program will begin in September,
and our objective will be to hire as many qualified
young women as we can find for the vacancies.

2. Our training program will run for one full year.
The first three months will be devoted to the orien-
tation of new employees.
```

The flush left style is a little easier to key, but most people prefer the appearance and readability of the hanging-indent style.

Computer Printouts, Tables, and Graphs

Computer printouts, tables, and graphs can be incorporated into the body of a report. Explanations of these graphics precede their placement in the text. Alternative placement is in an appendix at the end of the report. Placing items in the appendix, however, runs the risk that the reader may overlook them.

Tables and graphs can be reduced on some copiers. If this is the plan, make the reductions before keying the manuscript, so that appropriate space is allowed for each. Too many computer tables or graphs detract from the readability of the discussion. Unless absolutely necessary to the discussion, lengthy computer printouts or tables should be placed in the appendix.

Page Numbering

The title page of a report is considered the first page and is not numbered. Subsequent preliminary pages are numbered in small Roman numerals (ii, iii) at the bottom center. Arabic numerals without periods are used to number the body of the report and supplementary parts (appendix, bibliography, index). Arabic numbers can be keyed at the top right corner or centered at the bottom on the page. If footnotes are used in the manuscript, numbering at the top of the page is more practical. Numbers are keyed 1 inch (on line 6) from the top in the upper right corner; double-space beneath the page number to begin keying text. Numbering the first page of a report is optional. If it is numbered, the number is centered 1 inch from the bottom of the page. After page 1, pages are numbered consecutively throughout the report.

Numbering manuscript pages is automatic with computer software programs. The operator can choose between using headers (numbers at the top of the page) or footers (numbers at the bottom of the page).

PREPARING AND KEYING OTHER PARTS

The order in which the other parts of a report are prepared varies, but inserting page numbers in the table of contents is necessarily one of the final steps. This section discusses in alphabetical order the introductory and supplementary parts of a report.

Appendix

In a formal report, an appendix contains supporting tables, statistics, and similar reference materials. Items in an appendix are numbered Appendix A,

Appendix B, and so forth, and are listed in the table of contents. All items in the appendix should have a descriptive title; for example, Survey Questionnaire. In some reports the appendix materials are labeled Exhibit A, Exhibit B, and so forth. The appendix usually follows the bibliography.

Bibliography/Reference List

All references cited in a report should be included in a traditional bibliography. References used in the study, but not specifically cited, should also be included. A report based on a study of published materials frequently includes a bibliography of source material. Such a bibliography is called a *selected bibliography*. Many business reports are based on factual information compiled within the company, and there is no need to refer to outside source material.

Sometimes the administrative assistant is asked to prepare a *comprehensive bibliography* of all material published on a subject during a designated period of time. An *annotated bibliography* contains an evaluation or a brief explanation of the content of each reference. An example of a reference in an annotated bibliography follows:

> Tilton, Rita Sloan, J. Howard Jackson, and Sue C. Rigby. The Electronic Office: Procedures and Administration. Cincinnati: South-Western Educational Publishing, 1996.
>
> This text is designed to prepare administrative assistants for job entry and advancement. It provides a comprehensive picture of present-day office technology. The Reference Guide at the back of the book is invaluable to administrative assistants in training and to those on the job.

A bibliography reference is similar to a footnote in that it cites the author's name, the title of the publication, the publisher, and the date. The name of an editor, a translator, or an illustrator may also be included. Specific chapters or sections and their inclusive page numbers may be given if the entry refers only to a certain part of the book or periodical; otherwise, page numbers are omitted.

The keying of a bibliography in the traditional (academic) style is described in this paragraph. (See APA and MLA manuals of style for their presentations.) Key the word "Bibliography" 1 1/2 or 2 inches from the top of the page in capital letters. References are given in alphabetic order by the last name of the first-named author, or references may be listed alphabetically within designated sections, such as chapters. The first line is keyed flush with the left margin; succeeding lines are indented (hanging-indent style). Each reference is single-spaced with a double space between references. The bibliography is placed directly after the main body of the report or, if endnotes are used, after that section. Refer to the Reference Guide for the proper presentation of a bibliography.

Index

An index is the last section of the report and is included only when it is felt that there will be occasion to use it. A detailed table of contents usually suffices. Many word processing applications offer automatic indexing features. When an index is necessary and this option is not part of the available software, the administrative assistant can use a manual method of indexing by following these steps:

1. Underline in colored pencil each item on each page that should be included in the index.
2. Write each underlined item and its page number on a separate slip, as shown in Figure 16-7.
3. Sort completed slips into alphabetic order.
4. Prepare index from slips.

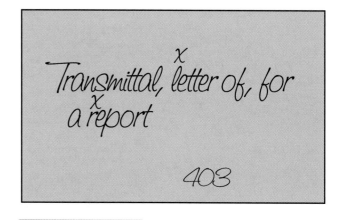

Fig. 16-7 This is an index slip for an item from this book. The X's indicate that cross-reference slips were made for *Letter of transmittal for report* and for *Report, letter of transmittal for.*

Letter or Memorandum of Transmittal

A letter or memorandum of transmittal is often bound into a report and performs a function similar to that of a preface. The letter or memorandum transmits the report and gives authorization for the report, its purpose, details of its preparation, the period covered by the report, acknowledgments, and similar information. A letter or memorandum of transmittal helps the reader understand the depth and breadth of a report and arouses interest in studying it (see Figure 16-8).

Letterhead stationery is used if the report is prepared for a person or persons outside the company. Memorandum stationery is used if the report is for internal distribution. The language of a letter/memorandum of transmittal is more personal than the objective style of a report.

Summary of the Report

The summary is a concise review of the entire report and its findings, and, by definition, no new material can be introduced. The summary is also sometimes called a synopsis, a precis, an abstract, or an executive summary.

The summary is prepared after the body of the report has been written. It includes a statement of the problem, its scope, the method of investigation, conclusions, and recommendations. It is objective in nature and is

CHALLENGE

Engineering Company
12204 Candelaria Road
Albuquerque, NM 87112-8709
(505) 555-3746

June 30, 19—

Mr. Douglas B. Hankins
Ultra Electronics Manufacturers, Inc.
20055 Coors Road, N.W.
Albuquerque, New Mexico 87114-1120

Dear Mr. Hankins:

The feasibility study you authorized on January 1, 19--, concerning the provision of an in-house cafeteria is enclosed.

The study included a thorough investigation of your company's buildings and possible areas for expansion. A series of conferences with employees of each department was held. In addition, a questionnaire was developed and administered to all employees.

As a result of our preliminary investigation of the company facilities and the information received from our discussions with company employees, we began the second step of our study. Our engineers developed refurbishing plans for the site selected for the cafeteria. Our plan will necessitate some expansion in the north wing of the headquarters building. We view the establishment of a company cafeteria as a positive move for the company and as logistically very possible. We believe that the cafeteria could be in full operation within six months.

Working with you and your staff has been a pleasure. Our gratitude is expressed to the many employees of the company who cooperated with us in completing this study. We are available to meet with you to discuss our recommendations at a time convenient for you.

Yours very truly,

Floyd C. Brock

Floyd C. Brock
Project Director

Enclosure

Fig. 16-8 A letter of transmittal may be less formal in style and tone than the body of the report.

written to give the reader a clear understanding of the facts in the report. The length of the report determines the length of the summary; however, recommended style is to limit the summary to one page. An executive summary, however, is longer than a synopsis and may contain headings and visual aids. An executive summary is considered a mini report and is most useful for documents longer than 30 pages.

The word "Summary" is keyed 1 1/2 or 2 inches from the top of the page. Double-space the summary; use the same side margins as are used in the report. An example of a summary appears in Figure 16-9. The first page of

SUMMARY

The feasibility study concerning the establishment of an in-house cafeteria at Ultra Electronics Manufacturers, Inc., indicates a very positive employee response to the implementation of this company facility. In addition, the study reveals a location that will require minimal refurbishing and expansion. The estimated time for completion at the site recommended is approximately six months.

The following recommendations are submitted:

1. Ultra Electronics Manufacturers, Inc., provide an in-house cafeteria for employees.

2. The location of the cafeteria be in the north wing of the headquarters building.

3. An 800-square-foot expansion be included to provide a private dining area for business lunches.

4. Bids be invited immediately to ensure that the cafeteria is completed before the end of the year.

In addition to the facilities analysis, the question of company management or a leasing arrangement for the cafeteria was investigated. Because of the number of leasing options available, the Human Resources Department will investigate and make recommendations regarding this subject.

iv

Fig. 16-9 The length of a summary varies with the length of the report, though one-page summaries are preferred.

the report for which this summary was prepared appears in Figure 16-10. The summary can precede or follow the main body of the report.

Table of Contents

After paginating a report, the administrative assistant prepares the table of contents. The table usually includes preliminary parts, the main division (if applicable), main topics or chapter titles, subheadings, and page numbers

Fig. 16-10   The first page of a report usually contains the title of the report and a short introduction.

(Roman and Arabic). The word used for a report's major divisions, such as "section" or "part," is keyed in all capital letters at the left margin after the preliminary parts. The alphanumeric or the decimal outline style can be used to present headings and subheadings. Another style allows the use of placement and form to signify headings and subheadings; with this arrangement main headings begin at the left margin and subheadings are indented two or three spaces. Leaders are commonly used in the table of contents. Rough out the table of contents to get an idea of its vertical and horizontal length before deciding on the final style. Figure 16-11 is an example of a typical table of contents.

TABLE OF CONTENTS

	Page
SUMMARY	iv
SECTION	
I. INTRODUCTION	1
A. The Problem	1
B. Purpose, Scope, and Limitations	2
C. Sources and Methods	3
D. Definitions	4
E. Organization of the Report	5
II. INSPECTION OF COMPANY FACILITIES	
A. The Buildings	5
B. Areas for Expansion	10
C. Utilities Analysis	13
III. CONFERENCES WITH COMPANY EMPLOYEES	
A. Meeting Agenda	20
B. Personal Interviews	23
C. Questionnaire	41
IV. COST ANALYSIS OF SITE SELECTION	
A. Refurbishing Costs	64
B. Construction of Expansion to New Wing	82
C. Time Estimates	95
V. RECOMMENDATIONS	106
APPENDIX	110

iii

Fig. 16-11 A table of contents uses leaders to enhance readability.

Title Page

Even a report of only five or ten pages is enhanced with a title page. The title page contains essential facts for identifying a report. Usually a title page contains the title, for whom it was prepared, by whom it was submitted, the date, and the place of preparation. An interoffice report may require only the title and the date.

An attractively arranged title commands attention—a respectable objective for a title page. Several arrangements of titles are possible. Traditionally, titles are formatted in all caps and underscored. Titles can be keyed in a spread, with extra space between letters and words. If boldface is used, underscoring is unnecessary. Titles of three or more lines may be distinctively framed.

The writer should be given the opportunity to review the content and the arrangement of the title page. Figure 16-12 shows a well-balanced title page.

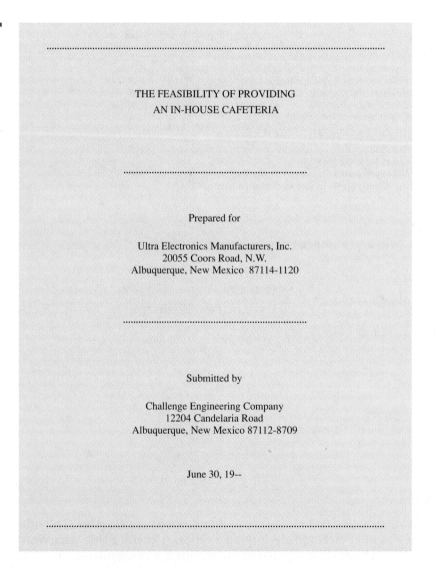

Fig. 16-12 A title page identifies essential facts concerning a report.

THE FEASIBILITY OF PROVIDING
AN IN-HOUSE CAFETERIA

Prepared for

Ultra Electronics Manufacturers, Inc.
20055 Coors Road, N.W.
Albuquerque, New Mexico 87114-1120

Submitted by

Challenge Engineering Company
12204 Candelaria Road
Albuquerque, New Mexico 87112-8709

June 30, 19--

FINAL PROOFREADING, FINAL CHECKING, COLLATING, AND BINDING

After all the keying is finished and the software's spell checker has been used, four important steps remain: final proofreading, checking of mechanics, collating, and binding. Use the report checklist (Figure 16-13) in reviewing the final copy of the report. If the report is prepared by an outside agency, these activities are performed by them. The originator's administrative assistant also proofreads the report.

Final Proofreading

Each page of the final copy of the report is proofread word for word and number for number. A practical plan is to use a copy for proofreading, marking all corrections prominently and filing the marked copy permanently. The careful proofreader goes through the material at least twice. In the first review, the copy is checked against the final draft for accuracy of keying and for omissions; in the second review, for consistency of style and form. The administrative assistant who uses electronic equipment to produce the report proofreads with every rekeying, comparing the draft paper copy with the manuscript appearing on the monitor. This same procedure is recommended for final proofreading. If possible, proofread the copy with the help of another person.

> **COMMUNICATION**
>
> *Proofreading is an important quality control step in report writing.*

Final Checking

After corrections have been made, make a final check. Many embarrassing errors have been caught during this final stage. Check the following items:

1. The last set of corrections
2. References to page numbers, tables, or figures
3. Sequence of pages (it is necessary to check page sequence for each set even when a copier has been used.)

Collating

The final report is submitted in complete sets. Assemble copied sets in reverse order; that is, the bottom page is laid out first, face-up. In this way, you can see any blank or mutilated pages during assembly. When you have collated a complete set, jog the pages until they are aligned precisely.

A REPORT CHECKLIST FOR THE ADMINISTRATIVE ASSISTANT

1. Title Page
   a. Include the title of the report; name, title, and address of the person/company for whom the report was written; name, title, address of person who prepared the report; and the date of submission of the report.
   b. Center all items for an attractive page layout.
2. Letter or Memorandum of Transmittal
   a. Select appropriate stationery.
   b. Maintain same left and right margins of the report body.
   c. Use single spacing; double-space between paragraphs.
   d. Use submission date.
   e. Do not number this page.
3. Table of Contents
   a. Center "Table of Contents" or "Contents" 1 1/2 or 2 inches from the top of the page consistent with beginning pages in the body of the report.
   b. Use leaders (periods every other space) to page numbers.
   c. Key main headings and subheadings according to established hierarchy.
   d. Use double spacing or a combination of single and double spacing.
   e. Center page number 1 inch from bottom of the page using lowercase Roman numerals.
4. Summary, Synopsis, Precis, Abstract, Executive Summary
   a. Center "Summary" or selected heading at top margin 1 1/2 or 2 inches as established for report.
   b. Double-space copy.
   c. Supply subheadings if Executive Summary.
   d. Center page number 1 inch from bottom of the page using lowercase Roman numerals if Summary follows Table of Contents.
   e. Maintain left and right margins set for body of the report.
5. Body of the Report
   a. Center title of report 1 1/2 or 2 inches from top of paper.
   b. Set left margin 1 1/2 inches if leftbound report, 1 inch if unbound report; use 1 inch right margin.
   c. Observe 1-inch bottom margin.
   d. Number first page of body of report or first page of a *chapter* or *part* 1 inch from the bottom at the center, or not at all.
   e. Number all other pages of the report using Arabic numbers keyed 1 inch from the top of the paper (line 6) at the right margin or centered 1 inch from the bottom.
   f. Double-space copy.
   g. Indent each paragraph at least five spaces.
   h. Follow hierarchy in keying headings and subheadings.
   i. Maintain consistency in the mechanical placement of headings and subheadings on the same level of hierarchy.

6. Tables, Charts, and Graphs
   a. Number consecutively throughout report or renew numbering with each chapter or part.
   b. Identify all graphics and tables with the word *Figure* or *Illustration,* or use the word *Table* for tables and the word *Figure* for graphics.
   c. Give each graphic or table a descriptive title.
   d. Place graphic or table as close after the text introduction as possible and refer to its placement in the manuscript.
   e. Provide reference source(s) and/or footnote(s) as necessary at the bottom of the table or graphic.
7. Footnotes/Endnotes
   a. Follow an acceptable style consistently in the manuscript. (APA, MLA, or traditional style)
   b. Place endnotes, if used, before the Bibliography.
8. Bibliography
   a. Follow style of bibliography consistent with the footnoting system used in the manuscript.
   b. Provide separate sections for books, articles, interviews, and governmental publications if bibliography is lengthy.
   c. Center title *Bibliography, References, Works Cited* 1 1/2 or 2 inches from top of paper.
   d. Maintain same right and left margins used in body of report.
9. Appendix
   a. Label each item in the appendix: A, B, and so forth.
   b. Provide a descriptive title for each item in the appendix.
10. Proofreading
   a. Use software functions to check spelling and grammar usage.
   b. Read the manuscript at least three times giving special attention to:
      correct spelling of proper names
      correct figures and statistics
      correct dates
      word omissions or word additions
      transposition of letters
      imperfect spacing
      errors in capitalization and word usage
      incomplete sentences
      improper shift from singular to plural in pronoun usage
      biased language
11. Collating
   a. Assemble copied sets in reverse order to identify blank or mutilated pages.
   b. Jog pages until they are aligned precisely.
12. Binding
   a. Place pages in proper order.
   b. Recheck to see that pages are numbered correctly.
   c. Select the proper binding and/or cover.

Binding

Binding is the last step in preparing a report. The most popular form of binding is the staple. When only one staple is required, position it diagonally in the upper left corner. When a wider margin has been allowed for binding at the top or at the left, use two or three staples along the wide margin, parallel with the edge of the paper. If a report that is to be stapled is thick, use a heavy-duty stapler.

Some offices prefer sturdier and more permanent types of binding. Some of these bindings require special supplies and equipment, such as metal eyelets, punches, wire spiral devices, or plastic combs. Convenient and attractive report covers in transparent plastic with snap-on spines are available from office supply stores.

PREPARING COPY FOR PUBLICATION

Most of the duties associated with preparing a manuscript for publication are assigned to the administrative assistant. (If an outside agency is available, the actual keying of the manuscript would be done by them.) Since a typesetter will set text in type exactly as it appears in manuscript, it is imperative that punctuation and spelling be correct. The administrative assistant always keeps a file copy for ready reference of all manuscripts that have been sent to a typesetter.

If you are not keying the document yourself, you should discuss the format with the person who is. Together you should develop a style sheet specifying how to key main headings and subheadings, footnotes, bibliography, and captions.

Manuscript

Publishers usually specify manuscript format. It then becomes your responsibility to see that the manuscript meets the publisher's standards. In general, a manuscript to be typeset should meet the following specifications:

1. Double-space all copy on one side of 8 1/2-by-11-inch sheets. Leave generous margins. Quoted material or other text to be set apart should be single-spaced and indented on both sides.

2. Code all copy to its exact position on a page layout.

3. Number all sheets in the upper right corner. Two or more compositors may work on the same assignment, so correct numbering is imperative.

4. Provide the publisher with a perfect final copy free of markings for even incidental changes.

5. Give explicit directions. With the help of a compositor, specify size and style of typefaces and the amount of leading (space between lines) desired.

6. Use a single underline to indicate italics and a triple underline for REGULAR CAPS. To indicate boldface, use a wavy underline. Most word processing software provides these options.

7. Number footnotes consecutively. They may be keyed on the page to which they pertain between full-width rules directly under the line in which the reference occurs or at the bottom of the page but separated from the text by a 1- or 1 1/2-inch rule. Footnotes may also be keyed in sequence on a separate sheet. If APA or MLA system of footnoting is used, follow the appropriate manual of style.

8. If a photograph is to be included, place the caption on a separate piece of paper and paste it on the bottom edge of the picture.

9. Provide titles. Number tables and illustrations consecutively with Arabic numerals. Send a full list of all tables and figures with the manuscript.

10. Include a title page showing the title, the author's name and address, and perhaps the date.

11. Include the author's resume if requested.

12. Send the manuscript by first-class or priority mail. Do not fasten the sheets together. Keep them flat by placing them between cardboard or in a strong box.

Magazine Articles and Press Releases

An executive may occasionally be asked to submit an article for magazine publication. The administrative assistant simplifies the editor's job of judging the amount of copy needed to fill the space for the article by keying a sample paragraph from a recent issue of the magazine line for line. In this way, the average line length and the number of lines to an inch of printed material are determined. Headings for the copy should be consistent with those used in the magazine; this information becomes the style sheet for the article. A cover letter giving the approximate number of words in the article also aids the editor.

If the approximate length requirements of the article are provided by the publisher, key a draft version with double spacing in the average line length of the magazine copy. This copy is given to the executive with a close estimation of the amount of space the article will fill. As revisions are made, the executive can lengthen or shorten the article. Copies of published material should be kept in an appropriately labeled file.

A company that submits numerous press releases uses a special letterhead. Otherwise, an item is typed on regular letterhead or on an 8 1/2-by-11-inch sheet of bond paper. If a plain sheet is used, the name, address, and telephone number of the company are keyed across the top. All press releases should carry the name and telephone number of a person the editor can contact for additional information. If the news stems from one of the executive's outside activities, the administrative assistant uses a plain sheet of paper and gives the executive's name as the contact. Other practices to observe are

1. Give the date when the news may be published—the release date.
2. Key the release date near the top. Express it in either of these ways: FOR IMMEDIATE RELEASE or FOR RELEASE TUESDAY, FEBRUARY 2, 19—.
3. Give the release a title, if possible. This gives the editor an idea of the contents at a quick glance.
4. Double-space the text. Leave generous margins for editorial use. Confine the release to one page, if possible.
5. Center each page number for second and succeeding pages on line 6.
6. Key -more- at the bottom of all pages but the last.
7. Center # # # a double space below the last line of the release.
8. Mail the release directly to the editor unless another person, such as the financial editor, is specified.

First and Second Proofs

It is customary for compositors to submit proofs. The administrative assistant usually checks the proof for errors, but the executive should be given an opportunity to approve revisions.

The first proof is usually in galley form. Galleys are long sheets containing columns of typeset copy. Each error or change to be made to the galley is indicated by a proofreaders' mark (illustrated in the Reference Guide on page 776). The place of the correction is indicated in the text, and the kind of correction to be made is written in the margin on the same line. If there is more than one correction in a line, proofreaders' marks in the margin are separated by conspicuous diagonal lines.

The compositor submits a second proof in page form. This new proof must be meticulously read and corrected. Page numbers and page headings are shown on this proof and are usually checked in separate, individual operations. The page proof stage is often the final opportunity for the author to catch errors and make changes.

PROCEDURES WRITING

Procedures writing has been called "verbal flowcharting." It lists the logical sequence of activities involved in a given task step by step. Procedures writing serves to control as well as to communicate. It controls how things are done as it instructs employees in the steps to follow in performing recurring tasks.

Writing good procedures sounds simple, but eliminating extraneous material can be surprisingly difficult. Effective procedures writing is one of the most valuable forms of writing because it enhances productivity and saves businesses time and money.

Writing procedures is a sophisticated process. Successful procedures writers do a great deal of research and involve management and support personnel in the process. In fact, some companies assign one person to write all procedures, thus maintaining uniformity. It is important that procedures be written in a simple, direct style, using terms that will be easily understood by all who will be expected to interpret and follow them.

Procedures for a department or for an operation are usually collected in a loose-leaf notebook that can be updated by adding and deleting pages as new procedures are issued. This notebook is commonly called a *procedures manual*. It is helpful to include an index in the manual for easy reference. Procedures can also be stored on the computer. In this form, an administrative assistant would review the procedures manual directory on the computer, then depress the key(s) for the desired procedure to be shown on the screen.

A Sample Procedure

As an administrative assistant, you may be asked to write some of the procedures that affect the work in your office. For instance, assume that you are the administrative assistant to the director of administrative services, and your office is in charge of scheduling the conference room. Within the last few months, several mixups have occurred in the use of the room. With the director's approval, you decide to develop a procedure for scheduling the office conference room. This procedure is to be sent to all office employees, outlining the steps to be taken in reserving and using the room. There are at least four formats that you can use in writing procedures: traditional, improved traditional, job breakdown, and playscript.

Traditional.   The traditional format is simply a series of sentences in paragraph form.

```
The person requesting use of the Conference Room
files a written request with the Director of
Administrative Services at least one week before the
date of the meeting, indicating the name of the
group involved, the exact time of the meeting, its
expected duration, the expected attendance, and the
room setup necessary.

The Director of Administrative Services immediately
notifies the applicant in writing whether the room
is available and, if so, notifies the custodial
staff in writing of the room setup necessary and the
```

duration of the meeting, giving instructions for any necessary special cleaning.

The person requesting the room checks the room one hour before the meeting, provides any special supplies needed, and checks lighting and temperature.

Improved Traditional.   The improved traditional format uses enumerations, tabulations, spacing changes, and underlinings to emphasize the importance of certain actions.

The person requesting use of the Conference Room files a written request with the Director of Administrative Services at least one week before the proposed meeting, indicating:

1. The name of the group involved
2. The exact time of the meeting
3. Its expected duration
4. The expected attendance
5. The room setup necessary

The Director of Administrative Services immediately notifies the applicant in writing whether the room is available and, if so, notifies the custodial staff in writing of:

1. The room setup necessary
2. The duration of the meeting
3. Instructions for any necessary special cleaning

The person requesting the room checks the room one hour before the meeting, provides any special supplies needed, and checks lighting and temperature.

Job Breakdown.   With the job breakdown format, the logical sequence of action is related in a series of steps. Key points caution employees where mistakes are likely to be made. The steps tell the employee what to do; the key points tell how to do it. Every step may not have a key point, but there may be more than one key point for any one step.

Steps	Key Points
1. File a written request with the Director of Administrative Services.	1a. Do this at least one week before the date of the proposed meeting.
	1b. List name of group to use room, time of meeting, the expected duration, expected attendance, and room setup necessary.

2. Receive clearance from the Director of Administrative Services.

2. Follow up if clearance is not received promptly.

3. On day of meeting, check the room one hour before the meeting.

3. Be sure that room is clean, the temperature is comfortable, and a sufficient number of chairs are positioned as requested for the participants. Check the lighting.

4. Distribute necessary supplies.

4. Provide water and paper cups or glasses, notepads, and sharpened pencils.

Playscript. The playscript format answers the question "Who does what?," using the team approach in completing office tasks. The actor is easily identified, and what the actor does starts with an action verb in the present tense. According to the developer of this technique, playscript is really a type of flowchart. Any step that flows backward rather than forward can be spotted immediately. Gaps in the logical sequence of steps can also be quickly detected.

<u>Responsibility</u>	<u>Action</u>
Requesting Employee	1. Prepares a written request at least one week before the date of the proposed meeting, including name of group, time of meeting, duration, expected attendance, and setup necessary.
	2. Sends request to Director of Administrative Services.
Director of Administrative Services	3. Notifies the applicant in writing whether the room is available.
	4. Notifies custodial staff in writing of room setup necessary, duration of meeting, and need for any special cleaning.

Requesting Employee	5. Checks the room one hour before the meeting for number of chairs, proper lighting, and temperature level of room.
	6. Distributes necessary supplies.

Selecting the Format

A traditional person or a traditional company will probably adopt the improved traditional format. A more venturesome author in search of an eye-catching arrangement will probably choose the job breakdown or the playscript. In a procedure involving one operator, the job breakdown might be chosen, for it has the advantage of cautioning against wrong moves. It looks more complicated than the playscript, however. The playscript probably will be selected for writing procedures involving more than one worker.

KEYING SPEECHES

Busy executives involved in professional and civic organizations will have many opportunities to make oral presentations. Some executives use only an outline of their ideas to assist them during their speeches. Some executives use cards on which they have written key ideas. Still others want their speeches keyed word for word, particularly if the topic is technical in nature. If only an outline is required, the administrative assistant follows the outline format shown in Figure 16-2. Several copies of the final outline or the speech should be made. One copy of a speech is retained in a topic file; one copy is for the media, if required; and another is for the executive to use during the delivery of the speech. Several software applications are available for speech writing. In general, when keying an entire speech for use during the presentation, you should use:

1. Triple or quadruple spacing
2. A 10-pitch type font or larger, if available
3. A four- or five-inch writing line
4. Top and bottom margins of at least one inch

To assist the executive in rapid comprehension of the keyed material, do not divide words or break up a sentence between pages. Also, be sure to number each page. Finally, place the final draft of the speech in a loose-leaf binder or a similar organizer so that pages will be kept in order during the presentation.

Speakers often provide handouts to the audience to supplement a presentation or provide copies of the speech itself. The administrative assistant would see that the material was prepared, copied, and assembled. Handouts can be color-coded, so the speaker can refer to them by color and avoid confusion. Most speakers recommend that handouts be distributed after the presentation or when the audience is to use them. If it is necessary to distribute material before a presentation, place it in envelopes with instructions not to open until a specified time.

To clarify or explain key points, speakers use visual aids, such as transparencies, flip charts, and electronic slides (see Figure 16-14). After being told what the executive wants, the administrative assistant either prepares the visuals (using desktop publishing software), asks a department within the company to prepare the visuals, or arranges for an outside graphic arts service to do the work. When other departments or outside agencies are performing work for the executive, an important contribution of the administrative assistant is to follow through to see that the work is ready on time.

Fig. 16-14 Presentations may incorporate computerized imagery projected onto an overhead screen. This handheld remote device attaches to a PC or notebook computer and allows a speaker to preview upcoming graphics and presentation notes.
Left: Photo courtesy of General Parametrics; right: Lanier Worldwide, Inc.

If transparencies are used, plastic sheets or frames can be used to protect the transparencies. Transparencies are put in plastic sheets and then placed in a loose-leaf binder. When frames are desired, tape each transparency to a frame. Number the frames according to the order of presentation. Notes also can be conveniently taped to these frames to cue the speaker. Highlight an outline or the text of a speech with a colored felt-tip pen to call attention to the point when a transparency is to be presented. Place transparencies and a copy of the speech in order in a box or a briefcase large enough to accommodate them. Bulky handouts should be wrapped or put in a box and delivered to the meeting location in advance of the presentation.

An additional contribution of the administrative assistant to an executive's speech-giving duties is to keep a file of poems, jokes, quotations, and cartoons that the employer may use in preparing a speech. Included in this file should be a list of speech topics for future presentations.

Summary

Executives depend on reports to provide information and to assist them in making business decisions. Written reports take the form of inter-office memorandums, letters, or bound manuscripts.

The report writer follows a set routine in gathering information and formulating the report. The administrative assistant's role follows closely the report-writing routine of the writer. In addition, the administrative assistant is responsible for producing an attractive manuscript, free of grammatical, spelling, and proofreading errors.

The preparation of a formal report begins with a topic outline. The second step is the draft, which may be edited and changed many times. The administrative assistant may produce the manuscript on a word processor or computer with word processing or integrated software. The equipment and software options available to the administrative assistant will determine the ease with which the manuscript is prepared. Just before keying the final document, the administrative assistant should determine the page layout and, if several persons will be working on the project, prepare a job instruction sheet. Three methods of footnoting are acceptable in business reports. When computer printouts, tables, and graphs appear in a report, explanations of these graphics must precede their placement in the text. Lengthy tables and graphs, unless they are absolutely necessary to understand the discussion, should be placed in an appendix. Preliminary pages are numbered in small Roman numerals; the body of the text, in Arabic numerals.

Parts of a formal report include the appendix, bibliography, index, letter or memorandum of transmittal, summary, table of contents, title page, and the body. The appendix is for supplementary documents. The bibliography should include all references cited in the study. A selected bibliography or a comprehensive bibliography may occasionally be compiled by the administrative assistant. If a report is very long, an index may be needed. The letter/memorandum of transmittal is more personal in style than the body of the report. It transmits the report, gives authorization for the report, its purpose, and other details of the report-writing process. A summary provides a concise review of the entire report and its findings. The title page must contain essential facts for identifying the report, including the title, for whom it was prepared, by whom it was submitted, the date, and the place of preparation. The last page to prepare is a table of contents.

After all the keying is completed, the manuscript must be proofread carefully, preferably with the help of another person. All numbers appearing in the manuscript should be checked. Finally, the manuscript is collated and bound.

When preparing copy for publication, a number of steps should be followed. For magazine articles, the administrative assistant keys material according to guidelines of the particular magazine. Press releases are addressed to the editor or another appropriate editor.

Office procedures change with technological advancements. The administrative assistant may be required to list the logical sequence of activities involved in new procedures. The administrative assistant can choose from the traditional format, the improved traditional format, the job breakdown style, or the playscript arrangement to write procedures.

When asked to key a speech, the administrative assistant should follow suggestions given in this chapter. If the executive requests transparencies, flip charts, or slides, the administrative assistant arranges for this work to be done. The same is true with any handouts to be distributed to an audience.

QUESTIONS FOR DISCUSSION

1. Why are business reports written in the third person?

2. If you were assigned the responsibility for keying a long report, which questions would you ask the writer and what items would you decide for yourself before you started the project?

3. Why is it important that reports follow a definite order of arrangement and that mechanical rules are followed to prepare them?

4. What is the relationship between the outline of a report and the placement of headings within the body of the report?

THINK IT
Through

THINK IT
Through

5. You are keying a long report with a number of footnote citations. The software you use has the superscript capability and footnote and bibliography options that make showing footnotes on the page of the citation a relatively simple matter. You consider the use of endnotes instead. What factors should you consider in making your decision?

THINK IT
Through

6. In what ways is the administrative assistant's role that of a facilitator when assisting the executive in preparing an oral presentation?

7. Do not confuse the dash with the hyphen. The dash is keyed as two hyphens with no space on either side (--). Rekey the following sentences and use a dash where appropriate. Check the Reference Guide to verify and correct your answers.

    a. Several items of furniture were marked down chairs, sofas, and beds.

    b. Torrential rain storms raged all night flooded the playing field.

    c. Robin is wealthy wealthy because she has good health, good friends, and a good job.

    d. Call Jack he's with Ace Warehouse and get his opinion.

    e. The actor is by the way, do you know the actor?

PROBLEMS

1. Key an outline of an article on the topic of the Americans with Disabilities Act appearing in a recent issue of a magazine.

2. Key each of the following titles twice (eight different arrangements). Divide the titles into two or more lines if necessary and center each line horizontally on the page. Allow six line spaces between titles. Indicate which of the arrangements you prefer.

    a. Career Opportunities for Administrative Assistants

    b. How Information Processing Creates Total Business Systems

    c. The Mature Woman Returns to Work in the Business Office

    d. The Importance of a Healthful Work Environment

3. As administrative assistant in a government procurement office, you are assigned the supervision of two young assistants. You have given them the responsibility of opening and sorting the office mail. You decide to prepare a procedural statement in playscript style covering this activity. Before you begin writing, analyze the cycle of the operation, determine the actors involved (the two assistants, mail messenger, and yourself), analyze each action in the operation, and identify any office forms used in the process. Write the statement of procedures. (You may wish to refer to Chapter 12.)

TECHNOLOGY APPLICATIONS

▶ **TA16-1**   In Chapter 14 you took notes and prepared a bibliography for a report on one of the following topics (or some other topic approved by your instructor):

1. Business Ethics: A Revived Interest in the Business Community
2. The Law in the Workplace
3. The Employee's Right to Privacy in the Workplace
4. Improving Personal Security in the Office
5. The Paperless Office: Myth or Reality?
6. Orientation Training for Office Workers
7. The Use of Job-Related Tests in the Selection of Office Employees
8. Privacy Laws and Office Records
9. How to Supervise Office Workers Effectively
10. The Career Path for the Administrative Assistant in the 1990s
11. Office Technology in the Year 2000

Using the information you collected for this assignment, prepare a business report. Use your word processing software; include any graphs or tables that will enhance your report and improve your presentation.

Part 4

Case Problems

Helen Gaines is administrative assistant to Phillip Milton, marketing director for Freeman Company, an air filter manufacturer in Seattle, Washington. Mr. Milton is to give a presentation before the National Association of Air Filter Manufacturers. Helen assisted him in researching information for his talk. Yesterday Helen finished the first draft of the handout material that will supplement Mr. Milton's speech and placed it on his desk. Today, Mr. Milton brings the handout to Helen and says, "This is ready to go to press. I'll need at least 100 copies for my session. You will note that I deleted three footnote citations. I really see no reason to clutter the copy with them. Let's take a chance that no one will miss them." After Mr. Milton leaves Helen's workstation, she studies the handout and is surprised to see which footnotes Mr. Milton deleted. One indicated where a number of questionable conclusions were taken, another referred to statistical results of a marketing survey, and the other cited recommendations for changes in a filter product made by a manufacturer in the field. Helen believes that deleting these footnotes amounts to plagiarism and could be a source of professional embarrassment for Mr. Milton. She certainly doesn't want this to happen.

What should Helen do?

Rhonda Reynolds, an administrative assistant to Dr. Johanna Spector, was put in charge of producing a 78-page medical report. Because she had other pressing duties to perform for Dr. Spector, she decided to assign the production of the report to three relatively new employees in the department. She met with each of the three employees and gave oral instructions as to the style to be followed in preparing the report. The work had to be completed within two days so that Dr. Spector could take it to a meeting at which she was to be the featured speaker. Rhonda received the completed work for assembling for presentation to Dr. Spector just two hours before the deadline.

When examining the report, she was horrified to discover that the type style for all the pages was not the same. Some of the pages had been printed in 10-pitch type and the remainder in 12-pitch type. In addition, footnotes in the first part of the report used the textual citation/reference method while the footnotes in the last fifty pages were in the traditional style and were keyed at the bottom of the page on which the citation was made. She noticed, too, that some first-level subheadings were keyed in all capital letters and underscored, while others were initial capital letters only and underscored.

She showed the variations to Dr. Spector and said, "I am just sick about the way this report looks. You would think that these operators could follow instructions. What can be done now?"

Dr. Spector replied icily, "Nothing, absolutely nothing. I will have to tell the people at the symposium that I will mail them a copy of the report next week. Heaven knows how I can get all their addresses. But, Rhonda, I am very unhappy with the way you handled this. After all, you were the one in charge. I had thought that you could handle a simple assignment like this one."

Was Rhonda at fault? What did she do wrong? If she talked with you about the problem, what advice would you give her for handling such a situation?

**Case 4-3
THE
IMPORTANCE OF
PROOFREADING**

When John Kelly asked his administrative assistant to arrange for transparencies for his speech at his professional organization's convention, he did so with confidence. Even though time was growing short, Mr. Kelly felt sure that his resourceful assistant, Abraham Green, would have no difficulty complying with his request. The numerical data called for a circle chart, a bar graph, a line chart, and several tables. Since the company did not have a computer graphics system, Abraham contracted with an outside organization to produce the transparencies. The transparencies were delivered the day before Mr. Kelly planned to leave for the convention. Abraham, under a great deal of pressure to complete the speech, decided to put the unopened box of transparencies in Mr. Kelly's office. That night Mr. Kelly took his copy of the speech and the transparencies home so that he could practice his delivery.

The next morning Mr. Kelly was in his office when Abraham arrived. Abraham entered Mr. Kelly's office saying, "Good morning, Mr. Kelly, are you ready for your big speech tomorrow?" There was a long pause. Then Mr. Kelly said, "Abraham, I wish you had checked these transparencies when they arrived. Two of them I cannot use. The numerical data do not agree with the information I gave you. The transparency outfit you used obviously misread the data. If you had checked the transparencies when they arrived yesterday, perhaps these errors could have been corrected. As it is, I will have to leave without two of the major transparencies. In the future, and particularly with something this important, will you please make proofreading one of your top priorities."

Is this situation entirely Abraham's fault? What explanation should Abraham give to Mr. Kelly? Should he apologize?

Part 5

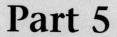

Travel and Conference Planning

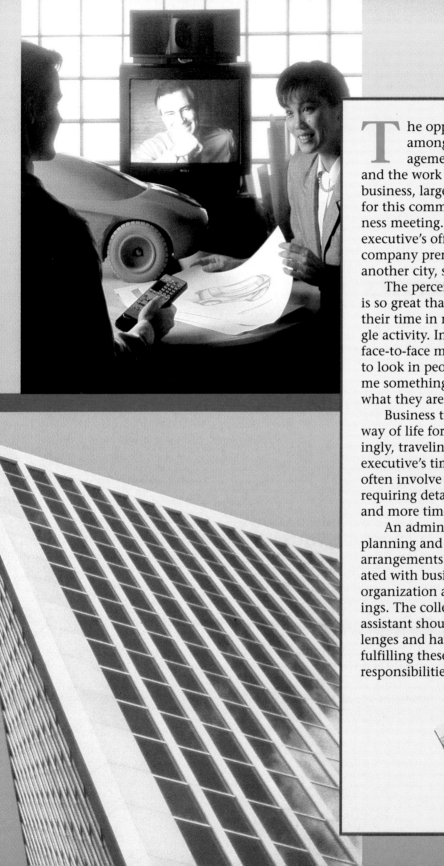

The opportunity to communicate—among individuals at all levels of management and between management and the work force—is essential for every business, large and small. One medium used for this communication process is the business meeting. Business meetings can be in the executive's office, in a conference room on company premises, or in a hotel or office in another city, state, or country.

The perceived value of business meetings is so great that many managers spend more of their time in meetings than in any other single activity. In discussing the importance of face-to-face meetings, one CEO states, "I want to look in people's eyes when they are telling me something. I can tell whether they know what they are talking about."

Business travel, therefore, has become a way of life for many executives. Not surprisingly, traveling is the second-biggest use of an executive's time. Business trips today more often involve travel to foreign countries, requiring detailed planning before the trip and more time away from the office.

An administrative assistant is involved in planning and following through with travel arrangements. Another responsibility associated with business travel is assisting in the organization and reporting of business meetings. The college-trained administrative assistant should welcome these challenges and have little difficulty fulfilling these responsibilities.

Chapter 17

Travel Arrangements

LEARNING OBJECTIVES

After studying this chapter and completing the activities, you will be able to:

1. Utilize the services of a company's travel department or an outside travel agency.
2. Plan and follow through with air travel, hotel, and rental car arrangements for the executive's domestic or international business trip.
3. Assist the executive in obtaining a passport, visa, travel funds, and trip insurance.
4. Prepare a detailed itinerary.
5. Complete appropriate follow-up activities upon the executive's return to the office.

INTRODUCTION

Over the past three decades many U.S. businesses have widened their operations to include international activities. Convenient air travel and telecommunications technology have contributed to this expansion. Large corporations whose operations were once totally domestic (within U.S. boundaries) now have offices in other countries. Employees of these corporations often travel to supervise various facets of operations or to meet with counterparts or clients.

Out-of-town meetings necessitate arrangements for airline flights, hotels, and ground transportation. By working with the company's travel department or a travel agent or by doing research independently, an administrative assistant secures travel information; obtains the executive's approval; then makes reservations that suit the executive's needs. These arrangements, of course, must conform with the company's established policies.

This chapter discusses domestic and international travel. The duties and responsibilities of the administrative assistant in planning and following through with travel arrangements are discussed in detail.

COMPANY POLICIES REGARDING TRAVEL ARRANGEMENTS

Travel arrangements may be handled by a travel department within the company, by an outside travel agency, or by the administrative assistant. The administrative assistant's first concern in handling these arrangements is to learn the company's policies. Who handles travel arrangements? What airline, hotel, and other credit cards are issued and what procedures are authorized for their use? How are employees reimbursed for travel expenses? What restrictions does the company have on per diem (per day) travel expenses? How are travel funds obtained? Which hotels and rental car companies offer corporate rates?

The Company Travel Department

Business travel is a big expense item for companies. Several years ago it was estimated that companies spend about $125 billion a year on business travel and entertainment, approximately 40 percent of it for air travel. A travel department can track a company's travel patterns and costs and thus have leverage in negotiating air and lodging discounts. A company travel department is also active in setting the travel policy for the organization. For example, a travel policy would include guidelines on who can travel, class of service, how much money can be spent with which vendor, which payment method to use, and how to report these expenses. In addition to making air travel arrangements, a company travel department also makes reservations for rail travel, lodging, and automobile rental. If the company maintains a fleet of cars, the travel department would coordinate reservations for their use.

Traditionally, travel is the third-largest expense item in a corporate budget.

When the executive tells the administrative assistant of a pending trip requiring air travel, a series of steps begins. The administrative assistant calls the travel department and informs them of the dates for the trip, the destination, and the executive's flight time preferences. The representative in the travel department then suggests possible schedules to be approved by the executive. The administrative assistant relays the flight times to the executive and a decision is made.

Computer on-line services exist where companies can make their own flight and hotel reservations and even issue tickets in-house. Most company travel departments, however, continue to use an outside travel agency for making the actual reservations and ticketing and for other services a travel agency provides. Assuming the executive's time preferences for flights are available, the administrative assistant would complete a transportation voucher. A signature by a higher ranking official of the company authorizing the trip may be required. If so, the signed form would then be sent to the travel department for its records. The department would then obtain the tickets and deliver them to the administrative assistant.

According to the U.S. Travel Data Center (Washington, DC), more than 33 million Americans travel on business every year.

Travel Agencies

In recent years the business world has turned increasingly to travel agencies to make its travel arrangements. By the very nature of its specialization, a reputable agency can cut through the maze of constantly changing fares, flight schedules, and classes of service that has emerged since the deregulation of the airline industry. They can book tickets (make reservations) and do it faster than a traveler acting independently. In addition, they have information on which airlines have the best record on departure and arrival times. It is estimated that 90 percent of all major corporations now use travel agencies.

Travel agencies are paid commissions by airlines, railroads, hotels, and other services booked for a client. Although travel agencies have a policy of not charging clients for their services, some agencies are beginning to do so, particularly for trips involving extensive planning.

Travel agencies offer their clients help in planning an itinerary, obtaining tickets, selecting and making hotel reservations, and arranging for rental cars (see Figure 17-1). Requests to them can be made by FAX or electronic mail and can be checked for continuity of client preferences. They develop a profile for each individual client noting seat preferences, special meal requirements, preferred departure times, payment method for rental cars, discount entitlements (senior citizen, for example), and the need for any other services. These instructions become a matter of record and are followed when additional trips are planned. Many agencies agree to monitor clients' requests for conformance with their companies' policies. Their service also includes free delivery of tickets to the traveler. Because of their contacts in the travel industry, agents may be successful in obtaining reservations when none are available to the public. Some agencies have hot lines; if a client has any problems, the client can call that number for assistance. While some agencies extend credit, nearly all of them will accept major credit cards.

If you are asked to choose a travel agency for your employer, determine which agencies specialize in business travel and seek a recommendation from a satisfied business traveler. Look for membership in the American Society of Travel Agents (ASTA) or the Association of Retail Travel Agents (ARTA).

Fig. 17-1 Travel agents offer many services to their clients.
Location courtesy of AAA World Wide Travel, Cincinnati, OH.

The Administrative Assistant

If a business organization has neither the services of an intracompany travel department nor the regular services of a travel agency, the administrative assistant either works directly with airlines, hotels, car rental agencies, etc., to make all travel arrangements or uses a personal computer and an electronic subscription service to gain access to all airline schedules, rates, and so forth. The alert administrative assistant will soon discover the employer's preferences for a hotel chain, an airline, and/or seat location. Consulting the executive about these preferences and remembering them from trip to trip results in effective trip planning.

AIR TRAVEL

Most people traveling on business prefer to fly, especially on long trips, because they save time. Today a traveler can breakfast in New York, lunch in Chicago, and dine in San Francisco. Supersonic transport planes cross the Atlantic from Washington to Paris in a little over three hours. One businessperson is reported to have had this workday: He left Germany at 7 a.m., flew to Paris and took the supersonic Concorde to New York. From New York he flew to Dallas for a luncheon meeting. After the meeting he took a flight to Las Vegas, where he had a dinner meeting. In the course of 24 hours he attended two business meetings, was on four airplanes and in five cities, and covered 6,500 miles. Yes, it is a small world.

Not only speed but comfort prompts many business travelers to fly. Wide-bodied jet aircraft that connect the large cities of the United States with each other and with foreign cities are equipped with large away-from-seat lounges. They also have in-flight movies and recorded entertainment. Some travelers prefer smaller jets, which provide similar comforts. On some flights, air-to-ground telephone service is available. Payment for these calls is by an approved credit card.

Most major airlines are supported by regional lines that fly to cities where passenger traffic does not support their service. A passenger traveling from a metropolitan area to a small city may fly to that destination on a small jet or on a propeller aircraft.

Classes of Flights

Most airlines have two kinds of flight classifications: first-class and coach. An additional section, business class, is also available on some flights.

> *First class* serves complimentary meals during conventional mealtimes and generous refreshments. Several attendants are available to provide personalized attention and to take care of passenger needs. Seats are wider, farther apart, and provide more legroom than those in the

coach section. Some aircraft have sleeper seats. First-class fares are considerably higher (50 percent or more) than regular unrestricted coach or economy fares.

Coach (or economy) serves a complimentary meal or snack when the plane is aloft at mealtime (on most airlines). Coffee, tea, or soft drinks are available at no charge. Coach passengers often sit three abreast, have less legroom, and occupy narrower seats than first-class passengers. The front row in the economy section allows more legroom.

Business class is available on some wide-bodied aircraft. Business-class seating is directly behind first class; seats, legroom, and complimentary meals are similar to those in first class. Some airlines provide a separate cabin for business-class passengers. More room is allotted for carry-on luggage, the trademark of the business traveler. Some have special check-in facilities, and use of VIP lounges is offered. Business-class fares are only slightly higher than the unrestricted coach fares.

Many organizations have a policy that only high-ranking executives travel first class. Some organizations require that all employees travel economy class. The administrative assistant should question whether there is a specific policy before making travel arrangements. Even though an executive may be entitled to first-class accommodations, business-class reservations, if available, will probably meet with the executive's approval.

Services Offered

Meal service differs among competing airlines. On certain domestic flights, a choice of entree is offered, and meals to accommodate special diets can be ordered. Some no-frills airlines may charge for meal service or provide only beverage service.

Shuttle service is available between certain cities, such as New York/Boston, New York/Washington, and San Francisco/Los Angeles. Passengers board the plane without reservations, and the flights leave at frequent intervals. Passengers can purchase tickets at shuttle locations at self-ticketing machines or pay their fares aloft with cash, a credit card, or personal check. Only carry-on luggage is accepted on some shuttle flights.

On most domestic flights, each passenger is allowed to check three pieces of luggage. Luggage can be checked at the airline curbside station or at the airline ticket counter. Allowable weight and dimensions of baggage vary among the airlines. Carry-on luggage is limited to two pieces, including a briefcase. One of the pieces may be a hanging garment bag. Other types of carry-on luggage must fit under a seat in front of the passenger or in an enclosed compartment overhead. Approximate dimensions for under-seat stowage are 9" × 13" × 23". Passengers who have luggage in excess of the allowed amount are charged excess baggage rates in addition to the regular fare.

Air Fares

Air fares are constantly changing. In addition to first-class, business, and regular unrestricted coach fares, domestic airlines offer special discount rates for night flights, for excursions that comprise a definite number of days, for certain weekend trips, and for tickets purchased in advance, from 2 to 14 days. Some airlines offer restricted nonrefundable Supersaver or MaxSaver fares requiring a 7-day advance purchase and a stay including a Saturday night. Reduced-rate night flights and restricted nonrefundable fares are not suitable for most business travel. When requesting fare quotations, ask for the lowest discounted fare.

In addition to the discounts cited above, major airlines also offer frequent-flyer incentive programs. A variety of rewards to passengers who accumulate travel mileage with an airline are available. Examples of such rewards include an upgrade in class of service (first-class seating), fare discounts, and free round-trip airline tickets. An added incentive to the business traveler is that many companies permit their employees to keep the frequent-flyer mileage rewards earned during business travel.

Flight Schedules

Airlines publish flight schedules and make them available in airports, major hotels, and travel agencies. Although schedules are not uniform in structure among airlines, Figure 17-2 (a sample schedule not intended to be valid) shows the ease with which flight schedules can be read. The example is a schedule of all Delta Air Lines flights between Atlanta, Georgia, and Los Angeles, California, airports.

Notice that there are nine flights daily from Atlanta to Los Angeles. Five flights operate nonstop to Los Angeles (Flights 117, 103, 157, 187, and 347). Flights 79 and 275 show a scheduled stop without a change of airplanes. These are called direct flights. The remaining two flights call for a change of airplanes at the Dallas/Fort Worth airport. All flights are given in boldface, indicating wide-body aircraft.

An executive from Atlanta planning a business trip to Los Angeles would most likely prefer either Flight 117 or 157. The 10:07 a.m. arrival time (local time) of Flight 117 gives the executive time to check into a hotel and make an appointment scheduled during the afternoon. Note that both are Royal Service Flights providing prestige catering in the first-class section and regular meal service in the coach section. Movies are also available during the flight. If the executive has an early morning appointment, the likely choice would be Flight 157 arriving in Los Angeles at 5:00 p.m. This schedule does not show that Atlanta is in the eastern time zone. A passenger gains three hours flying west from that time zone and loses three hours flying east from Los Angeles. Both flights give the executive an opportunity to adjust to the different time zone before business appointments.

In returning to Atlanta the executive has a choice of five nonstop flights. The most likely choice for the executive is Flight 134 arriving in

Fig. 17-2 This schedule of Delta Air Lines flights between Atlanta and Los Angeles can be interpreted easily. (Not intended to be valid.)

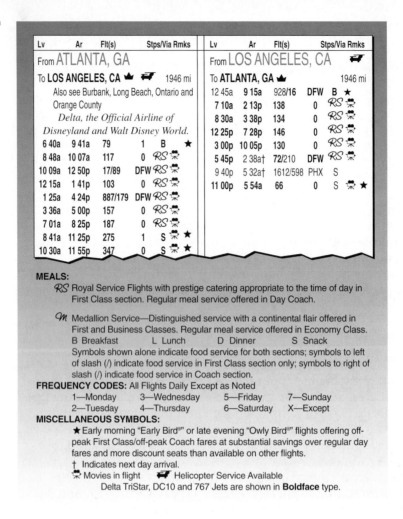

Lv	Ar	Flt(s)	Stps/Via Rmks
From ATLANTA, GA			
To LOS ANGELES, CA 🪑 🚁 1946 mi			
Also see Burbank, Long Beach, Ontario and Orange County			
Delta, the Official Airline of Disneyland and Walt Disney World.			
6 40a	9 41a	79	1 B ★
8 48a	10 07a	117	0 *RS* 🎬
10 09a	12 50p	17/89	DFW *RS* 🎬
12 15a	1 41p	103	0 *RS* 🎬
1 25a	4 24p	887/179	DFW *RS* 🎬
3 36a	5 00p	157	0 *RS* 🎬
7 01a	8 25p	187	0 *RS* 🎬
8 41a	11 25p	275	1 S 🎬 ★
10 30a	11 55p	347	0 S 🎬 ★

Lv	Ar	Flt(s)	Stps/Via Rmks
From LOS ANGELES, CA			🚁
To ATLANTA, GA 🪑			1946 mi
12 45a	9 15a	928/16	DFW B ★
7 10a	2 13p	138	0 *RS* 🎬
8 30a	3 38p	134	0 *RS* 🎬
12 25p	7 28p	146	0 *RS* 🎬
3 00p	10 05p	130	0 *RS* 🎬
5 45p	2 38a†	72/210	DFW *RS* 🎬
9 40p	5 32a†	1612/598	PHX S
11 00p	5 54a	66	0 S 🎬 ★

MEALS:

RS Royal Service Flights with prestige catering appropriate to the time of day in First Class section. Regular meal service offered in Day Coach.

M Medallion Service—Distinguished service with a continental flair offered in First and Business Classes. Regular meal service offered in Economy Class.
B Breakfast   L Lunch   D Dinner   S Snack
Symbols shown alone indicate food service for both sections; symbols to left of slash (/) indicate food service in First Class section only; symbols to right of slash (/) indicate food service in Coach section.

FREQUENCY CODES: All Flights Daily Except as Noted
        1—Monday   3—Wednesday   5—Friday   7—Sunday
        2—Tuesday   4—Thursday   6—Saturday   X—Except

MISCELLANEOUS SYMBOLS:
        ★ Early morning "Early Bird®" or late evening "Owly Bird®" flights offering off-peak First Class/off-peak Coach fares at substantial savings over regular day fares and more discount seats than available on other flights.
        † Indicates next day arrival.
        🎬 Movies in flight   🚁 Helicopter Service Available
                Delta TriStar, DC10 and 767 Jets are shown in **Boldface** type.

Atlanta at 3:38 p.m. Flight 146 is also a possibility, as it arrives in the early evening. Flight 138 leaves Los Angeles too early in the morning and the other two flights leave too late in the day. All of the nonstop flights use wide-body aircraft.

In researching information on flights, the administrative assistant should be aware that travelers normally have flight preferences in the following order:

1. Nonstop flights to the destination
2. Direct flights to the destination (flights that have intermediate stops but do not require a change of planes to the destination)
3. Connecting flights to the destination using the same airline
4. Connecting flights to the destination using another airline (Airplane gates may be a considerable distance from each other; in some airports, gates may be in different terminals.)

You should present possible flight schedules to the executive according to these preferences. You should also be aware that many cities have more than one airport. In making connecting flight reservations, be especially careful to book the connecting flight from the same airport. Also allow at least one hour between connecting flights. To reduce travel hassles, avoid peak travel times, early mornings, and late evenings if at all possible. Finally, when making reservations, be sure to get a seat assignment for each flight.

Official Airline Guides

The transportation department of a corporation may subscribe to the *Official Airline Guide Desktop Flight Guide, North American Edition* and its optional supplement on fares. A *Worldwide Edition* covering international schedules is also available. Published by Official Airline Guides, Inc., 2000 Clearwater Drive, Oak Brook, IL 60521-9953, these guides provide complete information on direct and connecting flights, departure and arrival times, stops en route, aircraft seating charts, and ground transportation availability. Other informative publications for the traveling executive are the monthly *OAG North American Pocket Flight Guide* and the quarterly *OAG North American Business Travel Planner Hotel/Motel Redbook.*

Subscribers receive updated materials automatically. Telecommunications technology permits subscribers to access the *OAG Electronic Edition* via computer terminals to compare schedules and fares, make airline reservations, and reserve rental cars and hotel rooms. This electronic edition updates airline schedules weekly.

Using the *OAG Desktop Flight Guide,* the administrative assistant can research the most convenient available flights and present alternative plans for the employer's approval before initiating the actual reservation. This publication (according to the edition used) also gives information about airport facilities, distances from airports to city centers, limousine service (time, fares, and pickup points), hotels, car rentals, and airport taxi service. The *Desktop Flight Guide* is simple to use once you understand the general method of presentation. Keys to the abbreviations and symbols used are listed on its preliminary pages. Flight information is listed alphabetically by the destination city, then alphabetically by cities from which flights to the destination city are available. For example, suppose your employer is to fly from Dallas/Fort Worth, Texas, to Milwaukee, Wisconsin. You would turn to the "TO MILWAUKEE" section in the guide. Under "TO MILWAUKEE," you would locate the "DALLAS/FT. WORTH" listings. You would find a flight schedule similar to that shown in Figure 17-3. Reading the boldface print at the top of the schedule, you learn the following:

1. Milwaukee is on central daylight time (CDT).
2. MKE is the city/airport code for Milwaukee.
3. Dallas/Fort Worth is on central daylight time (CDT).
4. DFW is the city/airport code for Dallas/Fort Worth.

```
To MILWAUKEE, WISCONSIN                    CDT   MKE
▲DALLAS/FT. WORTH, TEXAS                   CDT   DFW
        D-DFW   L-DAL   F-FTW   H-JDB
        9:30a  D   2:01p   AA    286  FYBMV    72S   S   2
X67    10:55a  D   1:05P   YX    305  YBQMV    DC9   L   0
                YX  305 PREMIUM SEATING & MEALS
X6      1:00p  D   3:10p   YX    307  YBQMV    DC9   L   0
                YX  305 PREMIUM SEATING & MEALS
X6      6:20p  D   8:30P   YX    309  YBQMV    DC9   D   0
                YX  305 PREMIUM SEATING & MEALS
                        CONNECTIONS
        6:50a  D   8:08a MEM NW   830  FYBMnQn  D9S   B   0
E- 6JUL 9:05a MEM 10:41a     NW   930  FYBQM    D95       0
        6:52a  D   8:10a MEM NW   830  FYBMnQn  D9S   B   0
E- 5JUL 9:05a MEM 10:39a     NW   930  FYBQM    D95       0
X67     7:00a  D   8:42a STL TW   538  FYBMBQ   D9S   B   0
        9:05a STL 10:42a     TW   517  FYMBQ    727       0
        8:20a  D  10:26a ORD UA   566  FYBMQ    72S   B   0
       11:15a ORD 11:48a     UA★ 2949  YBMQH    F27       0
        8:30a  D  10:12a STL TW   698  FYMBQ    DC9   B   0
       10:51a STL 11:56a     TW   406  FYMBQ    72S       0
       10:32a  D  11:50a MEM NW   882  FYBQM    D9S       0
E- 6JUL 12:25a MEM 2:00p     NW   932  FYBQM    D9S  L/S  0
       10:35a  D  11:55a MEM NW   882  FYBQM    D9S       0
D- 5JUL 12:30p MEM 3:45p     NW  1244  FYBQM    DC9       1
       10:41a  D  12:17p STL TW   636  FYBMQ    DC9       0
        1:33p STL  2:48p     TW   514  FYMBQ    DC9       0
7      11:00a  D   1:10p MSP NW   402  FYBQM    72S   L   0
        2:25p MSP  3:35p     NW   112  FYBQM    757       0
        1:04p  D   2:38p STL TW   668  FYMBQ    D9S   L   0
        3:20p STL  4:31p     TW   526  FYMBQ    D9S       0
        1:50p  D   3:58p ORD UA   964  FYBMQ    73S   S   0
        5:14p ORD  5:47p     UA★ 2959  YBMQH    F27       0
X67     2:56p  D   4:29p STL TW   118  FYMBQ    727       0
        5:43p STL  6:54p     TW   692  FYMBQ    D9S       0
7       2:56p  D   4:29p STL TW   118  FYMBQ    727       0
        6:00p STL  7:11p     TW   692  FYMBQ    DC9       0
        3:45p  D   5:02p MCI BN   576  YQLMK    72S   S   0
        5:40p MCI  7:04p     BN   150  YQLMK    B11   S   0
        4:55p  D   7:07p ORD UA   468  FYBMQ    727   D   0
        8:15p ORD  8:48p     UA★ 2965  YBMQH    F27       0
        5:30p  D   6:56p MEM NW   834  FYBQM    DC9   S   0
        8:20p MEM  9:55p     NW   936  FYBQM    72S       0
        5:30p  D   6:58p MEM NW   834  FYBQM    DC9   S   0
D- 5JUL 8:20p MEM  9:57p     NW   936  FYBQM    72S       0
        6:01p  D   7:40p STLI TW  600  FYMBQ    727  D/S  0
E- 6JUL 8:31p STL  9:43p     TW   484  FYMBQ    72S       0
```

Notice that three of the flights are nonstop, as indicated by the 0 at the far right. Select a flight based on your employer's time preference and the availability of the flight. Consider the following:

1. The first nonstop flight of the day is at 10:55 a.m. This flight does not operate on Saturdays and Sundays.

2. It arrives in Milwaukee at 1:05 p.m.

3. It is Midwest Express Airlines Flight 305.

4. A number of fares including coach/economy (Y), and coach/economy discounted (B, Q, M, and V) are available.

5. The aircraft is a McDonnell Douglas DC 9 (DC9).

Under "CONNECTIONS," you find a listing of connecting flights. If an executive wanted to go to St. Louis for a brief conference at the airport and then to Milwaukee, it could be arranged via a connecting flight. Notice that:

1. TWA Flight 636 leaves Dallas/Fort Worth at 10:41 a.m. and arrives in St. Louis at 12:17 p.m.

2. The connecting flight, TWA Flight 514, leaves St. Louis at 1:33 p.m. and arrives in Milwaukee at 2:48 p.m.

3. A number of fare options are available.

4. The aircraft on both flights is McDonnell Douglas DC 9-30, 40, 50 & 80 series.

5. Both flights are nonstop.

Flight Reservations and Ticketing

Flight reservations may be made by telephone, in person at the airport terminal, in an airline ticket office, at a travel agency, or in your office or home if you subscribe to the *OAG Electronic Edition.* After choosing a flight, the traveler asks the airline reservations agent, travel agent, or computer to check for the availability of space at the desired fare structure. Space is confirmed by means of computer equipment that records and stores flight reservations from all ticketing stations. Because of possible cancellation of flights, a traveler should avoid making a reservation on an airline that has filed bankruptcy or is in Chapter 11 (reorganization proceedings). If your employer prefers to travel coach/economy, and that particular section of the plane is booked, first class or business class may be available. If so, check with the executive to see which class to book.

A ticket for an in-person reservation is issued at once; otherwise, it is mailed to a specified address or held for pickup at the ticket office or at the airport. Payment can be made by cash, by check, or by credit card. A company with a travel department usually has the authority and the supplies for issuing tickets in-house. Travel agencies have this capability as well. Travelers who use the *OAG Electronic Edition* choose a ticketing option from among those shown on the ticketing options menu.

Even when a trip involves several destinations and several airlines, only one ticket is issued (by the airline on which the flight originates). Passengers who do not know their continuing flights can purchase an open ticket and make reservations later. Data for any changes in ticketed flights are merely attached to the original ticket.

When checking in for a flight, a passenger receives a boarding pass and, on most flights, is assigned a specific seat. On some airlines seat assignments are made when a ticket is purchased or after a specified date. For definitive information on airplane seating arrangements, refer to the *OAG* publications, Consumer Reports Travel Letter available in the local library (see *Consumer Reports*), or the book *Airline Seating Guide* published quarterly by Carlson Publishing Company, P.O. Box 888, Los Alamitos, CA 90720.

Airlines allow customers to make telephone reservations with credit cards. If payment is by credit card, the administrative assistant must know the credit card number and its expiration date. Many organizations issue corporate business cards to key personnel. Other companies maintain charge accounts with various airlines and are billed regularly for authorized travel.

For disabled passengers, special services and assistance for embarking, disembarking, and seating on the aircraft are offered by airlines. Such requests must be specified when making the reservation.

Redemption of Unused Plane Tickets

An unused ticket or unused portion of a plane ticket can be redeemed by submitting it to the issuing airline or travel agency, but may be subject to change or cancellation penalties. A travel agent or the airline can inform you of the redemption rules. If payment was made by credit card directly to an airline, the refund will appear as a credit on the charge account statement. If the ticket purchase was through a travel agency, the agent must process the refund for the traveler. In the case of lost tickets, a waiting period of 90 days to 6 months is imposed before a refund is made because there is the possibility that a lost ticket could be used by someone else. An airline processing charge is deducted from the refund. If the traveler paid for the lost ticket by credit card, the traveler has an additional record to support the ticket purchase. Payment by cash does not give the traveler this added documentation.

Airport Services

Airport limousines shuttle travelers between downtown locations and airports, usually at lower rates than taxi fares. In some cities, limousines call for passengers at key hotels; in others, they depart from downtown ticket offices or downtown airline terminals. If the limousine leaves from a downtown airport terminal, a passenger may check in for a flight at that terminal. If the limousine leaves from a point other than a terminal, passengers check in at the airport.

Limousines may also shuttle passengers between two or more airports serving one city. A handy reference for frequent flyers that outlines transit options, rates, and schedules between airports and city centers is Norman Crampton's *How to Get from the Airport to the City All Around the World,* published by M. Evans & Co., Inc., 216 E. 49 St., New York, New York 10017.

Helicopters may also be available at some airports to transport passengers to a nearby airport or to a downtown location. Check airline timetables for this information.

Major airlines also operate flight clubs. Travelers may join a flight club for a moderate annual fee. Many executives find it less tedious to wait for planes in flight club lounges than at busy airline gates.

Disabled passengers will find that many airports provide printed access guides that outline accessible services available in the airport. These brochures may be found at travelers aid stations, information counters, and airport administrative offices. A disabled passenger is shown boarding an airline flight in Figure 17-4. A comprehensive publication is *A Guide to Accessibility of Terminals Access Travel: Airports* is available free of charge from the Consumer Information Center, Pueblo, Colorado 81009.

Fig. 17-4 Airports provide special services, like this transport chair for narrow airplane aisles, to assist disabled passengers. *Photo courtesy of SeatCase, Inc.*

Company-Owned Planes

Many corporations own one or more planes. They do so to reduce travel time for executives more than is possible when commercial airline schedules have to be followed. Companies with branch offices or plants in hard-to-reach locations also find it necessary to maintain aircraft transportation for their personnel. Coordination of company planes is made by an in-house travel department. Many companies observe the precaution of limiting the number of top officials who can fly in the same plane (private or commercial) to protect continuity of management in case of an accident. Chartering planes is another option businesses have for transporting personnel to areas not served by regional airlines.

TRAIN TRAVEL

Traveling long distances by train takes time that many busy executives cannot afford to spend. Using commuter trains within metropolitan areas, however, is another matter. Amtrak, the nation's coast-to-coast railroad, offers Metroliner service between Boston and Washington, D.C. Improved service has enabled Amtrak to compete with airlines in this commuter market. Travelers can make reservations by telephone and pick up their tickets at an express window before departure. Travel agencies ticket Amtrak as well.

The administrative assistant can become familiar with rail services by consulting the *Official Railway Guide, North American Edition*. This guide is issued quarterly and contains schedules of all railway and steamship lines in the United States, Canada, Mexico, and Puerto Rico.

RENTAL CAR TRAVEL

Business executives often rent cars during out-of-town trips. Automobile rental companies publish directories of their rental agency locations both here and abroad, listing daily rates and mileage charges at each station. You can arrange for a rental car by calling the local office of a car rental agency or by using its toll-free number. It is also possible to arrange for a car rental through an airline. Since rates differ depending on the make of the car, the number of days leased, weekday or weekend travel, and anticipated mileage, check several agencies for the best price. Ask if the agency has corporate and government rates or senior citizen discounts, if applicable. Another consideration in car rental is that some agencies have arrangements with certain airlines through which car mileage can be added to frequent flyer plans.

When ordering a rental car, indicate the make and model of car wanted, where it will be picked up, the number of days the car is needed, and the method of payment. If possible, request a low-mileage car. Although a driver may be insured under a personal automobile policy, additional coverage is available through rental agencies for a daily charge. Many major credit cards also provide insurance coverage for the cardholder if the entire car rental is charged to the credit card, and most car rental agencies accept major credit cards. They also provide maps, dining guides, entertainment guides, etc., to clients who may be unfamiliar with the area.

The American Automobile Association (AAA) provides its members with travel guides for any contemplated trip. Several oil companies and insurance companies also map routes on request. In addition to these sources, bookstores and travel agencies also stock many handy dining and lodging guides.

HOTEL/MOTEL RESERVATIONS

There are several ways to make a hotel/motel reservation. Hotel chains, such as Hilton and Sheraton, have communication systems that reserve rooms in any of their hotels worldwide through local offices. Other major hotels maintain local offices in major cities. Toll-free 800 numbers for major hotels and motels can also be found in the telephone book. Reservations can be made by using voice mail capabilities or FAX machines. Most airlines make hotel and motel reservations for their passengers. Travel agencies and in-house travel departments, of course, make lodging arrangements as part of their service (see Figure 17-5).

Two factors play a role in the choice of a particular hotel or motel: the location with regard to where the traveler will be conducting business and the cost of the room. Some hotels have frequent-lodger programs that provide discounts or room upgrades; some offer corporate and government rates; some have arrangements with certain airlines as part of their frequent-flyer plans. Some corporations favor all-suite hotels where amenities include free breakfasts, complimentary newspapers, and airport shuttles. Reservations for lodging should include the following kinds of information:

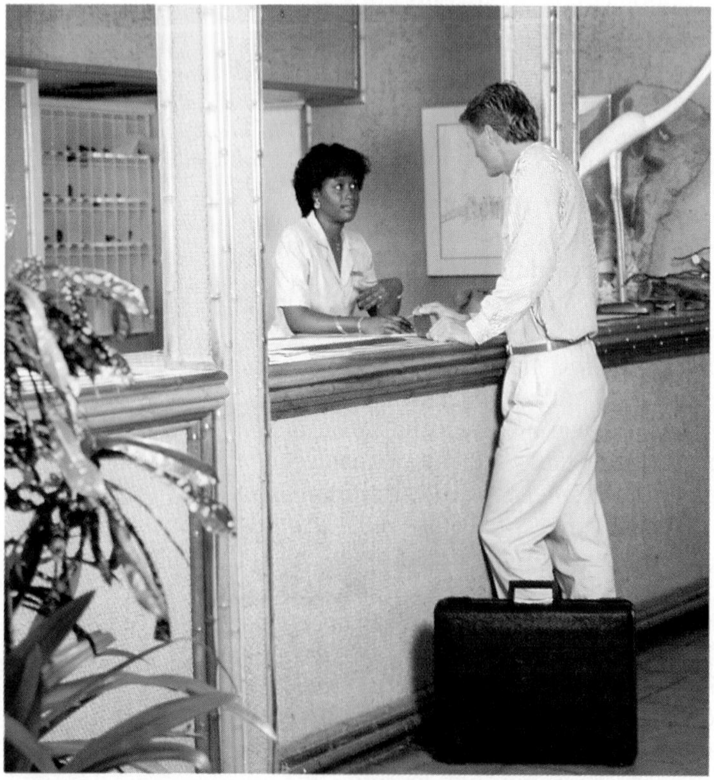

1. *Indicate the kind of room you desire.* Note whether you need one room, several rooms, or a suite of rooms. If you prefer a nonsmoking room and/or a certain room location (close to an elevator, for example), a certain floor, a room with a view, etc., say so.

2. *Indicate your choice of accommodations.* Do you prefer a queen- or king-sized bed?

3. *Indicate the approximate or relative rate.* Do you want a medium-priced or luxury-priced room?

Fig. 17-5 Business travelers rely on airlines, travel agencies, and in-house travel departments to make hotel reservations.
© *Superstock, Inc.*

4. *Give the names of the persons in your party.*

5. *Give the name of your company.* Commercial or convention rates may apply to business guests. In addition, older executives may be eligible for discount rates.

6. *Indicate the date of arrival and the approximate time of registration, if known.* Request a *guaranteed arrival* if you know that arrival will be after check-in time. The room will be held, but the guest will be billed even if the room is unoccupied. Generally, reservations must be canceled 24 hours ahead of time.

7. *Inquire about transportation services or parking availability.* Ask if the hotel has a courtesy car that provides transportation between the airport and the hotel. If so, indicate flight number and arrival time.

8. *Indicate the number of days lodging is needed.*

9. *Indicate the method of payment.*

After a reservation is made, request a confirmation record or a confirmation number that the executive can use when registering. Rooms are at a premium in many cities, and a confirmed reservation is a good precaution.

To simplify their accounting, some hotels and motels ask that a deposit *not* be sent. Small operations may require a deposit.

In canceling hotel reservations, obtain a cancellation number for your records, particularly if the reservation was guaranteed. It is also recommended to get the name of the hotel clerk, in case the cancellation request is not recorded. A guaranteed-arrival reservation must be canceled before 6 p.m. local time to avoid charges.

In making telephone calls from a hotel or motel room, a word of caution is in order. It is customary for hotels to add a surcharge to long-distance calls made from a room, sometimes at 200 to 300 percent. It is recommended that the hotel guest read instructions at or near the hotel telephone before making a long-distance call. Better still, it may be a good practice to bypass the hotel billing system entirely by using a public telephone for all calls. This is easy to do with a telephone credit card.

INTERNATIONAL TRAVEL

During the past three decades, U.S. business firms of almost every size have expanded their operations or their interests internationally. These multinational companies generally have an international division within their organization and branch offices in foreign cities. An administrative assistant to a top executive in a multinational firm probably will plan international as well as domestic travel.

General Considerations

Planning for foreign travel differs in several ways from planning for short, domestic trips. For instance, an executive traveling from New York to London

HUMAN RELATIONS

Five "Ps" are recommended for businesspeople heading to Japan: Patience, Presence (establishing relationship), Preparation, Product, and Protocol.

crosses five time zones. Travel experts estimate that it takes the human body one day to adapt fully for each time zone crossed. Body rhythms and cycles are disrupted, and changes in body temperature and heart rate occur. These changes are the effect of *jet lag.* If possible, an administrative assistant making international travel arrangements should schedule a flight that will allow an executive one day of rest before a scheduled meeting in London. For the return trip, two days are recommended for the traveler to adjust physically and psychologically to the time difference. If it is not possible to schedule a full day of rest before a London meeting, schedule a flight that arrives the night before. On the return, schedule a flight that arrives either on a Friday or a Saturday, giving the executive the weekend to rest.

Another difference between domestic and foreign travel is in arranging appointments. Because of the potential difficulties in getting around in a foreign city and because of the slower pace at which foreign business is conducted, the U.S. visitor will want to keep appointments to two or three a day.

Holidays are different in each country. In planning a trip, check to see if a holiday occurs during the period. For instance, in Italy many business firms close for vacation the entire month of August.

Learning the customs of the countries to be visited is important to the success of a business visit. An excellent reference is the *Countries of the World and Their Leaders Yearbook,* published by Gale Research Company. This yearbook gives background information about each country, health recommendations, methods of travel, and so forth. Most of the international airlines now publish guides for conducting business in Europe and the Far East. In addition, the U.S. Department of State publishes a series of pamphlets entitled *Background Notes on the Countries of the World,* which should be very useful to the administrative assistant of a traveling executive. This publication contains information about important trade fairs, holidays, time differences, climate, hotels and restaurants, office hours, important business contacts, currency exchange, business etiquette and customs, and invaluable hints for improving business contacts. *Background Notes on the Countries of the World* is available from the Superintendent of Documents, Government Printing Office, Washington, DC 20402.

The business card is an important adjunct to the business call. A card with English on one side and the appropriate foreign language on the reverse side would be an asset to a traveling executive. A card is always presented by a caller; therefore, a business visitor can easily use up a supply of 200 cards while attending a business fair. The European business fair has no counterpart in this country. An entire year's output of a product may be sold during such a fair.

Abroad, it pays to bring gifts—judiciously. There are many subtleties to the art of international gift-giving. Where possible, offer a gift that is company associated, such as a pen with a company logo. What pleases a customer in London may be offensive to a Tokyo counterpart. A gift to the wife of a business contact in Europe will be accepted graciously, but a gift to the wife of a Near Eastern businessman is offensive. The Registry Group, a subscription service, provides information and advice on international gift-giving; their toll-free number is 800-955-5077. As with gifts, the practice of tipping may not be appropriate. Asking advice of a resident of the country being visited may be helpful.

Services of a Travel Agency

In lieu of a well-established company in-house travel department, a travel agency can be of great help in planning a foreign trip. The administrative assistant to an executive who travels abroad frequently will find the following services of a travel agent almost indispensable:

Making hotel and rental car reservations

Listing available transportation

Suggesting itineraries and procuring tickets

Notifying you of the required travel documents and how to obtain them

Supplying currency conversion rates and obtaining foreign currency

Explaining baggage restrictions

Obtaining insurance for traveler and baggage

Listing port taxes (Most international airports levy a port tax. An international transportation tax is also imposed on each international passenger departing from the continental United States.)

Providing information about visas

Arranging for the traveler to be met by a representative or a limousine

Supplying information about vaccinations and inoculations

Explaining customs regulations

Giving average temperatures

HUMAN RELATIONS

From airlines and hotels to passports and foreign currency, travel agents are masters of all details that can make a trip successful.

Passports

The first requisite for foreign travel is a passport. A passport is an official document, issued by the Department of State, granting permission to travel. It authenticates a person's right to protection in the host country. For travel in most countries outside the United States, a passport is necessary. U.S. citizens are not required to carry passports in Canada, Mexico, Bermuda, the West Indies, or Central America, although proof of citizenship may be requested. For example, a visitor to Mexico must have a tourist card and carry proof of citizenship.

Passport application forms can be obtained from a travel agent; from passport offices in Boston, Chicago, Los Angeles, Miami, New Orleans, New York, Philadelphia, San Francisco, Seattle, Honolulu, and Washington; from the passport office in local federal buildings; or from designated post offices. For your nearest passport office, look in the White Pages. Most telephone directories list a number for passport information under "United States Government, Postal Service."

In order to obtain a passport for the first time, an applicant is required to appear in person before an agent of the passport office or before a clerk of a federal or state court authorized by law to naturalize aliens. The applicant must present the following papers:

The completed passport application

Proof of United States citizenship (birth certificate or certificate of naturalization)

Proof of identification bearing signature and description, such as a driver's license

Two signed duplicate photographs (meeting size and other specifications) taken by a photographer within the past six months

The passport fee

If the applicant is going abroad on a government contract, a letter from the employing company is required showing the applicant's position, destination, purpose of travel, and proposed length of stay.

As soon as a passport is received, it should be signed and the information requested on the inside cover should be completed. During overseas travel, a passport should be carried or kept in the hotel security box or safe, never left in a hotel room. It may be helpful to have a photocopy of the identification page of the passport kept separately to facilitate reissuance if the passport is lost. Loss of a passport should be reported immediately to the nearest passport office or, if abroad, to the nearest consulate. Business travelers should also carry a letter from the business they represent that describes the nature and the duration of their visit.

A person holding an expired passport must reapply for a current passport. A renewal application may be obtained from the nearest passport office or designated post office. The applicant completes the form, signs and dates the application, attaches two signed duplicate photographs taken within six months of the date of the application, and encloses the expired passport and the passport fee. These materials are mailed to the nearest passport office. Allow at least three weeks for delivery.

A passport is valid for ten years from date of issue. Since processing a passport application may take up to six weeks, persons contemplating foreign travel should keep their passports in order. Administrative assistants to traveling executives should note passport expiration dates in the tickler file. An example of a passport appears in Figure 17-6.

Visas

A **visa** is a permit granted by a foreign government for a person to enter its territory. It usually appears as a stamped notation in a passport indicating that the bearer may enter the country for a certain purpose and for a speci-

Fig. 17-6 This is a page from a valid passport. When a traveler enters a foreign country, an immigration officer may stamp the passport with a visa stamp (date of entry and allowable length of visit). When the visitor leaves the country, the passport is stamped with an embarkation stamp.

fied period of time. Take special note of the effective dates of a visa. Anyone unsure whether it is necessary to obtain a travel visa should contact the consulate of the particular country or a travel agent before leaving the United States. Consular representatives of most foreign countries are located in principal cities. Their addresses can be found in the *Congressional Directory,* available in many public libraries, or in the Yellow Pages of major cities under "Consulates." A traveler who intends to work in a foreign country should check to see whether a work permit is required.

Vaccination and Inoculation Requirements

When traveling to certain countries, the executive may be required to have certain vaccinations and inoculations to protect against a variety of diseases. A travel agent or the consulate of the country to be visited can supply information about required immunizations. (A vaccination record is no longer required for reentry to the United States.) Records of these vaccinations and inoculations are signed by the physician and validated by the local or state health officer on a card labeled "International Certificate of Vaccination." This form may be obtained from the travel agent, the passport office, the local health department, or in some cases, the physician. Even if the country being visited does not require immunizations, the international traveler is well advised to have had routine childhood vaccinations and booster shots every ten years. An excellent government booklet available from the Superintendent of Documents, Government Printing Office, Washington, DC 20402, is *Health Information for International Travel*. Published yearly, this booklet describes a number of possible travel ailments and includes health hints.

Overseas Flights

International plane travel is basically the same as domestic plane travel. Wide-body jets that seat more than 200 passengers usually are selected for international flights. Services include large passenger lounges, a choice from several entrees at mealtime, and containerized baggage compartments. Baggage is stored in an upright position and unloaded swiftly by bringing the containers to the customs area.

On international flights there are two classes of flights: first class and coach/economy. Business class is offered on some flights. Gourmet meals and beverages are served in first class. Beautiful china, crystal, and silver are used; and the service of flight attendants is outstanding. In coach/economy class, meals meet a lesser quality standard.

Baggage limitations vary, so the administrative assistant must check this information when making reservations. Passengers are advised to check in one and one-half hours before flight time. Reconfirmation of each international flight is essential.

Fares vary with the season of the year and according to the length of stay. The only way to keep abreast of air fares is to consult the international desk of the airline or your travel agent for special excursion rates. An international flight schedule of a foreign airline is more complicated than a domestic schedule, because timetables for foreign airlines are usually based on the 24-hour clock. Figure 17-7 explains the 24-hour clock.

a.m.—inner circle	
p.m.—outer circle	
12:00 a.m.—2400	
12:30 a.m.—0030	
9:00 a.m.—0900	
12:00 p.m.—1200	
9:00 p.m.—2100	

Fig. 17-7 The 24-hour clock assigns a number from 1 to 24 to each hour of the day.

Train Transportation

Most foreign railroads provide two classes of service: first-class accommodations seat four to six persons in a compartment; second-class accommodations seat six to eight persons. Reservations are necessary for first-class travel. Passengers carry on their luggage; therefore, it is recommended that passengers carry two small pieces of luggage rather than one large bag.

Sleeping accommodations on trains require first-class tickets. Reservations well in advance of the trip are recommended, for it is often difficult to obtain sleeping car accommodations. Extra-fare trains, carrying first- and second-class sleepers, are available only on the most important international routes.

A Eurailpass entitles the holder to unlimited train travel in over 15 European countries during the length of time specified on the ticket. All travel on a Eurailpass is in first class. A new option in rail travel in Europe is the Europass. This pass is good for unlimited train travel in three to five major western European countries. Several foreign railway systems maintain ticket and information offices in major cities in the United States. The Eurailpass must be purchased before a traveler leaves the United States. Great Britain offers a BritRail pass that entitles the holder to travel by rail in the British Isles for a specified period of time. Rail passes for use in Japan can be purchased through Japan Air Lines. Japanese National Railways has a reputation for providing fast, safe, and punctual service.

Hotel Reservations

Hotel reservations can be made through a travel agent or through the airline. Business travel guides indicate which hotels provide secretarial services and meeting rooms. When making a hotel reservation, ask if the hotel has a facsimile machine; and if so, obtain the FAX number. In addition, if you send a document by FAX, you will need the international access code, country code, and city code. If possible, determine the best ground transportation for your employer to use to meet appointments. If transportation is by train, request a train schedule.

Breakfast is often included in the hotel charge in Great Britain and frequently in the Netherlands. In other countries in Europe, a Continental breakfast, consisting of a hot beverage and a roll, may be included.

Automobile Rentals

Rented automobiles are as readily available in large foreign cities as in the United States. Flight schedules indicate whether this service is available at the airport. Rentals can be arranged by travel agents or airlines in this country. In most foreign countries, a U.S. driver's license is sufficient to operate an automobile; but to be on the safe side, travelers may obtain an international driving license from the American Automobile Association, either here or in Europe, for a small fee.

TRAVEL DETAILS HANDLED BY THE ADMINISTRATIVE ASSISTANT

The groundwork for a trip will probably be laid during a conference between the executive and the administrative assistant. For example, if your employer in Omaha were planning to visit a factory in Philadelphia on March 2, keep appointments in Brussels on March 4, meet with an executive in Paris on March 5, return to Omaha by way of New York, have a one-hour conference at the New York airport, and be back in Omaha on the evening of March 9, you would arrange all the details of the trip.

Planning the Trip

▶ *Procedure*

For the executive to take on international trips, the administrative assistant should prepare a photo-graph album illustrating the company products, the company premises, and representative company employees.

Planning a trip requires checking transportation schedules, researching hotel information, and making reservations. In the case just cited, you would route the executive by air to Philadelphia, from Philadelphia to Brussels, from Brussels to Paris, from Paris to New York, and from New York back to Omaha. If your company has a travel department, you should consult with someone in that department first. That department, in all likelihood, would handle all reservations and make suggestions concerning hotels as well. If your company does not have a travel department, you should contact a reputable travel agency, obtain and study current airline timetables, and discuss possible flight plans with airline reservation agents and with the travel agency. You should also obtain pertinent information about hotels and motels. Hotels provide a range of discounts and amenities. Travel agencies are especially knowledgeable about hotels. The *Hotel and Motel Red Book,* the *Hotel and Travel Index,* and directories published by the American Automobile Association are also good sources of hotel information. These sources list the number of rooms in a hotel, discuss rates, and indicate whether lodging is on the European or the American plan. Under the European plan, the rate represents the cost of the room only. Under the American plan, the rate includes the cost of meals as well. Most commercial hotels are operated under the European plan.

Room rates are quoted for one night's lodging, but many hotels offer reduced rates for daytime-only occupancy. If an executive will be in a city for a few hours for a short meeting, a hotel room makes a good headquarters. In order to be assured of accommodation before the afternoon check-in hour, it may be wise to reserve a room for the previous night and to pay in advance.

Always check the distance from the airport to the hotel and from the hotel to the meeting place. Nothing is more disconcerting than to find oneself across town from an appointment location.

A travel worksheet, such as the one shown in Figure 17-8, can be useful in accumulating information and finalizing trip plans. An executive's itinerary can be prepared from the information provided on this form.

Preparing an Itinerary

Preparing a comprehensive itinerary, a detailed outline of a trip, is an important administrative assistant responsibility. Foresight and analysis are required to prepare it. (The usual itinerary, which is prepared by a travel agency

TRAVEL WORKSHEET

Employee________________________ Date___________

Dates of Trip______________________

Mode of Travel: Commercial Air____ Company Plane____ Train____ Automobile____

Date	Destination	Time (Local) Departure	Arrival	Flight/Train No.	Class of Service	Meals	Date Confirmed

Ground Transportation Requirements (limousine, rental car, courtesy car):

Date	Time	Place	Type	Date Confirmed

Hotel/Motel Reservations:

Date	Destination	Estimated Arrival Time	Date of Departure	Name of Hotel/Motel	Date Confirmed

Travel Funds:

Cash Advance $__________ Company Credit Cards Required? Yes ___ No ___

Company Check $__________ Specify: ________________________________

Traveler's Checks $__________ ________________________________

Fig. 17-8 Travel worksheets are used to finalize trip plans.

if you use its services, covers only flight information for arrivals and departures.) A comprehensive itinerary serves as a daily appointment calendar and includes helpful reminders. Hotel reservations and ground transportation information are included in the chronological format. An itinerary for an international trip, in addition to giving the hotel names, should include their addresses, phone numbers, and FAX numbers. An executive may request a number of copies of an itinerary for associates and family so that mail and messages can be forwarded and emergencies reported. In addition to the office copy, the administrative assistant should keep a copy of the itinerary at home.

You should set up a file on a trip as soon as it enters the planning stage. In the file, place the travel worksheet, purchased tickets, reservations, confirmations, an appointment schedule, and any factual information that may be needed for scheduled meetings. Everything that pertains to the trip should be in this file. When it is time to prepare the itinerary, the file can be sorted into chronological sequence. Figure 17-9 shows the detail and thoroughness with which an itinerary should be prepared.

Fig. 17-9 This comprehensive itinerary is a combination of travel and appointment records and reminders.

ITINERARY FOR K. B. CUNNINGHAM
March 1 – 6, 19—

SUNDAY, MARCH 1   (Omaha to Philadelphia) No direct flights available.

4:15 p.m.   Leave Omaha on American Flight 23. Change in Chicago to United Flight 302 leaving at 6:15 p.m. Dinner served.

10:21 p.m.   Arrive in Philadelphia. Guaranteed arrival reservation at Warwick Hotel (confirmation attached).

MONDAY, MARCH 2   (West Chester Plant)

Take Southeastern Pennsylvania Transportation Authority Conrail commuter train from Penn Center Station. Frequent service. (Papers in briefcase.)

TUESDAY, MARCH 3   (En Route to Brussels)

9:00 a.m.   Leave Philadelphia on American Flight 2 to LaGuardia Airport (New York) to connect with Sabena Flight 34 to Brussels.

11:00 a.m.   Leave for Brussels.

5:00 p.m.   Arrive in Brussels. Reservation at Intercontinental Hotel (reservation attached).

WEDNESDAY, MARCH 4   (Brussels)

9:00 a.m.   Interview at La Societe Generale, Room 913, with Johann Schmidt about development of European office in Brussels (prospectus in briefcase).

1:00 p.m.   Lunch at La Maison du Cygne with Madame Helene Moal and three colleagues for same purpose (prospectus in briefcase). (Confirm by telephone after 11:00 a.m.)

5:00 p.m.   Leave for Paris on Sabena Flight 711 to Le Bourget Airport. Dinner served.

6:21 p.m.   Arrive in Paris. Reservation at the George V Hotel (reservation attached).

THURSDAY, MARCH 5   (Paris)

10:00 a.m.   Appointment with Martha Dillon at Citibank, 43 Rue de la Paix (financial statements in briefcase).

8:30 p.m.   Dinner at Maxim's with Roger Symonds (telephone 45-334).

FRIDAY, MARCH 6   (En Route to Omaha via New York)

12:00 Noon   Leave from Charles de Gaulle Airport on TWA Flight 803.

2:55 p.m.   Arrive at Kennedy Airport where Tom McQuiddy will meet your flight with a car. Conference at International Hotel at airport (daytime reservation enclosed). (Papers in McQuiddy folder.)

4:45 p.m.   Leave Kennedy Airport for Chicago on TWA Flight 347.

6:07 p.m.   Arrive at O'Hare Airport in Chicago.

6:45 p.m.   Leave Chicago on United Flight 779 for Omaha.

7:51 p.m.   Arrive at Omaha airport.

Background material for each appointment should be placed in individual file folders. Each file folder should be labeled with the time and date of the appointment.

Some executives prefer to carry an itinerary prepared by a travel agency and a separate appointment schedule, similar to the one shown in

Figure 17-10, on their business trips. An appointment schedule isolates appointments on one easy-to-read form. It should include the times of appointments, the persons involved, the means of contacting persons involved (telephone and FAX numbers), appointment locations, and other pertinent information.

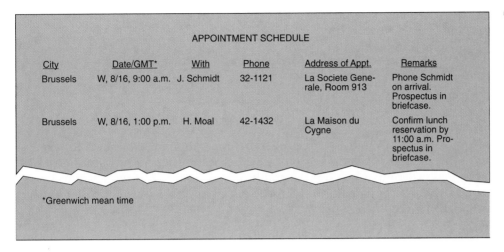

APPOINTMENT SCHEDULE

City	Date/GMT*	With	Phone	Address of Appt.	Remarks
Brussels	W, 8/16, 9:00 a.m.	J. Schmidt	32-1121	La Societe Gene-rale, Room 913	Phone Schmidt on arrival. Prospectus in briefcase.
Brussels	W, 8/16, 1:00 p.m.	H. Moal	42-1432	La Maison du Cygne	Confirm lunch reservation by 11:00 a.m. Prospectus in briefcase.

*Greenwich mean time

Fig. 17-10 An appointment schedule isolates appointments on one easy-to-read form.

Carrying Travel Funds

Ask the executive whether you are to get money for the trip from the company's cashier, the corporate credit card, or the bank. If it is an overseas trip, determine whether there are any restrictions on the amount of currency that may be taken. You can order packets of foreign currencies through the bank or a travel agent. Foreign currency can also be purchased from automatic vending machines in most international airports. To familiarize yourself with foreign currency, see Major Currencies of the World in the Reference Guide, pages 802–803.

Traveler's Checks.   *Traveler's checks* must be purchased by the person or persons who will use them and by nobody else. Therefore, the administrative assistant cannot perform this duty for the executive. Traveler's checks are sold in denominations of $10, $20, $50, and $100, for a small fee, depending on the amount purchased. Some banks issue them without charge, especially during certain times of the year. Figure 17-11 is a photograph of a traveler's check.

Each traveler's check is numbered and printed on a special kind of paper. The administrative assistant should prepare a record in duplicate of the numbers and the amounts of the checks issued, one for the files and one for the executive to carry so that reimbursement can be immediate in case the checks are lost or stolen.

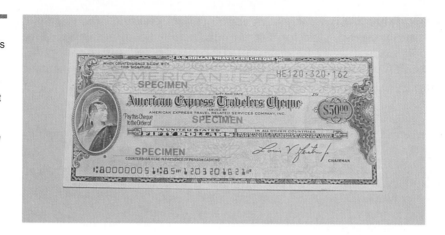

Fig. 17-11 The purchaser signs this traveler's check in the upper left-hand corner. On cashing this check, the purchaser countersigns the check at the bottom.
© American Express Company—reprinted with permission.

Money Orders. Administrative assistants may obtain travel funds for executives through money orders. A money order is a form sold by banks, post offices, express companies, and telegraph offices stating that money is to be paid to the person named on the form. An example of a money order appears in Figure 17-12.

Fig. 17-12 Money orders are convenient forms of payment because they can be purchased in so many places.
© American Express Company—reprinted with permission.

Letters of Credit. A letter of credit is used when extensive travel is involved or when the amount of funds required for a trip is relatively large. The cost of large amounts of money through a letter of credit is considerably less than the cost of traveler's checks. A letter of credit is obtained from a local bank. It indicates the amount the holder is entitled to draw on the issuing bank. To obtain funds, the holder presents the letter of credit to a designated bank in the foreign city. The amounts drawn are recorded on the letter so that the balance is always known. The disadvantage of carrying a letter of credit is that it can be used only during banking hours.

Credit Cards. General-purpose credit cards, such as American Express, VISA, MasterCard International, and Citicorp Diner's Club, permit holders to charge practically any service or goods, including air travel, to a personal or company charge account. Some companies use a corporate business card for transportation and other travel expenses. The administrative assistant's responsibility for credit cards involves requesting renewals on cards that expire and keeping serial numbers on file. Itemized bills for credit card purchases help you prepare expense reports and enable executives to verify expenses. Either method provides data for the company to use in determining its major suppliers and the suppliers that give better rates. Credit card statements are particularly useful in verifying meals and gratuities to meet Internal Revenue Service rules requiring receipts for expenditures of $25 or more.

Obtaining Insurance

Companies sometimes buy blanket insurance policies to cover executives while they are traveling on company business. In addition, companies usually have rules governing the purchase of travel insurance at airports. The administrative assistant is expected to investigate company policy about travel insurance and follow through to see that the executive is appropriately covered.

Assisting in Departure

The administrative assistant is frequently charged with packing the executive's briefcase. This is an important responsibility, for the effectiveness of any business trip is determined by the accessibility of relevant material.

As soon as you learn of an impending trip, start assembling materials and necessary papers that must be taken in order to avoid any last-minute crisis. Begin immediately to procure tickets and other documents for the trip. Check all calendars and ask how your employer wants to handle any scheduled appointments or meetings. Go through the tickler and the pending file and discuss matters to be handled in your employer's absence; determine who is responsible for making decisions. Notify people in the office who may be affected by the executive's absence. Check whether rent, insurance, or income tax payments will be due before the trip is over and get instructions for handling them. Write any letters that will increase the effectiveness of the trip. Decide how expected mail is to be handled. Find out who is responsible for what during the trip. Just before departure, hand the executive the following:

> Travel tickets (also a schedule of alternate flights or copy of *OAG Pocket Flight Guide*)
> Itinerary (a detailed one and a thumbnail copy on a card)

Hotel and motel confirmations

Car rental arrangements

Travel funds

Address book (including addresses of any people to be visited in the area)

A personal checkbook and expense account forms

A company telephone directory

A supply of business cards (in appropriate foreign language on the reverse side)

A supply of stamps (for domestic use only)

Completed address labels for letters to known correspondents, such as the executive's family, administrative assistant, or the president of the company

Notebook, pen, pencil

Dictation recorder and recording media

Laptop computer and diskettes, if requested

Small calculator, if appropriate

Small flashlight

Appointment papers (A separate file for each appointment is recommended. Include copies of relevant correspondence, list of people to be seen and their positions in their companies, and memorandums about matters to be discussed.)

Personal items, such as medication or extra eyeglasses

Favorite reading materials, crossword puzzles

Copies of company brochures, if requested

Extra camera film, chewing gum, mints

Luggage identification tags

Any maps and instructions that may be useful

In addition to the items above, the following should be included for foreign travel:

Money packets of foreign currency and traveler's checks

An international driving license (unless it has been determined that a U.S. driver's license is sufficient)

Notes about reconfirming reservations for foreign flights if required

Passport, International Certificate of Vaccination card, and baggage identification labels for foreign travel

As a precaution if important papers are lost or stolen, the administrative assistant should photocopy the executive's driver's license, passport identification page, credit cards, and airline tickets and keep the copies with the office copy of the itinerary.

AN OFFICE AWAY FROM HOME

Many hotels today in such cities as Boston, Houston, Chicago, and New York offer complete business centers, providing secretarial services for traveling executives. Hertz Rent-A-Car also has business centers around the country. Where a business center is not available, a hotel concierge can most likely find professional secretarial help.

An example of a business center is the Wall Street Journal Business Center, operated by Dow Jones & Co., Inc., located in the New York Hilton. This center offers travelers access to various types of computers, a printer plotter, software, office supplies, reference library, FAX equipment, and staff operators. A flat-rate charge by the hour or for the entire day is made. Business centers such as this have opened all over the country. As this type of service becomes well known, these conveniences will become more popular with the traveling public, and more offices away from home will be established.

Technology affords business travelers the opportunity to take their office with them. For instance, the traveler can work on a laptop/notebook/palm-top computer aboard an airplane. Upon landing, the traveler then can send messages to the office on a portable FAX machine or transmit the information on a portable modem.

Airport conference rooms are available, too, and can be reserved through the various airline companies. These rooms can serve as an office away from home.

WHILE THE EXECUTIVE IS TRAVELING

While the executive is on a trip, the administrative assistant assumes increased responsibility for smooth operation of the office. Members of the management team share the decision-making role for problems usually handled by the employer. It is better for administrative assistants to discuss a perplexing situation with an executive who has been designated to handle crises than to assume too much authority. Routine matters, of course, should be promptly taken care of by the administrative assistant.

The executive who wants to keep in touch with the home office usually telephones the office daily, especially if the company has 800 service. If the employer is in a time zone that precludes talking by telephone during business hours, FAX or voice mail will be used. If you expect your employer to call you, you should keep notes about situations you want to discuss. Many administrative assistants keep a daily log of incoming calls, letters, visitors, and any unusual events so that when the employer calls, they can be discussed.

Your performance while the executive is away is just as important as it is when the executive is present. Other employees may be quick to notice whether you are busy or frittering away time. A competent administrative assistant organizes work so that there is little idle time. During an employer's absence, complete tasks that you have not had time to do, such as reorganizing the files.

Upon return the executive will be grateful and pleased if you have taken care of routine matters, kept records of office activities for review, and arranged matters that require attention according to their importance. Materials that have accumulated for the executive's return should be separated into two groups: (1) matters to be handled by the executive personally and (2) matters already taken care of by you or by others.

You should place the first group in a folder marked "Important." The second group goes into a folder marked "Information Only." Just before presenting the folders, you should arrange materials in logical order, with the most important on top. A list of future appointments and engagements should be included in the "Important" folder.

If the trip is long, the executive may ask you to forward copies of documents that require personal attention (refer to pages 305–307 for instructions). FAX equipment, if available at the destination, can be used for this purpose.

FOLLOW-UP ACTIVITIES

After the executive returns to the office, a flurry of activity is required to wind up a trip. Follow-up activities include filing the expense report, composing thank-you letters, and updating the files.

Expense Reports

Some firms advance funds or provide corporate credit cards for travel. Periodically, or when a trip is over, the executive submits a complete report of expenses incurred. In other companies, executives advance their own funds and are reimbursed later. In either case, the executive must keep an accurate record of the dates and times of travel, the conveyances used, and the costs. Most organizations require receipts for hotel and other accommodations and for any expenses above an established minimum. The traveler's word is usually taken for the costs of taxis, meals, and tips, but usually these costs must be itemized. Receipts are required, however, for entertainment expenses. The date, cost, place, nature of the entertainment, the business purpose, and the names and business affiliations of the persons included must be specified. For further information on allowable business expenses, consult a current copy of the Internal Revenue Service bulletin, *Travel, Entertainment, and Gift Expenses* (see Chapter 21).

Expense report forms are usually provided by the company. Follow the company procedures manual in preparing expense reports, obtaining the necessary signatures, and submitting them to the financial division. The administrative assistant should check the executive's expenses against previous reports to make sure that the amounts for such items as taxis and meals are reasonable and that flight and rail fares are correct. Reimbursement is frequently held up until all expenses are approved by the auditor's office.

Letters

Thank-you letters must be sent to show appreciation for favors and occasions of hospitality during the trip. The need for other letters will be generated by the nature of the trip.

Files

After materials are unpacked and returned to the files, duplicate files can be destroyed. The administrative assistant updates files and business cards to reflect any changes resulting from the trip.

Summary

For most executives business travel is considered a necessary part of their responsibilities, and they generally travel by air. The administrative assistant is responsible for setting travel arrangements in motion by contacting either an in-house travel department, a travel agency, or airline reservation agents. Specific company policies regarding travel must be followed in making reservations.

Airline fares, flight schedules, and classes of service are constantly changing. Airlines publish flight schedules on a regular basis. For up-to-date information, however, consult the *Official Airline Guide Desktop Flight Guide, North American Edition, Worldwide Edition,* or *Electronic Edition.*

Hotel/motel reservations are made by telephone, voice mail, or FAX. Several hotel/motel directories are available that provide information on rates and services.

Planning for a trip abroad requires more time and preparation than a short, domestic trip. The service of an intracompany travel department or a travel agency is almost a necessity. The executive and the administrative assistant will have a number of questions concerning foreign travel that are best answered by a reputable travel agency. For travel in most countries outside the United States, a passport is necessary, and it takes time to acquire one.

When the administrative assistant becomes aware of an impending trip, a travel file is opened and a travel worksheet is prepared. Appointments are made and an itinerary is compiled. Travel funds are arranged and all necessary documents and files set aside.

While the executive is away, the administrative assistant is responsible for the smooth operation of the office. After the trip an expense report with the required receipts is prepared, follow-up letters are composed, and files are updated.

QUESTIONS FOR DISCUSSION

THINK IT
Through

1. If your employer asks you to make a hotel reservation for her in a distant city, what types of information would you ask before contacting the hotel?

2. In what ways can you inform yourself about changes in air and rail travel? Just to show that you are alert to such changes, report any recent travel plan not described in this chapter.

3. What are some of the services travel agencies provide to the business traveler?

4. What procedures should the administrative assistant follow to renew a passport and obtain the necessary visas and traveler's checks for an employer?

THINK IT
Through

5. If your employer were planning to visit five countries overseas on a business trip, what type of information about the countries would you provide?

6. Rekey the following sentences using the apostrophe correctly. Refer to the Reference Guide to verify or correct your answers.

   a. Mark has completed four years work, and he will soon receive his degree.

   b. You should dot your is and cross your ts to show that you are attentive to details.

   c. Its all right to change you're mind.

   d. We have only one position available. It is a secretaries' job.

   e. The company will hold it's annual picnic at the Thomases farm.

PROBLEMS

1. Your employment counselor, Heather Samuel, has arranged for you to interview for the position of administrative assistant for a well-known travel agency in your city. To prepare yourself for the interview, she suggests that you review the names of the capitals of each state and identify the time zone of each state. Using an atlas, you organize the information by making a listing of three columns: states (in alphabetical order), capi-

tals, and time zone. You key this listing and review it thoroughly prior to your interview.

2. Your employer, Edward L. Murray, has asked you to determine the flights he should take for a business trip from your community to the capital of each of three neighboring states. He prefers to travel after office hours so that he will have at least six hours in each city for appointments. He has no preference as to which city to visit first, but wants to make the most efficient use of his travel time. Determine the order in which Mr. Murray should visit the capital cities and then prepare what you consider to be the best flight schedule for him.

TECHNOLOGY APPLICATIONS

▶ **TA17-1**

As the administrative assistant to Jonathan Ames (President of Ames Industries, St. Louis, Missouri), you made travel arrangements for Mr. Ames beginning Monday, November 2. Key an itinerary—in proper format—for Mr. Ames.

Here is the travel data you will need for the itinerary:

TWA Flight 140 leaves St. Louis at 9:49 a.m., arrives La Guardia Airport at 12:50 p.m. Meal served on this flight. Reservation at Whitson Hotel; confirmation in briefcase. Appointment at 3:00 with Steven B. Hoover, Smith Oil Corporation, Rockefeller Plaza. Dinner and show with Aunt Rose at 7 p.m. She will meet Mr. Ames in his hotel lobby. Tuesday meeting at 10 a.m. with Mary Parker, Sales Manager, Larga Products, 243 Park Avenue. Lunch at the New York Club, 61 Central Park South at 1:00 with Arthur Lemont and Beth Arlington of J. Thomas Advertising Agency. All materials in briefcase. Dinner at 7 with the Hargroves in their apartment at 42 East 62nd Street. Wednesday Mr. Ames has a 9:30 interview with Ralph W. Carlson for production manager position. Application is in briefcase. Mr. Carlson is to call Mr. Ames to discuss a meeting place. At noon Mr. Ames is to give a speech at the Wire Products Manufacturers' Conference at the Whitson Hotel, Dining Room C. Speech in briefcase. At 3:30 take hotel limousine to La Guardia Airport for TWA Flight 495 leaving at 5:55 p.m., arriving St. Louis at 7:50 p.m. Meal served.

Chapter 18

eetings and Conferences

LEARNING OBJECTIVES

After studying this chapter and completing the activities, you will be able to:

1. Execute the planning and follow-up tasks associated with informal and formal office meetings, multinational meetings, and the executive's civic and professional meetings.
2. Prepare the order of business, resolutions, and minutes of a meeting.
3. Understand the responsibilities of a meeting participant.
4. Coordinate the planning and follow-up responsibilities associated with conferences and conventions.
5. Assume the administrative assistant's role in planning meetings involving teleconferencing.

INTRODUCTION

Ask executives how they spend most of their workday, and invariably their responses will be "In meetings." One projection is that executives spend at least one-third of their day in meetings. It is estimated that U.S. workers spend three years of their career lives in meetings. It is no wonder that businesses want to make these meetings as productive as possible.

American Express estimates that companies spend $46 billion a year on meetings.

Business meetings are planned for any of several reasons. Meetings take place to enable participants to exchange information, sell a product, solve a complex business problem, make a decision, or merely have an opportunity to get acquainted. Meetings may be informal, involving only a few employees, or they may be more structured and formal, involving a prepared agenda and many participants. A meeting can be face to face in a traditional office or conference room setting or in an electronic meeting room equipped with individual personal computers connected through a network. Business meetings with participants at different locations can take place over the telephone, via computer, or through a closed-circuit television hookup.

In addition to their business responsibilities, executives often assume leadership roles in the community. These responsibilities include membership and possibly the chairing of one or several civic committees. Executives also attend annual conventions, conferences, workshops, and symposia where they exchange ideas with people having similar interests and learn of new developments that will improve their job performance. Participation in these community and professional functions may require an executive to assume part or all of the responsibilities for planning a function.

This chapter discusses informal office or committee meetings, multinational meetings, formal meetings including computer-aided meetings, and conferences and conventions. Technological alternatives to face-to-face meetings are also discussed. The administrative assistant plays a significant role in making meetings effective. The administrative assistant is involved in planning and facilitating meetings, from the initial planning stage through the follow-up. In some cases the administrative assistant may be a meeting participant. All of these responsibilities are explained in detail in this chapter.

INFORMAL OFFICE OR COMMITTEE MEETINGS

Informal office meetings are held on company premises with company personnel and/or visitors. Informal meetings do not involve complicated arrangements and may be scheduled or unscheduled.

If an informal meeting is held on a regular basis (scheduled), participants should have a calendar notation to remind them of the time and place. Many companies provide employees with an annual calendar of meetings. All materials needed for the meeting should be given to the participants prior to the meeting. If a participant is late, the administrative assistant should call that person to determine if he or she plans to attend.

For unscheduled meetings, the administrative assistant follows these procedures:

1. Determines time and date convenient with participants using electronic calendaring, E-mail, or the telephone.
2. Notifies participants by telephone, E-mail, or FAX of the date, time, and location.
3. Informs participants of the meeting topics, and if appropriate, sends any materials that need to be reviewed.

The administrative assistant will follow the same procedures if the executive chairs a civic or professional committee and the meetings are of an informal nature. These meetings generally are held off the company premises.

If a meeting takes place in the executive's office, the administrative assistant makes sure that the room is in good order, enough chairs are available, and all the needed materials are assembled.

During the meeting, the administrative assistant may be asked to take notes. Recommended conference procedure suggests that the chairperson summarize actions and reiterate conclusions as they are reached. The administrative assistant taking notes of a meeting for such a chairperson is fortunate because the job of recording will be easier.

Many office conferences, however, are informal discussions where opinions are exchanged, conclusions are reached, and recommendations are made with no observance of protocol. In these cases the administrative assistant, working alone, is expected to summarize the meeting and to distribute copies of the report to all participants. If, during the meeting, it is agreed that certain conferees should take a specific action, the administrative assistant should send each a copy of the report *with the agreed-upon action underlined or highlighted.* For short, informal meetings, a summary may be made in memo form. An example appears in Figure 18-1.

Many departments have a weekly "stand-up briefing" on Monday mornings. Because these meetings are intended to be short, the administrative assistant need not make special provisions, unless told otherwise. Generally no report of this briefing is required.

MULTINATIONAL MEETINGS

A new experience for American businesses involves attending and conducting meetings where some of the participants do not speak English or English is their second language. Multinational meetings involving non-English-speaking management officials are likely to be formal in nature, requiring extensive planning and the preparation of a business agenda. It is important that the agenda be sent to attendees in advance of the meeting date. Having the agenda before the meeting gives the attendees an opportunity to prepare themselves for the topics to be discussed.

Rank (or protocol) may be an important concern with international visitors and should be carefully observed by the meeting hosts and administrative staff. Administrative assistants involved in the planning of a multinational meeting may arrange for an interpreter to attend the meeting and may also help the interpreter prepare special overhead visuals and handouts in the foreign language or languages. The length of a meeting doubles when an interpreter is used, so this needs to be considered in scheduling the meeting.

When English is a second language of some of the participants, their vocabularies may be limited, and they may be slow in understanding the material being presented. A detailed outline covering all the topics of the meeting should be prepared and given to participants or used as an overhead visual. English-speaking participants should speak slowly and clearly, using standard vocabulary without slang or regional expressions; they should be sensitive to cues that suggest misunderstanding. Finally, participants should resist any temptation to rush or assist people in expressing themselves in English. This practice might appear to be patronizing and could offend the visitor. These suggestions also apply to the administrative assistant who may have contact with international visitors.

Ensuring effective communication during multinational meetings takes a great deal of time and preparation on the part of the executive/administra-

```
                    MEMORANDUM

                              October 21, 19--

TO: ✔ R. Edison
      F. Marco
      J. Monroe
      S. Renberg

The Budget Committee met in Mr. Monroe's office on Monday, October
10, 19--, to discuss the group health plan and the parking lot
resurfacing.  All members were present.

Mr. Marco stated that the dental health plan is now in operation,
and the anticipated premium for the year is $6,000.

Mr. Renberg reviewed bids for resurfacing the company parking
lot.  The lowest bidder was Root Construction Company at $8,025.
The work will begin Saturday, October 25.

Mr. Edison agreed to develop guidelines for budget forecasts
and to present them at the next meeting of the Committee.




                    Joyce Anderson
                    ————————————————————
                      Joyce Anderson
                    Administrative Assistant
                       to Mr. Monroe
```

Fig. 18-1   A summary of an informal meeting is prepared and signed by the administrative assistant.

tive assistant team. If minutes of such a meeting are to be produced, the administrative assistant should use a tape recorder for a verbatim record. Afterward an interpreter and the executive should be consulted before keying the report. In addition to preparing the minutes in English, the executive may request that the interpreter prepare the minutes in the native language of the international visitors.

Not all multinational meetings require this type of preparation. Many foreign nationals speak English; however, in any multinational meeting, it is wise to use standard speech.

Administrative assistants may also facilitate a multinational meeting by developing packets of information for foreign visitors. Packets may include a list of ethnic restaurants, points of interest, important telephone numbers, a city map, and general information about the community.

FORMAL OFFICE MEETINGS

As soon as you know that a formal meeting is to be called, your responsibilities as a meeting facilitator begin. After you learn the purpose of the meeting and the names of the participants, you coordinate the selection of the date and time of the meeting, select and reserve the meeting location, prepare an agenda, assemble the required materials, and schedule any special equipment. After the meeting, you carry out the follow-up duties, such as preparing and distributing the minutes of the meetings. To keep meeting materials organized, you should set up a file folder. Use the name of the meeting and the date as the tab caption. Place into this folder every item of relevant information that crosses your desk during the planning stages.

Meeting Room Reservation

When the executive says, "Call a meeting on budget requests for next Wednesday afternoon at two o'clock," the first detail to take care of is reserving the meeting room. Since meetings of five or more people are customarily held in a room other than the executive's office, the administrative assistant asks if a standard conference room is suitable, and if so, checks to see if a conference room is available.

If the company has an electronic conference room, and the meeting requires this accommodation, the administrative assistant would check on the availability of that room. Electronic meeting rooms (see Figure 18-2) are equipped with individual personal computers with software (sometimes referred to as groupware), keyboards, and monitors connected to a network. Meeting participants talk through computers, and comments accumulate on a projection screen located at one end of the room. This meeting setup is particularly effective for group decision-making projects and brainstorming sessions. This technology gives everyone the opportunity to all talk at once, which could conceivably reduce some of the frustrations often associated with meetings. In addition, participants maintain anonymity, so even the shyest would not feel intimidated. At the end of the meeting a printed summary is given to all participants.

The next step is to reserve the selected meeting room. The administrative assistant makes the request through the designated company employee indicating the date, the number of people attending the meeting, and the

Fig. 18-2 Electronic meeting rooms like this one offer participants the latest in conference technology.
Photo courtesy of Ventana Corporation, Tucson, AZ.

time required. The administrative assistant should indicate the type of seating arangement preferred, such as rectangular or round tables or classroom seating configuration.

If the meeting is to be held in a hotel, the administrative assistant reserves an adequately sized room with seating facilities. The room should offer privacy, freedom from distractions, and easy access, particularly if a disabled person will attend. On the day of the meeting the location and hour of the meeting should be posted on the announcement board in the lobby and in the elevators. If a meal is included, the menu, the serving time, the method of payment, and the number of guests must be discussed with the hotel's banquet manager. Also, you should ask the executive whether seating place cards are needed. You will find that hotels do not normally charge for meeting rooms if the meeting includes meal service. In making these arrangements, keep a record of the names of hotel personnel you contact. If something must be done at the last minute, such as requesting additional chairs for the conference room or an additional place setting at the dining table, this list will be helpful.

Request for Special Equipment

Requesting equipment for use during the meeting is the administrative assistant's responsibility. Once the location, date, and time of the meeting are established, any special equipment can be ordered. For instance, flip charts, easels, and overhead or slide projectors with screens are often used by speakers in business meetings. Or a speaker may require an electronic chalkboard or whiteboard similar to that shown in Figure 18-3. Here, a speaker is explaining the information displayed on the whiteboard. With the press of a button, paper copies of the information can be produced for the participants to study. Other equipment used in business meetings include a VCR (videocassette recorder) connected to a television set. In this age of technology many configurations of electronic and telecommunications equipment are possible. A multimedia presentation might include a computer with animation, still images, full-motion video, and audio.

Fig. 18-3 This speaker is using an electronic chalkboard to explain material. This chalkboard has a feature that produces paper copies of the material appearing on the chalkboard.

Notices of Meetings

The administrative assistant's responsibility for notifying participants of a meeting frequently involves four steps:

1. Making calendar notations
2. Maintaining the mailing list
3. Composing and sending the notice
4. Handling the follow-up work

Most of these activities will be performed using a computer and appropriate software.

Making Calendar Notations. You should make notations on your computer calendar and your desk calendar to remind you to prepare and send a meeting notice. An E-mail or paper notice for an office conference of staff personnel could be delivered the day before a meeting, but an office conference of traveling salespeople might require two weeks' notice. You should also make the appropriate calendar notation to confirm your conference room reservation a few days before the meeting.

Maintaining the Mailing List. Mailing lists of persons outside your organization who are to receive meeting notices should be kept in a database file. The information may include only the person's name and address or give more detailed information as well, such as the person's telephone/FAX numbers and affiliations. For easy reference, the administrative assistant should have a computer printout or maintain a Rolodex file of the mailing list. Once the meeting notice is prepared, the mailing list can be merged with the notice. Envelopes would be prepared from the mailing list on the computer or by using address labels.

A mailing list must be kept up-to-date. In addition to making reported changes as they occur, you should verify the current addresses of members at least once a year.

Composing and Sending the Notice. Simple meeting notices can be composed by the administrative assistant for the executive's approval. Notices of meetings should answer the five Ws: Who? What? When? Where? Why? The notice of the previous meeting generally is a good model to follow. If required to prepare an agenda, the administrative assistant should send a request for agenda items along with the notice of the meeting.

For small meetings, participants are notified either with a keyed paper notice, an electronic message, or by telephone. For large meetings, a notice is reproduced and distributed.

A form notice (a skeleton notice) of meetings that recur on a regular basis should be stored in the computer memory or on diskette. When the meeting is called, pertinent information is keyed to complete the notice. If only a few participants are involved, a tabular listing of the names of those to receive the announcement may be keyed in place of the usual single name, address, and salutation. With the tabular listing, the salutation is a general one, such as *Dear Member* or *Dear Committee Member,* or the salutation can be omitted. Another method is to key an individual letter to each person. As a precaution, keep a file copy of the notice indicating the date of mailing.

For an internal company meeting, a paper notice or an electronic message is sent to participants. Figure 18-4 shows a paper notice sent to members of a finance committee, announcing the day, date, time, place, and purpose of a meeting. An electronic message takes the same form as a paper notice. Participants can confirm their attendance plans with an electronic message, by paper, or by telephone.

```
                                              November 19, 19--
To the Finance Committee

Donald Wang
C. B. Newman
✓Marian Sternberg

The Finance Committee will meet in the second-floor conference
room at 10 a.m. on Tuesday, November 24.

Please bring comparisons of last year's budget with actual
results in your division as of October 31 so that we can make
preliminary estimates of changes that will be necessary next
year.

                        J. J. J. Young
```

An administrative assistant who telephones participants to notify them of the meeting provides the same information that appears on a keyed notice. Attendance plans generally can be verified at that time.

Handling the Follow-up Work. Follow-up duties consist chiefly of recording who and how many will or will not attend the meeting. This information is necessary for several reasons. If it is a meeting of a professional or civic organization and business is to be transacted, the person chairing the meeting needs to know if a quorum will be in attendance. (A **quorum** is the number of voting members that when present is sufficient to transact business. That number is specified in the organization's constitution or bylaws.) For an internal company business meeting, having a quorum present probably would not be an issue. If a meal is part of the meeting, it is necessary to inform the hotel or restaurant of the number of reservations. If return postcards were furnished, follow-up is merely a matter of sorting the cards into the *will*'s and *will not*'s. But usually telephoning several persons for a definite yes or no is required.

With a fairly small group, the administrative assistant may call all persons expected, or their administrative assistants, to inquire if they plan to attend. A membership listing or a form similar to Figure 18-5 is used to record expected attendance.

Procedure

A quorum is the number of voting members that, when present, is sufficient to transact business.

Order of Business (Agenda)

Every formal meeting should follow a systematic program that has been planned and outlined in advance. This program is usually called the *order of business* (see Figure 18-6). It is called the *agenda* in academic and business meetings. The term *calendar* is used at meetings of some legislative bodies, such as a city council. A review of the bylaws and the minutes of previous

RECORD OF TELEPHONE VERIFICATION

Meeting *Production Manager* Date *Tuesday, October 15, 19--*

Time *10:00 a.m.* Place *Home Office, Conference Room 2*

Date Called	Name	Will Attend	Unable to Attend	Remarks
9/29	Angela Larsen	✓		
9/29	Sam Highland		conflicts with plant opening in Denver	

Fig. 18-5 This record is useful in determining the number of reservations to be made for a meeting and if a quorum will be present.

meetings (properly indexed for easy cross-reference) is an invaluable aid in preparing an order of business and in helping the presiding officer carry out the agenda effectively.

Sometime before the meeting you should remind the executive who is to preside over the meeting to prepare the order of business. If you know the

USUAL ORDER OF BUSINESS

1. Call to order by the presiding officer
2. Roll call (either oral or taken by the organization's secretary)
3. Announcement of quorum (not always done)
4. Reading of the minutes of the previous meeting (Sometimes the minutes are circulated before the meeting and this step is omitted.)
5. Approval of the minutes
6. Reports of officers
7. Reports of standing committees
8. Reports of special committees

   } Copies of these reports are usually given to the organization's secretary.

9. Unfinished business (taken from the previous minutes)
10. New business
11. Appointment of committees
12. Nominations and elections
13. Date of next meeting
14. Adjournment

Fig. 18-6 Every formal meeting should follow a consistent program.

purpose of the meeting, you can compose an agenda for the executive's approval following the order of business in general use by the organization. You would, of course, review the minutes of the last meeting to determine if any unfinished business should be included on the agenda. Then you would submit the agenda and a copy of the previous meeting's minutes to the executive for revision or approval. Any person responsible for an item of business on the agenda should be notified prior to the meeting.

In some organizations a tentative agenda is distributed to the membership for their information and additions. If no additional items are submitted, the tentative agenda becomes the final order of business and is redistributed to all members. If additional items are submitted for consideration, a final agenda is prepared and sent to the membership. If the agenda includes a discussion of a proposed plan, a copy of the proposal should accompany it. An example of an agenda is shown in Figure 18-7. Distribution of the agenda and any attachments, if within a company, can be done electronically.

A group that is meeting for the first time appoints a temporary chairperson and a temporary secretary. Later in the initial meeting, the group elects permanent officers or appoints a committee to nominate officers and to draw up a constitution and bylaws.

```
              AGENDA FOR THE REGULAR MEETING

                        of the

              COMMITTEE FOR A DOWNTOWN MALL

                     May 15, 19--

     I.  Call to Order . . . . . Randy Anderson, Chairperson

    II.  Reading of the Minutes  Alan Updike, Secretary

   III.  Treasurer's Report  . . Susan Novak, Treasurer

    IV.  Unfinished Business

              Government Regulations,  Walter Franks
              Special Funding Measures, Letitia Alberiche

     V.  New Business

              Architect's Concepts, William Chaney
              Rerouting Traffic, Officer Nelson
              The Tulsa Experience, Mayor LaFortune

    VI.  Adjournment
```

Fig. 18-7 To increase readability, a typical keyed agenda is double-spaced. Note that the numbering system used on this agenda will also be followed in preparing the minutes.

Last-Minute Duties

The administrative assistant's first duty on the day of the meeting is to check the meeting room to see that the air in the room is fresh; tables and chairs are appropriately placed; there are enough pens, pencils, paper, and paper-clips; and any requested equipment is in place.

Many small business meetings are recorded on tape. The administrative assistant makes arrangements for setting up the recording machine, often operating the tape recorder and taking notes as well. In order to identify voices on a tape during the meeting, use a form similar to the one shown in Figure 18-8 to record each speaker's initial comments.

Assemble materials in a file folder for the executive, arranging them in the order in which they will be needed as indicated by the agenda. Color-coding materials is also helpful. In addition, include the latest edition of *Robert's Rules of Order,* the organization's bylaws, a list of those who should attend the meeting, and a list of standing and special committees for the executive to take to the meeting.

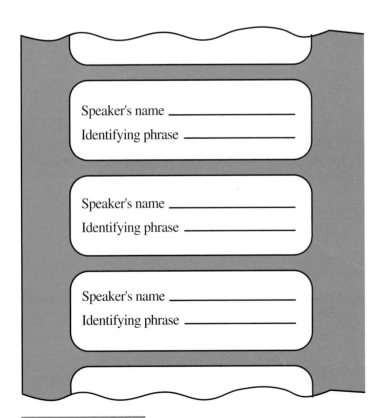

Fig. 18-8 To identify the speakers at a taped meeting, this form allows the administrative assistant to record the speaker's name and first phrase.

If you are to take the minutes, take a copy of the agenda, the attendance list, the minutes book, a seating chart (if necessary), ballots, and any other material that may be required during the meeting. Use the attendance list to mark off members' names as they enter the room and to record early departures. The attendance list can also be useful if you need to make introductions. You may wish to prepare a *minutes skeleton* from copies of the minutes of previous meetings to use as a guide in taking notes (see Figure 18-9). Study the agenda and become familiar with the names of those who are to present topics so you can easily record these names during the meeting. If you miss a name, jot down some distinguishing characteristics of that person and ask the presiding officer for help after the meeting.

Fig. 18-9 Administrative assistants who take minutes of meetings use minutes skeletons as guides to record all pertinent matters presented in a meeting.

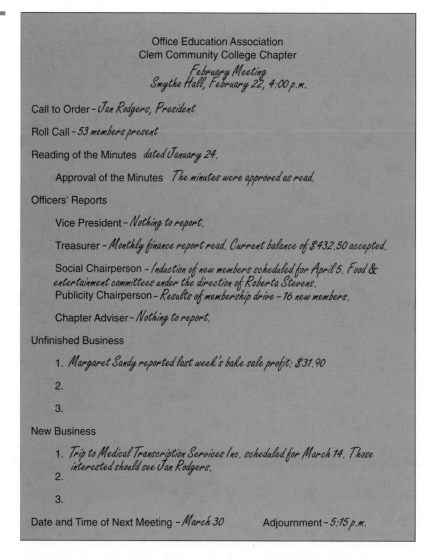

Office Education Association
Clem Community College Chapter
February Meeting
Smythe Hall, February 22, 4:00 p.m.

Call to Order – *Jan Rodgers, President*

Roll Call – *53 members present*

Reading of the Minutes   *dated January 24.*

    Approval of the Minutes   *The minutes were approved as read.*

Officers' Reports

    Vice President – *Nothing to report.*

    Treasurer – *Monthly finance report read. Current balance of $432.50 accepted.*

    Social Chairperson – *Induction of new members scheduled for April 5. Food & entertainment committees under the direction of Roberta Stevens.*
    Publicity Chairperson – *Results of membership drive – 16 new members.*

    Chapter Adviser – *Nothing to report.*

Unfinished Business

    1. *Margaret Sandy reported last week's bake sale profit: $31.90*

    2.

    3.

New Business

    1. *Trip to Medical Transcription Services Inc. scheduled for March 14. Those interested should see Jan Rodgers.*
    2.

    3.

Date and Time of Next Meeting – *March 30*   Adjournment – *5:15 p.m.*

Make arrangements so there will be no telephone interruptions during the meeting. Before leaving your desk to take the minutes, double-check to see that you have all necessary recording supplies and other materials with you. It is most embarrassing to leave a meeting for things that should already be there; it shows that you are not very thorough. On the other hand, offering to get records on subjects that arise unexpectedly shows your willingness to be of help. Before leaving a meeting room, however, get permission from the presiding officer.

Parliamentary Procedure

Robert's Rules of Order, the manual of parliamentary procedure, is an important reference for a meeting planner and/or meeting secretary. This manual provides guidelines for conducting orderly meetings and determining when a quorum is present. It explains types of motions, procedures for making motions, rules for voting, and other activities common to meetings. If you understand parliamentary procedure, you can report meetings more accurately. You can also unobtrusively call the attention of the chairperson to any violations of parliamentary rules. Therefore, you should review important points of parliamentary procedure before going to a meeting. You should also review the rules for handling motions outlined in Figure 18-10.

Parliamentary law has been defined as "common sense used in a gracious manner." Its purpose is to arrive at a group decision in an efficient and orderly fashion. Parliamentary procedure is based on four principles:

1. Courtesy and justice must be accorded to all.
2. Only one topic is considered at a time.
3. The minority must be heard.
4. The majority must prevail.

Most business is transacted through main motions, which require a majority vote for adoption. A member addresses the chairperson (by saying "Mr. Chairman" or "Madam Chair," as the case may be), is recognized, and makes a motion. Another member seconds the motion. After the motion has been made and seconded, the chairperson states the motion and calls for discussion. When the discussion ends, a vote is taken, usually by voice. The chairperson announces the result: "The motion is carried [or defeated]." If anyone calls "Division," the chairperson asks for a show of hands or a standing vote. If a majority demands it, the vote must be taken by ballot. Figure 18-11 on page 475 discusses several basic methods of voting.

After a main motion has been made, a member of the body can propose an amendment to the motion. If the proposal is seconded, it is discussed. The proposed amendment must be voted upon before the main motion can again be considered. After announcing the action on a proposed amendment, the chairperson states that the original motion plus the amendment is now

▶ Procedure

The National Association of Parliamentarians uses the term chairman *instead of* chairperson *to address the presiding officer.*

RULES FOR HANDLING MOTIONS

Types of Motions	Order of Handling	Must Be Seconded	Can Be Discussed	Can Be Amended	Vote Required[1]	Vote Can Be Reconsidered
MAIN MOTION						
To present a proposal to assembly	Cannot be made if any other motion is pending	Yes	Yes	Yes	Majority	Yes
SUBSIDIARY MOTIONS[2]						
To postpone indefinitely action on a motion	Has precedence over above motion	Yes	Yes	No	Majority	Affirmative vote only
To amend [improve] a main motion	Has precedence over above motions	Yes	Yes, when motion is debatable	Yes, but only once	Majority	Yes
To refer motion to committee [for special consideration]	Has precedence over above motions	Yes	Yes	Yes	Majority	Yes
To postpone definitely [to certain time] action on a motion	Has precedence over above motions	Yes	Yes	Yes	Majority	Yes
To limit discussion to a certain time	Has precedence over above motions	Yes	No	Yes	⅔	Yes
To call for vote [to end discussion at once and vote]	Has precedence over above motions	Yes	No	No	⅔	No
To table motion [to lay it aside until later]	Has precedence over above motions	Yes	No	No	Majority	No
INCIDENTAL MOTIONS[3]						
To suspend a rule temporarily [e.g., to change order of business]	No definite precedence rule	Yes	No	No	⅔	No
To close nominations[4]		Yes	No	Yes	⅔	No
To reopen nominations	These motions have precedence over motion to which they pertain	Yes	No	Yes	Majority	Negative vote only
To withdraw or modify a motion [to prevent vote or inclusion in minutes][5]		No	No	No	Majority	Negative vote only
To rise to a point of order [to enforce rules or program][6]		No	No	No	No vote, chairman rules	No
To appeal from decision of the chair [must be made immediately][6]		Yes	Yes, when motion is debatable	No	Majority	Yes
PRIVILEGED MOTIONS						
To call for orders of the day [to keep meeting to program or order of business][6]	Has precedence over above motions	No	No	No	No vote required[7]	No
Questions of privilege [to bring up an urgent matter—concerning noise, discomfort, etc.]	Has precedence over above motions	No	No	No	Majority	No
To take a recess	Has precedence over above motions	Yes	Yes, if no motion is pending	Yes	Majority	No
To adjourn	Has precedence over above motions	Yes	No	No	Majority	No
To set next meeting time	Has precedence over above motions	Yes	Yes, if no motion is pending	As to time and place	Majority	Yes
UNCLASSIFIED MOTIONS						
To take motion from table [to bring up tabled motion for consideration][8]	Cannot be made if any other motion is pending	Yes	No	No	Majority	No
To reconsider [to bring up discussion and obtain vote on previously decided motion][9]		Yes	Yes, when motion is debatable	No	Majority	No
To rescind [repeal] decision on a motion[10]		Yes	Yes, when motion is debatable	No	Majority or ⅔	Yes

1. A tied vote is always lost except on a motion to appeal from the decision of the chair [see "Incidental Motions"] when a tied vote sustains the decision of the chair.
2. Subsidiary motions are motions that pertain to a main motion while it is pending.
3. Most incidental motions arise out of another question that is pending and must be decided before the question out of which they arise is decided.
4. The chair opens nominations with "Nominations are now in order." Nominations may be made by a nominating committee, by a nominating ballot, or from the floor. A member may make a motion to close nominations, or the chair may declare nominations closed after assembly has been given a chance to make nominations. The voting is not limited to the nominees, as every member is at liberty to vote for any member who is not declared ineligible by the bylaws.
5. The mover may request to withdraw or modify his motion without consent of anyone before the motion has been put to assembly for consideration. When motion is before the assembly and if there is no objection from anyone in the assembly, the chairman announces that the motion is withdrawn or modified. If anyone objects, the request is put to a vote.
6. A member may interrupt the speaker who has the floor to rise to a point of order or appeal, call for orders of the day, or raise a question of privilege.
7. Orders of the day may be changed by a motion to suspend the rules. [See "Incidental Motions."]
8. Motion can be taken from the table during the meeting when it was tabled or at the next meeting.
9. Motion to reconsider may be made only by one who voted on the prevailing side. A motion to reconsider must be made during the meeting when it was decided or on the next succeeding day of the same session.
10. It is impossible to rescind any action that has been taken as a result of a motion, but the unexecuted part may be rescinded. Notice must be given one meeting before the vote is taken, or if voted on immediately, a two-thirds vote to rescind is necessary.

before the house if the amendment carried. If the amendment was defeated, the original motion is acted upon.

If a motion involves two actions rather than one, a member can move that the question be divided for voting; then each part becomes a separate motion. If a motion is so bogged down that further discussion

Fig. 18-11 There are four basic methods of voting.

BASIC METHODS OF VOTING

1. *Voice vote* is the most common voting method since it is the easiest and fastest way of determining a vote outcome. If the vote is in doubt, another voice vote or a show of hands may be taken. Responses in favor are either *yeas* or *ayes; against, nays* or *noes.*

2. *Show of hands* or *raising vote* is used when a motion requires a definite number of affirmative votes, such as two-thirds. The administrative assistant of the organization and possibly others appointed by the presiding officer are responsible for counting the votes.

3. *Roll call vote* may be required by the bylaws of an organization for particular motions or may be decided upon by a motion from a member. The presiding officer states the responses to be used in voting for or against the motion. Members not voting may be asked to respond by saying, "Present" or "Abstain." Names are called in alphabetical order and the vote is given. The presiding officer is named last and votes only if it would affect the result. The roll call record is made a part of the minutes of the meeting.

4. *Ballot vote* allows for a secret vote and is commonly used for elections or important matters brought before the organization. Printed ballots, as in the case of elections, generally are prepared before the meeting. For matters arising at the meeting requiring a ballot vote, slips of paper are distributed to the membership for voting use.

Announcement of Results: The affirmative vote is given first, followed by a statement to the effect that the motion passed or the motion was defeated.

would seem a waste of time, and if two-thirds of the voting members agree, a member can "move the question," forcing an immediate vote. If the motion to move the question loses, discussion continues. When it becomes obvious that further information is needed, a motion can be made to refer the matter to a committee, which is then named by the chairperson.

A motion can also be made to table a motion (to delay further discussion or action). A seconded motion to table must be voted upon at once. A successful motion to table permits the group to consider more important business and sometimes allows a motion to die, although a tabled motion may be taken from the table by a majority vote. (A surer way to kill a motion is to move that the motion be postponed indefinitely.)

Members may question the chairperson about the way business is being conducted at any time. If a member says, "I rise to a point of order," the chairperson must decide, without debate, whether a rule has been broken or rely on a parliamentarian for advice. By unobtrusively calling the attention of the chairperson to any violations in parliamentary procedure, the administrative assistant can prevent embarrassment. Slipping a brief, tactfully phrased note to the chairperson is sufficient to alert her or him to an error or an omission in procedure.

Privileged motions have precedence over others. One privileged motion is "to call for orders of the day." This motion, without debate, forces the chairperson to follow the agenda.

The Administrative Assistant as the Meeting Recorder

If you are asked to take notes at a meeting, familiarize yourself ahead of time with matters that may be discussed. Read the minutes of previous meetings, the agenda, proposals, and other information that might be brought before the membership. This background information will help you set up the order of your notetaking or supplement a recorder if the meeting is being taped. Select a place to sit next to the presiding officer and concentrate on taking notes as unobtrusively as possible.

Your first duty may be to report whether a quorum is present. A rapid check can be made by using a membership list. While taking notes, you may have to ask to have something repeated. The bylaws of some organizations require that the person making a motion submit the motion to the organization's secretary in writing so that it will be exactly phrased in the minutes. Some meeting recorders prepare blank motion forms and distribute them to members before the meeting begins (see Figure 18-12). Even with written motions, you should take the oral motion down verbatim to be sure that the written motion conforms to the oral one. Copies of complicated reports or presentations should be given to you to attach to the minutes.

You are not expected to take down the meeting word for word. Too many notes, however, are better than too few. You are responsible for getting everything important in your notes, especially motions, amendments, pertinent discussions, and decisions. If you cannot decide whether a statement is important, you should record it. It can be dropped from the final draft if it later seems inconsequential.

Some essential parts of the minutes may not be specifically announced at the time of the meeting. For example, the date,

Motion _____

_____

_____

Made by _____

Seconded by _____

Vote for _____ Vote against _____

Abstentions _____

Absent during voting _____

Summary of discussion _____

_____

_____

Fig. 18-12 If an organization's bylaws require motions to be submitted in writing, blank motion forms may be distributed before a meeting begins. Persons making motions record them on the forms and hand them to the meeting recorder. When a motion reaches the floor, the recorder uses the form to record all pertinent data—i.e., who made the motion, who seconded it, votes for and against, abstentions, and a summary of the discussion.

time, and place of the meeting and the name of the presiding officer may not be stated. The roll may be called; but if it is not called the *meeting recorder is expected to observe and to record* all details of attendance including who attended, who did not attend, who arrived late, and who left early. The last two items of information are important in recording action on measures voted upon. (Those not wishing to go on record with their votes may absent themselves from a part of the session for just that reason.) To report as present a person who left the meeting during an important transaction could have serious consequences.

If you are depending on a taped report of the meeting as the source for the minutes, you should have two recorders set up in the room. Activate the second recorder immediately after the first tape is used. In addition, you will need to make notes of *items that are not likely to appear in the recording*: the names of those attending, the official title of the speaker, who said what, the time of the meeting and adjournment, the names of those voting yes and no to motions, the names of those coming in late and leaving early, and possibly any difficult names and words that may cause confusion in transcription. If you outline the proceedings during the meeting, you can more easily make necessary insertions when you work with the taped report. Keep the tapes until the minutes have been signed and formally approved by the membership.

If it is the duty of the secretary of the organization to read the minutes of the last meeting, they should be read in an intelligible manner and in a voice loud enough for everyone in attendance to hear what matters were considered and what decisions were made. After the minutes are read, the presiding officer asks for corrections and additions. Usually this is a mere formality, and a voice vote approves the minutes as read. In some cases, however, corrections or additions are made. When this happens, the minutes should not be rekeyed. The changes should be made in red ink on the original copy of the minutes. Corrections and additions become a part of the minutes of the meeting at which they are made. Some organizations appoint a minutes committee to examine the minutes before the next meeting and report to the membership whether the minutes are in order or what changes should be made. Some organizations distribute minutes to the full membership for review prior to the meeting.

The order of business follows the agenda. The story of every motion, passed or defeated (as shown in Figure 18-12), must be recorded in the minutes. The name of the person making the motion, the complete motion exactly as stated, the name of the person seconding it, a summary of the pros and cons given, including the names of those speaking to the issue, and the decision by vote all must go into the recorder's notes. Motions written out by their originators and committee reports are important source documents.

After the business of the meeting is completed, the date of the next meeting is announced, usually just before adjournment. After the meeting has been adjourned, you as the meeting recorder collect copies of all papers read and all committee reports so that they can be made a part of the minutes. (Committee reports are attached to the minutes.) If in doubt, you should verify the correct spelling of names and the correct phrasing of motions before leaving the meeting room.

Follow-up Work after the Meeting

A great deal of work always follows a meeting. Aside from putting the meeting room back in order and preparing the minutes, the administrative assistant should note items that require future attention on office calendars. Individual letters to those newly elected to membership, to those appointed to serve on committees, and to those requested to perform certain tasks should be written. A check should also be made to see that appropriate thank-you letters are written. The administrative assistant should be especially diligent in processing all forms necessary for prompt payment of honoraria, fees, and expense accounts that the meeting's sponsors are obligated to pay.

Preparing Resolutions.   Often an organization wishes to formally express its opinion or will in the form of a resolution. A resolution may be presented at the meeting in writing, or afterward the organization's secretary may be instructed to prepare one. After a resolution is composed and keyed, it must be signed, distributed, and incorporated into the minutes. A resolution may express sympathy, voice approval of stated objectives, or recognize achievements. An example appears in Figure 18-13.

Fig. 18-13 A resolution is usually a formal statement. Each paragraph begins with WHEREAS or RESOLVED keyed in capital letters or underlined.

```
                          RESOLUTION
                    Adopted October 11, 19--

WHEREAS, Judith Monique has been a member of the legal firm of Killian,
    Longhill, Paganne, and Monique for the past twelve years and during this
    time has contributed significantly to the professional prestige of our
    company as well as to its monetary success; and

WHEREAS, Ms. Monique is leaving the organization to accept an appointment as
    judge of the district court of New Jersey; therefore, be it

RESOLVED, that the members of this firm go on record as expressing their sincere
    appreciation of Ms. Monique's services at the same time that they wish her
    well in the judgeship for which she is eminently qualified; and be it

RESOLVED FURTHER, that our Secretary send a copy of this resolution to the
    governor of the state of New Jersey.
```

Lucian Paganne
Lucian Paganne, Secretary

K. L. Killian
K. L. Killian, Senior Member

Preparing the Minutes.   Accurately reporting actions taken during a meeting is the most important part of preparing minutes, yet sometimes it is difficult to report what is done at a meeting when the record reports only what is said. It is a challenge for even an experienced administrative assistant as the meeting recorder to winnow the pertinent facts from a written or a taped record of a meeting.

The minutes of a meeting vary with the degree of formality required. The minutes of an office conference are often very compact and simple. If the administrative assistant finds that grouping the minutes around a central theme is clearer than preparing them in chronological order, the minutes of an informal meeting may be prepared in this fashion. The minutes of a meeting of a large organization are often complex. The efforts of individual members are often recognized and letters from former members may be read. Official minutes of a formal nature (corporate minutes, for example) must be prepared in the order of occurrence, contain complete details, and include the exact wording of all motions and resolutions.

Sometimes the original copy of the minutes is placed in the minutes book only. In other cases, copies of the minutes are made and distributed to members after they have been officially approved. Minutes should be ready for the secretary and presiding officer to sign within five days of the meeting. A summary of future actions agreed upon should be attached to the minutes along with names of the persons responsible. If it is known that the minutes will be referred to at another meeting, copies are often prepared with line numbers keyed in the left margin. It is easy for speakers to refer to *page 3, line 17,* and have the membership follow the discussion.

Sample formats for the preparation of minutes are presented in Figures 18-14 and 18-15. Notice that the minutes answer what, where, when, who, and why. Minutes should be written in complete sentences in the past tense. If the agenda used a numbering system such as that shown in Figure 18-7, the minutes would follow that same presentation. When preparing minutes, follow the suggestions given in Figure 18-16 on page 481.

Indexing the Minutes.   Because the membership of organizations is constantly changing, sometimes groups find themselves in embarrassing situations because they do not know the regulations the organization, as a body, has previously passed. They may take an action contrary to required procedure; they may violate their own regulations; or they may pass motions that contradict each other. Preparing and maintaining an index of an organization's minutes by subject, giving the year and page number of each action taken, helps to avoid this problem.

Writing captions in the margin of the minutes book facilitates preparing file cards for its index. File cards should be captioned with the titles of motions (and possibly their subtitles) on which action was taken, along with the year in which the group acted and the page on which decisions were recorded. An index card for an organization's minutes should look similar to the index card shown in Figure 18-17 on page 482. An index could also be electronically stored in a computer.

MEETING OF THE COMMITTEE TO STANDARDIZE OFFICE FORMS

February 17, 19--

The Committee held its organizational meeting in the private dining room in the company cafeteria at 12 noon.

Those present were Thomas Healey, L. D. Livovich, Denise Margolis, and Merville Perry. Madeleine Marshall was absent.

By unanimous vote Miss Margolis was elected chairperson, and Mr. Livovich was elected secretary.

The following actions were taken.

Collection of Forms Currently in Use. Using the corporation organization chart, Mr. Healey will assign each member of the Committee a definite number of departments from which to collect all forms presently being used. These forms are to be collected by March 1.

Research on Forms Control. Mr. Livovich will obtain from the company librarian a list of books already available in our library on forms control. He will bring these books to the next meeting of the Committee so that the members can volunteer to study those of greatest interest to them. He will also research Books in Print and request that the librarian purchase new books that would be useful. Mr. Perry suggested that the number of new books requested be kept to five, and the group concurred.

The meeting was adjourned at 1:15 p.m.

February 17, 19--
Date

L. D. Livovich
L. D. Livovich

PERSONNEL CLUB

Meeting of March 10, 19--

TIME AND
PLACE OF
MEETING

The regular monthly meeting of the Dayton Personnel Club was held on Tuesday, March 10, 19--, in the Regis Hotel. The meeting was called to order at 8:10 p.m. by the President, Alan Walker.

ROLL CALL

Thirty-four members were present.

READING OF
MINUTES

The minutes of the February meeting were approved as read by the Secretary.

TREASURER'S
REPORT

The Treasurer presented the monthly report showing a balance of $575.32. This report, a copy of which is attached, was accepted. Two small bills, totaling $5.20, were presented and approved for payment by the Treasurer.

COMMITTEE
REPORTS

The President called for special committee reports that were ordered for this meeting.

March 11, 19--
Date

Esther Sawhill
Esther Sawhill

SUGGESTIONS FOR PREPARING MINUTES

Fig. 18-16 Preparing clear and accurate minutes is an important responsibility.

1. Use plain white paper.

2. Capitalize and center the group's official title or the nature of its work.

3. Single- or double-space the minutes and allow generous margins. Indent paragraphs five to ten spaces.

4. Prepare the minutes with the agenda's subject captions. A numbering system can be followed. Record each different action in a separate paragraph.

5. Establish that the meeting was properly called and that members were properly notified. Indicate whether it was a regular or a special meeting.

6. Give the names of the presiding officer and the committee's official secretary.

7. Indicate whether a quorum was present; provide a roll of those present. At official meetings, list those absent.

8. Prepare the minutes while they are still fresh in your memory. If that is impossible, take the notes home and read through them, securing them in mind for accurate keying the next day. If the minutes for a meeting that you did not attend are dictated to you, be sure that you get all the pertinent data from your employer at the time of dictation.

9. Capitalize such words as Board of Directors, Company, Corporation, and Committee in the minutes when they refer to the group in session.

10. Use objective and businesslike language. Do not include personal opinions, interpretations, or comments. Record only business actions, not sentiments or feelings. Such phrases as "outstanding speech," "brilliant report," or "provocative argument" are out of place in the minutes. Where gratitude or appreciation is to be expressed, it should take the form of a resolution.

11. Give the name of each speaker. Try to summarize the gist of each person's discussion about a motion, including reasons presented for and against its adoption. (A recently formed organization interested in improving business records for historical purposes decries the lack of information in the minutes of company meetings at all levels. This organization stresses the value of summaries.)

12. End with date of the next meeting.

13. Number pages at the bottom.

14. Send official minutes to the secretary of the organization or to the presiding officer or both, for signatures. At the end of the minutes, key a line for recording the date of their approval.

Fig. 18-17 An index card concerning an organization's dental care plan might look like this.

```
Minutes of the Budget Comittee
Dental Care Plan



        January 13, 19--,    p. 1
        February 16, 19--,   p. 1
        March 16, 19--,      p. 1
```

Completing Other Duties. Some organizations require members to attend all meetings or a specified number of meetings per year. If attendance is required, the organization's minutes or other records are extremely important and will be periodically reviewed to determine which members should be replaced for violating the attendance requirement. If you are responsible for keeping a detailed record of attendance patterns, a form similar to the one shown in Figure 18-18 might be used for an organization that meets monthly. This form could easily be adapted for other time periods. This information also should be part of the organization's membership database and updated from the paper record.

Fig. 18-18 Administrative assistants often are responsible for keeping an accurate record of attendance patterns.

BUDGET COMMITTEE MEETING
Attendance Record 19--

Name	J	F	M	A	M	J	J	A	S	O	N	D
Sylvia Adams	✓	✓										
Brian Edison	✓	X										
Alan Gunderson	A	✓										
Leo Hunter	✓	✓										
Edmond Matson	✓	✓										
Larry Spitzmueler	✓	✓										
Carol Trudeau	✓	✓										

(Monthly Meeting)

✓   Present
X   Excused (ill or out of town)
A   Absent

The Administrative Assistant as a Meeting Participant

If you are to attend a meeting as a member of the committee or group, you have certain responsibilities. First of all, you must contribute to the discussion. In order to do this, you must be informed. Study the background material of the topics that will be discussed during the meeting. Arrive at the meeting location early and select a seat so you can have eye contact with the meeting leader. During the meeting listen attentively. Jot down any questions that need to be clarified. Before speaking, organize your comments and restrict them to those that bear directly on the subject being discussed. If you are to present an idea, review mentally how to present an idea: main idea first, followed by explanations, and then a summary. Encourage collaboration when appropriate. Certain precautions concerning meeting behavior are advisable. For instance, do not interrupt when another person is speaking. Do not be hostile. Finally, never take your executive by surprise during a meeting by presenting an idea you have not cleared with him or her beforehand.

Corporation Meetings and Minutes

Corporations are required by law to keep minutes of stockholders' and directors' meetings. Stockholders usually meet once a year, but directors' meetings are held more frequently. These minutes are extremely important legal records.

The minutes of a corporation are kept by a corporation secretary, a full-time executive. Stockholders' and directors' minutes are usually kept in separate books. These minutes books must be carefully guarded against the substitution or removal of pages. Prenumbered pages signed and dated by the corporation secretary, watermarked pages, and keylock binders that can be opened only with carefully guarded keys are ways to protect corporate minutes from tampering.

Corrections resulting from the reading of the minutes at a subsequent meeting are written in, and the incorrect portions are ruled out in ink. These changes are initialed in the margin.

The minutes of a corporation identify the membership of the group, show the date and place of the meeting, tell whether the meeting is regular or special, give the names of those attending, and contain a complete record of the proceedings. The official secretary of the corporation has full responsibility for their completeness, accuracy, and legality even though an administrative assistant may key them.

CONFERENCES AND CONVENTIONS

Executives are likely to participate in numerous conferences and conventions. A **conference** is a discussion or consultation on some important matter, often in a formal meeting. A **convention** is usually a formal, annual meeting of the delegates or members of a professional group. Planning and executing an annual convention is so involved that meeting consultants are often hired to assist the membership in this process. These meeting consultants have their own professional organization, called Meeting Planners International. The discussion that follows, however, assumes that the administrative assistant to an executive who is in charge of a convention or is part of a convention program will be very active in the planning and follow-up phases of these events.

Planning Responsibilities

Preparations for some conferences and conventions require the full-time efforts of an administrative assistant for an entire year. Months of painstaking work are necessary to handle such details as selecting the meeting location, contacting speakers, preparing publicity and registration materials, and planning meals and social functions.

The Meeting Location.   An annual convention of a professional association or similar group requires special facilities. For this reason, conventions are often held in hotels or in civic centers. At least one room large enough to accommodate all registered participants is required. In addition, a number of small conference rooms for group discussions and adequate facilities for dining and social functions are needed. A block of rooms for housing out-of-town participants must also be reserved, usually at a special rate. Estimates of attendance are necessary and should be available from the previous year's attendance figures.

In selecting a meeting location, the executive and the administrative assistant seek the help of hotel or convention bureau staffs. Before meeting with the staff of prospective convention sites, prepare a comprehensive facilities checklist of convention requirements (number of rooms, size of meeting rooms, services offered, etc.). After each interview and tour of facilities, rate each according to its offerings. When it comes to selection of a convention site, you will find that hotels are very competitive. To entice conventions, hotels make special package plans available. As part of a package, for example, the hotel may provide the services of a hotel staff member to coordinate events, a car and a driver for convention officials, or an office to serve as the meeting's headquarters.

Session Speakers.   You may be asked to make the initial contact with prospective speakers. If you have plenty of time before the convention program is printed, you may communicate with them by letter; otherwise, phone calls are necessary. The date and the location of the convention, the name of the convention, the expected attendance at the speaker's session, the preferred topic, and the length of the presentation should be discussed in the initial contact with a prospective speaker. Finally, the matter of fees and expenses must be addressed. If the speaker agrees to make a presentation, ask about the type of audiovisual equipment and room arrangement desired. The form shown in Figure 18-19 would be useful for gathering this information. Also, ask the speaker to send a biographical sketch and, if required, a recent photograph. Confirm final arrangements by letter. (The administrative assistant to an executive who makes several conference

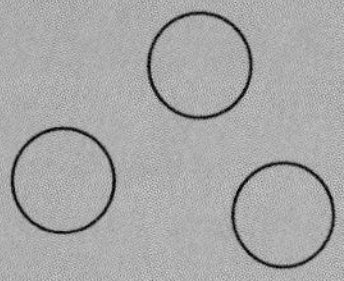

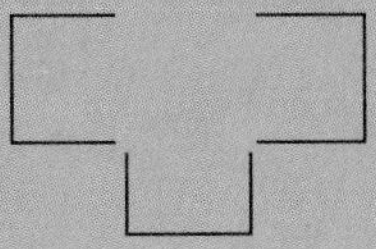

Fig. 18-19 This form helps gather information on the types of equipment and room arrangements speakers prefer.

EQUIPMENT REQUISITION

Session _____ Date _____ Time _____

Room _____ Room Capacity _____

Seating Accommodations:

Speaker's Table _____ Chairs _____

Number of Participants _____

Equipment Required	Date Ordered	Operator Required
Tape/Cassette Recorder	_____	_____
Chalkboard	_____	_____
Easel for Chart	_____	_____
Overhead Projector	_____	_____
35 mm Projector	_____	_____
Screen	_____	_____
Videocassette Recorder (VCR)	_____	_____
Slide Projector	_____	_____
8 mm Projector	_____	_____
Microphone	_____	_____
Lectern	_____	_____
Television Monitor	_____	_____
Computers/Monitors	_____	_____

Room Arrangement Preference (Check Preference):

Round Tables _____ Horseshoe _____ Classroom _____

Tables # _____ Chairs # _____

Desks # _____

presentations a year should have a packet of materials including a biographical sketch, photograph, requests for certain types of equipment, and a floor plan of a preferred room arrangement prepared in advance for conference coordinators.)

Publicity and Registration.   Publicity material, including the convention program and instructions for advance registration, must be prepared and mailed to prospective participants. You may be responsible for selecting the printer as well as proofreading and distributing publicity materials. Using desktop publishing software and a laser printer, you may decide to prepare some of the materials yourself. You may also be involved in preparing news releases. You may need to determine the proper advertising medium—newspapers, magazines, or spot radio announcements. In addition, you may be asked to collect and deposit registration fees.

When participants check in for a convention, they receive complimentary items (pens, pencils, notepads, etc.), a roster of participants, a name tag, meal tickets, and miscellaneous literature. You may be asked to obtain and assemble these materials into an attractive packet for distribution at convention time.

Other Preconvention Duties.   Some speakers may ask you to make hotel reservations for them. If so, ask the hotel to send the speaker a written confirmation. As a special courtesy, you may also arrange for each speaker to be met and escorted to the hotel.

The hotel staff assists the administrative assistant in deciding the menu for meals and other social functions. Generally, a budget has been determined for these functions, and menus are selected with the budget in mind. Be sure that menu decisions, price, seating arrangements, and number of meals are specified in writing. If there is to be a speaker's table, determine the proper seating order and prepare the necessary place cards.

Many conventions include displays and exhibits of the latest equipment and/or techniques of a particular profession. Floor space for each exhibit is assigned by contract; therefore, the administrative assistant may be responsible for keying and mailing contracts. A floor plan of the exhibit area is helpful in keeping track of assignments.

Duties at the Conference.   The administrative assistant is challenged at every turn to perform efficiently during the conference. Even with the best of planning, problems are bound to occur. Most last-minute problems can be avoided by alert, well-organized administrative assistants. Although you may not be involved in the registration process, you should check to see that registration tables are set up and that all the registration packets are conveniently arranged. A computer, printer, and stationery supplies should be available at the registration table. It is up to you to see that microphones work and that service people are on hand during presentations. This may involve checking union regulations. You must remember to send complimentary tickets to the spouse of the luncheon speaker, to position session signs, to direct traffic, to have ice water at the lectern, to check the number of chairs on the platform, to check that the table is draped, and to provide place cards for the speaker's table and arrange them according to protocol. As a general rule, arrange for the chairman or host of the meeting to sit at the center of the table. The most distinguished guest or speaker sits to the right of the chairman, and the next most distinguished person sits to the chairman's left. If there is a lectern at the table, seat the host and the most distinguished guest to one side of the podium. The remaining places at the table are filled according to rank.

For each speaker's session, you should verify that the equipment required is in the room and is in good working condition. You must see that the projectionist is available when the speaker wants to show films or slides. You make sure that the room is darkened during these presentations. If printed material accompanies a presentation, arrange to have it distributed. If there are not enough copies, make arrangements for additional copies to be made.

Procedure

Seating assignments at the speaker's table are determined by protocol.

Conference Follow-up

Administrative assistants are often responsible for conference groundwork and follow-up work. They should not, however, be concerned with the writing of the conference report, only with the processing of it.

Conference participants often want a copy of the proceedings. This service might be covered by the registration fee, or an additional charge might be made. In any case, the administrative assistant may be responsible for securing mailing addresses of those entitled to a copy.

If papers are read at a conference, each speaker is usually asked to submit the paper prior to (or at) the meeting so that it can be printed in its entirety or abstracted. Permission from the speaker must be obtained prior to publication. One of the administrative assistant's follow-up responsibilities is to obtain a copy of all papers for publication.

The conference reporter needs only to report the discussion following the presentation of a paper. Conference reports may be made from a tape recording or from summary notes. Sometimes the speaker is asked to prepare the summary. The conference reporter then becomes responsible for organizing the speaker's summary, editing it for uniformity of style, and writing introductions, conclusions, or recommendations.

Other follow-up duties include arranging for the return of any equipment on loan to the convention and picking up papers, supplies, and other things belonging to the convention that are left behind. The evaluation forms of the conference proceedings and facilities completed by attendees should be forwarded to the proper committee. Speakers and distinguished guests should be assisted in checking out of the hotel and in securing transportation. Thank-you letters must be sent and expense reports must be compiled and processed. A final task for the administrative assistant might be to compose recommendations for subsequent meetings, based on experience gained from this one.

TELECONFERENCING

Using today's technology, meeting participants do not even have to be in the same room to communicate effectively. In fact, they do not even have to be in the same city or country. *Teleconferencing* enables two or more persons in different geographic locations to communicate electronically. Teleconferencing is effective for informal meetings, sales meetings, and training sessions, and as an adjunct to formal, structured meetings, annual conventions, and other conferences. Audio (voice) transmission, video (pictorial) transmission with audio, and computer messages are forms of teleconferencing. Although there is often no substitute for a face-to-face meeting, companies that use teleconferencing, particularly videoconferencing, cite these benefits: reduction in travel costs; reduction in travel time, thus releasing this time for employees to use on other business activities; ease in organizing a meeting; quicker business decisions; and, finally, the opportunity to involve people who would not normally be included. Administrative assistants need to be familiar with the terms used in the telecommunication industry (freeze frame, for instance) in order to react quickly to the requests of the executive. Figure 18-20 shows several executives participating in a videoconference.

Fig. 18-20 These executives are participating in a videoconference. *Photo courtesy of Compression Labs, Inc. (CLI).*

Audio Conferencing

Audio teleconferences involve only the transmission of sound. Audio conferencing is also called *audio teleconferencing, voice teleconferencing, telephone conferencing,* and *conference calling.* Audio conferencing capabilities have been available since the 1950s. Speakerphones are generally used by conferees for this type of meeting. Conference call meetings can be arranged in several ways. With dial-out service, the conference call operator calls all participants at a specified time. When all participants are on the line, the operator connects to the meeting. With dial-in service, participants call in at a specified time and are connected by the conference operator to the meeting. If desired, operators can break in and divide participants into smaller meetings. Audio conferencing works well in sharing information, impromptu information gathering, making announcements, giving status reports, and making future plans.

While setting up a conference call meeting with the operator can be done in a matter of minutes, the administrative assistant's responsibilities in planning and executing a successful audio conference can be extensive. The administrative assistant may prepare and send an agenda and other handouts prior to the conference. In addition, the administrative assistant may have to reserve a conference room, determine whether to use dial-out or dial-in service, give instructions to the conference operator, introduce and establish the order of speakers, transmit graphics over facsimile equipment, arrange for special equipment such as a tape recorder or microphone, stand by until the conference is concluded, and take minutes of the meeting.

Videoconferencing

Videoconferencing, in addition to having audio capabilities, provides televideo pictures of participants at conference locations. When a still photograph of each participant is sufficient, *freeze frame* is used. The method most closely resembling a face-to-face conference is full motion (live) video. In addition to business meetings, videoconferencing is used by human resource managers to interview job candidates and by engineers to design and develop new products. A typical videoconference facility includes single or dual monitors, cameras, a control system, audio systems, optional peripherals such as a VCR or 35-mm slide system, and network connections.

In a videoconference the presenter is the person shown on the screen at the time, and attendees are those participating at different locations. During the pictorial and verbal interchange, text, graphics, and data can be sent back and forth via intelligent copiers (see page 126) and FAX equipment. If dual monitors are used, graphics or text can be visually displayed. Another device that can enhance a videoconference is the electronic blackboard or chalkboard (see also page 466). An electronic blackboard is used like an ordinary blackboard. When videoconferencing, chalk strokes are transmitted over

COMMUNICATION

An advantage of teleconferencing is the reduction in travel costs; a disadvantage is the lack of socialization by participants before and after the conference.

telephone lines and received on television monitors. As with an ordinary chalkboard, part or all of the information can be erased. The electronic blackboard is particularly effective in creating and displaying graphics.

The administrative assistant in charge of a videoconference must contact participants to schedule a time for the conference, arrange for the equipment and an operator, and schedule a conference room. Conference materials must be mailed and distributed prior to the conference. For reporting or summary purposes, the administrative assistant may be in attendance or replay a tape recording at a later time.

Computer Conferencing

Using linked computer terminals and software such as groupware, meetings can be held (either simultaneously or on a delayed basis) with groups of people in various geographic locations. Participants input messages to other members of the group on computer terminals that are linked by telephone on a national or international computer network. All records of discussions and document transmission are stored. Computer conferencing is like a business meeting except that not everyone is necessarily present at the same time. There may be discussion between two participants or a group discussion among several members, but all participants do not have to be in a group at the same time. One could arrive at 9 a.m. and see what another member did at 11 p.m. the previous evening. Computer conferencing may include a range of graphic capabilities, such as slides, transparencies, sketches, and handwritten notes. Computer conferencing appears to work best when tasks are clearly identified and users are comfortable using keyboards.

An administrative assistant's responsibilities with respect to computer conferencing may be to notify the executive when messages are received, to input messages, to obtain additional information, and to call other executives to ask for their input. Prior to the conference, the administrative assistant may be responsible for preparing graphics and other documentation.

Summary

Within a business organization, the majority of decisions are made during or as a result of business meetings. Meetings may be informal, involving two or more company employees, or they may be structured, involving many participants and a prepared agenda. Executives also attend community meetings and professional conferences and conventions. The administrative assistant to such an executive may be involved in conference preparation and follow-up. In addition, the administrative assistant may be responsible for recording the minutes of many different kinds of meetings, requiring different levels of office skills.

For informal scheduled meetings, the administrative assistant's responsibilities include reminding members of the meeting, preparing the meeting room, and preparing a summary of the meeting for distribution to members. If an executive calls an unscheduled meeting, the administrative assistant must quickly determine a mutually agreeable time for the meeting.

A special meeting situation arises if not all the participants speak English. The administrative assistant may be asked to contact an interpreter and assist in the preparation of visuals or handouts.

Formal meetings require scheduling a meeting room, sending meeting notices, preparing an agenda, and a number of last-minute duties. The administrative assistant who is to record the minutes of a formal meeting comes to the meeting prepared with an attendance list, the agenda, the minutes book, ballots, and any other material that may be required. For example, the latest edition of *Robert's Rules of Order* should be available for the executive's reference. If the administrative assistant is to read the minutes of the previous meeting, they should be read in an intelligible manner and in a voice loud enough to be heard. Any corrections to the minutes are made in red ink on the original copy. After the meeting, the administrative assistant is responsible for such follow-up activities as preparing resolutions, keying and indexing the minutes, and distributing the minutes for signatures. An administrative assistant who is a meeting participant must be prepared to be a contributor, must listen attentively, and present ideas in an organized fashion. A company officer, generally the corporation secretary, prepares the minutes of the corporation. The administrative assistant to a corporation secretary performs the planning and follow-up duties required for formal meetings.

Annual conferences or conventions can require the full-time services of an administrative assistant for an entire year. Many hours of work are involved in selecting the convention site, contacting speakers, preparing publicity and registration materials, and performing other pre-convention duties. During the conference, the administrative assistant makes sure that the equipment in the room is in good working order. The administrative assistant often assumes the role of a troubleshooter and attempts to solve problems before they occur. Responsibility for recording a convention's minutes is delegated to professional recorders. The administrative assistant may be in charge of the distribution of the minutes, however. Finally, a significant contribution an administrative assistant can offer to conference planning is making recommendations for next year's conference.

The time and expense involved in travel to and from meetings is making teleconferencing technology attractive to many business organizations. Teleconferencing (audio, video, computer) enables two or more persons in different geographic locations to communicate electronically without leaving their offices. Responsibilities of the administrative assistant differ with each teleconferencing method.

THINK IT
Through

1. Your employer is the presiding officer of a chamber of commerce committee. He is distressed because several members of the committee habitually arrive late for the committee meetings. He asks if you have any ideas how to cure this problem.

THINK IT
Through

2. Your employer has just told you to schedule a meeting with ten people in the company's electronic meeting room. What are your specific responsibilities at this point, and in which order would you execute them?

THINK IT
Through

3. How could an efficient administrative assistant have improved the last organized meeting you attended:

   a. Before the meeting?

   b. During the meeting?

   c. After the session?

4. Discuss methods of keeping a mailing list current.

5. What are some of the preliminary responsibilities of an administrative assistant to an executive in charge of an annual convention?

THINK IT
Through

6. How do the administrative assistant's responsibilities for arranging a meeting for an executive and two company employees differ in the following situations:

   a. Over the telephone

   b. In the executive's office

   c. When one of the employees does not speak English

   d. Via a computer network

7. Rekey the following sentences, using hyphens where appropriate. Consult the Reference Guide to verify and correct your answers.

   a. Karen has many childhood memories of the belllike building in the center of the neighborhood.

   b. The dress was made of close woven fabric produced on up to the minute looms.

   c. The 35 foot driveway was guaranteed for a two year period.

   d. The chair was recovered from the flood; I will recover it with a fine fabric.

   e. We made a house to house survey to find the highly informed voters in this precinct.

PROBLEMS

1. This chapter cited a professional organization of meeting planners known as Meeting Planners International. Visit the library and look up this organization in the Encyclopedia of Associations. Report to the class the background of this organization, its offices, number of members, its services, and its publications.

2. Your employer, Andrew Weir, has just informed you that he must select a convention site for his professional organization's convention two years from now. He wants you to assist him in this selection. He expects 3,000 attendees at the convention. He estimates that they will need one large meeting room for the entire membership plus ten small conference rooms. Three meal functions, one evening and two luncheons, are planned. Next week the two of you will tour three hotel facilities. For this tour you prepare a facilities checklist to use in evaluating each hotel.

3. You have been asked to prepare a resolution of appreciation for the services of Miss Janet Godfrey, who has just completed two terms as the first president of Phi Beta Lambda (PBL), a business education student organization. She was instrumental in getting the College of Business to award a PBL Member-of-the-Year plaque at the annual awards banquet. She also represented the organization on the Council of Student Groups on campus.

TECHNOLOGY APPLICATIONS

▶ **TA18-1**

Your company is responsible for setting up a convention for dealers and customers of Unique Auction Galleries, International. Mr. Long has asked you to prepare a checklist for use in evaluating various hotels and convention centers in your area. Your checklist will need to include the following items:

Name and address of facility and contact person
Dates of availability
Meeting room facilities—both large and small
Meal capabilities—menu planning
Parking
Restrooms
Elevators
Handicapped access
Overnight accommodations—discount or group rates?
Convention facilities—phones, registration, etc.   *continued*

continued

Price ranges:
    Meals
    Meeting rooms
    Accommodations
Other conventions hosted

▶ TA18-2   Your employer, Henry C. Campbell, is secretary of the Denver Credit Managers' Association. The regular monthly meeting of that organization was held on Thursday, June 22, at 6:30 p.m., at the Palace Hotel. Mr. Campbell gives you the following notes for the minutes of that meeting. You are to key the minutes in good form, using headings in the margins for each paragraph.

President Ralph Riopelle called the regular meeting to order at 8:00 pm. There were 16 present and the Vice-President, Charles Bavin was absent. The minutes of the May meeting approved as read by Secretary. The treasurer reported a balance of $572.68 and no bills presented for payment.

The Budget Committee, represented by Rene Betz, Chairperson, presented its report which was accepted by motion. Herbert Smith, Chairperson of the Membership Committee, introduced new members: T. E. Gary and R. C. Baldwin.

Donald Durst of Atlanta was speaker and was introduced by James Steer. The topic was "Trends in Installment Credit." Questions and answered followed.

The next meeting will be July 27. Meeting adjourned at 9:37 p.m.

Part 5

Case Problems

Case 5-1
ABUSING
EXPENSE
ACCOUNTS:
TO TELL OR
NOT TO TELL

Nancy Feldman has worked as administrative assistant for the past 15 years to the vice president of sales for the Kromack Company, a manufacturer of computer software. Nancy likes her job and is very loyal to the company. She began her career with the company after completing her secretarial training at a private business school. She has had several promotions and is well liked by employees at all levels. For five years Nancy worked for Ben Lee, who retired last year. In February of last year, Mark Allen was promoted from the sales staff to take Mr. Lee's position. Mr. Allen is in his late 30s, ambitious, and has a reputation for getting things done. Nancy has helped him adjust to the executive suite and, on several occasions, has saved him from serious blunders because of his lack of executive experience. Although Mr. Allen was a leading sales producer, he admits that the adjustment has been rough. He respects Nancy's opinion and her competence.

Because of his position, Mr. Allen travels extensively throughout the United States and abroad. Nancy makes all his travel arrangements, prepares his expense reports, and is generally aware of his whereabouts at all times.

Last year the company instituted a 1-800 number for employees to call if they become aware of excessive expense, exorbitant waste, or fraudulent activity within the company. A code number is given to each caller, and a reward is offered if the savings to the company amounts to $100 or more. Through the use of a code number, the employee is never identified.

Nancy has enjoyed a pleasant personal relationship with Mr. Allen; however, last month when his work took him to Honolulu, Mrs. Allen accompanied him. He paid for her airfare, but hotel and meals were billed to the company. On other occasions, when Mr. Allen mentioned that a friend took him to the airport from his home, Nancy has noticed taxi charges.

▬▬▬ **What should Nancy do? Are the actions of Mr. Allen dishonest? What are the risks involved in blowing the whistle on Mr. Allen?**

Case 5-2
LINES OF
AUTHORITY

Jessica Miller is the administrative assistant to Grayson Hill, manager of the insurance department of Jackson Industries, a conglomerate with offices in nine states. Mr. Hill travels an average of two weeks of every month visiting company locations. He is enrolled in the frequent-flyer program of Allied Airlines. Jackson Industries permits employees to keep their accumulated mileage credits on business trips with airlines as a fringe benefit.

After his last trip, Mr. Hill complained to Jessica about the travel arrangements she had made for him. His major complaint was that he did not fly on Allied Airlines. Jessica explained to him that she made the arrangements through the company's travel department. Mr. Hill suggested that from now on Jessica make his travel arrangements herself through a travel agency and request Allied flights exclusively. Unsure of company policy, Jessica reviewed the company's policies and procedures manual and learned that all travel arrangements should be made through the company's travel department. She pointed this out to Mr. Hill, but he brushed it off saying, "Several managers use their own travel agency; don't worry about it."

At the first indication of Mr. Hill's next trip, Jessica made reservations through an outside travel agency requesting Allied flights for the whole trip. Mr. Hill was satisfied with her arrangements.

After the trip Jessica prepared Mr. Hill's expense report and as usual submitted it to Mr. O'Halleran, vice president, administrative services, for his signature. Because the air fare seemed out of line, Mr. O'Halleran questioned Madeline Kapp, manager of the company's travel department, about the routing and the fare amount. Ms. Kapp said that Allied was not the direct routing for that particular trip, and because of this, the fare was higher than it should be. Ms. Kapp called Jessica to determine why this routing was used. Jessica responded that Allied Airlines was Mr. Hill's choice. Ms. Kapp reminded Jessica of the company's travel policy and the role of the travel department. "From now on, you make Mr. Hill's travel arrangements through my office. Your routing cost the company an additional $200 for this trip." Jessica apologized and the conversation ended.

At this point Jessica was extremely demoralized. She had done what Mr. Hill had asked her to do. She knew the company policy and prided herself on her ability to follow company procedures. She felt she had let the company down.

▬▬▬ **In reviewing her conversation with Ms. Kapp, she asked herself whether she should have mentioned the reason why Mr. Hill prefers Allied Airlines. She wondered also what she should say to Mr. Hill when he returns to the office. What principle should she follow in the future when making Mr. Hill's travel arrangements?**

Case 5-3
EXPANDING
DUTIES

Frank Larson was administrative assistant to Robert Holmes, manager of telecommunications for CXD. This multinational corporation had just purchased equipment for teleconferencing. Frank attended briefings on the use of the equipment and was given all the instruction manuals connected with its use. He did not study the manuals, however, because of the pressure of his other duties.

The first tryout was to be a conference between the president of the company and its five regional vice presidents. Mr. Holmes wanted this to be a stellar performance. Unfortunately, the full-motion video that was planned was unsatisfactory. Mr. Holmes asked Frank to supply freeze frames. Because he had not studied the material that had been given him, Frank did not know what a freeze frame was and had made no provision for obtaining the photographs.

After the pictureless conference, Mr. Holmes blamed Frank for not having had the backup pictures available. He pointed out that the instructions warn that they are necessary in case anything goes wrong with a conference as planned.

Frank replied, "I'm sorry, Mr. Holmes. However, I don't really think that I should be blamed. I'm an administrative assistant, not an engineer. I don't believe that I should have to know how to cope with that complicated equipment."

▆▆▆▆ **What principles are involved in Frank's reaction?**

Case 5-4 GETTING COOPERATION

Alexandria Bowman is administrative assistant to Paul Graham, vice president of a major soft drink bottling firm located in Atlanta, Georgia. Mr. Graham is very active in the professional organization of soft drink distributors. In fact, he has been appointed chairperson of the annual convention of that organization to be held in Atlanta in 1996. He has asked for Alexandria's assistance in registration and publicity for the convention. In requesting her help, he suggested that she form a committee of at least four of the administrative assistants with the company. They would work with her in preparing registration materials and complimentary items and in writing publicity. This work, of course, would be on company time, and therefore would not involve any overtime hours. Since all the officers of the company will be participating in the conference in one way or another, the participation of administrative assistants would not be questioned.

With this mandate, Alexandria makes her selection. She decides on her daily luncheon companions. At the first committee meeting, plans are made and assignments delegated. It is agreed that meetings will be held monthly. By the fourth meeting, it is obvious to Alexandria that no progress is being made. The members say they just don't have time to take on this added responsibility. Besides, it was mentioned that only the chairperson would get the credit, so why should they bother? This last comment disturbs Alexandria.

▆▆▆▆ **Had she deliberately created that impression with the other administrative assistants? How can she enlist their cooperation? Was she too hasty in selecting the members of the committee? Should she have cleared the membership names with her superior?**

Part 6

F

inancial
and Legal
Procedures

In discussing financial affairs with an assistant, William M. Vasey, a company president, made the following comment:

> There is no area of work that requires more diligence, more accuracy, and more confidentiality than that of handling the money of others. Few other tasks provide the opportunity to build a reputation of dependability as that of conscientiously handling company funds. Violation of this trust results not only in the loss of money to the company, but impugning this trust can result in occupational ruin for the employee who misuses company funds.

The extent to which the administrative assistant is involved in company banking and in the financial and legal affairs of the employer will depend upon the size of the company, the function of the division in which the administrative assistant is employed, and the scope of the employer's financial interests.

The chapters in Part 6 will not only contribute to your effective job performance but should also assist you in managing your own finances. No other aspect of your job will give you a greater opportunity for demonstrating your competence, your dependability, and your ability to keep a confidence than the "assist role" you will perform in handling your employer's financial and legal interests.

Chapter 19

Financial Responsibilities

LEARNING OBJECTIVES

After studying this chapter and completing the activities, you will be able to:

1. Understand standard financial practices.
2. Define and use various financial documents.
3. Understand electronic banking procedures.
4. Evaluate various services of banks and other financial institutions.
5. Interpret financial statements and reports.

INTRODUCTION

To be entrusted with financial responsibilities is evidence that your employer respects your ability to perform exacting work and trusts you to keep office matters confidential. Working with other people's money, however, is always an important responsibility. As an assistant to a busy executive, your understanding of basic financial services and procedures will enable you to handle this aspect of your job effectively. Your ability to make bank deposits, reconcile bank statements, handle petty cash, pay bills, and record incoming funds may be an important part of your job. Learning to perform these tasks for your employer will teach you to manage your own finances as well.

The type and size of the firm for which you work, in addition to your employer's preferences, define the extent of your financial responsibilities. For example, if you work for a large corporation, your responsibilities may be limited to approving bills for payment, handling petty cash, or arranging for foreign remittances. On the other hand, if you work for a small company or for a doctor or lawyer, handling all of the financial matters of the business may be one of your primary duties.

Although the total time spent each day performing financial duties may be comparatively small, their importance must not be underestimated. Financial responsibilities are exacting and confidential. Financial data are always highly restricted pieces of information.

STANDARD FINANCIAL PRACTICES

Because of the increasing need of businesses for financial services, banks and other financial institutions are constantly upgrading procedures to simplify banking tasks. Most bankers now transfer funds from one account to another electronically. Some bank customers, however, still insist on banking the traditional way; therefore, traditional practices and methods are still an important part of the administrative assistant's responsibilities.

Handling Checks

Accepting a check in person or through the mail requires precautions to ensure that the check is valid. Examine the date to see that the check is not postdated (dated later than the current date). Check the amount to determine that the amount of payment is correct. The amount written in figures must agree with the amount written in words. Finally, make sure that an endorsement, if required, has been properly made. To have a deposited check returned by the bank because it was improperly written is time-consuming and inconvenient. Before depositing a check, while details are still available, be sure to record information needed for accounting purposes on a receipt form or in a record book.

    If you have financial responsibilities, you must be identified at the bank as representing the employer. If you are to sign checks for the withdrawal or payment of personal or company funds or to endorse and cash checks, the bank must be authorized to honor your signature. The employer may be required to sign a special authorization form or to arrange for your signature to be added to the signature card on file at the bank. Some banks require that the administrative assistant be issued a *power of attorney* to perform these functions.

> ▶ *Procedure*
>
> *An endorsement is a signature and/or instructions written on the back of a check.*

> ▶ *Procedure*
>
> *A power of attorney is a legal instrument authorizing one person to act as an agent for another.*

Proving Cash

You may be responsible for receiving cash payments and making change and payments from a cash drawer. This responsibility will necessitate proving cash (that is, verifying the amount) at the beginning or end of each business day. Since you will be held personally responsible for this money, it is essential that you establish a system for protecting these funds. Should you relinquish custody of the cash drawer to another employee, prove the cash before doing so and ask for a receipt to protect yourself. To prove cash efficiently, use a form similar to the one shown in Figure 19-1.

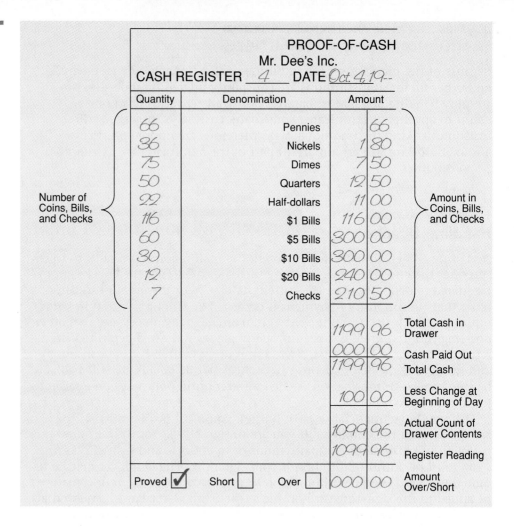

Fig. 19-1 A form for proving cash provides an accurate receipt of a cash drawer's contents.

Depositing Funds

To make a deposit, the administrative assistant presents a deposit ticket in duplicate (or a passbook) to the bank teller listing the amounts to be deposited. The deposit itself—currency, coin, endorsed checks, and money orders—should accompany the deposit ticket.

Coins and Bills for Deposit. If you are depositing a substantial quantity of coins and bills, banks prefer that you put them in money wrappers. Money wrappers can be obtained from any bank. Coins are packed in paper rolls as shown in Figure 19-2.

Bills of each denomination are made into packages of $50, $100, and so forth. The packages are separated into all-of-a-kind groups; each bill is laid right side up with the top edge at the top. Torn bills are mended with tape. A paper bill wrapper—a narrow strip with the amount printed on it—is wrapped tightly around the bills and securely glued.

The depositor's name or account number should be stamped or written on each roll of coins and package of bills. Receiving tellers do not count packaged money when taking deposits; rather, someone counts it later in the day. If the depositor's name or account number appears on each roll or wrapper, mistakes can be easily traced.

Loose bills are counted, stacked right side up with the largest denominations on the bottom and the smallest ones on top, and fastened with a rubber band. Extra coins are counted, placed in an envelope, identified, and sealed.

Fig. 19-2 Coins are packed in rolls designed to hold a specific quantity.
© *Superstock, Inc.*

Checks for Deposit. In order to deposit a check or money order, the payee (person to whom the check is written) endorses it on the back. Banks also accept checks for deposit that are endorsed by a representative of the payee. In fact, a bank may accept an occasional check that lacks an endorsement. Some banks stamp the back of such a check with a statement such as "Credited to account of payee named within—absence of endorsement guaranteed." Notwithstanding the last sentence, it is the administrative assistant's responsibility to endorse every check for deposit.

On August 10, 1987, Congress passed the Competition Equality Bank Act establishing standards for endorsement. This act requires that endorsements be placed at the payee end of the check (left end or trailing end of the check). When the check is turned over, the endorsement should be placed not more than 1 1/2 inches down from the edge of the check. An endorsement that extends farther than the prescribed 1 1/2 inches may overlap the processing bank's endorsement, causing delay in the clearing cycle. This act also established maximum holding periods that financial institutions can place on funds in demand accounts.

If the name of the payee is written differently from the account name, endorse the check twice: first, as the name appears on the face of the check and, second, the exact way the account is carried. A rubber-stamp endorsement (showing the name of the bank, the name of the account, and the account number) may be obtained from the employer's bank or from an office supplies store. Using a rubber stamp to endorse checks saves time. Companies that receive large numbers of checks can use a machine that endorses checks at a high rate of speed. A handwritten signature need not be added to a rubber stamp or machine endorsement. Three standard endorsements are shown in Figure 19-3.

1. A *restrictive endorsement* is one in which some condition restrains the negotiability of the check or renders the endorser liable upon a specified condition or conditions. "For deposit only" or "Upon delivery of contract" are two examples of restrictive endorsements. A restrictive endorsement is commonly used when checks are being deposited. Checks endorsed "For deposit only" need not be signed personally by the depositor but can be endorsed or stamped by the administrative assistant. The "For deposit only" qualification keeps the check from being used for any purpose other than for deposit to the account of the payee.

2. An *endorsement in full* or *special endorsement* gives the name of a specified payee, written before the endorser's signature. This endorsement identifies the person or firm to which the instrument is transferred. A check endorsed in this way cannot be cashed by anyone without the specified payee's signature. The words "Pay to the order of Dianne Ryke" in the example identify the person to whom the check is being transferred. For further transfer, Dianne Ryke must endorse the check again.

3. A *blank endorsement* consists simply of the signature of the payee and makes the check payable to any holder. This endorsement, therefore, should never be used except at the bank immediately before the check is deposited or cashed. A check should never be endorsed at the office or sent through the mail with a blank endorsement. If it is lost, the finder can turn it into cash.

For deposit and credit
TO THE ACCOUNT OF
THE CANDY SHOP
075-118095

Pay to the order of
Dianne Ryke
Jennifer Hardy

Jennifer Hardy

Fig. 19-3 Three standard endorsements are *restrictive, full or special,* and *blank.*

The person or business that accepts an endorsed check (unless stated otherwise in the endorsement) assumes (1) that the check is genuine and valid, (2) that the endorser has received value for it, and (3) that, if necessary, the endorser will reimburse the holder of the check if the bank refuses to process it.

Magnetic Ink Numbers. The American Bankers Association has adopted a uniform system of magnetic ink character recognition (MICR). This system allows a bank to preprint its bank number and the depositor's account number in magnetic ink characters in a fixed position at the bottom of checks and deposit tickets. When a bank receives a check, the date, amount of the check, and other coded information also are recorded in magnetic ink characters at the bottom of the check. Optical character recognition (OCR) equipment sorts the checks according to bank and account numbers, computes totals, and posts to depositors' accounts electronically. Figure 19-4 shows a preprinted deposit ticket for an MICR system; Figure 19-5 shows a check identified by magnetic ink characters.

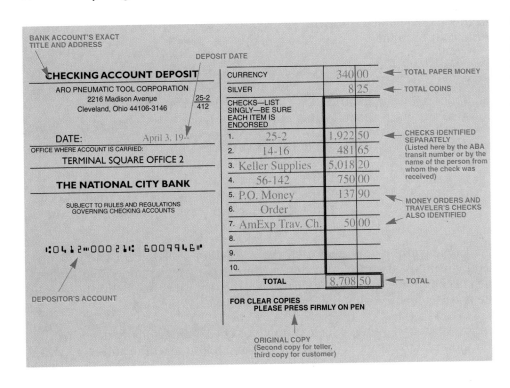

Fig. 19-4 A deposit ticket designed for automatic processing uses magnetic ink numbers to identify the depositor's account.

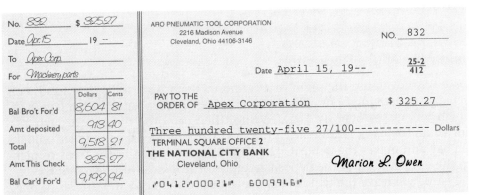

Fig. 19-5 Note that the series of magnetic ink identification numbers at the bottom of this check is the same as those on the preprinted deposit ticket in Figure 19-4.

Deposit Tickets. Many types of deposit tickets are used. Most banks have deposit tickets designed especially for use with automated equipment. The deposit ticket shown in Figure 19-4 is designed for automated processing.

If you wish to receive a portion of the total amount listed on the deposit slip as cash, you may "split" the deposit. This can be done, for example, when your employer asks you to deposit a salary check and bring back a specific amount of cash. Your employer should not restrict the endorsement in this case, since you are not depositing all the money.

Each depositor has an account number with which the bank's automated equipment identifies the depositor's account; therefore, the account number must appear on the deposit ticket. The bank provides the depositor with a supply of deposit tickets either preprinted with the account number in magnetic ink characters or with space provided for the depositor to record the account number.

ABA Transit Numbers. Each bank in the United States has an American Bankers Association (ABA) transit number. This number is usually printed in the upper right-hand corner of a check. It identifies the bank for clearinghouse functions in the following manner:

$\frac{25\text{-}2}{412}$	25	identifies the city or state
	2	identifies the specific bank in that city or state
	4	identifies the Federal Reserve district
	1	identifies the Federal Reserve branch in that district
	2	identifies the number of days required for the bank to clear the check

Some banks require that each check listed on a deposit ticket be identified by using the two top ABA transit numbers, in this example 25-2, unless the check is drawn on the bank in which the deposit is made. In this case, the check is identified by the name of the maker of the check.

Listing Checks. When a large number of checks are regularly deposited, common practice is to list the checks on an adding machine and to attach the tape to the deposit ticket. Only the total is recorded on the deposit ticket. Some banks prefer that all checks be shown on the deposit ticket and provide large deposit tickets for such use.

Using the Night Depository

Some businesses use the night or after-hours depository to deposit funds collected after banking hours. The bank provides the depositor with a bag in which to lock the deposit. The depositor then can drop the bag through a slot when the bank is closed. On the next banking day, a bank teller unlocks the bag and makes the deposit. The depositor later stops at the bank to pick up the empty bag and the deposit receipt. If the depositor prefers, however, the bank will leave the deposit bag locked until the depositor arrives to make the deposit personally.

Banking by Mail

Depositing by mail has become very popular because it saves time. The administrative assistant in a small office may make all or most deposits by mail. All checks must be endorsed "Pay to the order of [name of bank]" or "For Deposit Only," signed, and listed on a deposit slip. The deposit ticket and endorsed checks are placed in an envelope and mailed to the bank or are dropped in the night depository. Currency should never be deposited in this manner unless sent by registered mail. The bank sends the depositor a receipt by return mail, along with a new mail deposit ticket and envelope.

Using a Checking Account

Banks provide checks in a variety of forms. Checks with attached stubs, pads of checks with interleaved copy sheets, and checks with attached **vouchers** (forms used to record the purpose and other details of a payment) are a few of the forms available. In companies where all disbursements must be made by check, voucher checks, like the one shown in Figure 19-6, and a check register are used. A **check register** is a special journal containing a chronological and serial record of all voucher checks issued. Such a system ensures close control over cash disbursements. Many businesses use prenumbered checks

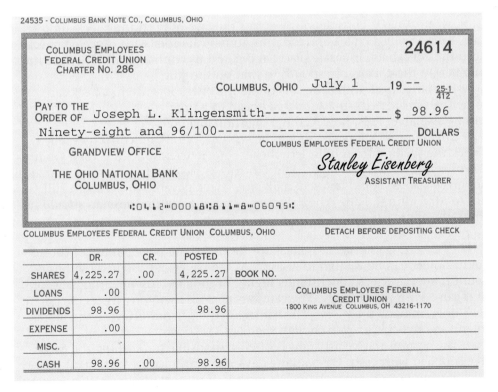

Fig. 19-6 A voucher check consists of the check and a detachable stub that shows the purpose of the check and various data necessary for recordkeeping.

imprinted with the name of the business. The administrative assistant is responsible for ordering a new checkbook before the old one is completely used. Banks usually enclose an order sheet in the back of these checkbooks to make reordering easy.

Completing Check Stubs. Complete the stub before you write the check. Failure to do so frequently results in the details of a check being forgotten. In addition to showing the number of the check, the date, the name of the payee, and the amount, the stub should provide other data for classifying or breaking down the disbursement for accounting or tax records. For example, if the check is a partial payment, an installment payment, or a final payment, that fact should be noted. If the amount covers several items (such as payment for two or more invoices), each should be listed. If the check is in payment of an insurance premium, the name of the insured and the policy number should be listed.

Writing Checks. A check is a negotiable instrument (can be substituted for cash) and imposes certain legal responsibilities on the maker. It must be written with care to ensure that no unintended liability is created. For example, an altered check is not cashable. If a bank honors such a check, it must assume any resulting loss. However, if it can be shown that the maker failed to use reasonable precautions in writing the check, thus making an alteration difficult to detect, the maker must assume any loss. Consequently, always type checks or write them in ink. Never use pencil.

Never cross out, erase, or change any part of a check. If you make an error, write "VOID" conspicuously across the face of both the check and the stub. Save a voided check and file it in numerical order with canceled checks. Keep the checkbook in a safe place, and guard its confidentiality. Be sure the number on the check corresponds to that on the stub.

Date the check using the exact date the check is written. Checks are sometimes postdated—that is, dated ahead to a time when sufficient funds will be available. This, however, is a questionable practice.

The name of the payee should be written in full and correctly spelled. Check the spelling from bills, letterheads, or the telephone directory. Omit titles of courtesy—Mr., Mrs., Dr., Rev. On checks payable to a married woman, her given name should be used; make the check payable to Elizabeth Hill, not to Mrs. John R. Hill. When signing a check, a married woman should use this same approach.

Writing Checks for Cash. A check for funds for the personal use of the account holder can be written to "Cash" (as the payee) and signed by the account holder. A check so written is highly negotiable. Anyone in possession of it can turn it into money. The cautious person, therefore, writes checks for cash only on bank premises. (The bank asks the person receiving the money to endorse the check, even though the payee is "Cash.")

The administrative assistant is often responsible for keeping the executive supplied with cash. On banking days, the administrative assistant simply asks the employer if he or she needs money. If so, the administrative assistant writes the check for cash and either presents it for the executive's signature or, if authorized to do so, signs it. To cash a check made out to "Cash" and signed by the employer, the administrative assistant endorses the check when it is presented at the bank. Unless the administrative assistant is well known at the bank, positive identification will be required. After cashing the check, the administrative assistant should keep the currency separate from personal funds. Place the money in an envelope, seal it, and protect it until delivery.

As a special service some banks provide depositors with a check-cashing or bank check guarantee card. This card, which is a form of identification, guarantees that the bank will honor the card holder's check up to a specified amount. Check-cashing guarantee cards facilitate the cashing of personal checks at stores and at other banks.

Checking Accounts That Pay Interest.   Funds deposited in checking accounts may draw interest. Banks and savings and loan associations nationwide offer NOW (negotiable order of withdrawal) accounts. Some credit unions pay interest on share-draft accounts, which are like NOW accounts. Some banks require a minimum balance to earn interest, and in some institutions a service charge is imposed on accounts that fall below that minimum balance.

Before depositing money in an interest-earning checking account, you should investigate the offerings of several financial institutions. Some of the questions to ask include the following: How much interest is earned? Is a minimum balance required? What if I go under the minimum? Will a traditional noninterest-bearing checking account serve my purposes just as well?

Stopping Payment on Checks

Unless a check has been cleared by the bank upon which it was drawn, payment can be stopped. It may be necessary to stop payment on a check that has been lost, stolen, or incorrectly written. Most banks charge for this service. Before placing a stop-payment order, ask about the fee. If the fee is more than the check, instituting stop-payment procedures would, of course, not be worthwhile.

To stop payment, go to the bank or telephone the bank's stop-payment desk. Give the name of the maker, the date, the number and amount of the check, the account number, the name of the payee, and the reason that payment is to be stopped. The bank teller will search the checks on hand or call up the account on a video display terminal (VDT) to see if it has cleared the bank. If it has not, the teller will process the stop-payment request. Some banks require either a letter of confirmation or a stop-payment form supplied by the bank. Others do not. When you are sure that the stop-payment request is in effect, write a replacement check, if necessary. Most banks will honor a request to stop payment for a limited time only. If additional time is needed, a new request must be filed with the bank.

Bank Overdrafts

Overdrafts happen occasionally, and they are embarrassing and expensive. Most banks levy a charge for checks returned because of insufficient funds. Overdrafts are usually the result of careless recordkeeping. They frequently occur when calculation errors have been made in the checkbook stub or when an electronic funds transfer (EFT) deduction has been overlooked. Overdrafts also occur when the employer makes a withdrawal from an automatic teller machine without notifying the person responsible for keeping the checkbook record.

To prevent the embarrassment, expense, and inconvenience of an overdraft, you should establish some procedure for having those with access to the account inform you of withdrawals. Automatic teller machines issue a receipt for each transaction. The administrative assistant should ask for these receipts daily.

► **Procedure**

An overdraft is an amount drawn from a bank account that exceeds the balance in the account.

Overdraft Protection

Banks offer various types of overdraft protection, ranging from special lines of credit to charging the overdraft to the depositor's credit card, if the card has been issued by the bank on which the overdraft is made. Some banks offer overdraft protection linked to money market or savings accounts. Usually, a small transfer fee is charged for these services, but it is usually much less than the overdraft charge.

Arrangements should be made with your bank for this protection, if you use a credit card issued by your bank. The procedure is simple. A signed authorization form is all that most banks require.

Reconciling the Bank Balance

Each month the bank returns canceled checks (checks that have cleared the bank during the month) to account holders with a statement that lists each deposit, each withdrawal, interest earned, and service charges. Account holders then check the accuracy of their checkbooks against the bank statement and file canceled checks as proof of payment.

When you receive a statement, compare the final balance on the statement against the checkbook balance. You must account for any difference between these two balances. This process is called *reconciling the bank balance*.

In order to reconcile a bank statement, you need the records of checks now outstanding. File reconciled bank statements chronologically. Canceled checks may be kept inside folded bank statements or filed numerically in a separate place. Canceled checks are evidence of payment and constitute legal receipts. The retention period for canceled checks should be established by company policy.

► **Procedure**

Many banks print instructions and provide a form for reconciling the bank balance on the back of the bank statement.

Some banks offer a check truncation, check retention, or check safekeeping service whereby the bank keeps your canceled checks instead of returning them to you. You receive a monthly statement listing the number and the amount of each check that cleared the bank. You have a right to a copy of any canceled check you may need; however, the bank usually assesses a fee to provide such a copy.

Following Up on Outstanding Checks

Investigate any check that has not cleared the bank within a few weeks of its date of issue. The payee may not have received the check or may have misplaced or lost it. A letter or telephone call to the payee will clarify the matter. If the check is lost, cancel the old check in the checkbook, forward a stop-payment order to the bank, and issue a new check.

Using a Safe-Deposit Box

A safe-deposit box may be rented from the bank. A safe-deposit box is a metal box that is locked by two keys into a small compartment in the bank's safe-deposit vault. The bank has very strict rules about access to safe-deposit boxes. The customer must register each time entry to the box is requested. A bank employee accompanies the customer to the box, opens one of the locks with the bank's key, and opens the other lock with the customer's key. The box itself is then removed from the vault and taken by the customer to a private room. Safe-deposit boxes may be used to store securities, wills, insurance policies, notes, gems, and other small, valuable articles. Rent is usually billed annually, sometimes as a deduction from the customer's checking account balance.

The executive must sign a special banking form if the administrative assistant is to have access to the safe-deposit box. The administrative assistant may have three responsibilities relative to safe-deposit boxes: (1) to maintain a perpetual inventory of the contents in duplicate (one copy is kept in the box, the other in the office); (2) to guard the key carefully; and (3) to add or remove items from the box as required.

ELECTRONIC BANKING

Because millions of checks are processed by banks in the United States each year, a number of new procedures have been developed by the banking industry to reduce dependence on checks. Most of these new procedures employ electronic fund transfers (EFTs), which permit cash withdrawals and the transfer of funds from one account to another without the use of checks. Computer and electronic technology has made EFT an acceptable substitute for checks and cash in many places. Each EFT service is designed to hold down the rising costs of handling checks and to provide a variety of banking conveniences. EFT services are available in many forms.

Automatic Teller Machines

At shopping centers and other convenient locations, automatic teller machines (ATM), like the one shown in Figure 19-7(a), provide 24-hour banking. Automatic teller machines are used to withdraw cash, transfer funds, make deposits, make payments on certain loans and bank credit card accounts, borrow funds in limited amounts, or obtain the current balance of an account. To use an ATM, the depositor inserts a plastic card and punches in a personal identification number (PIN), which has been assigned by the bank. This number or code is known only to the depositor and the computer, unless the depositor reveals it to others. Federal law requires all automatic tellers to issue receipts. Figure 19-7(b) shows a receipt for an ATM transaction.

Fig. 19-7(a)   Automatic tellers dispense cash to users electronically.

The magnetic strip on the back of the card should be protected against damage or accidental erasure. Discovering that a card is not functioning could be devastating to an executive needing cash on a business trip. Some banks provide a small envelope to protect the magnetic strip.

Many ATM cards can be used when traveling. Through the CIRRUS and MOST networks, for a modest fee, you can obtain cash and balance information. CIRRUS has 75,000 locations throughout the United States, Canada, Mexico, Europe, and Japan; MOST has 5,500 locations in the mid-Atlantic region of the United States. To use your ATM card at a location other than your own bank, follow the same procedure you would normally use to withdraw funds, make a deposit, or obtain information. Keep in mind that a fee is charged for each transaction, which will be deducted from your balance and shown on your next statement.

Direct Deposits or Withdrawals

You may authorize specific deposits, such as a paycheck or a social security check, to be credited to your account automatically on a regular basis. You can also arrange to have recurring bills, such as insurance premiums and utility bills, paid automatically. Employers may use EFT to deposit payroll checks directly to banks designated by employees, thus eliminating the need to write large numbers of payroll checks each pay period. This service also saves the employee a trip to the bank to make a deposit.

```
24-Hour    SKYWAY
CASH

   FOREST HILL
   RICHMOND VA

    DATE           TIME
  07/06/94       10:10 AM

      CARD NUMBER
  5608330042452514

   TRANSACTION TYPE
    WITHDRAWAL 2595

       FROM     TO
  CHK 6438

  AMOUNT      $200.00

  AVAILABLE BALANCE
       $569.20
    Update Your Records
```
Retain This Record. All Transactions Subject to Verification.
Skyway Bank, Skyway Bank MD, Skyway Bank N. A. Members FDIC
ATM-0017 (4/94)

Fig. 19-7(b) Automatic teller machines are required by law to issue a receipt for each transaction.

Pay-by-Phone Systems

After preauthorizing your bank to do so, you can call your bank and instruct it to pay certain bills or to transfer funds between accounts. To pay by phone, touch-tone telephone service is necessary. You must also provide the bank with your personal identification number (PIN) and an access code. Each pay-by-phone transaction appears on a monthly statement from your bank.

Point-of-Sale Transfers

Point-of-sale (POS) transfers let you pay for retail purchases with a debit card. This card is similar to a credit card with one important exception: the money for the purchase is immediately deducted from your bank account and transferred to the store's account. In other words, the amount of the purchase is deducted from the customer's checking account as soon as the customer's identity and the availability of funds are confirmed.

POS terminals permit transfer of amounts from a purchaser's bank account to the store's bank account without the use of a check. The terminal is connected by telephone circuits to the bank's computerized accounting data center. When a customer makes a purchase, the cash register operator inserts the customer's bank-issued debit card into the store's terminal. Using a telephone, the clerk dials the bank's computer storage facilities to connect the store's terminal to the bank's data center. The clerk then enters the amount of the purchase on the store's terminal keyboard. The customer keys in an individualized code number. The computer responds by authorizing the purchase, deducting the amount from the customer's checking account, and adding it to the merchant's account. Checkless transactions of this type appear on the customer's monthly bank statement.

Rights/Responsibilities

You will encounter EFT in one form or another as you transact routine banking for yourself or your employer. It behooves you to know your rights and responsibilities when handling EFTs. Each time you initiate an EFT at a terminal (automated teller machine or point-of-sale transfer), you get a receipt. Periodic statements must also be issued for all EFTs. Many banks use a single-statement system that reports all transactions—deposits, withdrawals, savings, and EFTs—on one form. You have 60 days from the date a problem or error appears on your statement or terminal receipt to notify your bank. If you fail to notify the bank within 60 days, you may find yourself without recourse. Under federal law the bank has no obligation to conduct an investigation once the 60-day deadline has passed.

If you report an error within 60 days, the bank must investigate the problem within 10 business days after notification to tell you the results of the investigation. If the bank needs more time, it may take up to 45 days to complete an investigation. In the meantime, the bank must replace the amount in dispute. The money is then available for the customer's use. It must be paid back to the bank if the investigation reveals that no error was made.

If an EFT card is lost or stolen, notify the issuing bank within two business days. You will then lose no more than $50 if someone else uses your card. If you do not notify the bank within two business days, you may lose as much as $500 if your card is used without your permission. The best way to protect yourself in case your card is lost or stolen is to notify your bank by telephone and to follow up the call with a letter.

When you use EFT, federal law gives you no right to stop payment. There is one case, however, when you can stop payment. If notice is given to the bank at least three days before a payment is scheduled, preauthorized payments, such as a regularly paid utility bill, can be stopped. This right does not apply to any payments, such as loan payments, that you owe your bank.

Smart Cards

Some banks are replacing traditional debit and credit cards with a new kind of computerized card with memory, a *smart card*.

Eventually, smart cards will be used to store patients' medical histories, to withdraw money from a bank account, to make retail purchases, and to record insurance information.

Retailers foresee that the smart card will enable a buyer to present a card containing a preset amount of money to a cashier. The amount of a purchase is deducted from the card. When the total preset amount in the card's memory is used, the customer takes the card to the bank to have another amount deposited into the card's memory. This system eliminates considerable paperwork, risk, and the time it takes to verify customers' credit cards at checkout counters.

Procedure

A smart card contains a tiny computer chip that makes the card almost fraud proof.

PAYING BILLS

An executive seldom turns over the task of paying personal bills to a new administrative assistant. It is one of the responsibilities that an administrative assistant acquires or assumes over a period of time. First, the administrative assistant may be asked to address envelopes. Then, when rushed, the executive may say, "Will you please write these checks for me." When asked, an administrative assistant should be ready to demonstrate the capability of handling this responsibility. Bill paying consists of the following:

1. Be sure that the bill has been approved for payment. Sometimes charges are made for purchases that have not been received. DO NOT pay a bill until such matters have been cleared with your employer.

2. Verify each charge and check the computations on each bill.

3. Fill in the check stub. (Be sure to itemize and identify the payment. Stubs are important for accounting purposes and in preparing income tax returns.)

4. Make out the check.

5. Write on the face of the invoice or the statement the date, the number, and the amount of the check.

6. Address the envelope.

7. Tear off the invoice or statement stub to be mailed with the check. Do not staple.

8. Attach the stub from the bill to the check and insert both under the flap of an addressed envelope to present to the executive for signature.

Verifying Bills

The administrative assistant should verify the price, the terms, the extensions, and the additions on all bills. The **invoice** (an itemized list of purchased goods) must be checked against quoted prices and terms or against records of previous prices paid. **Monthly statements** (details of an account showing the amount due at the beginning of the month, purchases and payments made during the month, and the unpaid balance) can be verified by comparison with invoices and sales slips, check stubs, and other records of payments made on the account.

Bills for services, such as utilities, are usually accepted as they appear, although the summary of long-distance charges with a telephone bill is checked very carefully. Explore the option of preauthorized bill payment service, if provided by your bank, to cut down on time spent writing checks for utility bills. Before paying bills for professional services, the administrative assistant should obtain the personal approval of the executive.

Cash Discounts

A **cash discount** is a premium allowed by the seller of goods to the buyer on the condition that the invoice is paid within a specified time. This enables the seller to ensure a steady cash flow to meet current expenses such as rent, payroll, and the like. Cash discounts are identified in terms such as 2/10, n/30, which means that the buyer may deduct 2 percent from the total amount of the invoice if the invoice is paid within 10 days from its date and the envelope is postmarked within the 10-day period. However, if the buyer does not pay within 10 days of the date of the invoice, the total is due in 30 days. Buyers who are financially able to take advantage of the discount may realize considerable savings from earned discounts in the course of a year. If you are responsible for paying bills, you will need to set up a tickler file to remind you of due dates. Such a file can prevent you from overlooking an important discount.

Credit Card Statements

To avoid carrying large amounts of cash or traveler's checks, many business and professional people use credit cards (such as American Express, Diner's Club, VISA, MasterCard, CHOICE, and Carte Blanche). Credit card statements also are helpful in preparing expense reports and in verifying travel and entertainment expenses for income tax reporting.

When making a purchase with a credit card, the purchaser signs a bill or receipt and receives a copy. A monthly statement for charges made to that card during the month is issued. The executive may delegate to the administrative assistant the responsibility for checking the monthly credit card statement. This requires careful inspection of the signature on each receipt and a comparison of the amount on the enclosed receipt with that on the receipt given at the time of purchase.

Lost or stolen credit cards can cause serious inconvenience for your employer; consequently, an easily accessible record should be available in case you need to report theft or loss. You should maintain a computerized list of your employer's credit card numbers, or place all cards face down on the glass of a copier with space between them to make a one-page record of all credit cards. On the copy, write the name of the contact you must notify if a card is lost or stolen. File for ready reference.

Credit card protection service is available from most credit card issuers to protect card holders in case of loss or theft. Numerous benefits are available, ranging from exemption from paying unauthorized charges over $50 to insuring the life of the holder during air travel—if the card is used to pay for the flight. You should note in your records any benefits that would accrue to your employer should something go wrong. Credit card protection is not automatic. It must be applied for and usually carries a charge in addition to the regular annual fee for the credit card privilege.

Filing Paid Bills

A logical system should be set up for filing paid bills, for they provide the key to canceled checks. If there are only 10 to 20 bills each month, the administrative assistant can place all of them in one file folder. If there are many, an alphabetic file may be set up; or subject files may be used to keep all utility bills, insurance bills, bills for supplies, and so on, together. Whenever a question arises concerning the payment of a bill, the administrative assistant should be able to locate the annotated bill on which the date, the check number, and the amount paid were written. Retrieving the canceled check from the files for evidence should not present a problem.

Using Other Cash Substitutes

Although most payments handled by the administrative assistant will probably be made by ordinary check or by electronic fund transfer, one of several special checks or money orders that can be obtained at the bank (usually at a nominal charge) may be used on occasion.

Certified Check. A regular depositor's check that is guaranteed by the bank on which it is drawn is called a **certified check.** To obtain such a check, the administrative assistant takes the employer's personal check to the bank and asks that it be certified. After seeing that sufficient funds are in the account to cover the check, a bank official stamps the check "CERTIFIED," adds an official signature, and immediately charges the account with the amount of the check. A certified check is often used when a sum of money is required to bind a contract, to guarantee fulfillment of a contract, or as payment to stockbrokers, bond dealers, etc. A stop-payment order cannot be issued on a certified check. An example of a certified check appears in Figure 19-8.

Official Check. A check written by the bank on its own funds is known as an **official check** (sometimes called a cashier's check or a treasurer's check). Official checks may be used by depositors and by persons who do not have

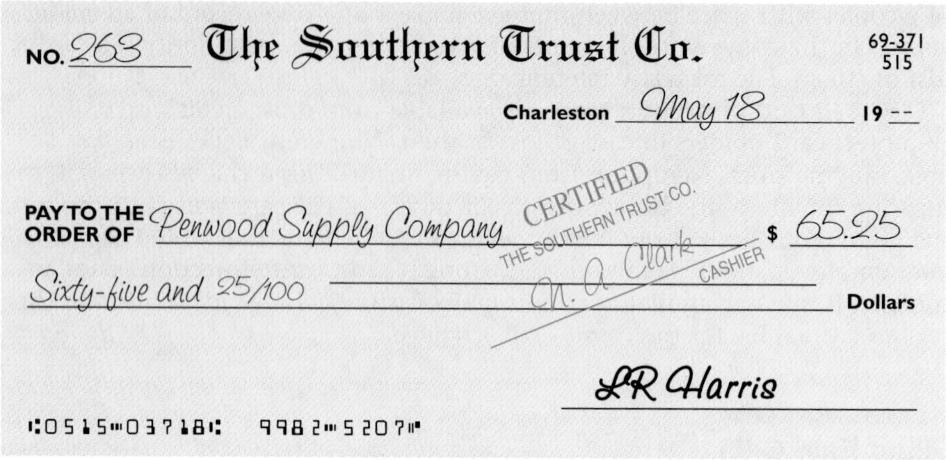
NO. 263 The Southern Trust Co. 69-371/515

Charleston May 18 19 --

PAY TO THE ORDER OF Penwood Supply Company $ 65.25

Sixty-five and 25/100 Dollars

CERTIFIED THE SOUTHERN TRUST CO. N. A. Clark CASHIER

LR Harris

⑆0515⑈03718⑆ 9982⑈5207⑈

Fig. 19-8 A certified check is guaranteed by the bank on which it is drawn.

checking accounts. The amount of the check plus a service fee is paid to the bank teller, who then writes the check to the specified payee. Recommended practice is to have the official check made payable to the purchaser, who must then endorse it in full to the ultimate payee. The canceled check is proof of payment. An example of an official check appears in Figure 19-9.

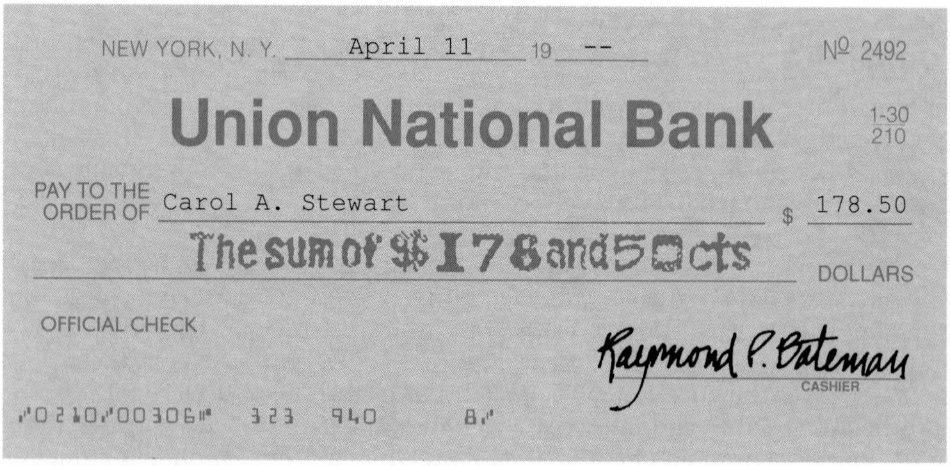
NEW YORK, N. Y. April 11 19 -- Nº 2492

Union National Bank 1-30/210

PAY TO THE ORDER OF Carol A. Stewart $ 178.50

The sum of $$178 and 50 cts DOLLARS

OFFICIAL CHECK

Raymond P. Bateman CASHIER

⑈0210⑈00306⑈ 323 940 8⑈

Fig. 19-9 An official check is also known as a cashier's check or a treasurer's check.

Bank Draft. A **bank draft,** as shown in Figure 19-10, is a check written by a bank on its account in another bank located in the same or another city. A purchaser pays the bank the exact amount of the draft plus a small fee for is-

Fig. 19-10 A bank draft is used primarily to transfer large sums of money from one city to another.

suing the draft. Properly endorsed, the bank draft can then be cashed at the bank on which it is drawn. It differs from an official check only in that the bank draft is drawn by the bank on funds it has on deposit in another bank; an official check is drawn by the cashier on funds in the cashier's own bank.

The bank draft is used primarily for the transfer of large sums from one city to another specific city. The recipient of the draft can then be sure that adequate funds are in hand before taking certain action, such as releasing a shipment of merchandise, signing a deed, or starting work on a contract.

When there is need to transfer funds quickly, the bank communicates with its corresponding bank and directs it to transfer funds to a designated person or company. This process provides a quick, convenient, and safe method of transferring large amounts of money.

Bank Money Order. A **bank money order** (also known as a *personal money order* or a *registered check*) is similar to the money order issued by the post office. It is sold primarily to persons without checking accounts who wish to send money through the mail. It can normally be cashed at any bank at home or abroad; it is negotiable and transferable by endorsement. The amount of a single bank money order generally cannot exceed $500, but there is no restriction on the number of bank money orders that may be issued to the same person to be sent to the same payee. The purchaser of a bank money order is given a receipt.

The bank money order is more frequently used than an official check or a bank draft when the amount of money transferred is relatively small. It differs from an official check in that the names of both the purchaser and the payee appear on the money order. An example of a bank money order appears in Figure 19-11.

Fig. 19-11 A bank money order is usually sold to persons who do not have checking accounts.

Fig. 19-11 A bank money order is usually sold to persons who do not have checking accounts.

THE PETTY CASH FUND

Payments of small amounts for postage, bus and taxi fares, donations, delivery charges, and incidental office supplies are frequently made from a petty cash fund. In many instances the fund is entrusted to the administrative assistant.

The size of the fund varies according to the cash demands, but can be any size desired. The fund should be kept in a locked cash box and stored in the office safe at night.

The petty cash fund is usually set up with a stipulated amount: $50, for example. Each replenishment of the depleted fund brings it up to $50 again. For example, after disbursements of $48 have been made from the fund, there should be $2 on hand. A reimbursement check to the petty cash fund would be for $48.

In replenishing the petty cash fund, the administrative assistant should prepare a summary report of all disbursements. Each disbursement should have a voucher for accounting purposes. If vouchers are consistently used, the total money in the cash box plus the total of the vouchers should equal the amount of the fund.

Keep a record of vouchers and disbursements. Balance the record whenever the funds get low, or periodically if the employer prefers. Some of the expenses itemized in a petty cash record may be tax deductible; therefore, file these records and examine them at tax-return time. Make petty cash entries at once, for they are difficult to recall later. A petty cash voucher is shown in Figure 19-12.

THE TREASURER'S REPORT

Although the responsibilities of a treasurer vary in different organizations, the primary responsibility of this officer is to act as banker. This officer's duties, whether as treasurer of a corporation or of a professional organization,

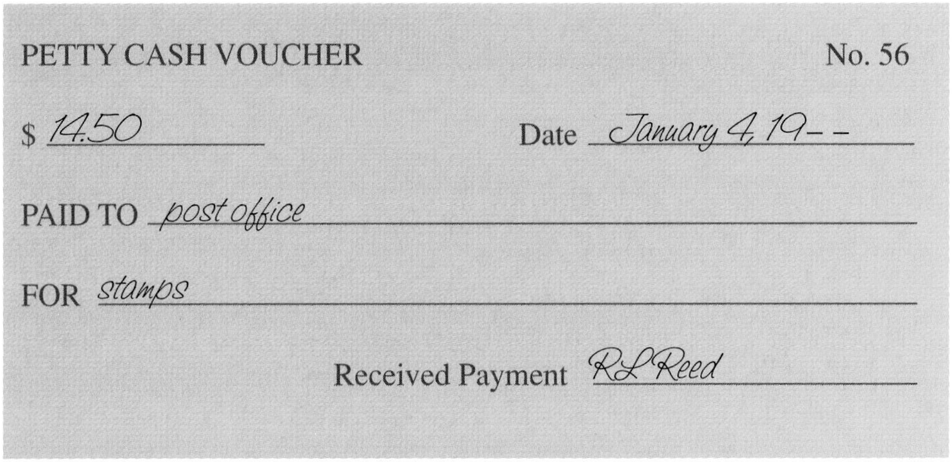

PETTY CASH VOUCHER	No. 56

$ *14.50*   Date *January 4, 19– –*

PAID TO *post office*

FOR *stamps*

Received Payment *R.L. Reed*

Fig. 19-12 Stationery stores sell pads of petty cash vouchers (or receipt forms).

are to receive and disburse funds and to report the financial condition of the organization.

In addition to keying the treasurer's report, the administrative assistant may also be given the responsibility of assembling the financial data required to complete the report. Prior to keying the report, you should file receipts for every payment in chronological order. Pay particular attention in accounting for money received. The treasurer's report consists of a statement of the amount of money on hand at the beginning of a designated period, the amount received during that period, the amount paid out, and the balance at the end of the period. The treasurer's report is prepared for general information. A detailed listing of separate payments is not necessary. Too much detail is useless and makes the report difficult to understand.

Examples of a treasurer's report are shown in Figures 19-13 and 19-14. These reports can be varied to fit the needs of most organizations. If the list of receipts and expenditures is extremely long, a separate listing can be attached to the report.

The treasurer's report may or may not be signed, but the treasurer's name should appear somewhere on the report. When the treasurer's report is submitted, it is referred to an auditing committee for examination and verification.

CREDIT AND COLLECTION INSTRUMENTS

The administrative assistant's financial responsibilities may extend to such credit and collection instruments as notes and drafts. Because these papers can be transferred or negotiated by the holder to someone else, they (together with checks and other substitutes for cash, such as money orders) are known as *negotiable instruments*. For an instrument to be classified as negotiable, it must:

1. be in writing and signed by the maker or drawer.
2. contain an unconditional promise or order to pay a definite sum.

TREASURER'S REPORT

As treasurer of the Richmond Chapter of PSI, I submit the following annual report:

The balance on hand at the beginning of the year was $1,150.76. Money received from all sources totaled $2,450.24. During the year expenses amounted to $1,250.00. The balance at the end of the year was $2,351.00.

An itemized statement of receipts and expenditures is attached.

Submitted by

Franklin P. Willis

Franklin P. Willis
Treasurer, PSI

FINANCIAL REPORT FOR FISCAL YEAR 19--

Kelly P. Barnes, Treasurer

Receipts and Disbursements

Beginning Cash Balance		$119,700
Receipts		
Cash Sales..	$ 19,200	
Collection on Accounts Receivable.............	134,908	
Interest Earned on Investments	1,300	
Total Receipts		155,408
Total Cash Available		$275,108
Disbursements		
Payments on Purchases of Merchandise ..	$125,740	
Selling Expenses	17,500	
Administrative Expenses	17,000	
Taxes	1,425	
Miscellaneous Expenses...............................	11,300	
Total Disbursements		$172,965
Ending Cash Balance		$102,143

3. be payable on demand or at a fixed or determinable future time.
4. be payable to the order of the payee or to the bearer.
5. identify the maker (person who signed the instrument) with reasonable certainty.

Notes

A **promissory note,** more commonly referred to as a note, is a promise by one person (known as the maker) to pay a certain sum of money on demand or at a fixed or determinable future date to another person or party (known as the payee). A promissory note is shown in Figure 19-15.

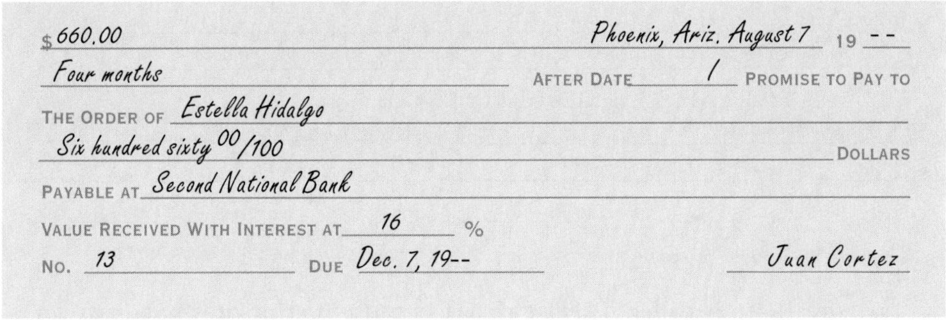
$660.00 Phoenix, Ariz. August 7 19 --
Four months AFTER DATE I PROMISE TO PAY TO
THE ORDER OF Estella Hidalgo
Six hundred sixty 00/100 DOLLARS
PAYABLE AT Second National Bank
VALUE RECEIVED WITH INTEREST AT 16 %
NO. 13 DUE Dec. 7, 19-- Juan Cortez

Fig. 19-15 With this promissory note, Juan Cortez (the maker) promises to pay Estella Hidalgo (the payee) $660 at the end of four months.

Frequently collateral is requested to pledge the payment of a note. In this case, the instrument is called a **collateral note.** Collateral can be salable securities (stocks, bonds), a real estate mortgage, or anything that represents ownership and is exchangeable. When an obligation is fully paid, the collateral is returned to the borrower. If the note is not paid, the creditor can convert the collateral into cash.

Some notes bear interest paid at maturity when the face of the note is due. On a discounted note, the loan-making agency deducts the interest in advance (known as the discount) from the face of the note. The remainder is called the proceeds. For instance, a borrower who takes out a three-month discounted note for $2,000 at 7 percent will receive $1,965 ($2,000 \times 0.07 \times 1/4 = \$35$). The full $2,000 must be paid when the note is due.

The amount and the date of a partial payment are written on the back of the note. When a partial payment is made, the administrative assistant should make certain that the payment is recorded on the back of the note, for the note is held by the lender until it is paid in full. If payment is made in full, the endorsed note should be turned over to the administrative assistant. It then becomes a legal record that the obligation has been discharged.

Commercial Drafts

A **commercial draft** is a written order by one person to another to pay a sum of money to a third person. It is generally used as a collection device. In the commercial draft shown in Figure 19-16, Huber and Stein owe $539.62 to Overman and McBrayer. Overman and McBrayer give this draft to their bank in Topeka for collection. The bank forwards the draft to its bank in Columbus, which presents it for payment to Huber and Stein. When the draft is paid, the proceeds are sent to the Columbus bank, and then to Overman and McBrayer.

Fig. 19-16 A sight draft is sometimes used by creditors to collect overdue accounts.

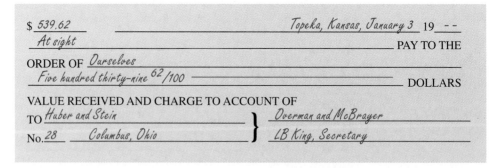

Figure 19-16 is called a **sight draft** because it stipulates payment "at sight." A **time draft** is payable at a future time and reads "thirty days after date" or some other stipulated period of time.

Drafts are frequently used as a means of collecting payment for goods shipped by freight before delivery. The merchandise is shipped on a **bill of lading** (a written account of goods shipped) prepared in triplicate and signed by a freight agent. A draft is attached to the original bill of lading and sent by the seller to the bank in the town of the buyer. When the merchandise arrives, the purchaser pays the draft at the bank, obtains the bill of lading, and then presents the bill of lading to the freight carrier to obtain possession of the goods held at the local freight office.

Foreign Remittances

Because of the dramatic changes that have occurred in the world in the past decade, financial transactions on a global basis are increasing. The fall of the Berlin Wall and the demise of communism in Russia and eastern Europe have opened new markets and new investment opportunities internationally. Expanding world markets for American-made products and increased investments of foreign firms in this country have added a new dimension to the work of the administrative assistant.

Responsibility for handling such transactions makes it essential for the administrative assistant to understand legal requirements and the available methods for making remittances to foreign countries. When a payment or a remittance is to be made to a person or business firm in a foreign country, currency, money orders, or a foreign bank draft may be used. Although the procedure is simple, some methods are more expensive than others. If speed is essential, your bank can arrange to wire money through a correspondent bank in a foreign country. This is the fastest method of sending money, but the fee for such a service ranges from $35 to $50. The service usually takes two days maximum. Both speed of delivery and cost of remittance should be considered by the administrative assistant.

 Procedure

The foreign exchange rate is the number of units of one nation's currency that can be exchanged for a unit of another nation's currency.

Currency.   U.S. currency or foreign currency purchased through your local bank may be sent abroad. Most foreign countries regulate the amount of currency that may be so transferred. Your bank will advise you of these legal restrictions. Currency payments, of course, should be sent by registered mail. The financial sections of major newspapers carry foreign exchange tables that show the value of foreign currency in U.S. dollars and vice versa for a specific day. A telephone call to major banks and travel agencies will provide an answer to most currency conversion questions. You should keep a recent

Fig. 19-17 Remittances to a person or firm in a foreign country may be made in U.S. or foreign currency purchased through your local bank.

currency conversion table if your job requires receiving or disbursing international currencies. Figure 19-18 shows a currency conversion table for some of the major currencies of the world. All the major currencies are listed in the Reference Guide on page 802–803. Keep in mind that the exchange rates fluctuate on a daily basis, and any calculations you perform should be based on the most recent figures.

Fig. 19-18 Newspapers in most cities publish a daily foreign exchange rate for the major world currencies.

FOREIGN EXCHANGE

MONDAY, OCTOBER 24, 1994

Currency	Foreign Currency in Dollars Mon.	Fri.	Dollars in Foreign Currency Mon.	Fri.	Currency	Foreign Currency in Dollars Mon.	Fri.	Dollars in Foreign Currency Mon.	Fri.
f-Argent (Peso)	1.0006	1.0006	.9994	.9994	Lebanon (Pound)	.000601	.000601	1663.00	1663.00
Australia (Dollar)	.7369	.7308	1.3570	1.3684	Malaysia (Ringgit)	.3918	.3915	2.5525	2.5540
Austria (Schilling)	.0952	.0947	10.507	10.558	z-Mexico (Peso)	.292826	.293040	3.4150	3.4125
c-Belgium (Franc)	.0324	.0326	30.89	30.71	N. Zealand (Dollar)	.6122	.6120	1.6335	1.6340
Brazil(Real)	1.1765	1.1765	.8500	.8500	Nethrlnds(Guilder)	.5946	.5983	1.6819	1.6714
Britain (Pound)	1.6298	1.6257	.6136	.6151	Norway (Krone)	.1532	.1540	6.5291	6.4927
30-day fwd	1.6291	1.6249	.6138	.6154	Pakistan (Rupee)	.0327	.0327	30.58	30.58
60-day fwd	1.6286	1.6245	.6140	.6156	y-Peru (New Sol)	.4545	.4545	2.200	2.200
90-day fwd	1.6286	1.6245	.6140	.6156	z-Philpins (Peso)	.0402	.0399	24.90	25.08
Canada (Dollar)	.7395	.7396	1.3523	1.3520	Poland (Zloty)	.000043	.000043	23067	23032
30-day fwd	.7395	.7396	1.3523	1.3520	Portugal (Escudo)	.006536	.006510	153.00	153.60
60-day fwd	.7395	.7396	1.3523	1.3521	a-Russia (Ruble)	.000333	.000333	3005.00	3005.00
90-day fwd	.7398	.7394	1.3517	1.3525	Saudi Arab (Riyal)	.2666	.2666	3.7503	3.7505
y-Chile (Peso)	.002486	.002486	402.26	402.26	Singapore (Dollar)	.6790	.6784	1.4728	1.4740
China (Yuan)	.1175	.1175	8.5113	8.5113	SlovakRep(Koruna)	.0328	.0326	30.51	30.68
Colombia (Peso)	.001199	.001199	834.31	834.31	So. Africa (Rand)	.2855	.2856	3.5030	3.5010
c-CzechRep(Koruna)	.0366	.0366	27.35	27.35	f-So.Africa(Rand)	.2519	.2528	3.9700	3.9550
Denmark (Krone)	.1705	.1714	5.8645	5.8357	So. Korea (Won)	.001255	.001254	796.80	797.50
ECU	1.26940	1.27380	.7878	.7851	Spain (Peseta)	.008035	.008000	124.45	125.00
z-Ecudr (Sucre)	.000445	.000445	2249.01	2249.01	Sweden (Krona)	.1413	.1402	7.0790	7.1315
d-Egypt (Pound)	.2957	.2956	3.3820	3.3830	Switzerlnd (Franc)	.8022	.8010	1.2465	1.2485
Finland (Mark)	.2200	.2177	4.5460	4.5940	30-day fwd	.8013	.8008	1.2479	1.2488
France (Franc)	.1956	.1945	5.1135	5.1420	60-day fwd	.8004	.7990	1.2494	1.2515
Germany (Mark)	.6691	.6669	1.4945	1.4995	90-day fwd	.7992	.7978	1.2513	1.2534
30-day fwd	.6691	.6668	1.4946	1.4996	Taiwan (NT $)	.0384	.0384	26.05	26.02
60-day fwd	.6689	.6666	1.4951	1.5002	Thailand (Baht)	.04011	.04011	24.93	24.93
90-day fwd	.6684	.6661	1.4962	1.5012	Turkey (Lira)	.000028	.000028	35316.51	35285.50
Greece (Drachma)	.004355	.004337	229.60	230.60	U.A.E. (Dirham)	.2723	.2723	3.6727	3.6727
Hong Kong (Dollar)	.1294	.1294	7.7268	7.7273	f-Uruguay (Peso)	.182482	.182482	5.48	5.48
Hungary (Forint)	.0094	.0093	106.64	107.05	z-Venzuel (Bolivar)	.0059	.0059	169.5700	169.5700
y-India (Rupee)	.0319	.0319	31.330	31.330					
Indnsia (Rupiah)	.000460	.000460	2173.02	2173.02					
Ireland (Punt)	1.6052	1.6006	.6230	.6248					
Israel (Shekel)	.3298	.3298	3.0320	3.0320					
Italy (Lira)	.000654	.000651	1529.00	1535.00					
Japan (Yen)	.010290	.010280	97.18	97.28					
30-day fwd	.010316	.010304	96.94	97.05					
60-day fwd	.010342	.010333	96.69	96.78					
90-day fwd	.010376	.010365	96.38	96.48					
Jordan (Dinar)	1.4745	1.4745	.67820	.67820					

ECU: European Currency Unit, a basket of European currencies. The Federal Reserve Board's index of the value of the dollar against 10 other currencies weighted on the basis of trade was 85.67 Friday, up 0.26 points or 0.30 percent from Thursday' 85.41. A year ago the index was 94.21

a-fixing, Moscow Interbank Currency Exchange
c-commercial rate, d-free market rate, f-financial rate, y-official rate, z-floating rate.
Prices as of 3:00 p.m. Eastern Time from Telerate Systems and other sources.

Money Orders. Either your bank, your local post office, Western Union, or an express company can arrange for money to be sent abroad. A money order is generally payable in the currency of the country to which it is sent. To obtain a foreign money order, present cash or a check to the teller. The teller will calculate the exchange rate and issue the money order in the currency of the country in which the payment is to be made. You are responsible for mailing the money order. This procedure is the same for obtaining currency or a foreign bank draft.

Foreign Bank Draft. A bank draft payable in a foreign currency can be purchased at your local bank. As with currency, most foreign countries limit the amount of money that may be transferred. The bank arranges for the transfer of the draft, or the purchaser may transfer it by mail or other means. This method of payment or transfer of funds should be used when large amounts are involved.

Methods of Expressing Foreign Moneys.   In many countries sums of money are written in much the same way as they are in the United States; that is, the abbreviation for the monetary unit is written before the figures, or the $ sign is used to designate the currency. Sometimes, however, the symbol "US$" is used to avoid confusion. The major difference in expressing amounts of money occurs when the period is used instead of the comma to indicate thousands, and the comma is used where we use a decimal point. In France, for example, Frs 75.987,20 means 75,987 francs and 20 centimes. In Austria the decimal point is raised—S ·75; in other countries a space is used instead of a decimal point, and the $ is placed between the unit and the fractional part. In Vietnam, for example, 6$75 means 6 piastres and 75 centimes.

FINANCIAL STATEMENTS

Because no two businesses are exactly alike, financial statements may vary. There are, however, two financial statements generally accepted by managers, owners, creditors, and investors that reflect the financial condition of a company. They are the balance sheet and the income statement.

The Balance Sheet

The **balance sheet** shows the financial condition of a firm at a specific time. It is called a balance sheet because the total items owned (assets) equal the total items owed (liabilities) plus the owners' or stockholders' equity (the owners' rights to the assets of the firm).

Assets may be classified as *current* (those that can be converted into cash in a short period of time) and *fixed* (those that will be used over an extended period of time in the operation of the business). Current assets include such items as cash, accounts receivable, notes receivable, and short-term securities that could readily be turned into cash should the need arise. Fixed assets include such items as buildings, equipment, land, and the like.

Liabilities are either current or long term. *Current* liabilities represent those debts which must be paid in one year or less. *Long-term* liabilities are those debts due over a period of time longer than one year. Mortgages, bonds, and notes payable are usually long-term liabilities.

The general format of a balance sheet may vary from company to company depending upon the amount of detail management wishes to include. The format should, however, remain constant from year to year to enable interested readers to discern trends. Figure 19-19 shows the balance sheet of the Autorama Sports Cars on a particular day (June 30, 19—).

Procedure

The major financial statements are the balance sheet and the income statement. The balance sheet shows the financial condition of a firm at a given time; the income statement is a summary of the company's income and expenses over a period of time.

Autorama Sports Cars
Balance Sheet
June 30, 19--

ASSETS

Current Assets

Cash		$26,450.00
Accounts Receivable	$45,600.00	
Less: Allowance for Bad Debts	2,600.00	43,000.00
Merchandise Inventory		90,000.00
Office Supplies		1,500.00
Prepaid Insurance		1,200.00
Prepaid Taxes		2,700.00
Total Current Assets		$164,850.00

Fixed Assets

Office Equipment	20,000.00	
Less: Depreciation	2,000.00	18,000.00
Warehouse Equipment	85,000.00	
Less: Depreciation	8,500.00	76,500.00
Building	95,000.00	
Less: Depreciation	9,500.00	85,500.00
Land		40,000.00
Total Fixed Assets		220,000.00
Total Assets		$384,850.00

LIABILITIES

Current Liabilities

Accounts Payable	$40,000.00	
Salaries and Wages Payable	3,000.00	
Interest Payable	2,000.00	
Total Current Liabilities		$45,000.00

Long-Term Liabilities

Mortgage Payable	75,000.00	
Notes Payable	2,000.00	
Total Long-Term Liabilities		77,000.00
Total Liabilities		$122,000.00

STOCKHOLDERS' EQUITY

Common Stock	$100,000.00	
Retained Earnings	162,850.00	
Total Stockholders' Equity		262,850.00
Total Liabilities and Stockholders' Equity		$384,850.00

Income Statement

The **income statement,** sometimes called the profit and loss statement, is a summary of a company's income and expenses over a period of time, such as a calendar quarter or a year. It also shows how much money was made or lost during that time. The income statement shows the total sales less the cost of merchandise sold. The difference is the gross profit on sales. Operating expenses for such things as advertising, insurance, and utilities are subtracted from the gross profit to obtain the net profit for the period. Figure 19-20 shows the income statement for Goldstar Bakery.

```
                        GOLDSTAR BAKERY, INC.
                            Income Statement
                      For the Year Ended June 30, 19--
Sales                                                              $ 375,000.00

   Cost of Goods Sold
      Merchandise Inventory, July 1    $  40,000.00
      Purchases                          250,000.00
      Merchandise Available for Sale     290,000.00
        Less:  Inventory, June 30         60,000.00
      Cost of Goods Sold                                            230,000.00
Gross Profit on Sales                                             $145,000.00

   Operating Expense
      Selling Expenses
         Sales Salaries                    31,000.00
         Advertising                       11,000.00
         Delivery Expense                   9,000.00
         Miscellaneous Selling Expense      1,000.00
      Total Selling Expenses                            $52,000.00

      General Expenses
         Office and Administrative Salaries  25,000.00
         Telephone                            4,800.00
         Utilities                            2,500.00
         Insurance                            2,300.00
         Rent                                 7,200.00
      Total General Expenses                             41,800.00
         Total Operating Expenses                                  $ 93,800.00
Net Income from Operations                                         $ 51,200.00
```

Fig. 19-20 The income statement for Goldstar Bakery, Inc., for the fiscal year ending June 30, 19—.

Interpreting Financial Statements

Before bankers lend money to a firm, or investors decide to buy stock, or management decides to borrow funds for expansion, a company's financial statements are usually analyzed. There are several tests that can be applied to a company's financial statements to determine the financial health of the firm. Three of the most frequently used tests involve the company's *working capital,* the *current ratio,* and the *acid test* or *quick ratio.*

Working Capital.   Working capital represents the total current assets after the current liabilities have been deducted. If a company's current assets are substantially greater than its current liabilities, the company will be able to meet its financial obligations on time.

Current Ratio.   By analyzing certain ratios, it is possible to determine the liquidity of the company—or its ability to meet current obligations. The current ratio is determined by dividing the firm's current assets (cash, accounts receivable, and marketable securities) by current liabilities (accounts payable, interest payable, and short-term notes payable). Bankers, for example, are interested in the company's current ratio when a short-term loan is being considered.

Acid Test or Quick Ratio.   Because it may be difficult to turn assets such as inventory and prepaid taxes into cash in a short period of time, the current ratio may not be an adequate measure of a firm's ability to satisfy current obligations. It may be supplemented by the acid test or quick ratio, which compares only the highly liquid or quick assets of cash, accounts receivable, and marketable securities with the firm's liabilities. To calculate the quick ratio, divide the quick assets by the current liabilities. A ratio of 1:1 is considered satisfactory for meeting current obligations. Examples of how these ratios are calculated are shown here using data from Figure 19-19:

$$\text{Current Ratio} = \frac{\text{(Current Assets) } \$164,850.00}{\text{(Current Liabilities) } \$45,000} = 3.66{:}1 \ \text{(excellent)}$$

$$\text{Acid Test or Quick Ratio} = \frac{\text{(Quick Assets) } \$69,450.00}{\text{(Current Liabilities) } \$45,000} = 1.54{:}1 \ \text{(good)}$$

Summary

Managing money is an exacting responsibility. Whether the funds handled by the administrative assistant are company funds or the employer's personal funds, an understanding of basic financial procedures and banking services is essential to the effective performance of this responsibility.

The degree of financial responsibility assigned to the administrative assistant depends upon the size of the firm and the personal preferences of the employer. In large companies, special departments are responsible for extending credit, collecting accounts, keeping financial records, and making decisions relating to services offered by financial institutions. On the other hand, an administrative assistant in a small firm, such as a doctor's or lawyer's office, may be responsible for all functions relating to the organization's bank accounts. In addition, you may be expected to assist your employer with personal financial records and banking services.

Whether your financial duties are extensive or limited, a basic knowledge of banking practices will help you understand the firm's financial operation. In almost every job, the administrative assistant will be expected to perform some, if not all, of these functions: make bank deposits, write checks, cash checks, pay bills, reconcile bank statements, handle petty cash, record incoming funds, and arrange for foreign remittances. Preparation of a treasurer's report, banking by mail, stopping payment on a check, using proper endorsements, filing canceled checks, using a safe-deposit box, handling credit card records, and selecting the proper credit and collection instrument may also be a part of the administrative assistant's duties. An awareness of transactions made possible by new technology and the ability to handle direct deposits and withdrawals, automatic teller machines, point-of-sale transfers, pay-by-phone systems, and other electronic banking services are often required.

A knowledge of financial practices and procedures offers the administrative assistant an opportunity to assume increased responsibilities and to improve career opportunities. Financial records and statements are vital to the survival of every organization. To be entrusted with them is an indication of the employer's confidence in the administrative assistant's ability.

QUESTIONS FOR DISCUSSION

1. Why is a knowledge of foreign exchange becoming an increasingly important facet of the administrative assistant's duties? What are the factors the administrative assistant should consider in making foreign remittances by mail?

2. Many top-level executives expect their administrative assistants to assist them with their personal financial records and banking. This may include writing checks to pay personal bills, keeping the executive's checking account, and keeping records of the executive's investments. Is this use of company-paid time of the administrative assistant on the part of the corporate executive ethical? Is it the administrative assistant's responsibility to conform or to refuse?
THINK IT *Through*

3. Your job requires that you accept cash payments and make change for customers. If a customer who made a payment earlier in the day returns to your office telling you that her change was $10 short, what action would you take before returning the money?
THINK IT *Through*

4. What is meant by electronic fund transfers? Why has EFT been introduced by banks? What is the bank's responsibility to depositors who use EFT?

5. If necessary, correct the following sentences. Use the Reference Guide to check your answers.

   a. We need 50 4 foot boards to complete the project.

   b. He lives at 1 Park Avenue.

   c. The team won four games in may, 14 in June, 21 in July, and eight in August.

   d. Take Interstate twenty from Monroe to Vicksburg.

   e. All accounts were closed by December 23d.

1. Interview an administrative assistant and write a report outlining the administrative assistant's banking responsibilities. Present your major findings to the class.

2. Assume that you are completing the year as treasurer of your chapter of Professional Secretaries International. You must submit your annual report to the board of directors at the next meeting. Prepare the report from the following data in statement form:

   You began the year with $522.42 in the bank. Receipts during the year consisted of $860 in dues ($516, national; $344, local); dinners, $232; seminar ticket sales, $208.40. Disbursements consisted of national dues, $516; printing, $46; postage, $25; paper and supplies, $25; jewelry, $41.81; dinners, $232; convention expenses, $400.40.

3. The following checks, bills, and coins are to be deposited:

   Checks

ABA 43-45	$ 225.80
ABA 19-24	19.50
ABA 63-785	1,346.00
ABA 2-77	7.50

   Bills

Five $20 bills	Sixteen $2 bills
Twelve $10 bills	One hundred ten $1 bills
Thirty-five $5 bills	

   Coins

21 halves	36 nickels
42 quarters	76 pennies
52 dimes	

   a. Determine the total amount of the deposit.

   b. Indicate specifically how the checks, bills, and coins should be prepared for deposit.

► **TA19-1.TEM** As treasurer of your local Professional Secretaries International organization (PSI), use the information below to key the annual report to the board of directors.

Money in the bank at the beginning of the year totaled $522.42.

Receipts during the year consisted of $860 in dues ($516 national; $344 local; dinners, $232; seminar ticket sales, $208.40.

Disbursements during the year consisted of national dues, $516; printing, $46; postage, $25; paper and supplies, $25; jewelry, $41.81; dinners, $232; convention expenses, $400.40

Access template file TA19-1.TEM for a treasurer's report in statement form. Fill in the missing figures on the report, and print a copy to be submitted.

Chapter 20

Investment and Insurance Documents

LEARNING OBJECTIVES:

After studying this chapter and completing the activities, you will be able to:
1. Understand the importance of keeping accurate and complete financial records.
2. Develop an awareness of the securities markets and the various types of securities.
3. Assess the advantages and disadvantages of the different kinds of investments.
4. Apply recordkeeping, computer, and mathematical techniques in processing investment information.
5. Expand your vocabulary with financial terminology.

INTRODUCTION

As an experienced administrative assistant, you may be required to maintain and supervise records pertaining to securities, real estate, and insurance. These records are needed to determine property values, to determine income and loss for tax purposes, and to settle insurance claims. Unless your employer's holdings are vast enough to justify the services of a professional portfolio manager, you will need to understand the language of investments and the workings of the financial markets. This chapter will acquaint you with the recordkeeping techniques and responsibilities required of the administrative assistant.

SECURITIES

A corporation can obtain capital (money to invest in equipment and merchandise and cash necessary for operating the business) by issuing stock or by borrowing money through bonds. **Stocks** are evidence of ownership in the corporation; **bonds** are evidence of creditorship, that is, of a loan to the corporation.

Stocks

Ownership in a corporation is divided into units known as *shares of stock*. A **stockholder** is an owner of one or more shares of stock. This ownership is signified by a paper known as a *stock certificate*. The stockholder receives **dividends** in return for an investment in the corporation. Dividends are paid from the earnings of the company either in cash or in additional stock known as a *stock dividend*.

A corporation can issue a designated number of stock shares. The term *authorized shares* refers to the maximum number of shares a corporation can issue. A corporation generally seeks authorization for more shares than it expects to issue. *Issued stock* represents the portion of authorized shares that has been issued and sold to investors. The remainder, consisting of the difference between authorized and issued stock, is called *unissued stock*.

From time to time a corporation may reacquire its stock from investors. If a corporation acquires stock either by gift, by purchase, or as compensation for certain actions, it is called *treasury stock*. Corporations can eventually either resell treasury shares or retire them. The number of a corporation's *outstanding shares* equals shares issued less treasury shares. Outstanding shares are shares in the hands of investors.

Kinds of Stock. Stocks fall into two general classes: **common** and **preferred.** Holders of common stock are usually the only ones who have the right to vote at stockholders' meetings. The rate of dividends paid on common stock is not fixed, but generally fluctuates with the company's profits.

Preferred stock usually has a fixed dividend rate and is senior to common stock in the first payment of dividends and in the first distribution of assets if the company is liquidated. Preferred stock may be *cumulative* or *noncumulative*. With cumulative preferred stock, any unpaid preferred stock dividends accumulate and must be paid before any distribution can be made to holders of common stock. Noncumulative preferred stock does not contain a provision to pay dividends in arrears.

Preferred stock also may be *participating* or *nonparticipating*. It is participating only if the stockholder is entitled to share with the holders of common stock in any additional dividend disbursement after an agreed rate is paid on the common stock.

Some preferred stock is *convertible;* that is, the owner has the privilege of converting it into a specified number of shares of common stock at any time. Most preferred stocks are *callable;* that is, they are redeemable at the option of the issuing corporation at the redemption price specified in the stock certificate.

Stock may be par value or no par value. **Par value** refers to the value ($1, $5, $10, $100) printed on the stock certificate. This printed value has no significance in determining the market price of the stock, which is measured by the stock's earning power—past, present, and future. Many companies today, therefore, do not print any value on their common stock. It is then known as *no par value* stock.

Stockholders' Meetings. Stockholders' meetings are held annually. Members of the board of directors are elected at this meeting by stockholders present or by proxy. A **proxy** is a legal instrument assigning one's voting privilege to a specified person or persons (see Figure 20-1). If directors of the corporation are to be elected, the proxy statement indicates the names of the persons nominated for whom the stockholder's proxy will be voted. The stockholder may vote in person by attending the meeting or vote by mail by signing the proxy. The board, in turn, elects the officers of the company at one of its regular meetings.

GE Proxy Form

The Board of Directors recommends a vote FOR the proposals regarding:
(A) ELECTION OF DIRECTORS:

FOR — all nominees listed on the reverse side (except as marked to the contrary to the right) ☐

WITHHOLD — Authority to vote for all nominees on the reverse side ☐

(INSTRUCTIONS: To withhold authority to vote for any individual nominee, write that nominee's name in the space provided below.)

	FOR	AGAINST	ABSTAIN			FOR	AGAINST	ABSTAIN
(B) KPMG Peat Marwick as Independent Auditors	☐	☐	☐	(C) Proposed 2-for-1 Stock Split and Increase in Number of Authorized Shares		☐	☐	☐

The Board of Directors recommends a vote AGAINST the share owner proposals regarding:

	FOR	AGAINST	ABSTAIN			FOR	AGAINST	ABSTAIN
(1) Political Contributions	☐	☐	☐	(3) NBC Programming		☐	☐	☐
(2) Economic Conversion	☐	☐	☐	(4) The CERES Principles		☐	☐	☐

If you wish to include any comments, please mark this box and then write your comments on the reverse side of this form → ☐

1000038747 646 - 1748   PLEASE MARK ALL CHOICES LIKE THIS ☒   0007650033

Please sign as registered. Executors, trustees, and others signing in a representative capacity should include their names and the capacity in which they sign.

SIGNATURE_____ DATE_____ HELEN J GORMAN

SIGNATURE_____ DATE_____

Fig. 20-1 A proxy form is sent to a stockholder for optional use. This form gives the stockholder the right to assign votes to someone else. In some cases, the stockholder may indicate a vote for or against certain proposals to be decided at the stockholders' meeting.

A notice of a stockholders' meeting, accompanied by a proxy form and a proxy statement, is sent to each stockholder entitled to vote. The notice gives a description of the business that is to be transacted.

If the executive usually attends stockholders' meetings, the dates of these meetings should be recorded on the administrative assistant's and the executive's calendars. It may also be necessary to request a ticket to the meeting from a broker.

Most companies send annual and, usually, quarterly reports to stockholders. Such reports usually include a review of the company's activities and its financial statements. Some executives study these reports carefully and then keep them. If this is your employer's habit, file them with other such reports or in a separate folder for that stock.

Bonds

A **bond** is a certificate containing a written interest-bearing promise to pay a definite sum of money at a specified time and place. Interest due on bonds must be paid to bondholders before stockholders can share in the profits of the company. For this reason, bonds are considered safer investments than stocks. The ownership of bonds does not give the investor voting rights in the company. The bondholder is an owner of a portion of the issuing company's debt, not a shareholder of its assets. When a corporation needs money, it sometimes sells bonds, promising to pay the bondholder the principal at some future time—in 5 years, 10 years, or even as long as 30 years. In addition, the issuer (the corporation) pays interest usually twice a year at a rate determined at the time the bond is issued. Bonds are rated as to their investment quality. The ratings of corporate bonds vary, ranging from high-quality bonds to low-grade "junk" bonds that pay a high rate of interest. The rating of a bond is an important consideration in selecting a bond for investment.

There are two general classes of bonds: coupon bonds and registered bonds. **Coupon bonds** are payable to any person holding them. **Registered bonds** are payable to the person in whose name the bond is registered. Coupons representing interest earned are cut from the bonds on or after their due date and presented at a local bank for collection. Coupon bonds are no longer issued; but if your employer holds bonds issued prior to the mid-1980s, you may encounter them in the investment portfolio. Some banks charge a small fee for this collection service. Bond coupons can be listed on a bank deposit ticket. If the bond or the interest coupons are lost or stolen, they can be converted into cash by the holder. Coupon bonds, therefore, present a security responsibility to the administrative assistant who is entrusted to care for them. Bonds should be kept in a safe-deposit box.

Registered bonds entail less responsibility for the administrative assistant. Such bonds are registered by the issuing organization, which mails the interest payments to registered holders. If the bond is lost, the owner still receives the payments, and the bond certificate can be replaced. The bonds discussed in the following paragraphs are all registered bonds.

Although corporate bonds are available in $1,000 units, they are usually issued in $5,000 units. The selling price, however, is quoted as a percentage of the par value. Thus, if a $5,000 bond is said to sell at 97 5/8, it actually sells at $4,881.25; that is, at a discount of 2 3/8 ($118.75) from its maturity value. Interest on bonds issued by a municipality, a state, or certain other political subdivisions is exempt from federal income tax. These bonds are known as *tax-exempt bonds*.

Another type of bond available to investors is the *mortgage bond.* Mortgage bonds are backed by mortgages on specific properties. A general mortgage bond is usually backed by a blanket mortgage on all the fixed capital assets of a corporation. *Convertible bonds* can usually be converted into common stock at a specific price or ratio. They are sometimes convertible to preferred stock or other types of bonds. *Guaranteed bonds* are guaranteed by firms other than the corporation that issues them. Principal (the original amount of money invested) or interest, or both, may be included in the guarantee. A *debenture bond* is a promissory note backed solely by the general credit of the issuing company; it is not secured by any specific property. Sometimes debenture bonds are issued with the provision that payment of interest will depend upon earnings. Such bonds are called *income bonds.*

One type of bond that has been popular with investors is the *zero-coupon bond.* This type of bond is different from other bonds because it pays no regular or semiannual interest. Instead, the bonds are offered at a discount and appreciate in value over a period of years. For example, a bond purchased today for $475 could be worth its face value, or *par,* of $1,000, in 2005. They are popular because they provide a specific value in a target year chosen by the investor.

Securities Trading

Most stocks and bonds are purchased and sold through a stock exchange, such as the New York Stock Exchange (see Figure 20-2), the American Stock Exchange (Amex), the Midwest (Chicago) Stock Exchange, the Pacific Coast Stock Exchange, or the Toronto Stock Exchange. A number of small organized exchanges are found in different parts of the country in large cities.

On the New York Stock Exchange, only securities listed on the exchange are traded; the American Stock Exchange and other exchanges permit trading in unlisted securities.

Buying and selling stocks and bonds on the stock exchange is handled through a broker. A broker is a professional financial agent who brings buyers and sellers together.

Stock certificates sold through brokers are not passed from owner to owner; rather, the seller turns in the certificates to the broker, who sends them to a transfer agent for cancellation.

The transfer agent employed by the corporation is usually a bank. The transfer agent keeps a record of the specific owners of stock certificates by name and number. The agent fills in a new certificate with the name of the new owner, writes in the number of shares the certificate represents, and has it signed and countersigned. It is then forwarded to the broker for delivery to the new owner or for deposit to the credit of the owner's account at the brokerage firm. Some brokerage firms hold all stocks and bonds owned by an investor and send a statement or inventory of holdings, listing the amounts received as dividends or interest, to clients each month.

Fig. 20-2   The New York Stock Exchange trades only listed securities.
© G. Martin/Superstock, Inc.

National Association of Securities Dealers Automated Quotations (NASDAQ).
Some stocks and bonds are purchased in the **over-the-counter** market. The
over-the-counter market is not a place but a method of doing business; that
is, transactions are handled privately through a bank, a broker, or a securities
dealer and do not go through any of the stock exchanges. A buyer or seller of
the security is located, and the sale price is arrived at through a process of
negotiation.

Most over-the-counter transactions are limited to unlisted securities
(stocks and bonds of relatively small local companies that are not listed on
an exchange). In the newspaper, over-the-counter stocks are listed under the
abbreviation NASDAQ. Not all of these stocks are listed every day because
there are so many. The daily NASDAQ listing reflects only the stocks most actively traded. Most newspapers that publish the quotations of the New York
Stock Exchange and the American Stock Exchange will carry the NASDAQ
quotations. See Figure 20-3.

NASDAQ originated in 1971 as a computerized communications network designed to provide automated quotations for the over-the-counter
market. This service enables brokers to obtain stock prices instantly and to
negotiate the best deal for their clients. Stockbrokers are agents who study
the fluctuations of the financial markets and bring buyers and sellers together. Stock transactions are handled through brokers because of their

*More than 40
percent of the
shares traded
in the United
States are traded
on the NASDAQ
market. This
electronic trading
market continues
to expand
internationally.*

NASDAQ NATIONAL MARKET ISSUES

52 Weeks HI	Lo	Stock	Sym	Div	Yld %	PE	Vol 100s	HI	Lo	Close	Net Chg
21¾	13½	AndowrBcp	*ANOB	.40	2.1	11	49	19½	19¼	19¼	– ¼
41⅜	17¹³⁄₁₆	AndrewCp	ANDW	...	...	30	2315	39½	38¾	39½	+ ⅝
21¼	13	Andros	ANDY	...	...	9	323	16¾	16¼	16¼	– ¼
8½	3¾	Anergen	ANRG	...	...	...	607	4	3½	3¾	– ⅛
13¼	6⅛	Anseta	INSTA	...	...	...	341	18½	9½	9¾	– ⅛
30¼	18½	ANTEC Cp	ANTC	...	...	...	587	25	24½	25	+ ½
4⅞	2⅜	ApertusTech	APTS	...	...	dd	540	4½	4⅜	4⅜	+ ⅛
27¾	16¼	Aphton	APHT	...	...	19	12⁹⁄₁₆	12½	12½	12½	– 1¼
17¾	11¾	ApogeeEnt	APOG	.30	2.2	36	192	13½	13	13½	– ¼
19½	16	Apogee	APGG	...	...	...	501	19¼	18¾	18¾	+ ⅜
39⅜	22	AppleCptr	AAPL	.48	1.7	dd	21835	28⁷⁄₁₆	26¾	28¼	+1¾
18½	9⁹⁄₁₆	AppleSouth	APSO	.02	.1	42	1968	15½	14¾	15	– ⅜
25¼	11	Applebee	APPB	.06	.4	30	784	14½	13½	14½	+ ½
16½	7	ApplncRecyc	ARCI	...	...	dd	500	8¼	6¾	6½	–1¾
7¾	3½	ApldBiosci	APBI	...	...	dd	772	6	5½	5¾	+ ⅛
25	13¾	ApldDigital	ADAX	...	...	...	90	23¼	22¼	22½	– ⅛
8¼	3¾	ApldExtr	AETC	...	...	dd	456	7¾	7½	7½	+ ⅛
21¾	6½	ApldImuSci	AISX	...	...	...	233	7	6½	7	– ¹⁄₃₂
33	9½	ApldInnovt	AINN	...	...	30	139	18¾	18	18¼	– ⅛
52	27¾	ApldMatl	AMAT	...	...	26	17998	48½	46	48½	+1
6½	3½	ApldMicbio	AMBI	...	...	41	3	3¼	3¼	3¼	– ¼
11½	4¾	ApldSciTech	ASTX	...	...	...	302	6¼	5¾	5⅞	...
1⅝	½	ApldSciTech wt		...	...	...	87	¾	½	¾	+ ⅛
7¾	4¼	ApldSignal	APSG	...	...	14	172	4¹³⁄₁₆	4¼	4¼	– ⅜
4¼	1¾	AraShld	ARSD	...	...	...	1	2¼	2¼	2¼	+ ¼
28¼	14½	Aramed	ARAM	...	...	...	500				
21	15½	ArborDrug	ARBR	.24	1.3	cc	65	19	18½	18½	– ½
25	12¾	ArborHlth	AHCC	...	...	...	128	21½	21	21½	+ ½
20¾	10¹¹⁄₁₆	ArborNtl	ARBH	...	...	10	1257	18½	18	18	– ⅜
19	11¾	ArchComm	APGR	...	...	dd	447	15½	15¼	15⅜	– ⅜
2½	1¾	ArchPetr	ARCH	...	...	cc	7⁽?	2⅜	2⁹⁄₁₆	2⁹⁄₁₆	...
½	18¼	Arctco	ACAT	.28	1.0	20	28	26½	28	+1	
	36	ArdenGp							39	4?		
									10½		

52 Weeks HI	Lo	Stock	Sym	Div	Yld %	PE	Vol 100s	HI	Lo	Close	Net Chg
2⅜	¾	BlackHwkGam wtB		...	...	...	24	¾	¾	¾	...
10¾	2⅜	Blimpielnt	BMPE	...	...	46	14	6¾	6¼	6¾	– ⅛
2⅞	1¼	BlocDev	BDEV	...	...	22	98	1½	1⁵⁄₁₆	1⁵⁄₁₆	...
44⅜	28⅞	BlockDrg	BLOCA	1.04b	3.4	12	29	31	30½	30¾	+ ⅛
18	3¾	BlythHldg	BLYH	...	...	dd	70	4⅛	4	4⅛	+ ⅛
35	26¾	BoatBksh	BOAT	1.24	3.8	10	1873	33	32⅝	32¾	– ⅛
23½	17¾	BobEvFrm	BOBE	.27	1.3	19	1187	21¾	21¾	21¾	...
10¼	5⅛	BocaResrch	BOCI	...	...	24	26	6¾	6¾	6¾	– ⁷⁄₃₂
14½	9	Bollingrlnd	BOLL	...	...	...	2	9¾	9¾	9¾	– ¼
10¾	5½	BonTonStr	BONT	...	...	10	40	9¾	9¼	9⁹⁄₁₆	+ ³⁄₁₆
25¾	17⅛	BooksMillion	BAMM	...	...	33	14	23¼	22¾	23¼	+ ⅜
30¾	22½	BooleBg	BOOL	...	...	13	1	25¼	25¼	25¼	...
27	13	Boomtown	BMTN	...	...	31	238	15½	15	15½	+ ⅛
26¾	16	Boral	BORAY	1.08e	5.7	...	1000	18⅜	18⅛	18¾	+ ⅛
22½	8½	Borland	BORL	...	...	dd	1783	10¾	10¼	10½	– ¼
12¾	7⅛	BorrerCp	BORR	...	...	...	18	7½	7½	7½	– ½
20¼	13½	BostnAc	BOSA	.40	2.9	13	10	14	14	14	...
41½	29	BostnBcp	SBOS	.76	2.3	6	100	33¼	32¾	33¼	...
51	32¼	BostonChick	BOST	...	...	...	2595	37½	36	37½	+1¾
14¾	6⅜	BostonTech	BSTN	...	...	28	2788	9	8½	8¾	...
27¾	9	BoxEngy A	BOXXA	...	...	...	66	11	11	11	+1½
14½	8½	BoxEngy B	BOXXB	...	...	...	1035	9¼	8¹³⁄₁₆	9	...
11½	10½	BoydBros	BOYD	...	...	...	37	10½	10	10¼	– ³⁄₁₆
4⁹⁄₁₆	1⅜	BradPharm	BPRXA	...	...	...	1298	2⁹⁄₁₆	2⁵⁄₁₆	2¼	– ⅛
3⁹⁄₁₆	½	BradPharm wtA		...	...	...	589	1½	1¼	1¹¹⁄₃₂	– ⁹⁄₃₂
1⁴⁄₁₆	⁹⁄₁₆	BradPharm wtB		...	...	...	755	⁹⁄₁₆	½	³¹⁄₆₄	– ¹⁄₆₄
2⁹⁄₁₆	½	BradPharm wtD		...	...	...	305	¹⁵⁄₃₂	⁹⁄₁₆	⁹⁄₁₆	...
48	34½	BradyWH	BRCOA	.68	1.4	19	31	47	46	47	+1
17½	9¼	BrantreeSvg	BTSB	.20	1.3	10	10	16	16	16	– ½
11¾	3¾	BraunFash	BFCI	...	...	12	10	4¾	4½	4¾	...
¼	¹⁄₁₆	BrkwatrR g	BWRLF	...	...	...	428	⅛	³⁄₃₂	³⁄₃₂	...
15	8¼	Brenco	BREN	.20	1.7	27	121	12	11¾	11¾	– ½
2¼	⅞	vjBrendts	BRDLQ	...	...	...	13	1¾	1⅝	1⅝	– ⅛
2?		BrentnBk	BRCK	.44	2.?	...	...	19½	19¼		

expertise in the market. They are generally paid a commission to arrange a purchase or sale of stock shares.

The NASDAQ market is innovative and technically sophisticated. It is rapidly expanding on a global basis, and experts believe that this type of brokerage will soon replace the traditional auction exchanges where brokers and financial specialists trade from the floors of the exchanges.

Foreign Markets.   Because of modern technology, financial markets never close. Somewhere in the world at any hour of the day or night, securities trading is taking place. From the world's major financial centers—London, Paris, Frankfurt, Zurich, Tokyo, Hong Kong, and Singapore—results are published daily in the *Wall Street Journal* under the title "Stock Market Indexes," as shown in Figure 20-4.

On-Line Trading

On-line trading permits investing by means of personal computer. Anyone with a personal computer and a modem can gain access to on-line services. A special software program that allows the PC to receive and send information is all that is needed. Once this equipment is installed, a user can dial a designated telephone number, enter a personal identification code or password, and be connected to the host computer that accesses the brokerage house. The order is forwarded to the floor of the exchange. It is then executed, and an electronic confirmation is issued.

Most on-line systems permit users to check current stock prices, place orders, and review their investment portfolio at no charge. Brokerage advice and analysis usually require a fee. Charges per minute for use of the system are also imposed, but on most systems fees are somewhat lower for nighttime use.

Mutual Funds

A **mutual fund** represents a pool of money contributed by investors and managed by professional money managers. Funds sell shares to investors and use the money raised to purchase securities. Stocks and bonds make up the portfolio of most funds. An individual investor in a mutual fund is offered a chance to own (indirectly) an interest in many companies and many types of securities. Mutual funds are also available to investors who want to purchase specialized securities, such as government bonds, health stocks, or gold stocks.

Shares in most mutual funds may be bought or sold at any time. The price of each share fluctuates daily. The investment is not insured; however, because most mutual fund portfolios are diversified, the risk of loss is minimized.

Stock Market Information. The financial pages of leading newspapers report daily stock transactions at major exchanges. The number of shares sold, the selling price for all stocks listed and traded that day on each exchange, and the net change in price from the previous day are reported. An example of a stock table appears in Figure 20-5. Sales and prices of bonds and the share price (or net asset value) of mutual funds are also reported in separate tables.

In addition to the daily stock market report and other financial news appearing in newspapers, information on security prices, trends, and business conditions may be obtained from such sources as the *Wall Street Journal*, *Business Week*, *Barron's*, *Financial World*, *Forbes*, the *New York Stock Exchange Monthly Review*, *American Investor*, Moody's handbooks, and the *Commercial*

Stock Market Indexes

EXCHANGE	7/12/94 CLOSE	NET CHG	PCT CHG
Tokyo Nikkei 225 Average	20400.48	− 72.61	− 0.35
Tokyo Nikkei 300 Index	299.47	− 1.27	− 0.42
Tokyo Topix Index	1647.15	− 9.01	− 0.54
London FT 30-share	2332.1	− 21.0	− 0.89
London 100-share	2963.9	− 19.9	− 0.67
London Gold Mines	223.3	+ 5.2	+ 2.38
Frankfurt DAX	2048.05	− 17.61	− 0.85
Zurich Swiss Market	2508.0	− 54.5	− 2.13
Paris CAC 40	1942.08	− 7.67	− 0.39
Milan MIBtel Index	10841	− 25	− 0.23
Amsterdam ANP-CBS General	259.4	− 2.8	− 1.07
Stockholm Affarsvariden	1383.8	+ 5.5	+ 0.40
Brussels Bel-20 Index	1395.03	− 13.14	− 0.93
Australia All Ordinaries	1972.9	+ 11.7	+ 0.60
Hong Kong Hang Seng	8591.45	+ 196.51	+ 2.34
Singapore Straits Times	2159.35	+ 8.10	+ 0.38
Taiwan DJ Equity Mkt	150.05	+ 0.37	+ 0.25
Johannesburg J'burg Gold	2111	+ 35	+ 1.69
Madrid General Index	298.72	+ 2.68	+ 0.91
Mexico I.P.C.	2288.28	− 3.72	− 0.16
Toronto 300 Composite	4131.72	+ 27.78	+ 0.68
Euro, Aust, Far East MSCI-p	1071.5	+ 1.6	+ 0.15

p-Preliminary
na-Not available

Fig. 20-4 Foreign stock market indexes are published daily in the *Wall Street Journal*.

Fig. 20-5 A New York Stock Exchange Composite Transaction.

52 wks 19-- High	Low	Stock 2	Sym 3	Div 4	% 5	P/E 6 Ratio	Vol 7 100s	High 8	Low 9	Close 10	Net 11 Chg.
34	**22 7/8**	**American Exp**	**AXP**	**.84**	**2.5**	**14**	**17306**	**34**	**32 7/8**	**34**	**+2 1/4**
33 1/2	19 3/8	Avonpdts	AVP	1.00	3.1	13	48112	32 5/8	30 7/8	32 1/4	- 3/4
15 5/8	10	Ashland Coal	ACI	.15e	1.0	7	176	15 3/4	15 1/4	15 1/4	- 1/4
7 5/8	5 1/4	Bank Amer pf	BAC	2.5	--	--	83	6 1/4	6 1/8	6 1/8	- 1/8
56 7/8	39 7/8	BauschLomb	BOL	1.16	2.0	17	1793	57 1/2	56 7/8	57 1/2	+5/8
51 7/8	40 1/2	Colgatepalm	CL	1.48a	2.8	11	3216	52 1/2	51 5/8	52 3/8	+7/8

NEW YORK STOCK EXCHANGE COMPOSITE TRANSACTION — Yield

1. To date this year, American Express common stock has sold at a high of $34.00 and a low of $22.875 (22 7/8).
2. Name of the issuing company is easily identifiable.
3. The ticker Symbol is essential for looking up information in electronic databases.
4. The rate of annual dividend paid per share based on the last quarterly, semiannual, or annual declaration was .84. Special and extra dividends are noted by a legend letter. In this illustration, the legend letters should be interpreted in the following manner:
     a--extra dividends or extras in addition to the regular dividends
     e--regular dividend declared and paid in the preceding 12 months
     pf--preferred stock
5. Yield is defined as the dividends paid by a company on its securities and is expressed as a percentage of price (American Express paid 2.5%).
6. The price-earnings ratio of 14 means that the current selling price for American Express is 14 times the annual earnings per share. P/E ratio is determined by dividing the price per share of stock by the company's earnings per share of stock.
7. During the day, 17,306 shares of American Express stock were sold.
8. The highest price the stock reached during the day was $34.
9. The lowest price the stock reached during the day was $32.875. (Stock quotations are in eighths of a point [$1.00]. Thus, 32 7/8 means a price of $32.875 per share.)
10. The last (closing) price for American Express was $34.00.
11. The difference between today's closing price and yesterday's closing price for American Express was up 2 1/4 (or up $2.25). (A plus sign indicates an increase, and a minus sign indicates a decrease).
12. Boldface notations indicate a price change of 5% or more (up or down) in the current trading session. Underlined quotations are those stocks with large changes in volume compared with the issue's average trading volume. (See Avonpdts.)

and Financial Chronicle. Several large brokerage firms and some banks also publish special reports on securities.

There are a number of investment advisory services. The most widely used services are those offered by Moody's Investors Service and Standard & Poor's Corporation. Most of these services analyze the stock market and provide investors with detailed information on companies, stocks to watch, stocks that represent good buys, and stocks to sell. These services are also available from the broker with whom an investor has an account (see also Chapter 19).

Market Averages. A number of stock averages are designed to serve as barometers of the stock market; that is, they indicate whether the market is rising or falling. Probably the best known are the Standard & Poor's index and the Dow Jones averages. The Standard and Poor's index is based on the price of 500 stocks and is computed hourly each trading day. The Dow Jones averages include three separate averages: one composed of 30 industrial stocks (stocks of industrial corporations), one based on 20 transportation stocks, and one comprising 15 utilities. A composite average of these 65 stocks is intended to measure trends in all divisions of the market. Market averages are published in leading newspapers and are reported on television and radio. The companies that make up the 30 Dow Jones industrial stocks are listed in the Monday issue of the *Wall Street Journal*.

Market Terminology.   Learning the language of the investment world requires a special effort. If you are new to the task of handling investments, you may find some terms and phrases puzzling. The following list of standard stock market terminology will help you handle this aspect of your job efficiently:

- A *bear market* is a declining market. A bear is someone who believes that the market will decline.

- A *bull market* is a rising market. A bull is someone who believes that the market will rise.

- *Bid and offer* is the price at which a prospective buyer will purchase and the price at which a prospective seller will sell.

- *Blue-chip stock* is the common stock of a company nationally known for high quality, wide acceptance of its products, service, and the ability to show a profit consistently and pay dividends in good times and bad. These stocks are relatively high priced and offer low yields (the measure of return in an investment) as compared to other stocks. Bonds issued by blue-chip companies are called *gilt-edged bonds*.

- A *day order* is good only for the day on which it is given. A *GTW* order is good for this week. A *GTM* order is good this month. A *GTC* order (or open order) is good until canceled.

- A *discretionary order* is an order that gives the broker the privilege of determining when to execute it.

- An *ex-dividend* is the term used when a company declares a dividend to be paid to all stockholders as of a given future date. Stock sold during the intervening period may be sold *ex-dividend*; that is, the seller, not the purchaser, receives the unpaid declared dividend.

- A *limited order* instructs the broker to buy or sell a security at a certain price only. If the transaction cannot be consummated at the designated price, the order is not executed.

- A *market order* instructs the broker to buy or sell a security at once. No price is designated and the order is executed "at the market"; that is, at the best price obtainable.

- Stocks that are listed on the stock exchanges and traded in 100-share units are called *round lots*. An order for anything less than 100 shares is known as an *odd lot*. A small additional commission is charged for handling odd lot transactions.

- A *short sale* occurs when an investor sells short; that is, the investor sells securities that she or he does not own in anticipation of buying them later at a lower price. To negotiate the sale, the broker borrows the stocks temporarily for the investor.

- *Stock rights* represent a corporation's plans to sell additional stock. Each existing stockholder may be given a stock warrant indicating the number of shares that he or she is entitled to purchase at a designated price, usually slightly below the market price. A stockholder who chooses not to exercise stock purchase rights has the option of selling the rights to another party.

- A *stock split* occurs when a company issues to each stockholder a specified number of additional shares for each share the stockholder now owns. For example, in a three-to-two split, the stockholder receives three shares in exchange for each two shares owned. A company may split its stock to lower its market value.

- A *stop order* instructs the broker to buy or sell "at the market" whenever a security moves to a specified quotation (price).

- The *yield* is the percentage of return for one year on one share of stock computed at the current market price or at the price paid by an owner.

A Brokerage Transaction.   To understand the procedure of a brokerage transaction, follow this hypothetical case:

1. The purchaser (or the purchaser's administrative assistant) places an order with a broker to buy 25 shares of Coca-Cola common at the market (generally by a telephone call). (The administrative assistant makes a full memorandum of the order. The date, the time, and the order placed are noted. The broker executes the order on that date—the trade date.)

2. When the broker makes the purchase through the stock exchange, an invoice (called a confirmation) for the purchase of the stock is sent to the buyer. (The invoice for the purchase or sale of securities is called a confirmation because the broker is acting as an agent and is confirming by means of the invoice the instructions received. The confirmation lists the name and description of the stock, the number of shares purchased or sold, the price per share, the extension [number of shares times the price], the commission charge, tax, postage, and total. The administrative assistant compares the confirmation with the memorandum to make sure the order has been carried out correctly.)

3. The purchaser or the administrative assistant sends a check to the broker by the settlement date (five business days after the trade date).

4. The broker arranges for the transfer of the stock to the purchaser. (If the executive has the brokerage company retain the stock, the executive's account is credited and the stock is reported on the next monthly inventory statement. The broker may also collect dividends and interest, which are also shown on a detailed monthly report. This simplifies income tax preparation. If the executive retains his or her own stock certificates, the certificate is forwarded by registered mail. If delivery is made to the executive, the administrative assistant, upon receipt of the stock, records the stock certificate number on the confirmation and transfers all information from the confirmation to the executive's permanent record. The administrative assistant may attach the confirmation to the stock certificate or file the confirmation chronologically under the broker's name so that it will be available when the stock is sold. The sales confirmation may be filed with the copy of the executive's income tax return.) A confirmation order is shown in Figure 20-6.

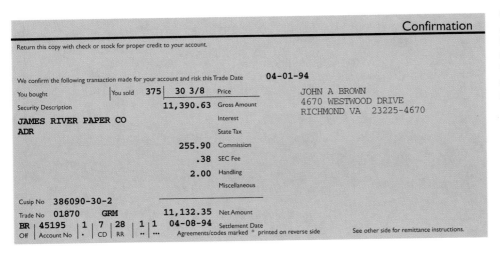

Fig. 20-6 A confirmation form shows the date and the type of transaction, a description of the security, the cost, commission, and fees, and the name and address of the shareholder.

Delivery of Securities. When securities held personally by the executive are sold, ordinarily the administrative assistant or a messenger delivers them to the broker's office; or they are insured and sent by registered mail with a cover letter describing the securities in full. Include the owner's name, the company name, the amount, and the certificate number for each stock certificate or bond enclosed. Request a return receipt. Keep in mind that stock certificates are valuable and should be treated as such.

Safeguarding Ownership of Securities. Banks and brokerage firms are now "fingerprinting" stock and bond certificates to prevent counterfeiting. With recent advances in color copying technology, counterfeiting has been a major concern of stockbrokers and investors. When the number of shares and the name of the owner are printed on a certificate to be issued, the fingerprinting system scans several tiny areas on the document to measure the light coming through. The paper on which the certificates are printed contains special fibers scattered throughout the paper. The location of these fibers varies enough from page to page to give each sheet a distinctive fingerprint.

The system combines the fingerprint information with the data printed on the security, encodes it, and prints it on a magnetic strip at the bottom of the document. When terminals read the strip and check it against the printed data and the certificate's fingerprint, counterfeiting is almost impossible. Bankers and brokers say such a system will cut costs and enable them to automate most security processing.

Records of Securities. One good rule for the administrative assistant to follow in keeping financial records for securities is to use a spreadsheet or a separate page or card for each lot. Figure 20-7 shows a card record of a common

Fig. 20-7 A card record of the purchase and sale of stock must be meticulously maintained.

JAN	FEB	MAR	APR	MAY	JUN	JUL	AUG	SEPT	OCT	NOV	DEC

(Dividend Date)

STOCK: Detroit Edison, common
BROKER: Merrill Lynch
FILED: Safe deposit box, City National

DIVIDENDS: Mar., June, Sept., Dec.

Date	Certificate Number	How Acquired	No. of Shares	Cost per Share	Total Cost*
1/18/--	H21601	Purchased	100	14 1/2	1,486.00
5/20/--	H29861	New cert. for H21601 after sale 40 shares	60		
12/4/--	H32504	5% stock dividend	3		

*Includes postage, insurance, and commission.

RECORD OF SALES

Trading Date	Shares Sold	Selling Price	Gross Amount	Int. or State Tax	Commission Paid	Net Amt. Received
5/20/--	40	16 3/4	670.00	2.43	33.75	636.25

stock. If your employer's stock holdings are extensive, consider storing this data on a computer. It will enable you to update information quickly and to retrieve vital investment data instantly. Otherwise, a separate record card or sheet for stock transactions should be kept for each lot of securities. Purchases and sales are recorded on the front of the card. Dividends are recorded on a ruled form on the back of the card. A metal tab can be used to indicate the dates on which to expect dividends. The card should show where the securities are kept. The "where kept" notation is important information that should be recorded for any valuable paper. Papers tucked away in unusual safekeeping spots known only to the owner can be difficult to find in the owner's absence.

Stock Certificate Numbers. When all the stock covered by one certificate is sold, the certificate is surrendered to the broker as part of the sale. When only a portion of a block of stock covered by one certificate is sold, the certificate is also turned over to the broker, but the investor receives a new certificate for the unsold shares. This sale requires a change in the certificate number on the stock records. For example, in Figure 20-7, the 40 shares sold were from the block of 100 shares covered by Certificate H21601. The new certificate number for the 60 unsold shares is also recorded.

If the executive and/or the administrative assistant keeps financial records on a PC, each should have at hand an alphabetical list of securities (see Figure 20-8). If this list is keyed, it is usually in triplicate: one copy for the executive's desk, one for the files, and one for the administrative assistant's records. Each purchase of stock for a given company made on different days or at different prices should be listed separately. If the employer's securities are stored in a computer and the list is kept current, an up-to-date computer printout can be obtained on request.

Securities Held by H. M. Gatz					
Stock	Date Purchased	Price	Commission	Total Cost	Exchange
100 shares Circuit City	10/10/90	$14.75	$ 65.36	$ 1,540.36	NYSE
200 shares CSX	4/26/91	40.88	189.48	8,365.48	NYSE
375 shares GrandMet	3/26/91	28.50	245.63	11,933.13	NYSE
500 shares Nissan	8/31/93	13.25	67.65	6,692.65	OTC
200 shares Reebok	3/23/90	17.50	116.61	3,616.61	NYSE
500 shares Tridex	9/12/93	10.25	94.87	5,219.87	AMEX
100 shares Wrigley	9/14/93	31.33	87.40	3,220.44	NYSE

Fig. 20-8 An alphabetical list of securities should be maintained on the administrative assistant's and the employer's computer. Keeping backup copies of these records is essential.

U.S. Treasury Securities

The U.S. Treasury raises funds to finance the debt of the federal government by selling securities to the public through the 12 Federal Reserve district banks and any of their branches. Treasury securities consist of bills, notes, and bonds and may be purchased at a Federal Reserve bank without charge. An application to purchase government securities must be accompanied by full payment. For a fee, Treasury securities may also be purchased from commercial banks, a broker, or other financial institutions.

Treasury securities are backed by the full taxing power of the federal government; therefore, interest and return of the principal (face value of the security) are guaranteed. Interest earned on Treasury securities is exempt from state and local income taxes but subject to federal income tax.

A Treasury bill is a short-term security sold at auction on a regular basis by the U.S. Treasury. Treasury bills mature in 13, 26, or 52 weeks. Bills are sold in minimum amounts of $10,000 and in multiples of $5,000 above the minimum. Purchasers receive a non-negotiable receipt. This receipt is evidence of a book entry at the Treasury that establishes an account for the purchaser.

Interest is earned by purchasing Treasury bills at a discount and redeeming them at face value. For example, if your employer purchased a 26-week, $10,000 (face value) bill on June 1 for $9,790, the discount would be $210. A check for the amount of the discount ($210) would be mailed by the Federal Reserve bank on the date the bills were issued or transferred electronically to the purchaser's personal bank account.

Every week on Monday, 13- and 26-week bills are auctioned. The bills are issued on the following Thursday. Bills having a 52-week maturity are auctioned and issued only once a month. At maturity, the Treasury mails a check (or makes an electronic transfer to the purchaser's account) for the face value of the bill, unless an automatic reinvestment of the face value at maturity has been requested. *Treasury notes* and *bonds* may also be purchased through the Federal Reserve bank. These securities have a longer maturity than Treasury bills and pay a fixed rate of interest twice a year, or every six months. Treasury notes and bonds are issued in denominations of $1,000, $5,000, $10,000, $100,000, and $1,000,000.

Complete information on investment opportunities in Treasury securities may be obtained from any Federal Reserve bank, stockbroker, or major commercial bank.

Investment Certificates

Investment certificates provide attractive alternatives for both individual and corporate investors. This form of investment is popular because the certificates are virtually risk free. Investment certificates provide a rate of return that varies with economic conditions. These certificates can be purchased without the payment of fees, commissions, or administrative costs. Institutions (commercial banks, for example) issuing investment certificates usually require that funds remain on deposit for a designated period of time. A substantial penalty is imposed for early withdrawal of the deposit. Interest is usually paid to the investor quarterly, semiannually, or annually. With some certificates, the interest is paid monthly. Once the certificate has been purchased, the rate of interest is fixed until the certificate matures.

A minimum investment ranging from $100 to $10,000 is required by most financial institutions. The minimum required depends upon the type of certificate and the issuing institution.

A negotiable *certificate of deposit* (CD) is a marketable receipt (can be sold to others) for funds that have been deposited in a bank for a specified time. Negotiable CDs are offered by banks in major money centers in denominations ranging from $25,000 to $10,000,000. The original maturity period can range from one to eighteen months, but most have a maturity date of four months or less. Income from negotiable CDs is taxable at all levels of government; the rate of return is similar to that of Treasury bills.

When the certificate matures, the owner receives the full amount deposited plus earned interest. CDs may be obtained from financial institutions without the cost of a commission. These certificates have been popular with investors because they are low risk, short term, and readily convertible to cash.

REAL ESTATE

An administrative assistant may be assigned tasks related to real estate holdings. These tasks include caring for valuable papers necessary to real estate transactions, completing the banking work, and keeping simple, complete records of income and expenses. Accurate records and a systematic method of following through all real estate transactions prevent costly errors and delays. Should you be responsible for following through on a real estate closing, you should check carefully to see that you have correctly calculated city and county taxes, insurance premiums, and commissions. To protect your employer, you should also check carefully all deeds, leases, checks, mortgages, and the like. Keep in mind that every record involving the transfer of real estate is vital to the completion of the transaction.

Buying Property

When real property is purchased, the title of ownership is transferred by means of a properly executed written instrument known as a **deed.** There are two types of deeds: warranty deeds and quitclaim deeds. In a **warranty deed** the grantor or seller warrants that he or she is the true and lawful owner with full power to convey the property and that the title is free, clear, and without any previous legal claim. In a **quitclaim deed,** the grantor quits claim to the property; that is, the grantor relinquishes claim but does not warrant or guarantee the title.

When a deed is transferred, it must be signed, witnessed, and acknowledged before a notary public. (See page 599 for a discussion of notary public.) It should be *recorded* on public record at the courthouse in the county where the property is located. Deeds, mortgages, and leases are valuable legal documents and should be kept in a bank safe-deposit box or in a fireproof vault or safe. Other terms frequently used when the title to real estate is transferred include the following:

1. The *abstract of title* is a history of the transfers of title to a given property briefly stating the parties to and the effect of all deeds, wills, and legal proceedings relating to the land.

2. *Amortization* is a mortgage or loan repayment plan that permits the borrower to retire the principal of the loan through regular payments at stated intervals.

3. *Appurtenances* are rights of way or other types of easements that are properly used with the land, the title to which passes with the land.

4. *Easements* are privileges regarding a special use of another person's property, such as right of way to pass over the land, to use a driveway, or to fish in a stream.

5. *Escrow* is the delivery of a deed or other property to a third party, who in turn makes final delivery to the transferee when specified conditions have been satisfied.

6. *Fixtures* are those articles permanently attached to real estate, such as buildings, fences, and the electrical wiring in a building.

7. *Foreclosure proceedings* are legal processes used to satisfy the claim of the lender in case of default in payment of interest or principal on a mortgage.

8. A *junior (second) mortgage* is a mortgage that is subordinate to a prior mortgage.

9. A *land contract* is a method of payment whereby the buyer makes a small down payment and agrees to pay additional amounts for the property at intervals. (The buyer does not get a deed to the property until a substantial amount of the price of the property is paid.)

10. A *mortgage* is a formal written contract that transfers interest in a property as security for the payment of the debt. (Mortgages must be signed, witnessed, and recorded in the public record just like a deed. The law considers the mortgagor [the borrower] the owner of the property during the period of the loan.)

11. An *option* is an agreement under which an owner of property gives another person the right to buy the property at a fixed price within a specified time.

If your employer invests heavily in real estate, you should be familiar not only with the terminology of real estate transactions but also with the means of protecting your employer's investments. Federal law requires the preparation of a **Federal Truth in Lending Statement** to be presented to loan applicants for the purchase of real property. This statement contains considerable detail including, among other things, the amount of the loan, the amount of the down payment, the amount to be financed, the escrow fee, the finance charges, the annual rate of interest, the method of payment, the due date of each installment, and the security for the loan. This statement, when presented to the loan applicant for signature, indicates that the disclosure statement has been received.

Property Records

Permanent records of property are kept for several reasons: to determine the value of the property, to show outstanding debt, to use in tax reporting, and to use as a basis for setting a satisfactory selling price. A record should be kept for each piece of property and should include information similar to that shown in Figure 20-9.

Type and Location of Property	Commercial Property 127 North Webster Avenue Tucson, AZ 85715-8635

Title in name of Robert C. and Mary K. Folley

Date Acquired	2/21/--
Purchase Price	$97,500
Mortgage (s)	Main Saving and Loan $40,000
	First Federal Bank 5,000
Assessed Evaluation for Taxes	$59,000
Remarks	Deed is filed in home safe

Income from Rentals			Mortgage Payments Interest & Principal			Expenses		
Date	Item	Amount	Date	Item	Amount	Date	Item	Amount
2/10	Rent	510.00	2/28	I&P	310.00	3/10	Taxes	500.00
3/10	Rent	510.00	3/31	I&P	310.00	3/10	Water	48.20
4/10	Rent	510.00	4/30	I&P	310.00	4/16	Plumb.	46.85

Fig. 20-9 Keep a record for each piece of property. At the end of each year, all income and expenses related to each piece of property can be conveniently organized for the preparation of the income tax report.

Investment Property. Property held for rental income or to be sold at a hoped-for profit is *investment property*. The administrative assistant's employer may own several pieces of investment property, or the business may be employed to manage property for other owners for a fee. Managing property means negotiating with tenants, keeping the building in repair, collecting rents, paying expenses, and so on.

An administrative assistant may prepare *leases* for tenants to sign. Printed lease forms are also available in stationery or legal supply stores. Pertinent facts must be filled in on these leases, and signatures must be affixed. These lease forms should be checked with an attorney to be certain they set forth the exact conditions desired.

The administrative assistant keeps detailed records of income and expenses on each piece of investment property because all income and deductible expenses must be reported on tax returns.

Although you might feel that a file folder gives you ready access to information concerning your employer's real estate holdings, storing the information in a word processor or a microcomputer greatly enhances the efficiency of handling such records. By storing the data on a diskette, you eliminate the tedium of updating records manually. All information relating to property can be recorded, stored, updated, retrieved, and printed or displayed on the screen at your workstation. Most large firms with extensive real estate holdings use computers to store property data of all types. Computers allow large quantities of data to be stored in a small space, and vital data are instantly available upon request.

Whether the administrative assistant uses a computer or a manual record system to ensure accurate data on each unit, he or she should follow the plan suggested here:

1. Set up an individual file for each rental unit; that is, each suite of offices, each apartment in a building, or each house. Identify each unit in the file by number or address. (An alphabetic index of tenants' names and their rental locations makes a helpful cross-reference.) Record everything pertaining to the rental unit, including correspondence, the lease, bills for repairs and improvements, lists of any special fixtures or furniture, and rental amount.

2. Use a miscellaneous file (or files) for the building in general to include items that cannot be charged to a specific rental unit, such as janitorial service, repairs to the exterior of the building or corridors, and taxes.

A record of all receipts and expenses paid can be keyed directly to each file, or pasted on a card or sheet filed inside a folder (if you are using a manual system). Preferably, such records should be kept on separate sheets in a loose-leaf book to reduce the chance of pages being lost.

Depositing money collected from investment property and paying bills for such property should be handled carefully. It is extremely important that deposit slips be completed so that every deposit can be identified. Every check stub should be labeled so that charges corresponding to a specific rental unit or building are accurately noted.

Personal Property Records.   To provide necessary information in event of death or other contingency, the administrative assistant is often asked to keep a file of the executive's personal property, an inventory of household goods, a description and the location of family jewels and heirlooms, insurance policies, and the names and addresses of certain key people involved in the executive's personal affairs. This information should be recorded on a diskette or in a file folder, placed in sealed envelopes, labeled, and kept in a safe-deposit box or a fireproof office safe.

Tickler File

There are many recurring expenses concerning property. Mortgage payments (usually due monthly), tax payments (due annually or semiannually), and insurance premiums (due annually) are a few of these recurring expenses. Income property rents are usually due on a certain day each month. To make sure that income is received when due and that recurring expenses are paid on time, tickler cards should either be prepared manually and continually refiled under the next pertinent date, or stored electronically on an electronic tickler system or any electronic calendar. In addition to interest and mortgage payments, use a tickler system to keep track of the following:

1. *Taxes.* Indicate for each kind of tax payment the kind of tax, the payment date, the amount, to whom the check is made payable, where to send the check, and whether or not a return must accompany the payment.
2. *Insurance premiums.* Indicate the renewal and due dates and the amount of the premium.
3. *Rent receipts.* For each rental unit show the location, the amount of rent, the name and mailing address of the tenant, and any special information regarding collection or interpretation of rent payments.

In companies where computers are used to store property records, automatic reminders of due dates for mortgages, rents, and taxes are built into the system. In some computerized tickler systems, when rents are due, the computer automatically prints out statements. Such systems also issue checks in payment of taxes and mortgages. All the administrative assistant has to do is mail the forms. Such a system relieves the administrative assistant of dependence upon manual devices for remembering dates. Whatever system is used, the administrative assistant should bear in mind that missing a due date can lead to financial loss, serious inconvenience, or both.

INSURANCE

Insurance guarantees the protection and safety of persons and property. There are many different kinds of insurance, as Figure 20-10 shows. An administrative assistant may have definite responsibilities for handling an

Fig. 20-10 There are many different kinds of insurance.

Barratry is a fraudulent breach of duty on the part of the master of a ship or of the mariners resulting in injury to the ship's owner or to the cargo.

TYPES OF INSURANCE

Personal insurance protects against the results of illness, accident, and loss of income due to illness, accident, or death.

Life: Universal life
Limited payment life
Ordinary life
Term

Health: Hospital care
Medical fees
Surgical fees
Loss of income

Property insurance protects the insured from financial loss resulting from damage to property.

Automobile collision
Burglary and employee theft
Fire
Fire—extended coverage—
    windstorm, lightning,
    riot, strike violence,
    smoke damage, falling
    aircraft and vehicle
    damage, most explosions
Plate glass
Standard boiler
Valuable papers
Vandalism

Marine: Barratry
Burning
Collision
Mutiny
Piracy
Sinking
Standing

Liability insurance (casualty) protects the insured against claim of other people if injury or property damage is done to others.

Automobile liability
Bailee insurance
Elevator insurance
Libel and slander

Premise and operations liability
Professional liability
Public liability
Product insurance
Workers compensation

Credit, fidelity, and surety insurance protect against losses from bad accounts (credit), employee embezzlement (fidelity), and title (surety).

employer's insurance. These responsibilities go beyond those assumed by the employer's insurance agent or broker and include the following:

1. Checking policies when received to determine if coverage is as agreed upon and (in some instances) to check conformity to the law
2. Maintaining adequate records of the payment of premiums, the follow-up of expirations, and a summary of the insurance coverage program

3. Canceling policies when necessary
4. Reporting claims
5. Storing policies and related documents in a safe place

Premium Payments and Renewals

Insurance premiums are payable in advance. Premiums on property insurance are usually paid annually or for a term of three to five years. Life insurance premiums may be paid annually or in monthly, quarterly, or semiannual installments.

Many life insurance policies allow a grace period of 28 to 31 days in making premium payments. If the premium is due and payable on August 16, for example, payment of the premium may be made any time before September 16. If the premium notice does not specify a grace period, the administrative assistant should ask the insurance company if a grace period is allowed.

Checks in payment of premiums must be drawn in sufficient time to have them signed and sent to the insurance company or agent before the expiration date. It is the administrative assistant's responsibility to avoid any insurance policy lapse caused by failure to make a premium payment.

In addition to seeing that premiums are paid, the administrative assistant should also arrange for the cancellation of policies when protection is no longer needed. A policy can be canceled by informing the insurance company or agent of the cancellation and returning the policy. The premium for the unexpired period of the policy is refundable. The administrative assistant should place a follow-up in the tickler file to check on the receipt of a premium refund.

All insurance-related correspondence should include the policy number. If the correspondence relates to a claim, include the claim number.

Insurance Records

A beginning administrative assistant may be fortunate enough to inherit a summary of the employer's personal insurance commitments. More likely, however, no records will be available. If necessary, compile a summary from insurance policies on file in the office and from notices of premiums due as they are received in the mail.

Methods of keeping insurance records vary; but, in general, these records consist of an insurance register and a premium payment reminder, usually a tickler card or computer reminder system. The register should contain information similar to that shown in Figure 20-11. Some administrative assistants record insurance policies on separate sheets in a small loose-leaf notebook; thus, when a policy is no longer in force, the sheet can be removed. Others prefer to use a separate register for each type of insurance (life, property, and liability) or to store the registers in a computer database or

Fig. 20-11 An insurance register should be kept either on the computer or in a loose-leaf notebook. Columns to provide appropriate information can be added to the insurance register as needed. When a policy expires, eliminate it from the register by drawing a line through it or deleting it from the computer database.

INSURANCE REGISTER

Company and Name of Agent	Policy No.	Type and Amount	Date Issued	Amt. of Premium	Date Due	Grace Period
N.Y. Life V. Getty	29 22 84	Ord. Life on Mr. B. $50,000	3/2/55	$563.00 Semian	2/2 8/2	30-day
N.Y. Life V. Getty	37 86 21	Term $25,000 on Mrs. B.	1/9/68	$107.25 Annual	5/6	30-day
Conn. Gen. T. Ramsey	H261 162	Fire on household goods $25,000	1/12/72	$249.00 Annual	12/12	

on a diskette. The executive's personal insurance and that of the business should be kept in separate registers.

Use a separate tickler card or set up a computer file for each policy according to premium payment date. This helps avoid letting a policy lapse or incurring a penalty for late payment. File data for each insurance policy in a tickler file. It provides a convenient record and serves as a reminder for renewals and premium payments.

Property Inventory

The importance of keeping an up-to-date property inventory can be fully appreciated only by someone who has experienced a loss from fire or theft. To present a claim for a loss, the insured must furnish a complete inventory of the destroyed, lost, damaged, and undamaged property with cost and actual cash value. This is difficult to do after the loss has taken place. A property inventory also serves a second important purpose: it shows how much insurance should be carried. Property values change; unless the inventory is updated periodically, property may be overinsured or underinsured.

The administrative assistant in a small office should assume the responsibility for compiling an inventory of the furniture and equipment in the office. In addition, the executive should be encouraged to provide details for an inventory of furniture and valuables at home. All inventories should be periodically updated. A computerized inventory is easy to update. Photographs or a videotape should be stored with an inventory to assist in the claims settlement in case of loss.

Storage of Policies and Inventory Records

Since insurance policies must be examined occasionally for data on coverage, beneficiaries, rates, cash value, endorsements, and the like, the policies should be readily available in a safe place. If the policies are kept in a file, you may find it convenient to remove them from their protective envelopes and place each policy in a separate folder. Label the front of the folder with the name, address, and telephone number of the agent and the policy number. This system makes it possible to file with each policy any important correspondence, itemized lists of property covered, endorsements, and other pertinent data that affect the conditions of the insurance contract. When insurance policies are stored in the office, there is always the possibility of their loss by fire. As a precaution, key a list of the policy numbers, the insuring company, the coverage, and the amount. Your employer should store this list in a safe at home or in a safe-deposit box. Thus, if office records are destroyed, they can be reconstructed.

Since an insurance policy is a contract, discard it when it has expired to keep your files cleared. First, however, call or write the agent to make certain that no claim on the policy is pending and that it has no continuing value. Some companies store expired policies in an inactive file. Referring to these policies is sometimes helpful in comparing coverages of policies currently in force.

Fidelity Bonds

A **fidelity bond** is insurance on an employee's honesty. Most employers carry this insurance on employees who handle large sums of money. The bonding company investigates the employee's character and the supervisory and control methods in force in the employer's business. No bond is sold if the applicant's character is questionable or if office conditions make it easy to embezzle company funds.

Blanket fidelity bonds covering all employees are bought by banks and other financial institutions. They protect against loss due to embezzlement, robbery, forgery, and so on. To be asked to take out a fidelity bond is not a bad reflection on your character. Actually, it indicates that you are considered competent to be entrusted with company funds.

Action in Emergency

When disaster strikes, you have an opportunity to prove that you are a cool-headed, responsible person who can think and act quickly. Others may be so excited and involved in the emergency that they fail to think of procedures. Insurance companies make these suggestions:

> After a fire, as soon as the situation is under control, notify the insurance company immediately by phone and confirm the call by letter. The insurance company may be able to have an inspector on the scene to witness the damage and save a lot of paperwork later on.
>
> Immediately report to the police any losses by theft.

Keep accurate and separate records for cleanup, repairs, and charges made by outside contractors. These charges become part of the insurance claim.

When an accident occurs, interview witnesses on the spot. Signed statements carry much weight and refresh memories when settling claims. If possible, take pictures or videotape.

WHERE-KEPT FILE

In the event of the sudden death of an executive, the family will need certain financial information immediately. The administrative assistant can be of great assistance in such an emergency if a folder containing up-to-date information has been maintained. The following information might be included in a where-kept file:

Bank accounts—the name and address of each bank in which an account is kept, the type of account, the exact name of the account, and the name of the bank contact (if the executive has one)

Birth certificate—where it can be found

Business interests—list of the executive's business interests

Combination to company safe or vault

Credit cards—record of names and account numbers

Income tax record—where past returns are filed; the name and address of the tax consultant

Insurance policies—location of insurance records. These records should contain detailed information on life, health and accident, hospitalization, and medical insurance policies. The name and address of the insurance adviser should be filed also.

Real estate investments—location of detailed property records

Passport—where it can be found

Safe-deposit box—the name of the bank, the box number, and location of key

Social security—the social security number

Stocks and bonds—location of detailed investment records

Tax accountant—name, address, and telephone number

Will—location of the original and copies of the will; date of the latest will; name of attorney who prepared the will; name and address of executor or executrix.

ADMINISTRATIVE FUNCTIONS

The administrative assistant may be expected to perform a number of administrative functions related to the company's and the executive's property, investments, and insurance coverage. The college-trained administrative assistant has a background of courses in economics, accounting, business law, and, in some cases, real estate and insurance. All these courses contribute to an administrative assistant's competency. You may be asked to do the following:

1. Prepare a prospectus on stocks that are under consideration for investment. This activity involves checking investment service reports to gather data on products, past performance, background of company officials, forecasts for the area and for the company, comparison with competitors, and so forth. Such data are also available in the business section of a public library and in special libraries.

2. Update the investment portfolio of the company or of the executive. The updating process involves analyzing the rate of yield on each investment, profit trends, and the outlook for the company. For some classes of stock, it may be necessary to prepare charts showing fluctuations in the market and to update them at regular intervals.

3. Supervise and follow through on repairs and improvements made to investment property. Frequent visits to the location of the property and careful study of repair and construction contracts are necessary.

4. Handle the details related to the sale or purchase of real estate. This activity involves such details as having the title searched, obtaining title insurance, and processing and recording the deed.

5. Review at regular intervals the insurance policies in force and arrange for revision in insurance coverage in keeping with changing values of property. The responsibility includes canceling unnecessary policies and being alert to new insurance needs.

6. Process an insurance claim. This responsibility involves compiling the records necessary to support a claim including cost records, appraisal of loss, and proof of loss.

Summary

Whether you are employed by a small firm with limited investments in stocks, bonds, real estate, and insurance, or a big corporation transacting business on a global basis, your understanding of investments and insurance is essential. Even the smallest enterprise requires the processing of insurance and investment documents.

Accurate records of all securities, real estate, and insurance transactions are extremely important. Although the services of a real estate agent, an insurance agent, and a stockbroker may be used, the administrative assistant may also keep records on property income, insurance coverage, and stock dividends.

In order for the administrative assistant to perform financial functions effectively, an understanding of the different kinds of stocks, bonds, and other securities held by the employer is necessary. Knowing how to prepare for stockholders' meetings and understanding the operations of securities markets are also essential. The ability to read and understand financial periodicals and stock quotations, trends, and business conditions depends upon the administrative assistant's awareness of market terminology and the process involved in brokerage transactions. Keeping records is necessary to determine which investments represent the most profitable investments.

An administrative assistant may also be commissioned to perform tasks related to the executive's real estate holdings. Caring for valuable papers necessary for real estate transactions, doing banking work, and keeping accurate, complete records of income and expenses are a few of the tasks the administrative assistant may regularly execute. A knowledge of legal terms, forms, and procedures frequently used in real estate transactions helps the administrative assistant handle these duties.

The insurance portfolio of an executive usually includes several types of insurance and may involve a number of policies. Accurate records are required to ensure that premiums are paid on time to avoid lapsing policies. The executive may delegate to the administrative assistant the responsibility for canceling policies and reporting claims.

The administrative assistant may be asked to take out a fidelity bond if large amounts of money are handled on the job. Such a request indicates the employer's confidence in the administrative assistant's competence to handle financial matters.

Should an emergency occur, the administrative assistant should know what action to take and where financial documents are kept. To provide quick access to the executive's financial records, the administrative assistant should keep an up-to-date folder of essential information concerning the employer's bank accounts, birth certificate, credit cards, safe combination, insurance policies, and the like.

The administrative assistant may also be expected to perform a number of administrative functions related to the property, investments, and insurance coverage of the company and the executive. Examples of these administrative duties include updating investment portfolios, preparing an investment prospectus, following through on a real estate closing, and processing insurance claims.

QUESTIONS FOR DISCUSSION

1. Why should the administrative assistant understand the Dow Jones industrial averages?

2. Why is NASDAQ considered the exchange of the future?

THINK IT *Through*

3. When the employer's automobile was involved in an accident, it was discovered that the insurance policy had lapsed because of nonpayment of premiums. The employer was extremely critical of the administrative assistant. The administrative assistant's defense was that the premium notices and follow-ups had been placed on the employer's desk. Furthermore, this was personal business and the employer's failure to act was not the administrative assistant's responsibility. Do you agree with the administrative assistant's position?

THINK IT *Through*

4. Your employer invests heavily in real estate and has given you complete charge of the collection of rent and the disbursement of funds for expenses related to the operation of various properties. You have been asked to complete the necessary forms for an application for a fidelity bond. What would be your reaction to such a request?

THINK IT *Through*

5. Complete the following statements by filling in the blank. Use the Reference Guide to verify your answers.

   a. The capital of Nova Scotia is _____.
   b. The basic monetary unit of North and South Korea is called the
      _____.
   c. The Roman numeral for 50 is _____.
   d. *First, second, third, fourth,* etc., are called _____ numbers.
   e. The numbers 1, 2, 3, 4, etc., are called _____ numbers.

1. Your employer owns all the following securities:

   200 shares of International Flavors and Fragrances (IFF)
   200 shares Disney, common (Disney)
   100 shares Coca-Cola, common (CocaCol)
   75 shares Consolidated Edison, 5% preferred (ConE pf 5)
   5 bonds of New York Telephone (NY Tel 4 1/2s 96)
   200 shares Procter & Gamble, common (P&G)
   500 shares Union Oil of Canada (Union Oil)

   a. Prepare a report showing the current market value of your employer's securities. (Use the closing price of the security on the date of the report.)

   b. Your employer purchased the shares of Disney at $35. A quarterly dividend of 26 cents per share is declared. Determine the rate of yield on the investment and the rate of yield at the current market price.

2. Your employer owns stock and carries several insurance policies. The insurance policies are on the employer's spouse, son, home, and automobile. You decide to set up a spreadsheet (tickler file) to keep track of the employer's stocks and insurance policies. Make a list of the type of information you would include on the spreadsheet for each of the following:

   a. Securities

   b. Insurance policies

3. When you obtain your first job, you may be able to participate in some form of employee insurance. So that you may know something about these arrangements and how they operate, investigate the employee insurance plan of a local company and report to the class the details of the plan.

   Include in your report the types of insurance available, how the premiums are paid, and the status of the insurance upon termination of employment with the company.

TECHNOLOGY APPLICATIONS

▶ TA20-1.TEM   Access the template disk, and select TA20-1.TEM file, which shows a screen for recording income and expenses on rental property.
   Your employer, Robert C. Foley, owns a professional building (located at 127 North Webster Avenue, Tucson, AZ 85715-8635), which

continued

continued

he purchased on April 21, 1990, for $219,000. Mortgage payments of $300 per month include interest and principal; the mortgage amount is $40,000; the mortgage is held by the First Federal Bank; payments are due on the 18th of each month. The assessed valuation for taxes is $110,000. The deed is kept in the office vault.

This building houses 18 offices. Six offices rent for $600 a month; ten, for $500; and two, for $350. All of the offices were rented during April except four of the $600 offices, which were vacant for three months while they were being redecorated. Rent is due on the 10th of each month. The management fee is 6% of the rental income. All bills are paid on the 15th of each month, unless otherwise indicated.

The following additional building-operation expenses were incurred during April:

Repairs (carpentry) April 10	$ 146
Maintenance service	980 per month
Supplies	400
Utilities	700
Taxes per year prorated each month	7,200
Painting	250
Miscellaneous expenses	975

Proceed as follows:

1. Using the template disk, fill in the spreadsheet information regarding the ownership of the building, including costs, mortgage, purchase, and tax assessment.

2. Construct a form so that you can conveniently record all income and expenses for the operation of this building.

3. Using the form, prepare a report showing the income, expenses, and net income for April.

Chapter 21

Payroll and Tax Documents

LEARNING OBJECTIVES

After studying this chapter and completing the activities, you will be able to:

1. Understand the importance of payroll records.
2. Compute earnings, deductions, and net pay.
3. Identify the various forms required for payroll maintenance.
4. Understand the importance of confidentiality and accuracy in the preparation of payroll and tax records.
5. Understand the administrative assistant's role in assisting the employer with income tax records.

INTRODUCTION

In a small firm, the administrative assistant may have complete responsibility for the payroll. This includes keeping time records, writing payroll checks, and filing the necessary forms and reports with the proper government agencies.

Payroll preparation in most firms has been computerized. In large companies a special payroll department handles most of this work; nevertheless, the administrative assistant is often responsible for some input to the payroll system. The extent of your payroll responsibilities, therefore, will depend on the size and function of the office in which you work. If your responsibilities include payroll work, you should be familiar with federal and state legislation governing payroll records.

Whether or not your work includes payroll responsibilities, your employer may depend upon your assistance in preparing annual income tax returns. This does not mean that you must be a tax expert. It does mean, though, that throughout the year you should collect pertinent income tax data so that they are available at tax time. Tax laws change with the economic and political climate, and these changes affect your employer's money management strategies. As an effective administrative assistant, you will want to update your knowledge of tax regulations to ensure that you, as well as your manager, have every tax advantage.

▶ *Procedure*

Keeping a record of income and deductible items throughout the year can be of inestimable help to your employer at tax time.

PAYROLL PROCEDURES

Because employees expect to be paid regularly, the administrative assistant in charge of payroll is responsible for the maintenance of essential payroll records. These records are necessary to determine pensions, vacations, seniority, eligibility for company benefits, wage and salary increases, promotions, and employment references. They also enable the executive to determine when to hold performance reviews and which employees to transfer, promote, or dismiss. In addition to maintaining these vital records, you should understand the forms and reports required by the Federal Insurance Contributions Act (social security) and the Fair Labor Standards Act as well as pertinent local legislation.

All payroll information is confidential. From the calculation of the first time card to the writing of the payroll check, payroll facts must be protected. Computation sheets and one-use ribbons must be destroyed to keep inquisitive persons from obtaining payroll information and possibly using it to damage morale. No matter how tempting, the professional administrative assistant never discusses payroll information and is adept at dealing with coworkers who persist in inquiring about the income of others. If you are interrupted while working on the payroll, do not leave your workstation until you have placed all confidential information in a locked drawer and have cleared your computer screen. If you key payroll data on a microcomputer, arrange your workstation in such a way that visitors cannot read the screen while you work. Computers containing payroll data should be equipped with a locking device to prevent another person from accessing this information. Examples of these locking devices are Nightwatch and Macintosh's MacGuardian. Diskettes containing payroll information should also be protected. See Figure 21-1.

Fig. 21-1 Locking devices for disk drives prevent computer access to confidential information. *Data Security from Qualtec Data Products.*

Fair Labor Standards Act

There are primarily two classes of remuneration: *wages* at a rate per hour and *salaries* at a rate per week or month. Persons receiving wages are usually paid only for the hours they work; salaried personnel are usually paid for the full pay period even though they may be absent from work for brief periods. To differentiate, employees are called *hourly* or *salaried.* Office employees are frequently paid salaries, although paying office employees on an hourly basis is also common.

Most hourly employees are covered by the provisions of the **Fair Labor Standards Act.** This act sets a minimum hourly wage and requires each employer to keep a record of the hours worked by each hourly employee. Also, every hourly employee must be paid at least 1 1/2 times the regular hourly rate for all hours worked in excess of 40 hours. For example, an employee who makes $10 an hour must be paid $15 an hour for overtime. Salaried employees are excluded from the provisions of the Fair Labor Standards Act. Some companies pay overtime for all work in excess of a specific number of hours worked per day. In other companies, no overtime is paid salaried workers; compensatory time off is given instead.

The Fair Labor Standards Act does not require the filing of overtime reports to any government office, but records must be kept on file for three years on hourly (or nonexempt) employees for perusal any time a government examiner chooses to inspect them. Detailed information about this legislation may be obtained from the nearest office of the Wage and Hour Division, Department of Labor.

Social Security

In 1935, Congress passed the Social Security Act to provide income when earnings are reduced due to retirement, disability, or death of a spouse. Social security is a tax based on earnings and, as such, represents a payroll deduction. Since 1935, the Social Security Act has been amended several times.

Under the social security system most business, farm, and household employees and self-employed persons receive an income in old age and survivor benefits in the event of death. Social security also provides a nationwide system of unemployment insurance and hospital and medical insurance benefits (Medicare) for persons age 65 and over.

To cover social security benefits, both employees and employers are taxed equally. Medical insurance (for persons age 65 and over) is optional and is financed jointly by contributions from the retired insured person and from the federal government.

Social Security Numbers.   Each employer and employee must obtain a social security number for government and accounting purposes. The number on your card is used to keep a record of your earnings. An employer's social security number is called an **employer identification number.** Under the provisions of the Tax Reform Act of 1986, everyone age 2 or older must now have a social security number.

To obtain a social security number, file an application with the nearest social security office or with the post office. You will receive a card stamped with your number. If the card is lost, a duplicate can be obtained. If you change your name or need to make other changes, contact the Social Security

Administration. The administrative assistant may find it convenient to have the following social security forms on hand:

Application for a Social Security Number (or Replacement of Lost Card)
Request for Change in Social Security Records
Request for Statement of Earnings

The Social Security Administration recommends that each employee request a statement of earnings every three years to make sure that individual earnings have been reported properly. This information can be obtained by sending a signed letter with your date of birth and social security number to P.O. Box 57, Baltimore, MD 20203, or by filing Form SSA-7004-PC with the Social Security Administration. A postcard with prepaid postage is also available for this purpose at any social security office.

 Procedure

The Social Security Administration suggests that each employee request a statement of earnings every three years to ensure that individual earnings have been reported properly.

FICA (Federal Insurance Contributions Act) Tax Deductions. Amounts withheld from employees' earnings (for social security) under this act are based on a percentage of earned wages. For the past few years, this percentage and the maximum wage base against which the FICA tax is applied have increased. Under the Social Security Act both the employer and the employee pay FICA *taxes* at the same rate. The tax rate, for example, was 7.15 percent in 1987 and 7.65 percent in 1992. Self-employed workers paid 15.30 percent of their earnings. Similarly, the wage base increased from $43,800 in 1987 to $60,600 in 1994. Prior to 1991, the social security and Medicare tax rates were combined and the wage bases were the same. In 1991, the tax rate for social security changed to 12.40 percent and the Medicare base to 2.90 percent.

To show you how this works, a person whose 1994 income was $63,600 earned $3,000 on which no social security tax was levied. Deductions for social security ended at $60,600, the wage base for that year. Should you have the responsibility for payroll preparation, you should check with your local social security office for current figures.

FICA tax is deducted from an employee's wage each payday; these amounts are accumulated and forwarded, together with the employer's FICA tax payments, to the Internal Revenue Service Center for the region. To illustrate, assume that an employee earns $200 a week and is paid at the end of each week. At the rate of 7.65 percent, $15.30 would be deducted from the employee's pay, and the employer would contribute an equal amount. At the end of the quarter (13 weeks), the employer would remit $397.80 to the government.

Self-employed persons (farmers, architects, and contractors, for example) contribute to social security at a higher rate than other wage earners because they are, in effect, employers and employees. Self-employed persons pay their FICA tax simultaneously with their income tax.

Unemployment Compensation Tax

Employers are subject to an unemployment tax. This tax provides funds from which unemployment compensation can be paid to unemployed workers. In most states unemployment taxes are paid only by the employer. The employer must pay both a federal tax and a state tax to provide funds for unemployment compensation. The state tax rate varies from state to state, but the federal portion of the tax is calculated at 6.2 percent on a wage base ($7,000 in 1994) paid to each employee per calendar year.

Employers can take a credit against the Federal Unemployment Tax (FUTA) for amounts they have paid into state unemployment funds. Consequently, the federal government receives a very small portion of the unemployment tax. This credit cannot exceed 5.4 percent of taxable wages.

In states where an unemployment tax is levied on employees as well as employers, it is deducted by the employer from the employees' wages. The amounts deducted from employees' pay and the employer's contribution are submitted to the state on a quarterly basis. Special forms are used to report these contributions.

Income Tax Deductions

The federal government requires employers to withhold an advance payment on income tax from an employee's wages. Amounts withheld are remitted to the regional Internal Revenue Service Center at the same time FICA taxes are paid. The term "wages" in this context incorporates wages, salaries, commissions, bonuses, and vacation allowances. The following forms are needed for income tax deduction purposes:

The Internal Revenue Service provides an order blank for ordering forms.

Form W-2	Wage and Tax Statement
Form W-3	Transmittal of Income and Tax Statements
Form W-4	Employee's Withholding Allowance Certificate
Form 940	Employer's Annual Federal Unemployment Tax Return
Form 941	Employer's Quarterly Federal Tax Return
Form 8027	Employer's Information Return on Tip Income and Tip Allocation
Form 8109	Federal Tax Deposit Coupon (to accompany employer's payment of quarterly taxes to the Internal Revenue Service)
Form 1099-MISC	Miscellaneous Income (This form is used to report payments of $600 or more per calendar year to people not treated as employees—consultants, subcontractors, and the like—for services performed.)

The amount of income tax withheld depends on earnings and the number of personal exemptions the taxpayer claims. Each employee must file an Employee's Withholding Allowance Certificate (Form W-4) with the employer immediately upon reporting for work to claim exemptions. In addition to one personal allowance, the following exemptions, subject to revision, may be claimed:

1. An allowance for a spouse (unless the spouse claims his or her own exemption)
2. An allowance for each dependent (unless the employee's spouse claims them)
3. An allowance if the taxpayer or spouse is 65 or older, or blind.

The amount of tax withheld is then computed from a table provided by the Internal Revenue Service.

A number of cities and states tax personal income. The percentage of deduction and the form of payment vary. One city may have the employer deduct 1 percent from every payroll check issued and remit these deductions at the end of each quarter. Some states and cities require individuals to file annual income tax returns.

Other Payroll Deductions

In addition to the deductions required by federal and state legislation, other payroll deductions for hospital care insurance (hospitalization), group insurance premiums, stock and bond purchases, etc., may be made. In most firms, these deductions are voluntary, and usually the authorization for these deductions may be canceled by the employee at any time.

A paycheck includes an itemized listing of all deductions taken from the employee's wages. This information is provided on a stub attached to the check which may be removed and retained by the employee when the check is cashed or deposited. By January 31 of each year the employer is required to furnish each employee with a Wage and Tax Statement (Form W-2) that shows the employee's total earnings and tax deductions for the preceding year. One copy of Form W-2 must be attached to the individual's income tax return form.

Time Records

Some hourly workers and some salaried workers use a time clock to punch in and out each time they enter and leave their places of employment. At the end of the payroll period, cards are collected and wages are computed from the time clock stampings. Figure 21-2 is an example of a time card.

Instead of using a time clock, salaried employees may sign in and out, or the administrative assistant may be responsible for checking each person

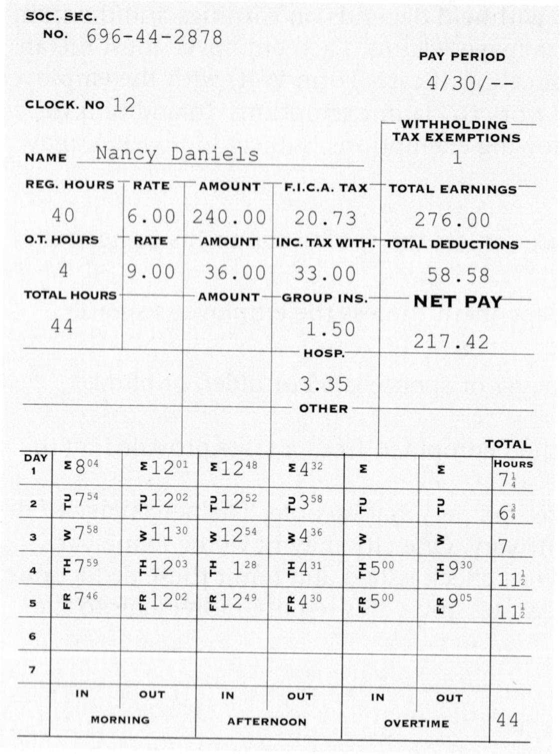
SOC. SEC. NO. 696-44-2878

PAY PERIOD 4/30/--

CLOCK. NO 12

WITHHOLDING TAX EXEMPTIONS 1

NAME Nancy Daniels

REG. HOURS	RATE	AMOUNT	F.I.C.A. TAX	TOTAL EARNINGS
40	6.00	240.00	20.73	276.00
O.T. HOURS	RATE	AMOUNT	INC. TAX WITH.	TOTAL DEDUCTIONS
4	9.00	36.00	33.00	58.58
TOTAL HOURS		AMOUNT	GROUP INS.	NET PAY
44			1.50	217.42
			HOSP.	
			3.35	
			OTHER	

DAY	MORNING IN	MORNING OUT	AFTERNOON IN	AFTERNOON OUT	OVERTIME IN	OVERTIME OUT	TOTAL HOURS
1	M 8^{04}	M 12^{01}	M 12^{48}	M 4^{32}	M	M	7$\frac{1}{4}$
2	TU 7^{54}	TU 12^{02}	TU 12^{52}	TU 3^{58}	TU	TU	6$\frac{3}{4}$
3	W 7^{58}	W 11^{30}	W 12^{54}	W 4^{36}	W	W	7
4	TH 7^{59}	TH 12^{03}	TH 1^{28}	TH 4^{31}	TH 5^{00}	TH 9^{30}	11$\frac{1}{2}$
5	FR 7^{46}	FR 12^{02}	FR 12^{49}	FR 4^{30}	FR 5^{00}	FR 9^{05}	11$\frac{1}{2}$
6							
7							
							44

Fig. 21-2 A time clock was used to stamp this card each time the employee arrived for and left work.

in and out daily on a time sheet. Time records are not always necessary for computing salaries, but such records may be the basis for paying overtime earnings or balancing compensatory time off with the overtime worked. There are various reports, however, that require records of the overtime and the compensatory time off for salaried employees.

This information, as well as the payroll register and the employees' earnings records, may be stored in a computer database so that the data may be retrieved when periodic reports are required. Some businesses use spreadsheet software for processing payroll reports.

Payroll Records

Federal legislation requires employers to keep payroll records. These records usually include a payroll register similar to those shown in Figures 21-3(a) and 21-3(b). In addition, an employee's earnings record (see Figure 21-4 on page 572) is usually kept for each employee for at least four years. (Pension records are usually retained permanently.) Data from the payroll register are transferred periodically to the employee's earnings record, preferably each pay period. The employee's earnings record provides quarterly totals for the

Fig. 21-3(a) Standard forms for payroll registers may be purchased at a stationery store.

PAYROLL REGISTER

FOR WEEK ENDING _March 31, 19--_

	NAME	M/S	EXEMPTIONS	TOTAL HOURS	HOURLY RATE	REGULAR EARNINGS	EARNINGS FOR OVERTIME	TOTAL EARNINGS	DEDUCTIONS F.I.C.A. TAX	INCOME TAX WITHHELD	HEALTH INS.	NET AMOUNT PAID
1.	Allen, Joanne	S	1	42	15.50	620.00	46.50	666.50	50.05	120.00	18.00	478.45
2.	Bauer, Thomas	M	2	40	14.00	560.00	—	560.00	42.06	64.00	28.00	425.94
3.	Chiang, Rhonda	S	1	40	12.00	480.00	—	480.00	36.05	73.00	18.00	352.95
20.	Scott, Martha	M	2	40	13.00	520.00	—	520.00	39.05	58.00	28.00	394.95
21.	Weyer, Luis	S	1	48	12.00	480.00	144.00	624.00	48.86	112.00	18.00	447.14
	YEARLY					12,640.00	1,866.00	14,506.00	1,089.40	1,980.00	460.00	10,976.60

Fig. 21-3(b) Payroll forms may be prepared using spreadsheet software and stored for future use.

Payroll Register

For Week Ending May 14, 19--

Name	M/S	Exemp	Total Hours	Hourly Rate	Regular Earnings	Overtime Earnings	Total Earnings	Deductions FICA	Income Tax	Health Insurance	Net Amount Paid
Bice, Bill	M	2	45	13.00	$520.00	97.50	617.50	47.24	43.00	23.00	504.26
Jessee, Bruce	M	3	38	11.55	$438.90		438.90	33.58	34.00	23.00	348.32
Jessee, Mark	M	5	46	12.85	$514.00	115.65	629.65	48.17	42.00	23.00	516.48
Collins, Linda	M	2	42	17.25	$690.00	51.75	741.75	56.74	40.00	23.00	622.01
Santana, Kelly	S	2	44	14.20	$568.00	85.20	653.20	49.97	56.00	13.00	534.23
Williams, Bill	S	0	41	9.50	$380.00	14.25	394.25	30.16	70.00	13.00	281.09
TOTAL					3110.90	364.35	3475.25	265.86	285.00	118.00	2806.39

required quarterly tax reports and for annual totals. Even though the laws affecting payroll taxes change from time to time, comprehensive records, similar to those illustrated, provide the basic data from which to compile almost any type of payroll tax report. A calendar of payroll procedures, suggested records retention schedules, and explanations of government requirements concerning payroll procedures are summarized in Figure 21-5 on page 573. If any due date falls on Saturday, Sunday, or a legal holiday, use the next regular workday for submitting quarterly tax payments.

EMPLOYEE'S EARNINGS RECORD

BARRINGTONS, INC.

EARNINGS RECORD

EMPLOYEE NO. 9-8970

NAME Scott, Martha   ADDRESS 261 Riverhill Dr. Atlanta, GA   EARNINGS RATE $13.00 hr.

SOCIAL SECURITY NO. 561-21-4800   OCCUPATION Word Processing Specialist   NUMBER OF ALLOWANCES 2   MARITAL STATUS M

NO.	WEEK ENDING	TOT. HOURS REG.	TOT. HOURS OVER.	EARNINGS REG.	EARNINGS OVER.	EARNINGS TOTAL	FICA	INCOME TAX	HEALTH INS.	TOTAL	NET PAY AMOUNT
1	1/15	40	—	520 00		520 00	39 05	58 00	28 00	125 05	394 95
2	1/31	40	—	520 00		520 00	39 05	58 00	28 00	125 05	394 95
3	2/15	40	2	520 00	39 00	559 00	41 98	62 00	28 00	131 98	427 02
4	2/28	40	—	520 00		520 00	39 05	58 00	28 00	125 05	394 95
5	3/15	40	—	520 00		520 00	39 05	58 00	28 00	125 05	394 95
6	3/31	40	—	520 00		520 00	39 05	58 00	28 00	125 05	394 95
7	QUARTER TOTALS					3159 00	237 23	352 00	168 00	757 23	2401 77
	YEARLY TOTALS										

Filing with Magnetic Media

The Internal Revenue Service, the Social Security Administration, and state tax departments encourage employers to use magnetic media to file reports. Details on how to file tax data electronically are available at most IRS and Social Security Administration offices. You may also obtain information on electronic filing by dialing a toll-free Tele-Tax telephone number in any state, the District of Columbia, and Puerto Rico. Toll-free numbers are listed at the end of the 1040 forms and instructions. Tele-Tax topic numbers designed to answer most federal tax questions are also listed.

The IRS now requires employers who file at least 250 returns, including W-2 forms, to use magnetic media. However, if filing on magnetic media causes undue hardship, the employer may be able to get a waiver of this requirement by filing Form 8508.

Employers who wish to file with magnetic media must obtain IRS approval for using their particular medium. To obtain this approval, write to Internal Revenue Service, Martinsburg Computing Center, P.O. Box 1359, Martinsburg, WV 25401-1359. Use this address for Forms 1099, 1098, 5498, or W-2G. Write to Social Security Administration, P.O. Box 2317, Baltimore, MD 21235, for Form W-2, Attention: Magnetic Media Group.

THE EXECUTIVE'S INCOME TAX

The Tax Reform Act of October 1986 lowered income tax rates and changed the tax structure. The act altered dramatically the laws that govern whether

CALENDAR OF PAYROLL PROCEDURES

On Hiring a New Employee

Have the employee complete *Form W-4*. Record employee's social security number and the number of his or her exemptions. File *Form W-4* in a safe place.

On Each Payment of Wages to an Employee

Withhold the proper amount of income tax and FICA tax by referring to instructions and tables supplied by the Internal Revenue Service and by the city and state (if necessary). Make all other authorized deductions. On a payroll check stub or on a separate statement, record total wages, amount and kind of each deduction, and net amount for each employee.

Within 15 Days after the Close of Any Month of Any Calendar Quarter

If withheld income tax and FICA tax totals $500 or more, but is less than $3,000, by the last day of any month in a calendar quarter, the full amount must be deposited in a Federal Reserve Bank or other authorized bank by the 15th of the following month. (Use *Form 8901*.) If the total amount of un-deposited tax is less than $500 by the last day of any month of a calendar quarter, the full amount may be paid with *Form 941*.

On or before Each April 30, July 31, October 31, and January 31

File *Form 941* or *Form 941-E* with the regional Internal Revenue Service Center. Remit with it the full amount due; that is, the total amount of income tax and FICA tax withheld during the quarter less the total deposited with *Form 8109*. State unemployment returns are usually filed at this time.

On or before January 31 and at the End of an Employee's Employment

Prepare *Form W-2* showing the total wages, total wages subject to withholding for income tax, the amount of income tax withheld, the total wage subject to FICA tax; and the amount of FICA withheld. The government-prepared *Form W-2* consists of four copies. Two copies are given to the employee, one copy to the Internal Revenue Service Center, and one copy to the employer. Some large firms print their own W-2 forms with five or six copies. These additional copies are given to the city and state (for records of income tax withheld) if they require them.

On or before January 31 of Each Year

File *Form 940* and *Form 940-EZ* to report payment of federal unemployment taxes. In general, employers are required to file state unemployment tax returns quarterly.

By February 28 of Each Year

File *Form W-3*. It is a summary of total income tax withheld and is used as a point of comparison between taxes withheld as reported on all W-2s and on all quarterly 941s—Employer's Quarterly Federal Tax Return.

Retain payroll records for a period of four years.

Fig. 21-5 Employers must file a number of forms throughout the year for income and FICA tax purposes.

income is taxable or nontaxable. Changes were also made in exemptions, deductions, filing requirements for dependents, and individual retirement accounts. Several provisions of prior tax laws were repealed by the act.

Receiving credit for political contributions, excluding certain dividend income, and deducting general sales taxes are no longer allowed.

Although the administrative assistant is not expected to be a tax expert, knowing what constitutes income and deductions will enable you to assist the executive in saving on taxes. Some of the ways you can assist your executive in the preparation of the annual income tax return are as follows:

Be alert to items that the executive must report as income and to items that may be taken as deductions, credits, and adjustments.

Accumulate such items throughout the year with supporting papers and records for use at income tax time.

Keep a supply of appropriate current tax forms and schedules.

See that returns are filed and payments made.

▶ *Procedure*

Should you have questions about tax-related problems, call the IRS toll-free number listed in Circular E—Employer's Tax Guide.

The performance of these duties demands a basic understanding of what constitutes taxable income, which deductions are allowable, and how to organize tax-related materials.

Income Tax Files

Income tax files generally consist of income and deduction records, supporting computations and memorandums, previous years' tax returns, and a current income tax file folder or portfolio. To avoid mixing current tax materials with those of previous years, use large expansion portfolios and file all income tax material related to a given year in that portfolio. Label the folder "Federal Income Tax, 19—." All supporting records for income tax returns should be retained for several years.

At the beginning of each year, set up a portfolio for tax data (bills, canceled checks, reports, itemized listings, receipts). Then, when it is time to prepare the executive's tax return, all the essential records and reference materials will have been accumulated.

Records of Taxable Income

Whether the record of the executive's personal income is maintained manually in a special record book or on a computer, each item must be individually recorded. Records of taxable income consist mainly of deposit slips to which identifying notations have been attached—receipts, statements of earnings and deductions, dividend distribution statements, statements of interest income on savings accounts, etc. Since personal income derives from many sources and accumulates at irregular intervals, the administrative assistant must be able to identify taxable income and see that a notation on each income item is entered in the tax portfolio or the computer.

Wages, Salaries, and Other Compensation. Gross earnings (earnings before deductions for income tax, retirement contributions, employee pensions, hospitalization, insurance, etc.) from wages, salaries, commissions, fees, tips, and similar sources of income are taxable. Awards and prizes of money or merchandise, amounts received in reimbursement for expenses in excess of actual business expenses incurred, and bonuses are also taxable income.

Dividends. Cash dividends are generally taxable. Stock dividends, however, may or may not be taxable. Since some dividends may be wholly or partially exempt from taxation, a complete record of all dividends should be maintained. Dividends that are not taxable can be eliminated when the tax return is prepared.

At the beginning of the year, corporations usually send stockholders a form (Form 1099-INT) to report the total amount of dividends paid to the addressed stockholder during the previous year. Watch for and file this information in the income tax portfolio. If your employer uses a broker to manage investments, the broker provides a detailed statement of reportable dividends and interest. These statements are helpful in keeping track of income from investments and determining what is reportable at tax time.

Interest. With the exception of interest on tax-exempt securities, all interest is taxable. Thus, interest received from corporate bonds, mortgage bonds, notes, bank deposits, personal loans, accounts in savings and loan associations, and most U.S. government bonds should be itemized and recorded.

If your employer has investments that earn tax-exempt interest, you should keep complete records of such interest. Under the Tax Reform Act, the tax return must show all tax-exempt interest received or accrued during the tax year. This is an information-reporting requirement and does *not* make the interest taxable.

Gains on Sale or Exchange of Property. Prior to 1986, one of the best ways to save tax dollars was to earn long-term capital gains on the sale of property—real estate, stocks, and other securities. (Long-term capital gains are those earned on investments held more than one year.) The full amount of long-term capital gains must be reported as income. In 1994 the maximum rate at which these gains were taxed was 28 percent. Profit from the sale of property (including real estate, stocks, and other securities) is fully taxable.

Fringe Benefits. Many company-provided fringe benefits must be reported as income. Included are such items as an employer-provided car, aircraft, vacation trip, country club membership, discounts on services or property, tickets to sporting events or other entertainment, and group life insurance premiums. The administrative assistant who keeps records of these items in the tax portfolio or in the computer can save his or her employer a great deal of frustration at tax time. Although it will be difficult for you to know which benefits should be reported, it is better to have too many records than too few.

Rents. Income received from rents is taxable. The owner of property from which rents are received is entitled to deductions for depreciation, mortgage interest, taxes, repairs, insurance, agents' commissions, and other ordinary and necessary operating expenses. Property records should be kept on each rental unit owned.

Royalties. Royalties include income received from writings, works of art, musical compositions, inventions, and patents. All expenses incurred in producing a property that provides a royalty income are deductible.

Income from a Profession or a Personally Owned Business. All income from a profession or a personally owned business is taxable after deductions for all ordinary, necessary operating expenses have been made. For example, if your manager owns a computer supplies store, operated by his or her parents, income from the store would be taxed after expenses for salaries, rent, utilities, etc., have been deducted.

Nontaxable Income. The administrative assistant should strive to keep as complete a record of all income as the working situation will permit. Incomes that are not taxable or incomes from which deductions can be made should be examined and properly excluded or recorded by the tax consultant at the time the tax return is prepared. The administrative assistant should not assume the responsibility of judging whether or not income is taxable.

Records of Tax Credits and Deductions

A detailed record of allowable tax credits and deductions should be kept in the tax portfolio. Allowable tax credits and deductions lower a taxpayer's taxable income and include such things as charitable contributions and child care expenses. Because tax laws change frequently, some existing authorized deductions may be eliminated, reduced, or modified.

Alimony. Alimony or other payments in lieu of alimony under a decree of divorce or of separate maintenance are allowable as a personal deduction. Such deductions are taken in the year of payment by the spouse making the payment but are taxable income to the spouse receiving the payment. Child support payments, however, are neither deductible nor taxable.

Bad Debts. Nonbusiness bad debt losses are deductible as short-term capital losses if they are supported by documentation and are nonfamily loans.

Casualty or Theft Losses. Losses resulting from fire, storm, flood, or theft of nonbusiness property are deductible if they are not reimbursed by insurance. The amount of damage to the taxpayer's automobile resulting from an accident or theft and not covered by insurance would be deductible. The taxpayer must absorb the first $100 of each casualty and theft loss. Your employer may deduct such losses only when the total amount lost in any year (less the $100 per casualty) exceeds 10 percent of the adjusted gross income. (*Adjusted gross income* is total earnings from wages plus other income, such as interest, dividends, royalties, and the like, less deductions for payments such as alimony and penalties for early withdrawals from certain savings accounts, for example.)

Child and Dependent Care Credit.   A tax credit is allowed under certain conditions for expenditures for child care. A deduction for disabled dependents is also possible up to a designated amount.

Contributions.   Contributions to organizations or institutions devoted primarily to charitable, religious, educational, scientific, or literary purposes are deductible. Examples are contributions to schools and colleges, churches, hospitals, American Cancer Society, Girl Scouts, Salvation Army, and United Way. Charitable gifts to individuals, political organizations, social clubs, or labor unions are not deductible.

Nonreimbursed expenses for the use of an automobile, postage, out-of-town telephone calls, etc., may be incurred while serving in a campaign to collect funds for a charitable, religious, or educational organization. These expenses are considered a contribution to the organization and are deductible as such.

IRAs.   An individual retirement account (IRA) is a personal savings plan that permits workers to set aside money for retirement. The Tax Reform Act of 1986 placed limitations on the deductions that may be allowed for these contributions. The deduction a person can take depends on whether he or she is covered by an employer-paid retirement plan and the amount of earned income. Contributions to IRAs may be wholly or partially deductible depending upon the circumstances. Nondeductible contributions may be made to an IRA.

Interest.   Not all interest paid on personal debts is deductible. Interest paid on bank loans, installment loans on automobiles, and credit card purchases is not deductible. Mortgage interest is deductible as long as it is on a person's main residence or a second home.

Medical and Dental Expenses.   Medical and dental expenses are not restricted to those of the taxpayer but may also include the taxpayer's family and dependents. Medical insurance premiums and medical expenses in excess of 7.5 percent of adjusted gross income are deductible. If premiums are paid by an employer, they cannot be deducted by the taxpayer. To claim these deductions the taxpayer is required to furnish the name and address of each person or agency to whom medical and dental expenses were paid, the amount, and the approximate date of payment.

Taxes.   Personal taxes (state, local, or foreign), income taxes, personal property taxes, and real estate taxes are deductible. State sales tax, however, is no longer deductible.

Business Expenses.   Traveling expenses incurred in connection with one's business or profession for which reimbursement is not received are deductible. These expenses include airline tickets, excess baggage charges, airport transportation services, car rentals, automobile expenses, bus and subway fares, taxi fares, meals (only if away overnight), hotel/motel expenses, tips, telephone/telegraph expenses, laundry, and secretarial services. These expenses are deductible only to the extent that they exceed 2 percent of a taxpayer's adjusted gross income. Figure 21-6 shows Schedule A—

Fig. 21-6 Taxpayers who itemize their deductions must complete Schedule A.

SCHEDULES A&B	Schedule A—Itemized Deductions	OMB No. 1545-0074
(Form 1040)	(Schedule B is on back)	**1993**
Department of the Treasury Internal Revenue Service (B)	► Attach to Form 1040. ► See Instructions for Schedules A and B (Form 1040).	Attachment Sequence No. **07**

Name(s) shown on Form 1040 | Your social security number

Medical and Dental Expenses		Caution: *Do not include expenses reimbursed or paid by others.*	
	1	Medical and dental expenses (see page A-1)	1
	2	Enter amount from Form 1040, line 32. [2]	
	3	Multiply line 2 above by 7.5% (.075)	3
	4	Subtract line 3 from line 1. If zero or less, enter -0- . . ►	4

Taxes You Paid (See page A-1.)	5	State and local income taxes	5
	6	Real estate taxes (see page A-2)	6
	7	Other taxes. List—include personal property taxes ►	7
	8	Add lines 5 through 7 . . . . ►	8

Interest You Paid (See page A-2.)	9a	Home mortgage interest and points reported to you on Form 1098	9a
	b	Home mortgage interest not reported to you on Form 1098. If paid to the person from whom you bought the home, see page A-3 and show that person's name, identifying no., and address ►	
Note: Personal interest is not deductible.		....	9b
	10	Points not reported to you on Form 1098. See page A-3 for special rules	10
	11	Investment interest. If required, attach Form 4952. (See page A-3.)	11
	12	Add lines 9a through 11 . . . . ►	12

Gifts to Charity (See page A-3.)		Caution: *If you made a charitable contribution and received a benefit in return, see page A-3.*	
	13	Contributions by cash or check	13
	14	Other than by cash or check. If over $500, you **MUST** attach Form 8283	14
	15	Carryover from prior year	15
	16	Add lines 13 through 15 . . . . ►	16

Casualty and Theft Losses	17	Casualty or theft loss(es). Attach Form 4684. (See page A-4.) . . . . . ►	17

Moving Expenses	18	Moving expenses. Attach Form 3903 or 3903-F. (See page A-4.) . . . . ►	18

Job Expenses and Most Other Miscellaneous Deductions (See page A-5 for expenses to deduct here.)	19	Unreimbursed employee expenses—job travel, union dues, job education, etc. If required, you **MUST** attach Form 2106. (See page A-4.) ►	19
	20	Other expenses—investment, tax preparation, safe deposit box, etc. List type and amount ►	20
	21	Add lines 19 and 20	21
	22	Enter amount from Form 1040, line 32. [22]	
	23	Multiply line 22 above by 2% (.02)	23
	24	Subtract line 23 from line 21. If zero or less, enter -0- . . ►	24

Other Miscellaneous Deductions	25	Other—from list on page A-5. List type and amount ►	25

Total Itemized Deductions	26	Is the amount on Form 1040, line 32, more than $108,450 (more than $54,225 if married filing separately)?	
		• **NO.** Your deduction is not limited. Add lines 4, 8, 12, 16, 17, 18, 24, and 25 and enter the total here. Also enter on Form 1040, line 34, the **larger** of this amount or your standard deduction.	► 26
		• **YES.** Your deduction may be limited. See page A-5 for the amount to enter.	

For Paperwork Reduction Act Notice, see Form 1040 instructions. | Cat. No. 12611D | Schedule A (Form 1040) 1993

Itemized Deductions, which must be completed by taxpayers who itemize deductions.

Travel expense reports are important tax-reporting documents. Expenses may be forgotten if they are not recorded promptly. At the completion of each business trip, the administrative assistant should obtain from the executive data needed to complete a report of travel expenses. Unless the expenses are reimbursed by the corporation, the report should be filed with receipts in an income tax portfolio.

Only 50 percent of entertainment expenses for business purposes (customers, clients, etc.) are deductible. Expenses for the spouse of an out-of-town guest may also be included. Meals, tips, and theater and other tickets are recognized entertainment costs. Even club dues are deductible, provided the club is used primarily for entertaining business guests. Deductions for entertainment, however, are subject to detailed examination by the Internal Revenue Service. Many companies place limits on travel expenses based upon management level. These limits include a daily amount for meals, lodging, and entertainment. Any verified amount spent by your employer for business purposes that is not reimbursed by the company is deductible. A detailed record, similar to the one shown in Figure 21-7, should be prepared and supported by receipts if the total cost is $25 or more. Guests and business connections should be identified. At the end of each day, the administrative assistant should check the appointment book and flag any appointment that involved deductible expenses. The next day, the needed information can be obtained from the executive. The report can be prepared and filed with attached receipts in the income tax portfolio.

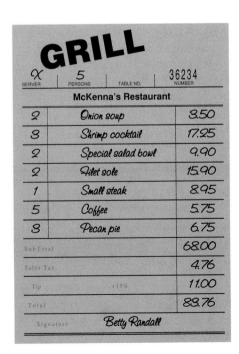

GUEST LIST

(Business Entertainment)

Date   April 10, 19--

Guest(s)   George Snyder
            Frank Fletcher
            Mary Lossi
            John Malinowski
            (All of V. M. Massey Co.)

Explanation Lunch at McKenna's to discuss
            contract renewal

Total cost $72.76 plus 15% tip, $83.76
            Receipt attached.

GRILL

X SERVER	5 PERSONS	TABLE NO.	36234 NUMBER
McKenna's Restaurant			

2	Onion soup	8.50
3	Shrimp cocktail	17.25
2	Special salad bowl	9.90
2	Filet sole	15.90
1	Small steak	8.95
5	Coffee	5.75
3	Pecan pie	6.75
SubTotal		68.00
Sales Tax		4.76
Tip	+15%	11.00
Total		83.76
Signature	Betty Randall	

Fig. 21-7 Entertainment expenses of $25 or more must be supported with a receipt.

Business gifts up to $25 in value per recipient per year are also deductible. Each gift deduction, however, must be supported by a record showing the date, the cost, the reason for giving, and the name and business connection of the recipient.

Most executives use credit cards to pay for travel and entertainment expenses. The administrative assistant should identify each travel and entertainment expenditure on the monthly credit card statement and file it, or a copy, in the income tax portfolio.

Other Deductions.   Other allowable deductions that apply in specific cases are safe-deposit box rentals (if income-producing items are stored in the box), subscriptions to investment publications, cost of uniforms and their upkeep, union dues, moving expenses (within certain limitations), and the cost of job-related educational expenses. These miscellaneous deductions are allowable only to the extent that they exceed 2 percent of adjusted gross income. The administrative assistant should keep a master list, either manually or in the computer, of deductible items that are pertinent to the executive's situation.

Assisting Your Executive with an IRS Audit

If your executive prepares his or her own tax return and is faced with an IRS audit, your "assist role" in financial matters will never be more needed nor more appreciated. If someone else prepares your executive's tax return, your involvement in an audit may be minimal; nevertheless, your efficiency in accumulating a complete and accurate record of tax-related items can save your executive time, money, and stress.

When returns are filed with the Internal Revenue Service Centers, they are first checked for mathematical and clerical errors. If such an error is detected, notice of the correction is sent to the taxpayer requesting payment of any tax due or enclosing a refund for any overpayment. This is a simple matter of correspondence, but your tax file could save your executive time in verifying IRS calculations.

The IRS uses a computerized system that identifies, through mathematical formulas, those returns containing claims for refunds over $200,000 and returns with mathematical errors that cannot be resolved without examining the taxpayer's records.

These are called high-level audit items. Average-level audit items that might initiate an audit include an increase of three or more exemptions, a capital loss over $10,000, and moving expenses exceeding $5,000.

The IRS randomly selects returns to be audited. This program is designed to evaluate taxpayers' compliance with tax regulations. For example, in cases where taxpayers deduct charitable contributions and medical expenses that are not allowable, the returns are sent to the IRS Regional Service Center for examination and correction by correspondence. Those returns judged to have the greatest need for audit are sent to the IRS district audit division, which will initiate one of two types of audits. The **office audit** may be made by correspondence or office interviews. With most of these returns, a short conversation will solve the problem. If the errors are more serious, IRS may conduct a **field audit** by inviting the taxpayer to the IRS office or by calling on the taxpayer at home or place of business.

Legally, IRS has three years after a return is filed to assess any additional taxes. If the taxpayer disagrees with the results of an audit, the case can be appealed.

Searching for substantiating documents, retrieving canceled checks, receipts, reports, and the like to satisfy an IRS audit are time-consuming, expensive, and stressful. Assistance in compiling tax data that are current, accurate, and complete provides the administrative assistant with a visibility that no other aspect of the job affords.

Tax Guides and Forms

Studying an income tax guide will help the administrative assistant be of more assistance to the executive in handling income tax materials. The administrative assistant should also become familiar with various tax forms, know how to choose the proper ones, and know where to find them. Two important individual income tax forms are shown in Figure 21-8. Form 1040 (shown in Figure 21-8a), also known as the long form, is a two-page return used for any amount of income. All deductions are listed in full, and all computations are made by the taxpayer. The appropriate schedules must also be filed with Form 1040. Available on request from the IRS, the schedules include:

Schedule A for reporting itemized deductions (already shown in Figure 21-6)

Schedule B for reporting interest and dividend income

Schedule C for reporting business and professional profits and losses

Schedule D for reporting capital gains and losses

Other special forms are available to report moving expenses, casualties and thefts, the sale or exchange of a principal residence, and employee business expenses.

Form 1040-ES is filed by every citizen who expects to owe at least $500 more in tax than is covered by withholding and credits. If tax withheld does not cover 90 percent of the tax shown on the previous year's tax return, estimated unpaid tax may be paid in full or in four equal quarterly installments.

Form **1040** Department of the Treasury—Internal Revenue Service (B) **1993**
U.S. Individual Income Tax Return

IRS Use Only—Do not write or staple in this space.

For the year Jan. 1–Dec. 31, 1993, or other tax year beginning _____, 1993, ending _____, 19____ | OMB No. 1545-0074

Label
(See instructions on page 12.)
Use the IRS label. Otherwise, please print or type.

Your first name and initial | Last name | Your social security number

If a joint return, spouse's first name and initial | Last name | Spouse's social security number

Home address (number and street). If you have a P.O. box, see page 12. | Apt. no.

City, town or post office, state, and ZIP code. If you have a foreign address, see page 12.

For Privacy Act and Paperwork Reduction Act Notice, see page 4.

Presidential Election Campaign (See page 12.)

Do you want $3 to go to this fund? . . . . | Yes | No
If a joint return, does your spouse want $3 to go to this fund? . . . .

Note: *Checking "Yes" will not change your tax or reduce your refund.*

Filing Status
(See page 12.)
Check only one box.

1 Single
2 Married filing joint return (even if only one had income)
3 Married filing separate return. Enter spouse's social security no. above and full name here. ▶
4 Head of household (with qualifying person). (See page 13.) If the qualifying person is a child but not your depend___ enter this child's name here. ▶
5 Qualifying widow(er) with dependent child (year spouse died ▶ 19____). (See page 13.)

Exemptions
(See page 13.)

If more than six dependents, see page 14.

6a ☐ **Yourself.** If your parent (or someone else) can claim you as a dependent on his or her tax return, **do not** check box 6a. But be sure to check the box on line 33b on page 2
b ☐ **Spouse** . . . .
c **Dependents:**
(1) Name (first, initial, and last name) | (2) Check if under age 1 | (3) If age 1 or older, dependent's social security number | (4) Dependent's relationship to you | (5) No. of mo___ lived in yr___

No. of box checked ___
38
39
40

d If your child didn't live with you but is claimed as your dependent unde___
e Total number of exemptions claimed . . . . .

Income

Attach Copy B of your Forms W-2, W-2G, and 1099-R here.

If you did not get a W-2, see page 10.

If you are attaching a check or money order, put it on top of any Forms W-2, W-2G, or 1099-R.

7 Wages, salaries, tips, etc. Attach Form(s)
8a **Taxable** interest income (see page 16).
b **Tax-exempt** interest (see page 17). DON___
9 Dividend income. Attach Schedule B ___ ___ne 40, enter -0-. . . . ▶
10 Taxable refunds, credits ___ ___ee line 25.
11 Alimony received
12 Business income or ___ ☐ Form 4255 b ☐ Form 8611 c ☐ Form 8828
13 Capital gain or (los___ ___ tip income not reported to employer. Attach Form 4137
14 Capital gain distri___ ___, including IRAs. If required, attach Form 5329 .
15 Other gai___ ___ayments from Form W-2 . . . . .
16a T___ ___s your **total tax** . . . . . . ▶
17 ___ ___is from Form(s) 1099, check ▶ ☐
___ ___ax payments and amount applied from 1992 return .
___ ___ne credit. Attach Schedule EIC
___ ___ with Form 4868 (extension request) . . . .
___ ___ security, Medicare, and RRTA tax withheld (see page 28) .
___ Deferral of additional 1993 taxes. Attach Form 8841
59 Other payments (see page 28). Check if from a ☐ Form 2439
b ☐ Form 4136 . . . . .
60 Add lines 54 through 59. These are your **total payments** . . . . . ▶

45
46
47
48
49
50
51
52
53
54
55
56
57
58a
58b
59
60

Refund or Amount You Owe

61 If line 60 is more than line 53, subtract line 53 from line 60. This is the amount you **OVERPAID**. ▶ | 61
62 Amount of line 61 you want **REFUNDED TO YOU.** . . . . . . ▶ | 62
63 Amount of line 61 you want **APPLIED TO YOUR 1994 ESTIMATED TAX** ▶ | 63
64 If line 53 is more than line 60, subtract line 60 from line 53. This is the **AMOUNT YOU OWE.** For details on how to pay, including what to write on your payment, see page 29 . . . | 64
65 Estimated tax penalty (see page 29). Also include on line 64 | 65

Sign Here
Keep a copy of this return for your records.

Under penalties of perjury, I declare that I have examined this return and accompanying schedules and statements, and to the best of my knowledge and belief, they are true, correct, and complete. Declaration of preparer (other than taxpayer) is based on all information of which preparer has any knowledge.

Your signature | Date | Your occupation

Spouse's signature. If a joint return, BOTH must sign. | Date | Spouse's occupation

Paid Preparer's Use Only

Preparer's signature | Date | Check if self-employed ☐ | Preparer's social security no.
Firm's name (for yours if self-employed) and address | E.I. No.
| ZIP code

*U.S. Government Printing Office: 1993 — 345-057

A packet of 1040-ES forms is mailed to taxpayers along with preprinted payment vouchers like the one shown in Figure 21-8(b) and a worksheet to help compute estimated tax. Keep the worksheet in the tax portfolio. Use the preprinted vouchers to speed the processing of estimated tax payments and reduce errors. File the vouchers in the tickler file.

Form **1040-ES (OCR)** Department of the Treasury Internal Revenue Service	**1994** Payment Voucher **4**	
		OMB No. 1545-0087

File only if you are making a payment of estimated tax. Return this voucher with check or money order payable to the "**Internal Revenue Service**." Please write your social security number (SSN) and "1994 Form 1040-ES" on your check or money order. Please do not send cash. Enclose, but do not staple or attach, your payment with this voucher.

Calendar year—
Due Jan. 17, 1995

286004141 TC GORM 30 0 9412 430 17

16 286-00-4141 TC 234-00-8876 8321

ROGER B & HELEN J GORMAN
2624 WESTERVILLE BLVD
CLEVELAND HTS OH 44121-2026

For Paperwork Reduction Act Notice, see instructions.   Cat. No. 61900V

Amount of payment $ _____

Change name or SSN if incorrect and **not previously corrected.** Cross out name and SSN of deceased or divorced spouse. Get **Form 8822**, Change of Address, to report a new address (see instructions).

Fig. 21-8(b) Form 1040-ES (Estimated Tax for Individuals) is filed by those whose tax will exceed withholding and credits by at least $500.

Tax Guides.   The following publications can be obtained from the Internal Revenue Service free or for a nominal charge: *Your Federal Income Tax, Tax Guide for U.S. Citizens Abroad and Alien Residents, Tax Information for Homeowners, Moving Expenses, Tax Guide for Small Business,* and *Child and Dependent Care Credit.* Also available are *Travel, Entertainment, and Gift Expenses; Tax Exempt Status for Your Organization; Tax Information for Older Americans; Tax Information for Divorced and Separated Individuals;* and *Tax Withholding and Estimated Tax.* Inexpensive tax guides can also be obtained at bookstores.

Tax Forms.   One set of blank tax forms in duplicate is mailed to each taxpayer; additional copies for drafting the return may be obtained from a local office of the Internal Revenue Service or from banks and post offices. They may also be reproduced on a copier. (The Internal Revenue Service has ruled that reproduction of tax forms, schedules, and supporting data on office copiers is acceptable.) Forms may be prepared in pencil and reproduced on a copier to avoid having to recopy or key the form.

Most employers use Form 1040; however, single taxpayers with no dependents, under age 65, who earn less than $50,000 and have taxable interest income of under $400 a year and no dividend income may use a simplified form, Form 1040-EZ. This form reduces filing complexities but permits taxpayers to claim only the standard deduction.

Copies of all supplementary information and supporting data, such as receipts, statements, expense reports, and other items that may be attached and mailed with the tax return, should be made on a copier and filed before a return is mailed.

Preparing and Mailing Tax Returns

Whether the tax return is computer generated using appropriate software or prepared on a typewriter or word processor, the tax return contains confidential information. It should be keyed by the administrative assistant, not by a subordinate. Before keying, each figure must be checked for accuracy; then the return must be keyed and proofread carefully. Before mailing the form, the administrative assistant should check to see that it has been properly signed and that materials to accompany the return have been securely attached to the finished form as directed.

Space is provided on federal tax forms for the signature of the preparer, if other than the taxpayer; this does not mean the signature of the administrative assistant who has collected tax data or keyed the form. This space is for the signature of the tax consultant or attorney who prepared the return and who assumes responsibility for its validity.

Since mailing tax returns is a very important responsibility, the administrative assistant should mail them personally. Do not put them in the regular office mail, send them through the mail department, or trust them to a clerk or anyone else to post. The administrative assistant should note on the file copy the exact time and place where each return was mailed. A certificate of mailing may be obtained from the post office as legal proof that the return was mailed. If such a certificate is obtained, attach it to the file copy of the return.

If a declaration of estimated tax was made, the administrative assistant must remind the employer when quarterly tax payments are due (April 15, June 15, September 15, and January 15). A good idea is to place cards in the tickler file at appropriate points.

Late Filing

The taxpayer who files a late tax return is assessed a penalty. However, an automatic four-month extension beyond the April 15 deadline may be obtained by submitting Form 4868, Application for Extension of Time. Additional extensions are granted only under special circumstances. A request for such an extension should be filed early so that, if refused, the return can be filed on time.

TECHNOLOGY

Tele-Tax is a recorded tax information service which includes about 140 topics of tax information that answer federal tax questions.

Tax Assistance

Should questions occur regarding the preparation of tax returns or while computing payroll deductions, the IRS has a problem-resolution program for taxpayers who are unable to solve problems through normal channels. By calling a toll-free number in your area and asking for the problem-resolution office, misunderstandings and misinterpretations can be cleared up.

Preparing Tax Documents for the Accountant

If your employer's taxes are complicated, you may be required to give the tax data you have collected and categorized to an accountant. If this is the case, there are several ways in which you may present the tax data. Following these procedures will expedite the preparation of your employer's taxes and will prevent needless telephone calls to verify questionable items. The more thorough your preparation, the less time the accountant will have to spend searching through receipts, canceled checks, and other papers. Disorganized paperwork may cause the accountant to overlook some deductions or omit some source of income, thus leading to a time-consuming tax audit.

The following procedures are recommended by tax accountants for submitting income tax data:

1. **The envelope method.** Submit a separate envelope for each category of income and deduction. Enclose all supporting documents in each envelope—W-2 forms, dividend statements, and the like, in the income envelopes and canceled checks, receipts, etc., in the deduction envelopes. Label each envelope and attach a tape showing the total of the enclosures in each envelope. Be extremely accurate. The accountant should not spend valuable time reading your receipts. Your documentation, however, may be spot-checked for accuracy.

2. **The notebook method.** Use a loose-leaf notebook with a separate page for each category of income—wages, bonuses, interest, rental income, etc.; and a separate page for each category of deduction—contributions, taxes, interest, and the like. Tab each section for quick identification. Total each notebook page. You may or may not submit the supporting documentation; it should, however, be kept on file. The description on each page of the notebook should satisfy the accountant and prevent needless poring over documentation.

3. **The worksheet method.** On a sheet divided into columns, label column headings for each source of income—wages, dividends, interest—and for each category. Total each column. Figure 21-9 shows an income tax worksheet. If you include the supporting documents with the worksheet, attach a tape showing the totals of the contents of the envelope as in the first method. Including documentation has the advantage of providing answers to questionable items for the accountant while the tax return is being prepared. This avoids bothersome phone calls to you and your employer. On the other hand, when the documentation is provided, some accountants feel it is necessary to check every item. This is a waste of valuable preparation time if you have reported accurately both income and deductibles.

INCOME TAX WORKSHEET

	INCOME					DESCRIPTION/ SOURCE	DEDUCTIONS					
Sal. & Wgs.	Int.	Div.	Bonus	Rent	Misc.		Taxes	Int.	Cont.	Med.	Trav.	Misc.
	188.00					Int. on CD-City Bank						
		17.50				Dividend-Merc, Inc.						
						Personal prop. taxes	285.00					
						St. Paul's Church			100.00			
						American Red Cross			100.00			
	188.00					Int. on CD-City Bank						
		17.50				Div. Merc, Inc.						
42,500.00						Annual salary						
				4,500.00		Rental income-Apt.						
			4,000.00			Year-end bonus						
						L.D. Sparks, D.D.S.				1,700.00		
						St. Mary's Hospital				2,680.00		
						Mortgage int. on home		1,100.00				
						Real estate taxes-Home	908.00					
					1,100.00	Royalty-Patent						
						Nonreimbursed bus. travel					475.00	
						Postage and tel. calls (Lions Club)						14.00
TOTALS												
42,500.00	376.00	35.00	4,000.00	4,500.00	1,100.00		1,930.00	1,100.00	200.00	4,380.00	475.00	14.00

Total Income	$52,511.00		Total Deductions	$7,362.00

Summary

Federal and state laws require all employers to keep detailed payroll records. Time records must be maintained, employee earnings and deductions must be recorded, payroll checks must be prepared, and tax reports must be submitted. In large firms, much of this work is done in a special payroll department. Unless employed in that department, an administrative assistant would have few, if any, of these duties to perform. In a small office, however, the administrative assistant may handle all payroll work. Obviously, then, the extent of an administrative assistant's payroll duties is determined by the size and type of office or company in which the administrative assistant works.

Payroll work is exacting and demands mathematical accuracy. In addition to the responsibility of safeguarding all payroll information, the administrative assistant must understand the forms and reports required by the Federal Insurance Contributions Act, the Fair Labor Standards Act, income tax laws, federal and state unemployment compensation acts, and pertinent local legislation.

Regardless of the extent of payroll responsibilities, every administrative assistant can help the employer in the preparation of annual income tax returns. Throughout the year, the administrative assistant can systematically collect income tax data so that facts and figures are readily available when income tax time comes. No employer expects the administrative assistant to be a tax expert, but the administrative assistant's willingness to assume a helpful role in the tax preparation process is appreciated by almost every employer.

To assist in the tax preparation process or an IRS audit, the administrative assistant should keep a supply of current tax forms and schedules on hand, maintain accurate records, file supporting documents, identify items that are deductible and items that must be declared as income, and see that returns are filed and payments are made on time. Knowing where to go for assistance with tax problems and the procedures for late filing and giving tax data to an accountant are also helpful.

QUESTIONS FOR DISCUSSION

1. Your employer, Ron Shefferd, holds a patent on recyclable insulation made from newspapers. Several companies have expressed interest in marketing the product; however, Mr. Shefferd does not have a contract. He travels regularly to make presentations to interested groups, and to meet with patent lawyers, designers, advertisers, and the like. All this travel is personal and in no way associated with the firm that employs you both. Mr. Shefferd pays you from his own funds to keep books, pay bills, handle his correspondence, file his taxes, and make his travel arrangements. Do you consider this assignment ethical? What can you do to assist Mr. Shefferd at tax time?

THINK IT
Through

2. Why should an administrative assistant not employed in a payroll department be familiar with payroll procedures and payroll taxes?

3. Assume you are employed in a small office (four employees) and your employer asks you to take complete charge of payroll records, including preparing and submitting all payroll tax reports. Where could you obtain assistance to help you prepare for and carry out this assignment?

THINK IT
Through

4. What precautions should the administrative assistant observe in keying and mailing the employer's income tax return?

5. If necessary, correct the following sentences. Use the Reference Guide to check your answers.

    a. Post-date the income statements and the bi-monthly expense vouchers that are in the Manila envelope marked exhibit A.

    b. In chapter 12 of bulletin 17, you will find the list of the CPA's in this state.

    c. Issue check 1056 as payment in full for this years dues.

    d. The non-deductible contributions will serve a multi-fold purpose.

    e. The burglar-proof vault contains a bell like compartment.

    f. We must reform the seat of the chair before it can be recovered with this fabric.

PROBLEMS

1. Obtain a Form 1040 and a Form 1040-EZ and examine them carefully. Assume that your boss, Martin Hebert, earns $44,000 annually and has no other income except interest on his savings account amounting to $390. Mr. Hobart is single and claims no dependents. During the year you have kept a tax file in which you have the following data:

Taxes on real estate (city and county)	$1,500.00
Contributions to St. Jude's Church	800.00
Contributions to Boy Scouts of America	100.00
Personal property taxes	564.00
Mortgage interest	2,976.00
Entertainment expenses	440.00
Medical fees (physical examination)	160.00
Glasses and eye examination	230.00
Prescription drugs	144.00
Contribution to United Way	300.00
Miscellaneous contributions (receipts)	250.00

    a. Is Mr. Hobart eligible to use Form 1040-EZ?

    b. What items in your tax file qualify for deduction?

    c. What are Mr. Hobart's total deductions?

2. Miguel Hernandez is paid $8.20 an hour and an overtime wage of 1 1/2 times his hourly rate. All hours over 40 are considered overtime. He worked 48 hours during the last week in March.

a. What are his gross earnings for the week?

b. If the FICA tax rate is 7.65 percent and a $40 federal income tax deduction and a 2 percent state income tax deduction are made, what are his net earnings?

3. Assume that you are administrative assistant to three executives in the same firm. All three have asked for your assistance in preparing their individual income tax returns. In order to submit the proper information to the CPA who will prepare their returns, design a questionnaire you could give to these executives to obtain vital information concerning their tax status.

TECHNOLOGY APPLICATIONS

▶ **TA21-1.TEM** Using your template disk, access the TA21-1.TEM file, which is a blank spreadsheet for income and deductions. Your employer has asked you to prepare a worksheet with his income and deductions so that he can submit it to his accountant.

Your employer's income sources are:

Interest on savings, certificates, First City Bank	$ 1,776.00
Dividends on IBM stock	427.00
Salary	52,000.00
Year-end bonus	4,500.00
Royalty on patent	2,700.00
Pay for jury duty	22.00

Your employer's deductions are:

Real estate tax	$1,700.00
Personal property tax	350.00
Interest on home mortgage (City Bank)	1,900.00
Dental expenses (daughter's)	3,100.00
Medical expenses	1,500.00
Eye examination and glasses	300.00
Sunglasses (prescription)	120.00
Nonreimbursed travel expenses	350.00

Proofread the document carefully. Print one copy for your instructor.

Chapter 22

L egal Responsibilities

LEARNING OBJECTIVES

After studying this chapter and completing the activities, you will be able to:

1. Understand the administrative assistant's responsibility concerning the most frequently used legal documents.
2. Prepare court and noncourt legal documents.
3. Understand the duties of the paralegal/legal assistant.
4. Interpret government regulations that impact upon the performance of the administrative assistant's duties.
5. Apply automated procedures in the legal office.

INTRODUCTION

The administrative assistant's work will inevitably involve some contact with legal documents, legal vocabulary, legal correspondence, and legal procedures. As an administrative assistant, you may enter into several legal activities daily. For example, should you call a vendor to repair the copier, you have made a contract. On the other hand, should you disclose too much information concerning a former employee's attendance record, you have inadvertently broken the law. People are more aware than ever of their rights and are prone to seek a remedy in the courts should their rights be violated. It is not surprising, then, that few management decisions are made that are not related in some way to local, state, and federal laws.

This chapter introduces the administrative assistant to the processing of the commonly used legal papers and outlines some legislation with which administrative assistants should be familiar. The roles of the notary public and the paralegal are also addressed.

FREQUENTLY USED LEGAL DOCUMENTS

Because many business transactions involve parties from different states, problems arise in preparing legal documents that cover conflicting laws of the federal government and the 50 states. To expedite legal procedures, a number of uniform statutes (laws) have been enacted. The most important one, from a business standpoint, is the Uniform Commercial Code. The legal documents described here conform to this code.

Contracts

Every buying and selling activity constitutes a contract between or among buyers and sellers. A **contract** is an enforceable agreement, either oral or written, that involves legal rights and responsibilities. A contract may be in the form of an oral agreement, a sales slip, a memorandum, a promissory note, or a letter. Some contracts, such as those for the purchase of real estate, must be in writing. See Figure 22-1. All important contracts should be written, although this is not a legal requirement.

Content.   In keying a contract, the administrative assistant should ensure that the following essential information is included:

Fig. 22-1   Some legal contracts are required to be in writing. © *Andy Sacks/Tony Stone Images.*

Date and place of agreement

Names of parties entering into the agreement

Purpose of the contract

Duties of each party

A statement of the money, the goods, or the services given in consideration of (as payment for) the agreement

Time element or duration involved

Signatures of the parties

Prepare enough copies of a contract to provide each party with a file copy. (If a contract is prepared in a law office, an additional copy is made for the law office files.) When an executive sells services by contract (as engineers, architects, builders, and real estate representatives do), the administrative assistant may use a standard form; but usually there are items peculiar to each contract that make it necessary to vary the blanks to be filled in each time. Printed forms are available for most common legal documents. Since some contracts must follow a statutory model or must contain specified provisions, it is recommended that the administrative assistant use a printed form or follow legal advice when preparing specific provisions of a legal document.

Care before Signing.   All contracts should be carefully read by all parties before they are signed. Not only will mistakes, misunderstandings, and fraud be avoided, but content will be clarified with regard to (1) what responsibilities are assumed by each party, (2) exactly what is offered at what price, (3) how payment is to be made, (4) whether or not material can be returned, and (5) when and how the contract can be terminated.

Contracts Made by the Administrative Assistant.   The administrative assistant often acts (in a legal sense) as an executive's deputy; that is, the administrative assistant knowingly—and sometimes unknowingly—executes contracts. The administrative assistant, therefore, should exercise caution in making commitments; in requesting work to be done by outside agencies; in quoting prices or making offers to purchase; and in signing purchase orders, repair orders, sales orders, or other agreements. Such commitments may be contractual.

When signing an agreement (contract) generated by the administrative assistant, the executive usually relies on the administrative assistant's recommendation. The mere fact that the administrative assistant presents a contract to an executive for signature implies the administrative assistant's endorsement of its content. For example, the administrative assistant may make all the arrangements for the purchase of a new machine. The executive signs the contract on the presumption that the administrative assistant has checked all details and has verified that the contract is correct, understood, and proper. By attaching an annotation of a contract's important points, the administrative assistant can save the employer the time of reading "the fine print."

A contract copy should be carefully filed. It is a legal instrument, necessary for prosecuting any deviation from the contract. It is a good idea to place a contract in a No. 10 envelope and mark plainly on the outside, "Signed contract between _____ ." The contract can be filed permanently under the appropriate name, in a separate file for signed contracts, or in a safe-deposit box. In some companies, legal papers are kept in fireproof envelopes as a protection against fire.

Legal firms store standard forms in memory on automated equipment. When a contract, deed, will, lease, or other standard document is needed, the stored document is retrieved, and the administrative assistant keys in the variables.

Proof of Claim in Bankruptcy

Our legal system provides a process by which honest but overextended debtors can be relieved of their financial obligations and start over. The process, called **bankruptcy,** was originally intended to benefit creditors (those to whom money is owed). Bankruptcy forces debtors (those who owe money) to pay creditors from property turned over to the court. This action prevents debtors from concealing their assets and paying only selected creditors. The Bankruptcy Reform Act of 1978 modernized bankruptcy laws. Today a bankruptcy petition can be initiated by the debtor or by creditors. Only federal courts may rule in bankruptcy matters.

Should your employer be involved in collecting money from a bankrupt debtor, you may be required to prepare a proof of claim (a written statement signed by the creditor or an authorized representative) stating the claim against the bankrupt and the basis for the claim. An example of a proof of claim appears in Figure 22-2. The proof of claim must be filed within six months after the first meeting of the bankrupt's creditors. Creditors may lose their claims if they fail to file on time.

Fig. 22-2 A proof of claim in bankruptcy must be presented to the court within six months after the first meeting of the creditors.

United States Bankruptcy Court

In re _____

Case No. _____

Debtor(s)   Claim No. *[For office use only]* _____

PROOF OF CLAIM

1. This proof of claim is made for the claimant named below by the undersigned individual who states that he is duly authorized to make this proof of claim on behalf of the claimant, which is: *(Check the appropriate line)*

    ____ An Individual   ____ A Partnership   ____ A Corporation   ____ Other

2. The correct name and address of the claimant, and the account number, if any, to which all notices and distribution checks should be mailed is stated below:

    _____ Account No. _____

    _____

    _____

3. This claim is based upon: *(Check the appropriate line)*

    ____ A note, contract, or other writing. The original or duplicate copies are attached, or, if not, an explanation is attached.

    ____ An open account. An itemized statement showing the date due is attached.

    ____ Other consideration (or ground of liability). Explain and attach documentation.

4. No judgment has been rendered upon the claim, except _____

5. The debtor was at the time of the filing of the petition, and still is, indebted (or liable) to the claimant as follows: [A detailed explanation of additional charges, including an itemization, basis for inclusion and computation, should be attached.]

    PRINCIPAL $_____
    PLUS ADDITIONAL CHARGES $_____
    TOTAL $_____
    LESS PAYMENTS/CREDITS $_____
    BALANCE DUE $_____

6. This claim is free from any charge forbidden by applicable law and excludes any interest accrued after the date the case was commenced.

7. This claim is an unsecured claim, except to the extent that the security interest, if any, described in paragraph 8 hereof is sufficient to satisfy the claim. (If priority is claimed, give amount and written explanation.)

8. NO SECURITY INTEREST IS HELD FOR THIS CLAIM EXCEPT: _____

    _____

    (If security interest in property of the debtor is claimed, it is claimed under the writing referred to in paragraph 3 or under a separate writing, the original or duplicate of which is attached hereto. If not attached, give written explanation. Evidence of perfection is also attached.)

9. The *FAIR MARKET VALUE* of the property on which the claimant has a lien is $ _____
    (Do NOT use balance due unless it is fair market value.)

File this form, *IN DUPLICATE*, with:

CLERK'S OFFICE, U.S. BANKRUPTCY COURT   Signed _____
Post Office Box 676   (Type or print name & title, if any)
Richmond, VA 23206   DATE: _____

Penalty for presenting fraudulent claim: Fine of not more than $5,000.00 or imprisonment for not more than five years, or both – Title 18, U.S.C. 152.

COPY 1 - COURT COPY

Within a reasonable time after a debtor has filed for bankruptcy, the bankruptcy court must call a meeting of unsecured creditors (those who do not have access to property or other assets that can be used to satisfy a debt). The debtor supplies the court with a list of creditors so that the court may notify them of the meeting. For example, a vendor can repossess office furniture to satisfy a debt, thereby securing the vendor's claim to the debtor's assets. On the other hand, a vendor supplying fuel oil to the bankrupt cannot repossess fuel oil that has been consumed; therefore, the oil vendor is an unsecured creditor.

The administrative assistant should also have some knowledge of the priority of claims. For example, creditors who hold a mortgage as security for payment are not affected by a debtor's bankruptcy. With the mortgage they hold, they may exercise their rights of foreclosure or repossession to obtain payment of their claims. Unsecured creditors share in the remaining assets of the bankrupt in priority order established by the court. The administrative assistant's ability to provide a proof of claim and to assist the employer in the timely presentation of evidence will result in considerable savings and reduce the stress associated with such litigation.

Wills and Codicils

Requirements regarding the drawing of wills and codicils are rather technical and vary among states. Hence, the documents should not be drawn without proper legal supervision or direction.

Wills.   A **will** is a legal instrument whereby a person provides for the disposition of property after death. A *testator* (man) or *testatrix* (woman) is one who makes a will. One who dies without having made a valid will is said to have died *intestate*. A *nuncupative* will is an oral will. It is valid only as to personal property; land may not be given or disposed of by a nuncupative will. A will in the handwriting of the testator is called a *holographic* will. A *joint* will is one executed by two or more persons. A will that sets forth provisions conditional upon the occurrence of a specified event is called a *conditional* will. Such a will might be written before a person undergoes a serious operation.

The *living* will is a relatively new type of will. Under its provisions, any adult of sound mind has the right to refuse medical treatment necessary to sustain life when there is no hope of recovery. A living will should be as specific as possible, and copies should be given to anyone who might have to speak for the writer. A copy should also be given to the family doctor to be placed in the writer's medical record. The living will should be signed and dated in the presence of two witnesses. State laws vary widely regarding the living will.

Another recent development is the *video* will. Many states have not yet passed specific legislation regarding these wills; however, such a will is usually considered evidence of the testator's intent and would be honored by the heirs. This type of will is videotaped with the picture and voice of the testator. After the testator's death, the will is played back on closed-circuit television by an attorney, close relative, or friend.

A will may be revoked by mutilation, alteration, cancellation, destruction, or the execution of a new will. Every will should contain a provision stating that any and all previous wills are revoked even though the testator does not remember ever having made an earlier will.

To *probate* a will is to prove its validity to the court for the purpose of carrying out its provisions. An *executor* (man) or *executrix* (woman) is named by the testator to carry out the provisions of a will. If a person dies intestate, the courts will appoint an administrator (man) or administratrix (woman) to settle the estate of the deceased.

Codicils. A **codicil** is a supplement that makes a change in, deletes or adds something to, or explains a will. It must be signed and witnessed with all the formalities of the original will.

A person asked to **attest** (witness) a will or codicil need not read the provisions and, of course, does not try. The attestant merely witnesses the signature of the testator and assures the beneficiaries that the testator was in sound mind when the will was signed. A will presented for witnessing should have only the signature area visible to prevent a chance reading of its contents.

Copyrights

Creative work reproduced for sale or public distribution may be *copyrighted*. Copyrighting applies not only to printed matter, such as books and periodicals, but also to photographs, drawings, musical compositions, maps, paintings, and movies.

To copyright is to register a claim with the federal government to a piece of original literary or artistic work. A copyright grants an exclusive right to reproduce a creative work or to perform it publicly. Registering is done either by the originator of the work or by the one reproducing and marketing copies. Copyrighting prevents a dishonest or careless person from stealing another's creative work and marketing it. A copyright endures for the life of the author plus fifty years after the author's death. It ensures that public broadcasters and others cannot use a copyrighted work without the originator's consent and provides guidelines under which classroom and library copying of material is permitted. A copyright can be obtained by filing an application for copyright with the Copyright Office, Library of Congress, Washington, DC 20559.

Petitions

Administrative assistants are often called upon to prepare petitions for employers or for organizations to which they belong. A **petition** is a document containing a formal written request. An example appears in Figure 22-3.

PETITION TO THE CITY COUNCIL

We, the undersigned residents of the city of Norwood, respectfully call your attention to the fact that automobile accidents are frequently occurring in areas where large recreational vehicles and business vans are parked on street corners, obstructing the view of drivers entering intersections.

Inasmuch as it has been the concern of city council for many years to reduce the number of accidents occurring on our city streets, we urgently request that a local ordinance be passed to prohibit the parking of large recreational vehicles and business vans of any type on street corners where the view could be obstructed.

NAMES	ADDRESSES
Mr. & Mrs. Greg C. Clements	902 Clarion Avenue
Anne Williams	3130 Smith Rd.

Writing a petition requires an orderly expression of ideas in clear, concise language. It should be forcefully presented in a respectful tone. Petitions are usually presented in one of the following styles:

1. The reasons for the petition are stated in the order of their importance and are followed by the request. Each reason is usually preceded by the words "inasmuch as" or "in view of the fact that."

2. An explanation of who is making the request is stated first. For example, "We, the undersigned residents of Colby Circle Apartments," would open the petition and be followed by the request and the reasons for the request.

Affidavits

An **affidavit** is a written declaration made under oath that the facts set forth are sworn to be true and correct. The word itself is Latin for "he or she has made an oath." An affidavit, made by an affiant, must be sworn to before a public officer, such as a notary, a judge, or a justice of the peace. For example, evidence of citizenship is required before an applicant can obtain a U.S. passport. If the person seeking a passport has no birth certificate, an affidavit from a relative declaring that the passport applicant was born in the United States may be used. An example of an affidavit appears in Figure 22-4.

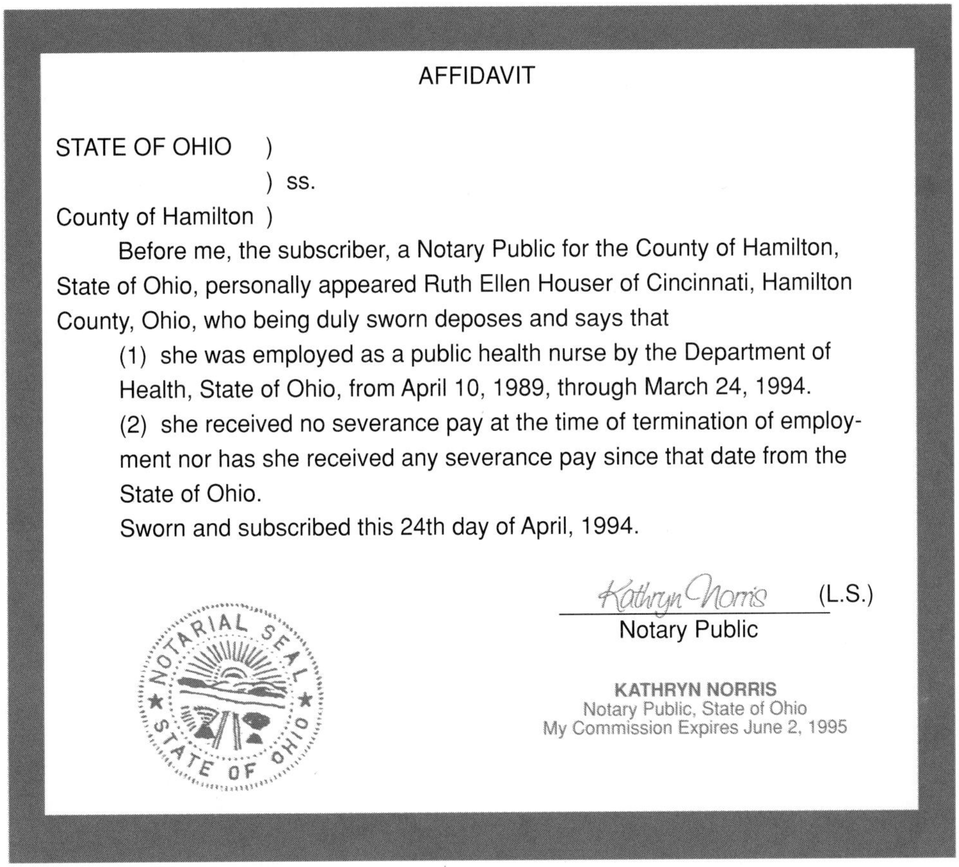

AFFIDAVIT

STATE OF OHIO)
) ss.
County of Hamilton)

Before me, the subscriber, a Notary Public for the County of Hamilton, State of Ohio, personally appeared Ruth Ellen Houser of Cincinnati, Hamilton County, Ohio, who being duly sworn deposes and says that

(1) she was employed as a public health nurse by the Department of Health, State of Ohio, from April 10, 1989, through March 24, 1994.

(2) she received no severance pay at the time of termination of employment nor has she received any severance pay since that date from the State of Ohio.

Sworn and subscribed this 24th day of April, 1994.

Kathryn Norris (L.S.)
Notary Public

NOTARIAL SEAL STATE OF OHIO

KATHRYN NORRIS
Notary Public, State of Ohio
My Commission Expires June 2, 1995

Fig. 22-4 An affidavit must be signed by a notary public, judge, or justice of the peace.

Power of Attorney

A legal instrument authorizing one person to act as an agent for another is known as a **power of attorney.** An example appears in Figure 22-5. Often an employer gives an administrative assistant power of attorney to perform certain specified functions. For example, the administrative assistant may be authorized to sign checks and other legal documents for the executive. A power of attorney may be made for an indefinite period, for a specific period, or for a specific purpose only. Only an administrative assistant with unquestionable professional integrity earns this decidedly weighty responsibility.

Should the executive have power of attorney for someone else, the administrative assistant sets up a special file and records all executions. These records will not only protect the employer, but will also serve as a vital source of information to the person granting the power of attorney.

Fig. 22-5 A power of attorney is notarized in a form similar to that shown in Figure 22-4.

Power of Attorney
Know All Men By These Presents

That Henry Thomas Aske of the City of Akron, Summit County, State of Ohio has made, constituted and appointed, and by these presents does make, constitute and appoint Raymond Henry Petroskey of the City of Seattle, State of Washington true and lawful attorney for me and in my name, place and stead to negotiate for the purchase of the structure and property situated at 112 West Third Street, City of Seattle, King County, State of Washington, known as Hidalgo Towers _____

giving and granting unto Raymond Henry Petroskey said attorney full power and authority to do and perform all and every act and thing whatsoever requisite and necessary to be done in and about the premises as fully, to all intents and purposes, as I might or could do if personally present, with full power of substitution and revocation, hereby ratifying and confirming all that Raymond Henry Petroskey said attorney or his substitute shall lawfully do or cause to be done by virtue hereof.

In Witness Whereof, I have hereunto set my hand and seal the Third day of October, in the year one thousand nine hundred and ninety-four.

Sealed and delivered in the presence of

.... } ....(L.S.)

....

Patents

A **patent** grants an inventor the exclusive right to make and sell a new and useful art, machine, manufacture, or composition of matter. Literature on the procedure for securing a patent can be obtained through the Office of Public Affairs, Patent and Trademark Office, Washington, DC 20231.

Legal specialists are usually employed to prepare a patent application. A patent application is the first step in negotiations between the Patent and Trademark Office and the inventor. A patent must be applied for by the inventor. After the patent has been granted, it can be sold outright or leased, in which case the inventor is paid a royalty for its use. A patent expires at the end of 17 years and can be renewed only by an Act of Congress.

Trademarks

The Patent and Trademark Office also registers trademarks for goods moved in interstate commerce, giving evidence of the validity and ownership of the mark by the registrant and of the right to use the mark. Examples of prominent trademarks are McDonald's Golden Arches, PSI, CPS, and 3M. The registration term covers 20 years. However, during the sixth year of registration, an affidavit must be filed with the Patent and Trademark Office showing that the trademark is being used or that its nonuse does not signify intention to abandon the mark.

RESPONSIBILITIES FOR LEGAL DOCUMENTS

The administrative assistant may key legal papers, fill in printed legal forms, and witness the signing of completed papers. It may be necessary to have legal papers notarized; that is, acknowledged by a notary public. A notary public attests that a document was actually executed by the person or persons who sign it. For convenience, it may be practical for the administrative assistant to become a notary public, thus avoiding the inconvenience of having to go outside the office for this service.

Becoming a Notary Public

Notarial commissions are issued by the secretary of state, the governor, or other designated state official. Application blanks are furnished upon request by the appropriate official in the state in which the commission is sought, or they may be purchased at a stationery store. Some states require a fee and an examination. Certain citizenship qualifications must also be met. Most states also require a fidelity bond, which may be applied for with the application.

Courts have held that a notary may be held liable for errors of omission of official acts, if a person is injured as a result of these omissions. Punishable crimes in some states include making a false statement on a certificate, charging exorbitant fees, or failing to make a report to the appropriate court or regulatory agency. A notary public can purchase *error and omission* insurance to protect against financial liability.

The notary's appointment states the county or counties in which authority to notarize has been granted. The commission's expiration date is also stated. It is necessary to buy a notary public seal and a rubber stamp. The former is used to emboss the document with a seal that shows the name of the state in which the notary is commissioned to act. The rubber stamp shows the date when the commission expires. Each notary receives a copy of local rules and instructions that must be observed.

A notary does not scrutinize the document being certified. The notary gives the oath and verifies that the signature or signatures are genuine. If you should become a notary, remember not to be curious about the content of the paper you are certifying.

Arranging for Notarization

If the administrative assistant is not a notary public, arranging to have papers notarized becomes his or her responsibility. The names of two or three notaries public convenient to the office should be obtained. Sometimes it may be necessary to arrange a meeting time with the notary public and to notify all parties involved.

The notary public witnesses affidavits and signs *acknowledgments* and *verifications* that are executed under oath. In an acknowledgment, like the one shown in Figure 22-6, the person swears that the signature appearing on a document is genuine and was made of free will. A verification is a sworn and signed statement of the truth and correctness of the content of a document. All necessary signatures must be completed before the notary public signs the document.

Fig. 22-6 An acknowledgment of a notary public attests that the signature on a document is genuine.

STATE OF OHIO   )
) ss.
County of Summit   )

    On October 3, 1994, before me, a Notary Public, in and for said County and State, personally appeared Henry Thomas Aske, known to me to be the person whose name is subscribed to the within instrument, and acknowledged that he executed the same.

    IN TESTIMONY THEREFOR I have hereunto subscribed my name and affixed my seal of office the day and year last above written.

                Lawrence E. Philpot
               —————————————— (L.S.)
           My commission expires June 10, 1995.

AUTOMATION IN THE LEGAL OFFICE

Most legal offices are equipped with computers. Standard paragraphs that have been court-tested make up a significant portion of many legal documents. These paragraphs can be keyed once, proofread and corrected, and then stored on the computer for quick retrieval as needed. This capability leaves the operator with only the task of filling in the variable information. Keying errors and erasures in critical places in a legal document can disqualify the document for court purposes. Using standard paragraphs can save many hours of proofreading time.

Computer networks have been established to serve legal offices. These networks carefully store and index legal material—cases, decisions, opinions, and reviews—in large computer banks. For a fee a legal office can access a vast amount of stored information and save hours of research. For example, the computer network can be instructed to print all court decisions dealing with a specific point of law. See Chapter 14 for a discussion of Lexis, a legal database used in legal research.

Preparation of Legal Documents

Legal papers can be divided into two classes:

1. *Court documents.* These vary considerably and must follow the specifications of the particular city, county, state, or federal court in which they are filed. They include such documents as *complaints, answers, demurrers, notices, motions, affidavits, summonses,* and *subpoenas.*

2. *Noncourt legal documents.* These include such legal papers as contracts, wills, leases, powers of attorney, agreements, and many others. They give formal expression to legal acts and are legal evidence if court action or litigation becomes necessary.

The form of legal papers is standardized in some respects; in others, it varies with the wishes of the court and with the personal preference of the employer.

Paper Size.   Traditionally all legal documents are keyed on 8 1/2-by-13- or 14-inch hard-to-tear white paper called *legal cap.* Legal cap is printed with a red or blue vertical double rule 1 3/8 inches from the left edge and a single rule 3/8 inch from the right edge. *Brief paper,* 8 1/2 by 10 1/2 inches, also with ruled margins, is used for legal briefs and memorandums; for some documents, each line on a sheet is numbered. Although legal cap is still used in some offices, there is a trend toward using standard 8 1/2-by-11-inch sheets because this size can be microfilmed easily for storage in court files. Most courts are accepting standard-size documents with or without the marginal rulings.

All federal courts now require 8 1/2-by-11-inch paper. In an effort to standardize, many city, county, and state courts are also adopting shorter papers for legal documents. Before keying a court document, the administrative assistant should learn the requirements of the particular court.

Copies.   Multiple copies of legal documents are usually required. For example, all parties to a contract receive a copy; file copies are necessary; and the attorney retains one or more copies for the office. Copies can be made on a copier; the administrative assistant keys only one original and makes copies from the original. In some offices, the administrative assistant keys an original and a file copy on color-coded paper. All other copies are made from the original on the copier. *Copies* can be used and referred to as *duplicate originals.* They must, however, be signed and made to conform in all respects to the original (to contain all the copy shown on the original).

After a paper has been executed (the original and duplicate originals have been made valid by necessary procedures, such as signing, witnessing, notarizing, and recording), all distribution copies and the office file copy must be *conformed* by keying in the signatures, dates, and all other data added in executing the paper.

Fonts.   For legal papers, pica type is preferred and may be required for court documents. In any case, do not use script, italic, or Gothic typefaces.

Margins, Spacing, and Centered Titles.   On paper with printed marginal rules, key within the rules by one or two spaces. On ruled paper, use 1 1/2-inch left and at least 1/2-inch right margins. Top margins are 2 inches on the first page and 1 1/2 inches on subsequent pages. Bottom margins are 1 inch.

For most legal papers, use double spacing. Very long documents are sometimes single-spaced to avoid exceptional bulkiness.

Two inches from the top of the first page, key the title of the paper in all capitals, and center it between the rules. A heading too long for one line should be divided at a logical point and double-spaced. Leave three blank lines below the title.

▶ *Procedure*

Once a will has been stapled, it becomes invalid if taken apart unless each page has been initialed in the handwriting of the one who makes the will.

Stapling and Punching.   Legal documents protected by legal backs should be stapled on each side at the lower edge on the top fold of the legal back about one inch from the side of the backing sheet. A legal back is the blue sheet backing the partnership agreement shown in Figure 22-7, and a folded legal back is shown in Figure 22-8 on page 604. A legal document prepared without a legal back, regardless of whether the document is an original or a copy, is stapled one inch from the top of the page on both corners (see Figure 22-9 on page 604). Try to avoid removing staples from documents fastened to a legal back. Once a will has been stapled, for example, it becomes invalid if taken apart unless each page is initialed in the handwriting of the maker of the will.

A two-hole punch with punches set 2 3/4 inches apart is used in legal offices to prepare documents for filing. All pages to be filed should be punched at the top center. Courts follow this practice; however, in many large law firms where frequent copying is required, documents are also side punched for loose-leaf notebooks.

Hyphenation.   Learn the preference of the office that employs you. Sometimes the last word on a page must not be hyphenated; sometimes a divided last word is recommended to make the unwarranted insertion of pages more difficult. Avoid dividing words at the end of other lines.

Paragraphs.   On most legal documents, indent ten spaces for paragraphs. To make any unwarranted insertion of pages difficult, do not end a page with the last line of a paragraph. Carry over two or more lines to the next page. Notice the format of the one-page contract in Figure 22-10 on page 605.

Quoted Matter and Land Descriptions.   For quoted matter and land descriptions, indent five to ten spaces from the left margin; retain the right margin if desired, or indent five spaces. Indent another five spaces for a new paragraph in the quoted material. Indented quotations may be single-spaced.

Page Numbers.   Legal documents frequently go through a series of drafts. Number and date each draft at the top of each page. Label the first by keying

PARTNERSHIP AGREEMENT

THIS AGREEMENT, made in the City of San Diego, State of California, on the 15th day of September, 19--, between KAY TAYLOR HOOD and JILL SMYTHE ROWE, both of San Diego, California.

WHEREIN IT IS MUTUALLY AGREED, AS FOLLOWS:

1. That the parties hereto shall, as partners, engage in and conduct the business of a worldwide travel agency.

2. That the name of the partnership shall be THE WORLDWIDE TRAVEL-EASE AGENCY.

3. That the capital of the partnership shall be the sum of Twenty Thousand Dollars ($20,000); and each party shall contribute thereto, contemporaneously with the execution of this agreement, the sum of Ten Thousand Dollars ($10,000) in cash.

4. That at the end of each calendar year the net profit or net loss shall be divided equally between the parties hereto, and the account of each shall be credited or debited as the case may be, with her proportionate share thereof.

Kay Taylor Hood
Kay Taylor Hood

Jill Smythe Rowe
Jill Smythe Rowe

Signed and delivered
in the presence of

Fig. 22-7 To protect a legal document, a single backing sheet (legal back or cover) with dimensions that are about 1 inch wider and 1½ inches longer than the document may be used. This sheet is a high-grade, heavy paper and is usually blue. Pages are inserted under the one-inch fold at the top of the sheet. An eyelet or staple is placed at each side. Backing sheets may be color coded to differentiate types of documents.

"first draft" and the date; the second, "second draft" and date it, etc. Keep all drafts and media until the final document has been keyed and processed.

Center page numbers one-half inch from the bottom edge. Always number the first and last page of every document.

Dates. Spell out single-digit ordinal dates and key the year to conform. For example, you would key "the first day of June, nineteen hundred and ninety-four"; but for a double-digit date, you would key "the 15th day of June,

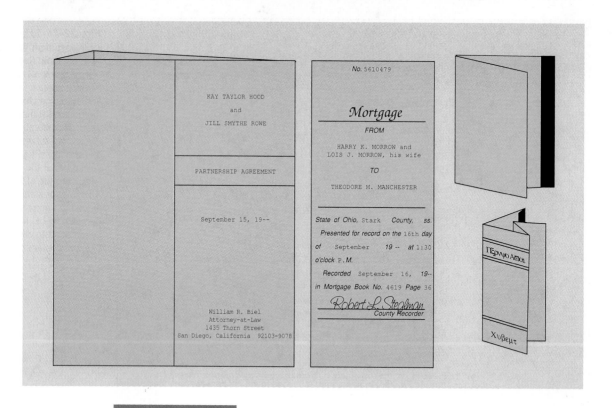

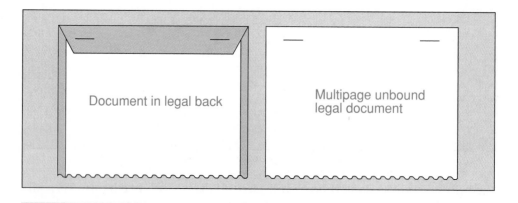

Document in legal back

Multipage unbound legal document

1994." Date every legal paper. If the last paragraph does not include the date, key the date on the last line immediately preceding the signature lines.

Numbers. Numbers with legal significance (amounts of money, periods of time) have traditionally been written in both words and figures.

Fig. 22-10 Observe that the copy is double spaced, that paragraphs have been indented ten spaces, that names of parties to the contract are in all caps, and that dates conform to suggested patterns for legal papers.

CONTRACT

THIS CONTRACT made and entered into this fourth day of October, nineteen hundred and ninety-four, by and between ROBERT LEYLAND ROBINS of the City of Tampa, County of Hillsborough, State of Florida, doing business under the name of ADORN MANUFACTURING COMPANY, and referred to as the firm in this contract, and JANICE WEBBER LOGAL of Bradenton, Manatee County, State of Florida, WITNESSETH:

1. JANICE WEBBER LOGAL shall enter the services of the said firm as a products representative for them in their business of manufacturing cosmetics for the period of one year from the 12th day of October, 1994, subject to the general control of said firm.

2. The said products representative shall devote the whole of her time, attention, and energies to the performance of her duties as such representative, and shall not either directly or indirectly, alone or in partnership, be connected with or concerned in any other business or pursuit whatsoever during the said term of one year.

3. The said products representative shall, subject to the control of the said firm, keep proper books of account and make due and correct entries of the price of all goods sold and of all transactions and dealings of and in relation to the said business, and shall serve the firm diligently and according to the best abilities of all respects.

4. The fixed salary of the said products representative shall be Thirty Thousand Dollars ($30,000) per annum, payable in equal semimonthly installments.

Date: October 4, 1994

/s/_____
          Adorn Manufacturing Company

/s/_____
          Janice Webber Logal

Figures follow words in parentheses. For example, Five Thousand Dollars ($5,000), or Ten (10) barrels of oil, or Sixty (60) days (but six-month period) would be keyed as shown here. Use the dollar sign with a number in conformity with the spelled-out version: Sixty Dollars ($60) or Sixty (60) Dollars. Capitalize all words of an amount: Three Hundred Seventy-Five and 45/100 Dollars ($375.45). Some offices key dollar amounts in all capitals.

Reference Notations. On the first page of a file copy in the upper left corner, key the full names of the recipients of all copies of the document. This facilitates the flow of paperwork and ensures that all parties are informed.

► *Procedure*

After preparing multiple copies of a legal paper that requires many signatures, attach a colored tag at the appropriate point for each signature. If signatures of several parties are required, use a different color for each signer.

Names and Signature Lines. If you know the exact signature that is to be used, key it in the body of the document in exactly that way. If you do not know the form of the signature, use the legal name. The full two or three names of the person without abbreviations or initials are the legal name. The legal signature of a married woman combines her maiden name with her married name, such as Dorothy Keller Brown, not Dorothy Ann Brown. Personal titles (Mr., Mrs., Ms., Miss) are not used; ordinarily, neither are professional titles. To permit easy reference and identification, it is common practice to key the names of individuals, businesses, agencies, and institutions named in a legal document in all capitals.

At the end of a legal paper, key the lines for required signatures. These signature lines cannot stand alone on a page; arrange the body so that at least two lines of text appear on the page with the signatures. The lines extend from the center to the right margin, with two or three blank lines between them. Signature lines for witnesses begin at the left margin and extend to the center.

Some administrative assistants lightly pencil in the respective initials on the lines where each is to sign. Other administrative assistants use a small *x* to mark the spot. In some jurisdictions, names must be keyed under signature lines. Names are keyed on signature lines after the word "signed" or the abbreviation "Sgd." on file copies.

Seals. The abbreviation "L.S." (for *locus sigilli,* meaning "place of the seal") frequently appears at the end of lines on which parties to a paper sign their names (see Figure 22-6). This abbreviation has the legal significance of a wax seal. State laws determine whether or not a legal paper requires a seal.

Insertions. At the signing of a legal paper, an insertion may be requested. An insertion is valid if the signers endorse it by writing their initials in ink near the insertion.

► *Procedure*

To ensure that no line of an original copy of a legal document has been omitted in rekeying, hold line-for-line keyed copy beside the original—or align the copy over the original and hold them up to a bright light.

Proofreading. The administrative assistant who is unfamiliar with legal work should be particularly careful in proofreading and questioning terms that are not understood. Novices have keyed "the plaintiff praise" for "the plaintiff prays," or the "Court of Common Please" or "Court of Common Police" rather than the "Court of Common Pleas." If you are not sure about a term, ask for assistance or consult an authoritative text.

Property descriptions, quoted material, and all figures and dates that appear in legal documents should be proofread twice, because a minor discrepancy can be the basis of litigation. Read a second time aloud to another person. Identify all capital letters, punctuation marks, and abbreviations.

Procedure

Some legal forms are purchased in pads. Insert a reorder reminder three-fourths of the way through each new pad.

Standard Legal Forms

Undoubtedly your employer will engage legal counsel when preparing important legal papers. If, however, certain types of papers are often used, such as leases or deeds, forms given in legal reference books can be used as guides. Avoid indiscriminate copying of such forms because laws vary from state to state, and laws also change.

Legal Forms.   Stationery stores that supply legal offices carry preprinted forms for such common documents as affidavits, agreements, deeds, leases, powers of attorney, and wills that concur with local laws. These are called legal forms or law blanks. Look in the Yellow Pages under "Legal Forms" for sources of supply. Some legal forms are purchased in pads.

Many legal forms consist of four pages, printed on both sides of one 8 1/2-by-28-inch sheet of paper folded once to make four pages 8 1/2 by 14 inches. The form for the endorsement is printed on the fourth page. With this arrangement, binding of pages at the top is unnecessary, and a cover is not used. When the front page (page 1) is turned, pages 2 and 3 read as one continuous page down the full inside length of the document.

To protect a legal document, a single backing sheet (legal back or cover) about 1 inch wider and 1 1/2 inches longer than the instrument may be used. This sheet is a high-grade, heavy paper and is usually blue. Pages are inserted under the 1-inch fold at the top of the backing sheet. An eyelet or staple is placed at each side.

Fill-Ins on Legal Blanks.   Fill-ins may range from inserting a single letter or figure to words, phrases, or long lines of text. Printed blank lines are usually not provided in the blank spaces; therefore, the typist must align the keyed insertion with the printed line of text. Use the printed margins for keying full lines. As a precaution, rule a "Z" in ink to fill deep unused space (see Figure 22-5).

Riders.   When the space allotted for filling in a conditional clause or other provision (called a **rider**) in a legal blank is not large enough to key the insert, leave sufficient space after the last line to permit a slip of paper containing the rest of the keyed material to be pasted to the document. Use legal cap for the rider, and cut off any unused part of the sheet. Fasten the rider securely to the document and fold the rider to fit neatly within the backing sheet.

Forms File.   Many legal documents that the administrative assistant keys are adaptations of existing documents. A forms file of commonly keyed legal documents, therefore, can be an important time-saver. Accumulate this file by making an extra photocopy of representative legal documents when they are first keyed. In the margin, add helpful notes regarding the number of copies to be prepared, the distribution of the copies, and other pertinent data. In time, the file will contain most, if not all, of the legal documents produced in the office. You can then consult the file to determine the exact procedure for any document contained therein. Legal secretaries consider their forms file to be their most valuable reference source.

THE PARALEGAL/LEGAL ASSISTANT

One of the fastest growing career fields in the nation has emerged in the legal field. Attorneys in private practice as well as those in larger law firms seek ways to improve the efficiency and reduce the costs of legal services. Increasing caseloads in the courts and the increased work loads brought on by more and more government regulations helped pave the way for a new member of the legal team—the paralegal/legal assistant. There is no difference in meaning between the two titles. The paralegal and legal assistant perform the same duties and work under the supervision of a licensed member of the legal profession. An attorney uses the services of a paralegal/legal assistant in much the same way as a doctor uses the services of a nurse. Some of the duties performed by paralegals/legal assistants include the following:

Conduct client interviews.

Follow up on an investigation of factual information.

Locate and interview witnesses.

Prepare various legal motions.

Handle exhibits used in court.

Prepare documents for the dissolution of marriage, for the collection of accounts, and for probating wills, handling claims, and transferring property.

Summarize depositions, testimony, and interrogatories for review by an attorney.

Compose and sign letters (provided the legal assistant's status is clearly indicated and that the correspondence does not contain legal advice or independent legal opinions).

Attend executions of wills, real estate closings, depositions, court or administrative hearings, and trials with the attorney.

Duties actually performed depend upon the law practice and the needs of the attorney. To be a legal assistant, you must be willing to accept responsibility, have an interest in and an aptitude for the law, and be oriented to serving the attorney who employs you. Your work must be of unquestionable accuracy.

The educational background required to become a paralegal/legal assistant varies widely. There are various programs designed to train paralegals/legal assistants, ranging from a few weeks to three or four years. Special courses and formal training classes are also available to those interested in becoming paralegals/legal assistants.

The American Bar Association's Standing Committee on Legal Assistants is conducting a program to approve those courses that meet its guidelines. When selecting a school offering this type of training, it would be wise to find out whether the program has been or is in the process of being approved by the American Bar Association, or if the school offers an internship program or assists in job placement for those who complete the training.

The National Association of Legal Assistants, Inc. (NALA), offers a voluntary certification program designed to promote high standards and professionalism among legal assistants. The certified legal assistant (CLA) program involves the successful completion of a two-day examination. The certifying board continually updates the content of the examination. Four one-hour specialty examinations administered during the same time as the full examination are available to those who want to certify in the areas of civil litigation, probate and estate planning, criminal law and procedure, corporate and business law, and real estate. The CLA examination tests the broad general skills required of all legal assistants. These skills include such areas as communications, legal research, ethics, judgment, and analytical ability. Specialty certification provides an avenue for recognition for excellence in a particular field.

Information on the CLA examination and the paralegal/legal assistant programs may be obtained from NALA Headquarters, 1601 S. Main Street, Tulsa, OK 74119-4464.

Because of the combined efforts of NALA and the American Bar Association, the field of paralegal/legal assistant is growing in demand and prestige. The field provides excellent job opportunities for the administrative assistant with a special interest in the law, as well as excellent preparation for law school. In addition to employment in private law firms, positions are often available in the courts, corporations, insurance companies, government offices, and trust departments of banks.

THE ADMINISTRATIVE ASSISTANT'S KNOWLEDGE OF THE LAW

Some elements of business law affect the day-to-day operation of every office. Because of the importance of your role as a guardian of information, a working knowledge of the laws that directly pertain to your company will add to your efficiency and prevent costly litigation. Business law is extensive and complex, and the administrative assistant is not expected to be an authority on legal matters. However, most companies have established policies that govern the handling of information pertaining to the company, its clients, and its employees.

It is not uncommon for executives and administrative assistants to unknowingly violate legislation safeguarding equal employment opportunities and the privacy of personnel information. It is essential that every administrative assistant be familiar with company policy and federal legislation regarding these areas.

Equal Employment Regulations

An administrative assistant who works closely with the human resources department of a company should be especially familiar with regulations concerning recruiting, screening, hiring, and terminating employees, since these regulations are frequently violated. If you share the responsibilities for interviewing and selecting employees, you should know about the discriminatory nature of certain questions. Before asking any preemployment question, consider these two points: Is the question job related? Does the question eliminate a disproportionate number of minorities? If the answer to this last question is yes or maybe, omit it.

Because regulations change rapidly, it is necessary that you keep up-to-date. The Equal Employment Opportunity Commission (EEOC) issues periodic employment regulation guidelines to employers. (For further information, check with your public library for the address of the Equal Employment Opportunity Commission.) As the work force becomes more diverse, the administrative assistant should seek guidelines for preventing discriminatory practices in hiring, promoting, and terminating employees. Although the EEOC is the primary government agency responsible for enforcing federal antidiscrimination laws, it has recently delegated some of its responsibility to state agencies known as *706 agencies*. Most major cities have a state 706 agency to review claims of discrimination.

As an administrative assistant, if you personally experience discrimination, it is best to try to resolve the problem in the workplace rather than involve the courts and other agencies. Practices that are offensive to you should be discussed with your employer before they expand into a serious violation of your civil rights. The significant regulations governing equal employment are as follows:

1. Every employer who is engaged in interstate commerce and employs at least 15 people is required to make employment decisions without consideration of race, creed, color, sex, religion, or national origin. In addition, an employer may not segregate or classify employees or applicants in any discriminatory way. This includes the advertisement of jobs as male jobs or female jobs.

2. All employers of 20 or more persons are prevented from making employment decisions based on age for persons between 40 and 70.

3. Employers must provide equal pay for men and women working in the same business at jobs requiring equal skill, effort, and responsibility under similar conditions.

4. The Rehabilitation Act of 1973 prevents discrimination by government contractors against disabled individuals. Discrimination against women because of pregnancy, childbirth, or other related medical conditions is forbidden by the Pregnancy Discrimination Act of 1978.

5. The Americans with Disabilities Act was passed in 1990. It requires that employers with 25 or more workers provide for the needs of people with disabilities. Under this law, businesses must have accommodations accessible to the physically challenged and eliminate all practices that discriminate against hiring disabled people.

The Americans with Disabilities Act has been criticized for its vague language and lack of specifics on how to comply. Many employers have faced charges of discrimination because they regarded only those in wheelchairs, deaf, or blind to be physically challenged. Individuals with chronic illnesses or injuries, including recovering alcoholics and those with epilepsy, HIV infections, heart conditions, and back injuries, are also covered.

Employee Information and Privacy Legislation

With the increasing sophistication of computerized recordkeeping systems, the public has become concerned about the kinds of information being collected, how the information is used, and who has access to it. The federal government responded to these concerns by passing the Freedom of Information Act (FOIA) in 1966 and amending it in 1974 with the Privacy Act. Both acts apply only to records kept by federal agencies, but it is possible that national legislation will be passed to ensure the privacy of employee records in private industry as well. Some states have already passed legislation to permit employees access to their own personnel records.

The collection, dispersal, and access of personnel information is usually covered by company policy. The administrative assistant should have a copy of these policies and be alert to requests for information from outsiders. Some companies give only directory information to outsiders. Directory information consists of the employee's job title and dates of employment.

Knowing what you are permitted to tell a caller about company employees can save your employer the cost and inconvenience of a lawsuit if the wrong information should be given. Personnel and payroll records should be made available only to authorized users. If in doubt about what information can or cannot be given, always refer to a higher authority.

Summary

Your work as an administrative assistant will inevitably involve contact with legal vocabulary, legal documents, legal correspondence, and legal procedures. The extent of this involvement depends upon several factors. The administrative assistant in a legal office spends a majority of the workday handling legal documents and procedures. An administrative assistant in a corporate office may deal with legal documents only occasionally.

Regardless of the legal responsibilities assigned to the administrative assistant, familiarity with commonly used legal documents—contracts, proofs of claim, wills and codicils, copyrights, petitions, affidavits, powers of attorney, and patents—is basic to the efficient performance of legal tasks. Responsibilities for the preparation of legal papers may include keying legal documents, filling in legal forms, and witnessing the signing of completed papers. The administrative assistant might find it convenient to become a notary public in order to witness affidavits, wills, acknowledgments, or verifications.

Preparation of legal papers involves work on two classes of documents: court documents (affidavits, demurrers, motions, and the like) and noncourt documents (leases, wills, contracts, powers of attorney, etc.).

Court requirements vary from state to state regarding the preparation of legal documents. The administrative assistant should learn the court's and the employer's standards for paper size, copies required, type styles, stapling and punching, hyphenation, paragraph indentation, page numbers, and handling of quoted matter and land descriptions. Understanding how to key dates, numbers, reference notations, and signature lines and how to handle insertions, erasures, and corrections is also necessary.

Proofreading is an essential skill. Administrative assistants unfamiliar with legal work should question unfamiliar terms. A knowledge of legal forms and how to appropriately fill in legal blanks, attach riders, and establish a forms file adds to the legal administrative assistant's effectiveness.

In many law offices, word processing technology is having a dramatic effect on the functions of the legal administrative assistant. Much of the repetitive keying, copying, and proofreading that formerly comprised a significant part of the work of a legal administrative assistant has been automated with word processors, computers, and copiers.

Some administrative assistants become legal assistants/paralegals. A certification program to become a certified legal assistant (CLA) has been established to professionalize the work of the legal assistant.

The daily operation of every business is in some way affected by the law. It is not uncommon for administrative assistants and executives to unknowingly violate legislation regulating equal employment opportunities and the privacy of personnel information. Most companies have policies to guide them in complying with legislation regarding employee rights. It is essential that the administrative assistant be familiar with these policies.

QUESTIONS FOR DISCUSSION

1. How does the administrative assistant's work relate to the law?

2. Why is the paralegal/legal assistant one of the fastest growing career fields in the country? What are the major duties performed by a paralegal/legal assistant?

THINK IT *Through*

3. Assume that you are a notary public. In what way do your responsibilities differ when you sign an agreement for monthly machine repair service and when you notarize an affidavit?

4. The administrative assistant in an adjacent office asks you to witness the signatures on a contract. When you reach the office, you find that the signatures have already been affixed. What would you do?

THINK IT *Through*

5. Many Latin words and phrases are used in legal documents. What is the English translation of each of the following Latin terms?

a. corpus juris

b. de jure

c. et al.

d. loco citato

e. prima facie

f. pro tempore (or pro tem)

g. quasi

h. quod erat demonstrandum (Q.E.D.)

i. scilicet (ss)

j. sic

6. Rekey the following sentences and eliminate the redundant expressions. Use the Reference Guide to verify or correct your answers.

a. Graduation at most colleges is held in the month of May.

b. The crew should continue on with its drill.

c. Mason is looking for a house in close proximity to a school.

d. The teacher refused to repeat the instructions again.

e. The property will depreciate in value during the next decade.

1. As administrative assistant to the vice president of General Services for a large manufacturing corporation, you receive frequent calls asking for information on employees who have left your company and applied for reemployment elsewhere. Questions concerning pay, family and marital status, age, race, religion, health, attendance, disciplinary action, and the like are almost a daily occurrence. Because there has been no company directive on how to handle such inquiries, you have used your best judgment. Recently, however, one caller threatened to have you fired because you refused (tactfully, of course) to reveal the reason why a food services employee left the company. Some of the callers have been very demanding, and some are customers of your firm. You are concerned with preventing a lawsuit and at the same time, maintaining the goodwill of your callers. Write a memorandum to your employer explaining your reasons for writing, ask for some direction, and make some suggestions based upon your knowledge of the law.

2. It has been recommended that an administrative assistant accumulate a file of legal forms for reference purposes. Prepare a keying instruction sheet that could be inserted in the front of such a file. Include keying instructions for:

    a. Setting margins

    b. Spacing

    c. Indenting paragraphs

    d. Writing dates

    e. Paging

    f. Writing figures

    g. Keying names

    h. Keying quoted matter

    i. Preparing forms for signatures

    j. Completing fill-ins for legal blanks

3. Assume that you wish to become a notary public in your state.

    a. From your library, from a notary public, or from some other source, obtain the name and address of the designated official in your state who issues notary public commissions.

    b. Obtain from the designated official the specific requirements for the commission in your state. Key a summary of the various requirements.

▶ **TA22-1.TEM**   Using your work processing software, access the TA22-1.TEM file, which is a template of an affidavit format.

For this exercise, pretend that you are a notary public commissioned in Storey County, Nevada. Mr. Toni Nuvamsa asks you to prepare an affidavit for his signature stating that he, Toni Nuvamsa, is a member of the Apache Indian tribe and has resided for the past 18 years at 2323 North Canyon Drive, Reno, Nevada.

Proceed as follows:

1. Sign the form as the notary public, using the current date.
2. Proofread the document carefully. Use your spelling checker to assist you.
3. Store the final document.

▶ **TA22-2**   In this assignment, you are to prepare and key a power of attorney, similar to the power of attorney illustrated in the textbook in Figure 22-5.

Proceed as follows:

1. Find Figure 22-5 in the text, and use this form as a guide.
2. Use the following explanation to complete the power of attorney:

    Mr. Ivan Colbert Rayzinski, who lives at 321 High Street, Cleveland, Ohio, owns a building located at 3150 Moore Street, Orlando, Florida. Mr. Rayzinsky wishes to give William Homer Parker of 76 Mulberry Drive, Orlando, authority to sell the building and the land for him and to execute in his behalf all papers necessary for the transfer of the property.

3. Key the current date.
4. Complete the notary public statement that constitutes part of the power of attorney.
5. Proofread the document carefully, make any corrections necessary, store the final form, print out one copy, and submit that final copy to your instructor.

▶ **TA22-3.TEM**   Using your word processing software, access the TA22-3.TEM file, which shows a template for a partnership agreement.

Using this form, prepare a partnership agreement for William Baylor Cross and Norma Farris Buchanan, both residents of Columbia,

continued

continued

South Carolina. They are forming a partnership to operate a tax accounting service to be known as the Star Tax Service. Each agrees to invest $15,000 in the business. Profits and losses are to be distributed annually and divided equally between the partners.

Proceed as follows:

1. Use the current date in completing the agreement.
2. Proofread your copy carefully.
3. Print two copies.
4. Store the file.
5. Submit both copies to your instructor.

Part 6

Case Problems

Anna Maples has worked as administrative assistant for Dr. John Lambrick, chairman of the Department of Biological Sciences at Crown Medical College. Dr. Lambrick often teaches the organic chemistry course. The course is rigorous, required of all medical students, and is the one course responsible for the greatest number of failures in the school. Anna has complete charge of all departmental records, and she has been extremely careful to guard the confidentiality of all information concerning students.

Last week, a person identifying himself as a registrar at another college called Anna asking for information on Pete Rowe, one of Dr. Lambrick's failures. The caller asked if Pete had attended Crown, what courses he had completed, and the grades he had made in each course. Anna confirmed Pete's attendance at Crown, but tactfully refused to give the caller any additional information. Anna told the caller he would have to request an official transcript from the registrar, and that this must be done with Pete's permission. She provided the registrar's telephone number. The caller became abusive, implying that Anna was giving him the runaround because she was too inefficient to find the information. The caller threatened to report the incident to the president of the college. The experience left Anna shaken, but she felt she had done the right thing.

▨▨▨ **What do you think? How can she justify withholding student information requested by another registrar?**

Norm Scurry is administrative assistant to Al Liang, a senior vice president. As part of his responsibilities, Norm organizes Mr. Liang's tax records to be turned over to his certified public accountant. He also pays his employer's personal bills. Mr. Liang is divorced, lives alone, and travels a good part of the year.

Recently, while Mr. Liang was on an extended business trip, a Mr. Edmunds, who introduced himself as Mr. Liang's investment counselor, came by the office. After introducing himself, he produced a questionnaire and asked Norm questions regarding Mr. Liang's income, investments, indebtedness, and bank balances. Mr. Liang had no appointment scheduled for Mr. Edmunds, and a quick check of his Rolodex revealed to Norm that Mr. Edmunds was not listed in any records.

▇▇▇ How should Norm handle this situation?

Ellen Landstrum has worked for the Klingman Corporation for ten years, and in that time she has had only one promotion. She is now administrative assistant to Gordon Johnson, vice president of Administrative Services. She has been in this position for eight years.

Ellen is competent, efficient, loyal, enthusiastic, and dependable. She has always willingly done whatever was necessary to ensure that her boss is the shining star of the executive suite. Ellen likes her job, is respected by her boss and his colleagues, and is considered helpful by her coworkers. Other than a small bonus two years ago, Ellen has had little more than verbal recognition in the past three years. She has not complained because the company was struggling to meet foreign competition in some markets, and profits had diminished.

Ellen is a single parent in her late thirties, and she is struggling to keep her bills paid.

The past year has been exceptional for the Klingman Corporation. Because of new product lines and new overseas markets, the company has enjoyed rapid expansion. Consequently, a new job as assistant chief administrator has recently been created; the company will actively begin recruiting next month. The salary is almost double what Ellen is presently making. Ellen has lots of contacts inside and outside the company, knows every aspect of the organization, and feels that she could make a genuine contribution in this position. She would supervise 12 other office employees and be responsible for the administrative functions of the corporation. She would report to Mr. Johnson.

Ellen will receive her university degree in management next May. She has attended evening classes at a local university for the past seven years as her family responsibilities would permit. Ellen successfully completed the CPS examination last May. Ellen feels that her experience and knowledge of the company should give her a competitive edge. Mr. Johnson will be responsible for selecting the new administrative officer.

This morning, Ellen approached her boss to let him know of her interest in the new position. He listened attentively, commented on the superior job she does in her present job, but made no commitment.

Later in the afternoon, while in the storeroom looking for some old files, she overheard her boss discussing her request with two other male executives. Mr. Johnson said, "My girl, Ellen, has expressed an interest in the new job, but I can't see giving this type of position to a female. Ellen will be much more valuable to me in the position she now holds." One of the other executives remarked, "You're right about that; she surely makes you look good. She has lots of ability, and I don't blame you for not wanting to lose her." Mr. Johnson replied, "She's much too valuable to me as a secretary; I wouldn't know where to turn to find a replacement." Ellen was livid!

▇▇▇ What advice would you give to Ellen?

Case 6-4
WHY CENTRALIZED FINANCIAL CONTROL? A QUESTION OF HONESTY

Sharon Strong is administrative assistant and office manager for a large medical practice owned and operated by Dr. David I. Hohenshill, Dr. Herman A. West, and Dr. Anita Petrelano. Dr. Hohenshill is the senior partner; Drs. West and Petrelano have been practicing for only a few years.

Sharon has complete charge of the firm's checking account, petty cash, office payroll, and accounts receivable. She signs all checks and is responsible for paying bills and collecting delinquent accounts. The office staff consists of Eva Broyles, who works only 20 hours per week. Eva is responsible for billing, correspondence, and the inventory of prescription drugs. The only other employee is a custodian, Anne Carpenter, who works five days a week. Anne sometimes helps with errands.

Sharon has been with the firm for ten years and has seen it grow from a few patients to as many as 110 patients a day. In the past ten years, the office has moved twice to accommodate larger numbers of patients. In that time, however, no new equipment has been purchased except an IBM Selectric typewriter on which Eva types bills and correspondence. The telephone system has been updated once in the past ten years.

Because of the large number of patients in and out of the office daily, most of Sharon's time is spent making appointments and updating patient records. Consequently, all billing, ordering of supplies, and collection of accounts has been left to Eva, who is woefully behind. Patients sometimes receive their bills as long as 45 days after their visits. Several patients have complained of errors. Because of some questionable charges to an insurance company for the treatment of a patient, Dr. Hohenshill hired an outside auditing firm to conduct an audit of the firm's records. The audit was completed last October. It is now February and the auditor's report arrived this morning containing the following notations:

1. Written procedures for handling petty cash are not being followed as outlined in the office manual. The account is seldom used, and Sharon often forgets to make a note of cash advances to Anne and Eva.
2. Some patients received bills for treatment 45 days after an office visit.
3. There is no evidence of executive approval of checks. Dr. Hohenshill countersigned all checks several years ago, but turned the entire responsibility over to Sharon last year.
4. Some accounts receivable are 60 days past due.
5. Several documents in the files bear no evidence of executive approval. Sharon has processed all insurance claims in the past without approval from the doctors.

These notations caused Sharon a great deal of concern inasmuch as she felt that they cast a negative reflection on her integrity and her efficiency. She feels that she is overworked and understaffed.

What action should Sharon recommend to the doctors?

Part 7

Employment and Career Advancement

A braham Lincoln said, "I will prepare myself and my chance will come." Now that you have completed the activities in this book, you should be prepared with the knowledge and skills that will enable you to successfully launch your career as an administrative assistant. Your opportunities are myriad. Information technology has opened many new career paths that should lead the competent administrative assistant into a position that will provide professional satisfaction and financial security. You should bear in mind, however, that there is much more to obtaining an administrative assistant's position than merely finding an employer. Finding a position that will offer you interesting and rewarding work and the future to which you aspire takes careful planning.

The traditional "secretarial" role in the office has undergone dramatic changes in the past two decades because of information technology, legislation, downsizing and restructuring, and the emergence of a global economy. As these influences continue to change the way we work and others are added as society changes, the role of the administrative assistant will take on new dimensions. Duties and responsibilities will expand to include management-related tasks and increased recognition and status for the administrative assistant as an integral part of the management team.

You will probably change positions and even careers during your work life, and you should do so if you become dissatisfied or find more challenging opportunities as the workplace changes. Your goal, however, should be to find the right position in the beginning.

Chapter 23

The Employment Process

LEARNING OBJECTIVES

After studying this chapter and completing the activities, you will be able to:

1. Evaluate the advantages and disadvantages of working in offices of different sizes and types.
2. Develop a list of prospective employers and identify the sources of job opportunities.
3. Prepare a resume and a letter of application.
4. Prepare for an employment interview.
5. Follow up the interview and look for advancement opportunities within the company.

INTRODUCTION

The administrative assistant working in today's office performs many tasks and assumes numerous responsibilities that go beyond the traditional "secretarial" role. Information technology has propelled the administrative assistant into a paraprofessional role that requires the use of management-related technologies as an important member of the management team.

The demand for competent, professional administrative assistants continues to increase. Salaries are on the rise; and as you are about to complete your final term of formal instruction, it is time to make some fundamental decisions about your career. Because there are so many career options available to you, you must exercise your best judgment in selecting the right position. For example, you must decide if you would prefer to specialize in a medical, legal, government, education, or technical field. You have the choice of working in a small company or a large one and of working for one person or several. The location of the office may also affect your career decision. You may prefer to work in the heart of town, in suburbia, or at home. You may want to work in your own hometown, in a distant city, or even overseas. It's really up to you. Well-qualified applicants have little difficulty getting the position they want in the office, location, and specialization of their choice.

This chapter will prepare you to make these career decisions. The important steps in the employment process are thoroughly discussed. The chapter concludes with suggestions of special interest to the part-time job seeker and to the experienced job applicant.

TYPES OF OFFICES

Business is conducted in offices of all types and sizes—in downtown areas of cities, in the suburbs, or on the near rural fringes of communities where many industries employ large forces of office workers and hundreds of factory workers in the same location.

The size of an office and its location determine the type and extent of benefits afforded employees. Although many administrative assistants work in the downtown areas of cities, where salaries are usually higher than in outlying districts, attractive positions are open in the suburbs and in smaller towns. From an administrative assistant's viewpoint each type of office and location offers certain advantages.

Small Offices

Many administrative assistants prefer to work in small offices because of the wide variety of duties they are responsible for performing. The small office is an excellent training ground for all facets of administrative support. There is usually no one but the administrative assistant to answer the telephone, greet callers, do the filing, handle the petty cash, duplicate materials, sort and send out the mail, and purchase supplies. Examples of offices that employ only one administrative assistant are those maintained by attorneys, architects, engineers, accountants, doctors, dentists, insurance agents, schools, and branch offices.

Research shows that 67 percent of all office workers begin their careers in small offices.

Personnel Policies.   One of the advantages of working in a small office is freedom. Working hours are usually established, but the administrative assistant in a small office knows the volume of work so thoroughly that when time permits, or personal circumstances require, a lunch hour may be extended or an early departure taken.

Small offices usually have general personnel policies rather than clearly defined ones. This may or may not be to the advantage of the administrative assistant. There may be no limit to sick leaves and emergency absences, or there may be no provision for them at all. There also may be no medical insurance or disability benefits, including retirement.

There are, however, a few definite disadvantages to working in a small office. Generally salaries have limits. The ceiling for salaries may be set by the circumstances of the business and not by the competence of the administrative assistant. Instead of giving specified salary increases at definite intervals, the employer is likely to consider each salary increase individually.

Another disadvantage is the absence of social opportunities in the work environment.

Administrative Opportunities.   In some small offices, the administrative assistant assumes a great deal of administrative responsibility but is rarely given an administrative title. Advancement is in terms of salary, not title. Small offices necessitate close working relationships; therefore, an employer soon learns the capabilities of the administrative assistant and will increasingly expand that position to include more and more responsibility. Depending upon the nature of the work, the employer may be out of the office much of the time, and the administrative assistant virtually runs the office.

An office with three or four administrative support employees frequently provides excellent opportunities to gain supervisory experience. In such situations, the senior administrative assistant may supervise the work of the office staff in addition to performing the other duties of the job.

Large Offices

Many administrative assistants deliberately choose to work in large offices because of the opportunities to meet interesting people and to have daily contact with other workers. The work of the administrative assistant in a large office tends to differ in many respects from that of the administrative assistant in the small office. In the large office, many business routines are performed by special departments. Postal and shipping chores are handled by mailing and shipping departments. A purchasing department may handle the ordering of equipment and supplies. On the other hand, the administrative assistant in the large office may handle travel details, research computer-based information for the executive, draft reports, attend conferences, and perform other important services.

The opportunity for advancement in a large organization to supervisory and administrative positions is good. Administrative assistants to top management in large firms are frequently administrative assistants in both duties and title.

Personnel Policies.   Personnel policies in large offices are clearly defined and must be followed. Singling out an individual employee for special privileges can be damaging to office morale. The personnel policies of a large company are usually very explicit about such matters as the following:

Hours of work, lunch hour, and rest periods

Overtime pay or compensatory time off

Eligibility for vacation, length of vacation

Number of days allowed annually for sick leave

Paid holidays

Salary range for each job, frequency and extent of salary increases

Fringe benefits

Job descriptions

Job classifications

Fringe Benefits.   Many businesses and government agencies offer fringe benefits to their employees. They are called fringe because they are outside the realm of salary, and sometimes outside the realm of taxable income. In some instances, these benefits cost an organization an additional 30 to 50 percent of wages paid. Common benefits include the following:

Group life insurance

Medical examinations

Medical and hospitalization insurance

Long-term disability benefits

Rehabilitation programs for alcohol and drug abuse

Counseling services for domestic problems

Company stock purchase plans

Profit-sharing plans

Pension fund

Bonuses

Employee credit union

Company educational seminars and conferences

Tuition refunds for job-related course work

Membership expenses in professional organizations

Company-subsidized cafeteria

Recreational facilities

Dental insurance

Child care services

Maternity benefits

A company may pay for all or part of an employee's insurance premiums, make substantial contributions to the pension fund, and provide office space for an employee-operated credit union. Some companies allow employees to choose their own package of benefits. Generous vacation, holiday, and sick-leave policies are becoming more and more common. Liberal maternity benefits have been written into many company policy manuals. Finally, some firms, such as retailers and commercial airlines, offer attractive purchase or travel discounts to their employees. A fringe benefit package can no longer be taken for granted and should be investigated carefully by the job seeker. The constantly rising cost of health care and the concomitant paperwork required of the employer make it necessary for companies to look for ways to decrease the cost of providing benefits to workers of all types.

OPPORTUNITIES FOR SPECIALIZATION

Few professions offer such a wide array of choices. There are unlimited opportunities for the qualified administrative assistant to specialize in a particular field. For most administrative assistants, a decision to specialize usually comes after having had some experience in general office work. Some office experience, training in business fundamentals and administrative support skills, and an interest in the area of specialization are prerequisite to making this decision. This chapter will discuss only a few of the many areas of specialization available to the administrative assistant.

The Administrative Assistant in a Medical Office

A long-established and rapidly growing area of specialization is that of the medical secretary/administrative assistant. With this specialty you may work in a doctor's or dentist's office, a clinic, a hospital, a pharmaceutical company, a public health facility, or even an insurance company.

Although desirable, special training is not essential; learning on the job is always possible. Good spelling skills and a good memory, however, are helpful in gaining familiarity with the terminology. Career schools, community colleges, technical colleges and institutes, and some four-year colleges and universities offer programs for training medical secretaries/administrative assistants. Besides training in office skills and medical dictation, curricula include a number of science courses, the study of medical terminology, records management, and accounting procedures. Specialized handbooks are available for the medical administrative assistant in the medical office. The administrative assistant who is contemplating this field would be wise to examine such a handbook.

In the one-doctor office, the administrative assistant may serve as receptionist, bookkeeper, transcriber of case histories, and office manager. Sterilizing instruments and taking temperatures may be required. Medical secretaries/administrative assistants must also observe the principles of medical ethics by keeping patients' records confidential.

In large medical offices and in hospitals, the administrative assistant's work consists of transcribing patients' records from machine dictation and handling patients smoothly, pleasantly, and sympathetically. Regardless of the size of the office or organization, the administrative assistant must be familiar with the meaning and the spelling of medical terms, with professional office procedures, and with medical and hospital insurance forms. Figure 23-1 shows an administrative assistant at work in a medical office.

To keep current in the field, the medical administrative assistant should join the American Association of Medical Assistants, a professional organization for office staff, nurses, technicians, and assistants employed by physicians or accredited hospitals. This organization sponsors a certification program, publishes a bimonthly magazine (*The Professional Medical Assistant*), and holds an annual convention.

Fig. 23-1 The work of an administrative assistant in a medical office is demanding. Keeping patients' records safe and confidential is an important aspect of this work. *Lanier Worldwide, Inc.*

To be eligible to take the certification examination, candidates must meet certain requirements. Training acquired in a medical assisting program and experience in the field are necessary. The examination has three categories. The general category tests knowledge of medical terminology, anatomy, physiology, behavioral science, medical law, and medical ethics. The basic administrative procedures category covers oral and written communication, bookkeeping, insurance, and office administration. The basic technical procedures category tests examination room techniques, sterilization procedures, knowledge of medications, and other clinical procedures.

The Administrative Assistant in a Legal Office

The administrative assistant in a legal office must have a superior command of the English language and excellent keyboarding and transcription skills. The work of a law office is exacting; an inaccurate record can be extremely expensive to the firm. Working long hours, most of them under pressure, a legal secretary/administrative assistant must have a thorough knowledge of legal procedures and a real interest in the law. Today law offices are equipped with word processors or computers with word processing capabilities; therefore, knowledge of these technologies is imperative.

The National Association of Legal Secretaries holds an annual convention and publishes the NALS *Docket* bimonthly. This organization sponsors through its chapters free training programs, an employment service, and a professional legal secretary (PLS) examination and certification program. To be eligible for the PLS examination, an applicant must have had at least five years' experience as a legal secretary and must provide the names of two attorneys as references. An applicant with a bachelor's or an associate's degree may file for a partial waiver of the experience requirement. The two-day examination consists of seven parts: written communication skills and knowledge; human relations and ethics; legal secretarial procedures; legal secretarial accounting; legal terminology, techniques, and procedures; exercise of judgment; and legal secretarial skills.

The legal secretary's work is highly varied and involves extensive contact with clients. Occasionally legal secretaries/administrative assistants become so fascinated with the profession that they prepare to be legal assistants (see Chapter 22) or go to law school.

The Administrative Assistant in Education

Every community offers employment opportunities for administrative assistants interested in working in an educational environment. Working for top school officials in a large city system involves duties similar to those of the administrative assistant in business and industry. On the other hand, the administrative assistant in the office of a small school performs vastly different duties, including taking dictation, keeping records, ordering materials and supplies, supervising student aides, scheduling facilities, working on master schedules, and planning group meetings. The educational administrative assistant also meets school visitors and has close contact with students, teachers, and parents.

The National Association of Educational Office Personnel (NAEOP) is the professional organization for personnel in this field. The organization seeks to upgrade the profession by sponsoring a continuing academic program, conducting conferences, and distributing three publications (*The National Educational Secretary, Beam,* and *Crossroads*). The NAEOP also sponsors a professional standards program that issues seven kinds of certificates (basic, associate professional, advanced I, II, III, bachelor, and master) based on education, experience, and professional activity. A college degree is required for the bachelor's certificate and a master's degree for the master's certificate. To be eligible for the examination, an applicant must be a member of the association.

The Administrative Assistant in a Technical Office

The administrative assistant working in a technical office serves engineers and scientists who are at home in the laboratory but not in the office. To conserve the time of highly paid scientific and engineering personnel, many companies provide each top-level scientist and engineer with assistants to perform routine functions, freeing the scientist for creative work. The administrative assistant in the technical office is a member of this support team, assuming the burden of office administration and minimizing distractions and interruptions.

The technical administrative assistant is probably as much an office manager as an administrative assistant. The work includes not only the usual administrative support duties but such additional responsibilities as handling all or most of the correspondence (from composition to mailing); maintaining the office technical library; gathering materials from libraries or computer databases; and proofreading, editing, and handling all details incident to the publication of scientific papers.

The technical administrative assistant prepares engineering reports, checks materials against specifications and standards, and orders materials in compliance with specifications. The work is demanding and exacting, but the pay is exceedingly rewarding. A strong background in mathematics, science, and technical terminology is a definite asset; advancement requires continued study. Figure 23-2 should give you an idea of the qualifications employers look for in a technical administrative assistant.

TECHNICAL
ADMINISTRATIVE ASSISTANT

Dynamic young medical research institute needs qualified technical administrative assistant to support quality control division. Highly proficient in all phases of office procedures with top skills. Must be able to work without supervision. Background in mathematics and sciences helpful. Salary commensurate with ability. Excellent benefits. Call Ms. Alvarez at 555-6782 for appointment.

TRIANGLE RESEARCH INSTITUTE
5770 Waycross Drive
Bala Cynwyd, PA 19004-2137

Fig. 23-2 An advertisement for a technical administrative assistant stresses that a background in science or mathematics is desirable.

When you work as an administrative assistant in a technical office, you can expect to undergo security clearance if you are employed in a company having contracts with the U.S. Department of Defense. The maintenance of strict security control is becoming important to other companies as well, because of the possibility of pirating formulas, research findings, advanced designs, and so forth. The technical administrative assistant must know how security is maintained for each classification from restricted data to top secret.

The Administrative Assistant Serving the Public

Some administrative assistants choose to go into business for themselves offering office support services to the public. People (usually traveling executives) often need someone for dictation and transcription or similar short-term jobs. For this reason, the office of a public administrative assistant is equipped with word processing and communication equipment and is usually located in a hotel, off the main foyer of a large office building, or at an airport facility. The administrative assistant charges by the hour or by the job and may work for as many as a dozen persons each day. The work ranges from taking highly technical dictation to recording speeches and testimony of witnesses, to keying legal documents, to running errands for a busy executive. The administrative assistant who serves the public is usually a notary public as well.

Highly qualified administrative assistants usually find this field gratifying and exciting. Only someone with a broad education, sufficient financial resources, a wealth of office experience, the temperament to cope with the pressure of deadlines, and the highest level of skills should attempt to enter the field. In the right location, the income is high; but much of the work is performed under pressure.

The Administrative Assistant in Government

More administrative assistants work for the government than for any other type of business or organization. Government positions offer certain advantages, such as assured annual salary increases, job security, a sound retirement system, and the opportunity for advancement based on merit. An administrative assistant trained in office administration, who has initiative and ambition, can advance to a position of great responsibility in government service. Being a government employee does not necessarily mean working in Washington, D.C., or for the federal government. Wherever there is a military installation, veterans' hospital, weather station, or federal bureau office, there are federal employees. State and local governments (combined) employ far more office workers than does the federal government. Government jobs are found in towns and cities in America and in foreign countries.

The federal government, all state governments, and many municipal governments have a civil service merit system in which jobs are classified and appointments made on the basis of examination results. As a student, you can obtain a certificate of proficiency in keying from your college, but you must take the written civil service examination on verbal and clerical abilities to qualify for these jobs. The federal government is now following the practice of self-certification in keying. An applicant who certifies a keying skill of 40 or more words a minute need not take the tests. The applicant is also graded on education, training, and experience.

Stenographic posts are classified in the federal government as GS3 (General Schedule 3) through GS6, and it is possible for an administrative assistant to advance to GS7 and GS8. There is a standard base salary, with annual increments, for each GS rating. For high-cost areas such as Alaska and Hawaii, cost-of-living increases are given.

For the first years of government service, an employee is considered *career conditional;* after three years, the status changes to *career permanent.* This latter classification means that you can apply to any federal agency without further testing. If you leave government service and return within three years from the date of your termination, you do not lose accumulated sick leave. In addition, unused sick leave hours count toward an early retirement date.

The United States is divided into ten regions with an Office of Personnel Management in each. There are also over 100 Federal Job Information Centers, listed in telephone directories under "U.S. Government." If a center is not listed in your directory, the toll-free number for a center in your area can be obtained by dialing 1-800-555-1212. To obtain information about a position, write to the Office of Personnel Management in the region in which you wish to obtain employment or telephone your local Federal Job Information Center. If you are interested in working in Washington, D.C., write to the Office of Personnel Management, 1900 E Street, NW, Washington, DC 20415.

The Administrative Assistant in Foreign Service

As the world rapidly becomes a global marketplace and executives take permanent and temporary assignments abroad, the prospect of serving as an administrative assistant in the American legation in South America, Africa, Singapore, or the capital cities of Europe offers the ultimate assignment in adventure, excitement, and cultural diversity. If you examine the employment opportunities in the Foreign Service, the U.S. Information Agency (USIA), the Agency for International Development (AID), and the Departments of the Army, Navy, and Air Force, you will discover challenging positions that require keen interpersonal skills in many parts of the world. The Department of State has Foreign Service offices in over 300 cities worldwide.

Work in a foreign country can be thrilling but also exacting. It calls for a special kind of person. Foreign Service personnel are on display 24 hours a day. Each staff member represents the United States and contributes to the success of our mission overseas. The Department of State, USIA, and AID, therefore, carefully screen all Foreign Service personnel, and requirements are high. The basic requirements for a position as an administrative assistant in the Foreign Service are as follows:

21 years of age

U.S. citizen

Pass a thorough background investigation for security clearance

High school graduate or equivalent

Passing grade from a qualifying examination requiring 60 words per minute keying speed and experience with word processing and/or computer equipment. The ability to take dictation is not required but is desirable.

Good health

Five years of general office administrative work of which two years must include progressively responsible secretarial experience. (Education beyond high school may be substituted for up to two years of the experience requirement.)

Competence in a foreign language is not required. If, however, you should have ambitions to advance to the position of a staff officer in the Department of State, the ability to speak and write a foreign language is required. Extensive study of a foreign language in college will be a strong plus factor when your application is evaluated.

The pay for Foreign Service administrative assistants is comparatively good, with additional allowances for housing and cost of living, and special compensation for hardship posts. For information, write to the Recruitment Division, Foreign Service Secretary Program, U.S. Department of State, P.O. Box 9317, Arlington, VA 22219-1317.

The Temporary Service Administrative Assistant

One of the fastest growing service industries today provides part-time office help. Kelly Services, Inc., Olsten Corp., and Manpower, Inc., are a few of the organizations specializing in temporary service. Others are listed in the Yellow Pages and are widely advertised in general publications. These organizations offer a corps of temporary workers to be deployed wherever required. It is estimated that over two million people work as temporaries each year. They help the office that experiences intermittent periods of heavy work load; they also fill in for employees who are on vacation or ill.

Many firms are staffed entirely with permanent temporary employees. In addition to rendering a service to business, some temporary service agencies provide their temporaries with training on word processors, computers, and related office equipment. These organizations also provide a means of organized part-time employment to a large number of persons who are unable, because of family obligations or other duties, to devote themselves to year-round, full-time jobs.

A temporary position permits a flexible schedule and a choice of job locations close to home. It also enables a person to acquire experience before applying for a full-time job or reentering the job market after a long absence. To be happy in temporary work, the administrative assistant must be skilled in the use of information technology, flexible, confident, and adaptable to change.

The work of a temporary administrative assistant is varied. Calls for assistance come from all types of offices. The agency attempts to match the requirements of the job with the competencies of the temporary worker. Temporaries can be selective in the jobs they accept; however, temporary services report that the majority of the calls for temporaries seldom request the short-term employee to perform routine filing, keying on a word processor, or other routine jobs. In contrast to the demands of ten years ago, the temporaries today must possess a myriad of skills ranging from word processing to spreadsheets. Computer literacy is a must. Today's temporary is retained for longer assignments, and familiarity with the various types of hardware and software has come to be expected by employers.

The flexible schedule that temporary work makes possible appeals to some professionals, and many a college student has found being an office temporary for the summer a good way to gain a wide variety of experience in a short time. At the same time, being a temporary helps an administrative assistant determine what type of company would be the most appealing to work for full-time.

SURVEY OF EMPLOYMENT OPPORTUNITIES

Even a cursory glance at the help-wanted advertisements in most newspapers reveals numerous options for the highly qualified, college-trained administrative assistant. You are in a position to pick and choose. The problem, then, is one of job selection. Before choosing a company, you should determine whether you want to work in your local community or a new location, in a small or a large office, what salary you need to meet your financial goals, and what type of job is most fitting for your skills and personality. Figure 23-3 shows that there are many dimensions to the selection process.

1. Do you want to work in your local community, or do you hope to find employment in a new location? in a large city? in a different part of the country? abroad?

2. Which organizations relate to your special interests in art, music, sports, medicine, accounting, social work, research, writing, politics?

3. How do your education and skills match the job requirements of your career goal?

4. Would you prefer to work in a one-administrative-assistant office or in a large organization?

5. What are you looking for in a job? Do you want a job that offers security? no pressure? competition? responsibility? advancement? prestige?

6. What is the average salary for the position you are seeking?

Psychologists say that the key elements of job satisfaction are interesting work, a feeling of achievement, opportunity for growth, recognition from one's employer, and a feeling of being needed. The right choice is not the result of luck but of careful analysis and action.

Before you begin your job search, take a few minutes to prepare a job prospect list. Decide how you will evaluate a company. Set goals and objectives for yourself. Then begin to execute your plan.

Developing a Job Prospect List

No good sales campaign is ready for action without a prospect list. Your job prospect list should include potential employers who can offer the kind of employment opportunity you are seeking in terms of salary, location, size, interest appeal, permanence, advancement, career development, company reputation in the community, and job satisfaction.

College Placement Office.   The placement office of your college can give you expert help in developing your prospect list and can assist you in making job contacts. Complete all forms necessary for registration promptly. Become acquainted with the placement office personnel. Discuss your employment needs with them freely and often. If they arrange a job interview for you, always report to them after the interview. Solicit their advice and let them know you appreciate their assistance.

Free Employment Agencies.   Employment agencies are a good source of prospective positions. Any person seeking employment may register without charge with a state employment office. Registration includes a comprehensive interview and a skills test so that you can be properly classified according to your abilities, personality traits, training, and experience. In order to keep on its active list, you must communicate with that office regularly. Consult the classified section of your newspaper for employment agency listings.

Private Employment Agencies.   A private employment agency performs three functions for a fee: It acts as an agent for the job seeker, as a recruiter for the employer, and as a job market information center. Many agencies have a computerized database of job candidates which they make available to employers. In about two-thirds of the jobs listed, employers pay the fee. In some states, regulatory bodies set limits on fees charged by agencies. An applicant registering with an agency signs a contract in which the fee terms are stated. (As with every written contract, read carefully before you sign. Be sure that you understand the conditions of the contract.) After a contract is signed, the applicant is assigned a counselor. Inform the counselor of all employers you have contacted before coming to the agency so that you will not be obligated for the fee if a job is offered from your previous contacts. A major advantage of a good agency is that it carries out a complete job hunt for the applicant, thus relieving the job seeker of much of the repetitive detail work involved in job hunting. Another advantage is that the agency serves as a third-party representative for the applicant with prospective employers. For example, an employee with a large medical supply house hears of an attractive opening with a competitor. Because the competition between the two firms makes the employee uncomfortable about applying for the position, an employment agency may be contacted to submit the employee's name as an applicant.

Private employment agencies perform a valuable service for the employer as well. The staff of the agency can expertly screen, test, and interview each applicant. The company then interviews only those who meet the company's specified qualifications. Because many businesses use private agencies exclusively, keep in mind that many desirable positions are available only through such agencies.

A private employment agency should be selected carefully. Don't hesitate to interview the agency to determine its professionalism. For a directory of reputable agencies, write to the National Association of Personnel Consultants, 3133 Mt. Vernon Avenue, Alexandria, VA 22305. This directory will be especially helpful in locating an agency in a distant city where you would like to obtain employment. Agencies listed in this directory subscribe to a code of ethical practices. Some agencies are a part of a recruiting network which can put you in touch with member agencies in other cities. You might also contact the Better Business Bureau to determine if any agency has been reported for unethical practices.

Newspaper Advertisements. The classified section of the newspaper is an excellent source of information for the job seeker. A glance at this section of any metropolitan newspaper will reveal the impact that information technology has had upon the traditional role of office support personnel. Practically every advertisement for administrative assistants indicates that word processing and familiarity with various software packages are in strong demand by employers.

Besides providing an employment picture of the community, skill requirements and current pay rates for administrative assistant positions are often stated. If a particular advertisement appeals to you, carefully follow the directions given for making an application.

In reviewing the help-wanted section, notice that these advertisements do not specify male or female or in any way indicate a preferred age range. Federal law prohibits employers and employment agencies from classifying jobs by gender (unless it is a realistic occupational qualification) or by preferred ethnic group or age level. In fact, some advertisements will state that the company is an equal opportunity employer.

Firms that advertise for help in the classified columns sometimes use a blind advertisement (see Figure 23-4). A **blind advertisement** is one in which a box number or letter is used for your reply and the firm name is not mentioned. A legitimate blind advertisement is used because the firm does not want to be bothered with interviewing large numbers of applicants. Most employers notify present employees before running a blind advertisement. This prevents the possibility of an employee answering a blind ad and being embarrassed for doing so. Be aware that blind advertisements are sometimes used improperly to get names of sales prospects by someone who has something to sell.

TOP DRAWER

Interested in art, music, theater, sports? A new magazine that will cover all aspects of life in the exciting city of Chicago is looking for an exceptional administrative assistant. You must have excellent skills, good judgment, be able to supervise the support staff, work effectively under pressure, and be eager to accept challenges and responsibility. Opportunities for creativity in the areas of writing, photography, graphics, and design abound. Strong background in English a must. This position offers you a ground floor opportunity to go as far as your abilities will take you. Send resume to Box 119, Sun Times, Chicago, IL 60651-5407

Fig. 23-4 Blind advertisements ask applicants to reply to a newspaper box number.

Friends, Relatives, and Associates. Include friends, friends of your family, businesspeople with whom you have had some kind of contact, student alumni groups, and former instructors to suggest names for your job prospect list. Inform them that you are seeking a position and that you would appreciate their help.

Another source of job leads is a professional organization such as the National Federation of Business and Professional Women's Clubs. This organization maintains a talent bank of members for referral to employers seeking women to fill middle to top-level management jobs. Special-interest groups also provide employment information to members. If someone tells you about a job opening, it is a matter of courtesy to let that person know the outcome.

Other Sources. The Yellow Pages of your telephone book provide a classified list of the local businesses to which you might apply. Make a list of those companies where you would like to work. Take the initiative to visit their personnel offices. This is a most effective way of securing employment. For instance, if you are interested in a position in an insurance company, look in the Yellow Pages for a listing of all local companies. Make an appointment for an interview or send your resume and a letter of application to the personnel department.

Another source of jobs often overlooked is the company that has employed you part-time while you were a student. Often, permanent jobs that represent a significant promotion are available and advertised to employees within a firm. You should, therefore, keep abreast of vacancies that match your skills, abilities, and career goals.

Do not forget that the government is a major employer. You will find federal and state employment offices listed in the telephone directory.

Become an avid reader of the daily newspaper and watch all news items that give clues to possible job contacts. New businesses are constantly opening, and articles relating to jobs, changes, or expansions often appear in the newspaper.

Job Prospects in Other Locations. A number of information sources may be used to obtain job prospects in a distant city or area. In addition to the directory of the National Association of Personnel Consultants (see page 635), copies of the leading newspapers from cities across the nation can be examined at your local library. Telephone directories for major cities are also kept in many public libraries. Trade association directories are helpful in providing addresses of companies, and chambers of commerce maintain directories of local employers.

Learning About a Company

After you have compiled a job prospect list, you should exhaust all means of getting information on each of the firms on your list. Telephone to find out the name of the human resources manager. Ask your friends, acquaintances, and instructors what they know about the firm. Check library reference materials and computer databases to learn of the company's financial condition. Examine the company's advertisements in papers and magazines. Study the annual report of the firm. A copy of an annual report can usually be obtained by sending a request to the company.

Many large companies publish brochures describing their job opportunities and employment policies. Your college placement office may have these brochures on file. If not, send a request to the company. If it is a small firm, consult the local chamber of commerce and the Better Business Bureau. Use separate file folders to accumulate pertinent material on each company.

Many firms will be eliminated from your list as you proceed in this information-gathering campaign. When your information is complete, group your prospects according to jobs you are best fitted to fill. Select prospects that offer the best chance for employment and that will provide an interesting future.

Evaluating a Company

Selecting a company in which you would like to begin your career is a highly significant decision that will have a long-lasting impact on your future. There is no foolproof test for evaluating a prospective employer, but the questions in Figure 23-5 may help.

Don't overlook opportunities in small offices—you may be happier there—or in a new company that is just getting under way. Being on the beginning team can be exciting and rewarding.

PREPARING AN APPLICATION

The first step in making an application for employment is to take an inventory of your knowledge, skills, strengths, and weaknesses in terms of the requirements of each particular position. What skills, understandings, and special qualities will the employer be seeking? What type of experience will be expected? Do you have unique qualities that would be an asset in the position? What weaknesses in your preparation or background might the employer note? What plan do you have to correct these weaknesses? The preparation of a resume will assist you in making this analysis.

Your Resume

Sometimes called a *personal data sheet* or *personal history,* a **resume** is a concise, positive summary of your background and abilities. Because your purpose is to gain a personal interview, your resume must arouse interest in your unique qualifications. It must be short, preferably one page; if too long, it dulls the interest. It must be a reflection of you. For the experienced applicant with a long work history, more than one page may be required.

Some large employment agencies and corporations code and enter information furnished on an applicant's resume in their computer system. When an opening occurs, the computer is searched for the names of applicants meeting the specific requirements of the job.

COMMUNICATION

The best resumes are written by people who know what they're looking for.

Fig. 23-5 Employers often criticize applicants who are not familiar with the company, its products, its markets, and its reputation.

EVALUATING A COMPANY AS A POTENTIAL EMPLOYER

1. *What is the reputation of the company in the community?* The community image of a company is the sum of many elements, including employee relationships, reputation for progressive management, sponsorship of community projects, fair employment practices, and general leadership in civic and business activities.

2. *Is the company an equal opportunity employer?* Is it known to discriminate in employment in the areas of race, creed, color, national origin, age, or gender?

3. *How satisfactory are employer-employee relationships?* Do employees seem to have a common bond of enthusiasm, or are there undercurrents of distrust and backbiting?

4. *Is the business financially stable?* A business that is not economically sound cannot give its employees a sense of financial security. Its wage policies and employee benefits will always depend on the profit picture.

5. *Is the company expanding?* A growing organization usually offers opportunities for advancement.

6. *What opportunities for training and advancement are provided?* Companies that provide special training programs or pay college tuition merit special consideration. Does the company have a reputation for promoting from within?

7. *Has the company recently undergone changes in top administration because of merger, buyout, or bankruptcy proceedings; and if so, has this affected employee morale and productivity?* Such changes sometimes result in reduction of the work force, drastic changes in the structure of the organization, low morale and productivity, or failure of the company to meet its financial obligations.

8. *Does the company have offices in other cities or overseas?* What are the requirements and/or opportunities for transferring to other locations?

9. *Is the company involved in any major litigation?* Are there lawsuits against the company for discrimination, environmental pollution, product liability, or the like that could affect profits and company image?

10. *What are the company's major products? competitors? markets?*

COMMUNICATION

Your resume is a highlight of your background, not a complete life history; it should be concise and to the point.

There are three types of resumes: chronological, functional, and targeted. The **chronological resume** lists your education and work experience in reverse chronological order. This means your most current degree and your most recent job are listed first. The **functional resume,** unlike the chronological resume, ignores historical sequence and stresses skills and abilities regardless of where they were developed or demonstrated. This format offers an opportunity to cluster your education, experiences, and activities into significant ability categories that support your career objective. The functional resume is recommended for those who have considerable work experience. The **targeted resume** focuses on a particular job or company. In other words, it targets a specific position or organization and presents the data in a way that shows the strengths needed to succeed in that particular company or in a specific job. Examples of the three types of resumes appear in Figures 23-6(a), 23-6(b) on page 640, and 23-6(c) on page 641.

You will use your resume in a number of ways. Send it with letters of application. Give copies to friends, relatives, and business acquaintances to pass on to prospective employers. Your college placement office will need one or more copies. Always take a copy to an interview. Use it to supplement an application form.

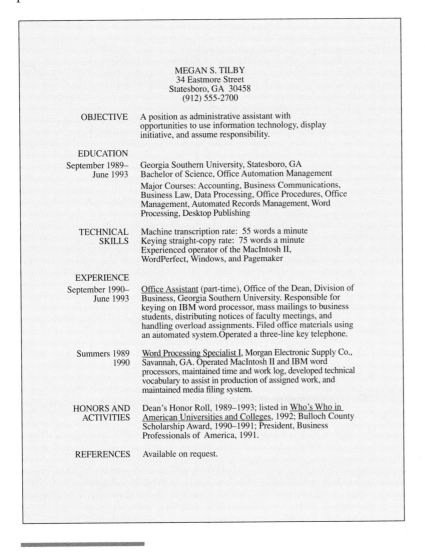

MEGAN S. TILBY
34 Eastmore Street
Statesboro, GA 30458
(912) 555-2700

OBJECTIVE   A position as administrative assistant with opportunities to use information technology, display initiative, and assume responsibility.

EDUCATION
September 1989–   Georgia Southern University, Statesboro, GA
June 1993   Bachelor of Science, Office Automation Management

Major Courses: Accounting, Business Communications, Business Law, Data Processing, Office Procedures, Office Management, Automated Records Management, Word Processing, Desktop Publishing

TECHNICAL   Machine transcription rate: 55 words a minute
SKILLS   Keying straight-copy rate: 75 words a minute
Experienced operator of the MacIntosh II, WordPerfect, Windows, and Pagemaker

EXPERIENCE
September 1990–   Office Assistant (part-time), Office of the Dean, Division of
June 1993   Business, Georgia Southern University. Responsible for keying on IBM word processor, mass mailings to business students, distributing notices of faculty meetings, and handling overload assignments. Filed office materials using an automated system. Operated a three-line key telephone.

Summers 1989   Word Processing Specialist I, Morgan Electronic Supply Co.,
1990   Savannah, GA. Operated MacIntosh II and IBM word processors, maintained time and work log, developed technical vocabulary to assist in production of assigned work, and maintained media filing system.

HONORS AND   Dean's Honor Roll, 1989–1993; listed in Who's Who in
ACTIVITIES   American Universities and Colleges, 1992; Bulloch County Scholarship Award, 1990–1991; President, Business Professionals of America, 1991.

REFERENCES   Available on request.

Fig. 23-6(a) A chronological resume.

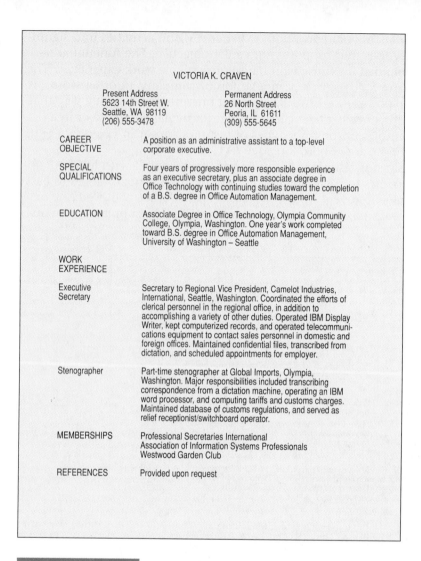

VICTORIA K. CRAVEN

Present Address	Permanent Address
5623 14th Street W.	26 North Street
Seattle, WA 98119	Peoria, IL 61611
(206) 555-3478	(309) 555-5645

CAREER OBJECTIVE
A position as an administrative assistant to a top-level corporate executive.

SPECIAL QUALIFICATIONS
Four years of progressively more responsible experience as an executive secretary, plus an associate degree in Office Technology with continuing studies toward the completion of a B.S. degree in Office Automation Management.

EDUCATION
Associate Degree in Office Technology, Olympia Community College, Olympia, Washington. One year's work completed toward B.S. degree in Office Automation Management, University of Washington – Seattle

WORK EXPERIENCE

Executive Secretary
Secretary to Regional Vice President, Camelot Industries, International, Seattle, Washington. Coordinated the efforts of clerical personnel in the regional office, in addition to accomplishing a variety of other duties. Operated IBM Display Writer, kept computerized records, and operated telecommunications equipment to contact sales personnel in domestic and foreign offices. Maintained confidential files, transcribed from dictation, and scheduled appointments for employer.

Stenographer
Part-time stenographer at Global Imports, Olympia, Washington. Major responsibilities included transcribing correspondence from a dictation machine, operating an IBM word processor, and computing tariffs and customs charges. Maintained database of customs regulations, and served as relief receptionist/switchboard operator.

MEMBERSHIPS
Professional Secretaries International
Association of Information Systems Professionals
Westwood Garden Club

REFERENCES
Provided upon request

Fig. 23-6(b) A functional resume.

Make sure that your resume is expertly keyed on good-quality white paper. Try to use an electronic typewriter or personal computer to give your resume a professional look. If you use a computer, a laser printer will give the most attractive results. Use wide margins and leave plenty of blank space between sections. Your resume's appearance says as much about you as its content does. Many an applicant has lost the opportunity for an interview because of messy corrections, poor format, misspelled words, or grammatical errors on a resume or on an accompanying application letter. Although interviewers prefer an original copy of a resume, a copy made on a good-quality copier is acceptable.

```
                    KATHRYN L. BANKS

                      272 Alamo Road
                    Peoria, IL  61614
                      309-555-9321

  JOB TARGET:   Administrative Assistant to CEO with Markham
                Advertising Agency

  CAPABILITIES:

    *Familiar with automated office technologies--Desktop Publishing,
      Graphics, Database, LANs, Electronic Mail, Teleconferencing, etc.
    *Analyze office procedures for increased productivity
    *Delegate routine work effectively
    *Write complete and clear reports and correspondence
    *Teach others to operate automated office equipment
    *Operate a variety of word processing equipment
    *Interact pleasantly with clients, coworkers, and executives
    *Speak and write German

  ACCOMPLISHMENTS:

    *Office Automation Management Student of the Year
    *Maintained Dean's List GPA of 3.8 for eight semesters
    *Served as Student Representative to the Dean's Council
    *Served as President of Phi Kappa Phi honor society

  EDUCATION:

    Virginia Commonwealth University, Richmond, VA  23284
      Will receive Bachelor of Science in Office Automation Management
      in May 1996
    J. Sergeant Reynolds Community College, Richmond, VA  23228
      Associate in Applied Science, Office Systems Technology, May 1994.
      Graduated magna cum laude.
    University of Freiberg, Germany
      Lived with German family and attended classes taught in German.
      Improved fluency in German and traveled throughout Europe, 1993.

  WORK EXPERIENCE:

    Administrative Assistant, Trust Department, Crestar Securities
      Corporation, 9191 E. Main Street, Richmond, VA  23219,
      September 1994-present
    Word Processing Operator, CreditCorp, Inc., 909 Cary Street,
      Richmond, VA  23219, October 1992-August 1994.

  REFERENCES:

    Available upon request
```

Fig. 23-6(c)   A targeted resume.

Personal Data.   You may omit the heading *Resume* or *Data Sheet* at the top. Every resume must include the job seeker's name, address, and telephone number. This identification should appear as a heading for the information that follows. If you mail your resume before you graduate, it is essential that you give a permanent address as well as a school address. It is not necessary to provide such personal information as age, height, weight, gender, marital status, or social security number.

Objective.   This section gives you the opportunity to identify the specific position you seek, your long-range career goals, or both. Some authorities believe, however, that this information belongs in a cover letter, thus leaving space on the resume for a summary of your accomplishments. If you have varied experience and can qualify for a number of different office jobs, you should not include a detailed objective that may disqualify you for positions for which you would like to be considered. From the reader's standpoint, an objective provides instant knowledge of the sort of job you are seeking. A well-written job objective can serve as a starting point for conversation during the interview; therefore, it should be practical, clear, and tailored to the company where you are seeking employment.

Education.   Include complete, pertinent information about your educational background. Begin with facts about your most recent educational experience.

Schools Attended.   Keeping in mind that the resume should generally be limited to one page, you may wish to list only the school from which you received your degree. If space permits and listing every school you attended will give you a competitive edge, list all colleges and universities you attended and those from which you graduated. List the most recent schools first and give dates of graduation, diplomas received, degrees conferred, awards, and scholarships.

Major Subjects.   If your resume is too brief, and you need to fill space, the business courses that you completed may be listed. Include also courses specifically related to the position for which you are applying. For example, in applying for a position as administrative assistant in an advertising office, you might list English, art, and psychology courses taken.

Skills and Abilities.   List your keying speed and the software packages you have mastered. Indicate by manufacturer's name the electronic equipment you have used in your work experience. List separately the business machines you can operate, and indicate your level of operating ability.

Work Experience.   List your work experience in reverse order (on a chronological resume) or in the order of its importance to the position in question (on a functional resume). For example, in applying for a position as an administrative assistant, list office experience (full- and part-time) first, giving inclusive dates of employment, the name and address (city and state only) of the employer, telephone number, the title of the position held, and a brief description of your job duties. Use action verbs to describe your duties. If your work involved the supervision of others, be sure to include that fact. And don't forget to mention promotions. Omit any reference to salary earned.

    If you are like most college students, with work experience limited to part-time and summer employment, you should include on your resume the dates and descriptions of your employment history. Even if your part-time and summer jobs did not involve office work, they should be listed. They are often indicative of your willingness to work and your ability to get along with other people.

Special Interests, Abilities, and Accomplishments. Your extracurricular activities, special interests, and achievements give the prospective employer an indication of what kind of person you are and how you would fit into the office; therefore, you should list:

1. *The extracurricular activities in which you have participated and the offices you have held.* Holding a responsible office in one organization may be more impressive than listing membership in virtually every organization on campus.

2. *Special honors received.* Awards and scholarships are evidence of your ability and perseverance.

3. *Special achievements if they have implications for the position you are seeking.* Your ability to read or speak a foreign language, awards for English composition or original writing, or special training in some field of science may be the specific point that influences an employer to grant you an interview.

References. You will need to have at least three references in mind when you begin your job search. The longer and better they have known you, the more valid will be their evaluation of your abilities.

If you have had no experience, consider using instructors of business subjects or administrators who have firsthand knowledge of your training and can evaluate your work potential. Avoid using the names of close relatives or your minister (unless the job is church related) for a work reference. You must secure permission to use anyone's name as a reference before submitting it to a prospective employer.

Upon leaving a job, request a letter of reference from your employer. This letter may be especially helpful to you if you are moving to another city or state.

Authorities do not agree on whether references should be included on the resume. The majority suggest that references be furnished upon request. An employer usually asks for the names and addresses of references during the interview or when you are completing an application blank. If you include your references on your resume, make clear their relationship to you (i.e., former employer or teacher).

Other Information. You may include on your resume the date that you will be available for employment and information about your willingness to relocate. Save matters concerning salary and your reasons for leaving previous employment for the interview.

Your Application Letter

An application letter is another document used by the job seeker to obtain a personal interview. It may be the only document to describe your qualifications, or a resume may be attached to it. Like the resume, the application letter should be individually and accurately keyed and limited to one page. It should highlight experience that is related to the job in question. Bear in mind, too, that your letter is one of many that the employer receives. Thus, it should be unique in order to set it apart from all the rest.

Solicited and Unsolicited Application Letters.   An application letter is *solicited* when a job opening is known to exist. If you are responding to a help-wanted advertisement or if you are writing at the request of an employer (frequently a part of the screening process), your application letter is solicited. A resume should accompany a solicited letter. The letter will expand on your special qualifications for the position and will indicate why you are interested in the company.

Unsolicited application letters can be written to discover whether an opening exists. An unsolicited letter format can be used repeatedly with carefully made adaptations to meet the special requirements of different types of jobs. Although an unsolicited application letter need not include a resume, most people do include a resume with an unsolicited letter. The letter should include a summary of your previous experience and a discussion of your capabilities and how they relate to the position you are seeking. If you are granted an interview, then you can present your resume tailored specifically to the available position.

Basic Parts of an Application Letter.   Whether solicited or unsolicited, your letter should include the following parts:

1. An interesting first paragraph that tells why you are writing commands attention. Three examples of interesting first paragraphs follow:

   Example 1
   Mr. Grant Lehman suggested that I write to inquire whether you have an opening for a technical administrative assistant in your Research and Development Division. (*unsolicited letter of application*)

   Example 2
   The position of administrative assistant described in your advertisement in today's issue of the *Sentinel* is a challenging opportunity. Please consider me an applicant for the position. (*solicited letter of application*)

   Example 3
   Mr. Ron Radtke, head of the Administrative Services Department at Eastern Community College, tells me that you have a position open for a graduate with administrative and word processing training. Please consider me an applicant. (*solicited letter of application*)

2. A statement indicating why you are interested in joining the company (if the name of the company is known), or in lieu of that, an expansion on what you know about the requirements of the position you are seeking. The use of quotation marks in the examples that follow indicates that the words appearing in the advertisement have been incorporated into the letter of application.

Example 1

```
Your company is well known in our community for its
superior products, recent plant expansion, and bene-
fits to employees. From reading about LKM's overseas
expansion, I would be proud to be part of your "fu-
ture growth."
```

Example 2

```
Words such as "responsible" and "administrative abil-
ity" in your advertisement's description of the avail-
able position immediately appealed to me. These words
mean that you are looking for an individual who can
show initiative, work without supervision, and assume
some of the administrative tasks of the employer. I
believe that my training at Madison Technical College
has qualified me to say, "I am up to the task."
```

3. A closing paragraph should ask for an appointment for an interview or other definite action.

Example 1

```
I will telephone your office on Friday morning to
arrange an appointment for an interview.
```

Example 2

```
I would like very much to come to your office to talk
with you about the position. When I telephone you on
Wednesday morning, will you please let me know a time
that would be convenient for you to see me?
```

Example 3

```
I would welcome the opportunity to meet you person-
ally to discuss my qualifications. Please call me at
603-555-1778 to arrange an interview.
```

Guides for Writing Application Letters.   There is no one formula for writing an effective application letter, but studying the sample letter of application in Figure 23-7 and observing the following guidelines should make the task less formidable:

1. *Address the letter to an individual.* A letter directed "To Whom It May Concern" may never concern anyone. Find out the name and title of

34 Eastmore Street
Statesboro, GA 30458
June 10, 19--

Mr. Phillip DeWitt, Director
Human Resources Department
Hart Manufacturing Company
1604 Gilmer Avenue
Atlanta, GA 30307-1604

Dear Mr. DeWitt:

TELLS WHY YOU ARE WRITING

The Placement Office at Georgia Southern University has told me of the opening in your office for a graduate with a background in WordPerfect and desktop publishing. I understand that the job requires a large volume of transcription in addition to routine office duties and provides an opportunity to assume administrative responsibilities. I believe I meet your requirements and would like to be considered for the position.

TELLS WHY YOU ARE INTERESTED IN THIS FIRM

While a student at Georgia Southern, I had an opportunity to tour a number of industrial firms in Atlanta. Of those I visited, your company, your operations, and the friendliness of your staff impressed me the most, and I would like to begin my career with your firm.

REFERS TO YOUR RESUME

You will see from the enclosed resume that I have acquired a high level of office administration and word processing skills. You will also note that I have supplemented my work at Georgia Southern with on-the-job experience during the summers and during my last year in school.

REQUESTS ACTION

Since it may be difficult to reach me by telephone during working hours, I shall call your office next Tuesday to schedule an appointment at your convenience. I am looking forward to discussing this position with you.

Sincerely yours,

Megan S. Tilby

Megan S. Tilby

Enclosure

---

the person in charge of employment from the switchboard operator of the company. The use of the name (correctly spelled) and title personalizes the letter and makes a favorable first impression. Obviously you cannot address your letter to an individual when you are replying to a blind advertisement. In this case, use the title of the position. The correct address form and salutation for such a letter is shown here:

```
Box H-816
Charlotte Observer
Charlotte, NC 28202-2555

Dear Human Resources Manager:
Ladies and Gentlemen:
        or
Good Morning!
```

2. *Use the "you" approach.* Your application letter is a sales letter, and the product is you. You must convince the prospective employer that you

can serve that company. Tell about yourself from the perspective of the employer. Avoid using these expressions: *I want, I did this, I did that.* Show that you understand the requirements of the position and demonstrate how your qualifications meet the employer's needs.

3. *Be honest, confident, and enthusiastic.* Your application letter should show a proper, not exaggerated, appreciation of your own ability. Above all, be honest. Your letter should be neither boastful nor deprecating. Employers are experts in detecting insincerity. Be specific about the position you want and the things you can do: You may be called upon to prove your claims. Do not be apologetic. If your experience is limited, you need not call attention to the fact. Concentrate on your positive qualities.

4. *Be concise.* If you enclose a resume, omit a detailed summary of your education and experience in your letter. Your letter should be an invitation to read the resume. The statement "I am enclosing information about my training and experience" does little to persuade the reader to continue to your resume. Stimulate interest. "An examination of my resume will show that my training and experience as an administrative assistant have prepared me for the position you advertised" or "My extracurricular activities, described in the enclosed resume, have prepared me to work with other people" are examples of sentences that arouse a reader's interest.

5. *Make action easy.* You are more likely to win an interview by saying, "I will call you on Friday morning to arrange a personal interview," than by saying, "May I hear from you?" The purpose of the application letter is to get an interview. If you obtain one, your letter has done as much as you can expect it to do.

6. *Give the letter eye appeal.* Make your letter attractive and absolutely faultless in conformity with the best rules of business letter writing. Anything you say will be worthless if your message contains an error. There must be no flaws in spelling, grammar, punctuation, keying, arrangement, spacing, placement, or wording. You should use a good-quality bond paper of standard letter size. Your envelope should match the paper in quality. Your name, complete address, and telephone number should be keyed as the heading.

7. *File a copy of each application letter that you write.* It is a good idea also to keep records of your interviews. A form similar to the one shown in Figure 23-8 is useful for keeping track of this information.

THE INTERVIEW

The interview is often the most important and the final obstacle in the job-hunting campaign. Everything else—the letter of application, the resume, your references and other resources—have all been directed toward this goal. Your performance during the interview will determine whether you receive a

APPLICATION LETTER AND RESUME MAILINGS

Date	Individual/Firm Name	Follow-up Date	Receipt Ack.	Interview Date	Follow-up Date	Action Plan
4/10	Howard Edmonds Harmon Manuf. Co.	4/16		4/23		

job offer. Keep in mind that the best candidate does not always get the job; many times, it is the person who was best prepared for the interview.

The hiring process usually involves two interviews. The first takes place in the human resources department; the second, within the department where the position is available. An invitation for an initial interview gives you an opportunity to learn more about the company and the position; and it also provides an opportunity to discuss your career aspirations, training, and specific skills. Go to the interview armed with information about the company, its products, and its reputation in the community.

The first interview typically lasts half an hour, which is ample time to exchange information and questions. During this interview, you must make a good impression. The interviewer will form opinions based on your general appearance, your voice, diction, posture, attitude, and personality. Enthusiasm for your career will be noted. The interviewer will evaluate how you answer questions and how your abilities match the company's requirements. In short, your performance during this first interview, plus your resume and application form, provide a volume of information about you. If you are interested in the position, aim for a second interview at the departmental level. A successful interview doesn't just happen. The job seeker must prepare to make a good first impression.

Guides to a Successful Interview

Tend toward the conservative side in dress and appearance (see Figure 23-9). Men should wear business suits; women, a suit or tailored dress. Nails should be clean and well manicured. Hair should be clean, trimmed, and simply styled. Make sure you are satisfied with your appearance before you leave for the interview. It is a good idea to get a good night's rest and to hold a dress rehearsal prior to the interview.

To assist you in contacting the person you need to see for the interview, a card, a letter, or a note of introduction to someone in the organization can be helpful. It may be a referral card from your placement or employment agency office or a note on the back of a business card from a reference. This communication can boost your confidence and provide a cue for opening conversation with your interviewer.

Anticipate questions the interviewer will ask. If you have thought through the possible questions, you will be less likely to be caught off guard during the interview. Plan your answers. Do not talk too much or too little; strive for the happy medium. Have a positive attitude. Remember, first impressions are extremely important. Before an interview, use the pre-interview checklist shown in Figure 23-10 on pages 650 and 651 to be sure you are well prepared. Guidelines for conducting yourself during an interview are also provided.

Fig. 23-9 A well-prepared interviewee conveys confidence and competence.

The Application Form. You may be asked to complete an application form before you are interviewed. The application form is a vital part of the hiring process. Many applicants are eliminated entirely on the basis of the way they fill out the application. Therefore, never treat it casually. Read it through carefully before you begin to complete it.

Application forms are usually planned with care. Every question serves a purpose for the interviewer. By law, you need not reveal your age, marital status, or the number of your dependents.

In completing an application, follow instructions carefully. For instance, print your name when the instructions tell you to print; put your last name first, if you are so requested. The way you fill out the form reveals far more about you than you realize.

The general neatness of the form is important. Good handwriting is desirable. No one in any office wants to decipher scrawly, illegible handwriting. An application form to be keyed may be disguised as a part of a keying test, so it should represent your best work.

The Interviewer's Method. The director of human resources or a member of that department usually conducts the preliminary interview. If a favorable impression is made, the interviewer sends the applicant to the supervisor who will oversee the job applicant's work (if hired) for a second interview.

An interview may be informal or structured. During a structured interview, the interviewer asks a series of questions in the same order to all applicants. This technique is often reserved for the second or third interview and

A PRE-INTERVIEW CHECKLIST

1. Have you checked the address, parking facilities, and traffic to ensure your prompt arrival?

2. Are you properly dressed and groomed?

3. Have you gathered all the information you need about the company concerning its products, policies, and status in the community?

4. Do you know the interviewer's name? If not, obtain it from the receptionist before the interview.

5. Have you mentally formulated answers to the interviewer's routine questions? Are you prepared for any unusual questions that the interviewer may ask?

6. Have you prepared a list of questions to ask the interviewer?

7. Have you practiced the interview with a friend?

8. Have you researched the salaries for comparable jobs in your locality in order to have some idea of what you are worth to the prospective employer?

9. Are you prepared for an interview? Be sure to take the following items:

   a. Your resume

   b. Your social security card

   c. A complete school transcript showing dates of attendance

   d. A tabulated summary of your college courses

   e. A record of your business skills and personal accomplishments (unless included on your resume)

   f. Letters of reference (Some personnel experts question the value of open letters of recommendation. You may decide to omit them.)

   g. List of personal references

   h. Your employment record including dates, names, addresses of employers, duties performed, names of immediate supervisors, and salaries

   i. A list of questions you wish to ask the interviewer

for administrative positions. The initial interviewer generally uses an informal method which follows this pattern:

1. Establishes rapport with the applicant.
2. Reviews the applicant's work experience record.
3. Asks questions related to the available job.
4. Indicates who will make the final selection.
5. Leads into the closing of the interview.

j. A pen and well-sharpened pencils

k. A small notebook for dictation (You may be asked to take an employment test.)

l. A good pocket-sized dictionary

m. Correction materials (in case you are required to take a keying test on a typewriter with no automatic lift-off correction device)

n. A personal appointment calendar

DURING THE INTERVIEW

1. Leave your coat in the reception area.

2. Wait to sit down until invited to do so.

3. Refrain from smoking or chewing gum.

4. Keep your voice well modulated.

5. Look directly at the interviewer when speaking or listening.

6. Control your nervous habits and maintain good posture.

7. Refrain from overtalking or undertalking.

8. Avoid interrupting the interviewer.

9. Be pleasant to everyone you meet in the office.

10. Listen to the interviewer and respond completely to all aspects of a question.

11. Be positive. Do not criticize your school, professors, past employers, or former colleagues.

12. Point out why you like the organization.

13. Remember that a person, not an organization, will hire you. The interview is your opportunity to gain this person's respect.

14. Determine what happens next. Will there be another interview? Is your file complete? When can you expect to hear the results of this interview?

15. At the end of the interview, thank the interviewer for her or his time and consideration. Also, thank the receptionist as you leave.

The interviewer will question you to encourage you to talk. Many of the questions will be routine and, although answered on your resume, may be asked again merely to put you at ease and to give you an opportunity to express yourself. Be sure to listen to questions. Ask for clarification if you do not understand the question. Some typical questions include:

Where did you attend college?

What is your special training for this work?

What business experience have you had? By what firms have you been employed? Why did you leave your last job?

Why do you want to work for this company? (What an opportunity to show that you know something about it!)

Two laws (Title VII of the Civil Rights Act and the Age Discrimination in Employment Act) prohibit the interviewer from asking questions of a personal nature concerning race, ethnic origin, religion, age, or marital status. You may, however, volunteer this information. A good rule to follow is to provide facts about your personality, education, and work history that are to your advantage.

The interviewer may ask a few questions to catch applicants off guard. Some of these questions may seem unusual and perhaps presumptuous, but they are all part of the interview technique and have a purpose. Some questions of this nature and examples of possible answers are given in Figure 23-11.

If you have had business experience, it is quite logical that your previous employment will be a point of discussion in the interview. You will probably be asked why you left your last position. Be prepared to answer this question and be sure to emphasize positive—not negative—factors. Be truthful but brief. It is tactless and unethical for you to say anything detrimental about any former employer or firm for which you have worked, regardless of any personal feelings you may have. Always speak well of former employers. Nothing is gained by doing otherwise. Other questions that an interviewer might ask include the following:

What do you expect your references to say about you when I call them?

How well do you work under pressure? Give an example.

What goals would you hope to achieve with our company?

How would you describe yourself?

What people have influenced your life? How?

Why should we hire you?

What two or three accomplishments have given you the greatest satisfaction?

Describe a typical day on your last job.

What do you consider your strengths? your weaknesses? (Give positive weaknesses, such as being too exacting, which are used by employers to describe good workers.)

The Salary Question.   Salary is always important, but don't pass up an interesting position for one that pays a few dollars more a week. If your work is challenging, your performance will soon merit a salary increase. Your college placement office can obtain information about salaries. The Department of Labor also makes an annual occupational wage survey. Survey results may be obtained from a regional office of the Bureau of Labor Statistics. Newspaper advertisements are excellent sources of local salary ranges. Finally, most large

Interview Questions and Answers

Questions	Possible Answers
Questions	*Possible Answers*
If you were starting college over again, what courses would you take?	I would major in the same field.
How much money do you hope to make by the age of 30?	At least 50 percent more than my entry-level salary today.
What do you plan to be doing in your career five to ten years from now?	I plan to hold a CPS, and be an administrative assistant to an executive.
Do you prefer to work with others or by yourself?	This depends on the nature of the work [then provide an example].
Do you think you have done the best scholastic work of which you are capable?	[This answer will vary. Be honest.]
What special interests do you have?	Sports, reading, cooking.
What have you learned from some of the positions you have held?	To work under pressure and to work with many types of individuals.
What are your future educational plans?	To prepare for the CPS examination.
What personal characteristics do you believe are important in your field?	Pleasant personality, cooperation, willingness to accept responsibility, and being a team player.
What do you think determines a person's progress within a company?	Performance on the job, attitude, and personality traits.
Why did you choose professional office work as a field?	I like the office environment; I enjoy using the office technology required in this field.

Fig. 23-11 Questions typically asked of interviewees with suggested answers.

businesses have a salary schedule about which you can become informed before applying for a position.

When the salary question comes up in the interview—and it usually does—the best response is, "I am willing to start at your scheduled salary for a person with my background." If, before leaving the interview, you are not told what the starting salary is, it is appropriate to ask, "What is the starting salary for this position?" If an application blank asks about desired salary, supply the standard range or bracket for your position. A range or bracket lists a minimum and a maximum for a particular position. The range or bracket is based upon years of experience, education, and other qualifications.

Salary is not always a negotiable item, but sometimes there is leeway. If there is some room to negotiate, some experts advise aiming slightly above realistic expectations on the assumption that employers seldom pay more than is asked for. You should, however, be cautioned that it is possible to price yourself out of the market. Carefully phrased questions regarding fringe benefits can indicate to the employer your financial astuteness and can also influence your decision on salary. In asking questions about benefits, phrasing and timing are important in determining whether the employer thinks you are intelligent or just materialistic.

Asking Questions.   An interview is a two-way street. You will be expected to ask questions. In fact, your failure to do so may be interpreted as a lack of genuine interest on your part. What will be the scope of your work? Is there a published job description? With whom will you be working? What opportunities will the position provide for advancement? Does the company promote from within? What is the rate of employee turnover? Is there on-the-job training? These are all thoughtful, intelligent questions that should concern you. Questions about working hours, vacation schedules, coffee breaks, and so forth are appropriate if you take care to give the impression that you are more interested in what you give to an employer than in what you will get.

Concluding the Interview.   You will probably know when an interview is coming to an end. Usually the interviewer will rise. If the interviewer has shown interest in your application and in any way encouraged you but has not made a definite commitment about a position, it is permissible to ask directly, "When will your decision be made?" If this does not seem to be a fitting question, you might ask, "May I call you on Friday at two?" If you are offered the job on the spot and you want it, accept the offer. If you need more time, ask for a delay. Do not say that you need time to discuss the job with your spouse or parents. That reply suggests that you are not a decision maker and could give the wrong impression to the interviewer.

When the interview is over, you should rise and thank the interviewer for the opportunity to discuss the position. Make no attempt to prolong the visit. Leave at once, pleasantly and with dignity. Remember to thank the receptionist as you leave.

Personnel Selection Practices

Those who are responsible for hiring employees rely on selection mechanisms in addition to application forms, resumes, cover letters, and personal interviews. Job-related tests and other considerations are also factors in the decision-making process.

Employment Tests.   If you made a favorable impression on an interviewer, you may be asked to take some type of employment test. By law, any test must be job related. For an administrative assistant's position, a job-related test may ask you to key a letter or to take notes in order to ascertain your shorthand, keying, and spelling abilities. You may be asked to operate an electronic typewriter or a personal computer with a specific software package. A test to determine your mathematical ability may be given. Some employers give tests to detect a wide variety of abilities. The main thing to remember when taking an employment test is to do what you are asked quietly, confidently, and efficiently.

For some positions, you may be asked to take a psychological test. You can refuse to take such a test; but, if you do, for all practical purposes you have removed yourself from any consideration for the position. Examples of types of employment tests and questions follow:

Type of Test	**Questions**
A personal preference test (also known as an occupational test) has no right or wrong answers. Employers try to es-establish an occupational preference from answers given to a series of statements.	Of these three activities, indicate which you like the most and which you like the least. Working with detail Operating office machines Selling office equipment
A clerical ability test consists of a series of problems that test basic skills, such as spelling, arithmetic, proofreading, vocabulary, and reasoning ability.	Is *accomodate* or *accommodate* the correct spelling of this word? What is 33 1/3% of 0.50? What do the following words mean: *ethics, principles,* and *etiquette.* Gray is to black as tan is to _____. (green, brown, or red)
A general employment test is very similar to a clerical ability test.	Which number does not belong in this series? 2, 4, 6, 8, 10, 11, 12 If three notebooks cost $2.25, how many can you buy for $10? What is the opposite of *sit*?

Other Considerations.   Personal habits of job applicants, if known, enter into hiring decisions. Discrimination against hiring smokers has been found not to be in violation of equal employment opportunity statutes, and managers of human resources are giving more and more preference to nonsmokers. Companies have found that smokers are twice as likely to be absent from work as nonsmokers. In addition, it is well known that smokers represent a health risk to nonsmokers. It is estimated that alcohol abuse costs American industry $43 billion a year in absenteeism, sick pay, and low productivity. The personal habits of employees in the form of drug use, smoking, and alcohol use have not only been found to cost industry in terms of productivity but also in terms of plant and office safety and security of information. It is little wonder that personnel directors probe for indications of negative personal habits.

Evaluation of the Interview

After leaving an interview, it is a good practice to evaluate your performance and attitude. Note any changes you will make in the future. Ask yourself the following questions:

Were your answers logical?

Did your conversation ramble?

Were you completely honest?

Were you convincing in your sales approach?

Did you keep your eyes focused on the interviewer?

Were you always courteous and positive in your replies?

What did you learn about the position?

Which questions did you handle well? poorly?

Can you do anything else to increase your chances of obtaining the position sought?

Besides evaluating your own behavior, it is important that you decide whether this is the best job for you. Refer to "Evaluating a Company" on page 638 to assist you in your decision.

Interview Follow-Up

If you decide you are interested in the position, a follow-up letter, arriving within two or three days after the interview, may put your application on top. A good follow-up letter includes an expression of appreciation for the meeting, a statement reaffirming your interest in the position, and additional selling points not completely covered during the visit. If you are offered and accept a position, notify your references and thank them for their help. At the same time, telephone or write other interviewers giving them this information.

You may decide not to accept a position that has been offered. This situation demands a prompt, courteous, and straightforward letter of explanation. The day may come when you need the goodwill of that company or person.

Job Hunting Within the Company

Most companies have internal policies covering promotions. These policies specify salary ranges and grade levels or titles for certain positions. In some companies, job vacancies are posted on bulletin boards. Generally, when a vacancy occurs, qualified personnel at the required job levels are notified and asked to interview. Other factors, such as education and seniority, are considered. For these reasons, you should make an effort to keep your personnel file up-to-date. Additional courses you have taken, offices you have held in a professional organization, and other pertinent information should be noted in your personnel file. Keeping a diary of your accomplishments in your current position will provide impressive information to bring to an interview.

If a job that represents a promotion for you becomes available, you should discuss it with your employer first, then make an appointment for the interview. An approach not recommended is to go directly to the executive or supervisor with whom the opening exists. When applying for a promotion, follow the procedures set up by the company so that you will not be subject to criticism from either your fellow workers or your present supervisor.

TERMINATION OF EMPLOYMENT

As you grow in your career, if you are like many office workers, you may decide to leave a position. Perhaps you become unhappy with your job, or your salary is not commensurate with your responsibilities or with local salary levels. Another reason may be that fringe benefits are better elsewhere. Never leave a job on impulse or for the wrong reasons.

Once you decide to resign, follow the rules of convention. If the company has a policy manual, you will find the proper procedures for resigning given there. Otherwise give notice first orally and then in written form (if requested). A resignation letter specifies the date of notice, the last day of employment, and the reason for leaving. It should also include a summary statement about the pleasant associations you have enjoyed with the firm. While still on the job, inquire about any benefits to which you are entitled, such as insurance options or unused vacation. Ask if any benefits, such as health insurance, can continue for a specified time. After the notice period (usually two weeks, unless you have made special arrangements), simply go pleasantly.

In the event that your employer initiates a termination, you should be entitled to advance notice or severance pay. Before you leave, request an exit interview to determine what benefits you have and whether you can expect a good reference from the company. If you suspect discrimination, you can turn to the Equal Employment Opportunity Commission for assistance, but be aware that relatively few firing decisions are reversed even if the employee wins the case. In addition, an employee who sues a former employer may have great difficulty securing another position.

Regardless of the reason for termination, your exit should be an amicable one. Avoid expressing ill will toward the company or attempting to make fellow workers dissatisfied with the company and their jobs.

FOR THE PART-TIME JOB SEEKER

Sometime in your working career you may decide to seek a part-time position because you have additional personal responsibilities. Perhaps your health does not permit full-time work, you plan to continue your education, your spouse's occupation requires mobility, or you are approaching retirement and do not want the responsibilities of a full-time job. Like other job seekers, an individual looking for part-time employment must be resourceful. Successful part-time job seekers offer this advice:

Visit firms that have part-timers on their payroll.

Apply at federal, state, and local government offices.

Visit smaller firms, because they are often more flexible and thus more responsive to part-time workers.

Do not ask for part-time employment on your application. Talk about this possibility during the interview.

Suggest a trial period to the employer.

Job sharing is becoming more accepted in professional ranks (see Chapter 1) and should be explored. If you can identify a potential partner, possibly an employee already on the payroll, both of you should present your plan to management. Many employers who would not normally hire part-timers will accept a job-sharing arrangement to keep a valued employee. If both you and your partner are unemployed, you should plan your strategy together by preparing joint resumes and application letters. Seeking a part-time job is a full-time proposition. It can be and is being done successfully.

FOR THE MATURE JOB SEEKER

The Age Discrimination in Employment Act of 1967 protects workers in the 40 to 70 age bracket. Basically, the act states that employers cannot discriminate against workers or applicants because of their age.

The mature job seeker has much to offer a company: work experience, the prospect of a good attendance record, and the ability to learn. An employer's only reservation probably concerns the cost of benefits for mature recruits. Retirement benefits, for instance, begin much sooner than for a young person.

If you are told you are overqualified for the job, the interviewer usually considers you too old or too high priced. You can turn this reaction into an advantage by emphasizing that your experience will lessen the training time required for the job. As for salary, you can stress that the salary designated is acceptable.

The reentry administrative assistant must devote some time to preparation for employment. Dormant office skills must be revitalized by taking a refresher course or an individualized instructional program. The next step is to make a survey of employment opportunities. Temporary service agencies and companies that use part-time workers should be included. Finally, the reentry job seeker should prepare a resume and letters of application. Include all your work experience, both paid and volunteer. In most cases the mature job seeker will use the functional resume (see Figure 23-6b).

A last word of advice for all job seekers: Don't be in a hurry to accept your first job offer. Evaluate each company and position in terms of your own goals and interests. Accepting a job you don't really want may prevent you from later accepting the very job you were seeking. The next interview just might be the right position for you. Choosing the company you want to work for can be both exciting and difficult. Your choice will have an immediate effect upon your personal lifestyle as well as affect your future opportunities. You should select your first job with your entire future in mind.

Summary

When seeking employment, the qualified administrative assistant has a number of decisions to make in selecting the right position. Decisions such as whether to work in a small office or a large organization and whether to specialize in a particular area or to work in a general office must be made. The small office offers the advantage of being an excellent training ground for all facets of administrative support. A large firm offers promotional opportunities, set personnel policies, and fringe benefits.

There are unlimited opportunities for the qualified administrative assistant to specialize in a particular field. The duties of the medical administrative assistant, the legal administrative assistant, and the educational administrative assistant will, of course, vary, and each specialty provides multiple opportunities for an exciting career. In addition, each area of specialization sponsors a professional organization and a certification program designed to encourage professional growth. The technical administrative assistant and the administrative assistant who serves the public have other opportunities for specialization.

Providing part-time office workers is big business. The opportunities for temporary workers are varied. Employment through a temporary agency is an excellent way to enhance skills after an absence from the job market. Working for the nation's largest employer, the government, or the Foreign Service also offers exciting career possibilities.

A job search begins with a survey of employment opportunities. College placement offices, free and private employment agencies, newspaper advertisements, friends, relatives, and associates should be contacted to compile a job prospect list. The next step in a job search is to gather information about every prospect on that list. This can be achieved by doing research at the library and by contacting the local chamber of commerce and the Better Business Bureau. Each prospect should be evaluated in terms of its reputation, fair employment practices, financial standing, and opportunities for training and advancement.

After taking an inventory of interests and capabilities, the job seeker prepares a resume. The major sections of a resume include a heading (name, address, telephone number), education, work experience, special interests (abilities and accomplishments), and references. An application letter can be solicited or unsolicited; its purpose is to expand on the applicant's qualifications in relation to the specific job in question and to gain a personal interview. For both the resume and an application letter, the use of action verbs is recommended.

A company's hiring process generally includes two interviews: one with the department of human resources and the other with the supervisor who will actually oversee the applicant's work. Interviewers ask specific job-related questions; some questions may take the applicant off guard. In order to have a successful interview, the applicant must be able to answer questions honestly, confidently, and with poise. The salary question is a delicate one; applicants should have some idea, prior to the interview, of an acceptable salary range. The applicant should go to an interview equipped with questions for the interviewer as well. Finally, when an interview is over, leave promptly. The hiring process may also include the administration of employment tests. Be aware that other considerations, such as negative personal habits, enter into a hiring decision. A follow-up letter is recommended, especially if the applicant is interested in the position.

The process of career development is likely to include, at some point, the need to develop strategies for resigning from a position and for seeking part-time employment. The mature job seeker must also develop unique employment strategies.

QUESTIONS FOR DISCUSSION

1. Why should you carefully choose your first job, knowing that you will probably change jobs or even careers several times during your work life?

2. What are the advantages of being an administrative assistant with the federal government?

THINK IT
Through

3. After carefully considering your training, interests, and special aptitudes, would you choose a specialization as an office professional (for example, legal, medical, technical, or educational)? If so, which one? Give reasons for your choice.

THINK IT
Through

4. What are the advantages of working through a temporary employment agency?

5. A compound word may be written as a solid word, joined with a hyphen, or written as individual words. Rekey the following sentences and make the necessary corrections. Consult the Reference Guide to verify and correct your answers.

   a. Several of the rioters who marched in the anti-war demonstrations are non-voters.
   b. Use a special stain-resistant fabric to recover the chair.
   c. The Greenbriar provides firstclass accommodations including an up to date gymnasium and a four mile hiking trail.

d. The preChristmas sales attracted many probritish customers who wanted to meet the exambassador from London.

e. We must reform the molds from which the precolumbian vases were made.

PROBLEMS

1. Assume that you work for a large company. The position of administrative assistant to the chief executive officer becomes vacant, and you and all your fellow administrative assistants are in line for the position. Make a list of the positive actions you could take to ensure your being selected for the job. Also list actions you would avoid to prevent antagonizing your fellow employees and your supervisor.

2. Interview an experienced administrative assistant in your community. Ask specific questions about the position concerning qualifications, duties, and promotional possibilities. Report your findings to the class.

3. When applying for a specific position, you are asked the following questions. Key your replies on a sheet of paper. In preparing your answers, try to analyze the motive behind the question.

   a. What are your career plans?
   b. How do you spend your spare time?
   c. Why do you want to work for this company?
   d. Are you willing to relocate?
   e. Do you like to work with office machines?
   f. Do your interests lie in the area of data processing?
   g. What do you consider a good starting salary for this position?
   h. Do you think your college grades reflect your true ability?
   i. Are you willing to work overtime when the situation warrants?
   j. What qualifications do you have that you believe will make you successful in your chosen career?
   k. Do you plan to join a professional organization?

4. Review the help-wanted advertisements in the newspaper for positions for administrative assistants. Select one for which you are qualified and that appeals to you. On a separate sheet of paper key two headings, *Requirements* and *Qualifications*. List each requirement, then specify your qualifications that meet each requirement.

TECHNOLOGY APPLICATIONS

▶ **TA23-1**   You notice a classified ad for an administrative assistant position that looks promising:

> **Needed: an administrative assistant with better-than-average communication skills; strong computer skills**

continued

continued

including knowledge of LOTUS 1-2-3 and WordPerfect software; keyboarding 60 wpm. Position involves maintaining a large volume of correspondence, telephone work, and customer assistance. Salary commensurate with ability. Reply Box 2100, JOURNAL.

You decide to apply! Proceed as follows:

1. Develop your resume. Devote extra time to preparing it, because (a) your resume is a very critical document and (b) this "base resume" will serve as a foundation for future resumes that you develop. Be sure to store the file copy for future use. Print two copies; save one in a permanent "Resume" file.
2. Draft an application letter.
3. Develop a list of local prospective employers, those companies and firms you would like to work for.
4. Using the merge function, individualize the letters to the potential employers you have identified.
5. Print a copy of each letter.

▶ TA23-2.TEM

Spend a few minutes considering "the perfect job." What duties would that job require of you?

Using your word processing software, access the TA23-2.TEM file, which sketches a three-column table.

Proceed as follows:

1. Under the DUTY heading, list at least ten duties of your "perfect job."
2. For each item entered in the DUTY column, rate yourself Poor, Fair, Good, or Superior (as appropriate) in the SELF-EVALUATION column. Be objective! Remember that the purpose of this exercise is to identify your specific strengths and weaknesses for the purpose of self-improvement.
3. In the IMPROVEMENT PLAN column, specify what action you should take to improve every Poor or Fair rating. Try to develop realistic strategies.
4. Review your document carefully. Are the duties listed appropriate and realistic? Are your self-evaluation comments on target? Are your evaluation plans achievable?
5. Print a final copy.

LEARNING OBJECTIVES

After studying this chapter and completing the activities, you will be able to:

1. Understand how to use your personal attributes to enhance your career.
2. Adjust to a new job quickly and effectively.
3. Locate sources of information about the company that employs you.
4. Develop a desk manual.
5. Identify methods of enhancing your professional growth.

Chapter 24

Your Professional Future

INTRODUCTION

If you set long-range goals, take advantage of professional growth opportunities, and perform competently on the job, career enrichment and upward mobility are available in most firms.

Your study of this text thus far has made you aware of the variety of career opportunities available to you, prepared you to perform various duties, and briefed you on how to get the position you seek. You should now consider how you will fulfill your long-range ambition of becoming a successful administrative assistant.

This chapter discusses the personal characteristics requisite to success as an administrative assistant and the means at your disposal for getting off to the right start and growing professionally. It deals with some of the difficulties you will encounter and how you can cope with them to assure the professional future to which you aspire.

USING YOUR PERSONAL ATTRIBUTES

New administrative assistants enter the job market with varying degrees of competence in the skills necessary to perform the job. The same is true of personal qualities. One administrative assistant may have all the characteristics that contribute to a successful career, while another may be weak in one or more of them.

Administrative assistants who are proficient in their work and enjoy satisfaction and recognition in their careers possess certain qualities and/or attributes necessary for achievement. Some are innate to the individual, and some can be learned on the job. They are as follows:

1. *Initiative* in performing your work
2. *Flexibility* in your approach to office needs and operations
3. *Awareness* of the business and of your employer
4. *Adeptness* in human relations

Displaying Initiative

A new administrative assistant may be reluctant to do work without being told or to assume new responsibilities not understood as part of the job description. Displaying initiative comes with confidence in one's ability to do the job. It may be difficult, however, to show initiative if you are assigned to a manager who expects no more than performance of habitual, routine tasks, or if you follow a predecessor who undertook only assigned jobs. Also, routinization of many office tasks reduces, if not eliminates, the opportunity to be enterprising or creative or to do anything out of the ordinary. You may have to start slowly, but you can overcome resistance if you demonstrate how much you can increase your effectiveness and that of your employer by extending your activities to include responsible tasks.

Taking initiative sometimes means taking risks. Use your judgment in taking action, then review with your employer what you have done. If you acted in error, you can profit from what you learn and apply this new knowledge to a similar situation in the future.

There are many opportunities in the administrative assistant's position to use initiative. In fact, making independent decisions and taking actions soon become a daily exercise. An administrative assistant who composes a reply to a letter without the employer having to request it is displaying initiative. An administrative assistant who obtains information for an employer before being asked to do so is using initiative. You, the college-trained administrative assistant, should feel comfortable in displaying your initiative. You have the background to be successful in making decisions on your own.

Being Flexible

You probably have heard that nothing is more certain than change. For years the functions of the office were accomplished in the same way and with the same equipment. Earlier chapters of this text discussed the ways in which technology has revolutionized the way we communicate, the way we calculate, and the way we send correspondence. Administrative assistants have to learn to cope with change. The look of the office has also changed. An ambitious person entering the business world must be flexible. That person must be able to adjust to tomorrow's office and tomorrow's duties quickly.

Offices usually have their own routines, their own ways of working with information and getting jobs done. A new administrative assistant must be willing to learn from others. On occasion the employer may request that you work a half hour longer or on a Saturday. Although this is a disruption of your regular schedule, if you are flexible you will be willing to make alterations in your work schedule and in your personal schedule.

One very sensitive area in an office community is the promotion or shift of personnel. The administrative assistant may be transferred to another department with a new set of coworkers and tasks, may be assigned a new employer or employers, may have to learn to operate new equipment or adopt new office procedures. These changes are a way of life in all organizations. Whether you like or dislike, approve or disapprove, you must maintain a positive attitude. A flexible employee makes the most of these changes.

Business is a constantly changing set of problems. Realize that you were hired to help solve these problems.

Developing Awareness

Being able to look at the office and its operations is one thing, but seeing what is there is quite another. Awareness is the capacity to draw accurate inferences from what is seen, heard, and learned. An administrative assistant must be aware of how each person fits into the work scheme. You must see quickly the part your employer plays in an organization and how your work contributes to the organization. "Listen and watch" would be a good motto for you during your initial weeks on the job.

As a college-trained administrative assistant, you should have little difficulty developing awareness. In college you studied business principles and organization, you understood office costs, and you learned the meaning of profit. With this background, see what you can do to assist the growth of your company, your employer, and yourself. (A word of caution is needed here: Temper any feelings of superiority you may have over your coworkers because of your college training.)

Building Positive Human Relations

To be happy and to grow in your position as an administrative assistant, you must feel good about going to the office each day. One reason you may feel content about working in an office is the people who work with you. Good working relationships with one's supervisor, coworkers, and subordinates will play an extremely important role in your well-being on the job. See Figure 24-1. Although you will like some of your colleagues better than others, assume a positive attitude toward all coworkers. You may have the highest level of technical skills to offer an employer. Yet, without the ability to maintain good working relationships, you could soon become dispensable. More workers lose their jobs because of poor human relations than because of lack of skills or ability.

The golden-rule approach with coworkers is worth considering. To be successful in establishing friendships throughout your life, you must be sensitive to the needs of others. Play a part in making a new office colleague feel like a member of the group. Cooperate with others. Treat each person courteously.

Your relations with executives, the ones to whom you report and others, are especially important to your success. Showing that you are a good team member enhances your opportunities to be a real member of the team. Be cheerful even when you are called on to go beyond the call of duty. Maintain a smiling countenance and a voice with a smile. Avoid being emotional, especially when you are under pressure. Remain calm. Respect confidentiality. Reveal neither organizational nor executive secrets. Never say anything in the office that you would not want displayed on the office bulletin board. People often repeat what is said in confidence.

Carry your good human relations attitudes over to the public. Every office or telephone visitor is important. Often the administrative assistant is the contact with the outside world that makes the difference in how a company is perceived.

BECOMING ACCLIMATED TO THE JOB

The first week or two on the job can be overwhelming. Everything will be new to you—the people, the office, and the work. This section gives you some clues on how to survive the first week of getting to know the office staff and learning about the company.

Some companies have well-planned programs for inducting new employees. If you obtain a position in such a firm, someone will be assigned to welcome you, introduce you to your colleagues, show you your work area, perhaps take you to lunch, discuss the history of the organization, possibly show you a video about your new company, and provide you with booklets describing company policies and benefits. Many companies, however, have no organized orientation program. If you are fortunate, the administrative assistant whose place you are taking will remain on the job for a few days to train you. In many cases, though, you will report to an employer whose administrative assistant has already left, and you sink or swim alone.

One of the first decisions you will have to make on the job is to determine priorities. You should decide what work must be done immediately, what must be done by the end of the day, and what can be done at some later time. Setting priorities will be especially difficult if you report to more than one executive.

Creating a Good First Impression

Everyone in the office forms first impressions of you, just as you will of them. Because you were hired, you can assume that you made a satisfactory impression on your employer. Now you must make a satisfactory impression on those with whom you work and make this impression a permanent one.

You will be under critical and detailed inspection that first day. Your clothing, your grooming, and everything you do and say will be observed. At this point, exercise good judgment by first being an attentive listener. It is a human trait to be defensive toward an outsider or a newcomer until that person wins one's goodwill and approval. Don't be disturbed by this; if you understand it, you will be encouraged to make your associates like and accept you. Remember that their approval is most important to your future welfare and your happiness on the job.

Begin your first day on time, allowing plenty of time for the things that fate seems to have in store for the first day on a new job! Being even a few minutes late will require an explanation to your employer, a situation that you will find uncomfortable.

There is no substitute for enthusiasm. The difference between a successful career and a mediocre one is the degree of enthusiasm you have for each job.

Learning Names

Certainly one way to create a good first impression is to learn promptly and pronounce correctly the names and titles of those with whom you work. Associate the name with a mental picture of the person when you are introduced. An effective plan is to write the name and practice pronouncing it, then address the person by name at every appropriate occasion. Drawing a floor plan to show the location of desks and the names of their occupants will help you through that first week.

Some of your coworkers and some executives may be sensitive to titles. An office manager may be offended at being referred to as a supervisor. A vice

Nothing is so pleasing to the ear as one's own name spoken with respect.

president may take exception to being called an assistant manager. To help you learn the titles and ranks of those with whom and for whom you work, study your company's organization chart.

Observing Ground Rules

New employees are expected to learn quickly a company's regulations relative to rest periods, lunch hours, personal telephone calls, coffee breaks, smoking, and other personal activities. Some of these rules may be in writing; others have been established by custom but are nonetheless binding. One of the surest ways to get off to a poor start is to be a rule breaker. Ignorance is a poor excuse. The only safe policy is to find out the rules and customs of the office and observe them. Some organizations even test new employees on the content of company manuals.

Developing a Code of Ethics

Many organizations have developed a code of ethics for members of their profession. Development of a code of ethics demonstrates that the members accept the obligation to engage in self-discipline and to uphold the standards of confidence and trust earned by practitioners throughout past generations.

Each member has a personal obligation to support and follow the code. Each member should recognize that the greatest penalty possible for its violation is loss of the respect of professional colleagues and the trust of employers, clients, and society. Most codes embody broad principles of moral conduct for those who earn their livelihood in the profession. A code of ethics applied to the office professional might include those shown in Figure 24-2.

Fig. 24-2 Ethical principles developed by Professional Secretaries International.

ETHICAL PRINCIPLES FOR THE ADMINISTRATIVE ASSISTANT

I. Competent performance of assigned duties and responsibilities, exercising professional knowledge and skill to promote the interests of the executive and the company.

II. Dedication to maintaining and enhancing the dignity, status, competence, and standards of the profession and its practitioners.

III. Achievement of continued employment, compensation, and promotion on the basis of professional knowledge, ability, experience, and performance.

IV. Dedication to the promotion and preservation of the safety and welfare of the public.

V. Loyalty to the company and to the executive.

VI. Protection of confidential matters affecting the image, profitability, and welfare of the company.

In addition to observing this code and company rules and policies, you should observe an unwritten work code. This code includes an appreciation of what belongs to your employer. For instance, you have agreed to work a certain number of hours a week. You have agreed also to the length of the workday.

Any abuse of time that should be devoted to your work is in violation of your work code. In addition, have respect for the equipment and the supplies that belong to your employer. This means a concerted effort to reduce waste and to maintain the security of these materials in the office.

Developing Office Friendships

Many administrative assistants make a distinction between their work lives and their personal lives. They try to avoid socializing with members of the office staff outside office hours. They believe this separation makes them immune to office gossip and office cliques.

Of course, these same administrative assistants recognize that office friendships are beneficial. Certainly, the administrative assistant who has friends throughout the company is better able to serve the employer. Through these friendships the administrative assistant gains a better understanding of the company as a whole and the functions of various departments.

Friendliness should extend to all employment levels. The goodwill of office messengers, custodians, and reprographics operators is important to your success.

Coping with Sexual Harassment

Administrative assistants work in close contact with employers and coworkers. Sometimes employers or coworkers engage in sexual harassment. In 1980 the Equal Employment Opportunity Commission (EEOC) defined sexual harassment and adopted guidelines for employers to deal with the problem. Sexual harassment, according to the EEOC, is "unwelcome sexual advances, requests for sexual favors, and other verbal or physical conduct of a sexual nature" that take place under any of the following circumstances:

1. When submission to the sexual advance is a condition of keeping or getting a job, whether expressed in explicit or implicit terms
2. When a supervisor or employer makes a personnel decision based on an employee's submission to or rejection of sexual advances
3. When sexual conduct unreasonably interferes with a person's work performance or creates an intimidating, hostile, or offensive work environment

Instances of sexual harassment, ranging from suggestive speech to actual physical attack, threats of withholding promotions, and threats of dismissal, have been widely publicized in the media. Women's groups, such as the National Organization for Women (NOW), have played an important role in alerting the public to these offenses.

Handling sexual harassment is especially perplexing for the young administrative assistant in a new position who is eager to please associates. The problem becomes more difficult because of the informality of today's office contrasted with the office of ten years ago. Cordial but not familiar relationships should be maintained. Ignoring suggestive words and actions often discourages them. Do not make an issue of one isolated incident. In case of continued infractions, however, you should speak unemotionally, asking the offender to refrain from such actions. If this does not stop the harassment, you should report the situation to your superior or ask for a transfer. You should keep a written record of exactly what occurred, as well as the time and place of each incident.

Preparing for Your Performance Appraisal

Most large firms have established procedures for rating employee performance periodically. If the company that employs you has such a procedure, you will want to understand the process and be prepared when the time comes for appraisal of your on-the-job performance.

Not all people are equal in ability or in the efforts they expend to do a good job. Some method is necessary that will provide an impartial rating of the employee's ability to handle the present job and to determine his or her potential for advancement.

An effective performance appraisal helps management in determining salary increases, selecting employees for promotion, developing supervisors, providing necessary training, recognizing good work, and setting guidelines for the selection of future employees. Productive employees believe that the performance appraisal is an indication of management's interest in their future with the company. Inasmuch as most employees like to know how they measure up, the performance appraisal is generally a boost to their morale.

When the time comes for your performance appraisal, you will sit down with your supervisor, who will complete a form that rates your performance in a number of areas: quality of work, quantity of work, cooperation, initiative, dependability, and the like. See Figure 24-3 for a performance appraisal form.

After your supervisor has completed the form, both of you will sign it. Signing the form does not mean that you agree with the rating but rather that your supervisor has discussed each item on the form with you. These periodic appraisals become a part of your personnel file and may be reviewed when you are being considered for a salary increase, a promotion, or some other reason. If you think that your appraisal has been unfair, most companies have an appeal process.

For the efficient administrative assistant who demonstrates those principles, skills, and abilities prescribed in the preceding chapters of this book and who displays a positive attitude, the performance appraisal will contain few,

Fig. 24-3 Performance appraisals serve many purposes for both management and employees.

THE NOBLE COMPANY
45 WEST 55TH STREET
RICHMOND, VA 23225-1119

PERFORMANCE APPRAISAL OF _____ (NAME OF EMPLOYEE)

DATE _____ JOB TITLE _____ DEPT. _____

I. QUALITY OF WORK--ACCURACY
How would you rate this employee with respect to quality of work produced, as well as its neatness and accuracy?
___ 1. Careless worker. Tends to repeat the same type of errors.
___ 2. Work is sometimes untidy--smudged, ragged, and contains errors.
___ 3. Work is usually acceptable. Makes few errors.
___ 4. Checks and proofs work carefully; can generally be depended upon for a high-quality finished product.
___ 5. Work is of highest quality. Very few errors.

II. QUANTITY OF WORK--VOLUME
The quality of work is not to be considered here. Merely rate the speed and volume only.
___ 1. Very slow. Unsatisfactory rate of performance.
___ 2. Has difficulty keeping up. Work tends to backlog.
___ 3. Moderate speed. Occasionally needs a pep talk.
___ 4. Gets work done promptly.
___ 5. Extremely rapid worker. Turns out a large volume of work and keeps up even under pressure.

III. RELIABILITY--THOROUGHNESS
___ 1. Extremely disorganized and careless; makes mistakes.
___ 2. Sporadic. Work is of an uneven quality.
___ 3. Does only what he/she is told. Requires frequent checking by supervisor.
___ 4. Very conscientious. Requires little supervision.
___ 5. Excellent worker, extremely reliable. Consistent high quality of work.

IV. ABILITY TO LEARN
___ 1. Slow learner. Needs constant repetition of instructions.
___ 2. Must practice new procedures over and over before becoming efficient.
___ 3. Average learner; sometimes resists change.
___ 4. Learns quickly and adopts new ideas and methods without repetitive instructions.
___ 5. Sharp mind. Willing and eager to learn.

V. RESPONSIBILITY
___ 1. Unwilling to take responsibility or takes unauthorized responsibility.
___ 2. Has apparent ability but does not use it beyond what he/she is told to do.
___ 3. Assumes responsibility only in matters relating to his/her job description.
___ 4. Assumes full share of responsibility within the scope of his/her authority.
___ 5. Goes the extra distance within the scope of his/her authority.

VI. ATTITUDE
___ 1. A chronic complainer. Works counter to company policy and procedures.
___ 2. Uninterested in the job or the organization.
___ 3. Satisfied with the job and the company.
___ 4. Always positive about the job and the company.
___ 5. Very enthusiastic about the job. Loyal to the company. Makes sound suggestions for improvement.

VII. INITIATIVE
___ 1. Does only what the job description calls for.
___ 2. Does a few extras with encouragement from the supervisor.
___ 3. Satisfactory. Alert to the possibilities for taking the initiative, but sometimes waits to be told what to do.
___ 4. Actively looks for ways to extend the effectiveness of his/her employer.
___ 5. Visualizes future procedures and is always one step ahead.

VIII. COOPERATION
___ 1. Is sometimes tactless in working with others. Prefers to work alone.
___ 2. Responds slowly to others. Suspicious and distrusting.
___ 3. Cooperates with others and elicits their cooperation as necessary.
___ 4. Cooperates willingly and, in turn, elicits cooperation from others.
___ 5. Outstanding ability to work with others and build a team spirit. Inspires others to get the job done.

IX. FLEXIBILITY
___ 1. Very rigid. Follows rules and procedures regardless of circumstances.
___ 2. Resists change. Must be "sold" on new procedures and policies.
___ 3. Changes as circumstances demand. Satisfactory.
___ 4. Changes willingly and promotes change among coworkers.
___ 5. Finds change exciting. Visualizes future methods and applications without abandoning tried-and-true methods that are still useful.

X. DECISIVENESS
___ 1. Lacks confidence. Reluctant to make decisions.
___ 2. Reluctant to make decisions or make decisions beyond the scope of his/her authority.
___ 3. Makes decisions only in matters relating to his/her job description.
___ 4. Makes logical decisions.
___ 5. Makes sound decisions appropriate to his/her authority. Uses common sense and is aware of the consequences of each decision.

Supervisor _____   Employee _____

RATING: Average the points allotted for each category.
The ratings are as follows: 5=SUPERIOR; 4=ABOVE AVERAGE; 3=AVERAGE; 2=BELOW AVERAGE; 1=UNSATISFACTORY

if any, surprises. That is not to say that there will be no weaknesses to report. You should realize that all employees can improve their performance. If your supervisor points out a weakness, discuss it objectively. Avoid placing blame or making excuses, but be determined to improve.

Learning About the Company

From your first moment on the job, learn as much as you can about the company as soon as you can. This is a sizable order for a new employee, but it can be done.

In some companies a job analysis, a job description, or job specifications for your new position are available in a company manual to give you an idea of the scope of your duties. To serve your employer effectively, you need to learn about the organization quickly so that you can interpret any request and carry out directions without asking for elementary information.

Learn as quickly as possible the names of customers, the names of your employer's close associates, frequently used telephone numbers, frequently used terminology in dictation, and the technical language of the company. The more you know and the more ready you are to apply what you know, the more quickly you will become valuable to your employer and to the organization.

Company Manuals. Most organizations have one or more company manuals or instruction sheets for office routines. A general office manual usually explains the organization of the company, the relationships of various offices and departments, general rules and regulations, and information that affects all employees. It may also include methods of distributing paychecks, company benefits, and a list of the holidays observed. Some manuals chart the work of all departments; others give directions for initiating and completing specific activities.

Operating manuals are often available for various office machines and other equipment. Most large companies have style manuals or other forms of direction for setting up correspondence and company forms. If your office has such a manual, spend many of your spare moments studying and thoroughly digesting everything that has a bearing on your work to the point of memorizing important facts.

If it is permissible for you to take some of these materials home for study, you should do so. Devoting an hour or so of quiet time at home studying an office manual may reduce considerably the amount of time it takes to learn a new job.

The Office Files. Office files offer a wealth of information to the new administrative assistant. Previous correspondence, incoming and outgoing, indicates the types of correspondence you can expect to execute. Office files are also an excellent source of terminology and technical language. As you look through the files, list the terms with which you are unfamiliar. Note your employer's letter-writing style and proper title. Note where and how to file letters and records. Become familiar with various company forms and types of stationery.

Other Sources of Information. Special types of records are often available to the administrative assistant. Scrapbooks or collections of clippings about the executive, the company, or its products are sources of background information. Many organizations publish a house organ, a periodical written by and about its employees. Back issues will tell you a great deal, as will industry journals.

One way to determine the actual scope of your position is to acquaint yourself with the duties of other company employees. Seeing how your job relates to theirs will help you understand not only your own job but also the total functions of the office.

Questions. Of course you must ask questions; but make them few and make them count. There are two kinds of questions—*learning* questions and *leaning* questions. Learning questions help you find out things you need to know; they are excellent questions. An example of a learning question is, "Who approves requisitions for office supplies?" If this information is not provided in the office manual, it is a legitimate learning question. Leaning questions, on the other hand, are those about something you really should know or can research yourself; they are the kind that you should avoid. An example of a leaning question is, "Should I keep a copy of all outgoing correspondence?"

There is a time and place for questioning. During the first few days on a new job, whenever possible, compile your problems and questions and ask them all at a logical time in one session with the employer or with your temporary mentor. As you compile your list, however, be sure that it does not include a problem that you should solve yourself.

The other employees usually help answer questions, but remember that they have full-time work to do themselves. Sometime later you will probably have an opportunity to repay those who helped you by returning the favor when they need extra help.

Developing a Desk Manual

A desk manual is a helpful organizer for the administrative assistant in a new job. If you have inherited one, you will find in it an explanation of company procedures, examples of company forms, and instructions for handling the duties specifically related to your job. If one is not available, begin at once to compile information for your desk manual.

You can start some sections such as correct letter formats and mailing procedures immediately. Accumulating other sections will require time and experience. You may want to break down your duties by time periods: daily, weekly, monthly, and annually. If you are always busy during the day, take the time to prepare the bulk of your desk manual after office hours. The first draft will be the most time-consuming; once written and thoughtfully indexed, the manual can be updated quickly and easily.

It will be impossible to remember everything you need to know about your job. You should, however, remember where to look for information.

Procedures Sections. Undoubtedly one of the first sections you will prepare is one that explains how to handle various duties of the administrative assistant. The topical outline in Figure 24-4 on pages 674 and 675 suggests a way to organize this part of the manual.

In addition to these procedural sections, include information of a general nature concerning the company and a directory of important employer contacts, customers, or projects. A personal data section about the employer is appropriate for the manual. If an administrative assistant

TOPICAL OUTLINE FOR PROCEDURES SECTION
OF THE DESK MANUAL

I. INCOMING MAIL
    A. Mail register
        1. Explanation of posting procedure
        2. Sample form
    B. Distribution of the mail

II. CORRESPONDENCE AND REPORTS
    A. Interoffice correspondence
        1. Model interoffice memorandum forms
        2. Number and distribution of copies
    B. Outside correspondence
        1. Model letter forms
        2. Stationery examples
        3. Number and distribution of copies
        4. Form letters and guide letter paragraphs
    C. Authorization for rush items and turnaround time
    D. Executive document format preferences
    E. Document backup procedures
    F. Dictation instructions
    G. Mail schedules

III. COMPANY FORMS
    A. Models of all forms
    B. Instructions for completing
    C. Number and distribution of copies
    D. Signature authorizations

IV. FILING
    A. Centralized filing system
        1. Materials that go to centralized file
        2. Procedure for release of materials for filing
        3. Procedure for obtaining materials from filing

    B. Administrative assistant's file (full explanation of filing system)
    C. Transfer and storage/retention policies

V. FINANCIAL DUTIES
    A. Bank account
        1. Procedure for making deposits
        2. Procedure for reconciling the bank statement
        3. Disposition of canceled checks and bank statements
        4. Location of bankbook and checkbook
    B. Payments of recurring expenses (membership dues and miscellaneous fees)
        1. Dates of payments
        2. Procedures for payments
    C. Petty cash
        1. Location of fund
        2. Regulations covering expenditures from fund
        3. Filing of receipts
        4. Procedure for replenishing fund

VI. INFORMATION SYSTEMS AND ELECTRONIC EQUIPMENT AVAILABLE WITHIN THE ORGANIZATION
    A. Locations
    B. Instructions for using services
    C. When to use

VII. OFFICE MACHINES
    A. Inventory of machines in office (serial numbers and purchase dates of all machines)
    B. Repair services (service contracts, name and telephone number of each service)
    C. Software programs

Fig. 24-4 A desk manual is a helpful organizer to the administrative assistant beginning a new job.

D. Directory of operations manuals
E. Service contracts and lease agreements
F. Machine codes and special functions

VIII. SUPPLIES
A. List of supplies to be stocked
  1. Quantities of each to be ordered
  2. Names and addresses (or telephone numbers) of suppliers
B. Procedure for obtaining supplies
C. Procedure for controlling supplies

IX. SUBSCRIPTIONS TO PUBLICATIONS
A. Names, number of copies, renewal dates
B. Procedure for renewal
C. Routing of publications in office

X. PUBLIC RELATIONS
A. News releases
B. Announcements

XI. TELEPHONE PROCEDURES
A. Types of services available
B. Regulations for use of various types of telephones
C. Procedures for reporting toll charges
D. Special instructions relating to use of equipment
E. Procedures for using voice mail

XII. TELECOMMUNICATIONS
A. Examples of FAX, electronic mail (E-mail)
B. Number and distribution of copies
C. Procedure for sending
  1. Determination of method used
  2. Time restrictions
D. Procedure for recording charges

XIII. REPROGRAPHICS
A. Types of equipment available
B. Procedures for using equipment
  1. Procedures for determining the method used
  2. Procedures for controlling confidentiality
  3. Procedures for controlling excessive copying
  4. Guidelines for requesting reprographic services
  5. Special instructions on selection of paper, color, reduction, enlargement, etc.
  6. Name, address, and telephone number of local vendor
  7. Copies of a repair order and service agreement
C. Examples of request forms

XIV. TRAVEL
A. Employer's travel and hotel preferences
B. Names and telephone numbers of persons in travel agency or airlines office
C. Locations of timetables
D. Model itinerary
E. Method of ticket pickup
F. Expense report form
  1. Number and distribution of copies
  2. Receipts required

XV. REFERENCE SECTION
A. Technical vocabulary
B. Product information
C. Price lists
D. Standard proofreaders' marks
E. Company information
  1. Organization chart
  2. Employee directory
  3. Holiday schedules, policies on absenteeism, safety, parking, etc.

reports to several executives, it is a good idea to have specific information for each in the manual.

Company Information.   One section of the manual should consist of pertinent company information, such as an organization chart showing the lines of authority and the names of persons in each executive and supervisory position. In addition, the following information should be helpful to an administrative assistant in a new job:

1. Addresses and telephone numbers of branch offices and subsidiaries
2. Names and titles of supervisory personnel at branch offices and subsidiaries
3. Company rules and regulations (hours of work, lunch hour, coffee breaks, and the like)
4. Company policies (vacation, sick leave, insurance, and other fringe benefits) in summary form
5. Telephone numbers of specific office services

Who's Who Directory.   Another section of the manual is likely to be a directory of the persons with whom the employer has frequent contacts. Individual circumstances determine whether to subdivide this directory into in-company and outside listings. At any rate, the list should include the following:

1. Clients with whom the employer frequently corresponds or holds telephone conversations
2. Frequent office visitors
3. Names of the executive's attorney, doctor, broker, automobile service, etc.

To build a list of names for the directory, jot down each one as it comes to your attention. Then prepare a card for each name with the following information: correct spelling, company affiliation and address, telephone number, and salutation and complimentary close for correspondence (you must learn when "Dear Charles" is more appropriate than "Dear Mr. Jones" as you learn the relationship of the correspondent to the executive). Cross-reference affiliations and identifications. For example, if you have Mr. Ericson's name as advertising manager of Acme Metal Company and Ms. Curry as sales manager of the same company, make a card for Acme and list the names of both executives. Likewise, if Ms. Roberta Nolan is your employer's attorney, make one card for Roberta Nolan, Attorney, and a cross-reference card for Attorney, Roberta Nolan. Copy the cards and insert in the manual. (Some administrative assistants prefer to use a card file; others store the information on the computer or word processor.) Updating changes is easier when the information is computerized; however, it is easy to update the card system by pasting over the original entry.

Clients and Projects Directory.   When your employer works with a succession of important clients, customers, projects, or jobs, a special section is necessary. Provide a page for each person or project, listing such information as the title of the job, the work to be performed, pertinent data, terms, and special procedures that the administrative assistant must follow. A list of all persons connected with the job is also helpful. Here, too, cross-referencing should be freely used.

Personal Data Section.   In addition to the major items that comprise the basic desk manual, many administrative assistants add a personal section. This section contains reminders—dates and events of special significance to the employer—and other personal information like that shown in Figure 24-5.

EMPLOYER'S PERSONAL DATA SECTION

Biography of employer or a complete list of educational achievements, employment records, awards, and community services

Important numbers (social security, passport, and credit cards)

Insurance policy numbers, amounts, and payment dates (unless already in an insurance register)

Memberships in professional and civic organizations, offices held, meeting dates, dues, committee assignments, and so on

Wedding anniversary

Family birthdays

College or school addresses of executive's children

Other birthdays the executive should remember

Expected retirement dates for company officials and other office personnel

Dates of important sports tournaments

Fig. 24-5   The personal data section of a desk manual contains reminders that are helpful to the administrative assistant.

MOVING UP IN YOUR POSITION

After you have demonstrated your competence, you can hope for promotion. Advancement depends on your performance and your professional growth while in your present position. If your career goals include moving up in the company, it is sometimes wise to let someone with influence know of your interest in a higher position. Should you be passed over for promotion, and you are confident that you are qualified, it is not improper to ask for a promotion when a suitable vacancy occurs.

Setting Personal and Professional Goals

Most successful organizations have established a mission statement and a set of goals and objectives that serve as a road map for their activities. Successful careerists also set personal and professional goals to give some focus on the future. As you begin your career as an administrative assistant, it is important that you give direction to your long-term and short-term professional efforts by outlining the major achievements you wish to realize during your career. Setting goals at the beginning of your career will help you target your efforts on the significant milestones you expect to reach. Successful goal setters recommend the goal-setting process shown in Figure 24-6.

Making Job-Enhancement Efforts

The position of administrative assistant is exactly what you make it. If you stay in your own little niche, doing only the work that has been assigned to you, you are likely to remain in the same position and at about the same salary indefinitely. Many employees who do not demonstrate the standards set throughout this textbook carry the title of administrative assistant. It is because of this that some employers do not recognize the potential of their administrative assistants and limit their activities to routine tasks. Therefore, advancement is very much up to you. Each time you find a way to free your employer of some task, you become more valuable. Each time you assume a new responsibility and prove yourself equal to the task, you become better qualified for advancement. This statement does not mean that you should use aggressive tactics or that you should infringe on the work of your coworkers—sure ways to ensure your being thoroughly disliked!—but it does mean that if you expect to get ahead, you must be a self-starter, alert to opportunities to prove your value by assuming more responsibility. In your rush to get ahead, don't overlook the fact that there is no substitute for competence. Competence comes at a high price—a price paid in hard work, study, and dedication. A capacity for growth must be coupled with the self-discipline necessary to carry out a sustained effort to grow with a job.

Build an impressive record of service to your employer and to others. Continue to promote your own individuality by maintaining a wholesome balance between business and social life, by developing interests and hobbies, and by cultivating friendships. Be well informed about business practices and the world around you.

Job Descriptions. You should work for the establishment and utilization of improved personnel practices. Most large organizations have adopted job descriptions that should be updated periodically by the executive and the administrative assistant. Have any expanded responsibilities put into writing; for example, setting up the conference room for a meeting may be your responsibility. But if you also organize the meeting, write the agenda, and prepare the report of the proceedings, make certain that these additional responsibilities are also included in your job description.

Upward mobility may be limited if you let a job description limit creativity and initiative. Performance beyond that called for in a job description often results in a salary increase greater than the standard increase given most employees.

THE GOAL-SETTING PROCESS

1. Put your goals in writing. This is the first step in committing yourself to achieving them, and writing them down will help you clarify them.
2. Be specific in your approach to goals. Instead of writing, "I will improve myself professionally," be specific. "I will pass the CPS examination next year," or "I will earn a degree," or "I will take an accounting course" are specific goals that can be easily measured.
3. Be realistic in selecting your goals, but don't underestimate your abilities. If you dislike working with figures, it would be unrealistic to choose the job as supervisor of payroll as one of your goals. On the other hand, if your mathematics background is weak but you enjoy accounting, this might be a worthy goal if you are willing to seek additional education. Recognizing your own limitations can save you from taking on jobs where your success will be limited and your efforts will only cause you frustration. For example, if you do not like being responsible for the work of others, a management position may not be a satisfying goal.
4. Set both intermediate and long-term goals. Ask yourself where you want to be in five years, in ten years, and even at the end of the first year on the job. Keep your list flexible. Achieving some goals will take longer than others. Interruptions occur that could delay the process.
5. Recognize the costs and the trade-offs involved in selecting certain goals. Suppose, for example, that your firm is willing to pay your tuition for night courses which are job related. You elect to go to night school and apply the courses you take towards a degree. The cost to you is lost personal time. Night classes take time away from social events, family, and other personal pursuits.
6. Identify the essential skills and knowledge required to attain your goals.

Suppose you have as one of your goals attainment of the position as executive assistant to the CEO of your firm when the person who presently holds the position retires in five years. Carefully study the attributes that person has that you don't have. Then concentrate your efforts on attaining those attributes.

7. Reexamine your goals periodically. What once seemed attractive as a professional goal may no longer hold interest for you.
8. Include on your list some personal goals. Such things as improvement of health and appearance, financial security, community service, marriage, and family should also be included because they affect the quality of your work life.
9. Measure your progress. In addition to reexamining your goals periodically, you should measure your progress to see if you are making any headway. If you are in a job that is taking you nowhere, or your executive limits your opportunities to expand your knowledge and responsibilities, you may wish to change jobs instead of altering your goals.
10. Tell someone about your goals. Once you have made a list of your goals, tell someone what they are. There is no better incentive than having to measure up. If, for example, you told your supervisor that you intend to prepare for the CPS examination, you will make the effort because someone else is either cheering you on or doubting that you will be successful—either way, you'll be motivated to achieve.
11. Don't be afraid to fail. Many potentially successful people remain in routine, mundane jobs because they are afraid of failure or are overly sensitive to their critics. Most people never achieve everything they expect to achieve from a career, but those who set goals and plan for the future generally achieve more than those who don't.

Fig. 24-6 Setting personal and professional goals will provide a road map for your career.

Authority for Giving Executive Orders.   Employers exercise a great deal of authority. Sometimes forgetting that their administrative assistants do not have the same authority, they may say, "Tell Ms. Montgomery to give me a report on the bid by Thursday." Unfortunately, your authority to give an order is not always established by your superior. Your request, although tactfully worded, may be resented by Ms. Montgomery. If you have a problem of this kind, ask the executive to establish your authority to make such requests.

Growing Professionally

As technology continues to make dramatic changes in the role of the administrative assistant, your role will become even more vital to the success of your employer. Becoming a pro at what you do is certainly a worthwhile career goal. Just as accountants, doctors, clergy, educators, and attorneys strive for certain hallmarks of professionalism, so should the administrative assistant. To qualify as a professional in any field, certain requirements must be met. These requirements are as follows: (1) mastery of a specific body of knowledge; (2) adherence to a code of ethics; (3) study of the literature in the field; (4) successful completion of a licensing or certification program; and (5) participation in a professional organization.

Your on-the-job activities shape your professional development. You need to learn all that you can on the job, but you can also make out-of-the-office activities contribute to your growth.

Participation in organizations is one way you can grow professionally. Taking part in professional groups is important to all employees. Many advancements are secured because of contacts made in both social and professional groups. Networking, the exchange of information among professionals in a social setting, often leads to advancement. Many professional organizations promote personal development by providing information, contacts, and support. They keep members updated on equipment and organizational changes, enabling them to work as part of a larger team and to learn new work styles.

Professional Organizations.   The largest professional organization for administrative assistants is Professional Secretaries International (PSI), which has chapters in the United States and foreign countries. Executive Women International, with membership comprised of executive secretaries and administrative assistants, is another organization that provides many opportunities for service and professional growth.

Certification Programs.   Several organizations sponsor rigorous certification programs. Anyone passing these examinations demonstrates superior competence in the field. The certification programs of the American Association of Medical Assistants (AAMA), the National Association of Legal Secretaries (International) (NALS), and the National Association of Educational Office Personnel (NAEOP) are described in Chapter 23.

Professional Secretaries International awards a Certified Professional Secretary (CPS) certificate to those who pass a one-day examination and have the required amount of verified secretarial experience (see Figure 24-7). About 40,000 secretaries have qualified for the certificate since its inception in 1951. The examination is divided into three sections testing management, office management procedures, and finance and business law. It is prepared by the Institute for Certifying Secretaries and is given in May and November at testing centers in the United States, Canada, Puerto Rico, Jamaica, Bahamas, Barbados, Hong Kong, and Malaysia. Testing centers are also available to military and civilian personnel in military installations overseas and within the United States through DANTES (Defense Activity for Non-Traditional Education Support), an educational activity of the Department of Defense.

Fig. 24-7 The CPS certificate is the hallmark of professional excellence for the administrative assistant.

Students may take the examination near the end of their college program; but if they pass all sections, they will not be certified until they complete the experience requirement. Specific information about qualifying is not included here since it changes from year to year. It is available from Professional Secretaries International, 10502 N.W. Ambassador Drive, P.O. Box 20404, Kansas City, MO 64195-0404. To prepare for the examination, you may obtain the following materials from PSI for a minimal fee: *CPS*

Outline and Bibliography; CPS, a Sampling of Questions; and *University/College Directory of Credits* granted for the CPS rating.

Unfortunately, management personnel are not as well informed about the CPS program as administrative assistants wish they were. There are notable exceptions, however. The governors of Indiana and Illinois have issued policy statements indicating that CPS holders will receive special consideration for promotions. A number of colleges grant college credit to holders of the CPS certificate.

Seminars and Courses for Administrative Assistants.   Several professional organizations offer seminars and courses to improve office skills. The local chapters of Professional Secretaries International conduct workshops, seminars, and CPS preparation courses. Private organizations such as the Dartnell Institute of Management sponsor seminars in major cities of the United States. Management organizations offer special seminars for administrative assistants. Colleges offer such programs through their adult education programs.

Many companies send their administrative assistants to these programs. If you are interested in attending any of them, request financial support from your immediate employer. If your request is granted, arrangements for time off from work and payment of registration fees can be made with your employer.

A study of companies with 500 or more employees shows that 75 percent of them offer some in-house courses, with one-eighth of all employees participating, mostly during working hours. Many of these courses are designed to improve on-the-job performance. It is obvious that educational opportunities are available to those ambitious enough to take advantage of them.

Promoting Your Employer

Few executives will be regarded as ordinary if they are supported by an extraordinary administrative assistant.

The more important your employer appears in the eyes of others—company executives, customers, clients, and friends—the more important you appear, too. Here are some suggestions which will help enhance your accomplishments.

1. Keep your employer's resume up-to-date. Many employers have a prepared resume which they submit when applying for membership in a professional organization or when supplying a biographical sketch in connection with a speech or an article accepted for publication. This information needs to be updated regularly.

2. Watch the newspaper and magazines for press notices that mention your employer. See that they are clipped, identified, and filed. They can be placed in a scrapbook. Many employers are too modest to handle or supervise such a task, so the administrative assistant should take the initiative. Posting clippings about your employer on

the bulletin board is one way of letting everyone in the office know that your employer is important.

3. Keep your employer's committee and project folders in good order and up-to-date to assure that your employer presents a good image in the eyes of other company personnel.

4. Watch the news for items concerning your employer's business associates and friends. When they are honored or promoted, draft a letter of congratulations for your employer's signature and submit it with the clipping.

5. Look for news reports about new firms or plants that may be potential customers. Your employer will watch for these items also, but it does no harm for you to say, "Did you happen to see this in yesterday's paper?"

There is no better way to promote a good image of your employer than to see that all work going out of the office is flawless and is turned out with dispatch. Mistakes, delays, and sloppiness are not the marks of a professional administrative assistant.

If you have worked with an executive for a period of time, you should be able to assess whether or not that person is on the way up the company ladder. Competition for executive positions is keen. It is a cruel fact that many bright young executives do not make the grade and are destined for dead-end jobs. People who get ahead in business are usually helped by a mentor (sponsor), someone who pushes for their advancement. If you are assigned to an executive whose promotional opportunities are nonexistent or to one who is not your mentor, you may decide that the best thing for you is to move out since you will probably not move up. Ask for a transfer or change to another organization.

Be aware that beginners are not always willing to wait until a sound assessment of an executive's potential situation can be made before deciding to seek greener pastures. Nothing is more questionable on your employment record than proof that you are a job hopper. However, an honest appraisal of your employer is valuable in planning your professional future. If you decide on a move after you have been in a position long enough to establish that you have been successful in it, leave with poise and dignity and without animosity. Any derogatory remarks could haunt you for a long time after you are gone. A letter of resignation will help to keep a good relationship intact.

Identifying Yourself with Management

Being an administrative assistant to a major official of a business is not a position that you step into or inherit because you have completed a degree or a technical program. These positions must be earned and are usually filled from the inside. Therefore, although you will probably start on a lower level, your goal is eventually to associate yourself with top management.

Fig. 24-8 Reading publications like the *Wall Street Journal* develops management thinking ability.

To work effectively at this level, the administrative assistant must develop the ability to look at problems from the management point of view. This trait requires an orientation toward management thinking. Read the same periodicals that management reads (see Figure 24-8), such as *Fortune, Nation's Business, Business Week,* the *Wall Street Journal, Forbes, The Office,* and others; become concerned with management problems; study management books and take management courses.

The emphasis of much of your training has been on following instructions, observing directives, carrying decisions through, and assuming the initiative in a relatively narrow range of operation. Management, however, involves determining courses of action, making decisions, giving directions, and delegating authority and responsibility. To shift to the management outlook, the administrative assistant must view problems basically from the other side of the desk. This transition requires a carefully planned program of self-education, orientation, and discipline.

You need to grow every day of your working life. If the time comes when you cannot keep up with your employer, be assured that you will be replaced by someone who can. If you continue to grow with the job, you will have a position as long as you want it; and possibilities for advancement become limitless.

As you grow into a management role, you will gradually perform more supervisory functions. The higher up the management ladder you climb, the greater your supervisory responsibilities will be. The final chapter in this text will discuss management and supervisory strategies.

Summary

Once you have decided on a company that you think will offer you a good starting point for your career, analyze the personal characteristics that will help you get off to the right start and to grow professionally on the job. Competent administrative assistants who achieve recognition and enjoy a high degree of job satisfaction suggest that initiative, flexibility in dealing with change, awareness of the needs of the business and the employer, and adeptness in human relations are prerequisites for their success.

The first week or two on the job can overwhelm the beginning administrative assistant. There is so much to learn—the people, the environment, and the work. During your first days on the job, everyone in the office forms first impressions of you. You will work under critical inspection. Strive to make a favorable first impression by being a good listener, learning names and titles quickly, observing the ground rules, and living up to a professional code of ethics. Develop a network of friends throughout the organization. Goodwill at all levels of an organization is essential to your effectiveness.

In addition to knowing the prerequisites for getting off on the right foot, you should also be aware of possible obstacles with which you will have to cope. Be aware of your rights in all situations. Learn how to handle problems when they occur. Keep in mind that your performance will be evaluated periodically, and work toward achieving a positive rating.

From the first day on the job, begin learning about the company that employs you—names of customers, your employer's close associates, and company terminology. The more you know about a company, its products, its people, and its customers, the more valuable you will be to your employer. Several sources of information are available to you: company manuals, office files, company publications, newsletters, trade journals, and the like.

Asking questions is a good way to learn, but they should be questions that count. Don't ask someone else a question when you can find the answer yourself.

A desk manual will help you organize your work. If one is not provided for you, make one. It should contain sections on procedures for handling certain duties, company information, a directory of those with whom your employer frequently interacts, a directory of clients and projects, and a personal data section on your employer.

After you have demonstrated your competence, you can hope for promotion. Advancement depends on your performance and professional growth in your present job. The position of administrative assistant is exactly what you make it, and you should establish some short-term and some long-term career goals to provide some focus for your efforts. Each time you assume a new responsibility and successfully see it through, you enhance your chances for promotion. There is no substitute for competence.

Update your job description periodically to include expanded responsibilities. Ask your executive to establish your authority for giving executive orders.

You also need to grow professionally by participating in activities outside the office. There are several avenues open for professional growth. One of the most effective is membership in professional organizations, such as Professional Secretaries International. Certificate programs, such as the Certified Professional Secretary (CPS) certificate, also give direction to your professional education. Seminars and special courses are also available from several professional organizations. Attend them. Very often, employers pay fees for their administrative assistants to attend.

To do an effective job of promoting the employer, the administrative assistant should produce flawless work. In addition, the employer's resume should be kept up-to-date. Keep a scrapbook of publicity relating to the employer's activities. Keep committee and project folders in good order. Look for publicity about your employer's customers, associates, and competitors that will help you stay informed of the changes that affect you and your employer.

Keep in mind that your employer can have a great deal of influence on your advancement. After you have worked for an executive for a period of time, you should be able to assess whether or not that person is on the way up the corporate ladder. Realize that people who get ahead in business are often helped by a mentor (someone who takes an interest in their advancement). If you sense that your employer is destined for a dead-end job, you may decide to move out or ask for a transfer. Don't build a reputation as a job hopper; but if you decide that your opportunities for advancement are limited in your present job and you have established a record of success in it, leave with poise and dignity.

QUESTIONS FOR DISCUSSION

1. Why is goal setting important for the professional? What are some goals you might set as a beginning administrative assistant?

2. What are the requirements for becoming a professional in any field? Does the field in which you will be working as an administrative assistant meet these requirements?

THINK IT
Through

3. Cite three examples, other than those mentioned in the text, of a new administrative assistant showing initiative in an appropriate way. Cite three examples in which you think that the administrative assistant exceeded his or her authority.

4. What recommendations would you make to a coworker who asks your advice on how to grow in your profession as an administrative assistant?

5. In what ways can an administrative assistant benefit from joining a local chapter of a professional organization?

6. Assume that you are employed to replace the administrative assistant to a department manager in a large company and that the administrative assistant has already left when you report. Where would you obtain the following information?

THINK IT
Through

a. Your job description

b. Your employer's proper title

c. The lines of authority in the office

d. The letter style preferred by your employer

e. The name of the company president's administrative assistant

f. The branch offices of the company

g. Your employer's professional memberships

7. Rekey the following sentences choosing the correct word from those in parentheses. Check the Reference Guide to verify and correct your answers.

a. We spent a large (number, amount) of dollars for the program.

b. The (ingenious, ingenuous) use of software has reduced the number of spelling errors.

c. We must take at least two members (off, off of) the project.

d. He (lead, led) the company in sales that month.

e. (Compared to, Compared with) the methods we (formerly, formally) used, we have come a long way.

PROBLEMS

1. Assume that the executive assistant to your company's chief executive officer is planning to retire in two years. The assistant is a college graduate and has held the position for 12 years. You want the job. Key a list of intermediate goals you hope to attain between now and the time the job becomes available.

2. Prepare a questionnaire suitable for mailing to a group of top administrative assistants to determine their professional outlooks. Base your questions on the five requirements for becoming a professional listed on page 680.

3. Prepare a report on one of the following topics:

a. What you believe are the personal contributions an administrative assistant makes to the office, to coworkers, and to the profession.

b. How you plan to meet the challenge of new office technology in your work as an administrative assistant.

4. Select a professional organization that has a chapter in your area. Make arrangements to attend one of the meetings or interview one of the members. Give an oral report to the class including a description of the organization, its objectives, activities, membership requirements, and services to members.

5. Write to the Institute for Certifying Secretaries or the National Association of Legal Secretaries and request information on requirements for taking the CPS or PLS examination. Prepare a written report outlining the requirements for after you graduate but before you have had any secretarial experience.

Chapter 25

Your Role as an Office Professional

INTRODUCTION

Probably no position in a business firm offers a better opportunity to observe the advantages and disadvantages of a managerial position than does the position of administrative assistant. As you grow in experience, in intellectual curiosity, and in your ability to solve problems and make decisions, you will find increased opportunities for jobs that will broaden your business perspective, increase your authority, and permit you to make major decisions. Increased knowledge and experience will strengthen your confidence in your ability to lead others in the achievement of common goals.

This chapter focuses on the fundamentals of the management process and on the basic qualifications necessary for effective administration and supervision. This chapter goes beyond the duties performed by the administrative assistant to outline the functions of management and gives some suggestions for continuing your professional growth as a manager.

Determine where you want to go and what you want to be. Then readjust your life to fit your goal.

APPRAISING YOUR MANAGEMENT POTENTIAL

The one characteristic that most successful people have in common is their capacity to pay the price to be better.

In many offices, administrative assistants perform a dual role; their duties include the supervision of other employees as well as the day-to-day responsibilities of their role as administrative assistant. The employees they supervise often work for and answer to someone other than the administrative assistant, whose authority is limited. Therefore, extreme tact and ability are required to keep work flowing smoothly. Because the administrative assistant's lines of authority are hazy under such an arrangement, frustration sometimes results. However, handling the administrative assistant/supervisor role successfully can prove your ability as a potential manager. As you expand your horizons beyond the support functions associated with your present position, focus on a particular management job and analyze it (see Figure 25-1).

ASSESSING YOUR MANAGEMENT POTENTIAL

___ Do I have managerial qualifications that are different from those required in my present job?

___ Am I willing to let go of the technical details of my present job and take on broader responsibilities?

___ Have I trained someone to take my place so that the transition will be a smooth one?

___ Do I want to devote more time and thought to my work than I do now?

___ Could I travel if the job required it?

___ Am I fully aware of the negative aspects of being a manager?

___ Could I make unpopular decisions and deal with criticism?

___ Could I build an effective team?

___ Could I cope with conflict and maintain discipline?

___ Do I have sufficient knowledge of my company—its people, its products, and its markets?

___ Would I rather move up than remain at the support level, retaining close associations with my peers?

___ Am I willing to give up most of the close associations with my peers?

UNDERSTANDING MANAGEMENT FUNCTIONS

Management is executive leadership, or the ability to obtain desired results through the use of an organization's resources and the efforts of others. The success of every organized activity depends on the managerial skills of its leaders. Although some managers seem to be born with the ability to lead, others must acquire management skills through reading, specialized courses and seminars, experience, and observation of successful executives.

The functions of management at all levels involve planning, organizing, controlling, and directing. To become an effective manager, you must understand these functions and how each contributes to the total organization.

Planning

Planning is the primary management function. It gives an organization a course of action. Before anything worthwhile can happen in an organization, goals must be set, objectives established, and checkpoints and target dates defined. This is the essence of planning.

Plans may be made for the long term (more than one year) or for the short term (one year or less). Long-range plans are general in nature. They must anticipate changes in social, economic, and political climates that can affect outcomes over a five-year or ten-year period. Short-range plans are spelled out in detail, and in some cases are devised to guide a specific, nonrecurring project. For example, a manager might make a short-range plan to conduct a feasibility study for installing desktop publishing in a company. Once the decision is made and the equipment is installed, there is no further need for the plan.

Good plans are not too rigid. Some flexibility is built in to allow for the uncertainties of the future. It should be possible to make slight adjustments without major deviation from the requirements of the plan.

Organizing

Once plans have been formulated, a structure must be developed within which the plans can be executed. Tasks must be divided among personnel. Each worker and supervisor must know who is to perform each task as well as when and how the work is to be done. The organizational function defines duties, assigns responsibilities (the obligation to perform a task), delegates authority (the power to make decisions related to the work), and establishes staff relationships (who reports to whom).

In an effective organization, employees answer to one supervisor. This is called **unity of command.** Imagine your dilemma, for example, in working as administrative assistant to four executives, each of whom feels that his or her work should be given priority. Violation of the unity of command principle, although not uncommon in many offices, is a cause of frustration, low morale, and high employee turnover.

Good organizational structure adheres to the principle of span of control. **Span of control** refers to the number of employees who report to a single supervisor. A manager who supervises too many employees will not be able to perform all supervisory duties effectively. On the other hand, supervision of too few employees is a waste of executive time. As a general rule, the lower the level of management, the larger the span of control can be. For example, a supervisor of a communications center might supervise 12 specialists effectively. It would be difficult, though, for an administrative manager to be responsible for more than five supervisors of such operations as communications, mail room, reprographics, records, and credit and collections because of the complex nature of these operations.

Business responsibilities may be organized in a number of ways. Two major types of organizational structures used in business are *line* and *line and staff,* but others are also in use.

Line Organization.   *Line organization* means that authority flows in a straight line from the top official in the company to the lowest administrative segment of the organization. A popular device for illustrating the line form of organization is an organization chart, which shows relationships among members of an organization and their areas of responsibility. An example of a line organization chart appears in Chapter 2 on page 21.

Line and Staff Organization.   The line and staff concept of organization originated in the military. Business adopted it as a means of coping with the expanding relationships that accompany growing organizations. Many large companies today use line and staff organization because the structure permits the use of staff specialists for advice and assistance. Staff specialists serve in an advisory capacity only; that is, they have no authority over line personnel. Their relationships to line personnel are indicated in Figure 25-2 by broken lines.

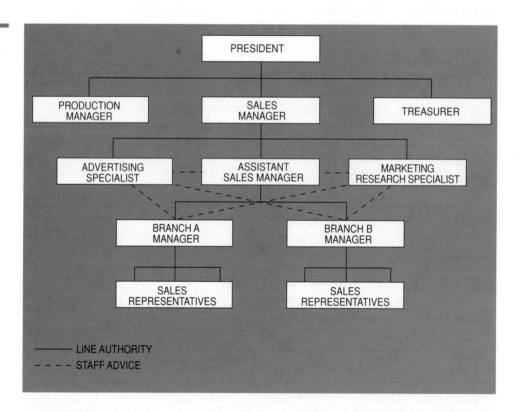

Fig. 25-2   A line and staff organization defines relationships between managers and staff.

Functional Authority.   The concept of *functional authority* is closely related to line and staff organization, but it violates the principle of unity of command. Functional authority delegates power to individuals or to departments over departments other than their own. For example, the president of your company decides to install microcomputers for payroll preparation and gives authority to a specialist from the management information systems department to supervise the accounting department in purchasing software, establishing procedures, and the like. The president has assigned *functional authority* to the data processing specialist.

Functional authority is usually concerned with when and how something is done rather than with what is to be done and who is to do it. Functional authority should be used only when specialists are needed; otherwise, it undermines the line manager's authority to organize, plan, staff, direct, and control. Functional authority does, however, save time and expedite the flow of information in complex situations.

Horizontal Organization.   In the traditional line or line and staff organization, the chief executive officer presides over a bureaucracy where orders are passed down the chain of command and decisions are passed up the chain. This is a slow process and work is segmented according to functions—marketing, manufacturing, finance, etc., with very little overlap.

Horizontal organization radically restructures the management hierarchy. Layers of management are eliminated, and workers are authorized to make decisions as far down in the organization as there is competence to solve a problem. For the administrative assistant moving into the position of office manager, this means that if the purchase of up-to-date information processing hardware and software is needed, the authority to make the decision on brands, configurations, software, and the like would rest with those who are closest to the information processing operation. Under the line or line and staff structure, such a decision would be referred up the chain of command through thick layers of middle management. Such an arrangement generates caution, slows decision making, and impedes efficiency.

The purpose of the horizontal structure is to find better ways for companies to respond to the marketplace, save time and money, generate ideas, and give workers a sense of their own value to the organization. Top management no longer commands and controls from the top, but, rather, responds to priorities set at lower levels in the organization. All activities, however, must conform to the objectives of the company. Figure 25-3 illustrates horizontal organization.

Committee Organization.   A **committee** is a group of people responsible for a specific project or situation. This form of organization is common to all types of institutions—religious, educational, governmental, and commercial. Committees are used to obtain the best judgment and thinking of a group. Those who advocate the use of this type of organization believe that groups are better at solving problems and guiding projects than individuals are. Because of the combined education, experience, and personal influence of a committee's members, better solutions to problems are possible. Committees are also used to avoid centering too much authority in one person. Because a committee involves several people, however, it has certain weaknesses: committee work is time-consuming and decisions are sometimes difficult to reach; meetings sometimes result in compromise rather than a solid solution; and some managers use committees to avoid making unpleasant decisions themselves. Employees who serve on committees, however, have an opportunity to get involved in large projects. Committees provide high visibility and an opportunity to influence decisions.

Fig. 25-3 In the horizontal structure, specialized workers make group decisions without going through a middle management hierarchy for approval.

Matrix (Project) Management. **Matrix management** is a form of organization that pools the skills and knowledge of teams of personnel from various departments throughout a company to complete major company projects. Employees from various departments may be assigned to a special project on a part-time or full-time basis until it is completed. Matrix management allows an organization to make the most effective use of its personnel.

Expertise that crosses departmental lines is often needed to handle complex problems brought on by increased government regulation and rapidly growing technology. Because word processing and telecommunications touch every aspect of a firm—personnel, production, marketing, and finance— experts in these areas are good candidates for matrix management.

To illustrate matrix management, consider a company planning to introduce a new brand of cake mix. Introducing the product would involve specialists from production, marketing, and finance working together as a team until the cake mix is on grocers' shelves. Because of the need for administrative support for the project, an information services specialist might be assigned to the project on a temporary basis to support the project team. When the project is completed, the specialist would return to his or her home department.

Members of a project team work in a climate unlike that in the traditional line and staff organization. As with any other management structure, matrix management has both advantages and disadvantages. On the positive side, it enables the firm to make more efficient use of skilled personnel. Because employees from different functional areas are required to work together for a common goal, the organization can respond quickly to special demands. On the negative side, matrix management violates the unity of command principle. Employees are responsible to home department managers as well as to the manager of the special project. Project managers find that employees borrowed from functional departments are extremely loyal to those departments. Therefore, it is frequently difficult to coordinate the efforts of employees on temporary assignments.

Controlling

Control is the monitoring function that ensures that work meets specifications. Control must be exercised to ensure that work is of the proper quality and produced in expected quantities at the most economical cost according to predetermined schedules, policies, and procedures.

Cost Control and Work Measurement. Two major types of control exist in every type of organized activity: cost control and production control. Effectiveness in cutting costs—the ability to reduce the cost of supplies, overtime, absenteeism, etc.—is one of the best measures of a manager's competence.

The other area of control in which the supervisor must be especially skillful is the area of production. Measurement techniques of several kinds are employed by supervisors as a basis for establishing production standards and arriving at pay scales for employees. Measuring the production of factory workers engaged in routine assembly line operations has been practiced for many years. Until recently, however, measuring office work had not been practiced on a large scale.

In evaluating your work and that of your subordinates, you need a set of criteria on which to base your judgments. Output in highly repetitive office operations has been successfully measured, and realistic quantitative standards have been established. In some offices, line and page counts are commonly used to measure worker productivity. In management literature you can find standards for keying straight copy, keying letters, addressing envelopes, or completing form letters. Determining qualitative standards is not as easy; just remember that the quality of all work from your department is your responsibility.

Corrective Action. In spite of adequate planning, efficient organization, and proper control, something will occasionally go wrong. A subordinate may not perform up to the expected standard, or external delays and errors may prevent the completion of a project on time. When this happens the supervisor must take corrective action. When taken promptly, corrective action can prevent more serious problems later on and help keep morale and productivity high. Problems such as computer downtime, failure of a printer to deliver forms, careless employees who make serious errors, and the like, must be dealt with by the supervisor decisively, calmly, and as quickly as possible.

Total Quality Management (TQM). Total quality management (TQM) is one of this decade's most discussed management strategies. TQM is a transformational process requiring a long-term commitment to quality. This theory is based upon the work of Dr. W. Edwards Deming, who helped revitalize Japanese industry after World War II. TQM involves instruction, tools, and techniques for improving quality at all levels of the organization. These techniques include (1) defining customers' needs, (2) improving the quality of products and services, (3) improving all work processes within the organization, (4) improving the services of suppliers and vendors, and (5) assessing the cultural elements of an organization. These elements include rewards for results, measurement of improvement, teamwork and cooperation, job security, authority commensurate with responsibility, and fair treatment.

Achieving TQM has become a priority for businesses around the world, and it requires the commitment of managers to these principles. If you aspire to a management position, you should explore opportunities to learn more about this important concept. Seminars, books, films, and classes are available to help you apply TQM to the workplace. Positive signs of TQM in the office are shown in Figure 25-4.

Fig. 25-4 The principles of total quality management (TQM) can be applied to the office.

TEN POSITIVE SIGNS OF TOTAL QUALITY MANAGEMENT IN THE OFFICE

1. A spirit of teamwork, service, and cooperation among employees.
2. A minimum of employee gripes and customer/client complaints.
3. Prompt and satisfactory service from vendors and suppliers.
4. Evidence of attention to detail at all levels, resulting in error-free work.
5. Regular attendance of employees working with a minimum of wasted time, materials, money, and effort.
6. Technical literacy of employees using state-of-the-art equipment and an awareness of office ecology, ergonomic principles, and employee safety.
7. Open lines of communication to all levels of the organization—upward, downward, and horizontal.
8. A program of training and professional development for office employees.
9. Evidence of meeting deadlines, setting appropriate priorities, and organizing paper flow to avoid backtracking, paper shuffling, and proliferation of forms and correspondence.
10. A protected records management system that is accurate, accessible to authorized personnel, complete without excessive backup, and organized for findability.

Directing

An effective manager leads employees in such a way that organizational goals are achieved. This is the function of directing. Expanding government regulations, new technology, and increased costs have magnified the importance of this management function. Employee turnover is expensive, and top management in every organization is aware that the key to managing through people is to have the best possible people through whom to manage. Leaders must motivate employees to work efficiently and attempt to boost morale by providing an environment conducive to job satisfaction.

SUPERVISING OTHERS

Effective supervision is the ability to get people to do *what* you want done, *when* you want it done, the *way* you want it done because they *want* to do it. Supervision is the first level of management. As you move up professionally, you will probably find yourself in a supervisory position. As a supervisor, you will be a member of the management team that is responsible for getting work done. What's more, you will be the communication link between top and middle management and those you supervise. Your job will be a multifaceted one. You will report to top and middle management, interpret management policies to those you supervise, and coordinate with other supervisors to facilitate the flow of work throughout the organization. You will be promoting teamwork.

The amount of supervision needed depends on several factors: the skills and attitudes of employees, the complexity of the tasks performed, the quality of the orientation process, and subsequent training on the job. If an employee receives in-depth orientation and adequate training, the need for supervision is considerably lessened. After the initial training period, the right amount of supervision becomes important. Too much supervision gives the employee the feeling of being policed; too little leads to confusion. A supervisor's major duties are shown in Figure 25-5.

Fulfilling the role of a successful supervisor requires more than job competence and hard work. It also requires the ability to recognize and select outstanding employees and to develop their potential for making a contribution to the company and the department to which they are assigned.

Recruiting

Recruitment of employees is usually the responsibility of the human resources department. Before any recruiting begins, however, a study of the complete job description and the educational background, work experience, and skill requirements for the position is made. Later, potential employees who meet screening standards are sent to the immediate supervisor for final approval or rejection. (Note the word "rejection." The supervisor, being close to the job, may recognize valid reasons why a proposed candidate would not be effective. It is best to say no now and avoid trouble later.)

An objective of every company is promotion from within. An effective supervisor or administrator makes the development of replacements and per-

HUMAN RELATIONS

If you would manage others, you must first get a firm grip on your own time, your own temper, and your own habits. But most of all, you must WANT to lead a winning team.

HUMAN RELATIONS

A good supervisor is able to get ordinary people to do extraordinary work.

SUPERVISORY DUTIES

Helping select the right people for the right job.
Controlling absences and tardiness.
Inspecting and proofing work.
Keeping workers informed.
Carrying out objectives and instructions of management.
Keeping track of hours worked.
Maintaining office discipline.
Planning, assigning, and scheduling work.
Controlling office costs.
Promoting teamwork and cooperation.
Listening to employees' problems.
Providing and caring for equipment and supplies.
Training employees.
Handling employee discipline problems.
Keeping records and making reports to management.
Maintaining high quality and quantity of production.
Maintaining high employee morale.
Improving work methods.
Maintaining safe, clean working conditions.
Evaluating employees for raises and promotions.
Orienting new employees to the job.
Handling matters of compensation.
Delegating work to others.
Resolving conflicts among employees.
Interpreting employees' needs to management.
Interpreting management's needs to employees.

sonnel for new jobs an important objective. In fact, without a well-trained replacement, you may not be considered for a promotion.

Assisting employees in reaching their potential begins with the orientation to the job. A thorough orientation process means less time required for supervision and more time for supervisors to accomplish their work.

Orienting

Many large organizations have formal orientation programs for new employees. Films, slides, and lectures acquaint new employees with the history, products, and fringe benefits of the company. Information related to the specific job, however, is left to the immediate supervisor. It is the supervisor's responsibility to explain and demonstrate the tasks of the job. If you are a supervisor, discuss how and when the employee will be evaluated and how this evaluation is tied to salary increases. The supervisor also introduces new employees to the other workers and conducts a tour of the office facilities. In a small organization, the administrative assistant/supervisor provides the entire orientation program, including general information about the company and specific information about the job.

Many supervisors develop an induction checklist to follow in orienting a new employee to the company and to the position. This list may include 50 to 100 items, whatever it takes to explain the job. Supplementary materials, such as an organization chart and an office telephone directory, are useful in outlining the office hierarchy and office procedures. Some companies provide an orientation package containing information that new employees will need in order to perform their routine activities. The orientation package is given to new employees during the induction process and should contain at least the information shown in Figure 25-6.

MINIMUM CONTENTS OF AN EMPLOYEE ORIENTATION PACKAGE

Internal telephone directory
Forms used regularly in the course of business
Glossary of terminology used in the company
List of recurring abbreviations/acronyms
Mail pickup and delivery schedule
Schedules of working hours and breaks
Schedule of paydays and paid holidays
Safety regulations and parking restrictions
Organization chart
Distribution lists—who gets copies of what
Security policies
Equipment and facilities available
Telephone procedures
Dress codes, smoking regulations, and the like

Fig. 25-6 An orientation package for new employees should contain this information.

The orientation package can be assembled in a loose-leaf binder or inserted in a large manila envelope. Regardless of the form it takes, it should be updated regularly to ensure its usefulness. Providing the orientation package helps make a good impression on the new employee and answers a multitude of questions every beginning worker must ask sooner or later.

In addition to providing a formal orientation program and a packet of information designed to answer the beginning employees' questions, many companies have found that assigning a mentor—an experienced employee who will be responsible for training the newcomer—adds a personal touch that contributes to shortening the time between induction and full productivity for the new employee. The experienced administrative assistant is often chosen as mentor for new office employees. Serving as a mentor to a new employee who is nervous, lacks confidence, and must ask numerous questions often provides an excellent springboard to supervision for the administrative assistant. An effective mentor should be patient, approachable, and a good communicator. Should you be assigned as a mentor for a new employee, consider the assignment an opportunity to demonstrate your supervisory skills and make a good impression for your employer.

Training

Before employees can perform effectively as team members, a basic understanding of procedures, policies, and technology is essential. Rarely can an employee learn a complex job merely by observing. One of your supervisory duties will be to provide sufficient training to make employees fully productive as soon after induction as possible. Too little training is expensive when it leads to errors, employee insecurity, and low productivity. On the other hand, training programs that prolong the time before an employee takes full responsibility for a job are also costly. To determine the types and length of training that an employee needs, a list of specific duties and responsibilities is helpful. It is also suggested that the supervisor follow the guidelines in Figure 25-7.

Fig. 25-7 Supervisors should follow these guidelines for training new employees.

GUIDELINES FOR EMPLOYEE TRAINING

1. Focus attention on what the employee is to do. First, have the employee observe as you complete a task. Then check the employee's understanding by having the trainee work through the process step by step. Allow more time for difficult tasks.
2. Discuss the purposes behind each task and encourage questions. Explain the *who, what, where, when, why,* and *how* of each task. Suggest that the employee compile a list of instructions. For more complicated tasks, it is a good practice for the supervisor to provide a written set of instructions. Use materials and office forms that are part of the job in your explanations.
3. Allow the employee some quiet time to digest information.
4. Assist the employee in understanding which tasks are important and which are not so important. Emphasize the key steps in each job task.
5. Provide feedback to the employee on work that has been done. You may have to reteach certain points that may have been misunderstood by the employee or overlooked in your explanation.

After an employee has been in the office long enough to learn an assigned job, continue your teaching responsibility by training the employee to do other jobs in the department. This technique is called **cross training.** Cross training has merit for the supervisor and for the employee. When an employee is absent because of sickness or vacation, another employee can assume the duties of the position. Cross training makes the employee more valuable to the department and increases the employee's job skills.

An example of cross training can be found in offices where a variety of information technology is used. Many companies train administrative assistants on *desktop publishing* and other sophisticated software to provide for better understanding of the equipment as well as to provide greater flexibility of personnel. Although computer operators are usually assigned to one specific piece of equipment, they might be trained on all equipment in the office for the same reason—staff flexibility.

Mentoring

As you advance in your career, you will find individuals in the workplace whose success, management style, and personality serve as a role model for your own career. These are usually senior executives—not necessarily your boss—whose advice, guidance, and support can provide momentum for your advancement. Their support can help you gain visibility through challenging assignments and influential contacts. Opportunities provided by a mentor can assist you in making noteworthy contributions to your company. These executives who coach, advise, and encourage employees of lesser rank are called **mentors.**

Informal mentoring in some form goes on in almost every organization. Younger workers who seek senior executives' advice on career-related matters, company policy, finances, promotions, and the like are, in essence, the recipients of informal executive mentoring (see Figure 25-8). Employees often find that such a relationship, although informal, can give focus to their work life, leading them to set higher goals, standards, and expectations for themselves.

Some companies have established formal mentoring programs. Under this formal arrangement, the mentor meets with the employee at regular intervals in either group or individual sessions. Employees find that such a relationship increases their confidence, their identity with the firm, and their sense of professionalism. The benefits that accrue to the company from a mentoring program include the following:

- Makes high-level managers known to employees
- Teaches managers and employees about the firm's culture
- Provides opportunities for discovering hidden talent
- Generates senior-executive support for younger employees
- Increases networking among employees
- Ensures sponsorship of senior executives for women and minorities

As you consider decisions that will significantly affect your career, the counsel of a mentor can help you affirm those decisions and assist you in seeking opportunities that will make the best use of your abilities. A good mentor can even protect you from company politics.

Fig. 25-8 A mentor can provide guidance and advice in a variety of professional areas.

If the company that employs you does not have a formal mentoring program, you will be on your own in finding the sponsorship of a senior executive. You can begin by showing initiative, going beyond your job description, taking on assignments with high visibility, and building a reputation for competence, service, and dependability.

Delegating

Supervisors must delegate to survive the avalanche of paperwork that characterizes the modern office and to get jobs done accurately and on time. As your supervisory responsibilities expand, you must let go of details and assign them to others. Working frantically from one crisis to another and attempting to do everything yourself lead to fatigue and inefficiency. These behaviors also do little to develop the potential of those you supervise. As a supervisor you will be judged by your ability to develop productive employees. By delegating some of your duties, you can give those you supervise added experience. Start your task of delegation simply. Delegate routine tasks, such as filling out reports and forms, checking materials and supplies, and composing routine correspondence.

As you begin your supervisory duties, you may find that you are not very skillful in delegating work to others. Many supervisors admit that, early in their careers, they labored under the false notion that it was easier to do a job than to explain it to someone else, or they were afraid to risk employee error on an important job. These are common misgivings; but if you are to become an effective supervisor, you must become effective at delegating work. Don't make the mistake of keeping busy with lots of routine details. Delegate routine jobs that can free you to perform major management functions—planning, organizing, controlling, and directing.

Motivating

A supervisor has an obligation to obtain the best results from employees. The ability to inspire people to undertake a job enthusiastically, to work as productive team members, and to exercise initiative is the hallmark of successful management. It is essential that you understand why some people do superior work while others do as little as possible. Hundreds of books have been written on the subject of motivation, and behavioral scientists are still seeking answers on how to motivate people effectively.

Closely allied to job motivation is the need for job satisfaction. Each individual has a set of needs that must be satisfied. In the past, money was used as the major motivation in the workplace. The assumption that people worked only for money has been debunked by recent motivational research. Studies reveal that, after a certain level of income, money ceases to be a significant motivator for many employees. Research studies by behavioral scientists Abraham Maslow and Frederick Herzberg have helped management personnel to determine the needs of employees. Maslow identified a *hierarchy* of human needs: *physiological* (food, clothing, shelter); *safety; belonging; esteem;* and *self-actualization* (see Figure 25-9). He indicated that once a lower need is fairly well satisfied, a worker can be motivated only by a desire to satisfy the next higher need. His work suggests that managers must help employees realize their upper level needs (belonging, esteem, self-actualization) before complete job satisfaction—and higher productivity—can be obtained. In the office, *belonging,* the third level of needs, refers to acceptance and

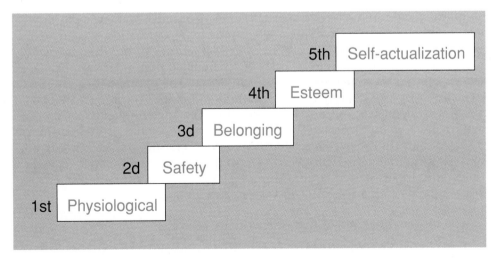

Fig. 25-9 Maslow's hierarchy of needs comprises five levels.

achievement of status with one's peers. The fourth level, *esteem,* is the need for prestige, recognition, and achievement. *Self-actualization,* the highest level, emphasizes becoming whatever a person can be, reaching one's full potential. The supervisor can assist subordinates in achieving these higher level needs in the following ways:

Give each employee complete responsibility for the preparation of one section of a report or one unit of work.

Grant increased authority in the accomplishment of office tasks.

Allow employees to participate in making decisions that affect their work.

Frederick Herzberg took another approach to understanding employee morale. His research on factors that result in employee satisfaction and dissatisfaction has helped managers in their attempts to reduce employee turnover and increase productivity.

Herzberg's major findings revealed that task-related experiences (achievement, recognition, interesting work, growth, advancement, and responsibility) led to job satisfaction. He called these experiences *satisfiers.* On the other hand, he found that experiences that caused employees to be unhappy were related to the job environment (working conditions, company policies and administration, supervision, pay, status, job security, and interpersonal relationships). Herzberg classified these as *dissatisfiers.*

Supervisors face problems of tardiness, absenteeism, carelessness, and errors. These are barriers to productivity. As a supervisor, you are the catalyst who motivates and inspires employees to overcome these barriers. Some of the ways you can help your subordinates become successful in their work are given in Figure 25-10.

Evaluating

Periodically the administrative assistant/supervisor must evaluate subordinates' work. In addition to being a job requirement, evaluation is both wanted and needed by the employee. Your evaluation can be either formal or informal. A *formal* evaluation consists of a scheduled performance appraisal review between the supervisor and the employee. The appraisal is written. After the supervisor completes the written appraisal, the comments are discussed with the employee, and both the employee and the supervisor sign it. Signing the appraisal merely signifies that the employee has been made aware of the contents of the evaluation. An *informal* evaluation, on the other hand, may consist of daily discussions with the employee on performance-related topics. Nothing is written, and nothing is signed. In order to assess an employee's job performance, you must observe the following:

Be thoroughly familiar with the work involved.

Have a set of job performance criteria.

SUGGESTIONS FOR OVERCOMING BARRIERS TO PRODUCTIVITY

1. Set specific objectives for each major undertaking. Set a reasonable standard and give clear instructions.
2. Make employees feel that every job is important.
3. Make employees feel that they are important contributors to your team.
4. Ask employees for assistance, advice, and suggestions.
5. Let employees express their own ideas.
6. Train your employees and then trust them by giving them the freedom to work on their own.
7. Judge your employees' actions by results obtained.
8. Suggest and request rather than demand.
9. Praise employees publicly when praise is deserved, but reprimand privately.
10. Give credit where credit is due.
11. Listen to learn what is important to your employees.
12. Reward those who achieve, and use their accomplishments to inspire others.
13. Look in on employees occasionally to check progress, offer help, answer questions, or boost confidence.
14. Don't assign a job that you don't know how to do yourself.
15. Find out why employees do poor work.
16. Don't do the work yourself if subordinates get into deep water; let them learn from the experience.
17. Remember that employees focus their best efforts where the supervisor places emphasis. Don't be a stickler for just one aspect of the job.
18. Put your critics to work. When you detect a complainer, delegate an important task to that person.

Fig. 25-10 Some ways a supervisor can help employees improve their work.

Be aware of individual differences in performing tasks required by the position.

Consider such factors as accuracy, neatness, and quantity of production.

Be able to communicate your evaluation clearly.

Criticize the work, not the person who performed it.

The importance of performance appraisal cannot be overstated. Assume that you are responsible for the yearly evaluation of a subordinate. It is time for the first-year performance appraisal, and you know that, in general, the person has done a good job. In the past few weeks, however, you have noticed a change in performance and attitude. The person is cooperative but sullen; the work is not up to former standards. Reluctant to make negative statements on record, you decide to disregard the last few weeks' performance and complete the form on the basis of the previous record. You are confident that something personal is bothering the person and that it will work out in time. Also, you decide not to mention these points in your conference with the person.

Is this the best course of action? Surprisingly, many supervisors in this situation react in exactly the same way. They tend to avoid potentially unpleasant incidents and, in general, do not want to become involved in the personal problems of employees. Yet it is the supervisor's responsibility to maintain quality and to assist the employee in every way to be a happy and effective worker. Unpleasant situations should be faced and an attempt should be made to resolve any problems as soon as possible.

As a supplement to a formal yearly performance appraisal, at specific points during the year a supervisor can evaluate an employee's cooperativeness. Such a checkup may point out problem areas for you to investigate. The result of such an approach might be to commend high performers, encourage the average group, and work more closely with those who appear to need help. Here are some activities you can review:

Does the employee accept instructions and assignments willingly?

Does the employee perform as directed?

Does the employee assume responsibility for work, inform the supervisor if something goes wrong, and call relevant matters to the supervisor's attention?

Does the employee volunteer for special assignments?

Does the employee give the job better than average attention?

Enriching the Job

Increased automation, the lack of diversity in many office jobs, and the monotony of some office tasks have brought a new challenge to the supervisor. More managers are beginning to give attention to the concept of job enrichment. Job enrichment attempts to bridge the gap between an employee's capabilities and job responsibilities. This is done by providing greater challenge, a greater sense of accomplishment, and more latitude in decision making. Flexible hours, job rotation, cross training, assigning full responsibility for an entire project, and establishing a pleasant working environment also provide job enrichment. In many companies, jobs are being redesigned to fill this need.

After all is said and done, unless actual benefits accrue to the worker, job enrichment techniques will become ineffective. Artificial measures cannot replace the need for training and promotions that move employees through the hierarchy of an organization.

Understanding and Respecting the Rights of Others

Our legal system provides employees with a variety of rights. Workers are keenly aware of these rights and are prone to seek court action when these rights are violated. Acquiring a knowledge of employees' rights helps you build a reputation for fairness. Should these rights be violated by the employer, legal action can be taken by an employee without fear of reprisal. Some of the more important employee rights are discussed throughout this book. In addition to the rights discussed in Chapter 22 (EEOC regulations, the Freedom of Information Act, and the Privacy Act, for example), legislation is pending in many states concerning drug testing, AIDS testing, the rights of smokers and nonsmokers, and the employment of handicapped and immigrant workers. Respecting the rights of employees you supervise and staying abreast of the legislation protecting these rights will help you establish guidelines for handling situations in which employer-employee interests sometimes collide.

Managing a Diverse Work Force

Modern business is no longer confined to national boundaries. Technology in almost every aspect of our work life has broadened our activities to include a global business community. As you move into management, it will not be unusual for you to have colleagues who represent a broad spectrum of race, religion, gender, age, physical and mental condition, and national origin (see Figure 25-11). Should you have the task of managing such diversity, keep in mind that the best measure of your success will be your ability to adjust to the different attitudes toward work, responsibility, time, customs, climate, language, and a host of other factors that affect the way workers conform to company policies and procedures. You should learn early that all employees are not motivated by the same rewards, and that change is more difficult for some than for others.

Keep in mind that you could be the "outsider." Consider, for example, how you might adjust to a different culture if your employer sent you overseas with the assignment to train support staff in the Asian branch of your company. Your success would depend upon your ability to win the confidence of these workers. You will, of course, be respected for your competence; however, the results you

Fig. 25-11 The global business community is made up of a multicultural work force.

get will depend upon your ability to blend the attitudes, skills, and abilities of your trainees with the goals and objectives of your employer. Successful managers of diversity are keen observers who are flexible and fair in executing management functions.

Downsizing

If you work for a large organization, you may experience a phenomenon called downsizing. **Downsizing,** in essence, means the elimination of some jobs, the restructuring of other jobs, and increased work loads for those who survive the cuts. Downsizing emerged as a management practice in the late 1980s. It resulted in early retirements for older employees, mergers of branch offices, reapportioning of company assets, and termination of surplus employees at all levels.

As an administrative assistant, should you find yourself in such an environment, you will probably make more decisions, represent your employer at meetings, manage resources, supervise more employees, and resolve conflicts. Because of downsizing, your job will become more varied, your responsibilities more visible, and your opportunities to make a broader contribution to your employer more significant.

As a manager, you will find that many of those you will supervise will consider the increased work load an added burden, the termination of colleagues unfair, and their job security threatened. A major part of your job will be to develop a cohesive team where morale and production are high.

Accepting downsizing as a challenge and an opportunity to prove your ability to perform beyond your present job description can, with the proper attitude, provide an excellent proving ground for your managerial skills.

Conducting an Exit Interview

Managers generally agree that the loss of competent employees is expensive, and that their reasons for leaving are not always obvious. For example, an employee may give insufficient pay as the reason for leaving a company when the real reason is the unfairness of the employee's supervisor. The exit interview is one of the most informative aspects of the termination procedure and should be carefully planned to ensure fairness to the employee and to protect the employer. In addition to uncovering the real reason for an employee's decision to terminate, the exit interview gives the alert manager insight into trouble spots within the company that may be causing high turnover among employees. Some companies have developed a form to be used as a guide in conducting the exit interview and as a record for the company files (see Figure 25-12). Supervisors of terminating employees should receive copies of the exit interview form or should be informed of feedback that affects their departments.

EXIT INTERVIEW FORM

Employee's name _____ Date of interview _____

Department _____ Termination date _____

Job title_____ Employment date _____

Name of interviewer _____ Title _____

Name of supervisor _____ Title _____

Reason for leaving company _____

1. List three things you liked most about your job.
   1.   2.   3.
2. List three things you disliked most about your job.
   1.   2.   3.
3. List three things you liked most about the company.
   1.   2.   3.
4. List three things you disliked most about the company.
   1.   2.   3.
5. Do you feel that you received adequate training for your job?   YES   NO
   If the answer is NO, what do you recommend in the future? _____
   _____
6. What one contribution do you think you made to the company? _____
   _____
7. Do you feel the company used your talents to the best advantage?   YES   NO
   If you answered NO, how could the company have better utilized your talents?
   _____
8. Did you receive adequate orientation to the job?   YES   NO
9. Was your supervisor patient in answering questions, demonstrating procedures, and
   making you feel that you were a member of the team? YES   NO
10. Would you like to discuss any point of disagreement that has not been settled to your
    satisfaction? YES   NO
11. What suggestions would you make that could lead to the improvement of the company?

Fig. 25-12 An exit interview form used as a guide for determining why employees desire to terminate their employment.

MAKING DECISIONS

One of the best gauges of your potential as a manager is the ability to make effective decisions. Decisions are a part of every manager's job. Your survival as a supervisor depends on your ability to weigh facts, consider alternative courses of action, foresee outcomes, and decide what to do. Deciding on day-to-day activities can be done quickly and without much thought. Major decisions, however, require much thought, time, and effort. Deciding what to do in a crisis can be a traumatic experience for a worker who has always referred problems to a superior. As you grow in your knowledge of your job, learn which decisions you can make on your own and which you should refer to your superior. To arrive at the proper course of action, successful decision makers do the following:

1. Determine exactly what the problem is and write it down.
2. Develop a list of alternative solutions to the problem.
3. Examine the advantages and disadvantages of each possible solution.
4. Select the best solution and review all the ramifications of this choice.
5. Implement (and later evaluate) the chosen course of action.

HUMAN RELATIONS

As a manager, your decisions will usually affect others. Ponder them carefully; but once they are made, move on.

Further evidence of your management potential is your reluctance to dump your problems in the lap of your superior for solution. In the army, all problems are handled on a "staff-work-accomplished" basis. The person with the problem is required to present all data and a recommendation for at least one solution to a superior. Preferably several alternative solutions should be provided. After a problem is identified, the person closest to it should be in the best position to work out a solution and recommend action.

MAINTAINING A COMMUNICATION NETWORK

It is estimated that 85 percent of a successful manager's job lies in the area of interpersonal communication skills. The ability to communicate effectively with employees is essential to the productivity of the office and to the well-being of the staff. Communication skills are also important for the administrative assistant/supervisor. The administrative assistant must develop channels of communication between and among subordinates, with other supervisors, and with company executives to maintain a flow of instructions, problem solving, work, and information. Understanding how communications are generated in the office is basic to the establishment of this network.

Organizational Communications

Very little work can be accomplished in an office without communication. Through communication, information is furnished to management for use in decision making and control. Communication also serves to motivate and influence employees to achieve higher productivity and meet company goals.

Organizational communication takes many forms. It can be oral—on a one-to-one basis or in a group. It can be written. Reports, forms, company magazines, newsletters, an employee suggestion system, and bulletin boards are all forms of written communication.

Organizational communication can take several different directions. It can flow upward through the company hierarchy; it can flow horizontally to those on the same managerial level; and it can flow downward to supervisees.

Barriers to Communication

No two people enter the office with exactly the same educational, economic, and ethnic background. Yet many office managers assume that, if an individual has the skills to do the job, adaptation to the work, people, procedures, and equipment will come in due time. The fallacy in this assumption is that it assumes all people communicate successfully with each other.

There are several reasons why communication between two people in the office can fail. Perhaps the most important reason rests in *semantics,* the fact that a speaker and a listener may attach very different concepts and feelings to the same word. *Lack of common knowledge* is another. An administrative assistant who uses words that can be easily misinterpreted or uses a technical vocabulary with a new employee is essentially wasting training time. Miscommunication can also occur because of the mere fact that the employee is new and the administrative assistant represents rank in the company.

Other barriers to effective communication are the physical distances between desks and offices, noise levels, and other distractions. The supervisor must recognize these as potential barriers and make changes to overcome them.

Communicating Effectively

In order to be successful in a supervisory role, you must communicate honestly, sincerely, and directly with your subordinates. Employees tend to be more responsive to managers who create an atmosphere of understanding and trust (see Figure 25-13).

Effective communication is a two-way street. Both the sender and the receiver must understand the message being transmitted. In a supervisory capacity you will learn quickly the advantages of listening to employees. Through listening, you establish a common ground on which to base further communications. You also get to know your subordinates so that a climate of mutual respect is possible. Two areas in which the administrative assistant can demonstrate interpersonal communication skills are

Fig. 25-13 Interpersonal communication requires honesty and sincerity to establish trust between supervisors and employees.

the explanation of work instructions and the interpretation of personnel policies to subordinates.

Work Instructions.   Work instructions can be given orally or in writing. Oral instructions have certain advantages over written ones. With oral instructions, the administrative assistant knows immediately whether a subordinate understands the instructions. An employee's facial expression and the questions asked provide clues. If the instructions are complicated, give them both orally and in writing.

Often the supervisor needs to write job instructions in order to update a procedures manual or ensure that instructions are available, understood, and followed. Two important points to include when giving job instructions are exactly what is to be done and why that specific type of procedure is desirable and important.

Personnel Policies.   Supervisors are responsible for interpreting management policy to workers in such a way that whatever conformity is needed is obtained. Usually, this means explaining the reasons behind a policy and the benefits that will accrue from its enactment. Whether you are in sympathy with the policy or not, you have an unavoidable obligation to support all company personnel policies. At the same time, you have an equal obligation to communicate suggestions for change—either from you or from those under your supervision—to management.

DEVELOPING A LEADERSHIP STYLE

HUMAN RELATIONS

You don't have to have a miraculous mind to be a successful manager; but you must use the one you possess, include in your circle of advisers those who are smarter than you, and continue to improve your mind, body, and personality.

In every business organization men and women rise to positions of leadership and responsibility only to find that their previous experience has not prepared them to deal comfortably with their new managerial roles. A significant number of these managers develop an effective leadership style by imitating those who supervised them. Because managers use different leadership styles to get the job done, you should be aware of the various styles and the advantages and disadvantages of each. A leadership style that works for one manager may be totally ineffective for another. Find a style that will help you exercise leadership in a manner compatible with your personality and temperament. See Figure 25-14 for a summary of some management styles that have been used effectively in the past. Some of these are still used. Others have been modified to conform to the changing legal, moral, and social climate in which modern business operates.

CONTINUING YOUR PROFESSIONAL GROWTH

Whether or not you seek a management position, you should continue your professional growth to ensure your job satisfaction and to increase your value to your employer. As a conclusion to this book, some additional suggestions are offered for improving your managerial skills and for growing professionally.

LEADERSHIP STYLES

THEORY X	Managers assume that the average worker is lazy, self-centered, lacks ambition, resists change, and works only for reward. Theory X managers believe that workers would rather be told what to do rather than think independently.
THEORY Y	Managers assume that all employees have potential for development, enjoy working, and will focus their behavior to achieve company goals. Theory Y managers believe that employees should participate in decisions that affect their work.
MANAGEMENT BY OBJECTIVES (MBO)	Managers and employees agree upon objectives they wish to accomplish within a specified time and the standards that will be used to measure performance. Once agreed upon, the objectives are put in writing and signed by the manager and the employee. The employee has complete freedom to accomplish the objectives. The manager checks at regular intervals to evaluate the employee's progress.
THE MANAGERIAL GRID	The managerial grid identifies two major concerns of managers: the concern for people and the concern for production. The grid identifies a technique for identifying managerial concerns by plotting managers' behavioral patterns on a grid. One axis represents the concern for people; the other represents the concern for production. Concerns are rated from 1 to 9, with 9 the highest score. By ranking managerial action on the grid, five categories emerge, illustrating to managers the need to merge their concern for production with concern for people.
SITUATIONAL LEADERSHIP	Situational leadership is based on the theory that the amount of leadership exercised by a manager varies from situation to situation. As the amount of authority exercised by the manager increases, autocratic leadership emerges. On the other hand, as the amount of participation by those supervised increases, democratic leadership is the focus.

Fig. 25-14 Various styles of leadership have been developed by management experts over the years. Although some of these are old, they provide an interesting insight into management thought.

Nurturing Creativity

Many people think that only a chosen few, those in artistic fields, are creative. They believe that creativity is a talent one must be born with. Every day in the business world these people are proved wrong.

Creativity can take many forms. Anyone who has an idea and develops it is being creative. Successful businesspeople have to be creative to be successful. You can be creative, too. You can become a contributor in the business office, a creator of ideas and actions.

Where to begin? Start by having an open mind. Ideas are born in imagination. Nonconformist alternatives to office problems are often creative solutions. Build a kit of ideas and experiment with them. A little idea can be expanded into a bigger or better idea.

Be an active observer of management functions. Look for *questions,* but also seek *answers.* Look for ways to improve work and information flow. Be a sounding board for your superior, and let ideas happen.

Most people have a certain time of the day when they operate at their best level. For some people it may be the early morning hours; for others, it may be at twilight. Determine when you operate best, then set your mind to action. A mind can be alert only if it is well rested. Adequate leisure time and proper eating habits are stimulants to creative brain activity.

Welcome new office experiences. In themselves, they enlarge visionary powers from which ideas and actions come. A person who wants to can be creative; therefore, it is up to you.

Improving Your Communication Skills

As you grow in your job, try to improve your communication skills. Even presidents of companies and countries continue to search for clearer and more persuasive ways of telling their stories. You may find yourself on a committee where you want to influence the actions of others. Keep in mind the staff-work-accomplished approach. Make sure that when you speak you are making a constructive suggestion.

Plan what you say before you put it in writing. A well-presented communication reduces your superior's reading time. Write and rewrite to reduce verbiage. Summarize material and present it graphically. Arrange material to highlight salient points. Become a master at presenting the heart of a matter in one succinct paragraph.

Consider the possibility of expressing your ideas in articles and talks. Too many people are afraid to attempt public speaking or to write for publication, yet these are tremendous aids to personal development and creativity. Public speaking teaches you to think on your feet; it makes you clarify and organize your thoughts effectively. Learn to judge the reactions of your listeners, and emphasize or rephrase a point according to your listeners' reactions.

Developing Personal Specialties

Work to develop one or more specialties for which you are known throughout the organization. For instance, become an expert in personnel work, state tax laws, or company pricing policies. Through your training of subordinates in your office, your reputation as a superior teacher may be known. Recognition creates opportunities. You may be asked to develop and teach a company-sponsored training course. Your desk manual may lead to the development of an office procedures manual. You may be considered a resource person, the person who knows the answers to questions frequently asked in the office. If you have become acquainted with information processing technology, you may be asked to participate in a feasibility study for your office. Whatever your inclination, your specialty or specialties can work to the company's advantage and to your own.

Taking Advantage of Professional Growth Opportunities

As you look at the management opportunities in the firm where you work, you may feel the need for additional education. Most colleges and universities offer a variety of evening courses that lead to advanced degrees in management, marketing, accounting, information systems, and economics. Should you want to specialize in an area that you feel promises a bright future, make your employer aware of your interest in additional education. In many cases, financial support for your efforts is available.

Special seminars sponsored by universities, consulting firms, equipment vendors, publishing houses, and your own company's training department offer excellent opportunities for self-improvement. Many of these seminars feature outstanding consultants in every major area of administration and management, and are helpful in keeping your management skills up-to-date.

Membership in a professional organization can provide valuable contact with those who share your business problems and professional interests. Through your association with other professionals, you enhance your management skills and strengthen your influence in the business community.

The spectrum of useful professional organizations broadens as you advance in your career. Every major segment of business activity (accounting, sales, personnel, records, etc.) has a professional organization structured to bring people together periodically to share new ideas and opportunities. The American Management Association, the Data Processing Management Association (DPMA), Executive Women International, and the Association of Records Managers and Administrators (ARMA) are just a few of the many organizations that offer opportunities for leadership, creativity, and professional growth. (Investigate the advantages of membership in a local chapter of an appropriate organization.)

Professional certification is another way to improve your upward mobility as a manager and to upgrade your management skills. In much the same way that the CPS rating represents the capstone of your professional preparation, other certification programs are also available to managers.

Only a few of the many opportunities for professional growth have been presented in this chapter. As you gain experience and improve your management skills, your opportunities for promotions will become more frequent and more attractive. Your professional growth, therefore, will be a continuing part of your work life.

Summary

At some point in an administrative assistant's career, the opportunity to move into a management position may arise.

In many offices, administrative assistants perform a dual role. Supervision of other employees is combined with their normal duties. Under such an arrangement, the administrative assistant's lines of authority can be hazy, and frustration sometimes results.

To move up in an organization, it is necessary to focus on a particular job and to analyze the requirements you must meet for the job. It is also necessary for the administrative assistant to understand the managerial functions of planning, organizing, controlling, and directing and to be familiar with the concepts of line and staff organization, horizontal organization, functional authority, committee organization, matrix management, total quality management, and corporate downsizing.

Since supervision is the first level of management, the administrative assistant must be aware of the duties of the supervisor, including recruitment, orientation, and training of employees. Making new employees productive as soon after orientation as possible is another responsibility of a supervisor. These tasks are accomplished in some companies by providing an orientation packet and assigning a mentor to the newcomer. The concept of mentoring and its advantages should be understood by the administrative assistant moving into management. A supervisor is also responsible for enriching the jobs of subordinates and blending the skills and abilities of a culturally diverse work force into a productive team. Supervisors should also be made aware of the information obtained through exit interviews with terminating employees.

Decision making is a primary management skill. To make effective decisions, it is necessary to maintain a communication network that provides essential information to all levels of the organization. Since 85 percent of a manager's time is spent communicating, an awareness of the many forms of organizational communication and knowledge of the barriers to and the techniques for effective communication are vital.

A study of various management styles will help an administrative assistant select and develop a management style that will be compatible with personality and temperament. A wide variety of management styles and philosophies have been researched and practiced with good results through the years.

Once a management position has been attained, it is necessary to continue to grow professionally. To do this, a new manager must nurture creativity, improve communication to ensure understanding, and develop a personal specialty to enhance visibility in the organization. Many opportunities for professional growth are available to managers. Membership in professional organizations, college courses, seminars, workshops, and professional certification programs can improve the upward mobility of new managers.

1. If you were offered the opportunity to go to Japan to manage the administrative services of your U.S.-based company employing mostly Japanese workers, what are some of the factors you would consider before accepting, and what are some of the cultural differences you would expect to encounter there?

THINK IT
Through

2. A manager must sometimes make decisions that are unpopular with subordinates. Give some examples of unpopular decisions that an office supervisor might have to make.

3. Why is supervision considered the first level of management, and why is it so important in the organizational structure?

4. As an administrative assistant eager to move into a management position, you are caught up in an intensive company effort to downsize. Your executive, a 55-year old department head with 14 years of company service, was terminated along with several other executives and their staffs. Your job is secure as an administrative assistant, but your duties have been increased, your responsibilities broadened, and your two assistants discharged. What would you do to cope with the effects of downsizing and improve your opportunities for moving into a management position should one become available?

THINK IT
Through

5. You believe that your experience and education as an administrative assistant have prepared you for a particular management position. What evidence could you give management to support your claim?

6. Rekey the following sentences. Capitalize the appropriate words in each line. Refer to the Reference Guide to verify and correct your answers.

   a. The new restaurant features french food on fine china in an atmosphere that is very bohemian.

   b. Every successful executive has studied accounting, marketing, finance, and economics.

   c. Take a Turkish towel and a Panama hat to the beach.

   d. If you understand latin or other languages, you will probably excel in english and spelling.

   e. During world war II, the department of justice opened an office in the old college of medicine at Upton university.

1. Assume that you have just returned from a total quality management (TQM) seminar. As a newly appointed office manager, key the steps you would consider to help you apply TQM to your company. Assume the following conditions exist which hampered your progress when you were an administrative assistant:

   > Company offices have a hodgepodge of information technology and software from almost every vendor in the city.

   > Support personnel are always the last to be invited to seminars, classes, and workshops.

   > Customers complain of delays in receiving responses to their inquiries, enclosures left out of correspondence, misaddressed mail, errors in their orders, invoices, etc.

   > No uniform records management system exists. Low morale among office workers results in absenteeism, unwillingness of employees to help each other in peak periods, and constant complaints about performance appraisals being unfair. You observed wasted time, supplies, and effort.

2. Assume that in your current position you have learned all you can about the job and see little possibility for advancement. You decide to seek another position. Before you begin, develop a career plan by compiling the following data, and key your analysis in memorandum form:

   a. A description of the next job you wish to hold

   b. Status of the job market

   c. The size of the organization that will best assist you in your professional development now, three years from now, and six years from now

   d. The working conditions of those organizations listed in (c).

3. Assume that you are required to conduct an eight-hour orientation program for new employees during their first week on the job with your company. Prepare an outline of the program you would present, including major topics and the time schedule you would follow in presenting such a program.

▶ TA25-1

Your firm has decided to automate its order processing department. Because your employer, Ms. Blanks, is vice president of administration, she is in charge of the organization, and you are assisting with a number of important details.

One detail involves how to determine how many employees will be needed to staff the department, once it is reorganized. Order processing now has 58 employees, as follows:

> 50 transcriptionists
> 5 record specialists
> 1 proofreader
> 1 messenger/mail clerk
> 1 supervisor

The order processing department does experience backlogs, but infrequently.

According to Edward Wynn, the representative of the equipment manufacturer from which your company plans to purchase all computers, the reorganized order processing department will require 20 percent fewer employees than it now has.

Working closely with Mr. Wynn, you and he perform some basic research and assemble the following data:

1. The department processes 1,700 orders daily.
2. Each order averages ten minutes to process.
3. 10,000 documents are filed each day.
4. Each document requires 0.5 minutes to file.
5. Office hours are from 8:30 a.m. to 4:30 p.m., with one hour for lunch and two 15-minute breaks.

Use the above data to determine how many employees will be needed to staff the department. Assume that Mr. Wynn's estimate is correct: 20 percent fewer employees will be needed. Prepare a memorandum to Ms. Blanks showing her your calculations. Keep in mind that this firm is moving steadily forward and that this reorganization could provide you with an opportunity to move into management! Do your best.

Case Problems

When Cheryl Forrest graduated from college, she took a job as administrative assistant to Morgan Whitlow, president of Oakland Oil Company. During the five years she has been in this position, she has developed a very solid relationship with Mr. Whitlow; he has become her mentor and friend. In fact, Mr. Whitlow has often referred to Cheryl as his other daughter. Needless to say, Cheryl has been very happy in her job and is well respected throughout the organization for her competence, dependability, and devotion to the company.

Six months ago, Mr. Whitlow retired. He had discussed his retirement with Cheryl, indicating that he would remain with the company as a consultant to the board of directors. He requested that Cheryl be assigned to handle his correspondence and other matters related to his new position.

Four months ago, the board of directors filled Mr. Whitlow's position with two young vice presidents who informed Cheryl that, because of her experience and competence, they would like her to serve as their administrative assistant. Mr. Whitlow's position as consultant required only one day of Cheryl's time each week and, because she had so much free time, she felt she could easily handle the work of the two new vice presidents and get Mr. Whitlow's work done, too. Cheryl's work went well for the first two months. She enjoyed the challenges of meeting the demands of the two young vice presidents and, at the same time, fulfilling her duties to her mentor, Mr. Whitlow. Then, just when she thought she had the best job in the world, two industrial planners were brought into the office. Mr. Gibson, one of the vice presidents, told Cheryl that she would be expected to handle the work of the two planners in addition to her other duties. Nothing was said about an increase in pay or the possibility of hiring another assistant. The same afternoon that she was told of her new responsibilities, Mr. Whitlow announced that he had been made chairman of the United Givers' Fund for the city of Oakland. He graciously asked Cheryl if she would assume the responsibility of establishing an accounting system for the incoming donations and handle the mailing of advertising, correspondence, receipts, and the like.

Suddenly, Cheryl is overwhelmed. She realizes that she cannot work with the same enthusiasm, accuracy, and efficiency to which her employers have become accustomed. For two weeks she has worked nights and weekends to complete her work. Her efficiency and morale are slipping, and she dreads going to work each morning. Cheryl is trying to maintain her professional attitude, but the tremendous overload is affecting her performance, her health, her attitude, and her social life.

▬▬ **What advice would you give Cheryl?**

Case 7-2
LIVING WITH A PROMOTION

Sylvia Murphy was promoted to administrative assistant to Paul Whitman, president of the Conners Manufacturing Company. Sylvia had expected that her coworker, Elizabeth Morgan, would get the promotion because of Elizabeth's excellent performance ratings. Elizabeth had also been with the company three years longer than Sylvia. The promotion came as a complete surprise to Sylvia. The only explanation she could offer for her promotion was that she had been taking night courses for two years and had successfully completed the CPS examination. She had also worked on a special assignment for Mr. Whitman.

Sylvia decided that the best way to prevent hard feelings would be to discuss the situation with Elizabeth before Elizabeth had time to brood and build resentment. Sylvia felt that, by winning Elizabeth's support, she would allay any resentment on the part of other members of the office staff.

▬▬ **If you were Sylvia, would you discuss your promotion with Elizabeth?**

Case 7-3
ASSUMING A NEW POSITION

For 12 years, Mark Gray served as administrative assistant to the personnel director at State University. Mark was a hard worker, always punctual, seldom complained about his work load, and had something nice to say to those who contacted him in person or by telephone. Last year he was selected as administrative assistant of the year by his chapter of PSI. He also received an outstanding employee award two years in a row at the university.

When the president's administrative assistant retired last year, Mark was appointed to the position. Mark was honored to receive the promotion because the job represented the highest administrative support job on campus. He also thought that the job would be much easier than his job in personnel. He thought that he would do little besides act as the president's receptionist.

During his first week on the job, Mark was astounded to find that the president's schedule required early arrival and late departure three times a week. The president's appointment calendar was a constant series of cancellations, substitutions, and rearrangements. Mark's telephone contacts, correspondence, and relationships with office visitors were extremely important. The job required him to make many decisions that he had relied upon his former boss to make. During his first week, he made several errors in judgment. Some technical foul-ups also left him feeling inadequate.

▬▬ **Although Mark likes the prestige and power that go with his new job, he misses the orderly, organized, regular work of his previous job. What should Mark do?**

Case 7-4
MANAGING A
MULTICULTURAL
STAFF

Lynn Wood is office manager for a large insurance corporation. At present the staff consists of 14 people representing a broad range of race, age, and gender. The group works as a team—always producing first-class work, working overtime when needed, and helping each other during peak loads. Matters of race or ethnic background have never been a problem. The company bowling and softball teams bring these workers together in many social and sporting events, where they seem to enjoy socializing outside the workplace.

Because of a terrific backlog in the medical claims section, Lynn interviewed and hired two Asian information processing specialists. Their work is flawless; they are polite, conscientious, thorough, prompt, and turn out more work in a day than any of the other staff members.

Lynn has noticed that they isolate themselves from the other workers. They bring their lunch, rather than eating in the cafeteria with the others. They take their coffee breaks at their desks, and they have never attended a ball game or a bowling tournament, although they have been invited.

Some of the staff have made critical remarks about their behavior, and Lynn finds herself reluctant to speak to them formally about their behavior.

▬▬ **What advice would you give Lynn?**

Case 7-5
DEVELOPING
POSITIVE
ATTITUDES

Apartment Furniture, Inc., has a buddy system under which selected experienced employees are assigned on a one-to-one basis to help new workers adjust to their jobs. This assignment is considered a compliment to experienced employees.

Blanche Woods, administrative assistant to J. W. Mills, was delighted when Ms. Mills said to her, "Blanche, will you help me out? Ben Falk, who is buddy to Martica Joyer, wants to give up his assignment. Martica is a griper. She takes a negative attitude toward other employees and toward work assignments. Her supervisor and she are almost at swords' points, and she is becoming a misfit among her colleagues. Yet she does the best work that we have had from a beginner in months. She could become a real asset and is definitely worth saving. Personally, I like her.

"Ordinarily, this situation would be handled by her supervisor, but you know as well as I do how rigid and inflexible Ms. Cruz is. I remember that you told me you are interested in psychology, so why not give this assignment a fling?"

▬▬ **Blanche decides to accept the challenge, but needs help in developing a plan. What recommendations would you make to her?**

**Case 7-6
ETHICS IN THE
OFFICE**

Janet Ying is administrative assistant to Carl Bachman, vice president of sales for the Morris Company, a manufacturer of office supplies. Mr. Bachman is well known locally, regionally, and nationally because of his position as president of the National Association of Sales Managers and his long service to the organization at local and regional levels. His work with the association requires considerable travel. Janet has worked with Mr. Bachman for seven years. When he is out of town, he leaves her in charge of the office.

Recently, while Mr. Bachman was out of town on an extended trip, Janet received a call from a sales manager in Detroit indicating that Mr. Bachman had agreed to send him the customer mailing list of all the companies holding membership in the National Association of Sales Managers. The caller indicated that he had paid $500 for the list and that he needed it immediately. Janet recognized the Detroit firm as a leading competitor and was surprised to receive such a request, since her employer's customers would be on that mailing list. In Janet's opinion releasing such a list could be potentially damaging to the Morris Company.

▬▬ If you were Janet's coworker, what would you advise her to do if she asks for your advice?

Part 8

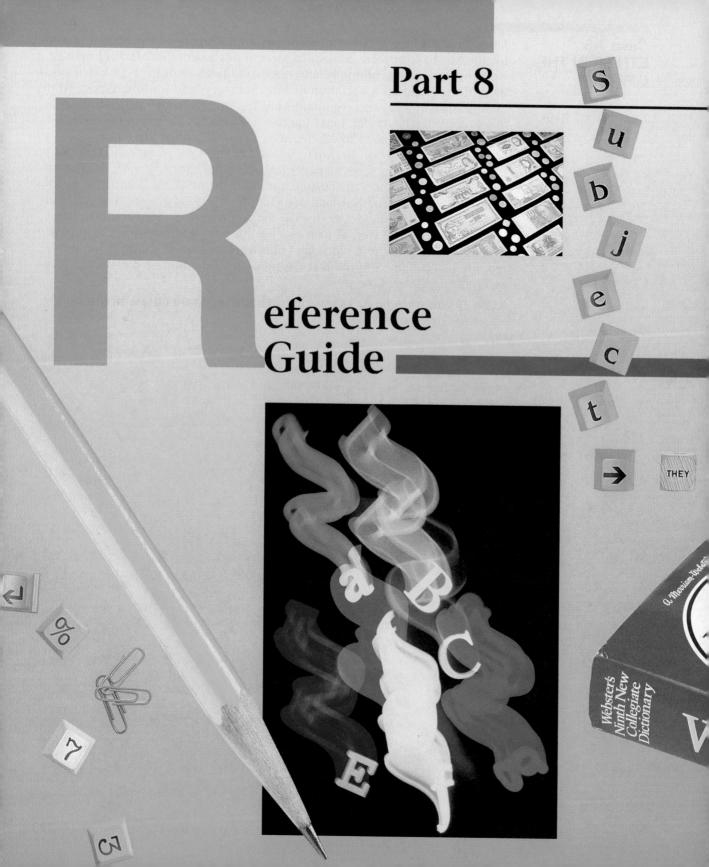

Reference Guide

"A well-educated gentleman," wrote John Ruskin, the master of English prose, "may not know many languages—may not be able to speak any but his own. But whatever language he knows, he knows precisely; whatever word he pronounces, he pronounces rightly."

Accuracy in the use of language is the foundation on which all effective writing and speaking rest. Mistakes in English reflect unfavorably on the writer and present stumbling blocks to the reader. It is, therefore, imperative that the administrative assistant master the principles of grammar, expand his or her vocabulary, and be constantly alert to the changes in language that arise from changes in technology, science, business, international trade, government, and cultural influences. Language evolves with continued usage. For example, twenty years ago, students were taught that a compound adjective should be hyphenated only when it precedes the noun it modifies. Today, most dictionaries show an exception to this rule with the word *up-to-date* hyphenated in any position—that is, before or after the noun.

Handbooks and dictionaries report language usage at different levels but are not definitive authorities. Nor does this guide purport to be the final authority. It, too, reports current, acceptable business usages. When more than one usage is reported in this Guide, it is because opinion is divided—dictionaries and handbooks do not agree. The administrative assistant, therefore, should not assume that one reference stands alone as the supreme authority on usage. But once a form has been selected, that form should be used consistently.

Because businesspeople are busy, business correspondence is often direct and to the point; brevity saves time for the writer and the reader. Frequently, however, the purpose of a business letter may be to obtain favorable action or create goodwill. Purposes such as these can best be served by using informal conversational English. Thus, colloquial English can be appropriate and at times even desirable in business writing.

With repeated usage, new meanings for common words creep into the language. *Cool, foxy,* and *chill* are words that have taken on different meanings as young people have used them in new ways. Similarly, words such as *software, byte, modem, laser,* and *flowchart* are additions to the dictionary that were coined by businesspeople. The administrative assistant should be familiar with new words and know not only their meaning but how to spell them and use them in a letter or report.

The trend in punctuation is toward less punctuation at the informal level; however, complete and accurate punctuation is still required at the formal level. Keep in mind that the purpose of punctuation is to make the meaning clear to the reader. Standard, accepted punctuation will attain this objective.

This Reference Guide should be the most helpful part of this text to the administrative assistant. It is designed to help you acquire expertise and confidence as you fulfill your responsibilities as an administrative assistant. It should become a permanent addition to your reference shelf.

Contents

■ Accepted Usage in Writing

Rules concerning capitalization, italics, abbreviations, acronyms, and numbers have evolved not from fundamental laws of language but from writing practices found to be efficient and clear to the reader. Although not all rules covering writing mechanics have the same degree of acceptance, those presented here are basically accepted and should be followed.

ABBREVIATIONS AND ACRONYMS

Although abbreviations are used infrequently in formal and general writing, advancing technology has resulted in an increased use of abbreviations and symbols in scientific and technical writing. This section treats only the general use of abbreviations and acronyms.

Acronyms are words formed from the initial letters or syllables of two or more words. They are not enclosed in quotes or underlined. The plural and possessive forms of acronyms are formed as for regular nouns.

DOS, radar, laser, UNICEF, modem
Order three modems for use in UNICEF's laboratories.

1. The personal titles *Mr., Mrs., Ms., Messrs., Dr.,* and *St.* or *Ste. (Saint)* are abbreviated with proper names, whether initials or first names are included.

Mr. Blalock	Messrs. Dutton and Franklin
Mrs. Connie Allen	Dr. E. E. Morton
Ms. Jennings	St. Paul

2. Other personal titles, such as *Rev., Hon., Prof., Gen., Col., Capt.,* and *Lieut.,* are abbreviated when they precede the full name—surname and given name. When only the surname is used, these titles should be spelled out.

   Prof. Robert G. Mitchell, A.B., Ph.D.
   Professor Mitchell
   General Taylor

   Note: *The titles Reverend and Honorable are spelled out if preceded by the.*

   the Reverend Mark Lowman
   Rev. Mark Lowman
   Hon. Charles E. Warden

3. Abbreviate titles and academic degrees used after a person's name.

   Michael Thorp, Jr.
   Ralph A. Farnsworth, Sr.
   Benjamin Randolph III, LL.D.
   Rev. Martin Hobart II

   Note: *Jr. and Sr. are preceded by a comma, but II and III are not.*

   (Personal preference as to the use of the comma between the name and the abbreviation should be respected.)

4. The abbreviations *B.C., A.D., a.m., p.m., No.* (for *number*), and the dollar sign *($)* may be used with numerals.

661 B.C. (before Christ) (*B.C.* follows the year cited.)
A.D. 44 (in the year of the Lord) (*A.D.* precedes the year cited.)

5. The abbreviations *Bro., Bros., Co., Corp., Inc., Ltd.,* and & are sometimes used as part of a company name; however, when possible, try to determine the official spelling of a company name and follow that usage.

6. Names of government agencies, network broadcasting companies, associations, fraternal and service organizations, unions, and other groups are often abbreviated. The first time the name of the organization is used in a manuscript or text it is spelled out with the abbreviation or acronym in parentheses—Federal Bureau of Investigation (FBI). Subsequently, use the abbreviation in all capitals with no periods and no space between the letters.

CIA	UNESCO	NATO
WRVA	AFL-CIO	USMC
BPOE	CBS	YMCA

Note: *Avoid abbreviating the following categories of words within text, except in tabulations or enumerations:*

1. Names of territories and possessions of the United States, countries, states, and cities

2. Names of months

3. Days of the week

4. Given names, such as *Chas.* for *Charles, Jas.* for *James*

5. Words such as *avenue, boulevard, court, street, drive, lane, parkway, place, road, square, terrace, building*

6. Parts of geographic names, such as *Ft. (Fort), Pt. (Port), Mt. (Mount)*

7. Parts of company names, such as *Bro., Bros., Co.,* and *Corp.,* unless they are abbreviated in the official company name.

8. Compass directions when they are part of an address—North, South, East, West (exceptions are *NW, NE, SE,* and *SW* after a street name).

CAPITALIZATION

The tendency today is to capitalize as little as possible; hence a good practice is not to use a capital letter unless a rule exists for its use.

1. Capitalize the first word of a sentence.

2. Capitalize the first word of a direct quotation.

3. Capitalize all proper nouns and adjectives.

   a. Names and initials of individuals (When a name includes a particle such as *de, du, la, l', della, von, van, van der,* and *ten,* observe carefully the way the name is written and extend the courtesy of spelling the individual's name accurately.)

Mary Van Reck	Lee De Forest
John von Bruckner	Pieter Ten Eyck
Charles de Gaulle	

b. Epithets, nicknames, and titles used as part of the name

Honest Abe	Babe Ruth
Blondy Gordon	Big Brother
Stonewall Jackson	Magic Johnson
Catherine the Great	

c. All words referring to the deity, the Bible, the books of the Bible, and other sacred books

God	Mohammed	the Koran
the Trinity	Catholic	Buddha
Talmud	Holy Spirit	Judaism
the Supreme Being		

d. Names of months, days of the week, holidays, holy days, and periods of history

November	Fourth of July	Yom Kippur
Thursday	Epiphany	the Ice Age

e. Names of organizations, political parties, and religious bodies

Girl Scouts	the Democratic party
the Republicans	the First Baptist Church

f. Names of geographic sections and places: continents, countries, states, cities, rivers, mountains, lakes, and islands

Mexico	Great Smoky Mountains; the Smokies
Jefferson City	Mississippi River
Portage Lake	Long Island
Lakes Erie and Superior	the West

Exceptions: *Directions are not capitalized, nor are political divisions when they precede the proper name.*

He drove south on I-81.
the city of Houston; the town of Litchfield

g. Names of divisions of a college or university

Department of Chemistry
the College of Medicine
the School of Business Administration

h. Names of specific historical events, specific laws, treaties, and departments of government

World War II	Treaty of Versailles
the Bill of Rights	Department of Justice

i. Titles that precede the names of individuals and abbreviations after a name

Dr. Walter Parrish
General Ridgeway
Professor Robinson, A.B., A.M., Ph.D.

the Reverend William Hammerstein
Father O'Toole
J. A. Hubbard, D.D.S.

j. Names of streets, avenues, buildings, churches, hotels, parks, and theaters

the DuBois Tower
First Avenue

St. Thomas Church
the Astor Hotel

k. Derivatives of proper nouns which are used as adjectives

Elizabethan play
Mexican music

Italian food
French literature

l. Personifications

Spring's warm touch   Winter's cold breath

4. Capitalize the first and last words and all other words—except articles, coordinate conjunctions, and prepositions—in titles of books, magazines, newspaper articles, stories, poems, musical compositions, theatrical productions, and chapters or subdivisions of books and periodicals.

Book Review Section of the *New York Times* (newspaper)
"Automation Is Here to Stay" (magazine article)
The Enjoyment of Drama (book)

5. Capitalize the words *Whereas* and *Resolved* in formal resolutions, and the first word following either of these.

6. Capitalize words before numerals (except *page, line, note, size,* and *verse.*)

Chapter 12	Article 5	Room 307
Figure 14	Column 1	Model 61
Check 213	Exhibit B	Lesson 24
Invoice 92A	Bulletin 19	Paragraph 2

Note: *The word* paragraph *may be capitalized or written in lowercase.*

7. Capitalize registered trademarks and trade names.

Coca-Cola   Orlon   Laundromat

8. When two independent clauses are separated by a colon and the second amplifies an idea presented in the first, capitalize the first word of the second independent clause.

Thomas Carlyle has said that he who first shortened the labor of copyists by devising movable type was disbanding hired armies, and cashiering most kings and senates, and creating a whole new democratic world: He had invented the art of printing.

Exceptions to capitalization rules:

Do not capitalize for emphasis.

Do not capitalize the names of the seasons of the year unless personified.

Register for the three courses offered in the fall semester.

Do not capitalize prefixes to proper names.

pre-Revolutionary colony
non-European country

Do not capitalize the names of college classes (*freshman, sophomore,* etc.) unless the class is referred to as a specific organization.

Do not capitalize words that were once proper nouns but have become common nouns through common usage.

macadam	anglicize
boycott	pasteurize
venetian blind	plaster of paris
turkish towel	bohemian
panama hat	manila envelope
china (dinnerware)	french fries
india ink	roman type

Do not capitalize academic degrees when they are referred to in general terms.

She earned a master's degree from State College.

ITALICS

Discretion should be exercised in the use of italics for emphasis. The trend among good writers is to attain emphasis through sentence structure rather than through the use of italics.

In preparing manuscript, indicate material that should be typeset in italics by <u>underlining</u> once.

1. Italicize to designate a key term in a discussion, a term with a special meaning, a technical term, or a term that is accompanied by a definition.

   In expectancy theory, *valence* refers to the value a person places on a particular outcome (consequence of an action).

2. Italicize titles of books, pamphlets, newspapers, magazines, plays, lengthy poems, musical compositions, motion pictures, paintings, drawings, and statues.

   Note: *Parts of complete works, such as chapters of a book or articles in a magazine, are placed in quotation marks.*

   The information is found in "The Management of Conflict and Stress" on page 346 of *Human Behavior in Organizations.*

3. Italicize letters used as letters and words used as words.

   Always dot your *i*'s and cross your *t*'s.
   The word *thane* refers to one of superior rank.

4. Italicize foreign words or phrases that have not yet been adopted into everyday English.

> Most businesses realize that a permanent clientele cannot be built upon the principle of *caveat emptor.*
> If demand rises, it is hypothesized that price will rise, *ceteris paribus.*

Exception: *Many scholarly Latin words and abbreviations that used to be italicized have become so familiar that italics are no longer used.*

c. or ca.	e.g.	i.e.	q.v.
et al.	ibid.	loc. cit.	viz.
etc.	idem	op. cit.	passim

Exception: *The word* sic *is Latin for "thus" or "so" and is used to show that an error in quoted material appeared in the original. It is italicized and enclosed in brackets.*

> His note read, "Order new stationary *[sic]* for the office."

5. Italicize the names of ships, trains, aircraft, and spacecraft.

> S.S. *Stella Solaris* (S.S. is not italicized.)
> Lindbergh's *Spirit of St. Louis*
> *Gemini VI*

6. Italicize the names of legal cases (plaintiff and defendant) but not *v.* (versus) when cited in text. Do not italicize the names of legal cases in footnote citations.

> Labor leaders were disappointed when in 1921 the Supreme Court held in *Duplex Printing Press Company* v. *Deering* that the Sherman Act applied to unions under certain conditions.

7. Italicize the word *Resolved* in formal resolutions.
8. Italicize the words *See* and *See also* in index cross-references.
9. Italicize such phrases as *Continued on page 321, Continued from page 321,* and *To be continued.*

NUMBERS

Since there is no simple, uniform style for the use of numbers, deciding when to use a figure rather than a word can sometimes be perplexing. This section presents general guidelines covering current usage and should answer most questions that may arise.

Addresses

1. Express federal, state, and interstate highways in figures.
   > U.S. Route 41 (U.S. 41)
   > Ohio 50
   > Interstate 64 (I-64)

2. Spell out numbered street names from *One* through *Ten.* When figures are used for numbered street names, a hyphen with a space on both sides

should separate the house number from the street name. Use *d, st,* or *th* where necessary with a numbered street name.

345 Fifth Street
345 West Fifth Street
345 - 22d Street
345 West 22d Street
345 West 21st Street
345 West 24th Street

3. Express house numbers in figures, except *One,* which is spelled out.

One Fourth Avenue

Adjacent Numbers

1. When one of two adjacent numbers is part of a compound adjective, spell out the smaller number.

50 twenty-nine-cent stamps
ten 29-cent stamps
twelve 25-inch pipes

2. Separate unrelated adjacent numbers by a comma.

In 1985, 2,560,479 fans attended the baseball games in the new stadium.

Dates

1. Use figures to designate the day and year after a month.

March 22, 1994

2. To express the day of the month, use a figure plus *d, st,* or *th* when it stands alone or precedes the month. It is also acceptable, although more formal, to spell out the day of the month.

On the 22d of July we will fly to Athens.
Her letter dated the 14th did not arrive until last Monday.
The events of the twenty-second of November, 1963, are still a source of controversy.

3. Spell out, in lowercase letters, references to particular centuries and decades.

twentieth century
during the sixties and seventies

But *the 1990s (Plurals of figures are formed by adding an* s *alone, unless used in a special context. See page 778.)*

Exact Numbers

1. Generally numbers from *one* through *ten* are spelled out unless the sentence contains a series of related numbers that are over ten.

Since only eight people gathered for the meeting, it was canceled.
The employees of that department include a manager, two supervisors, and seven clerks.
The team won 17 games in 1986, 14 games in 1987, 10 games in 1988, and only 8 games in 1989.

Exception: *If the numbers in a sentence or paragraph are in different categories, treat them consistently.*

In the past ten years, the company acquired three subsidiaries employing 212 people—one, 103; another, 99; and a third, 10—of whom 150 have at least eight years of service.

2. Spell out any number that begins a sentence; however, in most instances restructuring the sentence to avoid starting with a number is preferred.

One hundred fourteen applicants responded to the ad.
Preferred: The ad drew 114 responses.

Fractions, Decimals, and Percentages

1. Spell out isolated simple fractions in words. Write mixed fractions and decimals in figures. When a decimal fraction is not preceded by a whole number, a cipher (zero) is often used before the decimal point.

The bakery held one-half dozen doughnuts for us.
She was only 7 1/2 years old when she made her debut with the Dallas Symphony Orchestra.
Most of the students arrived at 0.611 as the answer.

2. A percentage is written as a number with the word *percent* spelled out. In statistical copy, the symbol % is used.

Only 3 percent of the loans were paid off.

Governmental Designations

The name of a governing body, political division, military unit, and the like is designated by a spelled-out ordinal number preceding the noun. Ordinals that require more than two words (ordinals over 100) are expressed in numbers.

Ninetieth Congress
Court of Appeals for the Tenth Circuit
Fifth Ward
Second Naval District
Fifth Army
Third Battalion, 122d Artillery

Money

1. Except in legal documents, sums of money (whether in dollars or foreign denominations) should be keyed in figures. Whole dollar amounts are set without ciphers (zeros) after the decimal point except when they appear in the same context with fractional amounts.

The book listed at $20.50, but the store offered a discount of $2.00.
The discount of $2 was a temptation the customer could not resist.

2. In legal documents use capitalized words to express sums of money followed by figures in parentheses.

> I agree to pay the sum of Seven Hundred Fifty-Five Dollars ($755).
> I agree to pay the sum of Seven Hundred Fifty-Five (755) Dollars.

3. Amounts of money less than one dollar are keyed or set in figures with the word *cents* spelled out.

> The lotion was on sale for 89 cents.

4. A sum of money used as an adjective should be spelled out and hyphenated.

> She bought a thirty-dollar purse.

Ordinal Numbers

Spell out isolated ordinal numbers of less than one hundred. Ordinals of one hundred or more should be written in figures. (See table on pages 774–775.)

The company is marking the twenty-fifth anniversary of its founding.
For the 120th time, an employee is retiring under the company's pension plan.
The 200th customer will receive a prize.

Quantities, Measures, Weights, and Dimensions

1. In mathematical, statistical, technical, or scientific text, express physical quantities such as distances, lengths, areas, volumes, pressures, and so on in figures.

55 miles	3 cubic feet
250 volts	6 meters

2. Designate measures, weights, and dimensions in figures without commas.

> 6 ft. 4 in.
> 7 lbs. 4 oz.
> The editor specified 8 1/2-by-11-inch paper. (In technical matter, the multiplication sign x is used instead of *by* to express dimensions.)

Round Numbers

Spell out round numbers that can be expressed in one or two words. Round numbers over one million may be expressed as a combination of words and numerals.

about two thousand employees
a population of three million
3.2 billion items of merchandise
$170 million

Note: *A round number such as 1,500 is expressed in hundreds rather than in thousands.*

fifteen hundred members (*not* one thousand five hundred members)

Time

1. To designate time, use a number with *a.m.* or *p.m.* When using *o'clock*, spell out the number.

   8:00 p.m.
   10:45 in the morning (Do not use *a.m.* or *p.m.* with *morning* or *evening*.)
   nine o'clock
   12:00 M (noon) or 12 noon (general usage)
   12:00 p.m. (midnight)

2. The time of day may be spelled out in textual matter.

   The executive left his office at five.
   The Senate hearing is expected to last until half-past six.

■ Alphabetic Filing

Definite rules are necessary for determining the order in which information is filed and located. These rules are known as alphabetic indexing rules. The rules developed by the Association of Records Managers and Administrators, Inc. (ARMA), are presented in this section. Minor variations from these rules are found in different organizations. Learn the established rules and procedures of your organization and follow them.

RULE 1: ORDER OF INDEXING UNITS

A. Personal Names

A personal name is indexed in the following manner:

1. the surname (last name) is the key unit;
2. the given name or initial is the second unit; and
3. the middle name or initial is the third unit.

Unusual names (frequently foreign names) are indexed in the same manner. If it is not possible to determine the surname, consider the last name as the surname. Cross-reference unusual names using the first name written as the key unit.

Index Order of Units in Personal Names

Name	Key Unit	Unit 2	Unit 3
Joan Ander	Ander	Joan	
Joan E. Ander	Ander	Joan	E
Louise Ander	Ander	Louise	
Adam Anders	Anders	Adam	
Anna Andersson	Andersson	Anna	
Alma Lee Andrews	Andrews	Alma	Lee
E. Bennett Andrews	Andrews	E	Bennett
Soo On Bee	Bee	Soo	On

B. Business Names

Business names are filed *as written* using letterheads and trademarks as guides. Business names containing personal names are indexed as written. Newspapers and periodicals are indexed as written. For newspapers and periodicals having identical names that do not include the city name, consider the city name as the last indexing unit. If necessary, the state name may follow the city name.

Index Order of Units in Business Names

Name	Key Unit	Unit 2	Unit 3	Unit 4
Ace Hardware Store	Ace	Hardware	Store	
Columbus News Leader	Columbus	News	Leader	
Times Herald (Seattle)	Times	Herald	(Seattle)	
Times Herald (Westchester)	Times	Herald	(Westchester)	
Vic Nobee News Corner	Vic	Nobee	News	Corner

RULE 2: MINOR WORDS IN BUSINESS NAMES

Each complete English word in a business name is considered a separate indexing unit. Prepositions, conjunctions, symbols, and articles are included; symbols *(&, $, cts., #, %)* are considered as spelled in full *(and, dollar, cents, number,* and *percent)*. All spelled-out symbols except *and* begin with a capital letter. When *The* is the first word in a business name, it is considered the last indexing unit.

Index Order of Units in Business Names

Name	Key Unit	Unit 2	Unit 3	Unit 4
The Antique Doll Shoppe	Antique	Doll	Shoppe	The
By the Lane Inn	By	the	Lane	Inn
$5 Bargain Store	5	Dollar	Bargain	Store
Flowers & Foliage	Flowers	and	Foliage	
Kate The Florist	Kate	The	Florist	

RULE 3: PUNCTUATION AND POSSESSIVES

All punctuation is disregarded when indexing personal and business names. Names are indexed with commas, periods, hyphens, and apostrophes omitted.

Index Order of Units in Names

Name	Key Unit	Unit 2	Unit 3	Unit 4
Harpers' Bakery	Harpers	Bakery		
Harper's Restaurant	Harpers	Restaurant		
John's Electric Company	Johns	Electric	Company	
Jenny K. Long	Long	Jenny	K	
Newton, Nesbitt, and Nash	Newton	Nesbitt	and	Nash
Old-Town Furniture Co.	OldTown	Furniture	Co.	

RULE 4: SINGLE LETTERS AND ABBREVIATIONS

A. Personal Names

Initials in personal names are considered separate indexing units. Abbreviations of personal names *(Jos., Thos., Wm.)* and brief personal nicknames *(Liz, Hank)* are indexed as they are written.

B. Business Names

Single letters in business names are indexed as written. If there is a space between single letters, each letter is indexed as a separate unit. An acronym (a word formed from the first, or first few, letters of several words) is indexed as one unit. Abbreviations are indexed as one unit regardless of punctuation or spacing *(BBB, C.P.A., Y M C A)*. Radio and television station call letters are indexed as one word. Cross-reference spelled-out names to their acronyms or abbreviations if necessary. For example: Certified Professional Secretary. *See* CPS.

Index Order of Units in Names

Name	Key Unit	Unit 2	Unit 3
BB Brakes	BB	Brakes	
Barbara Blaine Blake	Blake	Barbara	Blaine
J. P. Blake	Blake	J	P
Jos. Blake	Blake	Jos	
KNOX Radio Station	KNOX	Radio	Station
S.P.A.N., Inc.	SPAN	Inc	
VFW Auxiliary	VFW	Auxiliary	

RULE 5: TITLES

A. Personal Names

A personal title *(Miss, Mrs. Ms., Mr.)* is considered the last indexing unit when it appears. If a seniority title is required for identification, it is considered the last indexing unit in abbreviated form, with numeric titles *(II, III)* filed before alphabetic titles *(Jr., Sr.)*. When professional titles *(Rev., M.D., CPS, Dr., Governor)* are required for identification, they are considered the last units and are filed alphabetically as written. Royal and religious titles followed by either a given name or a surname only (Sister Angelica) are indexed and filed as written. When all units of identical names, *including titles,* have been compared and there are no differences, filing order is determined by addresses.

Note: *Titles are indexed as written without punctuation. For example:* Rev., M.D., Dr. *are indexed as* Rev, MD, Dr *without the period.*

B. Business Names

Titles in business names are indexed as written. *See* Rules 1 and 2.

Index Order of Units in Names

Name	Key Unit	Unit 2	Unit 3	Unit 4
Miss Leona Adams	Adams	Leona	Miss	
Mr. Jim's Steak House	Mr	Jims	Steak	House
Cyrus B. Nicholas II	Nicholas	Cyrus	B	II
Cyrus B. Nicholas, Jr.	Nicholas	Cyrus	B	Jr
Clinton W. Norton, M.D.	Norton	Clinton	W	MD
Prince Rainier	Prince	Rainier		
John B. Shawver, Governor	Shawver	John	B	Governor
Sister Mary Augusta	Sister	Mary	Augusta	

RULE 6: NAMES OF MARRIED WOMEN

A married woman's name is filed as she writes it. It is indexed according to Rule 1. If more than one form of a name is known, the alternate name may be cross-referenced.

Note: *A married woman's name in a business name is indexed as written and follows Rules 1B and 5B.*

Index Order of Units in Names

Name	Key Unit	Unit 2	Unit 3	Unit 4
Ms. Becky Jones Fritts	Fritts	Becky	Jones	Ms
Mrs. Becky Mae Fritts	Fritts	Becky	Mae	Mrs
Mrs. Lucien Fritts	Fritts	Lucien	Mrs	
Miss Becky Mae Jones	Jones	Becky	Mae	Miss
Mrs. Gerald V. Kingston	Kingston	Gerald	V	Mrs
Mrs. Kingston's Pies	Mrs	Kingstons	Pies	

RULE 7: ARTICLES AND PARTICLES

A foreign language article or a particle in a business or personal name is combined with the part of the name following it to form a single indexing unit. The indexing order is not affected by a space between a prefix and the rest of the name, and the space is disregarded when indexing. Examples of articles and particles are: *à la, D', Da, De, Del, De la, Della, Den, Des, Di, Dos, Du, El, Fitz, Il, L', La, Las, Le, Les, Lo, Los, M', Mac, Mc, O', Per, Saint, St., Ste., San, Santa, Santo, Te, Ten, Ter, Van, Van de, Van der, Von, Von der.*

Index Order of Units in Names

Name	Key Unit	Unit 2
Catherine Lemate	Lemate	Catherine
Francis LeMate	LeMate	Francis
Joan MacDowell	MacDowell	Joan
James McDaniel	McDaniel	James
Karen O'Bonner	OBonner	Karen
Edith St. Marner	StMarner	Edith

RULE 8: IDENTICAL NAMES

A. Personal Names

When the names of individuals are identical, their alphabetic order is determined by their addresses, starting with the city. Names of states and provinces are considered when the names of the cities are also alike. When the city names and the state or province names as well as the full names of the individuals are alike, the alphabetic order is determined by street names; next, house and building numbers, with the lowest number filed first. Seniority titles are indexed according to Rule 5 and are considered before addresses.

Name	Key Unit	Unit 2	Unit 3	Unit 4
Janice Hess 113 Elm Street Toledo, Ohio	Hess	Janice	Toledo	Elm
Janice Hess 92 Plum Avenue Toledo, Ohio	Hess	Janice	Toledo	Plum
Edward Iglecia Akron, Ohio	Iglecia	Edward	Akron	
Edward Iglecia Columbus, Ohio	Iglecia	Edward	Columbus	
Edward Iglecia Dayton, Ohio	Iglecia	Edward	Dayton	
Edward B. Iglecia	Iglecia	Edward	B	
Daniel Moore II Xenia, Ohio	Moore	Daniel	II	Xenia
Daniel Moore, Jr. Xenia, Ohio	Moore	Daniel	Jr	Xenia

B. Business Names

When identical names of businesses, organizations, and institutions occur, filing order is determined by the address, with address parts treated as identifying elements. If the names of cities are alike, filing arrangement depends upon names of states or provinces, followed by street names and house or building numbers, in that order.

When street names are written as figures (14th Street), the street names are considered in ascending numeric order and filed before alphabetic street names.

Street names with compass directions are indexed as written. Numbers after compass directions are considered before alphabetic names (East 8th would precede East Main).

House and building numbers written as figures are considered in ascending numeric order and placed together before spelled-out building names. If a street address and a building name are included in an address, disregard the building name. ZIP Codes are not considered in determining filing order.

Seniority titles are indexed according to Rule 5 and are considered before addresses.

Index Order of Units in Names

Name	Key Unit	Unit 2	Address
Janicki Stationers Decatur, Illinois	Janicki	Stationers	Decatur Illinois
Janicki Stationers Decatur, Indiana	Janicki	Stationers	Decatur Indiana
Janicki Stationers Topeka, Illinois	Janicki	Stationers	Topeka Illinois
Janicki Stationers Topeka, Kansas	Janicki	Stationers	Topeka Kansas
Kastner's 531 East Main	Kastners		531 East Main

Name	Key Unit	Unit 2	Address
Kastner's 2910 West Main	Kastners		2910 West Main
Lovington Lamps 55 - 14th Street	Lovington	Lamps	55 - 14th Street
Lovington Lamps 35 - 25th Street	Lovington	Lamps	35 - 25th Street
Lovington Lamps 2789 Beacon Street	Lovington	Lamps	2789 Beacon Street

RULE 9: NUMBERS IN BUSINESS NAMES

Numbers spelled out in a business name are considered as written, and filed alphabetically. Numbers written in digit form are considered as one unit. Names with numbers written in digit form as the first unit are filed in ascending order before alphabetic names. Arabic numerals are filed before Roman numerals *(2, 3, II, III)*. Names with inclusive numbers (33–37) are arranged by the first number only *(33)*. Names with numbers appearing in other than the first position (Pier 36 Cafe) are filed alphabetically within the appropriate section and immediately before a similar name without a number (Pier and Port Cafe). In indexing numbers written in digit form that contain *st, d,* or *th (1st, 2d, 3d, 4th)*, ignore the letter endings and consider only the digits *(1, 2, 3, 4)*.

Index Order of Units in Names

Name	Key Unit	Unit 2	Unit 3	Unit 4
8th & Walnut Cafe	8	and	Walnut	Cafe
8th Street Bldg.	8	Street	Bldg	
8th Street Garage	8	Street	Garage	
The 800 Club	800	Club	The	
5100 Condominiums	5100	Condominiums		
A 1 Garage	A	1	Garage	
Fortilla Flats	Fortilla	Flats		
Route 250 Market	Route	250	Market	
Route 250 Motel	Route	250	Motel	

RULE 10: ORGANIZATIONS AND INSTITUTIONS

The names of banks and other financial institutions, clubs, colleges, hospitals, hotels, motels, museums, religious institutions, schools, unions, universities, and other organizations and institutions are indexed and filed according to the names on their letterheads. If *The* is used as the first word in these names, it is considered as the last unit.

Index Order of Units in Names

Name	Unit 1	Unit 2	Unit 3	Address
Bank of Atlanta	Bank	of	Atlanta	
Bloomington Trust Co. Bloomington, Illinois	Bloomington	Trust	Co	Bloomington Illinois
Bloomington Trust Co. Bloomington, Indiana	Bloomington	Trust	Co	Bloomington Indiana
First Federal Savings Fairfield, California	First	Federal	Savings	Fairfield California

Name	Unit 1	Unit 2	Unit 3	Address

First Federal Savings
  Fairfield, Illinois
	First	Federal	Savings	Fairfield
				  Illinois

Newport High School
  Newport, Rhode Island
	Newport	High	School	Newport
				  Rhode Island

Newport High School
  Newport, Washington
	Newport	High	School	Newport
				  Washington

Petersburg Kiwanis Club	Petersburg	Kiwanis	Club	
United Methodist Church	United	Methodist	Church	
University of Idaho	University	of	Idaho	
Virginia State College	Virginia	State	College	
Yancey Motel	Yancey	Motel		
York Medical Center	York	Medical	Center	
The York Museum	York	Museum	The	

RULE 11: SEPARATED SINGLE WORDS

When a single word in a business name is separated into two or more parts, the parts are considered separate indexing units. If a name contains two compass directions separated by a space (South East Car Rental), each compass direction is a separate indexing unit. *Southeast* and *south-east* are considered as single indexing units. Cross-reference compound words if necessary. For example: South East. *See also* Southeast; South-East.

Index Order of Units in Names

Name	Key Unit	Unit 2	Unit 3	Unit 4
Semi Weekly Cleaning Service	Semi	Weekly	Cleaning	Service
Semi-Trailer Rentals Inc.	SemiTrailer	Rentals	Inc	
South Western Office Supplies	South	Western	Office	Supplies
Southwestern Machines	Southwestern	Machines		
South-Western Publishing Co.	SouthWestern	Publishing	Co	

RULE 12: HYPHENATED NAMES

A. Personal Names

Hyphenated personal names are considered one indexing unit and the hyphen is ignored. For example, *Reese-Melton* is a single indexing unit—*ReeseMelton*.

B. Business Names

Hyphenated business and place names and coined business names are considered one indexing unit, and the hyphen is ignored. *U-Haul* is a single indexing unit—*UHaul*.

Index Order of Units in Names

Name	Key Unit	Unit 2	Unit 3
A-1 Retail Markets	A1	Retail	Markets
Read-N-Sew Studio	ReadNSew	Studio	
Ready-Built Shelf Shop	ReadyBuilt	Shelf	Shop
Self-Service Laundry	SelfService	Laundry	
Self-Study Society	SelfStudy	Society	
South-East Plaza Cafe	SouthEast	Plaza	Cafe
Edith Spann-Corsa	SpannCorsa	Edith	
Jo-Belle Tunney	Tunney	JoBelle	

RULE 13: COMPOUND NAMES

A. Personal Names

When separated by a space, compound personal names are considered separate indexing units. *Mary Ann Snyder* is three units. Although *St. John* is a compound name, *St. (Saint)* is a prefix and follows Rule 7, which classifies it as a single indexing unit.

B. Business Names

Compound business or place names with spaces between the parts of the names follow Rule 11, and the parts are considered separate units. *New York* and *Mid Atlantic* are each considered two indexing units.

Index Order of Units in Names

Name	Key Unit	Unit 2	Unit 3	Unit 4
Miss Alice Ann Adams	Adams	Alice	Ann	Miss
Miss Aliceann Adams	Adams	Aliceann	Miss	
North South Transfer Co.	North	South	Transfer	Co
North-South Movers, Inc.	NorthSouth	Movers	Inc	
Post War Reclamation Co	Post	War	Reclamation	Co
Post-War Reclamation Co.	Post	War	Reclamation	Co
St. Gregory's Priory	StGregorys	Priory		

RULE 14: GOVERNMENT NAMES

Federal

The name of a federal government agency is indexed by the name of the government unit *(United States Government)* followed by the most distinctive name of the office, bureau, department, etc., as written. Such words as "Office of," "Department of," "Bureau of," etc., if needed in the official name are added and considered separate indexing units. If "of" is not a part of the official name as written, it is not added.

State and Local

The names of state, county, parish, city, town, township, and village governments/political divisions are indexed by their distinctive names. The words "State of," "County of," "City of," "Department of," etc., are added only if needed for clarity and if in the official name. They are considered separate indexing units *(Alaska/Transportation/Department of)*.

Foreign. The distinctive English name is the first indexing unit for foreign government names. This is followed, *if needed and in the official name,* by the balance of the formal name of the government. Branches, departments, and divisions follow in order by their distinctive or official names in English. Cross-reference the written foreign name to the English name, if necessary.

Name	Index Form of the Name
Bureau of the Census U.S. Department of Commerce	United States Government Commerce Department of Census Bureau of
Bureau of Indian Affairs U.S. Department of the Interior	United States Government Interior Department of Indian Affairs Bureau of
Department of Public Safety State of California	California State of Public Safety Department of
Board of Health Cincinnati, Ohio	Cincinnati Health Board of
Cook County Tax Collector	Cook County Tax Collector
Republique Française- Armée de l'Air	French Republic Air Force of
Estados Unidos Mexicanos Secretaria de Industrio y Commercia	Mexico Industry and Commerce Secretary

■ Communications Guide

This section contains a condensed guide for preparing business communications. Samples of letters keyed in block style with open punctuation, modified block style with blocked paragraphs and open punctuation, modified block style with indented paragraphs and mixed punctuation, and simplified style are shown in Figure 1. An example of a personal business letter keyed on executive letterhead appears in Figure 2. Figure 3 is an interoffice memo. Figure 4 describes the form and placement of envelope address parts. Figure 5 summarizes the form and arrangement of business letter parts. A summary of forms of address appears in Figure 6.

Letter 1 (top left):

International Business Consortium
308 Fifth Avenue   New York, NY 10001-4596

November 19, 19—

Mr. John B. McKee
Baltimore Chamber of Commerce
24 Fulton Street
Baltimore, MD 21224-2324

Dear Mr. McKee

This letter is keyed in block style with open punctuation. Every line begins at the left margin. Only essential punctuation marks are used in the opening and closing lines.

The distinctive feature is that the date, the letter address, and the salutation, the attention line (when used), all lines in the body, the complimentary close, and all signature lines begin at the left margin. No tabulator stops are necessary.

Keying time is accordingly reduced. First, time required to set tabulator stops and to use the tabulator is saved. Second, by omitting all but essential punctuation, the number of keystrokes is decreased.

The use of open punctuation is appropriate with this letter style.

Sincerely yours

Janet Margolis

Janet Margolis, Consultant

mos

BLOCK LETTER FORMAT, OPEN PUNCTUATION

Letter 2 (top right):

Recruitment Services, Inc.

900 Pump Street S.W.
Huntsville, AL 35801
Telephone (205) 555-8400

November 19, 19—

Mrs. Anna Wysong
Carlton-Higgins Associates
385 Redmon Tower
Columbia, SC 29206-3712

Dear Mrs. Wysong

This letter is keyed in modified block style with blocked paragraphs. Open punctuation is used in the opening and closing lines.

Contrast this style with the block style. Notice that the dateline has been moved to begin at the horizontal center (although it is also appropriate to end at the right margin). The closing lines have been blocked at the horizontal center of the letterhead as well. All other lines begin at the left margin. These modifications to the block style give this letter style its name--modified block.

When an attention line is used, it begins at the left margin. If a subject line is used, it begins at the left margin or is centered over the body of the letter a double space below the salutation.

Although open punctuation is used in this letter, it is equally appropriate to used mixed punctuation.

Sincerely yours

Leo Kapinsky

Leo Kapinsky, Director

mcm

MODIFIED BLOCK LETTER FORMAT, BLOCKED PARAGRAPHS, OPEN PUNCTUATION

Letter 3 (bottom left):

99 Detroit Avenue/Lakewood, Ohio 44107-1649 216-555-5045

LAZAROW & CO., INC

November 19, 19—

Mr. William Saunders
Magnaplastics, Inc.
One Riverview Plaza
Cleveland, OH 44224-5429

Dear Mr. Saunders:

This letter is keyed in modified block style with indented paragraphs. Mixed punctuation is used in the opening and closing lines. This punctuation style calls for a colon after the saluation and a comma after the complimentary close. All other end-of-the-line punctuation is omitted in the letter address, unless a line ends in an abbreviation that requires the usual abbreviation period.

Note that the dateline is centered (although it could have been keyed to begin at center or to end at the right margin). The first line of each paragraph is indented five spaces, although 10- to 15-space indentations are also commonly used. All other lines begin at the left margin. The closing lines are blocked at the horizontal center of the letterhead.

Although mixed punctuation is used in this letter, it is equally appropriate to use open punctuation.

Sincerely yours,

George R. Summers

George R. Summers

ck

MODIFIED BLOCK LETTER FORMAT, MIXED PUNCTUATION, INDENTED PARAGRAPHS

Letter 4 (bottom right):

Gemini International, Inc.

81 BROADWAY / NEW YORK, NY 10006-3217 / (212)555-4243

November 19, 19—

Office Manager
Office Services, Inc.
6700 Gilmer Street
Atlanta, GA 30307-6715

AMS SIMPLIFIED LETTER

There is a movement underway to take some of the monotony out of keying letters. The movement is symbolized by the simplified letter style.

What is it? You're reading a sample. Notice the left block and the general positioning of this letter. We didn't key "Dear . . ." nor will we key "Sincerely yours" or "Cordially yours." Are they really important? We feel just as friendly toward you without them.

Notice the formatting and location of the following points:

1. The date
2. The address
3. The subject
4. The name of the writer

Now examine the enclosed suggestions prepared for you. Talk them over with your employer, but don't form a final opinion until you have really tried the simplified letter. That's what our administrative assistants did. As a matter of fact, they finally wrote most of the suggestions themselves.

They say they are sold—and hope you'll have good luck with better (simplified) letters.

Arthur F. Avery

ARTHUR F. AVERY, STAFF DIRECTOR
TECHNICAL DIVISION

Enclosure

SIMPLIFIED BLOCK LETTER FORMAT

Fig. 1   Choosing an appropriate letter style can enhance the effectiveness of a business communication.

Fig. 2 Some writers personalize their communications by using the recipient's first name and placing the letter address at the end of the letter.

OMNIBUS CORPORATION

563 Opp Road
Evansville, IN 47708-6711

OFFICE OF THE PRESIDENT

October 24, 19–

Dear Jim:

The address keyed at the end of the letter removes the business tone and makes the letter more personal.

This letter style is also used for more formal letters, such as letters to public officials and honored individuals. In addition, letters of appreciation and congratulations are keyed in this form.

The reference initials are omitted. If the recipient knows the writer well, it is not necessary for the writer's name to be typed in full below the signature.

Cordially,

Bill

Mr. James Hill
4804 Riverwood Road
Atlanta, GA 30307

PERSONAL LETTER FORMAT
KEYED ON PERSONAL LETTERHEAD

Fig. 3 Interoffice memos are an important form of written communication within a company.

INTEROFFICE MEMORANDUM

Donaldson enterprises, inc.

TO: New Members of the Information Services Department

FROM: Judith L. Reeves, Supervisor J.L.R.

DATE: November 19, 19–

SUBJECT: Interoffice Correspondence

An interoffice or interdepartment letterhead is used for messages between offices or departments within acompany. One advantage of this form is that it can be set up quickly. This memorandum requires settings only for margins. Titles (Mr., Mrs., Dr., etc.), the salutation, the complimentary close, and the formal signature are usually omitted.

Double-space between the last line of the heading and the first line of the message. Short messages of no more than five lines may be double-spaced. Longer messages should be single-spaced.

Reference initials should be included. When enclosures are sent, the enclosure notation should appear below the reference initials.

jbm

ENVELOPE ADDRESS PARTS FOR OCR

PERSONAL AND FORMAL STYLE KEYED ON PERSONAL LETTERHEAD

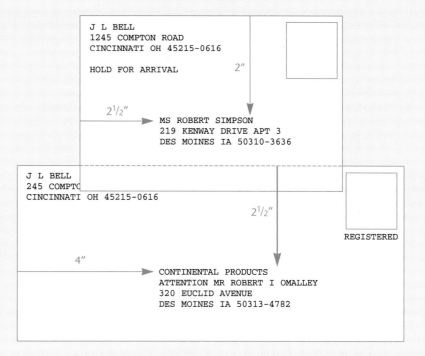

Post office optical character readers are programmed to scan a specific area, so the address must be completely within the read zone, blocked and single-spaced. Two-letter state abbreviations must be used. Apartment and room numbers should follow the street address on the same line. Acceptable placement for No. 10 and No. 6 3/4 envelopes are shown above. The U.S. Postal Service prefers the use of uppercase letters and no punctuation in envelope addresses.

Notations to Post Office

Type below the stamp at least three lines above the address in all caps. Underline if desired. Such notations include HAND STAMP, REGISTERED, and SPECIAL DELIVERY.

On-Receipt Notations

Type in all caps a triple space below the return address in three spaces from the envelope's left edge. Such notations include HOLD FOR ARRIVAL, PLEASE FORWARD, and CONFIDENTIAL.

Foreign Addresses

The last word in the address block should be the country name in all caps. If an address code is used, it should be placed at the left side of the last line or on the next-to-last line.

Fig. 5   FORM AND ARRANGEMENT OF BUSINESS LETTER PARTS

Line Position	Horizontal Placement	Points to Be Observed	Acceptable Forms
Date			
Floating Dateline: Keyed from 14 to 18 lines from the top, depending on the letter's length. Place the date on line 12 if a window envelope is used. *Fixed Dateline:* Keyed a double space below the last line in the letterhead.	*Block and Simplified Styles:* Even with the left margin. *Modified Block Style:* At center, to end flush with the right margin, or according to the letterhead.	1. Do not abbreviate names of months. 2. Unusual 2- or 3-line datelines are not commonly used. 3. Do not use *st, d, nd, rd,* or *th* following the day of the month. 4. Dates for government and military correspondence are often typed in this manner: 2 May 19—.	December 14, 19— 2 May 19—
Address			
With Floating Dateline: Keyed a quadruple space below the date. *With Fixed Dateline:* Keyed 3 to 9 lines below the date, depending on the letter's length. *Personal Letter:* Keyed at the left margin 5 or 6 lines below the letter's closing line.	Single-spaced at the left margin. Use at least three lines for an address. Place business titles at the end of the 1st line or at the beginning of the 2d line, whichever gives better balance. Break long company names at a logical point and indent the overrun 2 or 3 spaces.	1. Observe the addressee's letterhead style. 2. Do not abbreviate *Street* or *Avenue* unless it improves appearance. 3. Include the ZIP Code. 4. Spell out *In Care of;* do not use c/o. (This follows the name line.)	Miss Rose Bannaian Manager, Rupp Steel 2913 Drexmore Avenue Dallas, TX 75206-8116 Mr. Russell Rupp 68 Devoe Avenue Dallas, TX 75206-8116
Attention Line			
The preferred placement is a double space below the address and a double space above the salutation.	Even with the left margin, centered, or indented at the paragraph point.	1. Do not abbreviate *Attention.* 2. Do not use the expression *Attention of.*	Attention Mr. R.H. Rupp Attention Purchasing Agent Attention Mr. L. Cox, Agent

FORM AND ARRANGEMENT OF BUSINESS LETTER PARTS *(continued)*

Line Position	Horizontal Placement	Points to Be Observed	Acceptable Forms
Salutation			
Keyed a double space below the address or a double space below an attention line. (Interoffice correspondence and letters keyed in the simplified style omit the salutation.)		1. Use *Gentlemen* for a company, a committee, a post office box, or an organization made up entirely of men. 2. In addressing women, use *Ladies* or *Mesdames; Madam;* or *Miss, Mrs,* or *Ms.* 3. Use *Ladies and Gentlemen* for a company, a committee, a post office box, or an organization made up of women and men. 4. The salute opening is growing in popularity. It omits the traditional salutation and uses the reader's name in the first sentence: Thank you, Mrs. Williams, for your recent film order.	Dear Mr. Rupp Gentlemen Dear Russell Dear Miss Mason Dear Ms. Willis Dear Mrs. Cox Ladies and Gentlemen
Subject (or Reference) Line			
Keyed a double space below the salutation (Some letterheads indicate a position for the subject or a file number. Usually it is near the top of the letterhead.)	*Block Style:* Keyed at the left margin. *Simplified Style:* Keyed at the left margin in all caps a double space below the last line in the address. The word "Subject" is omitted. *Modified Block Style:* Keyed at the left margin, at paragraph point, or centered.	1. The word "Subject" is keyed in all caps, with an initial cap only, or it may be omitted. If used, the word "Subject" is followed by a colon. 2. Do not abbreviate the word "Subject." Capitalize important words in the subject.	Subject: Pension Plan SUBJECT: Pension Plan Pension Plan <u>Pension Plan</u> PENSION PLAN Your File 987 Reference File #586 Re: File 586

Line Position	Horizontal Placement	Points to Be Observed	Acceptable Forms
Body			
Keyed a double space below the salutation or the subject line.	*Block Style:* 1st line of each paragraph keyed at the left margin.	1. Keep right margins as even as possible. Avoid end-of-line hyphens.	
Simplified Style: Keyed a double space below the subject line.	*Modified Block Style:* 1st line of each paragraph keyed at the left margin or indented (commonly 5 or 10 spaces).	2. Indent enumerations 5 spaces from both margins; double-space between items. (Do not indent enumerations if using Simplified style. If indented material is not enumerated, it may be indented 5 spaces.)	
Second Page Heading			
Heading: Begin approximately 1" from the top (about line 6). Key the addressee's name, the page number, and the date in a 3-line block at the left margin, or use a 1-line arrangement and key the addressee's name at the left margin, center the page number, and position the date to end at the right margin. *Body:* Begin a double space below the heading, using the same margins used for the preceding page.		1. Key second and succeeding pages on plain paper. Do not use letterhead. 2. Do not begin a page with the last part of a hyphenated word. The last paragraph on a page should include at least 2 lines.	Mr. Jerry Robinson Page 2 (Current Date)

```
Mr. Jerry Robinson          2          (Current Date)
```

FORM AND ARRANGEMENT OF BUSINESS LETTER PARTS *(continued)*

Line Position	Horizontal Placement	Points to Be Observed	Acceptable Forms
Complimentary Close			
Keyed a double space below the last line of the body. (The complimentary close is omitted in the Simplified style and in interoffice correspondence.	Keyed at center. If a block style is used, the complimentary close may be keyed at the left margin.	1. Longest closing line should not extend noticeably beyond the right margin. 2. Cap first word only. 3. Avoid contractions.	Very truly yours, Sincerely yours, Cordially, Cordially yours, Respectfully yours,
Company Name			
Keyed flush with the complimentary close.	If used, keyed a double space below the complimentary close.	1. Cap all letters. 2. Use letterhead for correct spelling and punctuation.	RAND CLOTHING INC. JOHNSON SHOE CO.
Signature (Name and Title of Signee)			
Keyed a quadruple space below complimentary close (or company name, if used). If both the name and the title are used, key them on the same line, or key the title on the next line, whichever gives better balance. *Simplified Style:* Keyed in all caps at least 4 lines below body.	Keyed flush with the complimentary close (or company name, if used). *Simplified Style:* Keyed at the left margin.	1. Cap important words in title. 2. If dictator's name appears in the letterhead, use only the title. 3. Do not use a courtesy title (Mr.) when keying a man's name unless the name can be masculine or feminine: Chris, Dana, Lynn.	Harold A Wenchstern Director of Personnel Brenda Ryan, Manager Purchasing Department Mr. Lynn B. Carter Mrs. Beverly Fox LOUIS COX – AGENT
I.D. Notation			
Keyed a double space below or on the last closing line.	Keyed at the left margin.	1. Omit dictator's initials if his or her name appears in the closing lines.	jc JWR/jc jwr/jc JWR:jc JWRobinson/jc

Line Position	Horizontal Placement	Points to Be Observed	Acceptable Forms
Enc.			
Keyed a double space below the identification notation.	Keyed at the left margin.	1. Although *Enc.* and *Encl.* are not preferred forms, they are commonly used to save time.	Enclosures 3 Encs. 2 Enclosures: Stub Check
Postscript			
Keyed a double space below the identification notation or below the last typed line.	Indent or block according to paragraph style used in body.	1. Initials of the writer may be keyed below the postscript in place of a 2d signature. 2. The *P.S.* may be omitted, and the postscript may be written in the same form as paragraphs.	
Copy Notation			
Keyed a double space below the identification notation or below the last typed line. (If this notation is not to appear on the original, key at the top of the copy.)	Keyed at the left margin. (If typed on a copy, it may be centered or flush left.)	1. For *copy to*, key *c* or *Copy*. 2. For *blind copy to*, type *bc*, if notation is keyed on copies only. 3. For *photocopy to*, key *pc*.	c pc Copy bc Miss K. Neilen
Mailing Notation			
Keyed midway between date and first line of the address or 2 lines below the last keyed line.	Keyed at the left margin.	1. Key in all caps. 2. May be keyed on copies only.	SPECIAL DELIVERY REGISTERED MAIL CERTIFIED MAIL
Separate Mailing Notation			
Keyed a double space below the last keyed line.	Keyed at the left margin.	1. Used to indicate the method of transportation and the number of envelopes or packages sent.	Separate Mail-Express Separate Mail-2

Fig. 6

CORRECT FORMS OF ADDRESS AND REFERENCE

Person and Address (Envelope and Letter)	Salutation	Complimentary Close	In Referring to the Person: Informal Introduction	In Speaking to the Person
U.S. President				
The President The White House Washington, D.C. 20500	Dear President (Surname) Mr. President Dear Mr. President Dear Madam President	Respectfully yours Very truly yours	The President Mr. (Surname) Mrs. (Surname)	Mr. President Sir Madam President Madam
Spouse, U.S. President				
Mrs., Ms., *or* Mr. (Surname only) The White House Washington, D.C. 20500	Dear Mrs. (Surname only) Dear Mr. (Surname only) Dear Ms. (Surname only)	Respectfully yours	Mrs. (Surname only) Mr. (Surname only) Ms. (Surname only)	Mrs. *or* Ms. (Surname only) Mr. (Surname only)
U.S. Vice President				
The Vice President United States Senate Washington, D.C. 20510	Dear Vice President (Surname) Dear Mr. *or* Madam Vice President Mr. *or* Madam Vice President	Respectfully yours Very truly yours	The Vice President Mr. *or* Madam (Surname)	Mr. *or* Madam Vice President Mr. (Surname)
U.S. Chief Justice				
The Chief Justice The Supreme Court Washington, D.C. 20543	Mr. Chief Justice Dear Mr. Chief Justice	Respectfully yours Very truly yours	The Chief Justice	Mr. Chief Justice
U.S. Associate Justice				
Justice (Full Name) The Supreme Court Washington, D.C. 20543	Mr. Justice Madam Justice Dear Mr. Justice Dear Madam Justice Dear Justice (Surname)	Very truly yours Sincerely yours	Mr. *or* Madam Justice (Surname)	Mr. *or* Madam Justice Mr. *or* Madam Justice (Surname)
Cabinet Officer				
The Honorable (Full Name) Secretary of (Office) Washington, D.C. 20520 The Secretary of (Office) Washington, D.C. 20520	Dear Mr. Secretary Dear Madam Secretary Dear Secretary (Surname)	Very truly yours Sincerely yours	The Secretary of . . ., Mr., Mrs., Miss, *or* Ms. (Surname) The Secretary Mr., Mrs., Miss, *or* Ms. (Surname)	Mr. Secretary Madam Secretary Mr., Mrs., Miss, *or* Ms. (Surname)

Person and Address (Envelope and Letter)	Salutation	Complimentary Close	In Referring to the Person: Informal Introduction	In Speaking to the Person
Speaker of the House of Representatives				
The Honorable (Full Name) Speaker of the House of Representatives Washington, D.C. 20515	Dear Mr. *or* Madam (Surname) Mr. Speaker Madam Speaker Dear Madam Speaker	Very truly yours Sincerely yours	The Speaker, Mr., Mrs., Miss, *or* Ms. (Surname) Mr., Mrs., Miss, *or* Ms. (Surname)	Mr. Speaker Madam Speaker Mr., Mrs., Miss, *or* Ms. (Surname)
U.S. Senator, Senator-Elect				
The Honorable (Full Name) United States Senate Washington, D.C. 20510 The Honorable (Full Name) Senator-elect	Dear Senator (Surname) Dear Mr., Mrs., Miss, *or* Ms. (Surname)	Very truly yours Sincerely yours	Senator (Surname)	Senator (Surname) Mr., Mrs., Miss, *or* Ms. (Surname)
U.S. Representative				
The Honorable (Full (Name) House of Representatives Washington, D.C. 20515 Representative (Full Name) House of Representatives Washington, D.C. 20515	Dear Representative (Surname) Dear Mr., Mrs., Miss, *or* Ms. (Surname)	Very truly yours Sincerely yours	Representative (Surname) Mr., Mrs., Miss, *or* Ms. (Surname)	Mr., Mrs., Miss, *or* Ms. (Surname)
U.S. Government Official				
The Honorable (Full Name) Director of the Bureau of the Budget Washington, D.C. 20503 Librarian of Congress Washington, D.C. 20540	Dear Mr., Mrs., Miss, *or* Ms. (Surname)	Very truly yours Sincerely yours	Mr., Mrs., Miss, *or* Ms. (Surname)	Mr., Mrs., Miss, *or* Ms. (Surname)
American Ambassador				
The Honorable (Full Name) American Ambassador Paris, France	Dear Mr. Ambassador Dear Madam Ambassador Dear Ambassador (Surname)	Very truly yours Sincerely yours	The American Ambassador The Ambassador Mr., Mrs., Miss, *or* Ms. (Surname) Madam Ambassador	Mr., Mrs., Miss, *or* Ms. Ambassador Madam Ambassador Mr., Mrs., Miss, *or* Ms. (Surname)

CORRECT FORMS OF ADDRESS AND REFERENCE *(continued)*

Person and Address (Envelope and Letter)	Salutation	Complimentary Close	In Referring to the Person: Informal Introduction	In Speaking to the Person
American Minister to Another Country				
The Honorable (Full Name) American Minister Ottawa, Canada	Dear Mr., Mrs., Miss, *or* Ms. Minister Dear Minister (Surname) Dear Madam Minister	Very truly yours Sincerely yours	The American Minister, Mr., Mrs., Miss, *or* Ms. (Surname)† The Minister; Mr., Mrs., Miss, *or* Ms. (Surname)	Mr., Mrs., Miss, *or* Ms. Minister Mr., Mrs., Miss, *or* Ms. (Surname) Madam Minister
U.S. Representative to the United Nations				
The Honorable (Full Name United States Representative to the United Nations New York, New York 10017	Dear Mr., Mrs., Miss, *or* Ms. (Surname) **With Ambassadorial Rank:** Dear Ambassador (Surname)	Very truly yours Sincerely yours	Mr., Mrs., Miss *or* Ms. (Surname) Madam Ambassador Mr. Ambassador	Mr., Mrs., Miss, *or* Ms. (Surname) Madam Ambassador Mr. Ambassador
Foreign Ambassador in U.S.				
His/Her Excellency (Full Name) The Ambassador of France Washington, D.C. 20516	Excellency Dear Mr. Ambassador Dear Madam Ambassador Dear Ambassador (Surname)	Respectfully yours Sincerely yours Very truly yours	The Ambassador of . . ., Mr. *or* Madam (Surname) The Ambassador Mr. *or* Madam (Surname)	Mr. Ambassador Madam Ambassador Mr., Mrs., Miss *or* Ms. (Surname)
Foreign Minister in U.S.				
The Honorable (Full Name) Minister of Italy Washington, D.C. 20516	Dear Mr. Minister Dear Madam Minister (Surname) Dear Minister (Surname)	Respectfully yours Sincerely yours Very truly yours	The Minister of . . ., Mr. *or* Madam (Surname The Minister	Mr. Minister Madam Minister Mr., Mrs., Miss, *or* Ms. (Surname)
American Consul				
(Full Name), Esq. The American Consul United States Embassy (Foreign City, Country)	Dear Mr., Mrs., Miss, *or* Ms. (Surname)	Very truly yours Sincerely yours	Mr., Mrs., Miss, *or* Ms. (Surname)	Mr., Mrs., Miss, *or* Ms. (Surname)

†In presenting or referring to American ambassadors and ministers in any Latin American country, say "Ambassador of the United States" or "Minister of the United States."

CORRECT FORMS OF ADDRESS AND REFERENCE *(continued)*

Person and Address (Envelope and Letter)	Salutation	Complimentary Close	In Referring to the Person: Informal Introduction	In Speaking to the Person
Foreign Consul				
(Full Name), Esq. The French Consul (American City, State)	Dear Mr. (Surname) Dear Madam (Surname)	Very truly yours Sincerely yours	Mr. (Surname) Madam (Surname)	Mr. (Surname) Madam (Surname)
Governor of a State				
His/Her Excellency, the Governor of (State) *or* The Honorable (Full Name), Governor of (State) (Capital City, State)	Dear Governor Dear Governor (Surname)	Respectfully yours Very truly yours Sincerely yours	Governor (Surname) The Governor The Governor of (State)	Governor (Surname) Governor
Member, State Legislature				
The Honorable (Full Name) The State Senate *or* The House of Representatives (Capital City, State)	Dear Senator or Representative (Surname) Dear Mr., Mrs., Miss, *or* Ms. (Surname)	Very truly yours Sincerely yours	Mr., Mrs., Miss, or Ms. (Surname) Senator (Surname) Representative (Surname)	Mr., Mrs., Miss, or Ms. (Surname) Senator (Surname) Representative (Surname)
Mayor of a City				
The Honorable (Full Name) Mayor of the City of . . . (City, State)	Dear Mayor (Surname)	Very truly yours Sincerely yours	Mayor (Surname) The Mayor	Mayor (Surname) Mr. Mayor Madam Mayor
Judge of a Court				
The Honorable (Full Name) Judge of the . . . Court (Local address)	Dear Judge (Surname)	Very truly yours Sincerely yours	Judge (Surname)	Judge (Surname)
Military Personnel				
(Rank) (Full Name) Post or Name of Ship City, State	Dear (Rank) (Surname)	Very truly yours Sincerely yours	(Rank) (Surname)	(Rank) (Surname)

Person and Address (Envelope and Letter)	Salutation	Complimentary Close	In Referring to the Person: Informal Introduction	In Speaking to the Person
Clergy (Protestant)				
The Reverend (Full Name), D.D. or The Reverend (Full Name) Parsonage Address City, State	Dear Mr., Mrs., Miss, *or* Ms. (Surname) Dear Dr. (Surname) Dear Reverend (Surname)	Respectfully yours Sincerely yours Yours faithfully	The Reverend Doctor (Surname) Doctor (Surname) The Reverend (Surname) Mr., Mrs., Miss *or* Ms. (Surname)	Dr. (Surname) Sir Mr., Mrs., Miss, *or* Ms. (Surname)
Rabbi (Jewish Faith)				
Rabbi (Full Name) or Rabbi (Full Name), D.D. Local Address	Sir My dear Rabbi (Surname) My dear Rabbi	Respectfully yours Sincerely yours Yours faithfully	Dr. (Surname) Rabbi (Surname)	Dr. (Surname) Rabbi (Surname)
Priest (Roman Catholic)				
The Reverend (Full Name) (followed by comma and initials of order) Local Address	Reverend Father Dear Father (Surname)	Sincerely yours Respectfully yours Yours faithfully	Dr. (Surname) Father (Surname)	Dr. (Surname) Father (Surname)
Sister (Roman Catholic)				
Sister (Full Name) (followed by comma and initials of order) Local Address	Dear Sister Dear Sister (Religious Name)	Sincerely yours Respectfully yours Yours faithfully	Sister (Religious Name) Sister	Sister (Religious Name) Sister
President (College or University)				
Dr. (Surname) or President (Surname), (Degree) Name of University City, State	Dear President (Surname) Dear Dr. (Surname)	Very truly yours Sincerely yours	Dr. (Surname) President (Surname)	Dr. (Surname) President (Surname)

■ Footnote and Bibliography Entries

Typical footnote entries are illustrated below. Notice that in footnote 3, *Ibid.* (from the Latin word *ibidem,* meaning "in the same place") is used to refer to a single work cited in the note *immediately* preceding. Two related Latin abbreviations, *op. cit.* (from *opere citato,* "in the work cited") and *loc. cit.* (*loco citato,* "in the place cited"), were formerly in common use to refer to works cited earlier (but not immediately preceding). To make things clearer to the reader, these are now generally replaced by using a shortened form. For example:

Op. cit. (different page)

[12] Castilaw, *Court Reporting: Grammar and Punctuation,* p. 15.

Loc. cit. (same page)

[13] Castilaw, *Court Reporting: Grammar and Punctuation.*

One author ───────▶	[1]Diane Castilaw, *Court Reporting: Grammar and Punctuation* (2d ed.; Cincinnati: South-Western Publishing Co., 1993), p. 110.
Two authors ───────▶	[2]Jerry Moorman and James Halloran, *Entrepreneurship* (Cincinnati: South-Western Publishing Co., 1993), p. 116.
Ibid. ───────▶	[3]Ibid., pp. 158–160.
Three authors ───────▶	[4]Rita Tilton, J. Howard Jackson, and Sue Chappell Rigby, *The Electronic Office: Procedures and Administration* (Cincinnati: South-Western Publishing Co., 1991), p. 19.
Four or more authors ───────▶	[5]Jerry Robinson et al., *Basic Information Keyboarding Skills: A Collegiate Course* (Cincinnati: South-Western Publishing Co., 1988), pp. 115–117.
Author and editor ───────▶	[6]Douglas S. Sherwin, "The Meaning of Control," *Readings in Management,* edited by Max D. Richards (6th ed.; Cincinnati: South-Western Publishing Co., 1986), p. 255.

Editor ⟶ [7]Peter W. Bernstein (ed.), *The Arthur Young Tax Guide* (New York: Ballantine Books, 1988), p. 229.

Magazine article (no author) ⟶ [8]"1992 PSI Convention Highlights," *The Secretary,* 52, No. 7 (August/September 1992), p. 27.

Magazine article (one author) ⟶ [9]Robert Lyons, "Should You Try Temping?" *The Secretary,* 53, No. 2 (February 1993), pp. 10–12.

Newspaper article ⟶ [10]Laurie M. Grossman, "As Secretaries Buy More for Their Firms, Marketers Regard Them with Reverence," *Wall Street Journal* (March 10, 1993), p. B-1.

Unpublished material ⟶ [11]From the report by the County of Hanover, Virginia Schools on Teacher Certification Requirements, Richmond (March 3, 1993), p. 4.

Government publication ⟶ [12]U.S. Department of Commerce, Bureau of Economic Affairs, *Economic Indicators* (Washington: U.S. Government Printing Office, December 1988), p. 15.

Bibliography entries are alphabetized as illustrated below. Notice the difference between footnote construction and bibliography construction. Periods rather than commas are used between items in a bibliography. Footnotes use paragraph indentions; bibliographies use hanging indentions. Footnotes are listed by number; bibliographies are listed alphabetically.

Editor ⟶ Bernstein, Peter W. (ed.). *The Arthur Young Tax Guide.* New York: Ballantine Books, 1988, p. 229.

One author ⟶ Castilaw, Diane. *Court Reporting: Grammar and Punctuation.* 2d ed. Cincinnati: South-Western Publishing Co., 1993, p. 110.

Unpublished material ⟶ County of Hanover, Virginia Schools. A report on Teacher Certification Requirements, Richmond: March 3, 1993, p. 4.

Newspaper article ⟶	Grossman, Laurie M. "As Secretaries Buy More for Their Firms, Marketers Regard Them with Reverence." *Wall Street Journal,* March 10, 1993, p. B-1.
Magazine article (one author) ⟶	Lyons, Robert L. "Should You Try Temping?" *The Secretary,* 53, No. 2 (February 1993), pp. 10–12.
Two authors ⟶	Moorman, Jerry, and James Halloran. *Entrepreneurship.* Cincinnati: South-Western Publishing Co., 1993.
Magazine article (no author) ⟶	"1992 PSI Convention Highlights." *The Secretary,* 52, No. 7 (August/September 1992), p. 27.
Four or more authors ⟶	Robinson, Jerry, et al. *Basic Information Keyboarding Skills: A Collegiate Course.* Cincinnati: South-Western Publishing Co., 1988, p. 19.
Author and editor ⟶	Sherwin, Douglas S. "The Meaning of Control." *Readings in Management,* 6th ed., edited by Max D. Richards. Cincinnati: South-Western Publishing Co., 1986, p. 247.
Three authors ⟶	Tilton, Rita S., J. Howard Jackson, and Sue Chappell Rigby. *The Electronic Office: Procedures and Administration.* Cincinnati: South-Western Publishing Co., 1991, p. 19.
Government agency ⟶	U.S. Department of Commerce, Bureau of Economic Affairs. *Economic Indicators.* Washington: U.S. Government Printing Office, December 1988, p. 74.
Newspaper article ⟶	Zaslow, Jeffrey. "Not All Bosses Are Bossy." *Richmond (Virginia) Times Dispatch,* May 8, 1988, p. H-14.

■ Glossary of English Usage

This glossary is intended as a guide to acceptable usage. It is also a reference to which the reader may turn when a question of word choice arises. For the most part this glossary provides information not found in standard dictionaries.

A or an before h. Use *a* if the *h* is sounded; *an* if the word begins with a vowel sound: a historic novel, a humorous story, a hotel, a hysterical person; an hour's drive, an heir, an herb, an honest opinion.

Ability. Use *to* with *ability* plus a verb: ability to influence, not ability of influencing.

Accede, exceed. *Accede* means *to agree to* or *to yield to. Exceed* means *to go beyond.* The committee will accede to the demands of the majority. Do not exceed the speed limit.

Access, excess. *Access* means *permission, liberty,* or *the ability to enter, approach, communicate with,* or *pass to and from. Excess* means *more than enough.*

Accept, except. *Accept* is always a verb meaning *to receive; except* is a verb meaning *to exclude,* but is more often used as a preposition meaning *with the exception of.*

Acquiesce in (not *to*). He acquiesced in the matter of the bonus.

Adapt, adopt, adept. *To adapt* means to *change* or *to make suitable. To adopt* means *to accept* or *to put into practice. To be adept* means *to be expert.* They adapted to the harsh change in weather. They adopted the proposal. He is adept at training beginners. (*Adept* may be used with *at* or *in.*)

Adhere, adherent. *Adhere* (hold fast) *to:* adhere to our policy; an *adherent of:* an adherent of that policy.

Advice, advise. *Advice* is a noun meaning *recommendation; advise* is a verb meaning *to counsel.* I can advise you, but will you follow my advice?

Adverse, averse. *Adverse* means *antagonistic, hostile; averse* means *having a dislike or distaste for.* Adverse weather conditions delayed our flight. Joseph is averse to manual labor.

Affect, effect. *Affect* is a verb meaning *to influence. Effect* is a noun meaning *result* or *consequence. Effect* is also a verb meaning *to accomplish* or *to produce.* The weather affected our sales. The weather had an adverse effect on our sales. The delegates effected a compromise.

Aggravate, irritate. *To aggravate* means *to make worse; to irritate* means *to annoy.* Their constant bickering irritated me and aggravated my headache.

All, any, none, some, more, most. These words may be either singular or plural, depending on meaning. None of the money has been collected. None of the bills have been paid.

All of. Use *all; of* is redundant. If a pronoun follows *all,* reword the sentence. Check all the reports. They are all going (not: All of them are going).

All right. This is the only correct usage. *Alright* is incorrect.

All together, altogether. *All together* means *in a group; altogether* is an adverb meaning *entirely.* The correspondence is all together in one folder. He is altogether too casual in his manner.

Allude, elude. *Allude* means *to refer indirectly; elude* means *to avoid.* They alluded to a possible wage increase, but a real settlement eluded them.

Allusion, illusion. *Allusion* means *an indirect reference to; illusion* means *a false impression.* Most of us can appreciate her allusion to her college days. Many people suffer from the illusion that money is the only source of happiness.

Already, all ready. *Already* is an adverb meaning *previously; all ready* is an adverb-adjective compound meaning *completely ready.* Ms. Adams has already left. Are you all ready to go?

Altar, alter. An *altar* is a raised structure that serves as a center of worship or ritual. *Alter* is a verb meaning *to change.* They decorated the altar. The tailor altered Mr. Davis's suit.

Alternately, alternatively. *Alternately* means *one after the other. Alternatively* means *one or the other.* Arrange the red signs and the blue signs alternately along the parade route. The committee must alternatively use Oak Street or Lee Street for the parade route.

Alumna, alumnae, alumnus, alumni. An *alumna* is *a woman graduate* or *a former female student* (plural, *alumnae*). An *alumnus* is *a man graduate* or *a former male student* (plural, *alumni*). *Graduate, graduates,* or *former student* are good substitutes.

Among, between. *Between* implies two, whereas *among* implies more than two. There are frequent arguments between my brother and my sister. There is a great deal of rivalry among the women in the club.

Amount, number. *Amount* is usually used when referring to money and to that which cannot be counted; *number* generally refers to things that can be counted. A small number of soccer fans accounted for a large amount of damage.

Anxious, eager. *Anxious* connotes distress, fear, uneasiness, worry. *Eager* connotes enthusiasm, anticipation, impatient desire, or interest. We are anxious to meet your requirements (but worried that we may fail). We are eager to start on our trip.

Any. Use singular or plural verbs and pronouns according to the intended meaning. Was any of the dessert left? Are any of the students eligible for the prize?

Anyplace, everyplace, no place, someplace. These are colloquial expressions. In office communications, use *anywhere, everywhere, nowhere,* and *somewhere* instead.

Appraise, apprise. *Appraise* means *to set a value on; apprise* means *to inform.* The adjuster will appraise the damage and will apprise you of the estimate.

Apt, likely, liable. *Apt* means *unusually suitable* or *inclined; likely* emphasizes the idea of probability; *liable* means *susceptible to something unpleasant* or *responsible.* A shortsighted person is apt to make mistakes in financial planning. It is likely to rain tomorrow. She was liable for damages under the contract.

Ascent, assent. *Ascent* means *the act of upward movement.* His ascent in the organization has been rapid. *Assent* means *to agree to* or *to admit as true; to consent.* His reaction indicates his assent to the board's recommendations.

Awfully. As a synonym for *extremely* or *very* this word is overused. Avoid: She was *awfully* confused. Use instead: She was *very* confused.

Back of, in back of. Colloquial for *behind* or *at the back of.* The garden is behind the house (*not:* in back of the house).

Beside, besides. *Beside* means *next to*. He stood beside his sister at the reception. *Besides* means *in addition to*. I lost several items besides my billfold.

Bad, badly. *Bad* is a predicate adjective and should be used after verbs of sensing when used as linking verbs. *Badly* is an adverb. He feels bad about losing. She looks bad. The news sounds bad. He played badly in the tournament. He was injured badly in the accident. The home team played the game badly; the loss made them feel bad.

Bases, basis. *Bases* is the plural of *base* and *basis*.

Between. See *Among, between*.

Biannual, biennial, semiannual. *Biannual* means twice a year; *biennial,* every two years; *semiannual,* every half year or twice a year.

Bimonthly, semimonthly. *Bimonthly* means every two months; *semimonthly,* twice a month.

Blond, blonde. *Blond* is masculine; *blonde* is feminine.

Both, each. *Both* means two considered together. The twins are identical. *Both* wore blue. *Each* refers to individuals considered separately. *Each* would like a separate room.

Brunet, brunette. *Brunet* is masculine; *brunette* is feminine.

Can, may. *Can* means *to be able to; may* means *to have permission*. This model can be used for heating and air conditioning. Tell him that he may leave when he is finished.

Canvas, canvass. *Canvas* is a firm, closely woven fabric; *canvass* is a verb meaning *to survey* or *to solicit*. The cartons were covered with canvas. Mr. Lindsay will canvass the employees for their reactions.

Capital, capitol. Use *capital* unless you are talking about the building that houses a government. Capitalize *capitol* only when it is part of a proper name. The United States Capitol is located on Capitol Hill.

Cite, sight, site. *Cite* means *to quote* or *to refer to; sight* means *the act of seeing* or *an object or scene observed; site* means *location*. She cited some good examples in her lecture. They sighted another ship on the horizon. We chose the site for our new branch plant.

Comedian, comedienne. *Comedian* is masculine; *comedienne* is feminine.

Compare to, compare with. *Compare to* is used to equate or liken or put in the same category. *Compare with* is used to examine likenesses or differences. As a writer, he may be compared to Hemingway. Compared with last year's, this year's sales figures show great progress.

Complected, complexioned. *Complected* is a provincialism for *complexioned:* a dark-complexioned person.

Complement, compliment. *Complement* as a verb means *to complete, fill, or make perfect; complement* as a noun means *something that fills or completes; compliment* means *to praise*. Her attention to detail complements his energetic professionalism. He complimented Miss Shelley on her good work.

Confidant, confidante. *Confidant* is usually masculine; *confidante* is usually feminine.

Consist of, consist in. *Consist of* means *composed of; consist in* means *to lie, reside.* The mixture consists of four kinds of herbs. Contentment consists in the absence of frustrations.

Consul, council, counsel. A *consul* is a representative. A *council* is an assembly. *Counsel* as a noun means *advice* or *an attorney.* When used as a verb, *counsel* means *to advise.* The American consul served on the European Council for International Trade. Many members sought his wise counsel. He seemed eager to counsel them on legal matters.

Consult. *Consult about* something or merely *consult* (*consult with* is redundant). The heirs consulted the lawyer about the will.

Contact. Although business communicators use this term as a verb, its preferred usage is as a noun. Please contact the dealer's office. Preferred: We wish to establish a business contact in Brazil.

Continual, continuous. *Continual* means *occurring in close succession* or *frequently repeated; continuous* means *without break.* There were continual interruptions. The machine has been in continuous use for the past three hours.

Credible, creditable, credulous. *Credible* means *believable; creditable means praiseworthy; credulous* means *ready to believe on weak evidence.*

Data. *Data* is the plural form of the Latin *datum* and should be used with a plural verb. Data are processed electronically at incredible speeds.

Desert, desert, dessert. *Desert* (pronounced *dezert*) is an arid region lacking moisture; *desert (dizert)* means *to abandon; dessert* is a fruit or sweets served at the close of a meal.

Differ. One thing *differs from* another; persons *differ with* each other. One author's style differs from that of another in many ways. He differs with us on that point.

Different from. This usage is correct. *Different than* is incorrect. The circumstances were different from those he recalled.

Discreet, discrete. *Discreet* means *showing good judgment in conduct; discrete* means *separate; individually distinct.*

Disinterested, uninterested. *Disinterested* means *having an impersonal, unbiased, or unprejudiced interest; uninterested* means *having no interest.* Professional ethics requires accountants to be disinterested in the success of their clients. She is uninterested in fiction.

Doubt. To express doubt, use *if* or *whether.* To express lack of doubt, use a negative and *that.* I doubt if there is time. He doubts whether she will attend. I do not doubt that there is time. I have no doubt that there is time.

Due to. An adjective construction that should not be used as an adverb to introduce a prepositional phrase. Use *because of.* Incorrect: Due to faulty brakes, we drove slowly. Correct: Because of faulty brakes, we drove slowly.

Each other, one another. *Each other* refers to two persons; *one another,* to more than two. George and Mary are very fond of each other. All the men on the team like one another.

Each. See *Both, each.*

Eager. See *Anxious, eager.*

Effect. See *Affect, effect.*

Either, neither. Used as adjectives or as pronouns, these words usually take singular verbs. Either day is correct. Neither has replied to my letter.

Either . . . or, neither . . . nor. When these connectives join compound subjects, the subject that is nearer the verb determines whether a singular or plural verb is used. Usually place the plural subject near the verb. Either Mr. Lance or his associates are going. Neither the reports nor the book is here.

Eminent, imminent. *Eminent* means *high, lofty, distinguished; imminent* means *impending* or *threatening.* The eminent scholar predicted that recession is imminent in the next decade.

Ensure, insure. *Ensure* means *to make certain or safe; insure* means *to give, take, or procure insurance* (used in a financial sense). Snow tires will ensure safe driving in the snow. Every automobile owner should insure his or her vehicle in case of accident.

Ethics. *Ethics* is a plural noun but may be used in both plural and singular constructions. Professional ethics (singular) prohibits our advertising. His ethics (plural) have been questionable.

Exceed. See *Accede, exceed.*

Except. See *Accept, except.*

Excess. See *Access, excess.*

Farther, further. *Farther* refers to distance or space; *further* refers to time, quantity, or degree. The airport is a mile farther on this road. We can go into the matter further tomorrow.

Female. *Female* is used in records and statistics but is not acceptable as a synonym for *woman, lady,* or *feminine.*

Fewer, less. *Fewer* refers to number; *less,* to degree or quantity. There are fewer people living in single homes than formerly. She has less money this year.

Fiance, fiancee. A *fiance* (masculine) or a *fiancee* (feminine) is a person engaged to be married. Both words are pronounced *fee-on-say.*

Fine, well. *Fine* is used too often and too carelessly. Use *well* instead. The motor works well (not fine).

Flaunt, flout. *Flaunt* means *to wave; to display boastfully. Flout* means *to treat with contempt* or *to scorn.* He is resented by his colleagues because he flaunts his wealth and political connections. You will be a misfit in your new job if you flout the company rules.

Formally, formerly. *Formally* means *rigidly ceremonious* or *respectful of form. Formerly* means *previously.* I was formally introduced to Mr. Adams, who was formerly a member of the board of directors.

Good, well. To feel *good* and to feel *well* are not the same. Both *good* and *well* are adjectives; *well* is also an adverb. Used as adjectives, *feel good* and *feel well* have different meanings. I feel *good* implies an actual bodily sensation; I feel *well* simply means I am not ill.

Got, gotten. *Got* is preferred to *gotten* as the past participle of *get*. It is colloquial when used for *must* or *ought:* I've got to leave at once. Improved: I must leave at once.

Graduated. Use either *graduated from* or *was graduated from*. In letters of application, use the latter form—in case your reader is a purist. Formal: He was graduated from Indiana University. Informal: He graduated from Indiana University. Avoid the common error "graduated high school."

Hopefully. *Hopefully* is often misused. It is an adverb and should be used as such. It is not a synonym for *it is hoped, I hope,* or *we hope*. Use: We hope Miss James will do a good job. Avoid: Hopefully, Miss James will do a good job.

Hope phrases. Do not use *in hopes of* and *no hopes of*. Use the singular form. We sent the letter to Fairbanks, Alaska, in the hope of reaching Ms. Hanna.

However. Avoid starting a sentence with *however* when it is used as a transitional word. Used as an adverb, *however* can start a sentence. *Transitional:* We waited for hours; however, he . . . . *Adverb:* However you advised him, he did not . . . .

Identical with. To compare likeness, use *identical with*, not *identical to*.

Illusion, allusion. See *Allusion, illusion*.

Imply, infer. To *imply* means to give a certain impression; to *infer* means to receive a certain impression. Your question implies that you don't understand. I infer from your question that you don't understand.

In, into. *Into* is a preposition implying motion. *In* is a preposition implying place in which. She was diving into the pool (but was not yet in the pool). She was swimming in the pool (she is already in the pool).

Inconsistent. Use with *in* or *with*. He is inconsistent in his arguments. Her statements were inconsistent with her record.

Incredible, incredulous. *Incredible* means *unbelievable; incredulous* means *unbelieving*. The story is incredible; and, frankly, I'm incredulous.

Inferior to. Use *inferior to,* not *inferior than*.

Ingenious, ingenuous. *Ingenious* means *inventive; ingenuous* means *candid* or *artless*. She is ingenious in reducing office costs. His ingenuous reply to the interviewer's question was disarming.

Irregardless. Illiterate. Use *regardless* instead.

Its, it's. The possessive case takes no apostrophe. *It's* is a contraction of *it is*.

Job, position. Both words mean a post of employment, but with this distinction: A laborer who uses physical effort has a *job* and is paid wages at an hourly rate. A worker with special training or ability has a *position* and is paid a weekly or monthly salary. In personnel terminology, *job* is used for both because it is short; for example, a *clerical job.* (*Job* is also used to describe a unit of work.)

Junior, Senior, Jr., Sr. *Junior* is usually dropped after the death of the father of the same name. *Senior* or *Sr.* is unnecessary and is almost never used unless the two identical names are closely associated (such as business partners) or unless each is so well known that a distinction is needed.

Kind, kinds. Use singular verbs and pronouns with *kind;* plural verbs and pronouns with *kinds.* This applies also to *type, types; class, classes;* etc. That kind of machine performs well. The two types of machines used were suitable. Avoid: That kind of a machine performs well.

Later, latter. *Later* means *after a time; latter* means *the second of two things.* I shall reply later. I prefer the latter.

Latest, last. Although these words can be synonymous, a common distinction is to use *last* to mean *at the end in time or place; latest* is used to mean *following all others in time only, but not necessarily the end.* This is the latest edition of the book. It is not the last edition, because we have started to work on the next edition.

Lay, lie. *Lay* means *to put something in its place; lie* means *to recline* or *to rest on.* Principal parts of *lay* are *lay, laid, laid.* Principal parts of *lie* are *lie, lay, lain.* Lay the mail down. He laid the mail down. The mail lies on the table. It lay there yesterday.

Lead, led. The past tense of *lead* is *led.* He led the opposition.

Leave, let. *Leave* means *to depart; let, to permit* or *to allow.* When you leave the office after dark, let the security guard escort you to your car.

Less. See *Fewer, less.*

Like. *Like* should not be used for *as, as if,* or *as though.* Incorrect: The report looks like he took pains with it. Correct: The report looks as though he took pains with it.

Loan, lend. Although some writers use *loan* as a noun only, some dictionaries show both *loan* and *lend* as verbs. The principal parts are *loan, loaned, loaned; lend, lent, lent.*

Loose, lose. These words are frequently confused. *Loose* means *to be free of restraint; lose* means *to forget, to misplace,* or *to suffer a loss.* It is easy to lose a loose button.

Lots of. Colloquial for *many, much, a great many, a considerable number.*

Marital, martial, marshal. *Marital* means *pertaining to marriage; martial* means *warlike* or *military. Marshal* can be either a noun or a verb. As a verb, *marshal* means *to rally* or *to lead;* as a noun, *marshal* means *an official.* Poor money management is often the cause of serious marital problems. The strains of martial music were heard coming from the parade ground. We must marshal our voters if we are to elect a competent marshal.

May. See *Can, may*.

Neither . . . nor. See *Either . . . or*.

None. See *All, any, none, some, more, most*.

Not, and not. When either of these two introduces a phrase in contrast to the subject, the subject determines whether the verb is singular or plural. Results, not wishful thinking, count.

Not only . . . but also. In this construction, the noun closest to the verb determines whether the latter is singular or plural. When used with independent clauses, this construction is separated by commas. Not only the reports but also his report was due. Not only was it their first visit here, but also it was their first trip by air.

Off, off of. Use *off* only, not *off of*. The part fell off the machine. The girl jumped off the wall.

On, onto, on to. She drove *on* the expressway berm (implies position and movement over). He stepped *onto* the porch (implies motion). They went *on to* the next town. (*On* is an adverb in the verb phrase *went on; to* is a preposition.)

Oneself. Preferred to *one's self*. Taking oneself too seriously can cause problems.

Only. *Only* should be placed as close as possible to the word or clause that it modifies. Alan writes only form letters. Alan writes form letters only when he has spare time. Do not substitute *only* for *except* or *but*. Incorrect: No one is interested only Mr. Lane.

Other. Use *than* after *no other*. Incorrect: It was no other but Jane. Correct: It was no other than Jane.

Pair. The preferred plural of *pair* is *pairs*.

Passed, past, pastime. *Passed* is the past tense and past participle of the verb *to pass*. *Past* is a noun or an adjective meaning *a time gone by* or *by-gone*. It is also a preposition and an adverb. A *pastime* (often misspelled *passtime* or *pasttime*) is a *diversion*. They passed the time by reading. Go two blocks past Elm Street. In the past my favorite pastime was reading.

Percent, percentage. *Percent* is one word. *Percentage* is also one word and should not be used with a number. *Percentage* is a dubious colloquialism when used to mean *proportion*. A large proportion (rather than *percentage*) of the fish were cod.

Person, persons, individual, personage, party, people. A *person* is a human being; an *individual* is one apart from a group; a *personage* is a person of importance; *party* is a legal term for person. Use *persons* for small numbers and *people* for large masses.

Personal, personnel. *Personal* means *private*; *personnel* means *a body of persons, usually employed in a factory, office, or organization*. If you have a personal problem that is affecting your work, you may need to tell your employer. The personnel in our office often share career plans with our supervisor.

Personally, in person. These terms intensify meaning. Avoid using them in formal writing. I personally guarantee each one. Mr. Lane made the award in person.

Politics. This term is commonly used with singular verbs. Politics is the art or science concerned with guiding or influencing governmental policy.

Position. See *Job, position.*

Practical, practicable. *Practical* means *sensible, efficient,* or *useful. Practicable* means *capable of being put into practice.* My practical assistant suggested a practicable method for handling follow-ups.

Precedence, precedents, precedent. *Precedence* means *priority* or *preference; precedents* is the plural of the noun *precedent,* which means *an earlier occurrence; precedent* (preSEEdent) is an adjective meaning *earlier in order.* Completing the school year took precedence over her desire to take the trip. There are several precedents for that decision. The precedent decisions that apply to this case must be considered.

Preferable. Follow by *to,* not by *than.* Green is preferable to blue for the cover of our brochure.

Prerequisite. As a noun, *prerequisite* is used with *for;* as an adjective, it is used with *to* (to be prerequisite to).

Principal, principle. *Principal* may be a noun or an adjective. As a noun it means *a person who has controlling authority or is in a leading position.* It also means *a capital sum of money.* As an adjective, *principal* means *chief. Principle* is a noun meaning *a law, a doctrine, a rule,* or *a code of conduct.* The principals in the legal case are present. The principal actor was outstanding in his part. Mrs. Palmer invested the principal of the trust fund and used the interest for living expenses. Mr. Palmer was the principal of our school, and he was always a man of principle.

Proposition. Correctly used as a noun, *proposition* means *an assertion* or *a dignified proposal.* Do not use this word as a verb.

Proved, proven. Although either word may be used as the past participle of *prove, proved* is preferred. *Proven* is better confined to use as an adjective. You have proved your point. It was a proven fact.

Raise, increase, increment. In business, *raise* and *increase* may be used interchangeably when referring to wage or salary. *Raise* is the popular term, but *increase* is a more dignified term. *Increment* is generally used in personnel offices.

Real. *Real* should not be used for the adverb *very.* She had a very professional appearance (not real professional).

Respectfully, respectively, respectable. *Respectfully* means *in a courteous manner; respectively* refers to being considered singly in a particular order; *respectable* means *being of good name* or *fairly numerous.* He respectfully requested a letter of recommendation from his employer. Jan, Joan, and Edith were elected president, vice president, and treasurer, respectively. Each was elected by a respectable majority.

Retroactive. *Retroactive* is always used with the preposition *to* (not *from*). The price increase is retroactive to July 1.

Set, sit. *Set* means *to put or place something. Sit* means *to place yourself.* She set the cup and saucer on the table. She sits on the porch every evening.

Species. *Species* means *a class of individuals having common attributes and designated by a common name.* It is spelled the same in the singular and plural. *Specie* is money in the form of coins.

Stationary, stationery. *Stationary* means stable or fixed; *stationery* is writing paper.

Statistics. Use as a plural except when referring to the science of statistics.

Statue, stature, statute. *Statue* is *a sculptured or molded figure; stature* refers to height (as applied to people); *statute* refers to written law.

Stimulus, stimulant. *Stimulus* means *a mental goad; stimulant* means *a physical goad.* (In medicine, these two words are used synonymously.)

Superior. Use *superior to*, not *superior than*.

Sure, surely. *Sure* is an adjective; *surely* is a modifying adverb. Are you sure? That was surely record time.

These kind, those kind. Ungrammatical. Use *this kind* or *these kinds*.

Till, until. *Until* is preferred at the beginning of a sentence; although as prepositions and conjunctions, *until* and *till* are interchangeable.

Try and. This usage should be avoided. Use *to* with the infinitive: try to listen.

Uninterested. See *Disinterested, uninterested*.

Unique. *Unique* means *the only one of its kind.* It does not mean *rare* or *odd.* It is incorrect to say, "She is the most unique person I know."

United States. Use *the* before *United States,* rephrasing if necessary to avoid an awkward construction. (If necessary, substitute *American.*) *Poor:* According to United States laws. . . . *Preferred:* According to the laws of the United States. . . .

Unkempt, unkept. *Unkempt* means *unrefined, unpolished,* or *rough. Unkept* means *not maintained or preserved.*

Until. See *Till, until*.

Up. Avoid the use of *up* with verbs such as *connect, divide, end, open, rest, settle, finish*.

Very. *Very* should not be used to modify a past participle. It may modify an adjective directly. Incorrect: She was very interested in the position. Correct: She was very much interested in the position.

View. As a verb, use *to view* with *with*; as a noun, use *in view of* or *with a view to.* We view it with indifference. In view of the time, we will adjourn.

Well. See *Good, well*.

Where compounds. *Anywhere, everywhere, nowhere,* and *somewhere* are adverbs and are written as one word.

Whether. In indirect questions, *whether* is preferred to *if*. They asked whether he had come. Not: They asked if he had come.

Whether . . . or, whether or not. For alternatives, use *whether . . . or* or *whether or not*. State whether you will go or stay. State whether or not you will go. Avoid: State whether you will go or not.

While, awhile. Use *while* as a connective for time or as a noun. *Awhile,* an adverb, is written as one word. While Mrs. Lambert was out, her caller arrived. Once in a while, we find that. . . . He left awhile ago. *While* can be used for *although,* but it should not be used for *and*. While we see your point, we do not agree. Avoid: We order nails from the H & P Company, while we order hammers from Black and Burns.

■ The Greek Alphabet

The Greek alphabet is probably most familiar to college students in designations for fraternities, sororities, and honor societies—Phi Beta Lambda, Kappa Delta, Beta Gamma Sigma, Delta Pi Epsilon, and Pi Omega Pi are among the better known of these. However, with the rapid expansion of technology resulting from space exploration, nuclear engineering, and computer science, the Greek alphabet has become the most important foreign alphabet used in scientific work. Greek letters are used as symbols to represent physical qualities, quantities, and concepts. For example, electronic engineers refer to the wavelengths of a radio tube as its beta. Gamma rays describe nuclear radiation. Figure 7 will help you recognize and write the Greek alphabet should you have need for it in your work. Most manufacturers of word processing equipment make a special font containing the Greek alphabet; however, some English letters may be slightly modified on the typewriter for presentable copy if these symbols will be used too infrequently to justify the purchase of a special font.

Greek Letter	Greek Name	English Equivalent	Greek Letter	Greek Name	English Equivalent
A α	alpha	a	N ν	nu	n
B β	beta	b	Ξ ξ	xi	x
Γ γ	gamma	g	O o	omicron	ŏ
Δ δ	delta	d	Π π	pi	p
E ε	epsilon	ĕ	P ρ	rho	r
Z ζ	zeta	z	Σ σ ˢ	sigma	s
H η	eta	ē	T τ	tau	t
Θ θ ϑ	theta	th	Y υ	upsilon	u
I ι	iota	i	Φ φ φ	phi	ph
K κ	kappa	k	X χ	chi	ch
Λ λ	lambda	l	Ψ ψ	psi	ps
M μ	mu	m	Ω ω	omega	ō

Fig. 7 The Greek alphabet is the most important foreign alphabet used in scientific work.

■ Numerals—Cardinal (Arabic, Roman) and Ordinal

Two types of numerals are used in business—cardinal and ordinal. Cardinal numerals are used in simple counting: one (1), two (2), three (3). Ordinal numerals are used to show the order or succession in which such items as names, objects, and periods of time are considered (the seventh month, the fifth row of seats, the twentieth century). Arabic and Roman symbols distinguish cardinal numerals. Figure 8 shows the usual range of numbers that an executive or administrative assistant will need in business.

Fig. 8   **TABLE OF NUMERALS**

Cardinal Numbers			Ordinal Numbers	
Name	**Symbol**		**Name**	**Symbol**
	Arabic	**Roman**		
zero or naught or cipher	0			
one	1	I	first	1st
two	2	II	second	2d *or* 2nd
three	3	III	third	3d *or* 3rd
four	4	IV	fourth	4th
five	5	V	fifth	5th
six	6	VI	sixth	6th
seven	7	VII	seventh	7th
eight	8	VIII	eighth	8th
nine	9	IX	ninth	9th
ten	10	X	tenth	10th
eleven	11	XI	eleventh	11th
twelve	12	XII	twelfth	12th
thirteen	13	XIII	thirteenth	13th
fourteen	14	XIV	fourteenth	14th
fifteen	15	XV	fifteenth	15th
sixteen	16	XVI	sixteenth	16th
seventeen	17	XVII	seventeenth	17th
eighteen	18	XVIII	eighteenth	18th
nineteen	19	XIX	nineteenth	19th
twenty	20	XX	twentieth	20th
twenty-one	21	XXI	twenty-first	21st
twenty-two	22	XXII	twenty-second	22d *or* 22nd
twenty-three	23	XXIII	twenty-third	23d *or* 23rd
twenty-four	24	XXIV	twenty-fourth	24th
twenty-five	25	XXV	twenty-fifth	25th
twenty-six	26	XXVI	twenty-sixth	26th
twenty-seven	27	XXVII	twenty-seventh	27th
twenty-eight	28	XXVIII	twenty-eighth	28th
twenty-nine	29	XXIX	twenty-ninth	29th
thirty	30	XXX	thirtieth	30th

TABLE OF NUMERALS *(continued)*

Cardinal Numbers

Name	Symbol Arabic	Symbol Roman
thirty-one	31	XXXI
thirty-two, etc.	32	XXXII
forty	40	XL
forty-one, etc.	41	XLI
fifty	50	L
sixty	60	LX
seventy	70	LXX
eighty	80	LXXX
ninety	90	XC
one hundred	100	C
one hundred and one *or* one hundred one	101	CI
one hundred and two, etc.	102	CII
two hundred	200	CC
three hundred	300	CCC
four hundred	400	CD
five hundred	500	D
six hundred	600	DC
seven hundred	700	DCC
eight hundred	800	DCCC
nine hundred	900	CM
one thousand *or* ten hundred, etc.	1,000	M
two thousand, etc.	2,000	MM
five thousand	5,000	$\overline{V}$
ten thousand	10,000	$\overline{X}$
one hundred thousand	100,000	$\overline{C}$
one million	1,000,000	$\overline{M}$

Ordinal Numbers

Name	Symbol
thirty-first	31st
thirty-second, etc.	32d *or* 32nd
fortieth	40th
forty-first, etc.	41st
fiftieth	50th
sixtieth	60th
seventieth	70th
eightieth	80th
ninetieth	90th
hundred *or* one hundredth	100th
hundred and first *or* one hundred and first	101st
hundred and second, etc.	102d *or* 102nd
two hundredth	200th
three hundredth	300th
four hundredth	400th
five hundredth	500th
six hundredth	600th
seven hundredth	700th
eight hundredth	800th
nine hundredth	900th
thousandth *or* one thousandth	1,000th
two thousandth, etc.	2,000th
five thousandth	5,000th
ten thousandth	10,000th
hundred thousandth *or* one hundred thousandth	100,000th
millionth *or* one millionth	1,000,000th

■ Proofreaders' Marks

INSERT MARKS FOR PUNCTUATION

˅	Apostrophe	⌐	Move down; lower
[/]	Brackets	⌐	Move up; raise
⊙ :	Colon	⌐	Move to left
⋀ ˅	Comma	⌐	Move to right
⊠ ⊠ /	Ellipsis	⨍	Paragraph
! /	Exclamation point	no ⨍	No new paragraph
— /	Hyphen	out, s, c	Out; omit; see copy
⌃ ⌃	Inferior figure	↺	Reverse; upside down
.../	Leaders	rom	Roman, change to
(/)	Parentheses	↷	Run in material
⊙	Period	run in	Run in material on same line
? /	Question mark	#	Space, add (horizontal)
˅ ˅	Quotation mark	>	Space, add (vertical)
; ⊙	Semicolon	⌣	Space, close up (horizontal)
		<	Space, close up (vertical)

OTHER MARKS

//	Align type; set flush	sp	Spell out
bf	Boldface type	tr~	Transpose
X ⊗	Broken letter	?	Verify or supply information
≡ Cap	Capitalize	wf	Wrong font
⌐	Delete	#	All marks should be made inthe
⌐	Delete and close up	same	margin on the line in which
⋀	Insert (caret)	⅀/e	the error occurrs; if mor than one correction occurs in one line,they should appear
ital	Italic, change to	lc	in their Ørder separated by a slanting line.
bf ital	Italic, boldface		
stet	Let type stand		Errors should not be blotted out.
lc	Lowercase	sp/	Spell check

■ Punctuation

Effective writing expresses precisely the author's intended meaning. Punctuation helps the reader understand the meaning of a sentence through the use of a system of familiar symbols. While punctuation usage may vary in some instances, many fundamental rules are accepted and are generally adhered to in a precise yet simple manner.

APOSTROPHE

1. Use an apostrophe to designate the possessive of nouns and indefinite pronouns.

   a. To form the possessive of a singular or plural noun or an indefinite pronoun that does not end in a sibilant sound (*s, x, z*), add an apostrophe and an s.

bird's nest	Frank's coat
shopper's list	children's coats
man's coat	Marivaux's plays (silent *x*)
men's coats	one's coat
master's degree	bachelor's degree
a dollar's worth	a day's rest

   b. To form the possessive of a plural noun or an indefinite pronoun ending in a sibilant sound, add only an apostrophe.

dogs' leashes	three years' work
girls' coats	the Thomases' house
others' ills	ten dollars' worth
six hours' work	clients' evaluations

   c. To form the possessive of a singular noun ending in a sibilant sound, add an apostrophe and an *s*.

Burns's poems	the fox's tail
Jones's store	Liz's idea
Consolidated Service's truck	

   Exception: *If the singular noun has two or more syllables and if the last syllable is not accented and is preceded by a sibilant sound, add only the apostrophe for ease of pronunciation.*

Moses' law	Jesus' nativity
Ulysses' voyage	Demosthenes' oration
conscience' sake	

   d. To denote joint ownership, add the apostrophe or the apostrophe and *s* after the second noun only. Individual ownership is shown by making both elements possessive.

   Bob and Lou's store (one store, owned by Bob and Lou)
   Bob's and Lou's stores (two stores, one Bob's and one Lou's)
   Kinzers and Masons' annual picnic

e. To form the possessive of compound nouns and indefinite pronouns, add the apostrophe or apostrophe and *s* after the last element of the compound.

daughter-in-law's	daughters-in-law's
father-in-law's	fathers-in-law's
everyone else's	

2. Use an apostrophe to denote the omission of letters or figures.

It's too late to file your taxes.
They don't have time to visit.
The class of '85 had its reunion this year.
Where's Charlie?

3. Use an apostrophe to designate plurals of figures, letters, signs, and words to which special allusion is made.

If there are no 6's left in this type, use 9's turned upside down.
Your *T*'s and *F*'s are too much alike, and so are your *u*'s and *v*'s.
Use +'s and -'s to denote whether or not the sentences are correct.
When *and*'s and *the*'s are used in titles, they should not be capitalized, unless they are the first word.

COLON

The colon is a mark of introduction or anticipation. In general it denotes formality. The colon indicates a break in continuity that is greater than that requiring a semicolon and less than that requiring a period. It may be used to expand or emphasize a thought or to amplify in a second clause an idea contained in the first clause.

1. Use a colon to introduce a long or formal quotation.

Winston Churchill, in his opening statement as Prime Minister, declared to the House of Commons: "Victory at all costs, victory in spite of all terror, victory however long and hard the road may be; for without victory there is no survival."

John F. Kennedy, on conferring honorary citizenship on Sir Winston Churchill, said: "He mobilized the English language and sent it into battle."

2. Use a colon to introduce an example or a formal list; that is, a list preceded by a summarizing term.

Note: *An introductory expression preceding a colon should have a subject and a predicate and should cause the reader to expect an illustration or explanation following the colon.*

A check payable to a married woman should include her given name, not her husband's: Ruth Payne rather than Mrs. Larry Payne.

The following items are put on the check stub: the amount of the check, the date, the person or business to whom the check is payable, and the purpose of the check.

Exception: *Do not use a colon to introduce a brief, informal list when the colon would immediately follow a verb or a preposition.*

The only major types of coverage which cannot be written on an SMP policy are automobile, workers' compensation, surety bonds, and life or health insurance.

3. Use a colon between independent clauses or independent sentences when the second clause amplifies the first or when the second gives a concrete illustration of a general statement in the first. (Notice that the first word of an independent clause after a colon is capitalized.)

> In time, however, one of her favorite contentions was justified: In the long run people who are conscientious, set goals, and work diligently will achieve the position for which they are best qualified.

> George Washington, in a letter to the captains of the Virginia Regiment, said that discipline is the soul of an army: It makes small numbers formidable and procures success to the weak and esteem to all.

4. Use a colon after terms such as *the following* or *as follows* when these terms precede a list of enumerated items, a tabulation, a computation, etc.

> You will need the following:
>
> 1. Software
> 2. Printer
> 3. Keyboard

> Their actions were as follows: They went to the supermarket, purchased a number of items, returned to their car, and drove away.

> Each category of liability should be listed and the total amount of liabilities presented in the following manner:

> | | |
> |---|---|
> | Notes payable | $1,500 |
> | Accounts payable | 1,100 |
> | Salaries payable | 300 |
> | Total liabilities | $2,900 |

5. By common acceptance, a colon is used in the following instances:

   a. After the salutation in certain styles of formal or business letters

   > Ladies and Gentlemen: Dear Ms. McDaniel:
   > Dear Dean Roberts: Dear Professor Gordon:

   b. Between the hour and the minute when time is expressed in figures

   > 12:15 a.m.   2:30 p.m.

   c. Between chapter and verse in references to the Bible and between volume and page reference

   > *Proverbs* 16:9   *Papers of James Madison* 1:16

COMMA

Studies have indicated that three-fourths of all punctuation errors involve the use of the comma. Knowing the correct use of the comma is necessary in order to convey ideas clearly.

1. Use a comma to separate independent clauses that are linked by a coordinating conjunction (*and, but, for, or, nor*).

> June is a month of celebrations, and this family certainly has its share.
> The house had no central heating system, nor was it air conditioned.

Exception: *When the clauses are short and closely related, no comma is required.*

The chairperson called for order and everyone sat down.

2. Use a comma to separate each item when three or more elements form a series without linking words between the elements.

The florist advertised special discounts on roses, carnations, orchids, mums, and snapdragons.
The new administrative assistant is aggressive but not offensive, efficient but not officious, and friendly but not servile.
The student was either 21, 22, or 23 years old.

Note: *Although the use of* etc. *is discouraged in business communications, this abbreviation should be set off by commas when used.* Etc. *is never preceded by* and.

The store sold clothing, housewares, furniture, food, pharmaceuticals, linens, etc., at its Seventh Street location.

Exception: *When the elements in a series are simple and are joined by conjunctions, omit the commas.*

I cannot remember whether that symphony was composed by Bach or Beethoven or Brahms.

3. Use a comma to separate coordinate adjectives that modify a noun. (Adjectives are coordinate if *and* can be used between them.)

The gaudy, tasteless decorations detracted from the appearance of the room. (the gaudy *and* tasteless decorations)
An old straw hat was lying in the street. (NOT an old and straw hat)
The late Mayor Riley was a prominent public official. (NOT a prominent and public official)

4. Use a comma to separate elements that might be misread if the comma were omitted.

After all, the effort is secondary.
Abruptly the car stopped, throwing her forward.
In that office, organization is stressed.
Please call in, in a few days.

5. Use commas to set off nonrestrictive clauses, phrases, and appositives (clauses, phrases, and appositives that are not essential to the meaning of a sentence).

Dr. Roy Maris, the eminent scholar, was the principal speaker.
Understanding simple percentage, a major ingredient in banking and merchandising, is a concept often tested by employers.

Restrictive clauses, phrases, and appositives are necessary to the meaning of a sentence and are not set off by commas.

The person who composed that letter needs to develop tact.
Those executives planning to attend the conference must register in advance.
John Wayne the actor starred in many movies; John Wayne the doctor is my neighbor.

Note: *The conjunction* or *may appear with an appositive.*

The instructions, or information for correct use, were printed on the warranty card.

Note: *In some cases, only the writer knows if a clause is restrictive or nonrestrictive.*

My brother, who is on the team this year, is a senior. (The writer has only one brother.)
My brother who is on the team this year is a senior. (The writer has more than one brother.)

6. Use commas to set off complementary or antithetical (contrasting or opposing) elements.

   The unjust, though at the same time necessary, restriction was placed on all members of the class.

   a. Commas should set off an antithetical clause or phrase introduced by *not* if the modified element is complete without it.

      The dignitaries hoped that the president herself, not the vice president, would attend the ceremony.
      Betty went to the concert not to hear the orchestra but to observe the soloist.

   b. Commas should separate interdependent antithetical clauses.

      The more Maria read about Greece, the deeper became her resolve to visit that historic land.

   Exception: *Short antithetical phrases should not be separated by commas.*

   The bigger the better.
   The more the merrier.

7. Use a comma to separate an introductory adverbial clause or phrase from the rest of the sentence.

   Where the opportunities are available, first-line supervisors should be encouraged to move into higher management.
   Because of the unusual circumstances, the president of the company addressed the assembled employees.
   After leaving the store, he noticed the lights were on.

8. Commas set off an adverbial phrase or clause located between a subject and a predicate.

   Rita, after hearing the news, called home.

   Exception: *If a dependent adverbial clause follows a main clause and is restrictive, it should not be set off by a comma.*

   Louise was astonished when she received the award.

   Exception: *A comma is not used after a short introductory adverbial phrase if the clarity of the sentence does not suffer.*

   In December the class will visit the World Trade Center.

   Exception: *A comma is not used following an introductory adverbial phrase that immediately precedes the verb it modifies.*

   On the deck stood the captain, the first mate, and several crew members.

9. Use commas to set off introductory absolute, participial, infinitive, and gerund phrases.

Being a former member of the panel, she is familiar with the rules.
Remembering the appointment, Mr. Arnold left immediately.
After cashing the check, the customer left the bank.
In order to meet our quota, we must work overtime.
Keeping as close to our budget as possible, we will be able to complete the project without going over budget.

10. An omitted word or words are replaced by a comma.

   The Nordwell Corporation has long had a reputation for integrity and social responsibility; Blake and Beasley, for questionable methods. (The comma takes the place of the words *has long had a reputation.*)

11. Use commas with the following parenthetical elements:

   a. To separate items of address and geographical names

   The Smiths moved to 124 Oak Street, Pensacola, Florida, when they retired.
   Tulsa, Oklahoma, is served by several airlines.

   b. To separate elements in dates

   Thomas Jefferson and John Adams both died on July 4, 1826, after long careers in public service.

   c. To separate items in a reference

   In *Hamlet,* II, ii, 255, you will find the reference under discussion.

   d. To set off words used in direct address

   Did I hear, Mike, that you are going to England?

   e. To set off introductory expressions and those used to mark transitions

   If the facts were known, an investigation would follow.
   The merger, on the other hand, has increased the work of all employees.

   f. To set off parenthetical words, phrases, and clauses

   The new employee, I am told, is a graduate of your school.

12. Use a comma to separate a short direct quotation from the statement that precedes or follows it. (A long or formal quotation is introduced by a colon.)

   He shouted as he ran from the office, "No one in the building has a fire extinguisher."

   Note: *Do not use a comma to set off a quotation that is an integral part of the sentence.*

   He said that his credit rating is "A-1" and now is the time "to live it up."

13. A comma may be used to separate two identical words or phrases, even though the grammatical construction does not require the separation.

   The band played on, on key.
   They marched in, in pairs.
   When it's over, it's over.

14. Use a comma to separate unrelated adjacent numbers.

In 1994, 32 new stores were opened.

Note: *It is preferable to rewrite the sentence to avoid the foregoing construction.*

We opened 32 new stores in 1994.

15. Use commas with numerals in the following instances:

   a. With figures of 1,000 or more, between every group of three digits, counting from the right

      1,456
      11,420
      117,560,000

   Note: *The comma is frequently omitted in writing four-digit numbers not included in a set containing numbers of five or more digits. If a text contains a great quantity of numerical matter, it is advisable to choose a consistent use for that text.*

   b. With time divisions

      November 14, 1994
      New Year's Day, 1980

   Exception: *Do not use commas with numbers in historical references, page numbers, dimensions, weights, measures, time, policy numbers, room numbers, telephone numbers, and most serial numbers.*

2200 B.C.	3 feet 6 inches
page 1463	4 pounds 2 ounces
806423518	2 hours 4 minutes

16. Use a comma after *that is, i.e.,* and *namely.* The punctuation mark preceding such expressions is determined by the importance or length of the interruption. If the interruption is minor, use a comma. If the interruption is important or lengthy, use a semicolon. Always use a semicolon if the expression is followed by an independent clause.

   She is an expert in Colonial history, that is, colonial American history.
   The editor persuaded the author to change the direction of his manuscript; i.e., she convinced him that his book should appeal to management's interest in current ideas and practices rather than in historical methods of operating business firms.
   She wrote the article with three of her friends, namely, Jon, Randy, and Barbara.
   He said that he was going to give consideration to the three options the company presented to him; namely, to transfer to Duluth, to accept the production management position at the home office in Chicago, or to expand the branch office in Louisville.

DASH

The dash should not be confused with the hyphen. In keying a manuscript, the dash consists of two hyphens (--) placed together with no space preceding or following.

1. Use a dash when a sentence is interrupted abruptly and an entirely different sentence or thought is added.

> The old book of poetry—written in 1799—is being reprinted.
> The student read the paper carefully—but with confidence.

2. Use a dash to indicate the omission of words or letters.

> Drop out—minimum wages, you understand.
> Serious errors—dismissal, you get the picture.
> Mary J—, of C— Street, was the witness.

3. Use a dash before a word or statement that summarizes a preceding series or is an emphatic repetition of the preceding statement.

> Our annual clearance sale will include many items—furniture, bedding, housewares, and luggage.
> The editor stated that the author's work was original and scholarly—original and scholarly in the sense that it presented new information that had been well researched.

4. Use a dash to set off appositives that have internal punctuation or that are used for emphasis.

> We must consider all factors—the local labor market, the new tax laws, and our long-range plan—in order to make our factory productive.

5. When strong emphasis is desired, the dash may be used in place of the comma, the colon, the semicolon, or parentheses.

> Consultants rely heavily upon their authority of competence—the right of a person to influence others by virtue of recognized ability and expertise. (replaces a comma)
> The most realistic view of supervisors is that to varying degrees they are a special class of managers—they are strategically placed management representatives. (replaces a semicolon)

ELLIPSIS

The ellipsis mark—three periods with a space before and after each period (. . .)—is used to show the omission of a passage that is being quoted. If the omitted passage comes at the end of the sentence a period is added, making four periods.

In Illus. 13-3, if the calculations have been made correctly, the materials and parts needed . . . will be ready at the same time. Adequate time for delivery and production will be allowed, and in most cases . . . spare time must be allowed so that there will be no costly delay in assembling the final product simply because one part was not ordered early enough. . . . The problems outlined here are particularly true of certain types of products made on special orders for special purposes.

EXCLAMATION POINT

The exclamation point has two basic uses: after an exclamatory sentence and after words that express strong emotion. Exclamation points should be used sparingly; they should not be used in parentheses to express humor or irony.

Then the pilot shouted, "Bail out!"
Look out! You'll fall!

HYPHEN

The hyphen has two chief uses: to mark the division of a word that breaks at the end of a line and to designate certain compound words. As to the first use, words should be divided between syllables according to *Webster's New Collegiate Dictionary.* Never divide words of one syllable.

In keying manuscript, in order to avoid confusion for the typesetter, do not hyphenate words at the end of a line; let long words run into the right margin.

In forming compound words, it is always wise to consult *Webster's New Collegiate Dictionary,* since there are wide variations in styling compounds and numerous exceptions to the rules. For example, *vice-chancellor* is hyphenated, but *vice admiral* is two words; *vice-chancellorship* is hyphenated, but *viceroyalty* is one word. A few general rules apply to the use of hyphens in forming compounds.

1. Use a hyphen between a prefix and a root word under these circumstances:

    a. When the combination is a prefix and a proper name

    un-American
    pro-Canadian

    b. When the combination of the prefix and root word constitutes a word pronounced like another word but different in meaning

    recover, re-cover
    recreation, re-creation
    reform, re-form
    recollect, re-collect

    c. When the combination is a prefix ending in a vowel and a root word beginning with a vowel, if the omission of the hyphen will cause misreading

    re-echo
    re-ink
    co-op

    Note: *The prefixes* ex-, self-, half-, *and* all- *are often used with a hyphen.*

    ex-manager
    self-control
    half-baked
    all-around

    d. When figures, letters, or numbers are compounded with words to form a single idea

    two-year period
    25-foot stick
    L-shaped room
    U-turn

2. Use a hyphen between two or more words that precede a noun and act as a compound adjective.

    long-established custom
    coarse-grained wood
    well-known speaker
    up-to-date method
    up-to-the-minute technology

Exception: *This usage does not apply when one of the words is an adverb ending in* ly, *when the words form a comparative or superlative compound adjective, or, generally speaking, when the words follow the noun.*

highly paid executive
better known speaker

3. Some phrases used as adjectives are hyphenated in any position.

The equipment is up-to-date.
Up-to-date equipment has been installed.

4. Use a hyphen between the spelled-out numbers *twenty-one* through *ninety-nine.*

5. Use a hyphen in compounds formed from a noun or a verb and a preposition.

set-to
head-on
house-to-house
hands-on
in-service

6. Use a hyphen in writing fractions unless the numerator or the denominator already contains a hyphen.

a one-fourth share
a two-thirds majority vote
three-fourths of the population
two-thirds of a mile
twenty-one hundredths (21/100)
twenty one-hundredths (20/100)

7. Use a hyphen after each word or number in a series that modifies the same noun (suspended hyphenation). Notice the use of the space following the hyphen.

one-on-one conferences
six- or eight-cylinder engine
first-, second-, or third-class mail

8. Use a hyphen in compounding capitalized words: the Atlanta-Dallas flight.

9. Use a hyphen to indicate continuing or inclusive numbers—dates, times, or reference numbers.

1991-1995
June-July 1992
10:00 a.m.-5:00 p.m.
See pages 345-375.

PARENTHESES

1. Use parentheses to enclose nonessential information that interrupts the flow of a sentence or is incidental to the topic of a paragraph. Unlike dashes, parentheses usually de-emphasize information rather than emphasize it.

At 4:30 p.m. (the time when every member of the staff is free) is the best time for our committee meeting.

We have paid considerable installment interest this year. (It no longer qualifies as an income-tax deduction.)

2. Use parentheses to enclose letters or numbers in an enumeration that is not shown in list format.

The professor issued these instructions: (1) smoking is allowed only in designated areas, (2) punctuality in attending classes is expected of all students, and (3) assignments are to be submitted on time.

3. Use parentheses to enclose signs, numbers, and words when accuracy is essential.

Make out the check for the exact amount ($45.50).
The cash drawer was over by $200 (two hundred dollars).
An asterisk (*) was placed at the end of the sentence to indicate the footnote.

4. Parentheses are frequently used in text to enclose references to other parts of the text.

The current worth of this loss is $79,995 (see Table 31-1).
See Chapter 10 (pages 664–751) for complete coverage.

Note: *Before a parenthesis within a sentence, no punctuation mark is used. After parentheses within a sentence, no punctuation mark is used unless it would be required if the parenthetical material were removed; then whatever mark is required follows the closing parenthesis. Within parentheses inside a sentence, the punctuation is the same as if the material were a separate sentence. However, when it is a complete sentence, no capital is used at the beginning and no period at the end—although a question mark or exclamation point is used if one is required.*

Parentheses may enclose a separate sentence, in which case the ordinary rules for using the capital and period apply.

PERIOD

A period is used to mark the end of a declarative or imperative sentence, a legitimate fragmentary sentence, or a run-in heading. It is also used to mark an abbreviation.

1. When a period is used after an abbreviation, it is followed (except at the end of a sentence) by whatever punctuation mark would normally be used there.

Breakfast is served at 8:00 a.m., lunch at 12:30 p.m., and dinner at 6:30 p.m.

2. Examples of legitimate fragmentary sentences include the following:

a. A transition sentence

Now for the final vote.

b. Questions and answers

Who says this? The man who only four years ago said exactly the opposite.

c. Sentences reporting direct discourse where there is no chance of mistaking the speaker.

> "Ramona was at the meeting."
> "No!"
> "With her partner."
> "Not Pedro?"
> "No one else."
> "What a surprise!"

3. A period may be used after a rhetorical question.

> Will the audience please rise.
> May I congratulate you on your success.

4. A run-in heading is one that is followed on the same line by text material. A period or other appropriate end-of-sentence punctuation ends the run-in heading.

> *The Authority of Organized Labor.* The National Labor Relations Act of 1935 for the first time clearly legitimized at the national level the authority of organized labor. . . .

Note: *The design of a publication may call for the period to be omitted in typeset copy, but the author should always include the period in keyed manuscript.*

5. Use a period after each item in an enumerated list if the individual items are complete sentences. If the items are single words, short phrases, or incomplete sentences, use no periods.

> The main arguments for decentralized filing are as follows:
> 1. The confidential nature of the material suggests that it be kept from the majority of employees.
> 2. Unnecessary delay in getting papers from the centralized department is avoided.
> 3. The papers filed will not be required by any other department.
>
> The office manager should have available information about each of the following:
> 1. Principal types of furniture and equipment and reputable suppliers for each
> 2. Reliable statistics for comparing the effectiveness of competing brands of equipment and furniture
> 3. Suppliers' catalogs and current prices
> 4. Possibilities for standardizing equipment throughout the firm

QUESTION MARK

1. Use a question mark after a direct question.

> What are you doing?
> Where are you going?
> When will you return?

Note: *Do not use a question mark after an indirect question.*

> She asked what you are doing.
> He asked where you are going.

Note: *Placing a question mark at the end of a declarative or imperative sentence transposes the sentence into an interrogative remark.*

> That is what you intend to wear?

2. In a series of questions within an interrogative sentence, a question mark may follow each question. When used in this way, the question mark substitutes for a comma; the second and subsequent elements are preceded by one space and begin with a lowercase letter.

> Where is my desk? my computer? my software?
> Are you interested in a watch? a ring? a bracelet?

3. Use a question mark in parentheses (?) to express doubt or uncertainty.

> The tour of the house and gardens is scheduled for the first week in April(?).

Note: *Do not use a question mark to make a joke or to be ironical, since such usage questions the reader's intelligence.*

> Anne, you know, is the most popular (?) member of the royal family.

QUOTATION MARKS

The main function of quotation marks is to enclose matter quoted from any source, either spoken or written. Other functions are to enclose words used in a special way and to enclose certain titles.

1. Use quotation marks to enclose direct quotations.

> The manufacturing superintendent, in a heated discussion with the director of personnel, said: "I've had it with your job enrichment propaganda. It has taken me years to set up an assembly line that works smoothly and efficiently. Productivity is high, quality is on standard, and nobody is complaining. So why rock the boat?"

2. Use quotation marks to enclose the title of (a) a chapter in a book; (b) an individual poem, essay, or story in a volume; and (c) any item from a book or magazine. (Titles of books and magazines are italicized.)

> The poems "Emerson" and "Lands End" appear in the volume *More People* by Edgar Lee Masters.
> For information about the history of movies, read "Movies: Our 100-Year Love Affair" in *Modern Maturity,* March 1993.

3. Use quotation marks to enclose words used in a special way or words coined for special, limited use. Discretion should be practiced in using quotation marks in these instances. Only if readers are unfamiliar with the term should quotation marks be used to suggest that its status in the language is tentative.

> The Federal Reserve Board controls the amount of reserves by use of a tool known as the "open market operation."
> The speaker described his opponent's principal problem as the "ineptitude of innocence."

Note: *Quotation marks should be used sparingly for coined words, words used in a special way, colloquialisms, irony, and slang, and then only if the word is foreign to the reader.*

4. The following general rules should be observed with the use of quotation marks:

a. When several different speakers are quoted, each person's remarks are enclosed in quotation marks.

> When Mark returned from the football game, everyone shouted questions at once: "Who won?" "What was the score?" "What did Jim do?" "Was there much passing?"

b. When quoting a fragment of a sentence, do not begin the quotation with a capital letter unless the quoted passage began with a capital.

> Senator Margaret Hall said that "the machinations of a corrupt political machine will have to stop."

c. Quotations within quotations use single quotation marks. Quotations within single quotations use double quotation marks.

> In a letter the new student wrote: "I have been following the advice of my instructor who said, 'When I decide to write something, I first read Pope's "An Essay on Criticism" to inspire me to do my best'; but I find that it doesn't help me at all."

Exception: *Do not use quotation marks for proverbs, phrases, or figures of speech that are widely known.*

He was honest, not because he believed that honesty was the best policy, but because honesty was inherent in his character.
Absence makes the heart grow fonder, but out of sight out of mind was her usual experience.
Silence is golden when one has much studying to do.

Exception: *Do not use quotation marks for statements which are not quoted from someone else but are quotations in form only.*

She thought, Shall I wear gloves to go on my interview?
He said to himself, I think I'm going to make manager this year.

Exception: *Do not use quotation marks with the term* so-called. *Use of the term itself alerts the reader that a special usage is coming.*

The so-called easy way sometimes turns out to be the most difficult and longest way to get results.

Exception: *Do not quote the words* yes *and* no *except in direct discourse.*

Many persons have difficulty saying no, so they frequently answer yes against their better judgment.

Exception: *Do not use quotation marks where the name of a speaker introduces the speech.*

JEAN GROBE: It appears to me that we should give this experiment a chance before discarding the whole idea.
MARK WHITE: A good suggestion, except that we have spent entirely too much time and money already on trying to solve this problem.

Exception: *Do not use quotation marks to enclose material that is set off as a block quotation. Block quotations of one long paragraph or several short paragraphs are usually set indented in from the left and right text margins. Any quoted matter within a block quotation should be enclosed in double quotation marks, even if the source quoted uses single quotation marks.*

Exception: *Do not use quotation marks to enclose an indirect quotation.*

Cynthia said that she was leaving because she wanted to arrive home before dark.

OTHER PUNCTUATION WITH QUOTATION MARKS

The rules for punctuating sentences containing direct quotations are illustrated below.

1. Introductory expression preceding the quotation

   She called, "Where are you going?"

2. Explanatory expression interrupting the quotation

   "It is not," she interrupted, "my habit to change my mind so quickly."
   "This is my idea," Bob declared; "therefore, I won't have you stealing it."

3. Explanatory expression after the quotation

   "What are you going to do about it?" she inquired.

   Note: *Commas and periods precede closing quotation marks, including single quotation marks. Semicolons and colons follow closing quotation marks. The position of question marks or exclamation points depends on the content of the sentence: place them before inside closing quotation marks if they apply only to the quotation; place them after closing quotation marks if they apply to the entire sentence.*

   "Are you coming to the dance?" he asked.
   Have you ever heard her say, "I don't play bridge"?
   "What a wonderful day!" he exclaimed.
   How generous of her to say, "You may take my new car"!
   The professor was not shocked when the young instructor said, "I was dismayed at having one of my students define salutary as 'one who salutes.' "

SEMICOLON

If a comma indicates the smallest interruption in continuity of thought, the semicolon then stands midway between the functions of the comma and the period. The semicolon substitutes at times for the comma and at times for the period. But when it replaces either, there must be a logical basis for the substitution.

1. Use a semicolon to separate independent clauses of a compound sentence that have a close, logical relationship when they are not connected by a coordinate conjunction.

   The plane was overdue; it arrived three hours behind schedule.
   She did not let her emotions sway her; she considered the various alternatives objectively.

2. Use a semicolon between independent clauses when a conjunctive adverb joins the clauses. The semicolon precedes the conjunctive adverb. The most common conjunctive adverbs are *therefore, nevertheless, however, moreover, so, also, consequently, thus, hence, then, still, accordingly, besides,*

furthermore, likewise, and *otherwise.* These connecting words are generally followed by a comma.

> The buyers spent more time at the market; therefore, they had time to make better selections.
>
> All airports were closed until noon; consequently, all flights were delayed.

3. A semicolon precedes a coordinate conjunction (*and, but, for, or, nor*) between two independent clauses when either or both contain internal punctuation.

> There are many interesting places in Africa; but one must consider the time of year, the cost of airfare, and the time available for travel.
>
> Our office subscribes to four magazines, three newspapers, and a financial journal; but they are usually not read regularly by the staff.

4. A semicolon separates items in a series that are long and complex or that involve internal punctuation. (A comma is used between items in a series if a word or words are omitted.)

> The defendant, in justification of his act, pleaded that (1) he was despondent over the death of his wife; (2) he was without employment, a place to live, and warm clothing; (3) he was rejected by his only son, who had moved to Maine; and (4) he was under the influence of potent medication that had impaired his judgment.
>
> When the vote was tabulated, Ki won first place; Adams, secondplace; and Schmidt, third place.
>
> The speaker holds that democracy, although slow-moving and inefficient, is the best form of government; that the freedom we possess, although bought with war and death, is worth the cost; and that our form of government is worth living for, fighting for, and if need be, dying for.

5. A semicolon is used before such expressions as *for example (e.g.), for instance, that is (i.e.),* and *namely (viz.),* depending upon the importance and length of the interruption.

> Some pairs of words are bothersome to students; for example, *affect* and *effect, loose* and *lose, sit* and *set.*
>
> Every punctuation rule suggests three acts on your part; namely, learn it, use it, and check your writing to see if you have used it correctly.
>
> The professor spoke with authority; i.e., she set down the rules and stated that she expected them to be observed.

6. A semicolon follows a closing quotation mark if it would be used normally at the place the interruption comes.

> The president shouted, "The motion is carried!"; nevertheless, pandemonium erupted in the crowded hall.

■ Quick Grammar Reminders

These quick grammar reminders are not intended to be a substitute for a comprehensive grammar book. They are meant to jog a reader's memory or quickly clarify a point of confusion that may arise when composing letters, preparing reports, drafting speeches, or performing any of the multitudinous writing tasks that face an executive or administrative assistant.

ACTION VERBS

See "Transitive (Action) Verbs."

AND IN COMPOUND SUBJECTS

Compound subjects of two or more words joined by *and* take plural verbs and pronouns unless the words together comprise a single element.

Our secretary and our treasurer have mailed their reports.
Our secretary and treasurer has mailed his report.
A pen and a pencil were found after the meeting.
A matching pen and pencil makes a welcome gift.

COMPOUND WORDS

Compound words fall into three groups: hyphenated compounds, one-word compounds, and two-word compounds. Information about the two latter groups can generally be found in any standard dictionary. Compounds formed with prefixes and suffixes are treated under "Prefixes, Joined" and under "Suffixes." For information about hyphenated compounds, *see* "Hyphen," page 784.

EUPHEMISMS

Euphemisms are softened, tactful substitutes for blunt or harsh facts. Some common euphemisms are:

For *buried:* laid to rest
For *discharged:* left our employ
For *died:* passed away
For *claim:* think or believe
For *deaf:* hearing impaired

GERUNDS

1. A gerund is a verbal (ending in *-ing*) used as a noun. Gerunds can be used just like regular nouns.

   Subject: Collecting stamps is a rewarding hobby.
   Object: She learned stamp collecting several years ago.

2. In formal writing a possessive is used with a gerund.

   We appreciate your helping us with the project.
   The team's winning made the crowd happy.

   Exception: *The possessive form is not necessary with a compound or inanimate modifier.*

   The No. 2 mill breaking down caused a delay.
   The mill (or mill's) breaking down caused a delay.

IDIOMS

1. An idiom is an expression or phrase peculiar to a language—an arbitrary grouping of words that is often illogical in construction or whose meaning differs from the literal meaning of its parts. Some common American idioms are *to make ends meet, to take pains, laid up with a virus, by and large,* and *to catch a cold.*

2. A prepositional idiom is one in which the combination of words has a special meaning; for example, *to live up to, to live down* something, *to put up with* something, *to set up, to set about* something, *to hand over, to bring up* a point.

INFINITIVES

An *infinitive* is a verb form usually introduced by *to* and used as a noun, adjective, or adverb.

Noun, subject: To act upon your proposal requires a quorum.
Noun, object: He wants to talk with you.
Adjective: The place to go is Spain.
Adverb: He saved his graduation checks to go to Spain.

The *to* is usually omitted after the following verbs: *hear, feel, watch, let, dare, help, see, make, please, bid, need,* and *do.*

Help me (to) carry the luggage.
They bid us (to) leave immediately.
There was nothing to do but (to) read.

A *split infinitive* occurs when a word or phrase separates *to* from the verb. Use a split infinitive only when necessary for clarity or emphasis. Notice in the examples below how the meaning changes subtly with a shift of the infinitive.

The attorney invited them to *first* consider . . .
The attorney invited them to consider *first* . . .

INTRANSITIVE VERBS

See "Transitive (Action) Verbs."

LINKING VERBS

Linking verbs connect a subject with a predicate noun or adjective. *See also* "Transitive (Action) Verbs." Linking verbs include all forms of the verb *to be* and verbs that pertain to the senses:

to be (am, is, was, has been, etc.), act, appear, become, feel, get, grow, look, seem, sound, taste, turn

NUMBER OF

The meaning intended determines whether *number of* takes a singular or plural verb. When the word *number* is preceded by *the* and therefore expresses a unit, the verb should be singular.

The number of office workers is about ten.

When the word *number* is preceded by *a,* the plural form of the verb is required.

A number of employees are out of town today.

OR

When *or* joins two subject words, the verb agrees with the nearer word.

Only one or two are needed.
No pencils or paper was furnished.

PARALLEL CONSTRUCTION

If two or more sentence parts are joined by one or more conjunctions, the parts should be of like kinds; that is, all single words of the same part of speech, all phrases, or all clauses.

The shipment was returned not only because it was late but also because two items were incorrect. (*connecting two clauses*)

NOT: The shipment was returned not only for being late but also because two items were incorrect. (*connecting a phrase and a clause*)

A good administrative assistant not only is prompt but also shows initiative. (*connecting two verb phrases*)

NOT: A good administrative assistant is both prompt and shows initiative. (*connecting an adjective and a verb phrase*)

Our plan is to decide on the type of building, to choose an architect, and to let the contracts. (*connecting infinitives*)

NOT: Our plan is to decide on the type of building, choosing an architect, and letting the contracts. (*connecting an infinitive and participles*)

PARTICIPLES, DANGLING

A participial construction should modify a related, logical word except when the construction is absolute (modifying nothing).

Dangling: Leaving the office, the letter was dropped.
Logical: Leaving the office, I dropped the letter.
Absolute: The situation having developed, let's accept the changes it necessitates.

PLURALS

Since standard dictionaries give irregularly formed plurals of words, this section provides only that information pertaining to problems common in day-to-day business usage. Refer also to "Apostrophe," p. 777.

Abbreviations

1. For most, add *s*: gals, yds, Drs., bbls
2. For abbreviations in all caps, add *s*: CLUs, CPAs, R.N.s, RNs
3. For abbreviations consisting of single lowercase letters, add *'s*: btu's, pc's

Compound Nouns

1. The plurals of compound nouns are generally formed by adding *s* to the principal word in the compound: attorneys general, brides-to-be, judge advocates, notaries public, trade unions, assistant postmasters general.
2. Compound nouns containing prepositions form the plural by adding *s* to the principal word: chambers of commerce, attorneys-at-law, powers of attorney, points of view, bills of lading.
3. Hyphenated compounds composed of a noun and a preposition form the plural by adding *s* to the noun: lookers-on, hangers-on, runners-up, goings-on.
4. If there is no important word in the hyphenated compound noun, add an *s* to the end of the compound to form the plural: forget-me-nots, jack-in-

the-pulpits. If neither word in a compound is a noun, add *s* to the last word: also-rans, come-ons, follow-ups, go-betweens, higher-ups, trade-ins.

5. Some compounds form their plurals by making both parts plural: manservant, menservants; woman doctor, women doctors; Knight Templar, Knights Templars (or Knights Templar).

6. Compounds ending in *ful* form their plurals by adding *s* to the end of the compound: spoonfuls, cupfuls, handfuls, bucketfuls.

Foreign Words

Given a choice between a foreign and an English plural, use the English, or use the plural that is customary for the subject.

English Plural	Foreign Plural
appendixes	appendices
criterions	criteria
curriculums	curricula
indexes	indices
mediums	media
memorandums	memoranda
ultimatums	ultimata

Numbers

See "Numbers" under the "Accepted Usage in Writing" section, page 734.

Proper Names

To form the plurals of proper names add *s* or *es:* the Smiths, the Joneses, the Foxes, the Americas, the Eskimos, the Lillys, the Murrays, the Randolphs.

PREFIXES, JOINED

Compounds with the following prefixes are usually written as one word. When the second element is capitalized or is a figure, use a hyphen: anti-American, pre-Raphaelite, pre-1914, post-1945. Use a hyphen to distinguish homonyms: re-cover, re-form.

anti	antifreeze	*over*	overanxious
bi	bimonthly	*post*	postdate
co	coplanner	*pre*	prearrange
dis	disaffect	*pro*	procreate
extra	extracurricular	*pseudo*	pseudointellectual
fore	foreknown	*re*	restyle
hydro	hydrochloride	*semi*	semicircular
hyper	hypertension	*sub*	substandard
in	incapable	*super*	superstructure
infra	infrastructure	*supra*	supranational
inter	international	*trans*	transcontinental
intra	intramural	*tri*	tricity
mis	misread	*ultra*	ultrasound
non	noncombatant	*un*	unsuitable
out	outdistance	*under*	underestimate

PREPOSITIONS

Prepositions should end a construction only to avoid awkward phrasing or when used in a prepositional idiom.

A collective noun takes a singular verb when the *group* is thought of.
He left his car to be worked on.

REDUNDANCY

Redundancy is the needless repetition of words. In each redundant phrase below, the italicized word is sufficient for clarity. Two words joined by a conjunction that mean the same are called *doublets*. Either word in a doublet may be used for clarity.

Redundancies

both *alike*	*depreciate* in value
close *proximity*	month of *April*
continue on	*repeat* again
customary *practice*	two *twin sisters*

Doublets

first and foremost	each and every
basic and fundamental	courteous and polite
over and done with	assassinated and killed

SPLIT INFINITIVES

See "Infinitives."

SUBJUNCTIVE MOOD

In formal writing, the subjunctive mood is commonly used in contrary-to-fact clauses; clauses expressing doubt; and clauses expressing wishes, regrets, demands, recommendations, and the like.

If he *were* in town, you would not need an appointment.
If money *were* available, I would remodel the office.
If that *be* true, we must act now.
I wish I *were* confident of the outcome.
Even if the factory *were* located in China, the cost would be high.

SUFFIXES

Suffixes such as *-fold, -hood, -like, -proof,* and *-wide* are usually joined without a hyphen to the base word. But hyphens are used in compounds formed from proper names and word combinations where triple consonants come together.

threefold, multifold
childhood, motherhood
catlike, childlike
burglarproof, fireproof
nationwide, worldwide

BUT
Gandhi-like
bell-like
thrill-less

THAT, WHICH, WHO

1. *That* and *which* are not always interchangeable. *That* is preferred for introducing a restrictive clause.

    The phrasing that you suggest is good.
    The book that you recommend is excellent.

2. *Which* is preferred for introducing a nonrestrictive clause.

    The new phrasing, which seems clearer, is better.
    Your help, which we need badly, will save the day.

3. *Who* refers to persons and sometimes to animals. *Who* can introduce either restrictive or nonrestrictive clauses.

    The members who favored the amendment voted yes.
    Mr. Cortez, who was out of town, voted by proxy.
    Secretariat, who won the Kentucky Derby in 1973, went on to win the Triple Crown that year.

4. In formal writing, do not omit *that* as a conjunction.

    Formal: We think that this proposal is fair.
    Informal: We think this idea is a good one.

TRANSITIVE (ACTION) VERBS

Dictionaries designate verbs as *transitive (action)* or *intransitive* verbs.

1. Transitive verbs take objects. Intransitive verbs do not.

    Transitive: Send the letter today.
    Intransitive: She arrived this morning.

2. Some verbs are transitive or intransitive depending on content.

    Transitive: I wrote a full report.
                       She left her luggage at the hotel.
    Intransitive: I wrote yesterday.
                       She left yesterday.

VERBAL PHRASES

See "Infinitives" and "Participles, Dangling."

WHO, WHOM

Use *who* as the subject of a verb; *whom,* as the object of a verb or a preposition or as the subject of an infinitive.

Send it only to those *who asked* for it. (subject)
Who do you think *will be made* chairman? (subject)
Everyone *upon whom* I called accepted. (object of preposition)
Whom shall I *ask* first? (object of verb)
Whom did they ask *to be* chairman? (subject of infinitive)

WHOSE

Use *whose* as a possessive conjunction if *of which* is awkward. Most writers prefer to use *whose* because it is less cumbersome than *of which.*

Preferred: A large box, whose contents were unknown, stood on the loading dock.
Awkward: A large box, the contents of which were unknown, stood on the loading dock.

■ Supplemental Tables

ABBREVIATIONS AND CAPITALS OF THE UNITED STATES, THE CANADIAN PROVINCES, AND THE MEXICAN STATES

Name	Two-Letter Abbreviation	Capital
The United States		
Alabama	AL	Montgomery
Alaska	AK	Juneau
Arizona	AZ	Phoenix
Arkansas	AR	Little Rock
California	CA	Sacramento
Colorado	CO	Denver
Connecticut	CT	Hartford
Delaware	DE	Dover
District of Columbia	DC	Washington
Florida	FL	Tallahassee
Georgia	GA	Atlanta
Hawaii	HI	Honolulu
Idaho	ID	Boise
Illinois	IL	Springfield
Indiana	IN	Indianapolis
Iowa	IA	Des Moines
Kansas	KS	Topeka
Kentucky	KY	Frankfort
Louisiana	LA	Baton Rouge
Maine	ME	Augusta
Maryland	MD	Annapolis
Massachusetts	MA	Boston
Michigan	MI	Lansing
Minnesota	MN	St. Paul
Mississippi	MS	Jackson
Missouri	MO	Jefferson City
Montana	MT	Helena
Nebraska	NE	Lincoln
Nevada	NV	Carson City
New Hampshire	NH	Concord
New Jersey	NJ	Trenton
New Mexico	NM	Santa Fe
New York	NY	Albany
North Carolina	NC	Raleigh
North Dakota	ND	Bismarck
Ohio	OH	Columbus
Oklahoma	OK	Oklahoma City
Oregon	OR	Salem
Pennsylvania	PA	Harrisburg
Rhode Island	RI	Providence

ABBREVIATIONS AND CAPITALS OF THE UNITED STATES, THE CANADIAN PROVINCES, AND THE MEXICAN STATES *(continued)*

Name	Two-Letter Abbreviation	Capital
The United States		
South Carolina	SC	Columbia
South Dakota	SD	Pierre
Tennessee	TN	Nashville
Texas	TX	Austin
Utah	UT	Salt Lake City
Vermont	VT	Montpelier
Virginia	VA	Richmond
Washington	WA	Olympia
West Virginia	WV	Charleston
Wisconsin	WI	Madison
Wyoming	WY	Cheyenne
The Canadian Provinces		
Alberta	AB	Edmonton
British Columbia	BC	Victoria
Manitoba	MB	Winnipeg
New Brunswick	NB	Fredericton
Newfoundland	NF	St. John's
Northwest Territories	NT	Yellowknife
Nova Scotia	NS	Halifax
Ontario	ON	Toronto
Prince Edward Island	PE	Charlottetown
Quebec	PQ	Quebec
Saskatchewan	SK	Regina
Yukon Territory	YT	Whitehorse
The Mexican States		
Aguascalientes	AG	Aguascalientes
Baja California	BJ	Mexicali
Campeche	CA	Campeche
Chiapas	CH	Tuxtla Gutierrez
Chihuahua	CI	Chihuahua
Coahuila	CU	Saltillo
Colima	CL	Colima
Durango	DG	Durango
Guanajuato	GJ	Guanajuato
Guerrero	GR	Chilpancingo
Hidalgo	HG	Pachuca
Jalisco	JA	Guadalajara
Mexico	EM*	Toluca

*MX is the two-letter abbreviation for the country; EM is the two-letter abbreviation for the state.

ABBREVIATIONS AND CAPITALS OF THE UNITED STATES, THE CANADIAN PROVINCES, AND THE MEXICAN STATES *(continued)*

Name	Two-Letter Abbreviation	Capital
The Mexican States		
Michoacan	MH	Morelia
Morelos	MO	Cuernavaca
Nayarit	NA	Tepic
Nuevo Leon	NL	Monterrey
Oaxaca	OA	Oaxaca
Puebla	PU	Puebla
Queretaro	QA	Queretaro
Quintana Roo	QR	Chetumal
San Luis Potosi	SL	San Luis Potosi
Sinaloa	SI	Culiacan
Sonora	SO	Hermosillo
Tabasco	TA	Villahermosa
Tamaulipas	TM	Ciudad Victoria
Tlaxcala	TL	Tlaxcala
Veracruz	VL	Jalapa
Yucatan	YU	Merida
Zacatecas	ZT	Zacatecas
Distrito Federal	DF	Mexico City

FREQUENTLY USED ACRONYMS AND ABBREVIATIONS

The electronic work environment that has become so much a part of the administrative assistant's job is characterized by an increasing use of acronyms and abbreviations that relate to computers, software, and telecommunications. This list encompasses those the administrative assistant is most likely to encounter in publications, conversation, and software documentation. No attempt is made here to explain the functions of the equipment, software, or process that the acronym or abbreviation represents. Definitions of most of those listed here are given in various chapters throughout the text.

ASCII	American Standard Code for Information Interchange
ATM	Automatic Teller Machine
ATS	Administrative Terminal System
BASIC	Beginners's All-purpose Symbolic Instruction Code
CAD	Computer-Aided Design
CAI	Computer-Assisted Instruction
CAR	Computer-Assisted Retrieval
CBMS	Computer-Based Message System
CD	Compact Disk
CIM	Computer-Input Microfilm

COBOL	Common Business Oriented Language
COM	Computer-Output Microfilm
CPU	Central Processing Unit
CRT	Cathode Ray Tube
DBMS	Database Management System
DOS	Disk Operating System
DPMA	Data Processing Management Association
DSS	Decision Support Systems
EDP	Electronic Data Processing
EFTS	Electronic Funds Transfer System
FORTRAN	Formula Translation
I/O	Input/Output
IBM	International Business Machines Corporation
IT	Information Technology
KTS	Key Telephone Systems
LAN	Local Area Network
MICR	Magnetic Ink Character Recognition
MODEM	Modulate/Demodulate
OCR	Optical Character Recognition
OR	Operations Research
PABX	Private Automatic Branch Exchange
PBX	Private Branch Exchange
PC	Personal Computer
RAM	Random Access Memory
ROM	Read-Only Memory
RPG	Report Program Generator
UPC	Universal Product Code
VDT	Video Display Terminal
WATS	Wide-Area Telephone Service
WP	Word Processing

MAJOR CURRENCIES OF THE WORLD

Country	Symbol	Monetary Unit
Argentina	$a	austral
Australia	$A	dollar
Austria	S *or* Sch	schilling
Bahamas	B$	dollar
Belgium	BF	franc
Canada	Can$	dollar
China (Mainland)	$	yuan
China (Taiwan)	NT$	dollar or yuan

MAJOR CURRENCIES OF THE WORLD *(continued)*

Country	Symbol	Monetary Unit
Commonwealth of Independent States (formerly U.S.S.R.)	R *or* Rub.	ruble
Denmark	Kr *or* DKr	krone
Egypt	£	pound
France	Fr *or* FF	franc
Germany	DM	deutsche mark
Greece	Dr	drachma
Hong Kong	HK$	dollar
India	Re (*pl* Rs)	rupee
Ireland	£	pound
Italy	L *or* Lit	lira
Japan	Y *or* ¥	yen
Mexico	$	peso
New Zealand	NZ$	dollar
North Korea	W	won
Norway	Kr *or* NKr	krone
Poland	Zl	zloty
Saudi Arabia	R *or* SR	riyal
Singapore	S$	dollar
South Africa	R	rand
South Korea	W	won
Spain	Pta *or* P	peseta
Sweden	Skr *or* Kr	krona
Switzerland	SFr	franc
United Kingdom	£	pound
U.S.A.	$	dollar

WEIGHTS AND MEASURES WITH METRIC EQUIVALENTS

There are two commonly used methods of measurement. One, the English, or imperial, system, is used in the United States; the other is the metric system, which is used in most other parts of the world. In the English system, units used for measuring lengths are inches, feet, yards, and miles. The basic unit in the metric system for these measurements is the meter. The metric system is a decimal system, which means that you change from one measurement to another by merely moving a decimal point. For example: 10 decimeters = 1 meter. By moving the decimal point one place to the left, you have converted decimeters into meters. See the table on the following page.

English System	Metric System	Equivalents

Lengths

12 inches = 1 foot	10 millimeters = 1 centimeter	1 inch = 2.54 centimeters
3 feet = 1 yard	10 centimeters = 1 decimeter	1 foot = 30.48 centimeters
5,280 feet = 1 mile	10 decimeters = 1 meter	39.37 inches = 1 meter
	10 meters = 1 dekameter	1 mile = 1.609 kilometers
	10 dekameters = 1 hectometer	
	10 hectometers = 1 kilometer	

Weights

16 ounces = 1 pound	10 milligrams = 1 centigram	1 ounce = 28.35 grams
100 pounds = 1 hundredweight	10 centigrams = 1 decigram	1 pound = 453.6 grams
2,000 pounds = 1 ton	10 decigrams = 1 gram	1 ton = 907.2 kilograms
	10 grams = 1 dekagram	
	10 dekagrams = 1 hectogram	
	10 hectograms = 1 kilogram	

Dry and Liquid Measures

Dry Measure

2 pints = 1 quart
8 quarts = 1 peck
4 pecks = 1 bushel

Liquid Measure

2 pints = 1 quart
4 quarts = 1 gallon

Dry and Liquid Measure

10 milliliters = 1 centiliter
10 centiliters = 1 deciliter
10 deciliters = 1 liter
10 liters = 1 dekaliter
10 dekaliters = 1 hectoliter
10 hectoliters = 1 kiloliter

Dry Measure

1 pint = 0.550 liters
1 quart = 1.101 liters
1 peck = 8.809 liters
1 bushel = 35.238 liters

Liquid Measure

1 pint = 0.473 liters
1 quart = 0.946 liters
1 gallon = 3.785 liters

Temperature Conversion

	Celsius	Fahrenheit
Boiling point of water	100° C	212° F
Freezing point of water	0° C	32° F
Normal body temperature	37° C	98.6° F

To convert from Celsius to Fahrenheit:
$$F = 9/5\ C + 32$$

From Fahrenheit to Celsius:
$$C = 5/5\ (F - 32)$$

ndex

Desk manual, 50, 673–677
Desk readers, 161
Desk reference files, 52
Desktop publishing, 115–116, 134–138, 395
Dewey decimal system, 154, 348
Dictation, 233
   case problem on, 335–336
   dating transcription for, 245
   and forms of origination, 238–242
   giving, 242
   methods of, 233, 235–238
   number and kinds of copies for, 245
   on-the-spot, 240–241
   and order of transcription, 244–245
   predictation responsibilities, 234–235
   by telephone, 240
   transcription fundamentals, 242–245
Dictionaries, 243–244, 352
   electronic, 249
   and hyphenation, 785
Digest of incoming mail, 306
Digital dictation systems, 237
Digital laser technology, 141
Digital PBX, 184
Digital signals, 180
Direct deposits or withdrawals, 513
Direct-distance dialing (DDD), 194–195
Directing, 696–697
Direct inward dialing (DID), 184
Directional keys, 213
Directions, during dictations, 239–240
Directories, 352–353
   in desk manual, 676–677
   telephone, 191–194
Directory of Publications, 358
Directory of Special Libraries and Information Centers, 342
Directory of U.S. Government Depository Libraries, A, 354
Direct outward dialing (DOD), 184
Disabled employees:
   and Americans with Disabilities Act, 611
   and emergency procedures, 37
   workstation for, 28
Discount, cash, 516
Discrete media, 236
Discrimination:
   and employment termination, 657
   and equal employment regulations, 610–611
Disk drive, 103, 215
Disk operating system (DOS), 108–111
Disks:
   floppy, 103–104, 224
   hard, 104, 237
Display monitors, 105–106, 215
Diversified work force, 10, 707–708
   case problem on, 722

Dividends, 535
Divisions of company, 21–23
Documents, 233
   computer-generated, 157–158
   creating, 246
   formatting, 246–247
   inputting and editing, 247
   proofreading, 248–250
   See also Correspondence; Letters
Domestic Mail Manual, 312
Dot matrix printer, 216
Doublets (words), 204, 797
Downsizing, 20, 708
Draft, of report, 393–394
Drawer space, 40
Dress code, 5–6
Drucker, Peter R., quoted, 15
Duplication, commercial and in-house, 138–139. *See also* Reprographics
Duplicators, 130–131
   automated, 131

E

Easements, 550
Editing:
   of document, 247–248
   of document (technology application), 258
Editing, electronic, 130
Education, on resume, 642. *See also* Training
Education field, administrative assistant in, 628
800 numbers, 193–194
Electronic banking, 511–515
Electronic calendar, 41–42
Electronic dictionary, 249
Electronic editing, 130
Electronic mail (E-mail), 179, 198–199, 294–296
   messages to absent executive through, 305
   quick handling of, 292
   technology application for, 206
Electronic meeting rooms, 464, 465
Electronic messages, 260, 316–317
Electronic organizers, 41–42
Electronic shorthand, 238
Electronic telephone directories, 193
Electronic typewriter
   dictation on, 241
   and document creation, 246
   and envelope addressing, 251
Ellipsis, 784
E-mail. *See* Electronic mail
Emergency procedures, 33–34, 557–558
   in technology application, 37
Emery Air Freight Corp., 328
Employee evaluation, 48–50

Employee health and safety concerns, 28–33
Employee information and privacy legislation, 611
Employer, promoting of, 682–683
Employer identification number, 566
Employment agencies, 634–635
Employment opportunities for administrative assistant, 19, 622–623
   choosing among, 19–20, 633
   in education, 628
   in foreign service, 631–632
   in government, 630–631
   increasing number of, 3
   in legal office, 627–628
   in medical office, 626–627
   and perfect job (technology application), 662
   and size of office, 623–625
   in support services for public, 629–630
   in technical office, 628–629
   in temporary employment services, 632
   See also Job hunting
Employment tests, 654–655
Enclosure notations, 250
Enclosures, 251–252
Encyclopedias, 354, 359
End-of-day tasks:
   checking tickler file, 51
   clearing and securing, 40
   preparing work plan, 45
   reminding executive of unusual appointments, 57
Endless loop system, 236
Endnotes, 398–399, 411
Endorsement of check, 503–504
Engagements, canceling of, 287
English usage. *See* Usage, accepted
Enrichment, job, 706
Enumerations, in report, 400–401
Enunciation, 77
Envelopes:
   addressing, 251
   interoffice, 222
   opening, 298
   oversize, 222
   sealing and stamping, 255
   styles of, 245, 749
Equal Employment Opportunity Commission, 657, 669
Equal employment regulations, 610–611
Equipment:
   acquiring competence in, 228
   care of, 228–229
   common characteristics of, 213–218

Government, administrative assistant in, 630
Government names, indexing of, 745–746
Government offices, in alphabetical telephone directory, 192
Government publications, 354–355
Grammar, quick reminders on, 792–798
Grammar checks, 249
Grapevine, 10
Graphical user interface (GUI), 110, 120
Graphics, 106, 113–114, 380–383
  computer, 374–375
Graphs, 375
  bar, 376–377
  interpreting, 379–380
  limitations of, 378–379
  line, 376, 387
  in report, 401, 411
Gray zone, 139
Greek alphabet, 772–773
Greenwich time, 190
Ground rules of company, 668
Growth, professional, 680–682, 712–715

H

Handbooks, 358, 359
  office, 244
  of parliamentary procedures, 359
Handshaking, 74
Handwriting, 45–46
Hanging indent, 400
Harassment, sexual, 669–670
Hard disks, 104
  for digital dictation, 237
Hardware, computer:
  central processing unit, 99–100, 101–102
  information services on, 357
  input devices, 100–101
  output devices, 105–106
  storage devices, 103–105
Headings:
  in report, 396–398
  subject, 151
Health, and appearance, 6
Health and safety concerns, 28–33
Heating and cooling systems, 30–31
Help screens, in computer evaluation, 117
Hierarchy of human needs, 703–704
High-density mobile files, 163
Highlighting of material, 352
Highly confidential material, and dictation, 240
High-volume copiers, 125

Histogram, 376–377
Horizontal files, 164
Horizontal organization, 693
Hotel/motel reservations, 440–441, 448
  in foreign countries, 447
Human relations, 665–666. See also Relationships, office
Human resources department, 22. See also Personnel policies
Hyphen and hyphenation, 784–786
  and dictionary, 244
  in legal document, 602

I

Icons, 110
IDDD (international direct distance dialing), 189–190
"Idea bank," 41
Idioms, 793–794
Illness, in office, 33–34
Image, professional, 5–9
Image processing, 124
Imaging, 159
Impact printers, 215, 216
Income statements, 528, 529
Income tax deductions, 568–569
Income tax of executive, 572–580
  assistance with, 584–585
  and IRS audit, 580–581
  late filing of, 584
  preparation of documents for accountant, 585–586
  preparation and mailing of returns, 584
  tax guides and forms for, 581–584
  technology application on, 589
Incoming mail. See Mail, incoming
Incoming telephone calls, 78–85
  incoming toll-free calling, 186
Indentations, in report, 396
Index and indexing
  alphabetizing in, 738–746
  for files, 148–149, 166, 167
  of minutes, 479, 482
  phonetic, 150
  relative, 151
  for report, 403
  and uncertainty over key unit, 167
Infinitives, 794
Information. See Research
Information services, subscription, 355–357
Information services department, 22–23
Information technologies:
  in desk manual, 674
  information services on, 356
  integrated, 178
  local area networks, 178–180

Initiative, as administrative assistant attribute, 664
Ink cartridges, 220
Ink-jet printer, 217
Ink/toner cartridges, 221
Inoculations, for foreign travel, 445–446
Input devices, 100–101
Inputting, of document, 247–248
Inputting devices, 213
Inquiries, 272–273
  answers to, 273–274
Instruction booklets, 228
Instructions, during dictations, 239–240, 244
Insurance, 553–558
  and administrative assistant function, 559
  against error and omission (notary public), 599
  for travel, 453
Insured mail, 317
Integrated software packages, 115, 395
Integration of information technologies, 178
Intelligent copier/printer, 126–127, 198
Internal storage, 102
International correspondence, 281–283
  case problem on, 337
International financial markets. See Foreign financial markets
International mail, 327–328
International money orders, 326
International shipments, 330
International telephone service, 189–190
International travel, 441–447
  items to be given traveler, 454
International visitors, 71
  at meetings, 462–464
Interoffice correspondence, 279–280
Interoffice envelopes, 222
Interoffice letterheads, 222
Interoffice memorandum reports, 390–391
Interoffice relationships, 9–13
Interruption, of conference, 74–75
Interview, employment, 647–656
Introduction, letters of, 275–276
Introductions, of office visitors, 72–73
Inventory, property, 556
Investment certificates, 548–549
Investment property, 551–552
  and administrative assistant function, 559
Invitations:
  accepting, 285–286
  declining, 286–287
Invoices, 515
  enclosed, 304
  for office supplies, 227

Registration materials, for conference
  or convention, 486
Registry Group, 442–443
Regulations of company, 668
Rehabilitation Act (1973), 610
Relationships (friendships), office,
  9–13, 665–666, 669
  case problems on, 93–95, 207–208
  and first days on job, 666–668
  and help with peak loads, 47
  and professionalism, 9
  and socializing as time waster, 44
Relative index, 151
Relatives, and job prospects, 635
Reminder letters, 274
Remittances, foreign, 524–526
Rental car travel, 439–440
Reports, in desk manual, 674
Report writing, 388–390
  administrative assistant's
    responsibility in, 390
  appendix, 401–402, 411
  bibliography/reference list, 402, 411
  case problem on, 424–425
  checklist for, 410–411
  computer software for, 395
  developing body of report, 392–394,
    410
  final steps, 409–412
  and form of report, 390
  index, 403
  keying body of report, 395–401
  letter or memorandum of
    transmittal, 403
  preparation for publication, 412–414
  summary, 403–405, 410
  table of contents, 405–407, 410
  technology application on, 423
  title page, 407–408, 410
Reprographics, 124–125
  case problem on, 207–208
  and commercial or in-house
    duplication, 138–139
  in desk manual, 675
  future of, 140–141
  selecting method of, 139
Requests, 272–273
Requisition form, technology
  application on, 232
Requisitions, for office supplies, 227
Research, 339, 340–341
  bibliography cards, 349
  business information sources,
    355–359
  computer databases for, 343
  general information sources,
    352–355
  libraries for, 342–343, 343–349
  notetaking, 349–352
  objectives in, 341

secondary vs. primary data for,
    341–342
  technology applications on, 363
Research and development division, 22
Resignation. *See* Termination of
  employment
Respect, in office relationships, 10–11
Responsibilities of administrative
  assistant, 3–5
  administrative, 558–559
  areas of, 41
  financial, 500, 534
  future changes in, 621
  legal, 590
  paraprofessional, 622
  payroll, 564
  research, 340
  in technology application, 18
  timetables of, 340
  variation in, 38
Restrooms, and overtime work, 32–33
Resume, 637–643
Retention schedules, for paper
  documents, 171
Retrieval systems, 161–162
Reverse-charge toll number, 193–194
Ribbons, printer, 220–221
Rider, 607
Rights of others, 706–707
Robert's Rules of Order, 473
*Roget's International Thesaurus in
  Dictionary Form*, 264–265
Rolodex, 42
Romances, office, 10
Roman numerals, 773–775
Room reservations, for meetings,
  464–465
Rotary wheel files, 165
Routine duties, 41
Routing slip, technology application
  on, 232
Rulings (table), 372

S

Safe-deposit box, 511
Safety. *See* Security
Safety and health concerns, 28–33
Salary, and employment interview,
  652, 654
Sales representatives, for office
  supplies, 226
Salutation of letter, 268
Salute opening of letter, 268
Sans-serif typeface, 138
Satellite communication, 182
Scheduling:
  of appointments, 53–57
  of appointments (technology
    application), 63

Screening, of telephone calls, 79–80
Sealing envelopes, 255
Searching fees, 344–345
Secondary data, 341–342
Second-class mail, 314
"Secretary," vs. "administrative
  assistant," 3
Securities, 534
  and administrative assistant
    function, 559
  bonds, 534, 537–538
  and income tax, 575
  investment certificates, 548–549
  stocks, 534, 535–537
  trading in, 538–547
  U.S. Treasury, 547–548
  and where-kept file, 558
Security:
  for computers, 118–119
  for FAX messages, 201
  for files, 148
  for incoming mail, 296
  of office environment, 32–33
  and work code, 669
Self-evaluation chart, 11
  in technology application, 18
Semicolon, 791–792
Seminars, for administrative assistants,
  682
Sentence quality, 263–269
Serifs, 138
706 agencies, 610
Sexist words, 266, 267
Sexual harassment, 669–670
Shipping charges, technology
  application on, 334
Shipping services, 328–330
Shorthand, manual, 237
Sight draft, 524
Signature of executive, submitting
  correspondence for, 252–253
Signed mail. *See* Correspondence
Single-copy forms, 218
Situational leadership, 713
Sleeves (microfilm), 160
Small offices, 623–624
Smart cards, 514–515
Smoke-free environment, 30
Snap-out forms, 219
Socializing with coworkers, as time
  waster, 44
Social Security, 566–567
Software, 108
  applications, 111–116
  case problem on, 335
  desktop publishing, 134. *See also*
    Desktop publishing
  editing functions in, 248
  evaluation and selection of, 117
  information services on, 357